The Revels P
COMPANiuN
LIBRARY

E. A. J. HONIGMANN former editor
J. R. MULRYNE, R. L. SMALLWOOD and PETER CORBIN general editors

For over forty years *The Revels Plays* have offered the most authoritative editions of Elizabethan and Jacobean plays by authors other than Shakespeare. The *Companion Library* provides a fuller background to the main series by publishing worthwhile dramatic and non-dramatic material that will be essential for the serious student of the period.

Documents of the Rose Playhouse Chillington Rutter
Drama of the English Republic, 1649–60 Clare
'Art made tongue-tied by authority' Clare
Three Jacobean witchcraft plays eds Corbin, Sedge
Beyond 'The Spanish Tragedy': A study of the works of Thomas Kyd Erne
John Ford's political theatre Hopkins
The works of Richard Edwards King
Marlowe and the popular tradition: Innovation in the English drama before 1595 Lunney
Banquets set forth: Banqueting in English Renaissance drama Meads
Thomas Heywood: Three marriage plays ed. Merchant
Three Renaissance travel plays ed. Parr
John Lyly Pincombe
A textual companion to Doctor Faustus Rasmussen

Euphues: The Anatomy of Wit
and *Euphues and His England* John Lyly

THE REVELS PLAYS COMPANION LIBRARY

Euphues:
The Anatomy of Wit
and
Euphues and His England

John Lyly

AN ANNOTATED,
MODERN-SPELLING EDITION

edited by Leah Scragg

Manchester University Press

Manchester and New York

distributed exclusively in the USA by Palgrave

Published by Manchester University Press
Oxford Road, Manchester M13 9NR, UK
and Room 400, 175 Fifth Avenue, New York, NY 10010, USA
www.manchesteruniversitypress.co.uk

Distributed exclusively in the USA by
Palgrave, 175 Fifth Avenue, New York NY 10010, USA

Distributed exclusively in Canada by
UBC Press, University of British Columbia, 2029 West Mall,
Vancouver, BC, Canada V6T 1Z2

British Library Cataloguing-in-Publication Data
A catalogue record for this book is available from the British Library

Library of Congress Cataloging-in-Publication Data
A catalog record for this book is available from the Library of Congress

ISBN 13: 978 0 7190 6459 3

First published in hardback 2003 by Manchester University Press
This paperback edition first published 2009

Printed by Lightning Source

CONTENTS

GENERAL EDITORS' PREFACE

Since the late 1950s the series known as The Revels Plays has provided for students of the English Renaissance drama carefully edited texts of the major Elizabethan and Jacobean plays. The series includes some of the best-known drama of the period and has continued to expand, both within its original field and, to a lesser extent, beyond it, to include some important plays from the earlier Tudor and from the Restoration periods. The Revels Plays Companion Library is intended to further this expansion and to allow for new developments.

The aim of the Companion Library is to provide students of the Elizabethan and Jacobean drama with a fuller sense of its background and context. The series includes volumes of a variety of kinds. Small collections of plays, by a single author or concerned with a single theme and edited in accordance with the principles of textual modernization of the Revels Plays, offer a wider range of drama than the main series can include. Together with editions of masques, pageants and the non-dramatic work of Elizabethan and Jacobean play-wrights, these volumes make it possible, within the overall Revels enterprise, to examine the achievements of the major dramatists from a broader perspective. Other volumes provide a fuller context for the plays of the period by offering new collections of documentary evidence on Elizabethan theatrical conditions and on the performance of plays during that period and later. A third aim of the series is to offer modern critical interpretation, in the form of collections of essays or of monographs, of the dramatic achievement of the English Renaissance.

So wide a range of material necessarily precludes the standard format and uniform general editorial control which is possible in the original series of Revels Plays. To a considerable extent, therefore, treatment and approach are determined by the needs and intentions of individual volume editors. Within this rather ampler area, however, we hope that the Companion Library maintains the standards of scholarship that have for so long characterized The Revels Plays, and that it offers a useful enlargement of the work of the series in preserving, illuminating and celebrating the drama of Elizabethan and Jacobean England.

PETER CORBIN
J. R. MULRYNE
R. L. SMALLWOOD

ACKNOWLEDGEMENTS

The debts of gratitude incurred in the course of preparing this edition are many, and the help received of a variety of kinds. I am grateful to the Arts and Humanities Research Board (UK) and my own university for awarding me the year-long period of research leave that allowed me to bring the project to fruition; to the Master and Fellows of Trinity College, Cambridge, for affording me access to the only extant copy of the second edition of *The Anatomy of Wit*, and for their permission to reproduce the title page (p. 25); to the Harry Ransom Humanities Research Center, The University of Texas at Austin, for their assistance in enabling me to collate my text of *Euphues and His England* with the Pforzheimer Library copy of the first edition, and allowing me to reproduce the page which appears on p. 153; to the staff of Holborn Local History Library, London, for their help in locating the copy of *Euphues and His England* formerly in the possession of Professor Morley, and their ready assistance in making it available for me to consult; to the Bodleian Library, Oxford, for granting me access to their copy of the third edition of *The Anatomy of Wit*, affording me the opportunity to collate my text with the pages missing from the Trinity edition; to my colleagues in my own department at Manchester who have suggested solutions to some of the puzzles posed by Lyly's allusions, and to David Langslow of the Department of Classics and Ancient History for reading over and proposing some amendments to the Appendix; to William Duggan of St Paul's School, London, for his help with Lyly's encomium to Elizabeth, and James Diggle of Queens' College, Cambridge, for locating a hitherto untraced allusion to Euripedes. Above all I am grateful to Robin Griffin, formerly of Manchester Grammar School and the Cambridge School Classics Project, for his invaluable assistance in editing and translating Lyly's 'Iovis Elizabeth' (pp. 343–4 and 356–8) on my behalf, identifying the source of the poem, and supplying the material used on pp. 355–6. My debts to earlier editors are recorded in the 'Note on the texts'. The editor and the publisher would like to gratefully acknowledge the assistance of the *Ward* bequest in the publication of this volume.

Leah Scragg
University of Manchester

INTRODUCTION

Reader, I have, for the love I bear to posterity, digged up the grave of a rare and excellent poet, whom Queen Elizabeth then heard, graced and rewarded. These papers of his lay like dead laurels in a churchyard, but I have gathered the scattered branches up and by a charm gotten from Apollo made them green again, and set them up as epitaphs to his memory. A sin it were to suffer these rare monuments of wit to lie covered in dust. (Edward Blount, 1632)

The words of the first editor of Lyly's work[1] bear witness to both its prestige in the closing decades of the sixteenth century and the rapidity with which it fell from favour to neglect. Though combined editions of *Euphues: The Anatomy of Wit* and *Euphues and His England*, the two major prose works that had precipitated Lyly to public notice between 1578 and 1580, were still appearing on the book stalls when Blount was attempting to revive interest in the plays, the spate of editions that had turned their author into a literary phenomenon was finally coming to an end, leaving to Blount's successors the task of sweeping the dust from his pages for subsequent generations of readers. The undertaking has not proved an easy one. While many major writers have suffered a comparable period of neglect only to be rediscovered in course of time by a new audience, Lyly, for all the efforts of successive generations of scholars, has remained on the periphery of the literary canon, identified in the public mind with a peculiarly mannered style and remembered for the influence he exerted rather than the distinctive character of his own work. The brevity of his success would have come as no surprise to Lyly himself. The epistle 'To the Gentlemen Readers' prefacing *The Anatomy of Wit* remarks that 'we commonly see the book that at Midsummer lieth bound on the stationer's stall at Christmas to be broken in the haberdasher's shop' (p. 30),[2] a symptom of that inexorable process of change instanced throughout the Lylian corpus. Lyly's dictum that there is 'nothing' constant 'but inconstancy' (p. 236) has at last proved valid, however, in relation to the estimation of his own work. The cultural emphasis of late twentieth-century criticism has finally permitted his recuperation into a central position in the study of the English literary Renaissance, while contemporary interest in the process of signification has afforded his destabilization of meaning a new topicality.

Lyly's career was closely bound up with the reign of the monarch whose virtues he celebrates at the close of *Euphues and His England*, and to whom he clearly looked for preferment. Born around 1554, four years before Elizabeth came to the throne, he rose to the peak of his fortunes as the purveyor of highly sophisticated plays for the court, only to die in poverty in 1606, three years after the death of the Queen, as a result of her failure to respond to his petitions for financial help. It was not towards the court, however, that his aspirations were initially directed. Grandson of the grammarian William Lily (High Master of St Paul's), nephew of George Lily (secretary to the scholarly Cardinal Pole), and son of an official at Canterbury cathedral, he was born into a family with close connections with the humanist movement, and it was at the university rather than the court (an opposition set up in a number of his works) that he sought initially to make his career. Having received his early education, in all likelihood, at the King's School, Canterbury,[3] where his younger brothers were educated and Marlowe was later to be a pupil, he proceeded, like his uncle and grandfather before him, to Magdalene College, Oxford, where he obtained his B.A. in 1573 and his M.A. in 1575. His time at Oxford appears, however, to have been both intellectually and professionally disappointing. Complaints against the system of education he encountered run throughout *The Anatomy of Wit*, while the address 'To My Very Good Friends the Gentlemen Scholars of Oxford', introduced into the second edition, testifies to both the adverse response his comments attracted and his own resentment at the nature of his training (see pp. 151-2). His jaundiced stance towards the university may arise, in part, from the frustration of his hopes. In May 1574 he had petitioned Lord Burghley[4] to use his influence with the Queen to oblige his college to award him a fellowship, but the application came to nothing and he left Oxford after receiving his M.A.[5]

The avenue of academic preferment closed to him, Lyly took the path later to be followed by successive members of that generation that has come to be known as the 'university wits'.[6] Moving from Oxford to London, he sought to promote his fortunes by literary means, publishing his first composition, *Euphues: The Anatomy of Wit*, in 1578. The work, expanded in 1579 and followed by a sequel the subsequent year, was to prove the literary sensation of the age. By 1630 the two parts had run through more than thirty editions, and established their author as the principal exponent of a literary mode that informed the language of a generation. In the words of Edward Blount in 1632, 'Our nation are in his debt for a new English which he taught them. . . . All our ladies were then his scholars, and that beauty in court which could not parley Euphuism was as little regarded as she which now there speaks not French.'

Whereas the first part of *Euphues* was dedicated to a Lord Delaware of whom comparatively little is known, the sequel was addressed to a far more significant figure, the dedicatory epistle to the Earl of Oxford, Lord Great Chamberlain of England, signalling the author's entry into the service of a nobleman at the very centre of courtly life.[7] Through Oxford's patronage Lyly became a partner in the first Blackfriars theatre, turning from prose to drama to write a series of comedies for its company of boy actors, whose sophisticated productions were ultimately designed for performance at court. The new medium afforded Lyly the ideal channel for both his wit and structural gifts, and the remainder of his literary out-put, but for a brief excursion into pamphleteering (see p. 15), was written for the stage. In the course of the 1580s he produced a series of highly polished comedies for performance before the Queen, heightening his already considerable literary status and securing a promise of further preferment. The decade, which on the wider stage witnessed the defeat of the Spanish Armada, the publication of the first books of *The Faerie Queene*, and the first performance of Marlowe's *Tamburlaine*, constitutes the high-water mark of his achievement. With the suppression in 1590 of Paul's Boys (for whom he had written after the closure of the first Blackfriars in the mid-1580s) he abruptly found himself with no natural outlet for the highly specialized form of comedy he had evolved, and his attempts to find a new role in a changing culture seem to have been largely unsuccessful. A verse play, *The Woman in the Moon*, may well have been a failure, and he abandoned the attempt to compete in an arena dominated by Marlowe, and increasingly by Shakespeare. Having received only an honorary position at court, rather than the Mastership of the Revels for which he appears to have hoped,[8] he became a Member of Parliament for a succession of boroughs, but his political career was not financially rewarding, and he died in straitened circumstances in 1606, his numerous petitions to the Queen seemingly unregarded.

At the heart of both Lyly's achievement and the prolonged neglect suffered by his work is the literary style which has come to be known as euphuism or the euphuistic mode. Though the fundamental elements of the form did not originate with Lyly,[9] they were combined by him into the vehicle for a highly distinctive vision, the inseparability of style and subject distinguishing his deployment of the mode from that of his predecessors and the many imitators who sought to exploit his success. The style is rooted in antithetical balance, promoted by the use of schemes or figures of sound, notably isocolon (the repetition of clauses of the same length), parison (similarly structured sentences) and paramoion (sound patterning, e.g. syllabic repetition, assonance and alliteration). The see-saw oppositions of Eubulus' advice to Euphues in *The Anatomy of Wit* offer a straightforward example:

> Consider with thyself the great difference between staring and stark-blind, wit and wisdom, love and lust. Be merry, but with modesty; be sober, but not too sullen; be valiant, but not too venturous. Let thy attire be comely, but not costly; thy diet wholesome, but not excessive. (pp. 37–8)

Equally fundamental to Lyly's handling of the mode is the use of analogies drawn from proverbial wisdom, classical history, and mythology, particularly fables relating to the natural world. Like the schematically constructed sentences, the images are designed to enforce opposition, typically turning upon duality or the location of contrast. Euphues, in *The*

Anatomy of Wit, for example, having fallen in love with Lucilla, conducts an imaginary argument with her in the following terms:

> O my Lucilla, if thy heart be made of that stone which may be mollified only with blood, would I had sipped of that river in Caria which turneth those that drink of it to stones. If thine ears be anointed with the oil of Syria that bereaveth hearing, would mine eyes had been rubbed with the syrup of the cedar tree which taketh away sight. (p. 56)

The dialectical nature of the style originates, in part, in the scholastic disputations which formed a principal educational instrument in the sixteenth century, and debate (or the consideration of 'questions') supplies much of the incidental interest of both parts of *Euphues*, while informing the larger framework of the narrative. In *The Anatomy of Wit*, for example, Euphues and Eubulus dispute whether nature or education is of greater influence in shaping individual behaviour (pp. 35ff.), while in *Euphues and His England* Martius and the Lady Flavia debate whether unmarried young men and women should be permitted to meet (pp. 304ff.). These topics are enfolded, in turn, in a series of larger oppositions, most notably the conflicting claims of love and friendship, a widely disseminated Renaissance motif. Thus in *The Anatomy of Wit* Euphues is torn between his passion for Lucilla and his friendship for Philautus, a situation reversed in *Euphues and His England* in which Philautus chooses between his love for Camilla (and later Frances) and his devotion to Euphues. The love and friendship motif, traditionally employed to demonstrate the superiority of male comradeship to sexual passion, overlaps, moreover, with a second familiar story deployed as an educational instrument throughout the sixteenth century, and equally susceptible of treatment as debate, the parable of the prodigal son.[10] Thus in *The Anatomy of Wit*, Euphues, a gifted young man with his fortune in his own hands, rejects good counsel, falls victim to vice and, having suffered for his errors, repudiates his former conduct and embraces the pious life, a pattern repeated in one of the inset narratives of *Euphues and His England*, in which the wilful Callimachus rejects the advice of the wise Cassander, and descends into extreme penury before his patrimony is restored to him.

While the overall progress of the narrative in both *The Anatomy of Wit* and *Euphues and His England* appears to enforce the moral lessons conventionally inculcated by the author's inherited motifs (in the first part of the work, for example, Euphues learns through his misconduct, is reunited with Philautus and becomes the embodiment of piety), the pervasive ambivalence at the heart of the euphuistic mode endows Lyly's work with a far greater degree of ambiguity than its subject matter initially suggests. The opening debate between Euphues and Eubulus in *The Anatomy of Wit* is illustrative of the method at work throughout. Their encounter sets up a series of conventional oppositions. Euphues is a self-confident, inexperienced youth, Eubulus an old man with knowledge of the world. Euphues is intent upon pleasure, Eubulus conscious of moral danger. The assumptions

INTRODUCTION 5

encoded in the familiar didactic stories upon which Lyly draws, together with the interventions of the narrator, who here as elsewhere orchestrates the discussions through which the narrative evolves, invite endorsement, at first sight, of the older man's position and thus the acceptance of a stable universe governed by an immutable moral order. The position is complicated, however, by the medium through which the argument is advanced. The development through a series of antithetical propositions draws the reader not towards an irresistible conclusion, but into a series of branching avenues leading progressively further from an inevitable goal, frustrating the drive of the narrative towards finality and closure, and proliferating the positions from which a judgement might be reached.

At the core of the argument Eubulus advances is the seemingly unexceptionable proposition that it is the duty of the parent to train the child and that Euphues' waywardness is thus a product of some defect of his education. Rather than simply enunciating this viewpoint, however, the older man considers the possible causes of the younger's perversity, developing in the process an ever-widening circle of uncertainty:

> As thy birth doth show the express and lively image of gentle blood, so thy bringing up seemeth to me to be a great blot to the lineage of so noble a brute; so that I am enforced to think that either thou didst want one to give thee good instructions, or that thy parents made thee a wanton with too much cockering, either they were too foolish in using no discipline or thou too froward in rejecting their doctrine, either they willing to have thee idle or thou wilful to be ill-employed. (p. 35)

Here a variety of alternative childhoods are postulated for the hero, endowing him with a multitude of personalities rather than a single identity, and thus problematizing the assignment of blame for his present condition. The reader is left to speculate whether his parents were ignorant, over-indulgent, or neglectful, and whether he was a spoilt, wild or recalcitrant child. Whatever the causes of the young man's deficiencies, however, Eubulus is confident that it is childhood training that determines the nature of the man and that the natural world, classical precedent and daily experience all confirm that position:

> Did they [Euphues' parents] not remember that which no man ought to forget, that the tender youth of a child is like the tempering of new wax, apt to receive any form? He that will carry a bull with Milo must use to carry him a calf also, he that coveteth to have a straight tree must not bow him being a twig. The potter fashioneth his clay when it is soft, and the sparrow is taught to come when he is young. As, therefore, the iron being hot receiveth any form with the stroke of the hammer, and keepeth it being cold for ever, so the tender wit of a child, if with diligence it be instructed in youth, will with industry use those qualities in his age. (p. 35)

Unanswerable as this argument first appears, it is firmly rejected by Euphues, who in his turn co-opts the natural world to the support of his view:

> You bewray your own weakness in thinking that nature may anyways be altered by education; and as you have examples to confirm your pretence, so I have most evident and infallible arguments to serve for my purpose. It is natural for the vine to spread; the more you seek by art to alter it, the more in the end you shall augment it. It is proper for the palm-tree to mount; the heavier you load it, the higher it sprouteth. Though iron be made soft with fire it returneth to his hardness; though the falcon be reclaimed to the fist she retireth to her haggardness. (p. 39)

Not only do the examples cited run counter to those previously advanced, extending the antithetical structuring of sentences to the larger processes of the narrative as a whole, but the instances themselves evoke an unstable world in which actions lead to paradoxical outcomes and mutation is constantly at work. Thus cutting back a vine merely serves to promote its growth, while a hard substance may be transformed by heating into a malleable material.

Implicit in both the antithetical patterning of the narrative and the ambivalent illustrative phenomena is a 'doubleness'[11] which ultimately informs every aspect of Lyly's work. From the pun which exhibits the 'divers significations'[12] of which the single word is capable, through the balanced speeches articulating alternative positions, to the analogies locating duality and change, the work enforces the paradoxical conjunction of opposites, and the mutability of the human and natural worlds. Euphues, in *The Anatomy of Wit*, for example, expects Lucilla to remind him that

> hot love is soon cold; that the bavin, though it burn bright, is but a blaze; that scalding water, if it stand awhile, turneth almost to ice; that pepper, though it be hot in the mouth, is cold in the maw. (p. 64)

Lucilla's response, moreover, is couched in similar terms, promoting the reader's awareness of a universal equivocality through the insistent repetition of the same complex of ideas:

> What greater trial can I have of thy simplicity and truth than thine own request which desireth a trial? Aye, but in the coldest flint there is hot fire; the bee that hath honey in her mouth hath a sting in her tail; the tree that beareth the sweetest fruit hath a sour sap; yea, the words of men though they seem smooth as oil, yet their hearts are as crooked as the stalk of ivy. (pp. 68–9)

Similar passages, with the same emphasis, occur with equal frequency in *Euphues and His England*. Philautus, seeking to recover the friendship of Euphues, urges him to remember that 'there is no bone so hard but being laid in vinegar it may be wrought, nor ivory so tough but seasoned with zythum it may be engraven' (p. 285), while Euphues retorts that 'tilia hath a sweet rind and a pleasant leaf, but the fruit so bitter that no beast will bite it' (p. 286). Cassander tells Callimachus that 'the breath of the lion engendereth as well the serpent as the ant, and. . . . the self-same dew forceth the earth to yield both the darnel and wheat' (p. 173), only to have his advice rebutted with the observation that it would be folly not 'to cut one's meat with that knife that another hath cut his finger' (p. 178).

Though similar in their deployment of a style that implies in its polish the precise articulation of ideas, while simultaneously eroding semantic exactitude through its ambivalence, *The Anatomy of Wit* and *Euphues and His England* differ in structure. *The Anatomy of Wit* appears at first sight to fall into two distinct parts, the first (the most widely anthologized section of the work) consisting of a narrative dealing with the triangular relationship between Euphues, Philautus and Lucilla, while the second is made up of a warning against the wiles of the female sex, a treatise on the education of youth, a number of moralistic letters, and an encounter between Euphues and an atheist. The narrative section clearly exhibits the unity between style and subject characteristic of Lyly's work. As noted above, the story-line looks back to the love and friendship literature popular throughout Europe during this period, and superficially conforms, in large measure, to the expected pattern. Thus Euphues, having formed a friendship with Philautus, falls in love with Lucilla, the beloved of his friend, deceives him in order to win her affections, is repudiated in turn by Lucilla, repents and is reconciled with the man he betrayed. Though on one level the treatment of the story clearly invites interpretation in terms of the conventional assumptions of a patriarchal Christian society, on another it exhibits the maxim that lies at the heart of Lyly's work (and runs counter to the inculcation of universally accepted truths) that there is nothing 'but that hath his contraries' (p. 43). The progress of the narrative, for example, corresponds in its enactment of reversal to the antithetical structure of the style, while the protagonists conform in their conduct to the 'doubleness' of their world. Thus Euphues, having sought Philautus' friendship, becomes his enemy and rival only to embrace him once again as his friend; Lucilla's affections change from Philautus to Euphues, and from Euphues to Curio; Philautus moves from desiring Euphues' companionship to emphatically repudiating him; and Ferardo progresses from vesting his hopes in his daughter to wishing for her death. Similarly just as the imagery insists that 'in the most curious sepulchre are enclosed rotten bones, that the cypress tree beareth a fair leaf but no fruit, that the estridge carrieth fair feathers but rank flesh' (p. 49), so Euphues appears a faithful friend to Philautus while secretly betraying his trust, Lucilla plays the part of a discreet and honourable woman while encouraging a succession of lovers, and Ferardo feigns a readiness to endorse his daughter's choice of husband while in fact pursuing her marriage to Philautus. The changes undergone by the speakers, together with the oppositions set up both within and between the positions they adopt, robs the propositions they advance in the course of the narrative of their conventional moral force, even the narrator confessing to his partiality (p. 43) and limited understanding (p. 45). The tirade which Euphues delivers against women for their fickleness, for example, which taken out of context might be seen as a straightforward expression of Renaissance misogynism (pp. 83–4), takes on a very different character in the light of the infidelity of the speaker himself and the act of betrayal in which he is engaged. The sequence of reversals instigated by the conflict between love and friendship thus becomes symptomatic rather than exemplary, illustrative not of the inexorable consequences of moral failure but of an ambiguity that invades every aspect of experience and a relentless process of change.

While the deconstruction of Renaissance certainties in the first half of *The Anatomy of Wit* is not difficult to demonstrate, the latter half of the work appears to conform to the pieties of the period, forming an un-problematic coda completing Euphues' development from prodigality to probity and from lover to faithful friend. Though less attractive to the modern reader than the preceding narrative in both substance and tone, the second half of the work is not as straightforwardly didactic as it might seem at first sight. Having declared their undying devotion but simul-taneous unwillingness to defer to one another's wishes, Euphues and Philautus go their separate ways, the latter remaining at the court in Naples and the former returning to Athens to devote himself to the aca-demic life. The series of documents through which the eponymous hero's subsequent career is charted bear witness from one perspective to his growing piety, while sustaining from another the antithetical structuring of the narrative and emphasis on change. Since the reader has been encouraged to regard Euphues and Philautus as in some respects inter-changeable, or as two potentialites of the same personality (in choosing his friend, for example, Euphues looks for a man who will be 'the express image of mine own person' and elects one who will be 'at all times another I', p. 44), the progress of Philautus in the latter half of the work reflects upon that of Euphues himself, constituting a species of alternative career. Thus while Euphues is engaged in a process of intellectual development that leads him upwards towards the divine, Philautus, his alter ego, is moving in a contrary direction, a sequence of letters between Euphues, Livia and Philautus charting his moral descent. The treacherous friend of the first half of the work thus becomes the upholder of Christian piety in the second, while his 'other I' moves from fidelity to vice. At the same time, the various documents recording their progress chart the same see-saw process of reversal that informs the narrative as a whole, contribut-ing to the reduction of conventional certainties to temporary positions or points of view. Euphues, for example, does not simply devote himself to the academic life but undergoes an abrupt transformation in the course of his career, initially dedicating himself to the study of philosophy only to renounce this branch of study as wholly unsuited to the Christian soul, and to turn instead to theology (pp. 120–2). Similarly a committed atheist is converted by Euphues into a would-be martyr for the Christian faith (pp. 123ff.), Livia, once at home in the household of Lucilla, seeks to exchange her position at court for the retired life, while Euphues, having been reunited with Philautus, is threatening to repudiate him once again at the close of the work.

Whereas *The Anatomy of Wit* falls into two distinct but conceptually related halves, *Euphues and His England* constructs a series of frames, the narrative evolving through a process of regression. The dedicatory letter to the Earl of Oxford encourages the reader to view the work not as a sequel, but as an alternative potentiality, 'another face to Euphues, but yet just behind the other, like the image of Janus' (pp. 155–6). Thus although at the close of *The Anatomy of Wit* Euphues had arrived at middle age, having spent ten years studying philosophy and a further unspecified period immersed in divinity, when he arrives in England in the sequel he is still a young man (see p. 190), and Philautus, for all his career at the Emperor's court, is an impressionable youth. Rather than being of noble birth, the friends are now merely gentlemen, while Euphues' 'great patrimony' (p. 32) has dwindled to a bare sufficiency. In other respects, however, the narrative is a continuum, in that Euphues brings his learning and piety with him, and Philautus is tainted by his amatory experiences subsequent to his desertion by Lucilla. The competing perspectives, or alternative lives of the central figures, create a double-faceted framework for a narrative that itself evolves through the narration of tales within tales. Thus before the friends' arrival in England, Euphues narrates the story of Callimachus, which in turn enfolds the tale of the old hermit, both stories inviting the reader to imagine a series of transformations in the physical and mental states of their central figures. Similarly, having arrived at the house of the bee-keeper, Fidus, the friends are told the history of their host, an account which evolves, in part, through further stories in the form of 'questions', including, in the case of Iffida's questioning with Fidus, the extensive speeches of the Magnifico of Siena, a figure in a tale within a tale within a tale (pp. 205ff.). The process of regression at work here unsettles the reader's sense of actuality, the very length of Fidus' story, for example, serving to endow the characters of his narrative with a status comparable with that of many of the persons of the narrative proper. The subject matter of the inset stories, moreover, turns upon a limited number of themes, their overlapping interests affording the reader a variety of perspectives upon a complex of issues, problematizing the process of judgement in which the reader is encouraged to engage. At the same time, the stories (and analagous letters), while superficially didactic and thus unequivocal in tenor, acquire new meanings according to the standpoint of the listener and the context in which they are read. Thus Fidus' tale of his love for Iffida, told as a warning of the life-consuming nature of love (p. 223), is read by Philautus as a counter-history of his experience with Lucilla, signifying the possibility of an ideal amatory relationship (p. 226), while for Euphues its status is doubtful, dependent upon the reliance to be placed on the old man's veracity (p. 224). Similarly, the didactic force of Cassander's tale of his experience, told to warn Callimachus of the corrupting nature of travel, is qualified for the reader by the observations of Euphues, who proposes the possibility of a journey conducted to profitable ends (p. 180), and by the social reclamation of Philautus achieved through his voyage to England.

While the inset narratives contribute to an anatomy, or assemblage of perspectives upon a series of interrelated themes (notably the dangers to which youth is subject, the positive and negative aspects of love, and the nature of courtly life), the experiences of Euphues and Philautus constitute a progression which largely conforms to the traditional pattern of the two major inherited stories to which the work as a whole looks back, viz. the conflict between love and friendship and the tale of the prodigal son. Thus Philautus, like the misguided Euphues of *The Anatomy of Wit*, abuses his friend and surrenders himself to destructive passion, only to be reunited through painful experience with the companion he had repudiated, and reintegrated into the society he had threatened to disrupt. At the same time, his career approximates to that of the prodigal son, in that he arrives in England with a history of wanton behaviour, rapidly surrenders himself to reprehensible courses, brings himself to the point of physical and spiritual ruin, and is redeemed through good advice. Similarly, the career of Euphues appears to fulfil the assumptions of an audience familiar with the didactic materials invoked in the course of the work. Superior to love, and alert to moral danger, Euphues acts as a pious adviser to Philautus throughout, advocating the spiritual rather than the physical, and returning at the close to the life of the mind. The position achieved in the concluding pages of the work, however, fails to conform to audience expectation, the ultimate situation of the two friends deconstructing the moral absolutes implicit in the evolution of the narrative by its subversion of the anticipated outcome. Though Euphues has consistently operated on a higher level of awareness than Philautus, whose ultimate goal is the matrimonial bed, the final position of the friends is not indicative of the former's greater success, and thus of the richer rewards of the pious life. Whereas Philautus is happily integrated through marriage into a benificent society, Euphues is a lonely recluse in some 'uncouth place', 'tormented in body and grieved in mind' (p. 353). The precise cause of his 'cruelly martyred' condition remains, furthermore, uncertain. Grieved at leaving England, he is unable to reconcile himself to his native land, and his mental anguish may be attributed in part to his separation from Philautus and exclusion from a country that conformed to his vision of the ideal state. The closing comments of the narrator, however, invite the reader to place a very different construction on his condition. Declining to trespass further into the private lives of the two friends, the narrator speculates that 'Philautus would not have his life known which he leadeth in marriage, nor Euphues his love descried which he beginneth in solitariness; lest either the one being too kind might be thought to dote, or the other too constant might be judged to be mad' (pp. 353–4)—the concluding question that he poses turning on 'whether Philautus were a better wooer or a husband' and 'whether Euphues were a better lover or a scholar' (p. 354). The clear implication is that the hero is once again in love and that it is he rather than Philautus who ultimately proves the most constant lover. No indication is given of the object of his passion, but his encomium to the Queen in his 'Glass for Europe' invites the supposition that his unrequitable love may constitute a final tribute on the part of the author to Elizabeth herself.[13] The fresh conversion of the central figure from moralist to lover reverberates backwards throughout the work, radically destabilizing the positions advanced. Whereas in the course of the narrative Euphues had occupied a position of moral superiority, affording his pronouncements a particular weight, that status is eroded by his final transformation, encouraging the reconsideration of alternative standpoints, and lending fresh force to the doubts expressed by the narrator on the validity of the stances he adopts (e.g. on the superiority of Platonic to physical love, see pp. 293ff.). At the same time, the reversal of his position serves to sustain to the very last the emphasis on antithetical change, endowing the work with a circularity that militates against any sense of finality on either the narrative or conceptual levels.

The destabilization of meaning arising from the style and structure of the work is further promoted by the deployment of a range of source materials familiar to the sixteenth-century reader. Substantial sections of both *The Anatomy of Wit* and *Euphues and His England* are either direct translations of Latin texts or are borrowed (sometimes with minimal alteration) from contemporary writers. In *The Anatomy of Wit*, for example, Euphues' 'Cooling Card for Philautus' is heavily dependent upon Ovid's *Remedia amoris*, 'Euphues and His Ephebus' is adapted from Plutarch's *De educatione puerorum*, and 'Euphues to Botonio to take his exile Patiently' is abridged from the same author's *De exilio*—and this list is by no means exhaustive. Similarly, in *Euphues and His England*, the initial description of Britain is borrowed from Caesar's *Gallic Wars*, Fidus' account of the commonwealth of bees is from Pliny's *Historia naturalis*, and a large part of Euphues' 'Glass for Europe' is taken from William Harrison's 'Description of England', published in Holinshed's *Chronicle* (1577).[14] The name and character of Lyly's hero have their origins in Ascham's *The Schoolmaster* (1570), while the exemplary analogies which form such a distinctive feature of Lyly's style are derived from Pliny's *Historia naturalis*, or Erasmus' *Similia* and *Adagia*. A host of classical writers are invoked in the course of the work, Ovid's influence, in particular, being evident in both the Latin encomium to Elizabeth (see Appendix, pp. 355ff.) and the pervasive emphasis on change. Renaissance works are also pressed into service for narrative detail. Rebuking Philautus for his unjustified treatment of him, for example, Euphues refers him to Stephen Gosson's *Ephemerides of Phialo* (1579), and later reflects on the happiness of the English people in terms that look back to Abraham Fleming's version of Aelian's *Varia historia* (1576).

Whereas for the modern reader an extensive dependence upon the work of others smacks of plagiarism and a want of originality, for the cultivated Elizabethan a reliance on reputable sources is in line with a theory of creativity rooted in the concept of imitation.[15] Lyly does not, however, merely rework his schoolroom models in the manner endorsed by contemporary practice. The materials he brings together carry with them very different cultural assumptions, their juxtaposition instigating a species of trans-historical dialogue, contributing to the 'anatomy' or assemblage of perspectives with which the work as a whole is engaged, and thus encouraging the interrogation of the inherited texts. Ovid's views on the nature of women, for example, enunciated by the disillusioned Euphues in his 'Cooling Card', are immediately qualified by the accompanying letter to 'The Grave Matrons and Honest Maidens of Italy', which draws on Plutarch's *De mulierum virtutibus*, and later repudiated as the product of limited experience after Euphues' encounter with the Elizabethan state, defined through Harrison's 'Description of England' and celebrated in a poem indebted to Ovid's *Heroides* (see p. 355). Similarly, Pliny's harmonious commonwealth of bees, appropriated by Fidus and deployed as a metaphor for Elizabethan England (pp. 193ff.), sits uneasily beside the same speaker's 'Canterbury Tale' of the dangers of the Lion's den (p. 192), and the awareness Philautus exhibits of the Machiavellian realities of Renaissance political institutions (p. 252).

While qualifying the status of his co-opted texts through a swirl of competing voices, and the insistent 'doubleness' of the context into which they are transposed, Lyly simultaneously widens the scope of his narrative through the range of materials on which he draws. The Britain celebrated in *Euphues and His England*, for example, is first described by Euphues through the eyes of Julius Caesar, whose land inhabited by a people accustomed to paint their bodies with woad is sharply at odds with the sophisticated society described in Euphues' 'Glass for Europe', derived, as noted above, from Harrison's 'Description of England'. Two historical periods thus co-exist in the reader's mind (cf. the simultaneous youthfulness and maturity of the central figure), and this fusion of ages and cultures is characteristic of both parts of the work. Thus, whereas on one level *Euphues and His England* celebrates the new political era instigated by the reign of Elizabeth, on another it evokes a world in which fabulous creatures, classical deities, Old Testament patriarchs, Greek artists and philosophers, Roman soldiers and humanist scholars all co-exist, and in which the court of Alexander is as immediate as that of Henry VIII. The see-saw process of change that the narrative enacts thus emerges as a constant applicable to every age, while the intermeshing of times and places, like the texts within texts, contributes to the evocation of a pervasive ambivalence. Rather than functioning as the spokesmen for ultimate truths, Lyly's 'authorities' thus serve, paradoxically, to problematize the issues raised in the course of the work, universalizing the contention that 'he that seeketh the depth of knowledge is as it were in a labyrinth, in the which the further he goeth, the further he is from the end' (p. 122).

Though for the twenty-first-century reader the reliance upon now un-
familiar secondary material represents a further barrier to be overcome
in engaging with a work already difficult of access by virtue of its style,
for those to whom the two parts of *Euphues* were initially directed, the
author's eclecticism constituted an aspect of his topicality and thus of his
appeal. The commonplace book, in which quotations on a number of subjects were assembled from the compiler's reading to provide a reference
book for private use, was a popular instrument of self-improvement in
the Renaissance, and *The Anatomy of Wit* and *Euphues and His England*
might be viewed on one level as a commonplace book on a grand scale.
The topics around which views are assembled reflect many of the concerns of the second half of the sixteenth century, for example the
anxieties surrounding the acquisition of knowledge, the role of the
intelligentsia in a hierachical society, and the dangers of a divorce between
acuity and piety (cf. Marlowe's *Dr Faustus*).[16] The related issues of the
education of the young, the proper conduct of a gentleman and the poten-
tially destructive nature of sexual love are all the subject of contemporary debate (cf. Ascham's *The Schoolmaster*, Castiglione's *Il cortegiano*,
translated into English in 1561, and Brooke's *Romeus and Juliet*), while
in its celebration of Elizabeth as ruler, centre of patronage, and embodiment of the virtues of the female sex, the work intersects with a host
of contemporary texts (cf. Spenser's *The Faerie Queene*). Moreover, the
classical writers, philosophers and historical figures to whom Lyly refers,
though remote from a twenty-first-century audience, were as familiar to
a classically educated Elizabethan reader as Shakespeare, Bacon and
Raleigh today, while the easy exchange between Christianity and
Greek and Roman mythology is characteristic not merely of Lyly but of
Renaissance writers as a whole. The world that *Euphues* evokes in which
Stephen Gosson, Sir Thomas North and Erasmus function side-by-side
with Pliny and Homer, Xerxes and Alexander, Jezebel and Isaiah constitutes a reflection of the intellectual landscape of an era, exhibiting the
mental furniture with which the cultured Elizabethan was equipped and
thus, paradoxically, affording access for the modern reader, through its
superficially alienating allusiveness, to the consciousness of an age. From
the very outset Lyly stresses the contemporaneity of his work (p. 30), and
the field of reference is at one with a topicality signalled by allusions to
current events (e.g. a possible attempt on the life of the ambassador of
the Duke of Anjou, p. 335), references to contemporary figures (e.g. Lord
Burghley, pp. 327–8) and expressions of concern over the future of the
throne (p. 339).

The multifacetedness promoted by the style, structure and kaleido-
scopic assemblage of Renaissance concerns is heightened by an ambiguity of tone. While the subjects addressed all turn, fundamentally, upon
the serious issue of human conduct in the context of a universe in which
heaven and hell are ultimate realities, the mode in which the topics are

treated elicits amusement, the discrepancy between style and subject complicating the reader's response. The self-deprecatory stance and elaborate disclaimers of the introductory epistles (cf. the author's professed readiness to see his book turned to wrapping paper, or the assertion that he would prefer it to lie 'shut in a lady's casket [rather] than open in a scholar's study', pp. 30 and 162) militate against a high moral tone, while the insistent word-play invites both admiration of and delight in the author's linguistic dexterity even at moments of grave significance for the persons of the narrative. The pun with which Lucilla determines to renounce Philautus for Euphues, for example ('It is not his great manors but thy good manners that shall make my marriage', p. 70), or the antithetically balanced clauses through which Ferardo laments the unnaturalness of his child (pp. 85–6), unite intellectual pleasure with moral disapproval, encouraging enjoyment of that ambiguous 'wit' explored in the course of the work. The context in which the conventional pieties are located, moreover, frequently robs them of their full moral force. Euphues' encomium on friendship, for example, in *The Anatomy of Wit* (p. 44) is subverted by his subsequent betrayal of Philautus, while his instructive tale of the hermit in *Euphues and His England* is rendered ludicrous by the fact that as he is speaking Philautus is being seasick over the side of the ship (p. 182). The exhibition of the dangerous potential of Philautus' obsession with Camilla is undercut by the humorous review of love charms with which Psellus deflects him from his malign designs (pp. 257ff.), while the elevated Platonic love advocated by Euphues is diminished by the doubts of the narrator, and his arch expectation that his readers will not endorse his hero's views (p. 296). The situations engineered in the course of the narrative also generate an ambiguous response. The empty expostulations of Philautus in *The Anatomy of Wit* when betrayed by both his lover and his friend (pp. 77–8), the absurdity of his socially dangerous attempts to woo Camilla in *Euphues and His England*, and his surliness when being instructed by Euphues (e.g. p. 182), all serve to endow the work with a lightness of tone more in keeping with a novella than a serious moral tract. Even the euphuistic mode is satirized in Camilla's objection to Philautus' highly mannered courtship, which includes the use of a typically Lylian analogy involving a dove without a gall (p. 249). In short, just as the persons of the narrative and the natural phenonema of the universe that Lyly creates embody contrasting potentialities, so the work as a whole is both a serious disquisition on moral conduct and a light-hearted jeu d'esprit, capable of yielding different meanings according to the perspective from which it is viewed.

Euphues' response to Lucilla's highly ambiguous reception of his protestation of love, 'you have given unto me a true love's knot wrought of changeable silk' (p. 69), might thus be applied to *Euphues* itself, and the afterlife of the work bears witness to its capacity to yield 'divers significations'. Marginal comments in early editions testify to its edifying character and serious moral purport for some contemporary readers, and such passages as the encounter between Euphues and Atheos were no doubt influential in securing Lyly a commission from the Anglican bishops to enter the Martin Marprelate controversy with *Pappe with an Hatchet* (1589), a pamphlet designed to counter a series of presbyterian tracts. At the same time, it was patently not the improving character of the work that persuaded the cultured, brilliant and unstable Earl of Oxford that its author was an appropriate person to install as co-partner in the first Blackfriars theatre with a view to producing elegant plays for performance at court. Lyly's celebration of Elizabeth and English upper-class society patently constituted a bid for aristocratic rather than ecclesiastical patronage, and the testimony of Lyly's first editor (see p. 2) is indicative of his success in securing the attention of the courtly élite. Lyly's metamorphosis from prose writer to dramatist is not, furthermore, as unexpected as it might superficially appear. Just as the persons and properties of the universe he creates contain the potential to become their opposite, so *Euphues* is instinct with the dramatic potential later to be realized at the first Blackfriars theatre and the playhouse at St Paul's. Both *The Anatomy of Wit* and *Euphues and His England* largely consist of speeches, which clearly look forward to the debates and soliloquies of the plays (cf. *Campaspe*, II.ii.34–130 and III.v.13–68), while Lyly's capacity to write witty dialogue is evident in, for example, the courtship of Fidus and Iffida (pp. 202ff.), Philautus' attempts to woo Camilla (e.g. pp. 247ff.) or the quarrel between Euphues and Philautus (pp. 234ff.) The balanced oppositions of the euphuistic mode invite division between speakers, the opening scene of Lyly's first play, *Campaspe* (1583), exhibiting the ease of the transfer from the printed page to the spoken word:

Parmenio: Madam, you need not doubt; it is Alexander that is the conqueror.
Timoclea: Alexander hath overcome, not conquered.
Parmenio: To bring all under his subjection is to conquer.
Timoclea: He cannot subdue that which is divine.
Parmenio: Thebes was not.
Timoclea: Virtue is.

(I.i.49–55)[17]

The analogies that form a principal feature of Lyly's style also lend themselves to visual representation. The process of literalization at work in *Euphues and His England*, with the realization of the proverb, in the companionable habits of the old hermit's attendants, that it is a wily mouse that can sleep in a cat's ear (p. 171), is extended in the plays that follow, with stage properties embodying opposition, duality and change. The contrasting value systems of *Campaspe*, for example, are enforced by the on-stage juxtaposition of Diogenes' tub, representative of a life of privation, and Apelles' workshop, emblematic of the celebration of the senses; the tree that offers a sanctuary from the heat of the sun for the title figure of *Gallathea* is the site of the virgin sacrifice that threatens her life; while a small heap of pebbles in the opening scene of the same play denotes the metamorphoses at work in every aspect of the play world in that it was once a stately temple. The historical figures, philosophers and classical deities invoked in *Euphues* in support of intellectual positions emerge to people the stage in *Campaspe* (Alexander, Apelles and Diogenes), *Sappho and Phao* (Venus and Cupid), *Gallathea* (Neptune and Diana) etc., confronting the issues explored in the prose works (e.g. the conduct of the monarch, the pleasures and dangers of sexual passion, and the conflict between love and chastity). The dramatis personae, moreover, exhibit that fusion of opposite potentialities and capacity for change that distinguishes their prose progenitors. Just as Euphues repudiates passion in favour of the life of the mind, so Alexander, in *Campaspe*, renounces war and embraces love, only to reverse that decision at the close, the terms in which he does so conveying the possibility that he might once again become a lover (cf. Euphues' final position). Similarly the central figure of *Gallathea*, Lyly's most complex composition, having been disguised as a youth by her father, functions as both man and maiden for the duration of the play, and finally leaves the stage either to be changed into a man at the will of the gods, or to marry another woman transformed into masculine shape. The implied circularity of *Euphues* and development away from rather than towards intellectual closure (cf. 'he that seeketh the depth of knowledge is as it were in a labyrinth, in the which the further he goeth, the further he is from the end', p. 122) is also an increasingly self-conscious feature of the plays. The Epilogue to *Sappho and Phao*, for example, asserts the play's lack of finality in terms that might well be applied to *Euphues* itself:

> They that tread in a maze walk oftentimes in one path, and at the last come out where they entered in. We fear we have led you all this while in a labyrinth of conceits, divers times hearing one device, and have now brought you to an end where we first began. (lines 1–5)[18]

It is the self-conscious evasiveness of Lylian drama, however, that forges, perhaps, the strongest link between the dramatic and non-dramatic work. Just as the narrator of the two parts of *Euphues* constantly invites his readers to exercise their judgement, and hence to impose a meaning on the material he presents (e.g. pp. 45 and 296), so the Prologues and Epilogues with which the comedies are framed insist upon the fluidity of the dramatic spectacle, and the role of the spectator in determining its significance. The Prologue at Court, in *Campaspe*, for example, announces that

> whatsoever we present, we wish it may be thought the dancing of Agrippa his shadows, who, in the moment they were seen, were of any shape one would conceive (lines 13–16)

while the Epilogue at the Blackfriars transfers the process of signification from the text and its performers to the members of the audience:

Our exercises must be as your judgement is, resembling water, which is always of the same colour into what it runneth. (lines 5-7)

The statements imply that the corpus will inevitably yield up different meanings in the context of different understandings, a position enforcing the malleability of the material and the remoulding that it permits. The Epilogue at Court to *Campaspe* likens the artefact to the wax torches illuminating the playing space, affirming that it lies with the spectator (in the original context the Queen) to shape the work into 'doves or vultures, roses or nettles' (19-20). The terms Lyly employs here look back to the letter 'To the Gentlemen Readers' prefacing *Euphues and His England*, in which the writer encourages his audience to utilize his work, rather than to engage with it as a whole, culling from it those parts most relevant to their own concerns:

Lovers when they come into a garden, some gather nettles, some roses, one thyme, another sage, and everyone that for his lady's favour that she favoureth; insomuch as there is no weed almost but it is worn. If you, Gentlemen, do the like in reading, I shall be sure all my discourses shall be regarded. (p. 165)

The invitation to select and recreate extended by Lyly in both his prose and dramatic works was one to which his contemporaries were quick to respond. Just as Lyly himself appropriated the two parts of *Euphues* to his new dramatic career, so *The Anatomy of Wit* and *Euphues and His England* enjoyed an extended afterlife in the imaginations of the reading public and the works of fellow writers. As Edward Blount indicates in the prefatory material to his collected edition of the plays (see p. 2 above), the highly polished prose style became the model for courtly discourse, while the euphuistic mode, the names of the central characters and the concerns explored in the two parts of the work lived on in a host of sixteenth-century compositions designed to capitalize on Lyly's success. Melbancke's *Philotimus: The War Betwixt Nature and Fortune* (1583), Greene's *The Mirror of Modesty* (1584) and his later *Euphues, His Censure of Philautus* (1587), Lodge's *Rosalynde*, with its elaborate subtitle, *Euphues' Golden Legacy: found after his death in his cell at Silexedra, bequeathed to Philautus' sons nursed up with their father in England* (1590), all bear witness to the impact of *Euphues* on the imagination of Lyly's contemporaries and the multifacetedness that permitted its reworking. It was not merely Elizabethan prose, however, that bore the imprint of Lyly's work. The metamorphosis of *Euphues* into the court comedies opened a fresh channel by which *The Anatomy of Wit* and *Euphues and His England* informed the literature of the age. Just as the style, structure and content of the two parts of the work shaped the plays that Lyly produced for the first Blackfriars, so his comedies, in turn, were adapted by later dramatists writing for the public rather than the private stage. The elaborate parallelism of the two parts of *Euphues*, which gave

rise to the highly stylized plotting of the plays, fed into the work of
Shakespeare (cf. *Gallathea* III.i and *Love's Labour's Lost* IV.iii), while the
pervasive 'doubleness' that evolved into the evasive courtships, disguised
heroines and punning wit of the dramas lived on in the comedies of
Greene and Shakespeare, works considerably removed from the world
of theological polemic into which, in the eyes of the bishops, Lyly lent
himself to recruitment.

The adaptability of the Lylian corpus and variety of interpretations of
which it proved capable was matched by the diversity of opinions on its
success. The letter to 'My Very Good Friends the Gentlemen Scholars of
Oxford' in the second edition of *The Anatomy of Wit* (pp. 151ff.), and
the dedication to *Euphues and His England* (pp. 155ff.), are indicative of
the hostile reception accorded in some quarters to the content of the work,
and Gabriel Harvey was at pains to assert of the style, in a passage written
in 1589, that 'the finest wits prefer the loosest period in Master Ascham
or Sir Philip Sidney before the tricksiest page in *Euphues*'.[19] Other contemporaries, by contrast, were more favourable in their estimation. Lodge
celebrated Lyly's 'facility in discourse', classing him (with Spenser) among
those 'divine wits' that the period had produced, while for William Webbe
his achievement warranted comparison with that of the foremost classical writers:

> I think there is none that will gainsay but that Master John Lyly hath
> deserved most high commendations. . . . Whose works, surely in respect of
> his singular eloquence and brave composition of apt words and sentences,
> let the learned examine and make trial thereof through all the parts of
> rhetoric, in fit phrases, in pithy sentences, in gallant tropes, in flowing
> speech, in plain sense; and surely in my judgement I think he will yield
> him that verdict which Quintillian giveth of both the best orators, Demos-
> thenes and Tully, that from the one nothing may be taken away, to the
> other nothing may be added.[20]

Both positive and negative testimonies bear witness to Lyly's promi-
nence in the last quarter of the sixteenth century, and the imperative for
contemporary writers to engage with his work. The numerous parodies,[21]
often seen as confirming his current marginality, in fact bear witness to
the impact of *Euphues* on the imagination of the reading public, and the
universal familiarity with its style. Though the euphuistic mode itself,
moreover, ceased to be fashionable by the turn of the century, the works
that had given the term to the language continued to appear on the book
stalls, finding a new readership among the middle classes, rather than
the intelligentsia and cultured elite towards whom they were initially
directed.[22] Whether constructed as an index of vacuity (cf. Marston's
parody of euphuism in *Antonio and Mellida*, V.ii.117–25), as misogynis-
tic (cf. Joseph Swetnam's *Arraignment of Lewd, Idle, Froward and
Unconstant Women*, 1615), or a measure of creativity (cf. Ben Jonson's
prefatory poem to the First Folio of Shakespeare, 1623), the Lylian corpus

remained in the public mind into the early years of the new century, before suffering the neglect so poignantly lamented by the first editor of his plays.[23]

For the twenty-first-century reader *Euphues* continues to exhibit that 'doubleness' that lies at the heart of Lyly's achievement. On the one hand it is deeply enmeshed in the texts, tastes and aspirations of an age, affording a modern audience a means of access to a now-distant period of English cultural history. On the other hand, by contrast, the work is striking in its modernity, its radical destabilization of meaning speaking directly to contemporary concerns. The relentless word-play, the puns and homophones yoking disparate areas of experience, the syllabic repetition and half-rhymes challenging the relationship between signifier and signified, the ambiguity promoted by parison, isocolon and paromoion all contribute for the modern reader to an 'anatomy of wit' far more disturbing in its implications than the dangerous divorce of intelligence from piety that forms the ostensible subject of the work.

NOTES

1 *Six Court Comedies. . . . by the only rare poet of that time, the witty, comical, facetiously-quick and unparalleled John Lyly.* Spelling and punctuation have been modernized.
2 The seasons vary in different editions according to the month of publication. The first edition of 1578 reads 'the book that at Christmas. . . . at Easter to be broken'.
3 For the evidence to support this supposition, see G. K. Hunter, *John Lyly: The Humanist as Courtier* (London, 1962), pp. 37–8.
4 Possibly a distant relation on his mother's side: see Hunter, p. 46.
5 He was also awarded an M.A. by Cambridge (by incorporation) in 1579.
6 Peele (b. 1556), Greene (b. 1558), Marlowe (b. 1564), Nashe (b. 1567).
7 Though Oxford's patronage of Lyly was no doubt motivated by the success of the *Anatomy of Wit*, it may also have been a product of the influence of Burghley (see note 4 above), who was Oxford's father-in-law.
8 See Hunter, p. 77.
9 For a full account of the origins of euphuism see Morris William Croll and Harry Clemons (eds), *Euphues: The Anatomy of Wit / Euphues and His England* (London, 1916), pp. xv–lxiv, and Hunter, pp. 260–80.
10 For an account of the pervasiveness of this motif in sixteenth-century literature see Leah Scragg, *Shakespeare's Alternative Tales* (London, 1996), pp. 6ff.
11 For a full examination of the range of Lyly's antithetical devices, see Jonas Barish, 'The Prose Style of John Lyly', *English Literary History*, 23 (1956), pp. 14–35, from which the term 'doubleness' is derived.
12 The phrase occurs in *Campaspe* (III.ii.24–5) in the context of an exhibition of the 'doubleness' of words.
13 This interpretation is supported by a number of Lyly's plays in which the unrequitable love between a queen and a person of humble birth is a central motif (cf. *Sappho and Phao, Endymion*).
14 For works giving more detailed information on Lyly's sources see 'Further reading', pp. 23–4.
15 For an account of Renaissance attitudes to the creative process see Leah Scragg, *Shakespeare's Mouldy Tales* (London, 1992).
16 For the problems of self-definition experienced by the intelligentsia in the late sixteenth century see Hunter, pp. 1–35.

17 All references to Lyly's plays are to Leah Scragg (ed.), *John Lyly: Selected Prose and Dramatic Work* (Manchester, 1997), unless otherwise stated.

18 Quoted from George K. Hunter and David Bevington (eds), *Campaspe: Sappho and Phao* (Revels Plays, Manchester, 1991).

19 *Advertisement to Pap-Hatchet*. For a more extensive quotation see R. W. Bond (ed.), *The Complete Works of John Lyly*, 3 vols (Oxford, 1902), I, p. 80.

20 The passages from Lodge (*Wit's Misery and World's Madness*, 1596) and Webbe (*A Discourse of English Poetry*, 1586) are quoted from Edward Arber (ed.), *John Lyly: 'Euphues the Anatomy of Wit': 'Euphues and His England'* (London, 1868), pp. 13–16. Spelling and punctuation have been modernized for the purposes of the present edition.

21 See, for example, Shakespeare's *I Henry IV*, II.iv.393ff.

22 See Hunter, pp. 284–5.

23 The work enjoyed a fresh afterlife in the early years of the following century when an abridged version of *The Anatomy of Wit* was published in 1716 under the title of *Euphues and Lucilla: The False Friend and the Inconstant Mistress* and proved sufficiently popular to be republished in 1718.

NOTE ON THE TEXTS

Of the two parts of *Euphues*, the first (*The Anatomy of Wit*) is the more complicated in terms of its textual history. The first edition, published in December 1578, was swiftly followed by a second in the summer of 1579, and by a third at the end of the same year. The second edition differed significantly from the first, in that the narrative section was substantially longer, and it was this text that became the basis for subsequent sixteenth- and early seventeenth-century editions. Given that Elizabethan perceptions of the work were largely shaped by this version of the text, it is upon this edition, rather than that of 1578, that the first of the two items in the present volume is based. The single extant copy of the second edition, preserved in the library of Trinity College, Cambridge, is however, defective, in that it lacks the final leaf, and Euphues' last letter to Livia and the final observations of the narrator (pp. 147ff.) are consequently drawn from a copy of the third edition in the Bodleian Library, Oxford. The editorial position is further complicated by the letter 'To My Very Good Friends the Gentlemen Scholars of Oxford', introduced by Lyly into the second edition in response to the hostile reception accorded to his work by some members of the academic community. The letter appears with the prefatory material in the second edition, but is transferred in the third to the end of the book. Though later editions revert to the order of the Trinity text, the present edition follows the Bodleian copy, permitting the letter to form a link between the two parts of the work, and bringing it closer to the controversial matters with which it deals.

Euphues and His England was first published in 1580, its popularity leading to the appearance of two further editions in the same year. Only one perfect copy of the first edition is known to have survived, that in the Pforzheimer Library, Harry Ransom Humanities Research Center, University of Texas at Austin, and it is consequently upon that copy that the present edition is based – though the 'Morley' copy (formerly in Hampstead Public Library and now in Holborn Local History Library, London) has also been consulted.

With the minor exceptions noted above, the texts in this volume are derived exclusively from the earliest witnesses of the two works in their final form, i.e. the initial expanded version of *The Anatomy of Wit* (summer 1579) and the first edition of *Euphues and His England* (1580). Spelling and punctuation have been modernized, however, contractions expanded and obvious printing errors silently corrected. Paragraphing has been brought into conformity with current usage and consistency imposed upon the numerous proper names, which appear throughout in their modern forms (except in those instances where Latinization is a self-conscious feature of the text). The few instances of textual corruption are indicated by square brackets, and almost all emendations are drawn from later editions, the rare exceptions being signalled in the notes. The text thus differs significantly from that of both the seminal editions to which it inevitably looks back. On the one hand, unlike R. W. Bond's old-spelling *The Complete Works of John Lyly* (Oxford,

1902), it conforms to modern conventions, while on the other it departs from Morris William Croll and Harry Clemons's modern-spelling *Euphues: The Anatomy of Wit / Euphues and His England* (London, 1916), in that it reflects a single state of the two works. The nature of the annotation also differs from that of the two earlier editions. Rather than focusing upon the location of source material, the notes are largely explanatory, and are designed for the assistance of a reader lacking the classical and biblical knowledge assumed in the past as the cultural norm.

Though directed towards a twenty-first-century, rather than an early twentieth-century, readership (most notably, perhaps, in its layout with the typographical signalling of narrative levels and texts within texts), the present edition is, nevertheless, heavily indebted to its monumental predecessors. All readings have been checked against those of the two earlier major editions, and the notes to those works have informed the decisions reached at every stage. Though direct indebtedness is acknowleged, it would be impossible to record every instance at which a mark of punctuation or a reading of a particular word has been inspired by a previous editorial choice.

FURTHER READING

The study of Lyly in the modern period is founded upon three major early twentieth-century editorial and biographical works. R. Warwick Bond's old spelling edition, *The Complete Works of John Lyly* (3 vols, Oxford, 1902), remains the starting point for the study of the textual history of both the items in the present volume, and though the critical material is now largely outdated, the notes continue to be of value, particularly in relation to the study of Lyly's sources. The same decade that witnessed the appearance of Bond's edition saw the publication of Albert Feuillerat, *John Lyly: Contribution à l'histoire de la Renaissance en Angleterre* (Cambridge University Press, 1910), a monumental study that has yet to be superseded, drawing together all the materials pertinent to Lyly's life. The third major work of the period, Morris William Croll and Harry Clemons (eds), *Euphues: The Anatomy of Wit / Euphues and His England* (London, 1916), was the only modern-spelling edition of the two parts of *Euphues* to be published in the course of the twentieth century, and has consequently played a major part in shaping modern perceptions of the work. The notes, primarily concerned with Lyly's sources, and the introduction on the euphuistic mode, constitute a mine of information for those embarking upon the study of Lyly's prose.

Though Bond, Feuillerat, and Croll and Clemons may be said to have redefined Lylian studies in the early years of the twentieth century, they were not the only scholars working in the field. The degree of interest in Lyly's work at that period is evidenced by Hendrik de Vocht, *De invloed van Erasmus op de Englesche tooneelliteratur der XVIe en XVIIe eeuwen* (Ghent, 1908), exhibiting Lyly's indebtedness to Erasmus, and John Dover Wilson, *John Lyly* (Cambridge, 1905), an attempt to establish Lyly's importance to the development of English prose and the history of the drama. Less well known but more pertinent to modern perceptions of Lyly's work was a lecture delivered in Manchester, England, by the Earl of Crawford and Balcarres, subsequently published in the *Bulletin of the John Rylands Library*, 8 (1924), pp. 312–44. Though rooted (like John Dover Wilson's book) in now outdated critical positions, the article is significant in its emphasis on the precision of Lyly's prose and on the structural skills that distinguish the work.

Though in the early decades of the twentieth century Lyly appeared to have been rescued from the oblivion lamented by the first editor of his plays (see p. 1), no further significant advance took place in Lylian studies for a considerable number of years, and it was not until the appearance of an article by Jonas A. Barish, 'The Prose Style of John Lyly', *English Literary History*, 23 (1956), pp. 14–35, that the critical reassessment of Lyly's work was seriously resumed. Barish argues that an essential relationship exists between the style and vision of Lyly's work, and it is this perception that lies at the core of the re-evaluation of the Lylian corpus that took place in the latter half of the twentieth century. The most significant work of this period, and essential reading for any student of Lyly, is G. K. Hunter, *John Lyly: The Humanist as Courtier* (London, 1962), which reconsiders the life and work in the context of the humanist movement, and argues for the structural complexity of the plays. A second major study, Peter Saccio, *The Court Comedies of John Lyly: A Study in Allegorical Dramaturgy* (Princeton, 1969), remains the most detailed and perceptive analysis of the dramatic corpus that has so far appeared, emphasizing the insistent ambiguity of the writer's vision. The new impetus in Lylian scholarship proved, however, short-lived. A further book, Joseph Houppert, *John Lyly* (Boston, 1975), though including a useful bibliography, failed to build upon the work of previous scholars, and a lack of modern editions, with the exception of Merritt Lawlis (ed.), *Elizabethan Prose Fiction* (Indianapolis, 1967), and Anne B. Lancashire (ed.), *'Gallathea' and 'Midas'* (University of Nebraska, 1969), made the work inaccessible for the majority of students.

The closing years of the century witnessed a fresh dawn of interest in Lyly's work and a further attempt to demonstrate its centrality to the understanding of the English literary Renaissance. A number of new editions of the plays have been important in this respect. Carter A. Daniel (ed.), *The Plays of John Lyly* (London and Toronto, 1988), a modern-spelling edition of the plays with minimal annotation, has helped to make the work more readily available, while G. K. Hunter and David Bevington (eds), *Campaspe: Sappho and Phao* (Revels Plays, Manchester, 1991, revised 1999), David Bevington (ed.), *Endymion* (Revels Plays, Manchester, 1996) and G. K. Hunter and David Bevington (eds), *Galatea and Midas* (Revels Plays, Manchester, 2000) bring to bear a wealth of information to contextualize and elucidate the work. The prose has lagged behind the drama in the degree of editorial attention it has received. My own *John Lyly: Selected Prose and Dramatic Work* (Manchester, 1997), however, includes a modern-spelling edition of the narrative section of the 1578 version of *The Anatomy of Wit*, and the same portion of the 1579 version is now available in Paul Salzman, *An Anthology of Elizabethan Prose* (World's Classics, Oxford, 1987), which also has a helpful bibliography. (An old-spelling edition of the 1578 text may be found in J. Winny, *The Descent of Euphues*, Cambridge, 1957.) No edition of *Euphues and His England* other than that in the present volume has appeared since Croll and Clemons in 1916, but a complete concordance to both parts of *Euphues* was published by Harald Mittermann and Herbert Schendl in 1984 (The Elizabethan Concordance Series, vol. 2, Hildesheim).

Among recent critical contributions to Lylian studies, Michael Pincombe, *The Plays of John Lyly: Eros and Eliza* (Manchester and New York, 1996), has a chapter on *Euphues* in relation to Lyly's life, while my own 'John Lyly', *Dictionary of Literary Biography*, 62 (ed. Fredson Bowers, Detroit, 1987), pp. 196–211, offers an introduction to Lyly's life and work. A spectrum of views on the two parts of *Euphues* may be gained from Shimon Sandbank, 'Euphuistic Symmetry and the Image', *Studies in English Literature*, 11 (1971), pp. 1–13; Theodore L. Steinberg, 'The Anatomy of *Euphues*', *Studies in English Literature*, 17 (1977), pp. 27–38; Raymond Stephanson, 'John Lyly's Prose Fiction: Irony, Humour and Anti-Humanism', *English Literary Renaissance*, 11 (1981), pp. 3–21; and Richard A. McCabe, 'Wit, Eloquence, and Wisdom in *Euphues*', *Studies in Philology*, 81 (1984), pp. 299–324. Arthur Kinney's *Humanist Poetics: Thought, Rhetoric and Fiction in Sixteenth-century England* (Amherst, 1986) is also valuable in locating the works in their cultural context.

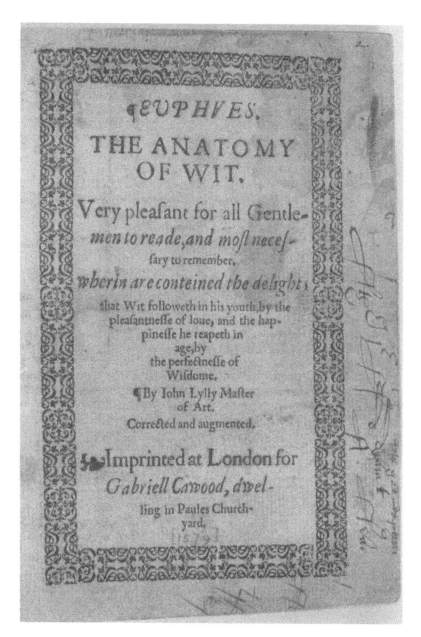

¶EVPHVES.

THE ANATOMY
OF WIT.

Very pleasant for all Gentlemen to reade, and most necef-
sary to remember,

wherin are conteined the delight,
that Wit followeth in his youth,by the
pleasantnesse of loue, and the hap-
pinesse he reapeth in
age,by
the perfectnesse of
Wisdome,

¶By Iohn Lylly Master
of Art.

Corrected and augmented,

Imprinted at London for
Gabriell Cawood, dwel-
ling in Paules Church-
yard,
1579

Title-page of *Euphues: The Anatomy of Wit* (1579)
Trinity College Library, Cambridge (classmark VI.11.16[2])

EUPHUES
THE ANATOMY OF WIT

TO THE RIGHT HONOURABLE MY VERY
GOOD LORD AND MASTER SIR WILLIAM
WEST, KNIGHT, LORD DELAWARE,
JOHN LYLY WISHETH LONG LIFE
WITH INCREASE OF HONOUR[1]

Parrhasius, drawing the counterfeit[2] of Helen, Right Honourable, made the attire of her head loose; who, being demanded why he did so, he answered she was loose.[3] Vulcan was painted curiously, yet with a polt foot;[4] Leda cunningly, yet with her black hair.[5] Alexander, having a scar in his cheek held his finger upon it that Apelles[6] might not paint it. Apelles painted him with his finger cleaving to his face. 'Why,' quoth Alexander, 'I laid my finger on my scar because I would not have thee see it.' 'Yea,' said Apelles, 'and I drew it there because none else should perceive it, for if thy finger had been away either thy scar would have been seen or my art misliked.' Whereby I gather that in all perfect works as well the fault as the face is to be shown. The fairest leopard is made with his spots, the finest cloth with his list,[7] the smoothest shoe with his last.[8] Seeing then that in every counterfeit as well the blemish as the beauty is coloured,[9] I hope I shall not incur the displeasure of the wise in that in the discourse of Euphues[10] I have as well touched the vanities of his love as the virtues of his life. The Persians, who above all their kings most honoured Cyrus,[11] caused him to be engraven as well with his hooked nose

---

1 *TO THE RIGHT HONOURABLE ... HONOUR*] The terms of the dedication suggest that Lyly may have been in the service of Lord Delaware (of whom very little is known) when the work was composed. His only known connection with the West family dates, however, from a later period when he and a Sir Thomas West were Members of Parliament for Aylesbury (see Hunter, pp. 67–8 and 79).
2 *Parrhasius / counterfeit*] celebrated Greek painter (fl. 400 BC) / picture
3 *Helen ... loose*] legendary Greek beauty, wife to Menelaus, whose flight with Paris (see p. 33n.) was the cause of the Trojan war (hence her 'looseness')
4 *Vulcan ... polt foot*] god of fire in Roman mythology who was born lame (hence his 'polt', i.e. deformed, foot). *curiously* = finely
5 *Leda / black hair*] wife of Tyndareus, King of Sparta, and beloved of Zeus who visited her in the form of a swan / not generally regarded in the Renaissance as a mark of beauty
6 *Alexander / Apelles*] outstanding military leader (356–323 BC) who promoted learning and the arts / the most important of the Greek painters, particularly favoured by Alexander, who would permit no one else to paint him
7 *list*] border of inferior material
8 *last*] blemish
9 *coloured*] depicted (for *counterfeit* see note 2 above)
10 *Euphues*] literally 'well-natured', i.e. with all the gifts of mind and body
11 *Cyrus*] founder of the Persian empire (d. 529 BC), renowned as a wise and just ruler

as his high forehead. He that loved Homer best concealed not his flattering,[1] and he that praised Alexander most bewrayed his quaffing.[2] Demonides must have a crooked shoe for his wry foot; Damocles[3] a smooth glove for his straight hand. For as every painter that shadoweth[4] a man in all parts giveth every piece his just proportion, so he that deciphereth the qualities of the mind ought as well to show every humour in his kind[5] as the other doth every part in his colour. The surgeon that maketh the anatomy[6] showeth as well the muscles in the heel as the veins of the heart.

If then the first sight of *Euphues* shall seem too light to be read of the wise or too foolish to be regarded of the learned, they ought not to impute it to the iniquity of the author but to the necessity of the history. Euphues beginneth with love as allured by wit, but endeth not with lust as bereft of wisdom. He wooeth women provoked by youth, but weddeth not himself to wantonness as pricked[7] by pleasure. I have set down the follies of his wit[8] without breach of modesty, and the sparks of his wisdom without suspicion of dishonesty. And, certes,[9] I think there be more speeches which for gravity will mislike the foolish[10] than unseemly terms which for vanity might offend the wise.

Which discourse, Right Honourable, I hope you will the rather pardon for the rudeness in that it is the first, and protect it the more willingly if it offend in that it may be the last. It may be that fine wits will descant upon[11] him that, having no wit, goeth about to make the Anatomy of Wit, and certainly their jesting, in my mind, is tolerable. For if the butcher should take upon him to cut the anatomy of a man because he hath skill in opening an ox, he would prove himself a calf; or if the horse-leech would adventure to minister a potion to a sick patient in that he hath knowledge to give a drench[12] to a diseased horse, he would make himself an ass. The shoemaker must not go above his latchet,[13] nor the hedger

---

1 *He that ... flattering*] possibly an allusion to Plutarch (see Bond, I, p. 328)
2 *quaffing*] heavy drinking. For *Alexander* see p. 27n. See pp. 32 and 34 for further references to his addiction to wine.
3 *Demonides / Damocles*] the cripple in Plutarch's *De audiendis poetis* who ironically hoped that the shoes stolen from him would fit the thief (see Croll and Clemons, p. 4n.) / possibly an Athenian youth noted for his beauty (see Bond, I, p. 328), but it is not clear to which Damocles this refers
4 *shadoweth*] draws
5 *humour in his kind*] quirk of his nature
6 *anatomy*] model of the body, showing the parts discovered through dissection
7 *pricked*] prompted
8 *wit*] quickness of mind
9 *certes*] truly
10 *for gravity ... foolish*] the foolish will dislike because of their seriousness.
11 *descant upon*] comment (adversely) on
12 *horse-leech / drench*] veterinary surgeon (literally, 'horse-doctor') / medicinal draught
13 *must not ... latchet*] should not meddle with things that do not concern him (proverbial). *latchet* = shoelace

meddle with anything but his bill.[1] It is unseemly for the painter to feather a shaft, or the fletcher to handle the pencil.[2] All which things make most against me, in that a fool hath intruded himself to discourse of wit. But as I was willing to commit the fault, so am I content to make amends. Howsoever the case standeth, I look for no praise for my labour, but pardon for my goodwill; it is the greatest reward that I dare ask, and the least that they can offer. I desire no more, I deserve no less. Though the style nothing delight the dainty ear of the curious sifter,[3] yet will the matter recreate the mind of the courteous reader. The variety of the one will abate the harshness of the other. Things of greatest profit are set forth with least price. Where the wine is neat there needeth no ivy-bush.[4] The right coral needeth no colouring. Where the matter itself bringeth credit, the man with his gloss winneth small commendation. It is therefore, methinketh, a greater show of a pregnant wit than perfect wisdom in a thing of sufficient excellency to use superfluous eloquence. We commonly see that a black ground doth best beseem a white counterfeit,[5] and Venus, according to the judgement of Mars, was then most amiable when she sat close by Vulcan.[6] If these things be true which experience trieth—that a naked tale doth most truly set forth the naked truth, that where the countenance is fair there need no colours, that painting is meeter for ragged walls than fine marble, that verity then shineth most bright when she is in least bravery[7]—I shall satisfy mine own mind, though I cannot feed their humours which greatly seek after those that sift the finest meal and bear the whitest mouths.[8] It is a world to see how Englishmen desire to hear finer speech than the language will allow, to eat finer bread than is made of wheat, to wear finer cloth than is wrought of wool. But I let pass their fineness, which can no way excuse my folly. If your Lordship shall accept my good will, which I have always desired, I will patiently bear the ill will of the malicious, which I never deserved.

Thus committing this simple pamphlet to your Lordship's patronage, and your honour to the Almighty's protection, for the preservation of the which, as most bounden, I will pray continually, I end.

Your Lordship's servant to command,

J. Lyly.

---

1 *bill*] lopping implement, bill-hook

2 *unseemly . . . pencil*] not fitting for the artist to fit a feather to an arrow, or an arrow-maker to use a pencil

3 *curious sifter*] over-scrupulous enquirer

4 *Where the wine . . . ivy-bush*] where the wine is unadulterated there is no need of advertisement (the ivy, sacred to Bacchus, was traditionally used to signal a tavern)

5 *black ground / white counterfeit*] dark background / light image

6 *Venus / Mars / Vulcan*] goddess of love / god of war (Venus' lover) / deformed husband of Venus and blacksmith of the gods (see p. 27n.)

7 *meeter / bravery*] more fit / finery

8 *that sift . . . mouths*] who seek the most sophisticated work and have the most fastidious tastes (literally, hold the bit most tenderly in their mouths)

I was driven into a quandary, gentlemen, whether I might send this my pamphlet to the printer or to the pedlar. I thought it too bad for the press and too good for the pack.[1] But seeing my folly in writing to be as great as others', I was willing my fortune should be as ill as any's. We commonly see the book that at Midsummer lieth bound on the stationer's stall at Christmas to be broken in the haberdasher's shop,[2] which, sith it is the order of proceeding, I am content this summer to have my doings read for a toy[3] that in winter they may be ready for trash. It is not strange whenas the greatest wonder lasteth but nine days that a new work should not endure but three months. Gentlemen use books as gentlewomen handle their flowers, who in the morning stick them in their heads and at night strew them at their heels. Cherries be fulsome[4] when they be through ripe because they be plenty, and books be stale when they be printed in that they be common. In my mind, printers and tailors are bound chiefly to pray for gentlemen; the one hath so many fantasies to print, the other such divers fashions to make, that the pressing-iron of the one is never out of the fire nor the printing press of the other any time lieth still. But a fashion is but a day's wearing and a book but an hour's reading; which seeing it is so, I am of the shoemaker's mind, who careth not so the shoe hold the plucking on, nor I so my labours last the running over. He that cometh in print because he would be known is like the fool that cometh into the market because he would be seen. I am not he that seeketh praise for his labour, but pardon for his offence; neither do I set this forth for any devotion in print, but for duty which I owe to my patron. If one write never so well he cannot please all, and write he never so ill he shall please some. Fine heads will pick a quarrel with me if all be not curious,[5] and flatterers a thank if anything be current.[6] But this is my mind—let him that findeth fault amend it, and him that liketh it use it. Envy braggeth but draweth no blood; the malicious have more mind to quip than might to cut. I submit myself to the judgement of the wise and little esteem the censure of fools: the one will

---

1 *pack*] bundle of goods carried by a pedlar
2 *stationer's stall / haberdasher's shop*] bookseller's stall / shop of dealer in small wares, usually for dressmaking (unsold books were commonly broken up to be used as wrapping paper)
3 *toy*] trifling amusement
4 *fulsome*] satiating
5 *curious*] highly wrought, ingenious
6 *flatterers ... current*] hangers-on will try to curry favour with me if it is popular

be satisfied with reason, the other are to be answered with silence. I
know gentlemen will find no fault without cause, and bear with those
that deserve blame. As for others, I care not for their jests, for I never
meant to make them my judges.

Farewell.

EUPHUES

There dwelt in Athens[1] a young gentleman of great patrimony and of so comely a personage that it was doubted whether he were more bound to Nature for the lineaments of his person or to Fortune for the increase of his possessions. But Nature, impatient of comparisons, and as it were disdaining a companion or copartner in her working, added to this comeliness of his body such a sharp capacity of mind that not only she proved Fortune counterfeit but was half of that opinion that she herself was only current.[2] This young gallant, of more wit than wealth, and yet of more wealth than wisdom, seeing himself inferior to none in pleasant conceits, thought himself superior to all in honest conditions,[3] insomuch that he thought himself so apt to all things that he gave himself almost to nothing but practising of those things commonly which are incident to these sharp wits—fine phrases, smooth quips, merry taunts—jesting without mean[4] and abusing mirth without measure. As therefore the sweetest rose hath his prickle, the finest velvet his brack,[5] the fairest flour his bran, so the sharpest wit hath his wanton will and the holiest head his wicked way. And true it is that some men write, and most men believe, that in all perfect shapes a blemish bringeth rather a liking every way to the eyes than a loathing any way to the mind. Venus had her mole in her cheek which made her more amiable; Helen her scar in her chin which Paris called *cos amoris*, the whetstone of love;[6] Aristippus his wart, Lycurgus[7] his wen. So likewise in the disposition of the mind, either virtue is over-shadowed with some vice or vice overcast with some virtue: Alexander valiant in war, yet given to wine; Tully eloquent in his glozes, yet vainglorious;[8] Solomon wise, yet too too wanton; David holy, but

---

1 *Athens*] university city, representative both of Greek learning (considerable emphasis is placed on Euphues' nationality) and of Oxford

2 *she proved . . . current*] she showed Fortune to be spurious and half-believed that she alone was of any influence (metaphor drawn from coining)

3 *conceits / conditions*] notions / qualities

4 *mean*] moderation

5 *brack*] flaw

6 *Helen . . . love*] see p. 27n.

7 *Aristippus / Lycurgus*] Greek philosopher (fl. circa 370 BC), hedonistic founder of the Cyrenaic school / founder (ninth century BC) of the Spartan constitution (including the training of youth), noted for his wisdom and integrity. No source has been found for either the former's wart or the latter's wen (i.e. cyst).

8 *Alexander / Tully . . . vainglorious*] see p. 27n. / Marcus Tullius Cicero, distinguished Roman orator (106–43 BC), notable for his eloquent expositions ('glozes') but absurdly vain in his later years

yet an homicide;[1] none more witty than Euphues, yet at the first none more wicked.

The freshest colours soonest fade, the teenest[2] razor soonest turneth his edge, the finest cloth is soonest eaten with moths, and the cambric[3] sooner stained than the coarse canvas. Which appeared well in this Euphues, whose wit being like wax apt to receive any impression, and bearing the head in his own hand either to use the rein or the spur,[4] disdaining counsel, leaving his country, loathing his old acquantance, thought either by wit to obtain some conquest, or by shame to abide some conflict; who, preferring fancy before friends and his present humour before honour to come, laid reason in water, being too salt for his taste,[5] and followed unbridled affection, most pleasant for his tooth.

When parents have more care how to leave their children wealthy than wise, and are more desirous to have them maintain the name than the nature of a gentleman, when they put gold into the hands of youth where they should put a rod under their girdle,[6] when instead of awe they make them past grace, and leave them rich executors of goods and poor executors of godliness, then is it no marvel that the son, being left rich by his father's will, become reckless by his own will.

But it hath been an old said saw,[7] and not of less truth than antiquity, that wit is the better if it be the dearer bought; as in the sequel of this history shall most manifestly appear. It happened this young imp[8] to arrive at Naples,[9] a place of more pleasure than profit, and yet of more profit than piety, the very walls and windows whereof showed it rather to be the tabernacle of Venus than the temple of Vesta.[10] There was all things necessary and in readiness that might either allure the mind to lust or entice the heart to folly—a court more meet for an atheist than for one of Athens, for Ovid than for Aristotle,[11] for a graceless lover than for a godly liver, more fitter for Paris than Hector,[12] and meeter for

---

1 *Solomon ... homicide*] kings of Israel, the first celebrated as the founder of the temple and noted for his wisdom but also known for his many concubines and wives, the second favoured by God but responsible for the death of Uriah

2 *teenest*] sharpest

3 *cambric*] fine white linen cloth

4 *bearing ... spur*] being in a position to determine his own course (metaphor drawn from horse-riding)

5 *laid reason ... taste*] set aside the unpalatable dictates of reason (a reference to the practice of soaking preserved meat in water to remove excess salt)

6 *rod under their girdle*] impose discipline

7 *saw*] maxim

8 *imp*] pun (offspring of a noble house / young devil)

9 *Naples*] sophisticated Italian city, partly identifiable with London, set in opposition to Athens (= Oxford)

10 *tabernacle ... Vesta*] a place dedicated to love (Venus) rather than chastity (Vesta)

11 *Ovid / Aristotle*] Roman poet (43 BC–AD 18), author of the *Ars amatoria* (*Art of Love*) / Greek philosopher (384–322 BC), concerned with ethics

12 *Paris / Hector*] sons of Priam, King of Troy, the first the seducer of Helen (see p. 27n.), the second the heroic defender of his father's city against the Greeks

Flora than Diana.[1] Here my youth (whether for weariness he could not, or for wantonness would not go any further) determined to make his abode; whereby it is evidently seen that the fleetest fish swalloweth the delicatest bait, that the highest soaring hawk traineth[2] to the lure, and that the wittiest brain is inveigled with the sudden view of alluring vanities.

Here he wanted[3] no companions, which courted him continually with sundry kinds of devices whereby they might either soak his purse to reap commodity or soothe his person to win credit; for he had guests and companions of all sorts. There frequented to his lodging as well the spider to suck poison of his fine wit as the bee to gather honey, as well the drone as the dove, the fox as the lamb, as well Damocles to betray him as Damon[4] to be true to him. Yet he behaved himself so warily that he singled his game wisely.[5] He could easily discern Apollo's music from Pan his pipe, and Venus' beauty from Juno's bravery, and the faith of Laelius from the flattery of Aristippus.[6] He welcomed all, but trusted none; he was merry, but yet so wary that neither the flatterer could take advantage to entrap him in his talk, nor the wisest any assurance of his friendship. Who, being demanded of one what countryman he was, he answered, 'What countryman am I not? If I be in Crete, I can lie; if in Greece, I can shift; if in Italy, I can court it.[7] If thou ask whose son I am also, I ask thee whose son I am not. I can carouse with Alexander, abstain with Romulus,[8] eat with the Epicure,[9] fast with the Stoic,[10] sleep with

1 *Flora / Diana*] goddesses of the spring and of chastity, the former associated with licentiousness through the nature of her festival
2 *traineth*] is drawn (The word is frequently used in this sense throughout.)
3 *wanted*] lacked. (The word is frequently used in this sense throughout.)
4 *Damocles / Damon*] archetypes of flattery and faithful friendship: Damocles the sycophantic companion of the tyrant Dionysius, Damon the comrade of Phintias (known as Pythias in the Renaissance) who was ready to sacrifice himself for his friend (see p. 45n.)
5 *singled his game wisely*] chose shrewdly from among the herd
6 *Apollo's music ... Aristippus*] all instances of true worth rather than ostentation or pretence. *Apollo's music / Pan's pipe*: divine harmony / rustic music. *Venus' beauty / Juno's bravery*: natural loveliness / ostentatious finery. *Laelius / Aristippus*: enduring friendship (see p. 45n.) / self-serving expediency (through his relationship with the tyrant Dionysius)
7 *Crete ... court it*] all references to traditional national characteristics. The mendacity of the Cretans is noted by Ovid in his *Ars amatoria* (see Croll and Clemons, p. 13n.); the association between Greeks and duplicity (i.e. 'shifting') may originate with the deception that brought about the fall of Troy; while the Italian city states were seen in the sixteenth century as patterns of courtly conduct (hence 'court it', i.e. play the courtier)
8 *Romulus*] legendary founder of Rome, noted for his sobriety
9 *Epicure*] follower of Epicurus (342–270 BC), who taught that pleasure is the highest good
10 *Stoic*] follower of the doctrine that the virtuous mind is indifferent to hardship and misfortune

Endymion,[1] watch with Chrysippus'[2] using these speeches and other like.

An old gentleman in Naples, seeing his pregnant wit, his eloquent tongue somewhat taunting yet with delight, his mirth without measure yet not without wit, his sayings vainglorious yet pithy, began to bewail his nurture and to muse at his nature, being incensed against the one as most pernicious and inflamed with the other as most precious. For well he knew that so rare a wit would in time either breed an intolerable trouble or bring an incomparable treasure to the commonweal; at the one he greatly pitied, at the other he rejoiced. Having, therefore, gotten opportunity to communicate with him his mind, with watery eyes, as one lamenting his wantonness, and smiling face, as one loving his wittiness, encountered him on this manner:

'Young gentleman, although my acquaintance be small to entreat you, and my authority less to command you, yet my good will in giving you good counsel should induce you to believe me, and my hoary hairs (ambassadors of experience) enforce you to follow me; for by how much the more I am a stranger to you, by so much the more you are beholding to me. Having, therefore, opportunity to utter my mind, I mean to be importunate with you to follow my meaning. As thy birth doth show the express and lively image of gentle blood, so thy bringing up seemeth to me to be a great blot to the lineage of so noble a brute;[3] so that I am enforced to think that either thou didst want one to give thee good instructions, or that thy parents made thee a wanton with too much cockering,[4] either they were too foolish in using no discipline or thou too froward[5] in rejecting their doctrine, either they willing to have thee idle or thou wilful to be ill-employed. Did they not remember that which no man ought to forget, that the tender youth of a child is like the tempering of new wax, apt to receive any form? He that will carry a bull with Milo[6] must use to carry him a calf also, he that coveteth to have a straight tree must not bow him being a twig. The potter fashioneth his clay when it is soft, and the sparrow is taught to come when he is young.[7] As, therefore, the iron being hot receiveth any form with the stroke of the hammer, and keepeth it being cold for ever, so the tender wit of a child, if with diligence it be instructed in youth, will with industry use those qualities in his age.

---

1 *Endymion*] mythical youth loved by the moon, who cast him into a profound sleep during which she visited him nightly
2 *Chrysippus*] Stoic philosopher (280–207 BC), renowned for his industry and thus accustomed to 'watch' (i.e. forgo sleep)
3 *brute*] person born of an illustrious line
4 *cockering*] indulgence
5 *froward*] recalcitrant
6 *Milo*] Greek athlete (sixth century BC) famous for feats of strength, including carrying a bull through the stadium at Olympia
7 *sparrow . . . young*] Sparrows were commonly kept as pets in the sixteenth century.

'They might also have taken example of the wise husbandmen, who in their fattest[1] and most fertile ground sow hemp before wheat, a grain that drieth up the superfluous moisture and maketh the soil more apt for corn; or of good gardeners, who in their curious knots[2] mix hyssop with thyme as aiders the one to the growth of the other, the one being dry, the other moist; or of cunning painters, who for the whitest work cast the blackest ground,[3] to make the picture more amiable. If, therefore, thy father had been as wise an husbandman as he was a fortunate husband, or thy mother as good a housewife as she was a happy wife, if they had been both as good gardeners to keep their knot as they were grafters to bring forth such fruit, or as cunning painters as they were happy parents, no doubt they had sowed hemp before wheat, that is discipline before affection, they had set hyssop with thyme, that is manners with wit, the one to aid the other; and to make thy dexterity more,[4] they had cast a black ground for their white work, that is they had mixed threats with fair looks.

'But things past are past calling again, it is too late to shut the stable door when the steed is stolen. The Trojans repented too late when their town was spoiled.[5] Yet the remembrance of thy former follies might breed in thee a remorse of conscience, and be a remedy against further concupiscence. But now to thy present time. The Lacedaemonians[6] were wont to show their children drunken men and other wicked men, that by seeing their filth they might shun the like fault, and avoid the like vices when they were at the like state. The Persians, to make their youth abhor gluttony, would paint an Epicure[7] sleeping with meat in his mouth and most horribly overladen with wine, that by the view of such monstrous sights they might eschew the means of the like excess. The Parthians, to cause their youth to loathe the alluring trains[8] of women's wiles and deceitful enticements, had most curiously carved in their houses a young man blind, besides whom was adjoined a woman so exquisite that in some men's judgement Pygmalion's image was not half so excellent,[9] having one hand in his pocket as noting her theft, and holding a knife in the other hand to cut his throat.

'If the sight of such ugly shapes caused a loathing of the like sins, then, my good Euphues, consider their plight and beware of thine own peril. Thou art here in Naples a young sojourner, I an old senior; thou a

---

1 *husbandmen / fattest*] farmers / heaviest
2 *knots*] formal, intricately patterned gardens, usually geometric in shape
3 *ground*] background
4 *to make thy dexterity more*] to promote your mental facility
5 *spoiled*] laid waste
6 *Lacedaemonians*] Spartans, noted for their austerity
7 *Epicure*] see p. 34n.
8 *trains*] snares
9 *Pygmalion's image . . . excellent*] statue of a woman made by Pygmalion, so beautiful that the sculptor fell in love with it

stranger, I a citizen; thou secure doubting no mishap, I sorrowful dreading thy misfortune. Here mayst thou see that which I sigh to see, drunken sots wallowing in every house, in every chamber, yea, in every channel;[1] here mayst thou behold that which I cannot without blushing behold, nor without blubbering utter, those whose bellies be their gods, who offer their goods as sacrifice to their guts, who sleep with meat in their mouths, with sin in their hearts, and with shame in their houses. Here, yea here, Euphues, mayst thou see, not the carved vizard[2] of a lewd woman, but the incarnate visage of a lascivious wanton, not the shadow of love, but the substance of lust. My heart melteth in drops of blood to see a harlot with the one hand rob so many coffers, and with the other to rip so many corpses. Thou art here amidst the pikes,[3] between Scylla and Charybdis,[4] ready if thou shun Syrtis to sink into Symplegades.[5] Let the Lacedaemonian, the Persian, the Parthian, yea, the Neapolitan cause thee rather to detest such villainy at the sight and view of their vanity.

'Is it not far better to abhor sins by the remembrance of others' faults than by repentance of thine own follies? Is not he accounted most wise whom other men's harms do make most wary? But thou wilt haply say that although there be many things in Naples to be justly condemned, yet there are some things of necessity to be commended, and as thy will doth lean unto the one, so thy wit would also embrace the other.

'Alas, Euphues, by how much the more I love the high climbing of thy capacity, by so much the more I fear thy fall. The fine crystal is sooner crazed than the hard marble, the greenest beech burneth faster than the driest oak, the fairest silk is soonest soiled, and the sweetest wine turneth to the sharpest vinegar. The pestilence doth most rifest[6] infect the clearest complexion, and the caterpillar cleaveth unto the ripest fruit; the most delicate wit is allured with small enticement unto vice, and most subject to yield unto vanity. If, therefore, thou do but harken to the Sirens thou wilt be enamoured, if thou haunt their houses and places thou shalt be enchanted.

'One drop of poison infecteth the whole tun of wine, one leaf of coloquintida[7] marreth and spoileth the whole pot of porridge, one iron-mole[8] defaceth the whole piece of lawn.[9] Descend into thine own conscience and consider with thyself the great difference between staring and

---

1 *channel*] gutter
2 *vizard*] mask
3 *pikes*] pointed rocks (i.e. equally perilous alternatives)
4 *Scylla and Charybdis*] a dangerous rock and a whirlpool (lying between Sicily and Italy)
5 *Syrtis / Symplegades*] sand bar (off the north coast of Africa) / group of wandering islands (thought to lie in the Black Sea)
6 *rifest*] readily
7 *coloquintida*] bitter apple (with purgative properties)
8 *iron-mole*] discoloration (caused by iron rust)
9 *lawn*] fine linen

stark-blind, wit and wisdom, love and lust. Be merry, but with modesty; be sober, but not too sullen; be valiant, but not too venturous. Let thy attire be comely, but not costly; thy diet wholesome, but not excessive; use pastime as the word importeth—to pass the time in honest recreation. Mistrust no man without cause, neither be thou credulous without proof. Be not light to follow every man's opinion, nor obstinate to stand in thine own conceit. Serve God, love God, fear God, and God will so bless thee as either heart can wish, or thy friends desire. And so I end my counsel, beseeching thee to begin to follow it.'

This old gentleman having finished his discourse, Euphues began to shape him an answer in this sort:

'Father and friend (your age showeth the one, your honesty the other), I am neither so suspicious to mistrust your good will, nor so sottish to mislike your good counsel; as I am therefore to thank you for the first, so it stands upon me[1] to think better on the latter. I mean not to cavil with you as one loving sophistry, nor to control[2] you as one having superiority; the one would bring my talk into the suspicion of fraud, the other convince[3] me of folly.

'Whereas you argue, I know not upon what probabilities but sure I am upon no proof, that my bringing-up should be a blemish to my birth, I answer and swear to that, you were not therein a little over-shot; either you gave too much credit to the report of others, or too much liberty to your own judgement. You convince my parents of peevishness[4] in making me a wanton, and me of lewdness in rejecting correction. But so many men, so many minds. That may seem in your eye odious which in another's eye may be gracious. Aristippus a philosopher, yet who more courtly? Diogenes a philosopher, yet who more carterly?[5] Who more popular than Plato, retaining always good company? Who more envious than Timon, denouncing all human society? Who so severe as the Stoics, which like stocks[6] were moved with no melody? Who so secure as the Epicures which wallowed in all kind of licentiousness? Though all men be made of one metal, yet they be not cast all in one mould. There is framed of the self-same clay as well the tile to keep out water as the pot to contain liquor, the sun doth harden the dirt and melt the wax, fire maketh the gold to shine and the straw to smother, perfumes doth refresh

---

1 *it stands upon me*] it is incumbent on me
2 *control*] rebuke
3 *convince*] convict
4 *peevishness*] folly
5 *carterly*] boorish. The references in this and the following sentences are to leading figures in Greek philosophy to whom Lyly frequently refers. For *Aristippus* see p. 32n; Diogenes (c. 412–323 BC), a leading Cynic, was renowned for his plain speaking and austerity of life; Plato (c. 428–347 BC), noted for his affability, originated the doctrine of *ideas*; Timon (c. 320–c. 230 BC) was a leading Sceptic, satirical in stance. For the Stoics and Epicures see p. 34nn.
6 *stocks*] tree stumps

the dove and kill the beetle, and the nature of the man disposeth that consent of the manners.[1]

'Now whereas you seem to love my nature and loathe my nurture, you bewray your own weakness in thinking that nature may anyways be altered by education; and as you have examples to confirm your pretence,[2] so I have most evident and infallible arguments to serve for my purpose. It is natural for the vine to spread; the more you seek by art to alter it, the more in the end you shall augment it. It is proper for the palm-tree to mount; the heavier you load it, the higher it sprouteth. Though iron be made soft with fire it returneth to his hardness; though the falcon be reclaimed to the fist she retireth to her haggardness;[3] the whelp of a mastiff will never be taught to retrieve the partridge; education can have no show where the excellency of nature doth bear sway. The silly[4] mouse will by no manner of means be tamed; the subtle fox may well be beaten, but never broken from stealing his prey; if you pound spices they smell the sweeter; season the wood never so well, the wine will taste of the cask; plant and translate the crab-tree where and whensoever it please you and it will never bear sweet apple—unless you graft by art, which nothing toucheth nature. Infinite and innumerable were the examples I could allege and declare to confirm the force of nature and confute these your vain and false forgeries, were not the repetition of them needless, having showed sufficient, or bootless,[5] seeing those alleged will not persuade you. And can you be so unnatural, whom Dame Nature hath nourished and brought up so many years, to repine as it were against Nature?

'The similitude you rehearse of the wax argueth your waxing and melting brain, and your example of the hot and hard iron showeth in you but cold and weak disposition. Do you not know that which all men do affirm and know, that black will take no other colour; that the stone asbestos being once made hot will never be made cold; that fire cannot be forced downward; that Nature will have course after kind;[6] that everything will dispose itself according to Nature? Can the Ethiop change or alter his skin, or the leopard his hue? Is it possible to gather grapes of thorns, or figs of thistles, or to cause anything to strive against Nature?

'But why go I about to praise Nature, the which as yet was never any imp so wicked and barbarous, any Turk so vile and brutish, any beast so dull and senseless, that could, or would, or durst dispraise or contemn? Doth not Cicero conclude and allow that if we follow and obey Nature we shall never err? Doth not Aristotle[7] allege and confirm that Nature

---

1 *nature ... manners*] the character of the individual determines his behaviour
2 *confirm your pretence*] support your position (*bewray* = betray)
3 *haggardness*] wild state
4 *silly*] simple, helpless
5 *bootless*] pointless
6 *course after kind*] will follow its natural bent
7 *Cicero / Aristotle*] see pp. 32 and 33nn.

frameth or maketh nothing in any point rude, vain, or unperfect? Nature was had in such estimation and admiration among the heathen people that she was reputed for the only goddess in heaven. If Nature, then, have largely and bountifully endued me with her gifts, why deem you me so untoward[1] and graceless? If she have dealt hardly[2] with me, why extol you so much my birth? If Nature bear no sway, why use you this adulation? If Nature work the effect, what booteth any education?[3] If Nature be of strength or force, what availeth discipline or nurture? If of none, what helpeth Nature? But let these sayings pass as known evidently and granted to be true, which none can or may deny unless he be false, or that he be an enemy to humanity.

'As touching my residence and abiding here in Naples, my youthly affections, my sports and pleasures, my pastimes, my common dalliance, my delights, my resort and company which daily use to visit me, although to you they breed more sorrow and care than solace and comfort because of your crabbed age, yet to me they bring more comfort and joy than care and grief, more bliss than bale,[4] more happiness than heaviness, because of my youthful gentleness. Either you would have all men old as you are, or else you have quite forgotten that you yourself were young or ever knew young days; either in your youth you were a very vicious and ungodly man, or now being aged very superstitious and devout above measure.

'Put you no difference between the young flourishing bay-tree and the old withered beech, no kind of distinction between the waxing and the waning of the moon, and between the rising and the setting of the sun? Do you measure the hot assaults of youth by the cold skirmishes of age, whose years are subject to more infirmities than our youth? We merry, you melancholy; we zealous in affection, you jealous[5] in all your doings; you testy without cause, we hasty for no quarrel; you careful, we careless; we bold, you fearful; we in all points contrary unto you, and ye in all points unlike unto us.

'Seeing, therefore, we be repugnant each to the other in nature, would you have us alike in qualities? Would you have one potion ministered to the burning fever and to the cold palsy; one plaster to an old issue[6] and a fresh wound; one salve for all sores; one sauce for all meats? No, no, Eubulus![7] But I will yield to more than either I am bound to grant, either thou able to prove. Suppose that which I will never believe, that Naples

---

1 *untoward*] backward
2 *hardly*] meanly
3 *what . . . education*] what point is there in education
4 *bale*] sorrow
5 *jealous*] suspicious
6 *issue*] discharge (usually of blood)
7 *Eubulus*] the name of the 'old gentleman' (signifying 'good or prudent in counsel'). For its possible origins see Croll and Clemons, p. 22n.

is a cankered store-house of all strife, a common stews[1] for all strumpets, the sink of shame, and the very nurse of all sin: shall it therefore follow of necessity that all that are wooed of love should be wedded to lust; will you conclude, as it were *ex consequenti*, that whosoever arriveth here shall be enticed to folly and, being enticed, of force[2] shall be entangled? No, no! It is the disposition of the thought that altereth the nature of the thing. The sun shineth upon the dunghill and is not corrupted, the diamond lieth in the fire and is not consumed, the crystal toucheth the toad and is not poisoned, the bird trochilus liveth by the mouth of the crocodile and is not spoiled,[3] a perfect wit is never bewitched with lewdness neither enticed with lasciviousness.

'Is it not common that the holm-tree springeth amidst the beech; that the ivy spreadeth upon the hard stones; that the soft feather bed breaketh the hard blade? If experience have not taught you this, you have lived long and learned little, or if your moist brain have forgot it, you have learned much and profited nothing. But it may be that you measure my affections by your own fancies, and knowing yourself either too simple to raise the siege by policy, or too weak to resist the assault by prowess, you deem me of as little wit as yourself, or of less force; either of small capacity, or of no courage. In my judgement, Eubulus, you shall as soon catch a hare with a tabor[4] as you shall persuade youth with your aged and overworn eloquence to such severity of life, which as yet there was never Stoic so strict, nor Jesuit so superstitious,[5] neither votary so devout, but would rather allow it in words than follow it in works, rather talk of it than try it. Neither were you such a saint in your youth that, abandoning all pleasures, all pastimes and delights, you would choose rather to sacrifice the first fruits of your life to vain holiness than to youthly affections. But as to the stomach quatted with dainties all delicates seem queasy,[6] and as he that surfeiteth with wine useth afterward to allay with water, so these old huddles,[7] having overcharged their gorges with fancy, account all honest recreation mere folly and having taken a surfeit of delight, seem now to savour it with despite.

'Seeing, therefore, it is labour lost for me to persuade you and wind vainly wasted for you to exhort me, here I found you and here I leave you, having neither bought nor sold with you but changed ware for ware.[8] If you have taken little pleasure in my reply, sure I am that by

---

1 *stews*] brothel
2 *ex consequenti / of force*] as an inevitable result / necessarily
3 *liveth by . . . spoiled*] sustains itself by means of [the pickings from] the crocodile's mouth and is not killed (which bird is referred to here is disputed)
4 *as soon . . . tabor*] proverbial (with reference to the hare's acute hearing), signifying to achieve the impossible (*tabor* = small drum)
5 *superstitious*] punctilious, extravagantly devoted
6 *quatted / queasy*] glutted / unsettling to the stomach
7 *huddles*] disrespectful term for the elderly
8 *changed ware for ware*] exchanged goods (here words)

your counsel I have reaped less profit. They that use to steal honey burn hemlock to smoke the bees from their hives, and it may be that to get some advantage of me you have used these smoky arguments, thinking thereby to smother me with the conceit of strong imagination. But as the chameleon though he have most guts draweth least breath, or as the elder tree though he be fullest of pith is farthest from strength, so though your reasons seem inwardly to yourself somewhat substantial, and your persuasions pithy in your own conceit, yet being well weighed without, they be shadows without substance and weak without force. The bird taurus[1] hath a great voice but a small body, the thunder a great clap yet but a little stone, the empty vessel giveth a greater sound than the full barrel. I mean not to apply it, but look into yourself and you shall certainly find it; and thus I leave you seeking it. But were it not that my company stay my coming, I would surely help you to look it—but I am called hence by my acquaintance.'

Euphues, having thus ended his talk, departed, leaving this old gentleman in a great quandary; who, perceiving that he was more inclined to wantonness than to wisdom, with a deep sigh, the tears trickling down his cheeks, said:

'Seeing thou wilt not buy counsel at the first hand good cheap, thou shalt buy repentance at the second hand at such an unreasonable rate that thou wilt curse thy hard pennyworth and ban[2] thy hard heart. Ah Euphues, little dost thou know that if thy wealth waste, thy wit will give but small warmth; and if thy wit incline to wilfulness, that thy wealth will do thee no great good. If the one had been employed to thrift, the other to learning, it had been hard to conjecture whether thou shouldst have been more fortunate by riches or happy by wisdom, whether more esteemed in the commonweal for wealth to maintain war or for counsel to conclude peace. But, alas, why do I pity that in thee which thou seemest to praise in thyself?'

And so saying he immediately went to his own house, heavily bewailing the young man's unhappiness.

Here ye may behold, gentlemen, how lewdly wit standeth in his own light, how he deemeth no penny good silver but his own,[3] preferring the blossom before the fruit, the bud before the flower, the green blade before the ripe ear of corn, his own wit before all men's wisdoms. Neither is that geason,[4] seeing for the most part it is proper to all those of sharp capacity to esteem of themselves as most proper.[5] If one be hard in conceiving they pronounce him a dolt, if given to study they proclaim him a dunce; if merry a jester, if sad a saint; if full of words a sot, if without speech a

---

1 *taurus*] bird said to imitate the lowing of oxen. Possibly the bittern.
2 *ban*] curse
3 *no penny ... own*] no coin current but his own (i.e. no ideas valid other than his)
4 *geason*] out of the ordinary
5 *proper / proper*] natural / admirable

cipher; if one argue with them boldly then is he impudent, if coldly an innocent; if there be reasoning of divinity the[y] cry, 'Quae supra nos nihil ad nos,' if of humanity, 'Sententias loquitur carnifex.'[1] Hereof cometh such great familiarity between the ripest wits when they shall see the disposition the one of the other, the 'sympathia' of affections, and as it were but a pair of shears to go between their natures.[2] One flattereth another in his own folly, and layeth cushions under the elbow of his fellow when he seeth him take a nap with fancy;[3] and as their wit wresteth them to vice, so it forgeth them some feat[4] excuse to cloak their vanity.

Too much study doth intoxicate their brains. 'For,' say they, 'although iron the more it is used the brighter it is, yet silver with much wearing doth waste to nothing; though the cammock[5] the more it is bowed the better it serveth, yet the bow the more it is bent and occupied[6] the weaker it waxeth; though the camomile the more it is trodden and pressed down the more it spreadeth, yet the violet the oftener it is handled and touched the sooner it withereth and decayeth. Besides this, a fine wit, a sharp sense, a quick understanding, is able to attain to more in a moment or a very little space than a dull and blockish head in a month. The scythe cutteth far better and smoother than the saw; the wax yieldeth better and sooner to the seal than the steel to the stamp; the smooth and plain beech is easier to be carved than the knotty box. For neither is there anything but that hath his contraries.'

Such is the nature of these novices that think to have learning without labour and treasure without travail; either not understanding, or else not remembering, that the finest edge is made with the blunt whetstone and the fairest jewel fashioned with the hard hammer. I go not about, gentlemen, to inveigh against wit, for then I were witless, but frankly to confess my own little wit. I have ever thought so superstitiously of wit that I fear I have committed idolatry against wisdom; and if Nature had dealt so beneficially with me to have given me any wit, I should have been readier in the defence of it to have made an apology, than any way to turn to apostasy. But this I note, that for the most part they stand so on their pantofles[7] that they be secure of perils, obstinate in their own opinions, impatient of labour, apt to conceive wrong, credulous to believe the worst, ready to shake off their old acquaintance without cause, and to condemn

---

1 *Quae supra nos nihil ad nos / Sententias loquitur carnifex*] that which is above us is nothing to us / the executioner pronounces sentence (i.e. no objective judgement is available)

2 *pair . . . natures*] proverbial. Cut from the same material (i.e. of the same disposition).

3 *layeth cushions . . . fellow / take a nap . . . fancy*] humours his companion (i.e. encourages him in his folly) / wrapped up in some idle conceit

4 *feat*] adroit

5 *cammock*] crook

6 *occupied*] used

7 *stand . . . pantofles*] stand so much on their high-heeled shoes (i.e. on their dignity)

them without colour.[1] All which humours are by so much the more easier to be purged, by how much the less they have festered the sinews. But return we again to Euphues.

Euphues having sojourned by the space of two months in Naples, whether he were moved by the courtesy of a young gentleman named Philautus[2] or enforced by destiny, whether his pregnant wit or his pleasant conceits[3] wrought the greater liking in the mind of Euphues, I know not for certainty, but Euphues showed such entire love towards him that he seemed to make small account of any others, determining to enter into such an inviolable league of friendship with him as neither time by piecemeal should impair, neither fancy utterly dissolve, nor any suspicion infringe. 'I have read,' saith he, 'and well I believe it, that a friend is in prosperity a pleasure, a solace in adversity, in grief a comfort, in joy a merry companion, at all times another I, in all places the express image of mine own person, insomuch that I cannot tell whether the immortal gods have bestowed any gift upon mortal men either more noble or more necessary than friendship. Is there anything in the world to be reputed—I will not say compared—to friendship? Can any treasure in this transitory pilgrimage be of more value than a friend, in whose bosom thou mayst sleep secure without fear, whom thou mayst make partner of all thy secrets without suspicion of fraud, and partaker of all thy misfortune without mistrust of fleeting,[4] who will account thy bale his bane,[5] thy mishap his misery, the pricking of thy finger the piercing of his heart? But whither am I carried? Have I not also learned that one should eat a bushel of salt with[6] him whom he meaneth to make his friend; that trial maketh trust; that there is falsehood in fellowship? And what then? Doth not the sympathy of manners make the conjunction of minds? Is it not a byword,[7] "Like will to like"? Not so common as commendable it is to see young gentlemen choose them such friends with whom they may seem, being absent to be present, being asunder to be conversant,[8] being dead to be alive. I will therefore have Philautus for my fere,[9] and by so much the more I make myself sure to have Philautus, by how much the more I view in him the lively image of Euphues.'

Although there be none so ignorant that doth not know, neither any so impudent that will not confess friendship to be the jewel of human joy, yet whosoever shall see this amity grounded upon a little affection will soon conjecture that it shall be dissolved upon a light occasion;

---

1 *colour*] show of reason
2 *Philautus*] self-love, see p. 136 below
3 *conceits*] fancies, ideas
4 *fleeting*] disloyalty
5 *thy bale his bane*] your misfortune his ruin
6 *eat a bushel of salt with*] spend considerable time in the company of (proverbial)
7 *byword*] proverbial saying
8 *being asunder . . . conversant*] being apart to be in communication
9 *fere*] comrade

as in the sequel of Euphues and Philautus you shall see, whose hot love waxed soon cold. For as the best wine doth make the sharpest vinegar, so the deepest love turneth to the deadliest hate. Who deserved the most blame in mine opinion it is doubtful, and so difficult that I dare not presume to give verdict. For love being the cause for which so many mischiefs have been attempted, I am not yet persuaded whether of them was most to be blamed, but certainly neither of them was blameless. I appeal to your judgement, gentlemen, not that I think any of you of the like disposition able to decide the question, but, being of deeper discretion than I am, are more fit to debate the quarrel. Though the discourse of their friendship and falling out be somewhat long, yet, being somewhat strange, I hope the delightfulness of the one will attenuate the tediousness of the other.

Euphues had continual access to the place of Philautus and no little familiarity with him, and finding him at convenient leisure, in these short terms unfolded his mind unto him:

'Gentleman and friend, the trial I have had of thy manners cutteth off divers terms which to another I would have used in the like matter.[1] And sithence[2] a long discourse argueth folly, and delicate words incur the suspicion of flattery, I am determined to use neither of them, knowing either of them to breed offence. Weighing with myself the force of friendship by the effects, I studied ever since my first coming to Naples to enter league with such a one as might direct my steps, being a stranger, and resemble my manners, being a scholar; the which two qualities as I find in you able to satisfy my desire, so I hope I shall find a heart in you willing to accomplish my request. Which, if I may obtain, assure yourself that Damon to his Pythias, Pylades to his Orestes, Titus to his Gysippus, Theseus to his Pirithous, Scipio to his Laelius,[3] was never found more faithful than Euphues will be to Philautus.'

Philautus by how much the less he looked for this discourse, by so much the more he liked it, for he saw all qualities both of body and mind in Euphues; unto whom he replied as followeth:

'Friend Euphues (for so your talk warrenteth me to term you), I dare neither use a long process, neither a loving speech, lest unwittingly I should cause you to convince me[4] of those things which you have already

---

1 *divers / the like matter*] many / a similar business
2 *sithence*] since
3 *Damon ... Laelius*] all examples of exemplary friendship familiar to a sixteenth-century reader. Damon contended with Pythias, who had stood surety for him, over which of them should die following the former's failure to return at the appointed time to face execution; Pylades assisted Orestes in revenging the murder of Agamemnon; Titus saved Gysippus by confessing to a murder to which his friend had also (falsely) confessed; Theseus assisted Pirithous in his battle against the Centaurs; the friendship between Scipio Africanus the younger (b. 185 BC) and Laelius (b. 186 BC) is celebrated in Cicero's *De amicitia*.
4 *convince me*] find me guilty of

condemned. And verily I am bold to presume upon your courtesy since you yourself have used so little curiosity,[1] persuading myself that my short answer will work as great an effect in you as your few words did in me. And seeing we resemble (as you say) each other in qualities, it cannot be that the one should differ from the other in courtesy; seeing the sincere affection of the mind cannot be expressed by the mouth and that no art can unfold the entire love of the heart, I am earnestly to beseech you not to measure the firmness of my faith by the fewness of my words, but rather think that the overflowing waves of goodwill leave no passage for many words. Trial shall prove trust. Here is my hand, my heart, my lands, and my life at thy commandment. Thou mayst well perceive that I did believe thee that so soon I did love thee, and I hope thou wilt the rather love me in that I did believe thee.'

Either Euphues and Philautus stood in need of friendship or were ordained to be friends. Upon so short warning to make so soon a conclusion might seem (in mine opinion), if it continued, miraculous, if shaken off, ridiculous. But after many embracings and protestations one to another, they walked to dinner, where they wanted neither meat,[2] neither music, neither any other pastime; and having banqueted, to digest their sweet confections, they danced all that afternoon. They used only one board,[3] but one bed, one book (if so be it they thought not one too many). Their friendship augmented every day, insomuch that the one could not refrain the company of the other one minute. All things went in common between them, which all men accounted commendable.

Philautus being a town-born child, both for his own countenance and the great countenance[4] which his father had while he lived, crept into credit with Don Ferardo, one of the chief govenors of the city, who, although he had a courtly crew of gentlewomen sojourning in his palace, yet his daughter, heir to his whole revenues, stained the beauty of them all, whose modest bashfulness caused the other to look wan for envy, whose lily cheeks, dyed with a vermilion red, made the rest to blush for shame. For as the finest ruby staineth the colour of the rest that be in place, or as the sun dimmeth the moon that she cannot be discerned, so this gallant girl, more fair than fortunate, and yet more fortunate than faithful, eclipsed the beauty of them all and changed their colours. Unto her had Philautus access, who won her by right of love and should have worn her by right of law, had not Euphues by strange destiny broken the bonds of marriage and forbidden the banns of matrimony.

It happened that Don Ferardo had occasion to go to Venice about certain his own affairs, leaving his daughter the only steward of his house-

---

1 *curiosity*] ceremony
2 *meat*] food
3 *board*] dinner table
4 *countenance / countenance*] bearing / reputation

hold, who spared not to feast Philautus her friend with all kinds of delights and delicates, reserving only her honesty[1] as the chief stay of her honour. Her father being gone, she sent for her friend to supper, who came not, as he was accustomed, solitarily alone, but accompanied with his friend, Euphues. The gentlewoman, whether it were for niceness or for niggardness of courtesy,[2] gave him such a cold welcome that he repented that he was come.

Euphues, though he knew himself worthy every way to have a good countenance,[3] yet could he not perceive her willing any way to lend him a friendly look. Yet, lest he should seem to want gestures[4] or to be dashed out of conceit with her coy countenance,[5] he addressed him to a gentlewoman called Livia, unto whom he uttered this speech:

'Fair lady, if it be the guise[6] of Italy to welcome strangers with strangeness, I must needs say the custom is strange and the country barbarous; if the manner of ladies to salute gentlemen with coyness, then I am enforced to think the women without courtesy to use such welcome, and the men past shame that will come. But hereafter I will either bring a stool on mine arm for an unbidden guest,[7] or a vizard on my face for a shameless gossip.'[8]

Livia replied:

'Sir, our country is civil and our gentlewomen are courteous, but in Naples it is counted a jest at every word to say, "In faith you are welcome".'

As she was yet talking, supper was set on the board. Then Philautus spake thus unto Lucilla:

'Yet, gentlewoman, I was the bolder to bring my shadow with me,' meaning Euphues, 'knowing that he should be the better welcome for my sake.'

Unto whom the gentlewoman replied:

'Sir, as I never when I saw you thought that you came without your shadow, so now I cannot a little marvel to see you so overshot[9] in bringing a new shadow with you.'

Euphues, though he perceived her coy nip,[10] semed not to care for it, but taking her by the hand said:

'Fair lady, seeing the shade doth often shield your beauty from the parching sun, I hope you will the better esteem of the shadow; and by so

---

1 *honesty*] chastity
2 *whether it were . . . courtesy*] whether through over-refinement or want of manners
3 *countenance*] reception
4 *want gestures*] lack the social graces
5 *dashed out . . . countenance*] abashed by her reserved manner
6 *guise*] custom
7 *bring . . . guest*] bring my own seat with me as if I were uninvited
8 *vizard . . . gossip*] mask on my face as if I were a shameless tittle-tattle
9 *overshot*] carried to excess
10 *coy nip*] disdainful jibe

much the less it ought to be offensive by how much the less it is able to offend you, and by so much the more you ought to like it by how much the more you use to lie in it.'

'Well, gentleman,' answered Lucilla, 'in arguing of the shadow we forgo the substance. Pleaseth it you, therefore, to sit down to supper?'

And so they all sat down; but Euphues fed of one dish which ever stood before him, the beauty of Lucilla. Here Euphues at the first sight was so kindled with desire that almost he was like to burn to coals.

Supper being ended, the order was in Naples that the gentlewomen would desire to hear some discourse, either concerning love or learning. And although Philautus was requested, yet he posted it over to Euphues, whom he knew most fit for that purpose. Euphues being thus tied to the stake[1] by their importunate entreaty, began as followeth:

'He that worst may is alway enforced to hold the candle; the weakest must still to the wall; where none will, the devil himself must bear the cross.[2] But were it not, gentlewomen, that your lust[3] stands for law, I would borrow so much leave as to resign mine office to one of you, whose experience in love hath made you learned, and whose learning hath made you so lovely. For me to entreat of[4] the one, being a novice, or to discourse of the other, being a truant, I may well make you weary but never the wiser, and give you occasion rather to laugh at my rashness than to like my reasons. Yet I care the less to excuse my boldness to you who were the cause of my blindness. And since I am at mine own choice either to talk of love or of learning, I had rather for this time be deemed an unthrift in rejecting profit than a Stoic in renouncing pleasure.

'It hath been a question often disputed, but never determined, whether the qualities of the mind or the composition of the man cause women most to like, or whether beauty or wit move men most to love. Certes, by how much the more the mind is to be preferred before the body, by so much the more the graces of the one are to be preferred before the gifts of the other; which if it be so that the contemplation of the inward quality ought to be respected more than the view of the outward beauty, then doubtless women either do or should love those best whose virtue is best, not measuring the deformed man with the reformed mind.[5] The foul toad hath a fair stone in his head,[6] the fine gold is found in the filthy

---

1 *tied ... stake*] constrained to comply (metaphor drawn from bear-baiting)
2 *He that ... cross*] all variations on proverbial sayings. *To hold the candle to one's shames*: to expose one's own failings. *The weakest goeth to the wall*: the feeblest are always exposed or obliged to give place. *Where none may the devil must bear the cross*: the least able must perform a task when there are no alternatives.
3 *lust*] wish
4 *entreat of*] expatiate on
5 *not measuring ... reformed mind*] not weighing the misshapen body and the elevated mind in the same scale
6 *foul toad ... head*] A reference to the popular belief that a precious stone with powerful medicinal properties was to be found in the head of a toad.

earth, the sweet kernel lieth in the hard shell. Virtue is harboured in the heart of him that most men esteem misshapen. Contrariwise, if we respect more the outward shape than the inward habit—good God, into how many mischiefs do we fall! Into what blindness are we led! Do we not commonly see that in painted pots is hidden the deadliest poison, that in the greenest grass is the greatest serpent, in the clearest water the ugliest toad? Doth not experience teach us that in the most curious sepulchre are enclosed rotten bones, that the cypress tree beareth a fair leaf but no fruit, that the estridge[1] carrieth fair feathers but rank flesh? How frantic are those lovers which are carried away with the gay glistering of the fine face, the beauty whereof is parched with the summer's blaze and chipped with the winter's blast, which is of so short continuance that it fadeth before one perceive it flourish, of so small profit that it poisoneth those that possess it, of so little value with the wise that they account it a delicate bait with a deadly hook, a sweet panther with a devouring paunch, a sour poison in a silver pot.

'Here I could enter into discourse of such fine dames as being in love with their own looks make such coarse account of their passionate lovers; for commonly, if they be adorned with beauty, they be so strait-laced and made so high in the instep[2] that they disdain them most that most desire them. It is a world to see[3] the doting of their lovers and their dealing with them, the revealing of whose subtle trains[4] would cause me to shed tears and you, gentlewomen, to shut your modest ears. Pardon me, gentlewomen, if I unfold every wile[5] and show every wrinkle[6] of women's disposition. Two things do they cause their servants to vow unto them, secrecy and sovereignty, the one to conceal their enticing sleights, by the other to assure themselves of their only service. Again—but ho there! If I should have waded any further and sounded the depth of their deceit, I should either have procured your displeasure or incurred the suspicion of fraud, either armed you to practise the like subtlety or accused myself of perjury. But I mean not to offend your chaste minds with the rehearsal of their unchaste manners, whose ears I perceive to glow and hearts to be grieved at that which I have already uttered; not that amongst you there be any such, but that in your sex there should be any such.

'Let not gentlewomen, therefore, make too much of their painted sheath,[7] let them not be so curious in their own conceit,[8] or so currish to their loyal lovers. When the black crow's foot shall appear in their eye,

---

1 *curious / estridge*] elaborate / goshawk
2 *high in the instep*] proud
3 *world to see*] wonder to behold
4 *trains*] tricks
5 *if I . . . wile*] if I do not reveal every contrivance
6 *wrinkle*] detail
7 *sheath*] physical exterior
8 *curious in their own conceit*] fine in their own imagination

or the black ox tread on their foot, when their beauty shall be like the
blasted rose, their wealth wasted, their bodies worn, their faces wrinkled,
their fingers crooked, who will like of them in their age who loved none
in their youth? If you will be cherished when you be old, be courteous
while you be young; if you look for comfort in your hoary hairs, be not
coy when you have your golden locks; if you would be embraced in the
waning of your bravery,[1] be not squeamish in the waxing of your beauty;
if you desire to be kept like the roses when they have lost their colour,
smell sweet as the rose doth in the bud; if you would be tasted for old
wine, be in the mouth a pleasant grape—so shall you be cherished for
your courtesy, comforted for your honesty, embraced for your amity; so
shall you be preserved with the sweet rose, and drunk with the pleasant
wine.

'Thus far I am bold, gentlewomen, to counsel those that be coy, that
they weave not the web of their own woe, nor spin the thread of their
own thraldom by their own overthwartness.[2] And seeing we are even in
the bowels of love, it shall not be amiss to examine whether man or
woman be soonest allured, whether be most constant the male or the
female. And in this point I mean not to be mine own carver,[3] lest I should
seem either to pick a thank with[4] men or a quarrel with women. If, therefore, it might stand with your pleasure, Mistress Lucilla, to give your
censure, I would take the contrary; for sure I am, though your judgement
be sound, yet affection[5] will shadow it.'

Lucilla, seeing his pretence, thought to take advantage of his large
proffer, unto whom she said:

'Gentleman, in my opinion women are to be won with every wind, in
whose sex there is neither force to withstand the assaults of love, neither
constancy to remain faithful. And because your discourse hath hitherto
bred delight, I am loath to hinder you in the sequel of your devices.'

Euphues, perceiving himself to be taken napping,[6] answered as
followeth:

'Mistress Lucilla, if you speak as you think, these gentlewomen present
have little cause to thank you; if you cause me to commend women, my
tale will be accounted a mere trifle and your words the plain truth. Yet
knowing promise to be debt, I will pay it with performance. And I would
the gentlemen here present were as ready to credit my proof as the
gentlewomen are willing to hear their own praises; or I as able to overcome as Mistress Lucilla would be content to be overthrown. Howsoever
the matter shall fall out, I am of the surer side: for if my reasons be weak,

---

1 *bravery*] fine looks
2 *thraldom / overthwartness*] servitude / cross-grained nature or behaviour
3 *be . . . carver*] introduce the topic myself
4 *pick a thank with*] seek to ingratiate myself with
5 *affection*] bias
6 *taken napping*] caught off guard

then is our sex strong; if forcible, then your judgement feeble; if I find truth on my side, I hope I shall, for my wages, win the good will of women; if I want proof, then, gentlewomen, of necessity you must yield to men. But to the matter.

'Touching the yielding to love, albeit their hearts seem tender, yet they harden them like the stone of Sicilia,[1] the which the more it is beaten the harder it is; for being framed as it were of the perfection of men, they be free from all such cogitations as may any way provoke them to uncleanness,[2] insomuch as they abhor the light love of youth which is grounded upon lust and dissolved upon every light occasion. When they see the folly of men turn to fury, their delight to doting, their affection to frenzy; when they see them as it were pine in pleasure, and to wax pale through their own peevishness;[3] their suits, their service, their letters, their labours, their loves—their lives seem to them so odious that they harden their hearts against such concupiscence, to the end they might convert them from rashness to reason, from such lewd disposition to honest discretion. Hereof it cometh that men accuse women of cruelty because they themselves want civility, they account them full of wiles in not yielding to their wickedness, faithless for resisting their filthiness. But I had almost forgot myself—. You shall pardon me, Mistress Lucilla, for this time, if this abruptly I finish my discourse. It is neither for want of good will, or lack of proof, but that I feel in myself such alteration that I can scarcely utter one word. Ah Euphues, Euphues!'

The gentlewomen were struck into such a quandary with this sudden change that they all changed colour. But Euphues, taking Philautus by the hand and giving the gentlewomen thanks for their patience and his repast, bade them all farewell and went immediately to his chamber.

But Lucilla, who now began to fry in the flames of love, all the company being departed to their lodgings, entered into these terms and contrarities:[4]

'Ah wretched wench Lucilla, how art thou perplexed! What a doubtful fight dost thou feel betwixt faith and fancy, hope and fear, conscience and concupiscence![5] O my Euphues, little dost thou know the sudden sorrow that I sustain for thy sweet sake, whose wit hath bewitched me, whose rare qualities have deprived me of mine old quality, [whose] courteous behaviour without curiosity,[6] whose comely feature without fault, whose filed[7] speech without fraud hath wrapped me in this misfortune. And canst thou, Lucilla, be so light of love in forsaking Philautus to fly to Euphues? Canst thou prefer a stranger before thy

---

1 *stone of Sicilia*] noted for making good whetstones (see Bond, I, p. 337)
2 *uncleanness*] impurity
3 *peevishness*] folly
4 *contrarities*] opposing arguments
5 *concupiscence*] desire
6 *curiosity*] over-refinement
7 *filed*] polished

countryman, a starter¹ before thy companion? Why, Euphues doth
perhaps desire my love; but Philautus hath deserved it. Why, Euphues'
feature is worthy as good as I; but Philautus his faith is worthy a better.
Aye, but the latter love is most fervent; aye, but the first ought to be most
faithful. Aye, but Euphues hath greater perfection; aye, but Philautus hath
deeper affection.

'Ah fond wench, dost thou think Euphues will deem thee constant to
him, when thou hast been unconstant to his friend? Weenest thou² that
he will have no mistrust of thy faithfulness when he hath had trial of thy
fickleness? Will he have no doubt of thine honour, when thou thyself
callest thine honesty in question? Yes, yes, Lucilla, well doth he know that
the glass once crazed will with the least clap³ be cracked, that the cloth
which staineth with milk will soon lose his colour with vinegar, that
the eagle's wing will waste the feather as well of the phoenix as of the
pheasant,⁴ that she that hath been faithless to one will never be faithful
to any.

'But can Euphues convince me of fleeting,⁵ seeing for his sake I break
my fidelity? Can he condemn me of disloyalty, when he is the only cause
of my disliking? May he justly condemn me of treachery, who hath this
testimony as trial of my good will? Doth not he remember that the broken
bone once set together is stronger than ever it was; that the greatest blot
is taken off with the pumice; that though the spider poison the fly, she
cannot infect the bee; that although I have been light⁶ to Philautus, I may
be lovely to Euphues? It is not my desire but his deserts that moveth my
mind to this choice; neither the want of the like good will in Philautus
but the lack of the like good qualities that removeth my fancy from the
one to the other.

'For as the bee that gathereth honey out of the weed when she espieth
the fair flower flieth to the sweetest; or as the kind⁷ spaniel though he
hunt after birds yet forsakes them to retrieve the partridge; or as we commonly feed on beef hungerly at the first, yet seeing the quail more dainty
change our diet; so I, although I loved Philautus for his good properties,
yet seeing Euphues to excel him I ought by nature to like him better. By
so much the more, therefore, my change is to be excused, by how much
the more my choice is excellent; and by so much the less I am to be
condemned, by how much the more Euphues is to be commended. Is not
the diamond of more value than the ruby because he is of more virtue?

---

1 *starter*] wanderer
2 *Weenest thou*] do you think
3 *clap*] knock, light blow
4 *eagle's wing . . . pheasant*] The feathers of the eagle were thought to destroy those
  of any other bird which came into contact with them.
5 *convince me of fleeting*] find me guilty of inconstancy
6 *light*] faithless
7 *kind*] true-bred

Is not the emerald preferred before the sapphire for his wonderful property? Is not Euphues more praiseworthy than Philautus being more witty?

'But fie, Lucilla, why dost thou flatter thyself in thine own folly? Canst thou feign Euphues thy friend, whom by thine own words thou hast made thy foe? Didst not thou accuse women of inconstancy? Didst not thou account them easy to be won? Didst not thou condemn them of weakness? What sounder arguments can he have against thee than thine own answer; what better proof than thine own speech; what greater trial than thine own talk? If thou hast belied women, he will judge thee unkind;[1] if thou have revealed the truth, he must needs think thee unconstant; if he perceive thee to be won with a nut, he will imagine that thou wilt be lost with an apple;[2] if he find thee wanton before thou be wooed, he will guess thou wilt be wavering when thou art wedded.

'But suppose that Euphues love thee, that Philautus leave thee, will thy father, thinkest thou, give thee liberty to live after thine own lust?[3] Will he esteem him worthy to inherit his possessions whom he accounteth unworthy to enjoy thy person? Is it like that he will match thee in marriage with a stranger, with a Grecian, with a mean man? Aye, but what knoweth my father whether he be wealthy, whether his revenues be able to countervail my father's lands,[4] whether his birth be noble, yea or no? Can anyone make doubt of his gentle blood that seeth his gentle conditions? Can his honour be called into question whose honesty is so great? Is he to be thought thriftless who in all qualities of the mind is peerless? No, no, the tree is known by his fruit, the gold by his touch,[5] the son by the sire. And as the soft wax receiveth whatsoever print be in the seal and showeth no other impression, so the tender babe, being sealed with his father's gifts, representeth his image most lively.

'But were I once certain of Euphues' good will I would not so superstitiously account of my father's ill will. Time hath weaned me from my mother's teat, and age rid me from my father's correction. When children are in their swath-clouts, then are they subject to the whip, and ought to be careful of the rigour of their parents. As for me, seeing I am not fed with their pap,[6] I am not to be led by their persuasions. Let my father use what speeches he list,[7] I will follow mine own lust. Lust, Lucilla? What sayest thou? No, no, mine own love, I should have said; for I am as far from lust as I am from reason, and as near to love as I am to folly. Then

---

1 *unkind*] unnatural
2 *won with a nut / lost with an apple*] won with a trifle / lost with something equally worthless
3 *lust*] In this context 'wish', but Lyly goes on in the following paragraph to play on the sexual connotations of the word.
4 *whether his revenues . . . lands*] whether his income counterbalances my father's property
5 *gold . . . touch*] A reference to the testing of gold by means of a touchstone.
6 *pap*] baby food
7 *list*] wishes

stick to thy determination and show thyself what love can do, what love dares do, what love hath done. Albeit I can no way quench the coals of desire with forgetfulness, yet will I rake them up in the ashes of modesty; seeing I dare not discover my love for maidenly shamefastness,[1] I will dissemble it till time I have opportunity. And I hope so to behave myself, as Euphues shall think me his own, and Philautus persuade himself I am none but his. But I would to God Euphues would repair hither, that the sight of him might mitigate some part of my martyrdom.'

She, having thus discoursed with herself her own miseries, cast herself on the bed. And there let her lie, and return we to Euphues, who was so caught in the gin[2] of folly that he neither could comfort himself nor durst ask counsel of his friend, suspecting that which indeed was true that Philautus was corrival with him and cockmate with[3] Lucilla. Amidst, therefore, these his extremities, between hope and fear, he uttered these or the like speeches:

'What is he, Euphues, that knowing thy wit and seeing thy folly, but will rather punish thy lewdness than pity thy heaviness? Was there ever any so fickle so soon to be allured; any ever so faithless to deceive his friend; ever any so foolish to bathe himself in his own misfortune? Too true it is that as the sea-crab swimmeth always against the stream, so wit always striveth against wisdom; and as the bee is oftentimes hurt with her own honey, so is wit not seldom plagued with his own conceit.[4]

'O ye gods, have ye ordained for every malady a medicine, for every sore a salve, for every pain a plaster, leaving only love remediless? Did ye deem no man so mad to be entangled with desire, or thought ye them worthy to be tormented that were so misled? Have ye dealt more favourably with brute beasts than with reasonable creatures? The filthy sow when she is sick eateth the sea-crab and is immediately recured;[5] the tortoise having tasted the viper sucketh origanum and is quickly revived; the bear ready to pine licketh up the ants and is recovered; the dog having surfeited to procure his vomit eateth grass and findeth remedy; the hart being pierced with the dart runneth out of hand to the herb dictanum[6] and is healed. And can men by no herb, by no art, by no way procure a remedy for the impatient disease of love? Ah well I perceive that love is not unlike the fig-tree, whose fruit is sweet, whose root is more bitter than the claw of a bittern;[7] or like the apple in Persia, whose blossom savoureth like honey, whose bud is more sour than gall.

---

1 *discover / shamefastness*] reveal / modesty
2 *gin*] trap
3 *cockmate with*] chosen companion of
4 *conceit*] devices
5 *recured*] made well
6 *origanum / dictanum*] wild marjoram / dittany (herb reputed to have medicinal properties)
7 *bittern*] marsh bird, eaten until recent times. (The pun is more pointed in the copy-text, which reads 'bitter', the more common form of the bird's name in the sixteenth century.)

'But oh, impiety! Oh broad blasphemy against the heavens! Wilt thou be so impudent, Euphues, to accuse the gods of iniquity? No, fond fool, no! Neither is it forbidden us by the gods to love, by whose divine providence we are permitted to live, neither do we want remedies to recure our maladies,[1] but reason to use the means. But why go I about to hinder the course of love with the discourse of law? Hast thou not read, Euphues, that he that loppeth the vine causeth it to spread fairer; that he that stoppeth the stream forceth it to swell higher; that he that casteth water on the fire in the smith's forge maketh it to flame fiercer? Even so, he that seeketh by counsel to moderate his overlashing[2] affections increaseth his own misfortune.

'Ah my Lucilla, would thou wert either less fair, or I more fortunate; either I wiser, or thou milder; either I would I were out of this mad mood, either I would we were both of one mind. But how should she be persuaded of my loyalty that yet had never one simple proof of my love? Will she not rather imagine me to be entangled with her beauty than with her virtue; that my fancy being so lewdly chained at the first will be as lightly changed at the last; that nothing violent can be permanent? Yes, yes, she must needs conjecture so, although it be nothing so; for by how much the more my affection cometh on the sudden, by so much the less will she think it certain. The rattling thunderbolt hath but his clap, the lightning but his flash; and as they both come in a moment, so do they both end in a minute.

'Aye but, Euphues, hath she not heard also that the dry touchwood[3] is kindled with lime; that the greatest mushroom groweth in one night; that the fire quickly burneth the flax;[4] that love easily entereth into the sharp wit without resistance, and is harboured there without repentance? If, therefore, the gods have endued her with as much bounty as beauty, if she have no less wit than she hath comeliness, certes, she will neither conceive sinisterly of my sudden suit, neither be coy[5] to receive me into her service, neither suspect me of lightness in yielding so lightly, neither reject me disdainfully for loving so hastily.

'Shall I not then hazard my life to obtain my love, and deceive Philautus to receive Lucilla? Yes, Euphues, where love beareth sway, friendship can have no show. As Philautus brought me for his shadow the last supper, so will I use him for my shadow till I have gained his saint. And canst thou, wretch, be false to him that is faithful to thee? Shall his courtesy be cause of thy cruelty? Wilt thou violate the league of faith to inherit the land of folly? Shall affection be of more force than friendship, love than law, lust than loyalty? Knowest thou not that he that loseth his honesty hath nothing else to lose?

---

1 *want remedies . . . maladies*] lack cures to treat our diseases
2 *overlashing*] immoderate
3 *touchwood*] easily combustible wood derivative, used for kindling
4 *flax*] material used for candle wicks
5 *sinisterly / coy*] adversely / reluctant

'Tush, the case is light where reason taketh place; to love and to live well is not granted to Jupiter.[1] Whoso is blinded with the caul[2] of beauty discerneth no colour of honesty. Did not Gyges cut Candaules a coat by his own measure; did not Paris, though he were a welcome guest to Menelaus, serve his host a slippery prank?[3] If Philautus had loved Lucilla he would never have suffered Euphues to have seen her. Is it not the prey that enticeth the thief to rifle;[4] is it not the pleasant bait that causeth the fleetest fish to bite; is it not a byword amongst us that gold maketh an honest man an ill man? Did Philautus account Euphues too simple to decipher beauty, or superstitious[5] not to desire it? Did he deem him a saint in rejecting fancy, or a sot in not discerning? Thought he him a Stoic that he would not be moved, or a stock that he could not?

'Well, well, seeing the wound that bleedeth inwardly is most danger-ous, that the fire kept close burneth most furious, that the oven dammed up baketh soonest, that sores having no vent fester secretly, it is high time to unfold my secret love to my secret friend. Let Philautus behave himself never so craftily, he shall know that it must be a wily mouse that shall breed in the cat's ear; and because I resemble him in wit, I mean a little to dissemble with him in wiles.

'But, O my Lucilla, if thy heart be made of that stone which may be mollified only with blood,[6] would I had sipped of that river in Caria[7] which turneth those that drink of it to stones. If thine ears be anointed with the oil of Syria that bereaveth hearing, would mine eyes had been rubbed with the syrup of the cedar tree which taketh away sight. If Lucilla be so proud to disdain poor Euphues, would Euphues were so happy to deny Lucilla; or if Lucilla be so mortified[8] to live without love, would Euphues were so fortunate to live in hate. Aye, but my cold welcome foretelleth my cold suit. Aye, but her privy glances signify some good fortune. Fie, fond fool Euphues, why goest thou about to allege those things to cut off thy hope which she perhaps would never have found, or to comfort thyself with those reasons which she never meaneth to propose?

---

1 *the case . . . Jupiter*] both proverbial. (i) The grief is slight that can be eased by good counsel. (ii) Even the gods behave badly in love.

2 *caul*] net-like membrane, veil

3 *Gyges . . . prank*] instances of betrayal motivated by lust. Gyges killed King Candaules and married his wife, having been forced by her husband to spy on her beauty. For *Paris* see pp. 27 and 33nn.

4 *rifle*] rob

5 *superstitious*] governed by scruple

6 *stone . . . blood*] the diamond (fabled, amongst other fabulous properties, to be softened by blood)

7 *river in Caria*] tentatively identified by Croll and Clemons (p. 47n.) with the river Pactolus which had the power to turn anything dipped in it to gold

8 *mortified*] dead to feeling

'Tush, it were no love if it were certain, and a small conquest it is to overthrow those that never resisteth. In battles there ought to be a doubtful fight and a desperate end; in pleading a difficult entrance and a diffused determination;[1] in love a life without hope and a death without fear. Fire cometh out of the hardest flint with the steel; oil out of the driest jet by the fire; love out of the stoniest heart by faith, by trust, by time. Had Tarquinius used his love with colours of continuance,[2] Lucretia would either with some pity have answered his desire, or with some persuasion have stayed her death. It was the heat of his lust that made her haste to end her life, wherefore love in neither respect is to be condemned, but he of rashness to attempt a lady furiously, and she of rigour to punish his folly in her own flesh—a fact, in mine opinion, more worthy the name of cruelty than chastity, and fitter for a monster in the deserts than a matron of Rome. Penelope, no less constant than she yet more wise, would be weary to unweave that in the night she spun in the day if Ulysses had not come home the sooner.[3] There is no woman, Euphues, but she will yield in time. Be not, therefore, dismayed either with high looks or froward[4] words.'

Euphues having thus talked with himself, Philautus entered the chamber, and finding him so worn and wasted with continual mourning, neither joying in his meat nor rejoicing in his friend, with watery eyes uttered this speech:

'Friend and fellow, as I am not ignorant of thy present weakness, so I am not privy of the cause; and although I suspect many things, yet can I assure myself of no one thing. Therefore, my good Euphues, for these doubts and dumps of mine either remove the cause or reveal it. Thou hast hitherto found me a cheerful companion in thy mirth, and now shalt thou find me as careful with thee[5] in thy moan. If altogether thou mayst not be cured, yet mayst thou be comforted. If there be anything that either by my friends may be procured, or by my life attained, that may either heal thee in part or help thee in all, I protest to thee by the name of a friend that it shall rather be gotten with the loss of my body, than lost by getting a kingdom. Thou hast tried me, therefore trust me; thou hast trusted me in many things, therefore try me in this one thing. I never yet failed, and now I will not faint. Be bold to speak and blush not. Thy sore

---

1 *difficult entrance / diffused determination*] complex opening / expansive close
2 *Tarquinius / colours of continuance*] last king of Rome, whose rape of Lucretia, wife of Collatinus, induced her to take her own life / some pretence of perseverance
3 *Penelope . . . sooner*] Beset by suitors after Ulysses' failure to return from the Trojan war, Penelope promised to take a new husband when she had completed a tapestry on which she was working, unweaving during the night the work she had done in the day. Ulysses returned after a ten-year journey, having been away for twenty years.
4 *froward*] contrary
5 *careful with thee*] ready to share your care

is not so angry but I can salve it; the wound not so deep but I can search it; thy grief not so great but I can ease it. If it be ripe it shall be lanced, if it be broken it shall be tainted,[1] be it never so desperate it shall be cured. Rise, therefore, Euphues, and take heart at grass.[2] Younger thou shalt never be! Pluck up thy stomach! If love itself have stung thee, it shall not stifle thee. Though thou be enamoured of some lady, thou shalt not be enchanted. They that begin to pine of a consumption without delay preserve themselves with cullises;[3] he that feeleth his stomach inflamed with heat cooleth it eftsoons with conserves.[4] Delays breed dangers; nothing so perilous as procrastination.'

Euphues, hearing this comfort and friendly counsel, dissembled his sorrowing heart with a smiling face, answering him forthwith as followeth:

'True it is, Philautus, that he which toucheth the nettle tenderly is soonest stung, that the fly which playeth with the fire is singed in the flame, that he that dallieth with women is drawn to his woe. And as the adamant[5] draweth the heavy iron, the harp the fleet dolphin, so beauty allureth the chaste mind to love, and the wisest wit to lust. The example whereof I would it were no less profitable than the experience to me is like to be perilous. The vine watered with wine is soon withered, the blossom in the fattest[6] ground is quickly blasted, the goat the fatter she is the less fertile she is; yea, man the more witty he is the less happy[7] he is. So it is, Philautus (for why should I conceal it from thee of whom I am to take counsel?), that since my last and first being with thee at the house of Ferardo, I have felt such a furious battle in mine own body as, if it be not speedily repressed by policy, it will carry my mind (the grand captain in this fight) into endless captivity. Ah Livia, Livia, thy courtly grace without coyness, thy blazing beauty without blemish, thy courteous demeanour without curiosity,[8] thy sweet speech savoured with wit, thy comely mirth tempered with modesty, thy chaste looks yet lovely, thy sharp taunts yet pleasant, have given me such a check that, sure I am, at the next view of thy virtues I shall take the mate.[9] And taking it not of a pawn but of a prince the loss is to be accounted the less. And though they be commonly in a great choler that receive the mate, yet would I willingly take every minute ten mates to enjoy Livia for my loving mate.

---

1 *ripe / tainted*] ready to burst / anointed
2 *take heart at grass*] pluck up your spirits
3 *cullises*] rich broths
4 *cooleth . . . conserves*] immediately cools it with medicinal preparations
5 *adamant*] magnet
6 *fattest*] most fertile
7 *happy*] fortunate
8 *curiosity*] undue nicety
9 *take the mate*] All early editions read 'take thee mate', but the sense is clearly 'be checkmated by you' rather than 'take you as my partner'. The chess imagery is sustained in the following lines.

'Doubtless, if ever she herself have been scorched with the flames of desire, she will be ready to quench the coals with courtesy in another; if ever she have been attached of[1] love, she will rescue him that is drenched in desire; if ever she have been taken with the fever of fancy, she will help his ague who by a quotidian fit[2] is converted into frenzy. Neither can there be under so delicate a hue lodged deceit, neither in so beautiful a mould[3] a malicious mind. True it is that the disposition of the mind followeth the composition of the body; how then can she be in mind any way imperfect who in body is perfect every way?

'I know my success will be good, but I know not how to have access to my goddess; neither do I want courage to discover my love to my friend, but some colour[4] to cloak my coming to the house of Ferardo. For if they be in Naples as jealous[5] as they be in the other parts of Italy, then it behoveth me to walk circumspectly, and to forge some cause for my often coming. If, therefore, Philautus, thou canst set but this feather to mine arrow, thou shalt see me shoot so near that thou wilt account me for a cunning archer. And verily, if I had not loved thee well, I would have swallowed mine own sorrow in silence, knowing that in love nothing is so dangerous as to participate the means thereof to another, and that two may keep counsel if one be away.[6] I am, therefore, enforced perforce to challenge that courtesy at thy hands which erst[7] thou didst promise with thy heart, the performance whereof shall bind me to Philautus, and prove thee faithful to Euphues. Now, if thy cunning be answerable to thy good will, practise some pleasant conceit upon thy poor patient: one dram of Ovid's art, some of Tibullus' drugs, one of Propertius' pills,[8] which may cause me either to purge my new disease or recover my hoped desire. But I fear me where so strange a sickness is to be recured of[9] so unskilful a physician, that either thou wilt be too bold to practise or my body too weak to purge. But seeing a desperate disease is to be committed to a desperate doctor, I will follow thy counsel and become thy cure,[10] desiring thee to be as wise in ministering thy physic as I have been willing to put my life into thy hands.'

Philautus, thinking all to be gold that glistered and all to be gospel that Euphues uttered, answered his forged gloze with this friendly close:[11]

---

1 *attached of*] seized by
2 *quotidian fit*] intermittent fever, recurring daily
3 *mould*] physical form
4 *colour*] excuse
5 *jealous*] suspiciously vigilant
6 *two . . . away*] no one can keep a secret (proverbial)
7 *erst*] previously
8 *Ovid's . . . pills*] All references to works on the subject of love. For *Ovid* see p. 33n. Tibullus (circa 54–18 BC) wrote a series of elegies to Delia. Propertius (b. circa 51 BC) wrote elegies to Cynthia. ·
9 *recured of*] remedied by
10 *cure*] patient
11 *forged gloze / friendly close*] disingenuous eloquence / supportive response

'In that thou hast made me privy to thy purpose, I will not conceal my
practice; in that thou cravest my aid, assure thyself, I will be the finger
next thy thumb[1]—insomuch as thou shalt never repent thee of the one or
the other, for persuade thyself that thou shalt find Philautus during life
ready to comfort thee in thy misfortunes and succour thee in thy necessity. Concerning Livia, though she be fair yet is she not so amiable as
my Lucilla, whose servant[2] I have been the term of three years—but lest
comparisons should seem odious, chiefly where both the parties be without comparison, I will omit that. And seeing that we had both
rather be talking with them than tattling of them, we will immediately
go to them. And truly, Euphues, I am not a little glad that I shall have
thee not only a comfort in my life but also a companion in my love. As
thou hast been wise in thy choice, so I hope thou shalt be fortunate in
thy chance. Livia is a wench of more wit than beauty, Lucilla of more
beauty than wit; both of more honesty than honour, and yet both of such
honour as in all Naples there is not one in birth to be compared with any
of them both. How much, therefore, have we to rejoice in our choice.
Touching our access, be thou secure. I will flap Ferardo in the mouth with
some conceit,[3] and fill his old head so full of new fables that thou shalt
rather be earnestly entreated to repair to his house than evil entreated[4]
to leave it. As old men are very suspicious to mistrust everything, so
are they very credulous to believe anything. The blind man doth eat many
a fly.'
'Yea, but,' said Euphues, 'take heed, my Philautus, that thou thyself
swallow not a gudgeon,'[5] which word Philautus did not mark until he
had almost digested it.
'But,' said [Philautus], 'let us go devoutly to the shrine of our saints,
there to offer our devotion; for my books teach me that such a wound
must be healed where it was first hurt, and for this disease we will use a
common remedy, but yet comfortable. The eye that blinded thee shall
make thee see, the scorpion that stung thee shall heal thee, a sharp sore
hath a short cure. Let us go.' To the which Euphues consented willingly,
smiling to himself to see how he had brought Philautus into a fool's
paradise.
Here you may see, gentlemen, the falsehood in fellowship, the fraud in
friendship, the painted sheath with the leaden dagger, the fair words that
make fools fain.[6] But I will not trouble you with superfluous addition,
unto whom I fear me I have been tedious with the bare discourse of this
rude history.

---

1 *finger next thy thumb*] chief assistant
2 *servant*] acknowledged admirer
3 *flap Ferardo . . . conceit*] tell Ferardo some story
4 *evil entreated*] injuriously required
5 *swallow not a gudgeon*] don't take the bait (i.e. are not tricked)
6 *fain*] glad

Philautus and Euphues repaired to the house of Ferardo, where they found Mistress Lucilla and Livia, accompanied with other gentlewomen, neither being idle nor well employed, but playing at cards. But when Lucilla beheld Euphues she could scarcely contain herself from embracing him, had not womanly shamefastness, and Philautus his presence, stayed her wisdom. Euphues, on the other side, was fallen into such a trance that he had not the power either to succour himself or salute the gentlewomen. At the last, Lucilla began—as one that best might be bold— on this manner:

'Gentlemen, although your long absence gave me occasion to think that you disliked your late entertainment, yet your coming at the last hath cut off my former suspicion. And by so much the more you are welcome, by how much the more you were wished for. But you, gentleman,' taking Euphues by the hand, 'were the rather wished for, for that your discourse being left unperfect caused us all to long (as women are wont for things that like them) to have an end thereof.'

Unto whom Philautus replied as followeth:

'Mistress Lucilla, though your courtesy made us nothing to doubt of our welcome, yet modesty caused us to pinch courtesy[1] who should first come. As for my friend, I think he was never wished for here so earnestly of any as of himself, whether it might be to renew his talk or to recant his sayings I cannot tell.'

Euphues, taking the tale out of Philautus' mouth, answered:

'Mistress Lucilla, to recant verities were heresy, and renew the praises of women flattery. The only cause I wished myself here was to give thanks for so good entertainment, the which I could no ways deserve, and to breed a greater acquaintance if it might be to make amends.'

Lucilla, inflamed with his presence, said:

'Nay, Euphues, you shall not escape so; for if my courtesy, as you say, were the cause of your coming, let it also be the occasion of the ending your former discourse, otherwise I shall think your proof naked, and you shall find my reward nothing.'

Euphues, now as willing to obey as she to command, addressed himself to a further conclusion, who, seeing all the gentlewomen ready to give him the hearing, proceeded as followeth:

'I have not yet forgotten that my last talk with these gentlewomen tended to their praises, and therefore the end must tie up the just proof— otherwise I should set down Venus' shadow without the lively substance.

'As there is no one thing which can be reckoned either concerning love or loyalty wherein women do not excel men, yet in fervency above all others they so far exceed that men are liker to marvel at them than to imitate them, and readier to laugh at their virtues than emulate them. For

---

1 *pinch courtesy*] be over-punctilious over

as they be hard to be won without trial of great faith, so are they hard to be lost without great cause of fickleness. It is long before the cold water seethe, yet being once hot it is long before it be cooled; it is long before salt come to his saltness, but being once seasoned it never loseth his savour.

'I, for mine own part, am brought into a paradise by the only imagination of women's virtues; and were I persuaded that all the devils in hell were women, I would never live devoutly to inherit heaven, or that they were all saints in heaven, I would live more strictly for fear of hell. What could Adam have done in his Paradise before his fall without a woman, or how would he have rise again after his fall with[out] a woman? Artificers are wont in their last works to excel themselves: yea, God, when he had made all things, at the last made man as most perfect, thinking nothing could be framed more excellent, yet after him he created a woman, the express image of eternity, the lively picture of Nature, the only steel glass[1] for man to behold his infirmities by comparing them with women's perfections. Are they not more gentle, more witty, more beautiful than men? Are not men so bewitched with their qualities that they become mad for love, and women so wise that they detest lust?

'I am entered into so large a field that I shall sooner want time than proof, and so cloy you with variety of praises that I fear me I am like to infect women with pride, which yet they have not, and men with spite, which yet I would not. For as the horse if he knew his own strength were no ways to be bridled, or the unicorn his own virtue[2] were never to be caught, so women, if they knew what excellency were in them, I fear me men should never win them to their wills or wean them from their mind.'

Lucilla began to smile, saying:

'In faith, Euphues, I would have you stay there,[3] for as the sun when he is at the highest beginneth to go down, so when the praises of women are at the best, if you leave not, they will begin to fail.'

But Euphues, being rapt with the sight of his saint, answered:

'No, no, Lucilla—'

But whilst he was yet speaking Ferardo entered, whom they all dutifully welcomed home; who, rounding Philautus in the ear,[4] desired him to accompany him immediately without further pausing, protesting it should be as well for his preferment as for his own profit. Philautus consenting, Ferardo said unto his daughter:

'Lucilla, the urgent affairs I have in hand will scarce suffer me to tarry with you one hour. Yet my return, I hope, will be so short that my absence

---

1 *steel glass*] mirror (commonly made of steel)
2 *virtue*] peculiar property (in this case, that it could only be caught by a virgin)
3 *stay there*] stop at that point
4 *rounding . . . ear*] speaking privately to Philautus

shall not breed thy sorrow. In the mean season, I commit all things into thy custody, wishing thee to use thy accustomable courtesy. And seeing I must take Philautus with me, I will be so bold to crave you, gentleman, his friend, to supply his room,[1] desiring you to take this hasty warning for a hearty welcome, and so to spend this time of mine absence in honest mirth. And thus I leave you.'

Philautus knew well the cause of this sudden departure, which was to redeem certain lands that were mortgaged in his father's time to the use of Ferardo, who, on that condition, had beforetime promised him his daughter in marriage. But return we to Euphues.

Euphues was surprised with such incredible joy at this strange event that he had almost swooned; for seeing his corrival to be departed, and Ferardo to give him so friendly entertainment, doubted not in time to get the good will of Lucilla. Whom finding in place convenient without company, with a bold courage and comely gesture he began to assay[2] her in this sort:

'Gentlewoman, my acquaintance being so little, I am afraid my credit will be less, for that they commonly are soonest believed that are best beloved, and they liked best whom we have known longest. Nevertheless, the noble mind suspecteth no guile without cause, neither condemneth any wight[3] without proof. Having, therefore, notice of your heroical heart, I am the better persuaded of my good hap.[4]

'So it is, Lucilla, that coming to Naples but to fetch fire, as the byword is, not to make my place of abode,[5] I have found such flames that I can neither quench them with the water of free will, neither cool them with wisdom. For as the hop, the pole being never so high, groweth to the end, or as the dry beech kindled at the root never leaveth until it come to the top, or as one drop of poison disperseth itself into every vein, so affection having caught hold of my heart, and the sparkles of love kindled my liver,[6] will suddenly, though secretly, flame up into my head and spread itself into every sinew. It is your beauty (pardon my abrupt boldness), lady, that hath taken every part of me prisoner, and brought me unto this deep distress. But seeing women, when one praiseth them for their deserts, deem that he flattereth them to obtain his desire, I am here present to yield myself to such trial as your courtesy in this behalf shall require.

---

1 *supply his room*] take his place
2 *assay*] try, attempt
3 *wight*] person
4 *hap*] fortune
5 *but to fetch . . . place of abode*] to visit rather than to stay (proverbial expression drawn from the practice of going to a neighbour's house for live coals in order to light a fire)
6 *liver*] traditional seat of the passions

'Yet will you commonly object this to such as serve you and starve[1] to win your good will: that hot love is soon cold; that the bavin,[2] though it burn bright, is but a blaze; that scalding water, if it stand awhile, turneth almost to ice; that pepper, though it be hot in the mouth, is cold in the maw;[3] that the faith of men, though it fry in their words, it freezeth in their works. Which things, Lucilla, albeit they be sufficient to reprove the lightness of some one, yet can they not convince every one of lewdness; neither ought the constancy of all to be brought in question through the subtlety of a few. For although the worm entereth almost into every wood, yet he eateth not the cedar-tree; though the stone cylindrus at every thunderclap roll from the hill, yet the pure sleek-stone mounteth at the noise;[4] though the rust fret the hardest steel, yet doth it not eat into the emerald; though polypus change his hue, yet the salamander[5] keepeth his colour; though Proteus transform himself into every shape, yet Pygmalion[6] retaineth his old form; though Aeneas were too fickle to Dido, yet Troilus[7] was too faithful to Cressid; though others seem counterfeit in their deeds, yet, Lucilla, persuade yourself that Euphues will be always current in his dealings.

'But as the true gold is tried by the touch, the pure flint by the stroke of the iron, so the loyal heart of the faithful lover is known by the trial of his lady. Of the which trial, Lucilla, if you shall account Euphues worthy, assure yourself he will be as ready to offer himself a sacrifice for your sweet sake, as yourself shall be willing to employ him in your service. Neither doth he desire to be trusted any way until he shall be tried every way, neither doth he crave credit at the first, but a good countenance till time[8] his desire shall be made manifest by his deserts. Thus not blinded by light affection, but dazzled with your rare perfection, and boldened by your exceeding courtesy, I have unfolded mine entire love; desiring you, having so good leisure, to give so friendly an answer as I may receive comfort and you commendation.'

Lucilla, although she were contented to hear this desired discourse, yet did she seem to be somewhat displeased. And truly I know not whether

---

1 *starve*] die (specifically of cold)
2 *bavin*] bundle of brushwood
3 *maw*] stomach
4 *stone cylindrus . . . noise*] No source has been found for these allusions. A sleek-stone is used for polishing.
5 *polypus / salamander*] fish reputed to adapt its colour to its environment / creature thought to be capable of living, unchanged, in fire
6 *Proteus / Pygmalion*] mythological figure able to change his shape at will / sculptor associated with constancy through his devotion to one of his own statues (see p. 36n.)
7 *Aeneas / Troilus*] types of inconstancy and constancy. Aeneas left Dido, Queen of Carthage, in order to found Rome / Troilus, a brother of Paris (see p. 33n.), remained faithful to Cressida, who transferred her love to his enemy, Diomedes.
8 *till time*] until such time as

it be peculiar to that sex to dissemble with those whom they most desire, or whether by craft they have learned outwardly to loathe that which inwardly they most love. Yet wisely did she cast this in her head, that if she should yield at the first assault he would think her a light huswife,[1] if she should reject him scornfully a very haggard.[2] Minding, therefore, that he should neither take hold of her promise, neither unkindness of her preciseness, she fed him indifferently[3] with hope and despair, reason and affection, life and death. Yet in the end, arguing wittily upon certain questions, they fell into such agreement as poor Philautus would not have agreed unto if he had been present, yet always keeping the body undefiled. And thus she replied:

'Gentleman, as you may suspect me of idleness in giving ear to your talk, so may you convince me of lightness[4] in answering such toys. Certes, as you have made mine ears glow at the rehearsal of your love, so have you galled my heart with the remembrance of your folly. Though you came to Naples as a stranger, yet were you welcome to my father's house as a friend. And can you then so much transgress the bonds of honour (I will not say of honesty) as to solicit a suit more sharp to me than death? I have hitherto, God be thanked, lived without suspicion of lewdness, and shall I now incur the danger of sensual liberty? What hope can you have to obtain my love, seeing yet I could never afford you a good look? Do you, therefore, think me easily enticed to the bent of your bow because I was easily entreated to listen to your late discourse; or seeing me (as finely you gloze) to excel all other in beauty, did you deem that I would exceed all other in beastliness?

'But yet I am not angry, Euphues, but in an agony; for who is she that will fret or fume with one that loveth her—if this love to delude me be not dissembled? It is that which causeth me most to fear; not that my beauty is unknown to myself, but that commonly we poor wenches are deluded through light belief, and ye men are naturally inclined craftily to lead your life. When the fox preacheth the geese perish; the crocodile shroudeth greatest treason under most pitiful tears; in a kissing mouth there lieth a galling[5] mind. You have made so large proffer of your service, and so fair promises of fidelity, that were I not over chary of mine honesty you would inveigle me to shake hands with chastity. But, certes, I will either lead a virgin's life in earth (though I lead apes in hell),[6] or else follow thee rather than thy gifts. Yet am I neither so precise to refuse thy proffer, neither so peevish[7] to disdain thy good will; so excellent

---

1 *huswife*] hussy
2 *very haggard*] person of wholly untractable disposition
3 *indifferently*] even-handedly
4 *convince me of lightness*] find me guilty of wantonness
5 *galling*] corrosive
6 *lead apes in hell*] proverbial fate of old maids
7 *precise / peevish*] over-scrupulous / foolish

always are the gifts which are made acceptable by the virtue of the giver.

'I did at the first entrance discern thy love, but yet dissemble it. Thy wanton glances, thy scalding sighs, thy loving signs caused me to blush for shame and to look wan for fear, lest they should be perceived of any. These subtle shifts,[1] these painted practices, if I were to be won, would soon wean me from the teat of Vesta to the toys of Venus.[2] Besides this, thy comely grace, thy rare qualities, thy exquisite perfection were able to move a mind half-mortified[3] to transgress the bonds of maidenly modesty. But God shield, Lucilla, that thou shouldst be so careless of thine honour as to commit the state thereof to a stranger. Learn thou by me, Euphues, to despise things that be amiable, to forgo delightful practices; believe me, it is piety to abstain from pleasure.

'Thou art not the first that hath solicited this suit, but the first that goeth about to seduce me; neither discernest thou more than other, but darest more than any; neither hast thou more art to discover thy meaning, but more heart to open thy mind. But thou preferrest me before thy lands, thy livings, thy life; thou offerest thyself a sacrifice for my security; thou profferest me the whole and only sovereignty of thy service. Truly I were very cruel and hard-hearted if I should not love thee. Hard-hearted albeit I am not, but truly love thee I cannot, whom I doubt to be my lover.

'Moreover, I have not been used to the court of Cupid, wherein there be more sleights[4] than there be hares in Athos, than bees in Hybla,[5] than stars in heaven. Besides this, the common people here in Naples are not only both very suspicious of other men's matters and manners, but also very jealous over other men's children and maidens. Either, therefore, dissemble thy fancy or desist from thy folly. But why shouldst thou desist from the one, seeing thou canst cunningly dissemble the other? My father is now gone to Venice, and as I am uncertain of his return so am I not privy to the cause of his travel. But yet is he so from hence that he seeth me in his absence. Knowest thou not, Euphues, that kings have long arms and rulers large reaches? Neither let this comfort thee, that at his departure he deputed thee in Philautus' place. Although my face cause him to mistrust my loyalty, yet my faith enforceth him to give me this liberty; though he be suspicious of my fair hue, yet is he secure of my firm honesty.

'But alas, Euphues, what truth can there be found in a traveller, what stay in a stranger, whose words and bodies both watch but for a wind, whose feet are ever fleeting,[6] whose faith plighted on the shore is turned

---

1 *shifts*] devices
2 *Vesta / Venus*] see p. 33n.
3 *half-mortified*] half dead to human feeling
4 *sleights*] deceits
5 *Athos / Hybla*] wild, mountainous peninsula in Macedonia / town in Sicily noted for its honey
6 *fleeting*] constantly moving

to perjury when they hoist sail? Who more traitorous to Phyllis than Demophon, yet he a traveller? Who more perjured to Dido than Aeneas, and he a stranger? Both these queens, both they caitiffs. Who more false to Ariadne than Theseus, yet he a sailor? Who more fickle to Medea than Jason,[1] yet he a starter?[2] Both these daughters to great princes, both they unfaithful of their promises. Is it then likely that Euphues will be faithful to Lucilla, being in Naples but a sojourner?

'I have not yet forgotten the invective (I can no otherwise term it) which thou madest against beauty, saying it was a deceitful bait with a deadly hook, and a sweet poison in a painted pot. Canst thou then be so unwise to swallow the bait which will breed thy bane; to swill the drink that will expire thy date;[3] to desire the wight that will work thy death? But it may be that with the scorpion thou canst feed on the earth, or with the quail and roebuck be fat with poison, or with beauty live in all bravery.

'I fear me thou hast the stone continens[4] about thee, which is named of the contrary; that though thou pretend faith in thy words, thou devisest fraud in thy heart; that though thou seem to prefer love, thou art inflamed with lust. And what for that? Though thou have eaten the seeds of rocket[5] which breed incontinency, yet have I chewed the leaf cress which maintaineth modesty. Though thou bear in thy bosom the herb araxa, most noisome[6] to virginity, yet have I the stone that groweth in the mount Tmolus,[7] the upholder of chastity.

'You may, gentleman, account me for a cold prophet, thus hastily to divine of your disposition. Pardon me, Euphues, if in love I cast beyond the moon,[8] which bringeth us women to endless moan. Although I myself were never burnt, whereby I should dread the fire, yet the scorching of others in the flames of fancy warneth me to beware; though I as yet never tried any faithless, whereby I should be fearful, yet have I read of many that have been perjured, which causeth me to be careful; though I am able to convince[9] none by proof, yet am I enforced to suspect one upon probabilities. Alas, we silly souls, which have neither wit to decipher the wiles of men, nor wisdom to dissemble our affection, neither craft to train in[10] young lovers, neither courage to withstand their encounters, neither

---

1 Demophon ... Jason] all travellers who deserted (or were thought to have deserted) the women who fell in love with them in the course of their journeys
2 starter] rover
3 expire thy date] end your life
4 stone continens] No stone of this name has been traced, though others were reputed to have similar properties.
5 rocket] plant used in salads
6 noisesome] harmful
7 mount Tmolus] mountain in Asia Minor where many precious commodities were produced
8 cast beyond the moon] speculate too wildly
9 convince] condemn
10 train in] inveigle

discretion to discern their doubling, neither hard hearts to reject their complaints—we, I say, are soon enticed, being by nature simple, and easily entangled, being apt to receive the impression of love.

'But alas, it is both common and lamentable to behold simplicity entrapped by subtlety, and those that have most might to be infected with most malice. The spider weaveth a fine web to hang the fly, the wolf weareth a fair face to devour the lamb, the merlin striketh at the partridge, the eagle often snappeth at the fly, men are always laying baits for women which are the weaker vessels. But as yet I could never hear man by such snares to entrap man. For true it is, that men themselves have by use observed, that it must be a hard winter when one wolf eateth another. I have read that the bull being tied to the fig-tree loseth his strength; that the whole herd of deer stand at the gaze if they smell a sweet apple; that the dolphin by the sound of music is brought to the shore. And then no marvel it is that if the fierce bull be tamed with the fig-tree, if that women (being as weak as sheep) be overcome with a fig; if the wild deer be caught with an apple, that the tame damsel is won with a blossom; if the fleet dolphin be allured with harmony, that women be entangled with the melody of men's speech, fair promises and solemn protestations.

'But folly it were for me to mark their mischiefs. Sith[1] I am neither able, neither they willing, to amend their manners, it becometh me rather to show what our sex should do than to open what yours doth. And seeing I cannot by reason restrain your importunate suit, I will by rigour done on myself cause you to refrain the means. I would to God Ferardo were in this point like to Lysander,[2] which would not suffer his daughters to wear gorgeous apparel, saying it would rather make them common than comely. I would it were in Naples a law, which was a custom in Egypt, that women should always go barefoot, to the intent that they might keep themselves always at home, that they should be ever like to the snail which hath ever his house on his head. I mean so to mortify myself that instead of silks I will wear sackcloth; for ouches[3] and bracelets, lear and caddis;[4] for the lute, use the distaff;[5] for the pen, the needle; for lovers' sonnets, David's psalms.

'But yet I am not so senseless altogether to reject your service; which if I were certainly assured to proceed of a simple mind, it should not receive so simple a reward.[6] And what greater trial can I have of thy simplicity and truth than thine own request which desireth a trial? Aye, but in the coldest flint there is hot fire; the bee that hath honey in her mouth hath a sting in her tail; the tree that beareth the sweetest fruit hath a sour

---

1 Sith] since
2 Lysander] Spartan leader (d. 395 BC) noted for his aloof austerity
3 ouches] brooches (set with precious stones)
4 lear and caddis] plain tape and coarse worsted bindings
5 distaff] cleft stick wound with wool or flax, used for spinning
6 simple mind / so simple a reward] undesigning mind / such a poor return

sap; yea, the words of men though they seem smooth as oil, yet their hearts are as crooked as the stalk of ivy. I would not, Euphues, that thou shouldst condemn me of rigour in that I seek to assuage thy folly by reason; but take this by the way, that although as yet I am disposed to like of none, yet whensoever I shall love any I will not forget thee. In the mean season account me thy friend, for thy foe I will never be.'

Euphues was brought into a great quandary and as it were a cold shivering to hear this new kind of kindness—such sweet meat, such sour sauce; such fair words, such faint promises; such hot love, such cold desire; such certain hope, such sudden change—and stood like one that had looked on Medusa's head[1] and so had been turned into a stone. Lucilla, seeing him in this pitiful plight and fearing he would take stand if the lure were not cast out,[2] took him by the hand and, wringing[3] him softly, with a smiling countenance began thus to comfort him:

'Methinks, Euphues, changing so your colour upon the sudden, you will soon change your copy.[4] Is your mind on your meat?[5] A penny for your thought.'

'Mistress,' quoth he, 'if you would buy all my thoughts at that price, I should never be weary of thinking; but seeing it is too dear, read it and take it for nothing.'

'It seems to me,' said she, 'that you are in some brown study[6] what colours you might best wear for your lady.'

'Indeed, Lucilla, you level shrewdly at my thought by the aim of your own imagination. For you have given unto me a true love's knot wrought of changeable silk, and you deem that I am devising how I might have my colours changeable also that they might agree. But let this with such toys and devices pass. If it please you to command me any service, I am here ready to attend your leisure.'

'No service, Euphues, but that you keep silence until I have uttered my mind, and secrecy when I have unfolded my meaning.'

'If I should offend in the one I were too bold, if in the other too beastly.'

'Well then, Euphues,' said she, 'so it is that for the hope that I conceive of thy loyalty and the happy success that is like to ensue of this our love, I am content to yield thee the place in my heart which thou desirest and deservest above all other; which consent in me, if it may any ways breed thy contentation, sure I am that it will every way work my comfort. But as either thou tenderest mine honour or thine own safety, use such secrecy

---

1 *Medusa's head*] head of one of the Gorgons that had the power to turn those that looked at it to stone
2 *take stand ... cast out*] remain arrested unless attracted by the lure (metaphor drawn from falconry)
3 *wringing*] squeezing
4 *change your copy*] alter your behaviour
5 *Is your ... meat?*] Are you thinking about your food (i.e. your dinner)?
6 *brown study*] reverie

in this matter that my father have no inkling hereof before I have framed his mind fit for our purpose. And though women have small force to overcome men by reason, yet have they good fortune to undermine them by policy. The soft drops of rain pierce the hard marble, many strokes overthrow the tallest oak, a silly woman in time may make such a breach into a man's heart as her tears may enter without resistance; then doubt not but I will so undermine mine old father as quickly I will enjoy my new friend. Tush, Philautus was liked for fashion sake, but never loved for fancy sake; and this I vow by the faith of a virgin and by the love I bear thee (for greater bands[1] to confirm my vow I have not) that my father shall sooner martyr me in the fire than marry me to Philautus. No, no, Euphues, thou only hast won me by love, and shalt only wear me by law.[2] I force not[3] Philautus his fury so I may have Euphues his friendship, neither will I prefer his possessions before thy person, neither esteem better of his lands than of thy love. Ferardo shall sooner disherit me of my patrimony than dishonour me in breaking my promise. It is not his great manors but thy good manners that shall make my marriage. In token of which my sincere affection, I give thee my hand in pawn and my heart for ever to be thy Lucilla.'

Unto whom Euphues answered in this manner:

'If my tongue were able to utter the joys that my heart hath conceived, I fear me though I be well beloved, yet I should hardly be believed. Ah my Lucilla, how much am I bound to thee, which preferrest mine unworthiness before thy father's wrath, my happiness before thine own misfortune, my love before thine own life! How might I excel thee in courtesy, whom no mortal creature can exceed in constancy? I find it now for a settled truth, which erst[4] I accounted for a vain talk, that the purple dye will never stain, that the pure civet[5] will never lose his savour, that the green laurel will never change his colour, that beauty can never be blotted with discourtesy. As touching secrecy in this behalf, assure thyself that I will not so much as tell it to myself. Command Euphues to run, to ride, to undertake any exploit be it never so dangerous, to hazard himself in any enterprise be it never so desperate.'

As they were thus pleasantly conferring the one with the other, Livia (whom Euphues made his stale)[6] entered into the parlour, unto whom Lucilla spake in these terms:

---

1 *bands*] pledges
2 *thou only . . . law*] you alone have won me by love and [you] alone shall legally possess me
3 *force not*] care nothing for
4 *erst*] until now
5 *civet*] substance derived from a species of cat, used in perfumes
6 *stale*] decoy

'Dost thou not laugh, Livia, to see my ghostly father[1] keep me here so long at shrift?'

'Truly,' answered Livia, 'methinks that you smile at some pleasant shift.[2] Either he is slow in enquiring of your faults, or you slack in answering of his questions.'

And thus, being supper time, they all sat down, Lucilla well pleased, no man better content than Euphues; who after his repast, having no opportunity to confer with his lover, had small lust[3] to continue with the gentlewomen any longer. Seeing, therefore, he could frame no means to work his delight, he coined an excuse to hasten his departure, promising the next morning to trouble them again as a guest more bold than welcome, although indeed he thought himself to be the better welcome in saying that he would come.

But as Ferardo went in post,[4] so he returned in haste, having concluded with Philautus that the marriage should immediately be consummated, which wrought such a content in Philautus that he was almost in an ecstasy through the extremity of his passions. Such is the fullness and force of pleasure that there is nothing so dangerous as the fruition. Yet knowing that delays bring dangers, although he nothing doubted of Lucilla whom he loved, yet feared he the fickleness of old men, which is always to be mistrusted. He urged, therefore, Ferardo to break[5] with his daughter, who, being willing to have the match made, was content incontinently[6] to procure the means. Finding, therefore, his daughter at leisure, and having knowledge of her former love, spake to her as followeth:

'Dear daughter, as thou hast long time lived a maiden, so now thou must learn to be a mother; and as I have been careful to bring thee up a virgin, so am I now desirous to make thee a wife. Neither ought I in this matter to use any persuasions, for that maidens commonly nowadays are no sooner born but they begin to bride it; neither to offer any great portions, for that thou knowest thou shalt inherit all my possessions. Mine only care hath been hitherto to match thee with such an one as should be of good wealth able to maintain thee, of great worship[7] able to compare with thee in birth, of honest conditions to deserve thy love, and an Italian-born to enjoy my lands. At the last I have found one answerable to my desire, a gentleman of great revenues, of a noble progeny, of honest behaviour, of comely personage, born and brought up in Naples – Philautus, thy friend as I guess, thy husband, Lucilla, if thou

---

1 *ghostly father*] priest (*ghostly* = spiritual)
2 *shift*] jest (with a pun on *shrift* = confession, in the previous sentence)
3 *lust*] desire
4 *in post*] in a hurry
5 *break*] raise the matter
6 *incontinently*] without delay
7 *worship*] honour and respect

like it; neither canst thou dislike him who wanteth nothing that should cause thy liking, neither hath anything that should breed thy loathing. And surely I rejoice the more that thou shalt be linked to him in marriage whom thou hast loved, as I hear, being a maiden, neither can there any jars[1] kindle between them where the minds be so united, neither any jealousy arise where love hath so long been settled.

'Therefore, Lucilla, to the end the desire of either of you may now be accomplished to the delight of you both, I am here come to finish the contract by giving hands, which you have already begun between yourselves by joining of hearts; that as God doth witness the one in your consciences, so the world may testify the other by your conversations.[2] And therefore, Lucilla, make such answer to my request as may like[3] me and satisfy thy friend.'

Lucilla, abashed with this sudden speech of her father, yet boldened by the love of her friend, with a comely bashfulness answered him in this manner:

'Reverend sir, the sweetness that I have found in the undefiled estate of virginity causeth me to loathe the sour sauce which is mixed with matrimony, and the quiet life which I have tried being a maiden maketh me to shun the cares that are always incident to a mother. Neither am I so wedded to the world that I should be moved with great possessions, neither so bewitched with wantonness that I should be enticed with any man's proportion,[4] neither (if I were so disposed) would I be so proud to desire one of noble progeny, or so precise to choose one only in mine own country, for that commonly these things happen always to the contrary. Do we not see the noble to match with the base, the rich with the poor, the Italian oftentimes with the Portingale?[5] As love knoweth no laws, so it regardeth no conditions; as the lover maketh no pause where he liketh, so he maketh no conscience of these idle ceremonies.

'In that Philautus is the man that threateneth such kindness at my hands and such courtesy at yours that he should account me his wife before he woo me, certainly he is like, for me, to make his reckoning twice, because he reckoneth without his hostess.[6] And in this Philautus would either show himself of great wisdom to persuade, or me of great lightness to be allured. Although the loadstone draw iron, yet it cannot move gold; though the jet gather up the light straw, yet can it not take up the pure steel; although Philautus think himself of virtue sufficient to win his lover, yet shall he not obtain Lucilla. I cannot but smile to hear that a marriage

---

1 *jars*] disagreements
2 *conversations*] public behaviour
3 *like*] please
4 *proportion*] shape
5 *Portingale*] Portuguese
6 *make his reckoning . . . hostess*] be forced to reassess his position because he has left the principal factor out of account (metaphor drawn from inn-keeping)

should be solemnized where never was any mention of assuring,[1] and that the wooing should be a day after the wedding. Certes, if when I looked merrily on Philautus he deemed it in the way of marriage, or if seeing me disposed to jest he took me in good earnest, then sure he might gather some presumption of my love, but no promise. But methinks it is good reason that I should be at mine own bridal,[2] and not given in the church before I know the bridegroom.

'Therefore, dear father, in mine opinion, as there can be no bargain where both be not agreed, neither any indentures sealed[3] where the one will not consent, so there can be no contract where both be not content, no banns asked lawfully where one of the parties forbiddeth them, no marriage made where no match was meant. But I will hereafter frame myself to be coy, seeing I am claimed for a wife because I have been courteous, and give myself to melancholy, seeing I am accounted won in that I have been merry. And if every gentleman be made of the metal that Philautus is, then I fear I shall be challenged of as many as I have used to company with, and be a common wife to all those that have commonly resorted hither.

'My duty therefore ever reserved, I here on my knees forswear Philautus for my husband, although I accept him for my friend. And seeing I shall hardly be induced ever to match with any, I beseech you, if by your fatherly love I shall be compelled, that I may match with such a one as both I may love and you may like.'

Ferardo, being a grave and wise gentleman, although he were throughly angry, yet he dissembled his fury to the end he might by craft discover her fancy. And whispering Philautus in the ear (who stood as though he had a flea in his ear),[4] desired him to keep silence until he had undermined her by subtlety, which Philautus having granted, Ferardo began to sift[5] his daughter with this device:

'Lucilla, thy colour showeth thee to be in a great choler, and thy hot words bewray[6] thy heavy wrath; but be patient, seeing all my talk was only to try thee. I am neither so unnatural to wrest thee against thine own will, neither so malicious to wed thee to any against thine own liking; for well I know what jars,[7] what jealousy, what strife, what storms ensue where the match is made rather by the compulsion of the parents than by the consent of the parties. Neither do I like thee the less in that thou likest Philautus so little, neither can Philautus love thee the worse in that thou lovest thyself so well, wishing rather to stand to thy chance than to the choice of any other.

---

1 *assuring*] betrothal
2 *bridal*] wedding ceremony
3 *indentures sealed*] apprenticeship contract ratified
4 *as though . . . ear*] as if confounded by what he had heard
5 *sift*] sound out
6 *bewray*] reveal
7 *jars*] quarrels

'But this grieveth me most, that thou art almost vowed to the vain order of the vestal virgins, despising—or at the least not desiring—the sacred bands of Juno her bed.[1] If thy mother had been of that mind when she was a maiden, thou hadst not now been born to be of this mind to be a virgin. Weigh with thyself what slender profit they bring to the commonwealth, what slight pleasure to themselves, what great grief to their parents, which joy most in their offspring and desire most to enjoy the noble and blessed name of a grandfather. Thou knowest that the tallest ash is cut down for fuel because it beareth no good fruit, that the cow that gives no milk is brought to the slaughter, that the drone that gathereth no honey is contemned, that the woman that maketh herself barren by not marrying is accounted among the Grecian ladies worse than a carrion, as Homer reporteth.[2] Therefore, Lucilla, if thou have any care to be a comfort to my hoary hairs or a commodity to thy commonweal,[3] frame thyself to that honourable estate of matrimony which was sanctified in paradise, allowed of the patriarchs, hallowed of the old prophets, and commended of all persons.

'If thou like any, be not ashamed to tell it me, which only am to exhort thee, yea and as much as in me lieth to command thee, to love one. If he be base, thy blood will make him noble; if beggarly, thy goods shall make him wealthy; if a stranger, thy freedom may enfranchise him; if he be young, he is the more fitter to be thy fere;[4] if he be old, the liker to thine aged father. For I had rather thou shouldst lead a life to thine own liking in earth than to thy great torments lead apes in hell.[5] Be bold, therefore, to make me partner of thy desire, which will be partaker of thy disease, yea, and a furtherer of thy delights, as far as either my friends or my lands or my life will stretch.'

Lucilla, perceiving the drift of the old fox her father, weighed with herself what was the best to be done. At the last, not weighing her father's ill will but encouraged by her love, shaped him an answer which pleased Ferardo but a little and pinched Philautus on the parson's side[6] on this manner:

'Dear father Ferardo, although I see the bait you lay to catch me, yet I am content to swallow the hook; neither are you more desirous to take me napping, than I willing to confess my meaning. So it is that love hath

1 *almost vowed to . . . bed*] all but committed to a life of chastity, repudiating the holy bonds of the goddess of married love
2 *the woman that . . . Homer reporteth*] Lyly's source here is not, in fact, Homer, but North's *Dial of Princes* (1557), from which the ascription to Homer is derived (see Bond, I, p. 343).
3 *commodity . . . commonweal*] something of use to your country
4 *fere*] partner
5 *lead apes in hell*] see p. 65n.
6 *pinched . . . side*] robbed Philautus of his marriage (from the proverb 'to pinch the parson', i.e. to save money by withholding the parson's tithes)

as well inveigled me as others which make it as strange as I.[1] Neither do I love him so meanly that I should be ashamed of his name, neither is his personage so mean that I should love him shamefully. It is Euphues that lately arrived here at Naples that hath battered the bulwark of my breast and shall shortly enter as conqueror into my bosom. What his wealth is, I neither know it nor weigh it; what his wit is, all Naples doth know it and wonder at it; neither have I been curious to enquire of his progenitors, for that I know so noble a mind could take no original but from a noble man. For as no bird can look against the sun but those that be bred of the eagle, neither any hawk soar so high as the brood of the hobby,[2] so no wight can have such excellent qualities except he descend of a noble race, neither be of so high capacity unless he issue of a high progeny. And I hope Philautus will not be my foe, seeing I have chosen his dear friend, neither you, father, be displeased in that Philautus is displaced. You need not muse that I should so suddenly be entangled; love gives no reason of choice, neither will it suffer any repulse. Myrrha was enamoured of her natural father, Byblis of her brother, Phaedra[3] of her son-in-law. If nature can no way resist the fury of affection, how should it be stayed by wisdom?'

Ferardo, interrupting her in the middle of her discourse, although he were moved with inward grudge, yet he wisely repressed his anger, knowing that sharp words would but sharpen her froward[4] will, and thus answered her briefly:

'Lucilla, as I am not presently to grant my good will, so mean I not to reprehend thy choice. Yet wisdom willeth me to pause until I have called what may happen to my remembrance, and warneth thee to be circumspect lest thy rash conceit bring a sharp repentance. As for you, Philautus, I would not have you despair, seeing a woman doth oftentimes change her desire.'

Unto whom Philautus in few words made answer:

'Certainly, Ferardo, I take the less grief in that I see her so greedy after Euphues; and by so much the more I am content to leave my suit, by how much the more she seemeth to disdain my service. But as for hope, because I would not by any means taste one dram thereof, I will abjure all places of her abode, and loathe her company whose countenance I have so much loved. As for Euphues—.'

And there staying his speech, he flung out of the doors, and repairing to his lodging uttered these words:

---

1 *make it as strange as I*] repudiate it as I have done
2 *against / hobby*] into / a species of falcon
3 *Myrrha / Byblis / Phaedra*] all examples of unnatural love. Myrrha neglected her duties to Aphrodite and was punished by being made to fall in love with her father; Byblis pursued her brother Caunus until she was changed into a fountain; Phaedra, rejected by her stepson Hippolytus, accused him of attempting to dishonour her.
4 *froward*] refractory

'Ah most dissembling wretch Euphues! O counterfeit companion! Couldst thou under the show of a steadfast friend cloak the malice of a mortal foe; under the colour of simplicity shroud the image of deceit? Is thy Livia turned to my Lucilla, thy love to my lover, thy devotion to my saint? Is this the courtesy of Athens, the cavilling of scholars, the craft of Grecians? Couldst thou not remember, Philautus, that Greece is never without some wily Ulysses, never void of some Sinon,[1] never to seek of some deceitful shifter? Is it not commonly said of Grecians that craft cometh to them by kind,[2] that they learn to deceive in their cradle? Why then did his pretended courtesy bewitch thee with such credulity? Shall my good will be the cause of his ill will? Because I was content to be his friend, thought he me meet to be made his fool? I see now that as the fish scolopidus in the flood Araris[3] at the waxing of the moon is as white as the driven snow, and at the waning as black as the burnt coal, so Euphues, which at the first increasing of our familiarity was very zealous, is now at the last cast become most faithless.

'But why rather exclaim I not against Lucilla, whose wanton looks caused Euphues to violate his plighted faith? Ah wretched wench, canst thou be so light of love as to change with every wind, so unconstant as to prefer a new lover before thine old friend? Ah, well I wot[4] that a new broom sweepeth clean, and a new garment maketh thee leave off the old though it be fitter, and new wine causeth thee to forsake the old though it be better; much like to the men in the island Scyros which pull up the old tree when they see the young begin to spring, and not unlike unto the widow of Lesbos[5] which changed all her old gold for new glass. Have I served thee three years faithfully, and am I served so unkindly? Shall the fruit of my desire be turned to disdain?

'But unless Euphues had inveigled thee thou hadst yet been constant; yea, but if Euphues had not seen thee willing to be won he would never have wooed thee. But had not Euphues enticed thee with fair words thou wouldst never have loved him; but hadst thou not given him fair looks he would never have liked thee. Aye, but Euphues gave the onset; aye, but Lucilla gave the occasion. Aye, but Euphues first brake his mind; aye, but Lucilla first bewrayed her meaning.[6] Tush, why go I about to excuse any of them, seeing I have just cause to accuse them both? Neither ought

---

1 *Ulysses / Sinon*] exemplars of Greek cunning. Ulysses devised the stratagem of the wooden horse that brought about the fall of Troy. Sinon persuaded the Trojans to take it into their city.
2 *craft . . . kind*] they are born crafty
3 *fish scolopidus / flood Araris*] mythological creature said to change colour with the waxing and waning of the moon / river Saône (see Bond, I, pp. 343–4)
4 *wot*] know
5 *Scyros / Lesbos*] islands in the Aegean sea. No source has been found for either reference.
6 *brake his mind / bewrayed her meaning*] disclosed his thoughts / revealed her intentions

I to dispute which of them hath proffered me the greatest villainy, sith that either of them hath committed perjury. Yet although they have found me dull in perceiving their falsehood, they shall not find me slack in revenging their folly. As for Lucilla, seeing I mean altogether to forget her, I mean also to forgive her, lest in seeking means to be revenged mine old desire be renewed.'

Philautus, having thus discoursed with himself, began to write to Euphues as followeth:

Although hitherto, Euphues, I have shrined thee in my heart for a trusty friend, I will shun thee hereafter as a trothless foe; and although I cannot see in thee less wit than I was wont, yet do I find less honesty. I perceive at the last (although, being deceived, it be too late) that musk, though it be sweet in the smell, is sour in the smack;[1] that the leaf of the cedar tree, though it be fair to be seen yet the syrup depriveth sight; that friendship, though it be plighted by shaking the hand, yet it is shaken off by fraud of the heart.

But thou hast not much to boast of, for as thou hast won a fickle lady so hast thou lost a faithful friend. How canst thou be secure of her constancy, when thou hast had such trial of her lightness; how canst thou assure thyself that she will be faithful to thee, which hath been faithless to me?

Ah Euphues, let not my credulity be an occasion hereafter for thee to practise the like cruelty. Remember this, that yet there hath never been any faithless to his friend that hath not also been fruitless to his God. But I weigh the treachery the less in that it cometh from a Grecian in whom is no troth. Though I be too weak to wrestle for a revenge, yet God, who permitteth no guile to be guiltless, will shortly requite this injury; though Philautus have no policy to undermine thee, yet thine own practices will be sufficient to overthrow thee.

Couldst thou, Euphues, for the love of a fruitless pleasure violate the league of faithful friendship; didst thou weigh more the enticing looks of a lewd wench than the entire love of a loyal friend? If thou didst determine with thyself at the first to be false, why didst thou swear to be true; if to be true, why art thou false? If thou wast minded both falsely and forgedly to deceive me, why didst thou flatter and dissemble with me at the first; if to love me, why didst thou flinch at the last? If the sacred bands of amity did delight thee, why didst thou break them; if dislike thee, why didst thou praise them? Dost thou not know that a perfect friend should be like the glaze-worm[2] which shineth most bright in the dark; or like the pure frankincense which smelleth most sweet when it is in the fire; or, at the least, not unlike to the damask rose which is sweeter in the still[3] than on the stalk? But thou, Euphues, dost rather resemble the swallow which in the summer creepeth under the eaves of every house and in the winter leaveth nothing but dirt behind her; or the humble-bee which having sucked honey out of the fair flower doth leave it and loathe it; or the spider which in the finest web doth hang the fairest fly.

---

1 *smack*] taste
2 *glaze-worm*] glow-worm
3 *still*] distilling apparatus

Dost thou think, Euphues, that thy craft in betraying me shall any whit cool my courage in revenging thy villainy, or that a gentleman of Naples will put up such an injury at the hands of a scholar? And if I do, it is not for want of strength to maintain my just quarrel, but of will which thinketh scorn to get so vain a conquest. I know that Menelaus for his ten years' war endured ten years' woe,[1] that after all his strife he won but a strumpet, that for all his travail he reduced[2] (I cannot say reclaimed) but a straggler; which was as much, in my judgement, as to strive for a broken glass, which is good for nothing. I wish thee rather Menelaus' care[3] than myself his conquest; that thou, being deluded by Lucilla, mayst rather know what it is to be deceived, than I, having conquered thee, should prove what it were to bring back a dissembler. Seeing, therefore, there can no greater revenge light upon thee than that, as thou hast reaped where another hath sown, so another may thresh that which thou hast reaped, I will pray that thou mayst be measured unto with the like measure that thou hast meten[4] unto others; that as thou hast thought it no conscience to betray me, so others may deem it no dishonesty to deceive thee; that as Lucilla made it a light matter to forswear her old friend Philautus, so she may make it a mock to forsake her new fere[5] Euphues. Which, if it come to pass, as it is like by my compass, then shalt thou see the troubles and feel the torments which thou hast already thrown into the hearts and eyes of others.

Thus hoping shortly to see thee as hopeless as myself is hapless,[6] I wish my wish were as effectually ended as it is heartily looked for. And so I leave thee.

Thine once,
Philautus.

Philautus, dispatching a messenger with this letter speedily to Euphues, went into the fields to walk there, either to digest his choler or chew upon his melancholy. But Euphues, having read the contents, was well content, setting his talk at naught and answering his taunts in these jibing terms:

I remember, Philautus, how valiantly Ajax boasted in the feats of arms yet Ulysses bare away the armour;[7] and it may be that though thou crake[8] of thine own courage, thou mayst easily lose the conquest. Dost thou think Euphues a dastard that he is not able to withstand thy courage, or such a dullard that he cannot descry[9] thy craft? Alas, good soul! It fareth with thee as with the hen which when the puttock[10] hath caught her chicken beginneth to cackle; and thou, having lost thy lover, beginnest to prattle.

---

1 *Menelaus . . . woe*] see p. 27n.
2 *reduced*] brought back
3 *care*] suffering
4 *meten*] measured
5 *fere*] favourite
6 *hapless*] unfortunate
7 *Ajax . . . armour*] A reference to the contest between Ajax and Ulysses for the armour of Achilles, won by Ulysses because of his superior eloquence in vaunting his deeds.
8 *crake*] boast
9 *descry*] perceive
10 *puttock*] kite

Tush, Philautus, I am in this point of Euripides his mind, who thinks it lawful for the desire of a kingdom to transgress the bonds of honesty,[1] and for the love of a lady to violate and break the bonds of amity. The friendship between man and man as it is common so is it of course, between man and woman as it is seldom so is it sincere; the one proceedeth of the similitude of manners, the other of the sincerity of the heart. If thou hadst learned the first point of hawking, thou wouldst have learned to have held fast;[2] or the first note of descant, thou wouldst have kept thy *sol fa* to thyself.[3]

But thou canst blame me no more of folly in leaving thee to love Lucilla than thou mayst reprove him of foolishness that having a sparrow in his hand letteth her go to catch the pheasant, or him of unskilfulness that seeing the heron leaveth to level his shot at the stock-dove, or that woman of coyness that having a dead rose in her bosom throweth it away to gather the fresh violet. Love knoweth no laws. Did not Jupiter transform himself into the shape of Amphitryon to embrace Alcmene; into the form of a swan to enjoy Leda; into a bull to beguile Io; into a shower of gold to win Danae? Did not Neptune change himself into a heifer, a ram, a flood, a dolphin, only for the love of those he lusted after? Did not Apollo convert himself into a shepherd, into a bird, into a lion, for the desire he had to heal his disease? If the gods thought no scorn to become beasts to obtain their best beloved, shall Euphues be so nice in changing his copy[4] to gain his lady? No, no; he that cannot dissemble in love is not worthy to live. I am of this mind, that both might and malice, deceit and treachery, all perjury, any impiety may lawfully be committed in love, which is lawless.

In that thou arguest Lucilla of lightness, thy will hangs in the light of thy wit.[5] Dost thou not know that the weak stomach, if it be cloyed with one diet, doth soon surfeit; that the clown's[6] garlic cannot ease the courtier's disease so well as the pure treacle; that far fet and dear bought is good for ladies;[7] that Euphues being a more dainty morsel than Philautus ought better to be accepted?

Tush, Philautus, set thy heart at rest, for thy hap[8] willeth thee to give over all hope both of my friendship and her love. As for revenge, thou art not so able to lend a blow as I to ward it, neither more venturous to challenge the combat than I valiant to answer the quarrel. As Lucilla was caught by fraud so shall she be kept by force, and as thou wast too simple to espy my craft, so I think thou wilt be too weak to withstand my courage; but if thy revenge

---

1 *Euripedes his mind / lawful for the desire . . . honesty*] the same opinion as Euripedes (celebrated Greek dramatist, b. 480 BC) / adapted from the words of Euripedes' Eteocles, 'If one may be unlawful, it is best to be unlawful for absolute rule' (*Phoenissae*, 524–5)
2 *held fast*] not to let go of your bird (metaphor drawn from falconry)
3 *first note of descant / kept thy* sol fa *to thyself*] first principles of singing in harmony / kept your part to yourself
4 *nice in changing his copy*] over-scrupulous about shifting his position
5 *thy will . . . wit*] your wishes are clouding your judgement
6 *clown's*] peasant's
7 *far fet . . . ladies*] women like novelties that are difficult and expensive to obtain (*fet* = fetched)
8 *hap*] fate

stand only upon thy wish, thou shalt never live to see my woe or to have thy will.

And so farewell.
Euphues.

This letter being dispatched, Euphues sent it and Philautus read it; who, disdaining those proud terms, disdained also to answer them, being ready to ride with Ferardo.

Euphues, having for a space absented himself from the house of Ferardo because he was at home, longed sore to see Lucilla, which now opportunity offered unto him, Ferardo being gone again to Venice with Philautus. But in this his absence one Curio, a gentleman of Naples of little wealth and less wit, haunted Lucilla her company, and so enchanted her that Euphues was also cast off with Philautus; which thing being unknown to Euphues caused him the sooner to make his repair to the presence of his lady, whom he finding in her muses began pleasantly to salute in this manner:

'Mistress Lucilla, although my long absence might breed your just anger (for that lovers desire nothing so much as often meeting), yet I hope my presence will dissolve your choler (for that lovers are soon pleased when of their wishes they be fully possessed). My absence is the rather to be excused in that your father hath been always at home, whose frowns seemed to threaten my ill fortune, and my presence at this present the better to be accepted in that I have made such speedy repair[1] to your presence.'

Unto whom Lucilla answered with this gleek:[2]

'Truly, Euphues, you have missed the cushion,[3] for I was neither angry with your long absence, neither am I well pleased at your presence; the one gave me rather a good hope hereafter never to see you, the other giveth me a greater occasion to abhor you.'

Euphues, being nipped on the head,[4] with a pale countenance as though his soul had forsaken his body, replied as followeth:

'If this sudden change, Lucilla, proceed of any desert of mine, I am here not only to answer the fact but also to make amends for my fault; if of any new motion or mind to forsake your new friend, I am rather to lament your inconstancy than revenge it. But I hope that such hot love cannot be so soon cold, neither such sure faith be rewarded with so sudden forgetfulness.'

Lucilla, not ashamed to confess her folly, answered him with this frump:

'Sir, whether your deserts or my desire have wrought this change it will boot[5] you little to know; neither do I crave amends, neither fear revenge.

1 *made such speedy repair*] made my way so quickly
2 *gleek*] jibe
3 *missed the cushion*] are in error
4 *nipped on the head*] brought to a stand
5 *frump / boot*] derisive retort / avail

As for fervent love, you know there is no fire so hot but it is quenched with water, neither affection so strong but is weakened with reason. Let this suffice thee, that thou know I care not for thee.'

'Indeed,' said Euphues, 'to know the cause of your alteration would boot me little, seeing the effect taketh such force. I have heard that women either love entirely or hate deadly, and seeing you have put me out of doubt of the one, I must needs persuade myself of the other. This change will cause Philautus to laugh me to scorn, and double thy lightness in turning so often. Such was the hope that I conceived of thy constancy that I spared not in all places to blaze[1] thy loyalty, but now my rash conceit will prove me a liar and thee a light huswife.'[2]

'Nay,' said Lucilla, 'now shalt thou not laugh Philautus to scorn, seeing you have both drunk of one cup. In misery, Euphues, it is great comfort to have a companion. I doubt not but that you will both conspire against me to work some mischief, although I nothing fear your malice. Whosoever accounteth you a liar for praising me, may also deem you a lecher for being enamoured of me; and whosoever judgeth me light in forsaking of you, may think thee as lewd in loving of me. For thou that thoughtst it lawful to deceive thy friend must take no scorn to be deceived of thy foe.'

'Then I perceive, Lucilla,' said he, 'that I was made thy stale[3] and Philautus thy laughing-stock, whose friendship (I must confess indeed) I have refused to obtain thy favour. And sithence another hath won what we both have lost, I am content for my part; neither ought I to be grieved seeing thou art fickle.'

'Certes, Euphues,' said Lucilla, 'you spend your wind in waste, for your welcome is but small and your cheer is like to be less. Fancy giveth no reason of his change, neither will be controlled for any choice. This is, therefore, to warn you that from henceforth you neither solicit this suit, neither offer any way your service. I have chosen one (I must needs confess) neither to be compared to Philautus in wealth, nor to thee in wit, neither in birth to the worst of you both. I think God gave it me for a just plague for renouncing Philautus and choosing thee; and sithence I am an example to all women of lightness, I am like also to be a mirror to them all of unhappiness; which ill luck I must take by so much the more patiently, by how much the more I acknowledge myself to have deserved it worthily.'

'Well, Lucilla,' answered Euphues, 'this case breedeth my sorrow the more in that it is so sudden, and by so much the more I lament it, by how much the less I looked for it. In that my welcome is so cold and my cheer so simple it nothing toucheth me, seeing your fury is so hot and my misfortune so great that I am neither willing to receive it nor you to bestow

---

1 *blaze*] proclaim
2 *light huswife*] wanton
3 *stale*] lover made a target of ridicule for the amusement of others

it. If tract of time or want of trial had caused this metamorphosis, my grief had been more tolerable, and your fleeting[1] more excusable; but coming in a moment, undeserved, unlooked for, unthought of, it increaseth my sorrow and thy shame.'

'Euphues,' quoth she, 'you make a long harvest for a little corn, and angle for the fish that is already caught. Curio, yea Curio, is he that hath my love at his pleasure, and shall also have my life at his commandment; and although you deem him unworthy to enjoy that which erst you accounted no wight[2] worthy to embrace, yet seeing I esteem him more worth than any, he is to be reputed as chief. The wolf chooseth him for her make[3] that hath or doth endure most travail for her sake; Venus was content to take the blacksmith with his polt foot;[4] Cornelia here in Naples disdained not to love a rude miller.[5] As for changing, did not Helen, that pearl of Greece, thy countrywoman, first take Menelaus, then Theseus, and last of all Paris?[6] If brute beasts give us examples that those are most to be liked of whom we are best beloved, or if the princess of beauty, Venus, and her heirs, Helen and Cornelia, show that our affection standeth on our free will, then am I rather to be excused than accused. Therefore, good Euphues, be as merry as you may be, for time may so turn that once again you may be.'

'Nay, Lucilla,' said he, 'my harvest shall cease seeing others have reaped my corn; as for angling for the fish that is already caught, that were but mere folly. But in my mind, if you be fish, you are either an eel which as soon as one hath hold on her tail will slip out of his hand, or else a minnow which will be nibbling at every bait but never biting. But what fish soever you be, you have made both me and Philautus to swallow a gudgeon.[7]

'If Curio be the person, I would neither wish thee a greater plague, nor him a deadlier poison. I, for my part, think him worthy of thee, and thou unworthy of him; for although he be in body deformed, in mind foolish, an innocent born, a beggar by misfortune, yet doth he deserve a better than thyself, whose corrupt manners have stained thy heavenly hue, whose light behaviour hath dimmed the lights of thy beauty, whose unconstant mind hath betrayed the innocency of so many a gentleman.

'And in that you bring in the example of a beast to confirm your folly, you show therein your beastly disposition, which is ready to follow such beastliness. But Venus played false! And what for that? Seeing her light-

---

1 *fleeting*] inconstancy
2 *erst . . . wight*] formerly you thought no person
3 *make*] mate
4 *Venus . . . polt foot*] see above pp. 27 and 29nn.
5 *Cornelia . . . miller*] A reference to the kind of tale found in Boccaccio's *Decameron*, but no specific source has been found.
6 *Helen . . . Paris*] see p. 27n.
7 *swallow a gudgeon*] see p. 60n.

ness serveth for an example, I would wish thou mightst try her punishment for a reward, that being openly taken in an iron net all the world might judge whether thou be fish or flesh—and certes, in my mind no angle[1] will hold thee, it must be a net. Cornelia loved a miller, and thou a miser. Can her folly excuse thy fault? Helen of Greece, my countrywoman born, but thine by profession, changed and rechanged at her pleasure, I grant. Shall the lewdness of others animate thee in thy lightness? Why then dost thou not haunt the stews because Lais[2] frequented them? Why dost thou not love a bull seeing Pasiphae[3] loved one? Why art thou not enamoured of thy father knowing that Myrrha[4] was so incensed? These are set down that we, viewing their incontinency, should fly the like impudency, not follow the like excess; neither can they excuse thee of any inconstancy.

'Merry I will be as I may; but if I may hereafter as thou meanest, I will not. And therefore farewell Lucilla, the most inconstant that ever was nursed in Naples; farewell Naples, the most cursed town in all Italy; and women all, farewell.'

Euphues, having thus given her his last farewell, yet, being solitary, began afresh to recount his sorrow on this manner:

'Ah Euphues, into what misfortune art thou brought! In what sudden misery art thou wrapped! It is like to fare with thee as with the eagle, which dieth neither for age nor with sickness but with famine,[5] for although thy stomach hunger, yet thy heart will not suffer thee to eat. And why shouldst thou torment thyself for one in whom is neither faith nor fervency? Oh the counterfeit love of women! Oh inconstant sex! I have lost Philautus; I have lost Lucilla; I have lost that which I shall hardly find again, a faithful friend.

'Ah foolish Euphues, why didst thou leave Athens, the nurse of wisdom, to inhabit Naples, the nourisher of wantonness? Had it not been better for thee to have eaten salt with the philosophers in Greece than sugar with the courtiers of Italy? But behold the course of youth, which always inclineth to pleasure. I forsook mine old companions to search for new friends. I rejected the grave and fatherly counsel of Eubulus to follow the brainsick humour of mine own will. I addicted myself wholly to the service of women, to spend my life in the laps of ladies, my lands in maintenance of bravery, my wit in the vanities of idle sonnets. I had thought

---

1 angle] fish-hook. The reference is to the public shaming of Venus by Vulcan, who caught her with her lover (Mars) in an invisible net, exposing her to the laughter of the gods.
2 Lais] celebrated Corinthian courtesan (stews = brothel)
3 Pasiphae] wife of King Minos of Crete and mother, by a bull, of the Minotaur, a monster with the body of a man but a bull's head
4 Myrrha] see p. 75n.
5 eagle . . . famine] Eagles were believed to die from hunger because their beaks grew too long to permit them to feed.

that women had been as we men, that is, true, faithful, zealous, constant; but I perceive they be rather woe unto men by their falsehood, jealousy, inconstancy. I was half-persuaded that they were made of the perfection of men and would be comforters, but now I see they have tasted of the infection of the serpent and will be corrosives. The physician saith it is dangerous to minister physic unto the patient that hath a cold stomach and a hot liver, lest in giving warmth to the one he inflame the other; so verily it is hard to deal with a woman, whose words seem fervent, whose heart is congealed into hard ice, lest trusting their outward talk he be betrayed with their inward treachery.

'I will to Athens there to toss[1] my books, no more in Naples to live with fair looks. I will so frame myself as all youth hereafter shall rather rejoice to see mine amendment than be animated to follow my former life. Philosophy, physic,[2] divinity shall be my study. Oh the hidden secrets of nature, the express image of moral virtues, the equal balance of justice, the medicines to heal all diseases, how they begin to delight me! The axioms of Aristotle, the maxims of Justinian, the aphorisms of Galen,[3] have suddenly made such a breach into my mind that I seem only to desire them, which did only erst detest them.

'If wit be employed in the honest study of learning, what thing so precious as wit; if in the idle trade of love, what thing more pestilent than wit? The proof of late hath been verified in me, whom Nature hath endued with a little wit which I have abused with an obstinate will. Most true it is that the thing the better it is the greater is the abuse, and that there is nothing but through the malice of man may be abused. Doth not the fire (an element so necessary that without it man cannot live) as well burn the house as burn in the house if it be abused; doth not treacle[4] as well poison as help if it be taken out of time; doth not wine if it be immoderately taken kill the stomach, inflame the liver, mischief the drunken; doth not physic destroy if it be not well tempered; doth not law accuse if it be not rightly interpreted; doth not divinity condemn[5] if it be not faithfully construed? Is not poison taken out of the honeysuckle by the spider, venom out of the rose by the canker, dung out of the maple-tree by the scorpion? Even so the greatest wickedness is drawn out of the greatest wit if it be abused by will, or entangled with the world, or inveigled with women.

'But seeing I see mine own impiety, I will endeavour myself to amend all that is past and to be a mirror of godliness hereafter. The rose, though a little it be eaten with the canker, yet being distilled yieldeth sweet water; the iron, though fretted with the rust, yet being burnt in the fire shineth

---

1 *toss*] turn over
2 *physic*] medicine
3 *axioms of . . . Galen*] tenets of philosophy, law and medicine
4 *treacle*] medicinal compound, derived from venom
5 *condemn*] damn

brighter; and wit, although it hath been eaten with the canker of his own conceit and fretted with the rust of vain love, yet being purified in the still of wisdom and tried in the fire of zeal, will shine bright and smell sweet in the nostrils of all young novices.

'As, therefore, I gave a farewell to Lucilla, a farewell to Naples, a farewell to women, so now do I give a farewell to the world, meaning rather to macerate myself[1] with melancholy than pine in folly, rather choosing to die in my study amidst my books than to court it in Italy in the company of ladies.'

Euphues, having thus debated with himself, went to his bed; there either with sleep to deceive his fancy, or with musing to renew his ill fortune or recant his old follies. But it happened immediately Ferardo to return home, who, hearing this strange event, was not a little amazed, and was now more ready to exhort Lucilla from the love of Curio than before to the liking of Philautus. Therefore, in all haste, with watery eyes and a woeful heart, began on this manner to reason with his daughter:

'Lucilla (daughter I am ashamed to call thee, seeing thou hast neither care of thy father's tender affection nor of thine own credit), what sprite hath enchanted thy spirit that every minute thou alterest thy mind? I had thought that my hoary hairs should have found comfort by thy golden locks, and my rotten age great ease by thy ripe years. But, alas, I see in thee neither wit to order thy doings, neither will to frame thyself to discretion; neither the nature of a child, neither the nurture of a maiden; neither (I cannot without tears speak it) any regard of thine honour, neither any care of thine honesty.[2] I am now enforced to remember thy mother's death, who I think was a prophetess in her life; for oftentimes she would say that thou hadst more beauty than was convenient for one that should be honest, and more cockering[3] than was meet for one that should be a matron.

'Would I had never lived to be so old, or thou to be so obstinate; either would I had died in my youth in the court, or thou in thy cradle; I would to God that either I had never been born, or thou never bred. Is this the comfort that the parent reapeth for all his care? Is obstinacy paid for obedience, stubbornness rendered for duty, malicious desperateness for filial fear? I perceive now that the wise painter saw more than the foolish parent can, who painted love going downward, saying it might well descend but ascend it could never. Danaus,[4] whom they report to be the father of fifty children, had among them all but one that disobeyed him in a thing most dishonest; but I that am father to one more than I would be, although one be all, have that one most disobedient to me in a request

---

1 *macerate myself*] waste myself away
2 *honesty*] virtue
3 *cockering*] pampering
4 *Danaus*] father of fifty daughters, all of whom, with the exception of Hypermnestra, murdered their husbands at his command

lawful and reasonable. If Danaus seeing but one of his daughters without awe became himself without mercy, what shall Ferardo do in this case who hath one and all most unnatural to him in a most just cause?

'Shall Curio enjoy the fruit of my travails, possess the benefit of my labours, inherit the patrimony of mine ancestors, who hath neither wisdom to increase them, nor wit to keep them? Wilt thou, Lucilla, bestow thyself on such an one as hath neither comeliness in his body, nor knowledge in his mind, nor credit in his country? Oh I would thou hadst either been ever faithful to Philautus or never faithless to Euphues, or would thou wouldst be most fickle to Curio. As thy beauty made thee the blaze of Italy, so will thy lightness make thee the byword[1] of the world. O Lucilla, Lucilla, would thou wert less fair or more fortunate, either of less honour or greater honesty, either better minded or soon buried!

'Shall thine old father live to see thee match with a young fool; shall my kind heart be rewarded with such unkind hate? Ah Lucilla, thou knowest not the care of a father nor the duty of a child, and as far art thou from piety as I from cruelty. Nature will not permit me to disherit my daughter, and yet it will suffer thee to dishonour thy father. Affection causeth me to wish thy life, and shall it entice thee to procure my death? It is mine only comfort to see thee flourish in thy youth, and is it thine to see me fade in mine age? To conclude, I desire to live to see thee prosper, and thou to see me perish.

'But why cast I the effect of this unnaturalness in thy teeth, seeing I myself was the cause? I made thee a wanton, and thou hast made me a fool; I brought thee up like a cockney, and thou hast handled me like a coxcomb[2] (I speak it to mine own shame); I made more of thee than became a father, and thou less of me than beseemed a child. And shall my loving care be cause of thy wicked cruelty? Yea, yea, I am not the first that hath been too careful, nor the last that shall be handled so unkindly. It is common to see fathers too fond and children too froward.[3]

'Well, Lucilla, the tears which thou seest trickle down my cheeks, and my drops of blood (which thou canst not see) that fall from my heart, enforce me to make an end of my talk. And if thou have any duty of a child, or care of a friend, or courtesy of a stranger, or feeling of a Christian, or humanity of a reasonable creature, then release thy father of grief and acquit thyself of ungratefulness. Otherwise thou shalt but hasten my death and increase thine own defame; which if thou do, the gain is mine, and the loss thine, and both infinite.'

Lucilla, either so bewitched that she could not relent, or so wicked that she would not yield to her father's request, answered him on this manner:

---

1 *blaze / the byword*] glory / proverbial (for a particular kind of behaviour)
2 *cockney / coxcomb*] spoiled child / fool
3 *froward*] wilful

'Dear father, as you would have me to show the duty of a child, so ought you to show the care of a parent, for as the one standeth in obedience, so the other is grounded upon reason. You would have me, as I owe duty to you, to leave Curio; and I desire you, as you owe me any love, that you suffer me to enjoy him. If you accuse me of unnaturalness in that I yield not to your request, I am also to condemn you of unkindness in that you grant not my petition. You object I know not what to Curio; but it is the eye of the master that fatteth the horse,[1] and the love of the woman that maketh the man. To give reason for fancy were to weigh the fire and measure the wind. If, therefore, my delight be the cause of your death, I think my sorrow would be an occasion of your solace. And if you be angry because I am pleased, certes I deem you would be content if I were deceased; which if it be so that my pleasure breed your pain and mine annoy your joy, I may well say that you are an unkind father and I an unfortunate child. But, good father, either content yourself with my choice, or let me stand to the main chance;[2] otherwise the grief will be mine, and the fault yours, and both untolerable.'

Ferardo, seeing his daughter to have neither regard of her own honour nor his request, conceived such an inward grief that in short space he died, leaving Lucilla the only heir of his lands and Curio to possess them. But what end came of her, seeing it is nothing incident to the history of Euphues, it were superfluous to insert it, and so incredible that all women would rather wonder at it than believe it; which event being so strange, I had rather leave them in a muse what it should be than in a maze in telling what it was.

Philautus, having intelligence of Euphues his success and the falsehood of Lucilla, although he began to rejoice at the misery of his fellow, yet seeing her fickleness could not but lament her folly and pity his friend's misfortune, thinking that the lightness of Lucilla enticed Euphues to so great liking. Euphues and Philautus having conference between themselves, casting discourtesy in the teeth each of the other, but chiefly noting disloyalty in the demeanour of Lucilla, after much talk renewed their old friendship, both abandoning Lucilla as most abominable. Philautus was earnest to have Euphues tarry in Naples, and Euphues desirous to have Philautus to Athens, but the one was so addicted to the court, the other so wedded to the university, that each refused the offer of the other. Yet this they agreed between themselves, that though their bodies were by distance of place severed, yet the conjunction of their minds should neither be separated by the length of time, nor alienated by change of soil. 'I, for my part,' said Euphues, 'to confirm this league give thee my hand and my heart.' And so likewise did Philautus.

And so, shaking hands, they bid each other farewell.

---

1 *eye of . . . horse*] the watchfulness of the owner that ensures the well-being of the horse (proverbial)
2 *stand to the main chance*] abide by my major gamble (dicing term)

Euphues, to the intent he might bridle the overlashing[1] affections of Philautus, conveyed into his study a certain pamphlet, which he termed, 'A Cooling Card[2] for Philautus', yet generally to be applied to all lovers, which I have inserted as followeth.

A COOLING CARD FOR PHILAUTUS
AND ALL FOND LOVERS

Musing with myself, being idle, how I might be well employed, friend Philautus, I could find nothing either more fit to continue our friendship or of greater force to dissolve our folly than to write a remedy for that which many judge past cure, for love, Philautus, with the which I have been so tormented that I have lost my time, thou so troubled that thou hast forgot reason, both so mangled with repulse, inveigled by deceit, and almost murdered by disdain, that I can neither remember our miseries without grief nor redress our mishaps without groans. How wantonly, yea, and how willingly, have we abused our golden time and misspent our gotten treasure! How curious were we to please our lady, how careless to displease our Lord! How devout in serving our goddess, how desperate in forgetting our God! Ah, my Philautus, if the wasting of our money might not dehort[3] us, yet the wounding of our minds should deter us; if reason might nothing persuade us to wisdom, yet shame should provoke us to wit.

If Lucilla read this trifle she will straight proclaim Euphues for a traitor, and, seeing me turn my tippet,[4] will either shut me out for a wrangler, or cast me off for a wiredrawer;[5] either convince me of malice in bewraying their sleights,[6] or condemn me of mischief in arming young men against fleeting minions.[7] And what then? Though Curio be as hot as a toast, yet Euphues is as cold as a clock;[8] though he be a cock of the game,[9] yet Euphues is content to be craven and cry creak;[10] though Curio be old huddle and twang 'ipse, he',[11] yet Euphues had rather shrink in the wetting than waste in the wearing.[12] I know Curio to be steel to the back, standard-bearer to Venus'

---

1 *overlashing*] intemperate
2 *Cooling Card*] something designed to lower the spirits (term drawn from sixteenth-century card game). The advice in the 'pamphlet' that follows is largely derived from Ovid's *Remedia amoris*.
3 *dehort*] dissuade
4 *turn my tippet*] become a turn-coat
5 *wrangler / wiredrawer*] squabbler / quibbler (literally a manufacturer of wire by a process of stretching)
6 *convince me . . . sleights*] find me guilty of malice in revealing their deceits
7 *fleeting minions*] inconstant flirts
8 *hot as a toast / cold as a clock*] proverbial expressions for the extremes of ardour and frigidity
9 *cock of the game*] the winner
10 *craven / cry creak*] a coward / concede defeat
11 *old huddle and twang 'ipse, he'*] bosom friend and sing 'I am the one'
12 *shrink in the wetting / waste in the wearing*] be instantly discarded (as unserviceable) / slowly wear away

camp, sworn to the crew, true to the crown, knight marshal to Cupid, and heir apparent to his kingdom.[1] But by that time that he hath eaten but one bushel of salt with Lucilla,[2] he shall taste ten quarters[3] of sorrow in his love. Then shall he find for every pint of honey a gallon of gall, for every dram of pleasure an ounce of pain, for every inch of mirth an ell[4] of moan.

And yet, Philautus, if there be any man in despair to obtain his purpose, or so obstinate in his opinion that having lost his freedom by folly would also lose his life for love, let him repair hither and he shall reap such profit as will either quench his flames or assuage his fury, either cause him to renounce his lady as most pernicious or redeem his liberty as most precious. Come, therefore, to me all ye lovers that have been deceived by fancy, the glass of pestilence, or deluded by women, the gate to perdition; be as earnest to seek a medicine as you were eager to run into a mischief. The earth bringeth forth as well endive to delight the people as hemlock to endanger the patient; as well the rose to distil as the nettle to sting; as well the bee to give honey as the spider to yield poison. If my lewd life, gentlemen, have given you offence, let my good counsel make amends; if by my folly any be allured to lust, let them by my repentance be drawn to continency. Achilles' spear could as well heal as hurt;[5] the scorpion, though he sting, yet he stints the pain;[6] though the herb nerius poison the sheep, yet is [it] a remedy to man against poison; though I have infected some by example, yet I hope I shall comfort many by repentance.

Whatsoever I speak to men, the same also I speak to women. I mean not to run with the hare and hold with the hound,[7] to carry fire in the one hand and water in the other,[8] neither to flatter men as altogether faultless, neither to fall out with women as altogether guilty—for as I am not minded to pick a thank[9] with the one, so am I not determined to pick a quarrel with the other. If women be not perverse they shall reap profit by remedy of pleasure. If Phyllis were now to take counsel she would not be so foolish to hang herself, neither Dido so fond to die for Aeneas, neither Pasiphae so monstrous to love a bull, nor Phaedra so unnatural to be enamoured of her son.[10]

---

1 *steel to the back ... kingdom*] all expressions denoting total commitment to the cause of love

2 *eaten ... Lucilla*] spent any time with Lucilla (for a comparable use of the expression, see p. 44)

3 *ten quarters*] eighty bushels (measure of grain: 1 quarter = 8 bushels)

4 *ell*] measurement of length (45 inches)

5 *Achilles' ... hurt*] An allusion to the story of Telephus who was healed by the verdigris from Achilles' spear by which he had been wounded (see Bond, I, p. 347).

6 *scorpion ... pain*] A compound made from the body of the scorpion was believed to relieve the pain of its sting (see Croll and Clemons, p. 53n.). The *herb nerius* in the next clause is derived from Pliny.

7 *run with ... hound*] seem to support each side against the other

8 *carry fire ... other*] operate between two extremes

9 *pick a thank*] see p. 50n.

10 *Phyllis ... son*] all examples of destructive passion. Phyllis believed herself to be deserted by Demophon and hanged herself. For *Dido*, *Pasiphae* and *Phaedra* see notes to pp. 64, 83, and 75 respectively.

This is, therefore, to admonish all young imps and novices in love not to blow the coals of fancy with desire but to quench them with disdain. When love tickleth thee, decline it lest it stifle thee; rather fast than surfeit; rather starve than strive to exceed. Though the beginning of love bring delight, the end bringeth destruction—for as the first draught of wine doth comfort the stomach, the second inflame the liver, the third fume[1] into the head, so the first sip of love is pleasant, the second perilous, the third pestilent. If thou perceive thyself to be enticed with their wanton glances or allured with their wicked guiles, either enchanted with their beauty or enamoured with their bravery, enter with thyself into this meditation. 'What shall I gain if I obtain my purpose, nay rather what shall I lose in winning my pleasure? If my lady yield to be my lover, is it not likely she will be another's leman?[2] And if she be a modest matron my labour is lost. This therefore remaineth, that either I must pine in cares or perish with curses. If she be chaste, then is she coy;[3] if light, then is she impudent. If a grave matron, who can woo her; if a lewd minion who would wed her? If one of the vestal virgins, they have vowed virginity; if one of Venus' court they have vowed dishonesty.[4] If I love one that is fair, it will kindle jealousy; if one that is foul, it will convert me into a frenzy. If fertile to bear children, my care is increased; if barren, my curse is augmented. If honest, I shall fear her death; if immodest, I shall be weary of her life. To what end then shall I live in love, seeing always it is a life more to be feared than death? For all my time wasted in sighs and worn in sobs, for all my treasure spent on jewels and spilt in jollity, what recompense shall I reap besides repentance, what other reward shall I have than reproach, what other solace than endless shame?'

But haply thou wilt say, 'If I refuse their courtesy I shall be accounted a meacock,[5] a milksop, taunted and retaunted with check and checkmate, flouted and reflouted with intolerable glee.' Alas, fond fool, art thou so pinned to their sleeves[6] that thou regardest more their babble than thine own bliss, more their frumps[7] than thine own welfare? Wilt thou resemble the kind spaniel which the more he is beaten the fonder he is, or the foolish eyas which will never away?[8] Dost thou not know that women deem none valiant unless he be too venturous, that they account one a dastard if he be not desperate, a pinchpenny if he be not prodigal, if silent a sot, if full of words a fool? Perversely do they always think of their lovers, and talk of them scornfully, judging all to be clowns which be no courtiers, and all to be pinglers[9] that be not coursers.

Seeing, therefore, the very blossom of love is sour, the bud cannot be sweet. In time prevent danger, lest untimely[10] thou run into a thousand perils. Search

---

1 *fume*] rise (used of noxious vapours)
2 *leman*] mistress
3 *coy*] modest, reserved
4 *vestal virgins . . . dishonesty*] For other examples of this opposition see pp. 33 and 66.
5 *haply / meacock*] perhaps / weakling
6 *pinned to their sleeves*] dependent on them (cf. tied to their apron-strings)
7 *frumps*] mocks
8 *eyas . . . away*] young bird of prey that won't fly from the perch
9 *clowns / pinglers*] country bumpkins / heavy-goers (used of horses)
10 *untimely*] prematurely

the wound while it is green;[1] too late cometh the salve when the sore festereth, and the medicine bringeth double care when the malady is past cure. Beware of delays. What less than the grain of mustard seed; in time almost what thing is greater than the stalk thereof? The slender twig groweth to a stately tree, and that which with the hand might easily have been pulled up will hardly with the axe be hewn down. The least spark if it be not quenched will burst into a flame; the least moth in time eateth the thickest cloth; and I have read that in a short space there was a town in Spain undermined with conies,[2] in Thessalia with moles, with frogs in France, in Africa with flies. If these silly worms[3] in tract of time overthrow so stately towns, how much more will love which creepeth secretly into the mind (as the rust doth into the iron and is not perceived) consume the body, yea, and confound the soul. Defer not from hour to day, from day to month, from month to year, and always remain in misery. He that today is not willing will tomorrow be more wilful.

But alas, it is no less common than lamentable to behold the tottering estate[4] of lovers who think by delays to prevent dangers, with oil to quench fire, with smoke to clear the eyesight. They flatter themselves with a fainting[5] farewell, deferring ever until tomorrow, whenas their morrow doth always increase their sorrow. Let neither their amiable countenances, neither their painted protestations, neither their deceitful promises allure thee to delays. Think this with thyself, that the sweet songs of Calypso were subtle snares to entice Ulysses,[6] that the crab then catcheth the oyster when the sun shineth, that hyena when she speaketh like a man deviseth most mischief,[7] that women when they be most pleasant pretend[8] most treachery. Follow Alexander which, hearing the commendation and singular comeliness of the wife of Darius, so courageously withstood the assaults of fancy that he would not so much as take a view of her beauty. Imitate Cyrus, a king endued with such continency that he loathed to look on the heavenly hue of Panthea, and when Araspus told him that she excelled all mortal wights in amiable show, 'By so much the more,' said Cyrus, 'I ought to abstain from her sight, for if I follow thy counsel in going to her, it may be I shall desire to continue with her and by my light affection neglect my serious affairs.'[9] Learn of Romulus to refrain from wine, be it never so delicate; of Agesilaus to despise costly apparel, be it never so curious; of Diogenes[10] to detest women, be they never so comely. He that

---

1 *search . . . green*] probe the wound while it is fresh
2 *conies*] rabbits
3 *silly worms*] inconsiderable creatures
4 *estate*] condition
5 *fainting*] half-hearted
6 *sweet songs . . . Ulysses*] Calypso, in love with Ulysses who was shipwrecked on her island, sought to entice him to remain with her by means of her music
7 *hyena . . . mischief*] A reference to the belief, recorded by Pliny, that the hyena lured its victims by adopting human speech (see Bond, I, pp. 348–9).
8 *pretend*] intend
9 *Follow Alexander . . . affairs*] For *Alexander* and *Cyrus* see p. 27nn. Darius, King of Persia was conquered by Alexander in 330 BC. Panthea, wife of King Abradatus of Susa, was so honourably treated by Cyrus after his capture of her that her husband became his ally. Araspus and Cyrus were friends.
10 *Romulus / Agesilaus / Diogenes*] For *Romulus* and *Diogenes* see pp. 34 and 38nn. Agesilaus (d. 360 BC) was a celebrated king of Sparta.

toucheth pitch shall be defiled, the sore eye infecteth the sound, the society with women breedeth security in the soul and maketh all the senses senseless.

Moreover, take this counsel as an article of thy creed, which I mean to follow as the chief argument of my faith, that idleness is the only nurse and nourisher of sensual appetite, the sole maintenance of youthful affection, the first shaft that Cupid shooteth into the hot liver of a heedless lover. I would to God I were not able to find this for a truth by mine own trial, and I would the example of others' idleness had caused me rather to avoid that fault than experience of mine own folly. How dissolute have I been in striving against good counsel; how resolute in standing in mine own conceit![1] How forward to wickedness; how froward[2] to wisdom! How wanton with too much cockering;[3] how wayward in hearing correction! Neither was I much unlike these abbey-lubbers[4] in my life (though far unlike them in belief), which laboured till they were cold, eat till they sweat, and lay in bed till their bones ached. Hereof cometh it, gentlemen, that love creepeth into the mind by privy craft and keepeth his hold by main courage.

The man being idle, the mind is apt to all uncleanness; the mind being void of exercise, the man is void of honesty. Doth not the rust fret the hardest iron if it be not used? Doth not the moth eat the finest garment if it be not worn? Doth not moss grow on the smoothest stone if it be not stirred? Doth not impiety infect the wisest wit if it be given to idleness? Is not the standing water sooner frozen than the running stream? Is not he that sitteth more subject to sleep than he that walketh? Doth not common experience make this common unto us, that the fattest[5] ground bringeth forth nothing but weeds if it be not well tilled, that the sharpest wit inclineth only to wickedness if it be not exercised? Is it not true which Seneca reporteth, that as too much bending breaketh the bow so too much remission[6] spoileth the mind? Besides this, immoderate sleep, immodest play, unsatiable swilling of wine doth so weaken the senses and bewitch the soul that before we feel the motion of love we are resolved into lust. Eschew[7] idleness, my Philautus, so shalt thou easily unbend the bow and quench the brands of Cupid.[8] Love gives place to labour. Labour and thou shalt never love. Cupid is a crafty child, following those at an inch[9] that study pleasure, and flying those swiftly that take pains. Bend thy mind to the law, whereby thou mayst have understanding of old and ancient customs, defend thy clients, enrich thy coffers and carry credit[10] in thy country. If law seem loathsome unto thee, search the secrets of physic, whereby thou mayst know the hidden natures of herbs, whereby thou mayst gather profit to thy purse and pleasure to thy mind. What can be more exquisite in human affairs than for every fever be it never so hot, for every palsy be

---

1 *standing in mine own conceit*] adhering to my own views
2 *froward*] averse
3 *too much cockering*] over-indulgence
4 *abbey-lubbers*] idle monks
5 *fattest*] most fertile
6 *remission*] relaxation
7 *Eschew*] avoid
8 *brands of Cupid*] flaming torches of the god of love
9 *at an inch*] closely
10 *carry credit*] be held in good estimation

it never so cold, for every infection be it never so strange, to give a remedy? The old verse standeth as yet in his old virtue: that Galen giveth goods, Justinian honours.[1]

If thou be so nice that thou canst no way brook[2] the practice of physic or so unwise that thou wilt not beat thy brains about the institutes of the law, confer all thy study, all thy time, all thy treasure to the attaining of the sacred and sincere knowledge of divinity; by this mayst thou bridle thine incontinency, rein thy affections, restrain thy lust. Here shalt thou behold, as it were in a glass, that all the glory of man is as the grass, that all things under heaven are but vain, that our life is but a shadow, a warfare, a pilgrimage, a vapour, a bubble, a blast; of such shortness that David saith it is but a span long, of such sharpness that Job noteth it replenished with all miseries, of such uncertainty that we are no sooner born but we are subject to death, the one foot no sooner on the ground but the other ready to slip into the grave. Here shalt thou find ease for thy burden of sin, comfort for thy conscience pined with vanity, mercy for thine offences by the martyrdom of thy sweet Saviour. By this thou shalt be able to instruct those that be weak, to confute those that be obstinate, to confound those that be erroneous, to confirm the faithful, to comfort the desperate, to cut off the presumptuous, to save thine own soul by thy sure faith, and edify the hearts of many by thy sound doctrine.

If this seem too strait[3] a diet for thy straying disease or too holy a profession for so hollow a person, then employ thyself to martial feats, to jousts, to tourneys, yea, to all torments, rather than to loiter in love and spend thy life in the laps of ladies. What more monstrous can there be than to see a young man abuse those gifts to his own shame which God hath given him for his own preferment? What greater infamy than to confer the sharp wit to the making of lewd sonnets, to the idolatrous worshipping of their ladies, to the vain delights of fancy, to all kinds of vice as it were against kind[4] and course of nature? Is it not folly to show wit to women, which are neither able nor willing to receive fruit thereof? Dost thou not know that the tree silvacenda beareth no fruit in Pharos; that the Persian trees in Rhodes do only wax green but never bring forth apple; that amomus and nardus will only grow in India, balsamum only in Syria; that in Rhodes no eagle will build her nest; no owl live in Crete;[5] no wit spring in the will of women?

Mortify, therefore, thy affections and force not Nature against Nature to strive in vain. Go into the country. Look to thy grounds, yoke thine oxen, follow the plough, graft thy trees, behold thy cattle, and devise with thyself how the increase of them may increase thy profit. In autumn pull[6] thine apples, in summer ply thy harvest, in the spring trim thy gardens, in the winter thy woods; and thus, beginning to delight to be a good husband, thou shalt begin

---

1 *Galen . . . honours*] see p. 84 and n.
2 *nice / brook*] fastidious / tolerate
3 *strait*] strict
4 *kind*] natural propensity
5 *Dost thou . . . Crete*] examples, drawn from Pliny, of natural phenomena peculiar to a specific place. Amomus, nardus and balsamum are aromatic plants, silvacenda appears to arise from a misreading of the source (see Croll and Clemons, pp. 100–1nn.).
6 *pull*] pick

to detest to be in love with an idle huswife.[1] When profit shall begin to fill thy purse with gold, then pleasure shall have no force to defile thy mind with love. For honest recreation after thy toil, use hunting or hawking, either rouse the deer or unperch the pheasant; so shalt thou root out the remembrance of thy former love and repent thee of thy foolish lust. And although thy sweetheart bind thee by oath alway to hold a candle at her shrine and to offer thy devotion to thine own destruction, yet go, run, fly into the country; neither water thou thy plants[2] in that thou departest from thy pigsney,[3] neither stand in a mammering[4] whether it be best to depart or not, but by how much the more thou art unwilling to go, by so much the more hasten thy steps—neither feign for thyself any sleeveless[5] excuse whereby thou mayst tarry. Neither let rain nor thunder, neither lightning nor tempest, stay thy jouney; and reckon not with thyself how many miles thou hast gone (that showeth weariness), but how many thou hast to go (that proveth manliness).

But foolish and frantic lovers will deem my precepts hard and esteem my persuasions haggard.[6] I must of force confess that it is a corrosive to the stomach of a lover but a comfort to a godly liver to run through a thousand pikes to escape ten thousand perils. Sour potions bring sound health, sharp purgations make short diseases, and the medicine the more bitter it is the more better it is in working. To heal the body we try physic, search cunning, prove[7] sorcery, venture through fire and water, leaving nothing unsought that may be gotten for money, be it never so much, or procured by any means, be they never so unlawful. How much more ought we to hazard all things for the safeguard of mind and quiet of conscience!

And certes, easier will the remedy be when the reason is espied. Do you not know the nature of women, which is grounded only upon extremities? Do they think any man to delight in them unless he dote on them? Any to be zealous except they be jealous? Any to be fervent in case he be not furious?[8] If he be cleanly then term they him proud, if mean in apparel a sloven; if tall a lungis,[9] if short a dwarf; if bold blunt, if shamefast[10] a coward—insomuch as they have neither mean in their frumps[11] nor measure in their folly.

But at the first the ox wieldeth not the yoke, nor the colt the snaffle, nor the lover good counsel; yet time causeth the one to bend his neck, the other to open his mouth, and should enforce the third to yield his right to reason. Lay before thine eyes the sleights and deceits of thy lady, her snatching in jest and keeping in earnest, her perjury, her impiety, the countenance she showeth to thee of course, the love she beareth to others of zeal,[12] her open malice, her dissembled mischief. Oh, I would in repeating their vices thou couldst be

---

1 *husband* / *huswife*] husbandman (i.e. farmer) / hussy
2 *neither water ... plants*] do not weep
3 *pigsney*] sweetheart
4 *mammering*] state of hesitation
5 *sleeveless*] insubstantial
6 *haggard*] wild and unsociable
7 *prove*] try
8 *case ... furious*] unless he is frantic
9 *lungis*] a tall, thin, awkward fellow
10 *shamefast*] retiring
11 *mean in their frumps*] moderation in their jeers
12 *of course* / *of zeal*] by habit / with enthusiasm

as eloquent as in remembering them thou oughtst to be penitent! Be she never so comely, call her counterfeit; be she never so straight, think her crooked; and wrest all parts of her body to the worst, be she never so worthy. If she be well-set then call her a boss,[1] if slender a hazel twig; if nut-brown as black as a coal, if well-coloured a painted wall; if she be pleasant then is she a wanton, if sullen a clown; if honest then is she coy,[2] if impudent, a harlot. Search every vein and sinew of their disposition. If she have no sight in descant, desire her to chant it;[3] if no cunning to dance, request her to trip it; if no skill in music, proffer her the lute; if an ill gait, then walk with her; if rude in speech, talk with her; if she be gag-toothed, tell her some merry jest to make her laugh, if pink-eyed,[4] some doleful history to cause her weep—in the one her grinning will show her deformed, in the other her whining, like a pig half-roasted.

It is a world to see how commonly we are blinded with the collusions of women, and more enticed by their ornaments, being artificial, than their proportion, being natural. I loathe almost to think on their ointments and apothecary drugs, the sleeking of their faces and all their slibber-sauces,[5] which bring queasiness to the stomach and disquiet to the mind. Take from them their periwigs, their paintings, their jewels, their rolls,[6] their bolsterings, and thou shalt soon perceive that a woman is the least part of herself. When they be once robbed of their robes, then will they appear so odious, so ugly, so monstrous that thou wilt rather think them serpents than saints, and so like hags that thou wilt fear rather to be enchanted than enamoured. Look in their closets and there shalt thou find an apothecary's shop of sweet confections, a surgeon's box of sundry salves, a pedlar's pack of newfangles. Besides all this, their shadows, their spots, their lawns,[7] their lyfkies,[8] their ruffs, their rings, show them rather cardinals' courtesans than modest matrons, and more carnally affected than moved in conscience. If every one of these things severally be not of force to move thee, yet all of them jointly should mortify thee.

Moreover, to make thee the more stronger to strive against these sirens and more subtle to deceive these tame serpents, my counsel is that thou have more strings to thy bow than one. It is safe riding at two anchors, a fire divided in twain burneth slower, a fountain running into many rivers is of less force, the mind enamoured on two women is less affected with desire and less infected with despair. One love expelleth another and the remembrance of the latter quencheth the concupiscence of the first.

Yet if thou be so weak, being bewitched with their wiles, that thou hast neither will to eschew[9] nor wit to avoid their company, if thou be either so wicked that thou wilt not, or so wedded that thou canst not, abstain from

---

1 *boss*] lump
2 *honest / coy*] chaste / too reserved
3 *sight in descant / chant it*] skill in singing in harmony / sing
4 *be gag-toothed / if pink-eyed*] has a projecting tooth / has narrow or squint eyes (associated with petulance)
5 *sleeking of their faces / slibber-sauces*] smoothing of their cheeks / oily compounds used for cosmetics
6 *rolls*] padding used in hair dressing
7 *lawns*] fine linens
8 *lyfkies*] bodices
9 *eschew*] forgo

their glances, yet at the least dissemble thy grief. If thou be as hot as the Mount Etna, feign thyself as cold as the hill Caucasus; carry two faces in one hood,[1] cover thy flaming fancy with feigned ashes, show thyself sound when thou art rotten, let thy hue be merry when thy heart is melancholy, bear a pleasant countenance with a pined conscience, a painted sheath with a leaden dagger. Thus, dissembling thy grief, thou mayst recure[2] thy disease. Love creepeth in by stealth and by stealth slideth away.

If she break promise with thee in the night or absent herself in the day, seem thou careless and then will she be careful.[3] If thou languish, then will she be lavish of her honour, yea, and of the other strange beast—her honesty. Stand thou on thy pantofles and she will vail bonnet;[4] lie thou aloof and she will seize on the lure.[5] If thou pass by her door and be called back, either seem deaf and not to hear, or desperate and not to care. Fly the places, the parlours, the portals, wherein thou hast been conversant with thy lady. Yea, Philautus, shun the street where Lucilla doth dwell, lest the sight of her window renew the sum of thy sorrow.

Yet although I would have thee precise in keeping these precepts, yet would I have thee to avoid solitariness that breeds melancholy, melancholy madness, madness mischief and utter desolation. Have ever some faithful fere with whom thou mayst communicate thy counsels, some Pylades to encourage Orestes, some Damon to release Pythias, some Scipio to recure Laelius.[6] Phyllis in wandering the woods hanged herself; Asiarchus, forsaking company, spoiled himself with his own bodkin; Biarus, a Roman more wise than fortunate, being alone destroyed himself with a potsherd.[7] Beware solitariness. But although I would have thee use company for thy recreation, yet would I have thee always to leave the company of those that accompany thy lady; yea, if she have any jewel of thine in her custody, rather lose it than go for it, lest in seeking to recover a trifle thou renew thine old trouble.

Be not curious to curl thy hair, nor careful to be neat in thine apparel; be not prodigal of thy gold, nor precise in thy going;[8] be not like the Englishman, which preferreth every strange fashion before the use of his country; be thou dissolute,[9] lest thy lady think thee foolish in framing thyself to every fashion for her sake. Believe not their oaths and solemn protestations, their exorcisms and conjurations, their tears which they have at commandment,

---

1 *carry two ... hood*] disguise your feelings with a false show
2 *recure*] heal
3 *careless / be careful*] to be indifferent / care the more
4 *stand thou on thy pantofles / vail bonnet*] stand on your dignity (cf. p. 43n.) / show you respect
5 *lie thou aloof / seize on the lure*] keep your distance / take the bait
6 *Pylades ... Laelius*] For the first two examples see p. 45n. Though the friendship between Laelius and Scipio Africanus the younger is well attested (as is that between his father and Scipio Africanus the elder), it is not clear to what incident Lyly alludes here (*fere* = friend)
7 *Phyllis / Asiarchus / Biarus*] instances of suicide. For *Phyllis* see p. 67. The references to Asiarchus and Biarus remain obscure. (*potsherd* = piece of broken earthenware)
8 *precise in thy going*] over-scrupulous about your appearance
9 *dissolute*] careless of your appearance

their alluring looks, their treading on the toe, their unsavoury toys.[1] Let everyone loathe his lady and be ashamed to be her servant. It is riches and ease that nourisheth affection; it is play, wine and wantonness that feedeth a lover as fat as a fool. Refrain from all such meats as shall provoke thine appetite to lust, and all such means as may allure thy mind to folly. Take clear water for strong wine, brown bread for fine manchet,[2] beef and brewis[3] for quails and partridge, for ease labour, for pleasure pain, for surfeiting hunger, for sleep watching, for the fellowship of ladies the company of philosophers.

If thou say to me, 'Physician heal thyself,' I answer that I am meetly[4] well purged of that disease, and yet was I never more willing to cure myself than to comfort my friend. And seeing the cause that made in me so cold a devotion should make in thee also as frozen a desire, I hope thou wilt be as ready to provide a salve as thou wast hasty in see[k]ing a sore.

And yet, Philautus, I would not that all women should take pepper in the nose[5] in that I have disclosed the legerdemains[6] of a few, for well I know none will wince except she be galled, neither any be offended unless she be guilty. Therefore I earnestly desire thee that thou show this 'cooling card' to none, except thou show also this my defence to them all. For although I weigh nothing the ill will of light huswives,[7] yet would I be loath to lose the good will of honest matrons.

Thus, being ready to go to Athens, and ready there to entertain thee whensoever thou shalt repair thither, I bid thee farewell—and fly women.

Thine ever,
Euphues.

TO THE GRAVE MATRONS AND HONEST MAIDENS OF ITALY

Gentlewomen, because I would neither be mistaken of purpose,[8] neither misconstrued of malice, lest either the simple should suspect me of folly, or the subtle condemn me of blasphemy against the noble sex of women, I thought good that this my faith should be set down to find favour with the one and confute the cavils of the other. Believe me, gentlewomen, although I have been bold to inveigh against many, yet am I not so brutish to envy[9] them all; though I seem not so gamesome as Aristippus to play with Lais,[10] yet am I not so

---

1 *toys*] dallyings
2 *manchet*] white bread
3 *brewis*] bread soaked in the broth in which salt beef was boiled
4 *meetly*] fittingly
5 *take pepper in the nose*] be offended
6 *legerdemains*] deceits
7 *weigh nothing . . . huswives*] care nothing for the hostility of hussies
8 *of purpose*] deliberately
9 *envy*] disapprove of
10 *Aristippus . . . Lais*] The hedonistic life style of Aristippus (see p. 32n.) included enjoying the company of the celebrated courtesan Lais.

dogged as Diogenes[1] to abhor all ladies; neither would I you should think me so foolish (although of late I have been very fantastical) that for the light behaviour of a few I should call in question the demeanour of all. I know that as there hath been an unchaste Helen in Greece, so there hath been also a chaste Penelope; as there hath been a prodigious Pasiphae, so there hath been a godly Theocrita;[2] though many have desired to be beloved as Jupiter loved Alcmene, yet some have wished to be embraced as Phrigius embraced Pieria;[3] as there hath reigned a wicked Jezebel, so hath there ruled a devout Deborah;[4] though many have been as fickle as Lucilla, yet hath there many been as faithful as Lucretia.[5] Whatsoever, therefore, I have spoken of the spleen against the sleights and subtleties of women, I hope there is none will mislike it if she be honest, neither care I if any do if she be an harlot. The sour crab[6] hath the show of an apple as well as the sweet pippin, the black raven the shape of a bird as well as the white swan, the lewd wight the name of a woman as well as the honest matron. There is great difference between the standing puddle and the running stream, yet both water; great odds between the adamant[7] and the pumice, yet both stones; a great distinction to be put between vitrum[8] and the crystal, yet both glass; great contrariety between Lais and Lucretia,[9] yet both women. Seeing, therefore, one may love the clear conduit water[10] though he loathe the muddy ditch, and wear the precious diamond though he despise the ragged brick, I think one may also with safe conscience reverence the modest sex of honest maidens though he forswear the lewd sort of unchaste minions. Ulysses though he detested Calypso with her sugared voice, yet he embraced Penelope with her rude distaff;[11] though Euphues abhor the beauty of Lucilla, yet will he not abstain from the company of a grave maiden. Though the tears of the hart be salt, yet the tears of the boar be sweet; though the tears of some women be counterfeit to deceive, yet the tears of many be current to try their love. I, for my part, will honour those always that be honest and worship them in my life whom I shall know to be worthy in their living, neither can I promise such preciseness that I shall never be caught again with the bait of beauty; for although the

---

1 *dogged as Diogenes*] pun on the meaning of Cynic (Greek, *kunikos* = dog-like), the school of philosophy to which Diogenes belonged

2 *Helen . . . Theocrita*] For *Helen, Penelope* and *Pasiphae*, see pp. 27, 57 and 83nn. The reference to Theocrita remains obscure.

3 *Jupiter . . . Pieria*] types of adulterous and faithful love. Jupiter embraced Alcmene in the guise of her husband. The enduring love between Phrigius and Pieria brought peace between their cities.

4 *Jezebel / Deborah*] infamous wife of Ahab who encouraged his offences against God / prophetess and judge of Israel who brought about the defeat of the Canaanites

5 *Lucretia*] see p. 57n.

6 *crab*] wild apple

7 *adamant*] legendary stone, often associated through its impenetrability with the diamond

8 *vitrum*] common glass

9 *Lais and Lucretia*] a courtesan and a faithful wife

10 *conduit water*] piped (i.e. clean) water

11 *Ulysses . . . distaff*] For *Ulysses* and *Calypso* see pp. 57 and 91nn. Penelope (see p. 57n.) is usually associated with weaving rather than spinning.

falsehood of Lucilla have caused me to forsake my wonted dotage, yet the faith of some lady may cause me once again to fall into mine old disease. For as the fire-stone in Liguria though it be quenched with milk yet again it is kindled with water, or as the roots of anchusa[1] though it be hardened with water yet it is again made soft with oil, so the heart of Euphues inflamed erst with love although it be cooled with the deceits of Lucilla yet will it again flame with the loyalty of some honest lady, and though it be hardened with the water of wiliness yet will it be mollified with the oil of wisdom. I presume, therefore, so much upon the discretion of you gentlewomen that you will not think the worse of me in that I have thought so ill of some women, or love me the worse in that I loathe some so much. For this is my faith: that some one rose will be blasted in the bud, some other never fall from the stalk; that the oak will soon be eaten with the worm, the walnut tree never; that some women will easily be enticed to folly, some other never allured to vanity. You ought, therefore, no more to be aggrieved with that which I have said than the mint-master to see the coiner hanged, or the true subject the false traitor arraigned, or the honest man the thief condemned.

And so farewell.

You have heard, gentlemen, how soon the hot desire of Euphues was turned into a cold devotion—not that fancy caused him to change, but that the fickleness of Lucilla enforced him to alter his mind. Having, therefore, determined with himself never again to be entangled with such fond delights, according to the appointment made with Philautus he immediately repaired to Athens, there to follow his own private study. And calling to mind his former looseness and how in his youth he had misspent his time, he thought to give a caveat[2] to all parents how they might bring their children up in virtue, and a commandment to all youth how they should frame themselves to their fathers' instructions; in which is plainly to be seen what wit can do if it be well employed. Which discourse following, although it bring less pleasure to your youthful minds than his first course, yet will it bring more profit—in the one being contained the race[3] of a lover, in the other the reasons of a philosopher.

EUPHUES AND HIS EPHEBUS[4]

It is commonly said, yet do I think it a common lie, that experience is the mistress of fools; for in my opinion they be most fools that want[5] it. Neither am I one of the least that have tried this true,[6] neither he only that

---

1 *fire-stone in Liguria* / *anchusa*] possibly amber (see Bond, I, p. 351) / alkanet
2 *caveat*] warning
3 *race*] career
4 *Ephebus*] boy, youth. The following treatise on the education of the young is largely drawn from Plutarch's *De educatione puerorum*.
5 *want*] lack
6 *tried this true*] found the truth of this by experience

heretofore thought it to be false. I have been here[1] a student, of great wealth, of some wit, of no small acquaintance; yet have I learned that by experience that I should hardly have seen by learning. I have thoroughly sifted the disposition of youth, wherein I have found more bran than meal, more dough than leaven,[2] more rage than reason. He that hath been burned knoweth the force of the fire, he that hath been stung remembereth the smart of the scorpion, he that hath endured the brunts of fancy knoweth best how to eschew[3] the broils of affection. Let, therefore, my counsel be of such authority as it may command you to be sober, your conversation of such integrity as it may encourage me to go forward in that which I have taken in hand. The whole effect shall be to set down a young man so absolute as that nothing may be added to his further perfection. And although Plato hath been so curious in his commonweal, Aristotle so precise in his happy man, Tully[4] so pure in his orator, that we may well wish to see them, but never have any hope to enjoy them, yet shall my young imp be such an one as shall be perfect every way, and yet common, if diligence and industry be employed to the attaining of such perfection. But I would not have young men slow to follow my precepts or idle to defer the time, like St George who is ever on horseback yet never rideth.[5]

If my counsel shall seem rigorous to fathers to instruct their children, or heavy for youth to follow their parents' will, let them both remember that the ostrich digesteth hard iron to preserve his health,[6] that the soldier lieth in his harness to achieve conquest, that the sick patient swalloweth bitter pills to be eased of his grief, that youth should endure sharp storms to find relief.

I myself had been happy if I had been unfortunate,[7] wealthy if left meanly, better learned if I had been better lived. We have an old proverb, 'Youth will have his course.' Ah, gentlemen, it is a course we ought to make a coarse account of, replenished with more miseries than old age, with more sins than common cut-throats, with more calamities than the date of Priamus.[8] We are no sooner out of the shell but we resemble the cocyx which destroyeth itself through self-will,[9] or the pelican which pierceth a wound in her own breast;[10] we are either led with a vain glory of our proper personage or with self-love of our sharp capacity, either entangled with beauty or seduced by idle pastimes, either witched with vicious company of others or inveigled with our

---

1 *here*] Athens
2 *leaven*] substance added to dough to produce fermentation
3 *brunts / eschew*] assaults / avoid
4 *Plato / Aristotle / Tully*] all writers who defined an ideal, Plato in the *Republic* (the ideal state), Aristotle in the *Nicomachean Ethics* (the happy man), Tully (i.e. Cicero) in the *De oratore* (the perfect orator)
5 *St George ... rideth*] A reference to a common inn sign showing St George on horseback (i.e. the promise of action without progression).
6 *ostrich ... health*] See Bond, I, p. 353, for the sources of the belief that the ostrich eats iron for the good of its health.
7 *happy ... unfortunate*] lucky if I had been less fortunate
8 *date of Priamus*] lifetime of King Priam (which witnessed the fall of Troy)
9 *cocyx ... self-will*] cuckoo, which destroys itself through wilfulness (no source has been found for this example of perverse behaviour)
10 *pelican ... breast*] the pelican was thought to feed or renew its offspring with its own blood

own conceits.[1] Of all these things I may the bolder speak, having tried it true to mine own trouble.

To the intent, therefore, that all young gentlemen might shun my former looseness, I have set it down; and that all might follow my future life, I mean here to show what fathers should do, what children should follow, desiring them both not reject it because it proceedeth from one which hath been lewd, no more than if they would neglect the gold because it lieth in the dirty earth, or the pure wine for that it cometh out of a homely press, or the precious stone aetites which is found in the filthy nests of the eagle, or the precious gem draconites[2] that is ever taken out of the head of the poisoned dragon. But to my purpose.

THAT THE CHILD SHOULD BE TRUE BORN AND NO BASTARD

First, touching their procreation, it shall seem necessary to entreat of whosoever he be that desireth to be the sire of an happy son or the father of a fortunate child, let him abstain from those women which be either base of birth or bare of honesty. For if the mother be noted of incontinency or the father of vice, the child will either during life be infected with the like crime, or the treacheries of his parents as ignomy to him will be cast in his teeth—for we commonly call those unhappy children which have sprung from unhonest parents.

It is, therefore, a great treasure to the father and tranquillity to the mind of the child to have that liberty which both nature, law and reason hath set down. The guilty conscience of a father that hath trodden awry causeth him to think and suspect that his father also went not right, whereby his own behaviour is, as it were, a witness of his own baseness; even as those that come of a noble progeny boast of their gentry. Hereupon it came that Diophantus, Themistocles[3] his son, would often and that openly say in a great multitude that whatsoever he should seem to request of the Athenians he should be sure also to obtain, 'For,' saith he, 'whatsoever I will, that will my mother; and what my mother saith, my father sootheth;[4] and what my father desireth, that the Athenians will grant most willingly.' The bold courage of the Lacedaemonians is to be praised, which set a fine on the head of Archidamus their king for that he had married a woman of small personage, saying he minded to beget queens not kings to succeeed him. Let us not omit that which our ancestors were wont precisely to keep, that men should either be sober or drink little wine that would have sober and discreet children, for that the fact[5] of the father would be figured in the infant. Diogenes, therefore, seeing a young man either overcome with drink or bereaved of his wits,

---

1 *inveigled . . . conceit*] misled by our own fancies
2 *aetites / draconites*] pebble of argillaceous oxide of iron, thought to have medicinal properties / precious stone reputedly found in the brains of dragons
3 *Themistocles*] celebrated leader (b. circa 514 BC) to whom the Greeks were indebted for their victory over Xerxes, and to whose wishes they were therefore ready to defer
4 *sootheth*] assents to
5 *fact*] behaviour

cried with a loud voice, 'Youth, youth, thou hadst a drunken father!' And
thus much for procreation. Now how the life should be led I will show briefly.

HOW THE LIFE OF A YOUNG MAN SHOULD BE LED

There are three things which cause perfection in man—nature, reason, use.
Reason I call discipline, use exercise. If any one of these branches want, certainly the tree of virtue must needs wither. For nature without discipline is of
small force, and discipline without nature more feeble. If exercise or study be
void of any of these, it availeth nothing. For as in tilling of the ground and
husbandry there is first chosen a fertile soil, then a cunning sower, then good
seed, even so must we compare nature to the fat earth, the expert husbandman[1] to the schoolmaster, the faculties and sciences to the pure seeds. If this
order had not been in our predecessors, Pythagoras, Socrates, Plato, and
whosoever was renowned in Greece for the glory of wisdom, they had never
been eternized for wise men, neither canonized, as it were, for saints among
those that study sciences. It is, therefore, a most evident sign of God's singular favour towards him that is endued with all these qualities, without the
least of the which man is most miserable.

But if there be any one that thinketh wit not necessary to the obtaining of
wisdom after he hath gotten the way to virtue by industry and exercise, he is
an heretic, in my opinion, touching the true faith of learning; for if nature
play not her part in vain is labour, and (as I said before), if study be not
employed in vain is nature. Sloth turneth the edge of wit, study sharpeneth
the mind; a thing be it never so easy is hard to the idle, a thing be it never so
hard is easy to the wit well employed. And most plainly we may see in many
things the efficacy of industry and labour. The little drops of rain pierceth
hard marble, iron with often handling is worn to nothing. Besides this, industry showeth herself in other things. The fertile soil if it be never tilled doth
wax barren, and that which is most noble by nature is made most vile by negligence. What tree if it be not topped beareth any fruit? What vine if it be not
pruned bringeth forth grapes? Is not the strength of the body turned to weakness through too much delicacy? Were not Milo his arms brawnfallen for
want[2] of wrestling? Moreover, by labour the fierce unicorn is tamed, the
wildest falcon is reclaimed, the greatest bulwark is sacked. It was well
answered of that man of Thessaly, who, being demanded who among the
Thessalians were reputed most vile, 'Those,' said he, 'that live at quiet and
ease, never giving themselves to martial affairs.' But what should one use
many words in a thing already proved? It is custom, use, and exercise that
bring a young man to virtue, and virtue to his perfection.

Lycurgus, the law-giver of the Spartans, did nourish two whelps, both of
one sire and one dam, but after a sundry[3] manner; for the one he framed to
hunt and the other to lie always in the chimney's end at the porridge pot.
Afterward, calling the Lacedaemonians into one assembly, he said, 'To the
attaining of virtue, ye Lacedaemonians, education, industry, and exercise is

---

1 *fat earth / expert husbandman*] rich soil / skilful farmer
2 *brawnfallen / want*] less muscular / lack (for *Milo* see p. 35n.)
3 *Lycurgus / sundry*] see p. 32n. / different

the most noblest means, the truth of which I will make manifest unto you by trial.' Then bringing forth the whelps and setting down there a pot and a hare, the one ran at the hare, the other to the porridge pot. The Lacedaemonians scarce understanding this mystery, he said, 'Both of these be of one sire and one dam, but you see how education altereth nature.'

OF THE EDUCATION OF YOUTH

It is most necessary and most natural, in mine opinion, that the mother of the child be also the nurse, both for the entire love she beareth to the babe, and the great desire she hath to have it well-nourished; for is there anyone more meet to bring up the infant than she that bore it, or will any be so careful for it as she that bred it? For as the throbs and throes in childbirth wrought her pain, so the smiling countenance of the infant increaseth her pleasure. The hired nurse is not unlike to the hired servant which, not for good will but gain, not for love of the man but the desire of the money, accomplisheth his day's work. Moreover, Nature in this point enforceth the mother to nurse her own child, which hath given unto every beast milk to succour her own. And methinketh Nature to be a most provident foreseer and provider for the same, which hath given unto a woman two paps,[1] that if she conceive two she might have wherewith also to nourish twain, and that by sucking of the mother's breasts there might be a greater love both of the mother towards the child and the child towards the mother, which is very likely to come to pass, for we see commonly those that eat and drink and live together to be more zealous one to the other than those that meet seldom. Is not the name of a mother most sweet? If it be, why is half that title bestowed on a woman which never felt the pains in conceiving, neither can conceive the like pleasure in nursing as the mother doth? Is the earth called the mother of all things only because it bringeth forth? No, but because it nourisheth those things that spring out of it. Whatsoever is bred in the sea is fed in the sea; no plant, no tree, no herb cometh out of the ground that is not moistened and, as it were, nursed of the moisture and milk of the earth. The lioness nurseth her whelps, the raven cherisheth her birds, the viper her brood, and shall a woman cast away her babe?

I account it cast away which in the swath-clouts[2] is cast aside, and little care can the mother have which can suffer such cruelty. And can it be termed with any other title than cruelty, the infant yet looking red of the mother, the mother yet breathing through the torments of her travail,[3] the child crying for help, which is said to move wild beasts, even in the self-said moment it is born, or the next minute, to deliver to a strange nurse, which perhaps is neither wholesome in body, neither honest in manners, which esteemeth more thy argent,[4] although a trifle, than thy tender infant, thy greatest treasure? Is it not necessary and requisite that the babe be nursed with that true

1 *paps*] breasts
2 *swath-clouts*] baby clothes (literally, the cloth in which a new-born infant is wrapped)
3 *travail*] labour
4 *argent*] money (literally, silver)

accustomed juice and cherished with his wonted heat, and not fed with counterfeit diet? Wheat thrown into a strange ground turneth to a contrary grain,
the vine translated into another soil changeth his kind. A slip[1] pulled from
the stalk withereth, the young child as it were slipped from the paps of his
mother either changeth his nature or altereth his disposition. It is prettily said
of Horace[2] a new vessel will long time savour of that liquor that is first poured
into it, and the infant will ever smell of the nurse's manners having tasted of
her milk. Therefore let the mother, as often as she shall behold those two
fountains of milk as it were of their own accord flowing and swelling with
liquor, remember that she is admonished of Nature, yea, commanded of duty,
to cherish her own child with her own teats—otherwise when the babe shall
now begin to tattle and call her 'Mamma,' with what face can she hear it of
his mouth unto whom she hath denied mamma?[3] It is not milk only that
increaseth the strength or augmenteth the body, but the natural heat and
agreement of the mother's body with the child's: it craveth the same accustomed moisture that before it received in the bowels, by the which the tender
parts were bound and knit together, by the which it increased and was suc-
coured in the body.

Certes, I am of that mind that the wit and disposition is altered and changed
by the milk, as the moisture and sap of the earth doth change the nature of
that tree or plant that it nourisheth. Wherefore the common byword[4] of the
common people seemeth to be grounded upon good experience, which
is, 'This fellow hath sucked mischief even from the teat of his nurse.' The
Grecians, when they saw anyone sluttishly fed, they would say 'Even as
nurses,'[5] whereby they noted the great disliking they had of their fulsome
feeding. The etymology of mother among the Grecians may aptly be applied
to those mothers which unnaturally deal with their children: they call it 'meter
a meterine,' that is, 'mother of not making much of,' or of not nourishing.
Hereof it cometh that the son doth not with deep desire love his mother,
neither with duty obey her, his natural affection being, as it were, divided and
distraught into twain, a mother and a nurse. Hereof it proceedeth that the
mother beareth but a cold kindness towards her child when she shall see the
nature of her nurse in the nurture of her child. The chiefest way to learning
is if there be a mutual love and fervent desire between the teacher and him
that is taught; then, verily, the greatest furtherance to education is if the
mother nourish the child and the child suck the mother, that there be, as it
were, a relation and reciprocal order of affection.

Yet if the mother, either for the evil habit[6] of her body or the weakness of
her paps, cannot, though she would, nurse her infant, then let her provide
such a one as shall be of a good complexion, of honest condition, careful to
tender the child, loving to see well to it, willing to take pains, diligent in
tending and providing all things necessary, and as like both in the lineaments

---

1 *slip*] cutting
2 *Horace*] Roman poet (65–8 BC). The reference is to the first book of the *Epistles*
   (ii. 70).
3 *mamma*] the breast
4 *byword*] saying
5 *Even as nurses*] just like wet-nurses
6 *for the evil habit*] because of the sick condition

of the body and disposition of the mind to the mother as may be. Let her forslow[1] no occasion that may bring the child to quietness and cleanliness; for as the parts of a child as soon as it is born are framed and fashioned of the midwife, that in all points it might be straight and comely, so the manners of the child at the first are to be looked unto, that nothing discommend[2] the mind, that no crooked behaviour or undecent demeanour be found in the man.

Young and tender age is easily framed to manners, and hardly are those things mollified which are hard.[3] For as the steel is imprinted in the soft wax, so learning is engraven in the mind of an young imp. Plato, that divine philosopher, admonished all nurses and weaners of youth that they should not be too busy to tell them fond fables or filthy tales, lest at their entrance into the world they should be contaminated with unseemly behaviour. Unto the which Phocylides, the poet, doth pithily allude,[4] saying, 'Whilst that the child is young let him be instructed in virtue and literature.'

Moreover, they are to be trained up in the languge of their country, to pronounce aptly and distinctly, without stammering, every word and syllable of their native speech, and to be kept from barbarous talk as the ship from rocks, lest, being affected with their barbarism, they be infected also with their unclean conversation.

It is an old proverb that if one dwell the next door to a cripple he will learn to halt;[5] if one be conversant with an hypocrite he will soon endeavour to dissemble. When this young infant shall grow in years and be of that ripeness that he can conceive learning, insomuch that he is to be committed to the tuition of some tutor, all diligence is to be had to search such a one as shall neither be unlearned, neither ill-lived, neither a light person.

A gentleman that hath honest and discreet servants disposeth them to the increase of his seigniories;[6] one he appointeth steward of his courts, another overseer of his lands, one his factor in far countries for his merchandise, another purveyor for his cates[7] at home. But if among all his servants he shall espy one either filthy in his talk or foolish in his behaviour, either without wit or void of honesty, either an unthrift or a wittol,[8] him he sets not as a surveyor and overseer of his manors but a supervisor of his children's conditions and manners; to him he committeth the guiding and tuition of his sons, which is by his proper[9] nature a slave, a knave by condition, a beast in behaviour. And sooner will they bestow an hundred crowns to have a horse well broken than a child well taught, wherein I cannot but marvel to see them so careful to increase their possessions when they be so careless to have them wise that should inherit them.

---

1 *forslow*] neglect
2 *discommend*] reflect adversely on
3 *hardly . . . hard*] those things that are already hard are softened with difficulty
4 *Phocylides . . . allude*] Ionian poet (b. 560 BC), writer of gnomic verses (hence 'pithily'). For *Plato* in the previous sentence see p. 38n.
5 *halt*] limp
6 *seigniories*] domains
7 *purveyor for his cates*] buyer of his provisions
8 *unthrift / wittol*] spendthrift / fool
9 *proper*] own

A good and discreet schoolmaster should be such an one as Phoenix was, the instructor of Achilles, whom Peleus[1] (as Homer reporteth) appointed to that end that he should be unto Achilles not only a teacher of learning but an example of good living. But that is most principally to be looked for and most diligently to be foreseen, that such tutors be sought out for the education of a young child whose life hath never been stained with dishonesty, whose good name hath never been called unto question, whose manners hath been irreprehensible before the world. As husbandmen hedge in their trees, so should good schoolmasters with good manners hedge in the wit and disposition of the scholar, whereby the blossoms of learning may the sooner increase to a bud.

Many parents are in this to be misliked which, having neither trial of his honesty nor experience of his learning to whom they commit the child to be taught, without any deep or due consideration put them to one either ignorant or obstinate; the which if they themselves shall do of ignorance the folly cannot be excused, if of obstinacy their lewdness[2] is to be abhorred. Some fathers are overcome with the flattery of those fools which profess outwardly great knowledge and show a certain kind of dissembling sincerity in their life; others, at the entreating of their familiar friends, are content to commit their sons to one without either substance of honesty or shadow of learning. By which their undiscreet dealing they are like those sick men which reject the expert and cunning physician and, at the request of their friends, admit the heedless practiser, which dangereth the patient and bringeth the body to his bane;[3] or not unlike unto those which, at the instant and importunate suit of their acquaintance, refuse a cunning pilot and choose an unskilful mariner, which hazardeth the ship and themselves in the calmest sea. Good God, can there be any that hath the name of a father which will esteem more the fancy of his friend than the nurture of his son!

It was not in vain that Crates[4] would often say that, if it were lawful, even in the market place he would cry out, 'Whither run you, fathers, which have all your cark[5] and care to multiply your wealth, nothing regarding your children unto whom you must leave all?' In this they resemble him which is very curious about the shoe, and hath no care of the foot. Besides this, there be many fathers so inflamed with the love of wealth that they be as it were incensed with hate against their children, which Aristippus, seeing in an old miser, did partly note it. This old miser asking of Aristippus what he would take to teach and bring up his son, he answered, 'A thousand groats.'[6] 'A thousand groats! God shield!' answered this old huddle,[7] 'I can have two

---

1 Peleus] King of the Myrmidons, who entrusted his son Achilles, ultimately the greatest of the Greek warriors, to the care of Phoenix, King of the Dolopes. Phoenix subsequently accompanied Achilles to the Trojan war.
2 lewdness] viciousness
3 bringeth . . . bane] imperil the body
4 Crates] Cynic philosopher (fl. circa 320 BC), given to visiting the citizens of Athens individually to rebuke them for their vices
5 cark] pains
6 groats] coin worth 4d in pre-decimalization English currency. For Aristippus see p. 32n.
7 huddle] miser

servants of that price!' Unto whom he made answer, 'Thou shalt have two servants and one son, and whether wilt thou sell?'

Is it not absurd to have so great a care of the right hand of the child to cut his meat that if he handle his knife in the left hand we rebuke him severely, and to be secure of[1] his nurture in discipline and learning? But what do happen unto those parents that bring up their children like wantons? When their sons shall grow to man's estate, disdaining now to be corrected, stubborn to obey, giving themselves to vain pleasures and unseemly pastimes, then with the foolish truants they begin to wax wise and to repent them of their former folly. When their sons shall insinuate themselves in the company of flatterers (a kind of men more perilous to youth than any kind of beasts), when they shall haunt harlots, frequent taverns, be curious in their attire, costly in their diet, careless in their behaviour, when they shall either be common dicers with gamesters, either wanton dalliers with ladies, either spend all their thrift on wine or all their wealth on women, then the father curseth his own security and lamenteth too late his child's misfortune. Then the one accuseth his sire as it were of malice that he would not bring him up in learning, and himself of mischief that he gave not his mind to good letters. If these youths had been trained up in the company of any philosopher, they would never have been so dissolute in their life or so resolute in their own conceits.[2]

It is good nurture that leadeth to virtue and discreet demeanour that planeth[3] the path to felicity. If one have either the gifts of fortune, as great riches, or of nature, as seemly personage, he is to be despised in respect of learning. To be a nobleman it is most excellent, but that is our ancestors',[4] as Ulysses said to Ajax; as for our nobility, our stock,[5] our kindred, and whatsoever we ourselves have not done, I scarcely account ours. Riches are precious, but fortune ruleth the roast,[6] which oftentimes taketh away all from them that have much and giveth them more that had nothing. Glory is a thing worthy to be followed, but as it is gotten with great travail, so is it lost in a small time. Beauty is such a thing as we commonly prefer before all things, yet it fadeth before we perceive it to flourish. Health is that which all men desire, yet ever subject to any disease. Strength is to be wished for, yet is it either abated with an ague or taken away with age; whosoever, therefore, boasteth of force[7] is too beastly, seeing he is in that quality not to be compared with beasts—as the lion, the bull, the elephant. It is virtue, yea, virtue, gentlemen, that maketh gentlemen, that maketh the poor rich, the base-born noble, the subject a sovereign, the deformed beautiful, the sick whole, the weak strong, the most miserable most happy.

There are two principal and peculiar gifts in the nature of man, knowledge and reason; the one commandeth, the other obeyeth. These things neither the whirling wheel of fortune can change, neither the deceitful cavilling of

---

1 *secure of*] unconcerned about
2 *resolute in their own conceits*] wedded to their own views
3 *planeth*] smooths
4 *that is our ancestors'*] that is a property belonging to our predecessors
5 *stock*] lineage
6 *ruleth the roast*] overrides everything else
7 *force*] strength

wordlings separate, neither sickness abate, neither age abolish. It is only knowledge which, worn with years, waxeth young; and when all things are cut away with the sickle of time,[1] knowledge flourisheth so high that time cannot reach it. War taketh all things with it even as the whirlpool, yet must it leave learning behind it. Wherefore it was wisely answered in my opinion of Stilpo the philosopher: for when Demetrius[2] won the city and made it even to[3] the ground, leaving nothing standing, he demanded of Stilpo whether he had lost anything of his in this great spoil; unto whom he answered, 'No, verily, for war getteth no spoil of virtue.' Unto the like sense may the answer of Socrates be applied, when Gorgias[4] asked him whether he thought the Persian king happy or not. 'I know not,' said he, 'how much virtue or discipline he hath, for happiness doth not consist in the gifts of fortune but in the grace of virtue.'

But as there is nothing more convenient than instruction for youth, so I would have them nurtured in such a place as is renowned for learning, void of corrupt manners, undefiled with vice, that seeing no vain delights they may the more easily abstain from licentious desires. They that study to please the multitude are sure to displease the wise; they that seem to flatter rude people with their rude pretences level at great honour, having no aim at honesty.

When I was here a student in Athens it was thought a great commendation for a young scholar to make an oration extempore, but certainly in my judgement it is utterly to be condemned, for whatsoever is done rashly is done also rawly. He that taketh upon him to speak without premeditation knoweth neither how to begin nor where to end, but falling into a vein of babbling uttereth those things which with modesty he should have concealed, and forgetteth those things that before he had conceived. An oration, either penned either premeditated, keepeth itself within the bonds of decorum. I have read that Pericles,[5] being at sundry times called of the people to plead, would always answer that he was not ready. Even after the same manner Demosthenes, being sent for to declaim amidst the multitude, stayed and said, 'I am not yet provided.' And in his invective against Midias[6] he seemeth to praise the profitableness of premeditation. 'I confess,' saith he, 'ye Athenians, that I have studied and considered deeply with myself what to speak; for I were a sot if without due consideration had of those things that are to be spoken I should have talked unadvisedly.'

But I speak this not to this end to condemn the exercise of the wit, but that I would not have any young scholar openly to exercise it. But when he shall

---

1   *sickle of time*] cf. the representation of time as an old man with a scythe
2   *Stilpo / Demetrius*] celebrated philosopher of Megara, who taught that the wise man is not subject to evil / Macedonian king (d. 283 BC) distinguished by the brilliance of his military campaigns who spared Stilpo's house when Megara was sacked
3   *even to*] level with
4   *Socrates / Gorgias*] the founding father of speculative philosophy (d. 399 BC) / celebrated orator (b. circa 480 BC), and participant in one of the dialogues with Socrates recorded by Plato
5   *Pericles*] outstanding Athenian statesman (d. 429 BC), noted for his eloquence
6   *Demosthenes / Midias*] greatest of the Athenian orators (b. circa 385 BC) / enemy of Demosthenes, whom he assaulted in 354 BC, leading to the orator's 'invective against' (i.e. formal indictment of) him

grow both in age and eloquence, insomuch as he shall through great use and good memory be able aptly to conceive and readily to utter anything, then this saying extempore bringeth an admiration and delight to the auditory, and singular praise and commendation to the orator. For as he that hath long time been fettered with chains, being released, halteth through the force of his former irons, so he that hath been used to a strict kind of pleading, when he shall talk extempore will savour of his former penning. But if any shall use it as it were a precept for youth to tattle extempore, he will in time bring them to an immoderate kind of humility.[1] A certain painter brought to Apelles the counterfeit of a face in a table,[2] saying, 'Lo, Apelles, I drew this even now,' whereunto he replied, 'If thou hadst been silent I would have judged this picture to have been framed of the sudden.[3] I marvel that in this time thou couldst not paint many more of these.'

But return we again. As I would have tragical and stately style shunned, so would I have that abject and base phrase eschewed; for this swelling kind of talk hath little modesty, the other nothing moveth. Besides this, to have the oration all one in every part, neither adorned with fine figures, neither sprinkled with choice phrases, bringeth tediousness to the hearers and argueth the speaker of little learning and less eloquence. He should, moreover, talk of many matters, not always harp upon one string; he that always singeth one note without descant breedeth no delight, he that always playeth one part bringeth loathsomeness to the ear. It is variety that moveth the mind of all men, and one thing said twice, as we say commonly, deserveth a trudge.[4] Homer would say that it loathed him to repeat anything again though it were never so pleasant or profitable.[5] Though the rose be sweet, yet being tied with the violet the smell is more fragrant; though meat nourish, yet having good savour it provoketh the appetite. The fairest nosegay is made of many flowers, the finest picture of sundry colours, the wholesomest medicine of divers herbs. Wherefore it behoveth youth with all industry to search not only the hard questions of the philosophers but also the fine cases of the lawyers, not only the quirks and quiddities of the logicians but also to have a sight in[6] the numbers of the arithmeticians, the triangles and circles of the geometricians, the sphere and globe of the astrologians, the notes and crotchets of the musicians, the odd conceits of the poets, the simples[7] of the physicians, and in all things, to the end that when they shall be willed to talk of any of them they may be ignorant in nothing. He that hath a garden-plot doth as well sow the pot-herb as the marjoram, as well the leek as the lily, as well the wholesome hyssop as the fair carnation; the which he doth to the intent he may have wholesome herbs as well to nourish his inward parts as sweet flowers to please his outward desire, as well fruitful plants to refresh his senses as fair shows

---

1 *immoderate . . . humility*] an extremely unambitious style
2 *counterfeit . . . table*] the picture of a face in a design (for *Apelles* see p. 27n.)
3 *framed of the sudden*] drawn quickly
4 *deserveth a trudge*] obscure. Possibly 'deserves to be sent packing' (from *trudge* = to go or be sent away)
5 *Homer . . . profitable*] a comment made in the *Odyssey*, bk xxii (see Bond, I, p. 358)
6 *have a sight in*] have some knowledge of
7 *simples*] medicinal herbs

to please his sight. Even so whosoever that hath a sharp and capable wit, let him as well give his mind to sacred knowledge of divinity as to the profound study of philosophy, that by his wit he may not only reap pleasure but profit, not only contentation in mind but quietness in conscience. I will proceed in the education.

I would have them first of all to follow philosophy as most ancient, yea, most excellent; for as it is pleasant to pass through many fair cities but most pleasant to dwell in the fairest, even so to read many histories and arts it is pleasant, but as it were to lodge with philosophy most profitable. It was prettily said of Bion[1] the philosopher, 'Even as when the wooers could not have the company of Penelope they ran to her handmaidens, so they that cannot attain to the knowledge of philosophy apply their minds to things most vile and contemptible.' Wherefore we must prefer philosophy as the only princess of all sciences and other arts as waiting-maids. For the curing and keeping in temper of the body, man by his industry hath found two things, physic and exercise, the one cureth sickness, the other preserveth the body in temper; but there is nothing that may heal diseases or cure the wounds of the mind but only philosophy. By this shall we learn what is honest, what dishonest, what is right, what is wrong; and that I may in one word say what may be said, what is to be known, what is to be avoided. How we ought to obey our parents, reverence our elders, entertain strangers, honour magistrates, love our friends, live with our wives, use our servants; how we should worship God, be dutiful to our fathers, stand in awe of our superiors, obey laws, give place to officers; how we may choose friends, nurture our children, and (that which is most noble) how we should neither be too proud in prosperity, neither pensive in adversity, neither like beasts overcome with anger.

And here I cannot but lament Athens, which, having been always the nurse of philosophers, doth now nourish only the name of philosophy. For to speak plainly of the disorder of Athens, who doth not see it and sorrow at it? Such playing at dice, such quaffing of drink, such dalliance with women, such dancing, that in my opinion there is no quaffer in Flanders so given to tip-pling, no courtier in Italy so given to riot,[2] no creature in the world so misled as a student in Athens. Such a confusion of degrees that the Scholar knoweth not his duty to the Bachelor, nor the Bachelor to the Master, nor the Master to the Doctor. Such corruption of manners, contempt of magistrates, such open sins, such privy villainy, such quarrelling in the streets, such subtle prac-tices in chambers as maketh my heart to melt with sorrow to think of it, and should cause your minds, gentlemen, to be penitent to remember it.

Moreover, who doth know a scholar by his habit?[3] Is there any hat of so unseemly a fashion, any doublet of so long a waist, any hose so short, any attire either so costly or so courtly, either so strange in making or so mon-strous in wearing, that is not worn of a scholar? Have they not now instead of black cloth, black velvet; instead of coarse sackcloth, fine silk? Be they not more like courtiers than scholars, more like stage-players than students, more like ruffians of Naples than disputers in Athens? I would to God they did not

---

1 *Bion*] Cyrenaic philosopher (fl. 250 BC) noted for his pointed sayings
2 *quaffer . . . riot*] allusions to stereotypical national characteristics. Residents of the low countries were thought to be inordinately given to drink. For *Italy* see p. 34n.
3 *habit*] style of dress

imitate all other nations in the vice of the mind as they do in the attire of their body, for certainly as there is no nation whose fashion in apparel they do not use, so there is no wickedness published in any place that they do not practise. I think that in Sodom and Gomorrah there was never more filthiness, never more pride in Rome, more poisoning in Italy, more lying in Crete, more privy spoiling[1] in Spain, more idolatry in Egypt than is at this day in Athens; never such sects among the heathens, such schisms amongst the Turks, such misbelief among the infidels as is now among scholars. Be there not many in Athens which think there is no God? No redemption? No resurrection? What shame is this, gentlemen, that a place so renowned for good learning should be so shamed for ill living; that where grace doth abound, sin should so superabound; that where the greatest profession of knowledge is, there should also be the least practising of honesty!

I have read of many universities, as of Padua in Italy, Paris in France, Wittenberg in Germany, in England of Oxford and Cambridge, which if they were half so ill as Athens they were too too bad; and as I have heard, as they be they be stark nought. But I can speak the less against them for that I was never in them, yet can I not choose but be aggrieved that by report I am enforced rather to accuse them of vanity than excuse them any way. Ah, gentlemen, what is to be looked for, nay, what is not to be feared, when the temple of Vesta,[2] where virgins should live, is like the stews, fraught with strumpets; when the altar where nothing but sanctity and holiness should be used is polluted with uncleanness; when the universities of Christendom, which should be the eyes, the lights, the leaven,[3] the salt, the seasoning of the world are dimmed with blind concupiscence, put out with pride, and have lost their savour with impiety?

Is it not become a byword amongst the common people that they had rather send their children to the cart[4] than to the university, being induced so to say for the abuse that reigneth in the universities? Who, sending their sons to attain knowledge, find them little better learned but a great deal worst lived than when they went, and not only unthrifts of their money but also bankrupts of good manners. Was not this the cause that caused a simple woman in Greece to exclaim against Athens, saying, 'The Master and the Scholar, the tutor and the pupil, be both agreed; for the one careth not how little pain he taketh for his money, the other how little learning.'

I perceive that in Athens there be no changelings[5] when, of old, it was said to a Lacedaemonian that all the Grecians knew honesty, but not one practised it. When Panathenaea[6] were celebrated at Athens, an old man going to take a

---

1 *privy spoiling*] covert injuries (a reference to the contemporary association between Spaniards and revenge). For the Cretans and lying see p. 34n. The equation of Italy with poisoning relates to the activities of such notorious Italian families as the Borgias.

2 *temple of Vesta*] see p. 33n.

3 *leaven*] fermenting agent

4 *byword / cart*] common saying / gallows (literally the cart bearing them to the gallows)

5 *there be no changelings*] the people run true to type (literally, there are no elf-children substituted by the fairies at birth)

6 *Panathenaea*] national festival of Athens, involving gymnastic games and musical competitions

place was mockingly rejected. At the last, coming among the Lacedaemonians, all the youth gave him place, which the Athenians liked well of. Then one of the Spartans cried out, 'Verily, the Athenians know what should be done, but they never do it.' When one of the Lacedaemonians had been for a certain time in Athens, seeing nothing but dancing, dicing, banqueting, surfeiting, and licentious behaviour, returning home he was asked how all things stood in Athens; to whom he answered, 'All things are honest there,' meaning that the Athenians accounted all things good and nothing bad.

How such abuses should or might be redressed in all universities, especially in Athens, if I were of authority to command, it should soon be seen, or of credit to persuade those that have the dealings with them, it should soon be shown. And until I see better reformation in Athens, my young Ephebus shall not be nurtured in Athens.

I have spoken all this that you gentlemen might see how the philosophers in Athens practise nothing less than philosophy. What scholar is he that is so zealous at his book as Chrysippus, who, had not his maid Melissa thrust meat in his mouth, had perished with famine, being always studying?[1] Who so watchful as Aristotle, who going to bed would have a ball of brass in his hand, that if he should be taken in a slumber it might fall and awake him? No, no, the times are changed, as Ovid saith, and we are changed in the times. Let us endeavour every one to amend one, and we shall all soon be amended; let us give no occasion of reproach, and we shall more easily bear the burden of false reports; and as we see by learning what we should do, so let us do as we learn. Then shall Athens flourish, then shall the students be had in great reputation, then shall learning have his hire[2] and every good scholar his hope. But return we once again to philo[sophy].

There is amongst men a trifold kind of life: active, which is about civil function and administration of the commonweal; speculative, which is in continual meditation and study; the third a life led, most commonly a lewd life, an idle and vain life, the life that the Epicures[3] account their whole felicity, a voluptuous life replenished with all kind of vanity. If this active life be without philosophy, it is an idle life, or at the least a life evil employed which is worse; if the contemplative life be separated from the active, it is most unprofitable. I would, therefore, have my youth so to bestow his study as he may be both exercised in the commonweal to common profit and well employed privately for his own perfection; so as by his study the rule he shall bear may be directed, and by his government his study may be increased. In this manner did Pericles deal in civil affairs, after this sort did Archytas Tarentine, Dion the Syracusian, the Theban Epaminondas govern their cities.[4]

---

1 *Chrysippus ... studying*] a story originally associated with Carneades, founder of the New Academy at Athens, but attributed by Lyly to Chrysippus (see p. 35n.) both here and in *Campaspe*. For *Ovid* and *Aristotle* in the following sentences see p. 33n.
2 *hire*] reward
3 *Epicures*] see p. 34n.
4 *Pericles / Archytas Tarentine / Dion the Syracusian / Epaminondas*] all civic leaders of outstanding intellectual stature. For *Pericles* see p. 108n. Archytas of Tarentum (fl. 400 BC), distinguished statesman and general, belonged to the Pythagorean school and was a notable mathematician. Dion (d. 353 BC) was a disciple of Plato. Epaminondas (d. 362 BC), a celebrated Theban general, was an ardent student of philosophy and attempted to carry its teachings into everyday life.

For the exercise of the body it is necessary also somewhat be added: that is, that the child should be at such times permitted to recreate himself when his mind is overcome with study, lest dulling himself with overmuch industry he become unfit afterward to conceive readily; besides this, it will cause an apt composition and that natural strength that it before retained. A good composition of the body layeth a good foundation of old age; for as in the fair summer we prepare all things necessary for the cold winter, so good manners in youth and lawful exercises be as it were victuals and nourishments for age. Yet are their labours and pastimes so to be tempered that they weaken not their bodies more by play than otherwise they should have done by study, and so to be used that they addict not themselves more to the exercise of the limbs than the following of learning. The greatest enemies to discipline, as Plato recounteth, are labours and sleep. It is also requisite that he be expert in martial affairs, in shooting, in darting,[1] that he hawk and hunt for his honest pastime and recreation.

And if after these pastimes he shall seem secure,[2] nothing regarding his books, I would not have him scourged with stripes[3] but threatened with words, not dulled with blows like servants, the which the more they are beaten the better they bear it and the less they care for it. For children of good disposition are either incited by praise to go forward or shamed by dispraise to commit the like offence; those of obstinate and blockish behaviour are neither with words to be persuaded, neither with stripes to be corrected. They must now be taunted with sharp rebukes, straightways admonished with fair words, now threatened a payment,[4] by and by promised a reward, and dealt withal as nurses do with the babes, whom after they have made to cry they proffer the teat. But diligent heed must be taken that he be not praised above measure, lest standing too much in his own conceit[5] he become also obstinate in his own opinions.

I have known many fathers whose great love towards their sons hath been the cause in time that they loved them not; for when they see a sharp wit in their son to conceive, for the desire they have that he should outrun his fellows they loaden him with continual exercise, which is the only cause that he sinketh under his burden and giveth over in the plain field. Plants are nourished with little rain, yet drowned with much; even so the mind with indifferent[6] labour waxeth more perfect, with much study it is made fruitless. We must consider that all our life is divided into remission[7] and study. As there is watching,[8] so is there sleep; as there is war, so is there peace; as there is winter, so is there summer; as there be many working days, so is there also many holidays. And if I may speak all in one word, ease is the sauce of labour, which is plainly to be seen not only in living things but also in things without life. We unbend the bow that we may the better bend him, we unloose the

---

1 *darting*] throwing the javelin
2 *secure*] careless
3 *scourged with stripes*] whipped
4 *payment*] punishment
5 *standing too much in his own conceit*] becoming too confident of his own judgement
6 *indifferent*] moderate
7 *remission*] relaxation
8 *watching*] waking

harp that we may the sooner tune him, the body is kept in health as well with fasting as eating, the mind healed with ease as well as with labour.

Those parents are in mind to be misliked which commit the whole care of their child to the custody of a hireling, neither asking, neither knowing how their children profit in learning. For if the father were desirous to examine the son in that which he hath learned, the master would be more careful what he did teach; but seeing the father careless what they learn, he is also secure what he teacheth. That notable saying of the horsekeeper may here be applied which said, 'Nothing did so fat the horse as the eye of the king.'[1] Moreover, I would have the memory of children continually to be exercised, which is the greatest furtherance to learning that can be. For this cause they feigned in their old fables memory to be the mother of perfection.

Children are to be chastised if they shall use any filthy or unseemly talk, for, as Democritus[2] saith, the word is the shadow of the work. They must be courteous in their behaviour, lowly[3] in their speech, not disdaining their cock-mates[4] or refraining their company. They must not live wantonly, neither speak impudently, neither angry without cause, neither quarrelous without colour.[5] A young man, being perverse in nature and proud in words and manners, gave Socrates a spurn,[6] who being moved by his fellows to give him another, 'If,' said Socrates, 'an ass had kicked me, would you also have me to kick him again?' The greatest wisdom in Socrates in compressing his anger is worthy great commendation. Archytas Tarentine, returning from war and finding his ground overgrown with weeds and turned up with moles, sent for his farmer, unto whom he said, 'If I were not angry, I would make thee repent thy ill husbandry.' Plato,[7] having a servant whose bliss was in filling of his belly, seeing him on a time idle and unhonest in behaviour, said, 'Out of my sight, for I am incensed with anger.' Although these examples be hard to imitate, yet should every man do his endeavour to repress that hot and heady humour which he is by nature subject unto.

To be silent and discreet in company, though many think it a thing of no great weight or importance, yet is it most requisite for a young man and most necessary for my Ephebus. It never hath been hurtful to any to hold his peace; to speak, damage to many. Whatso is kept in silence is hushed, but what-soever is babbled out cannot again be recalled. We may see the cunning and curious work of Nature which hath barred and hedged nothing in so strongly as the tongue, with two rows of teeth and therewith two lips; besides, she hath placed it far from the heart, that it should not utter that which the heart had conceived. This also should cause us to be silent, seeing those that use much talk though they speak truly are never believed. Wine, therefore, is to

---

1 *Nothing . . . king*] the watchfulness of the king ensures the well-being of his horse. (For another example of the same proverb, see p. 87n.)

2 *Democritus*] Greek philosopher (circa 460–361 BC), noted for his upright charac-ter. The quotation is from his *Protesilaus* but derived by Lyly from Plutarch's *De edu-catione puerorum*.

3 *lowly*] unassuming

4 *cockmates*] playmates

5 *colour*] cause

6 *spurn*] kick (for *Socrates* see p. 108n.)

7 *Archytas Tarentine / Plato*] see pp. 112 and 38nn.

be refrained, which is termed to be the glass of the mind, and it is an old proverb, 'Whatsoever is in the heart of the sober man is in the mouth of the drunkard.' Bias, holding his tongue at a feast, was termed there of a tattler to be a fool; who said, 'Is there any wise man that can hold his tongue amidst the wine?' Unto whom Bias answered, 'There is no fool that can.'[1] A certain gentleman here in Athens invited the king's legates to a costly and sumptuous feast, where also he assembled many philosophers; and talking of divers matters, both of the commonweal and learning, only Zeno said nothing. Then the ambassadors said, 'What shall we show of thee, O Zeno, to the King?' 'Nothing,' answered he, 'but that there is an old man in Athens that amidst the pots[2] could hold his peace.' Anarcharsis, supping with Solon, was found asleep, having his right hand before his mouth, his left upon his privities; whereby was noted that the tongue should be reined with the strongest bridle. Zeno, because he would not be enforced to reveal anything against his will by torments, bit off his tongue and spit it in the face of the tyrant.

Now, when children shall by wisdom and use refrain from over much tattling, let them also be admonished that when they shall speak they speak nothing but truth. To lie is a vice most detestable, not to be suffered in a slave, much less in a son.

But the greatest thing is yet behind: whether that those are to be admitted as cockmates[3] with children which love them entirely, or whether they be to be banished from them. Whenas I see many fathers, more cruel to their children than careful of them, which think it not necessary to have those about them that most tender them, then I am half as it were in a doubt to give counsel. But when I call to my remembrance Socrates, Plato, Xenophon, Aeschines, Saebetes,[4] and all those that so much commend the love of men, which have also brought up many to great rule, reason and piety, then I am encouraged to imitate those whose excellency doth warrant my precepts to be perfect. If any shall love the child for his comely countenance, him would I have to be banished as a most dangerous and infectious beast; if he shall love him for his father's sake, or for his own good qualities, him would I have to be with him always as supervisor of his manners. Such hath it been in times past, the love of one Athenian to the other and of one Lacedaemonian to the other.

But having said almost sufficient for the education of a child, I will speak two words how he should be trained when he groweth in years. I cannot but mislike the nature of divers parents which appoint overseers and tutors for their children in their tender age, and suffer them when they come to be young

---

1 *Bias . . . can'*] story derived from Plutarch's *De garrulitate*. The tales concerning Zeno and Anarcharsis that follow are derived from the same source (see Bond, I, p. 361).
2 *pots*] drinking vessels
3 *cockmates*] companions
4 *Socrates . . . Saebetes*] For *Socrates* and *Plato*, see pp. 108 and 38nn. Xenophon (b. circa 444 BC) wrote the *Symposium* in which, among other matters, love and friendship are discussed. Aeschines (b. 389 BC) was an Athenian orator, founder of a school of eloquence at Rhodes. Saebetes (= Cebes), a disciple of Socrates, was the author of a popular work showing that happiness lies in the development of the virtuous mind.

men to have the bridle in their own hand knowing not that age requireth rather a hard snaffle than a pleasant bit,[1] and is sooner allured to wickedness than childhood. Who knoweth not the escapes[2] of children, as they are small, so they are soon amended? Either with threats they are to be remedied or with fair promises to be rewarded. But the sins and faults of young men are almost or altogether intolerable, which give themselves to be delicate in their diet, prodigal in their expense, using dicing, dancing, drunkenness, deflowering of virgins, abusing wives, committing adulteries, and accounting all things honest that are most detestable. Here, therefore, must be used a due regard, that their lust may be repressed, their riot abated, their courage cooled; for hard it is to see a young man to be master of himself which yieldeth himself as it were a bondslave to fond and overlashing affections.[3] Wise parents ought to take good heed, especially at this time, that they frame their sons to modesty, either by threats or by rewards, either by fair promises or severe practices, either showing the miseries of those that have been overcome with wildness or the happiness of them that have contained themselves within the bands of reason; these two are as it were the ensigns of virtue—the hope of honour, the fear of punishment.

But chiefly parents must cause their youths to abandon the society of those which are noted of evil living and lewd behaviour, which Pythagoras[4] seemed, somewhat obscurely, to note in these his sayings. First, *that one should abstain from the taste of those things that have black tails*: that is, we must not use the company of those whose corrupt manners do as it were make their life black. *Not to go above the balance*: that is, to reverence justice, neither for fear or flattery to lean unto anyone partially. *Not to lie in idleness*: that is, that sloth should be abhorred. *That we should not shake every man by the hand*: that is, we should not contract friendship with all. *Not to wear a strait[5] ring*: that is, that we should lead our life so as we need not to fetter it with chains. *Not to bring fire to a slaughter*: that is, we must not provoke any that is furious with words. *Not to eat our hearts*: that is, that we should not vex ourselves with thoughts, consume our bodies with sighs, with sobs, or with care to pine our carcasses. *To abstain from beans*: that is, not to meddle in civil affairs or business of the commonweal (for in the old times the election of magistrates was made by the pulling of beans). *Not to put our meat in scapio*:[6] that is, we should not speak of manners or virtue to those whose minds are infected with vice. *Not to retire when we are come to the end of our race*: that is, when we are at the point of death we should not be oppressed with grief but willingly yield to nature.

But I will return to my former precepts; that is, that young men should be kept from the company of those that are wicked, especially from the sight of

---

1 *bridle in their own hand / requireth rather … bit*] control of their own affairs / needs to be curbed rather than allowed to take its own course (metaphor drawn from horse-riding)
2 *escapes*] transgressions
3 *overlashing affections*] ungoverned passions
4 *Pythagoras*] Greek philosopher (fl. circa 540–510 BC), who aimed to raise his followers to a more elevated mode of life through a strict regime of religious observance and esoteric instruction (hence his maxims or gnomic 'sayings')
5 strait] tight-fitting
6 *scapio*] the chamber-pot

the flatterer. For I say now, as I have oftentimes before said, that there is no kind of beast so noisome[1] as the flatterer, nothing that will sooner consume both the son and the father and all honest friends. When the father exhorteth the son to sobriety, the flatterer provoketh him to wine; when the father weaneth them to continency, the flatterer allureth them to lust; when the father admonisheth them to thrift, the flatterer haleth them to prodigality; when the father encourageth them to labour, the flatterer layeth a cushion under his elbow[2] to sleep, bidding them to eat, drink, and to be merry, for that the life of man is soon gone and but as a short shadow, and seeing that we have but a while to live, who would live like a servant? They say that now their fathers be old and dote through age like Saturnus.[3]

Hereof it cometh that young men, giving not only attentive ear but ready coin to flatterers, fall into such misfortune; hereof it proceedeth that they haunt the stews, marry before they be wise, and die before they thrive. These be the beasts which live by the trenchers[4] of young gentlemen and consume the treasures of their revenues; these be they that soothe[5] young youths in all their sayings, that uphold them in all their doings with a yea or a nay; these be they that are at every beck, at every nod, freemen by fortune, slaves by free will. Wherefore, if there be any fathers that would have his children nurtured and brought up in honesty, let him expel these panthers, which have a sweet smell but a devouring mind.

Yet would I not have parents altogether precise or too severe in correction, but let them with mildness forgive light offences, and remember that they themselves have been young. As the physician by mingling bitter poisons with sweet liquor bringeth health to the body, so the father with sharp rebukes seasoned with loving looks causeth a redress and amendment in his child. But if the father be throughly angry upon good occasion, let him not continue his rage, for I had rather he should be soon angry than hard to be pleased; for when the son shall perceive that the father conceiveth rather a hate than a heat[6] against him, he becometh desperate, neither regarding his father's ire, neither his own duty. Some light faults let them dissemble as though they knew them not, and seeing them let them not seem to see them, and hearing them let them not seem to hear. We can easily forget the offences of our friends, be they never so great; and shall we not forgive the escapes of our children, be they never so small? We bear oftentimes with[7] our servants, and shall we not sometimes with our sons? The fairest jennet is ruled as well with the wand[8] as with the spur; the wildest child is as soon corrected with a word as with a weapon. If thy son be so stubborn obstinately to rebel against thee, or so wilful to persevere in his wickedness that neither for fear of punishment neither for hope of reward he is any way to be reclaimed, then seek out some

---

1 *noisome*] harmful
2 *layeth a cushion . . . elbow*] encourages him (for a comparable use of the phrase see p. 43)
3 *Saturnus*] identified by the Romans with Cronos, father of the Olympian gods, who was deposed by his son, Zeus
4 *trenchers*] platters
5 *soothe*] agree with
6 *heat*] fit of anger
7 *bear oftentimes with*] often overlook the mistakes of. For *escapes* in the previous sentence see p. 116n.
8 *jennet / wand*] small Spanish horse / riding switch

marriage fit for his degree, which is the surest bond of youth and the strongest chain to fetter affections that can be found. Yet let his wife be such a one as is neither much more noble in birth or far more richer in goods, but, according to the wise saying, choose one every way as near as may be equal in both—for they that do desire great dowries do rather marry themselves to the wealth than to their wife.

But to return to the matter. It is most requisite that fathers, both by their discreet counsel and also their honest conversation, be an example of imitation to their children; that they seeing in their parents, as it were in a glass, the perfection of manners, they may be encouraged by their upright living to practise the like piety. For if a father rebuke his child of swearing and he himself a blasphemer, doth he not see that in detecting his son's vice he also noteth his own? If the father counsel the son to refrain wine as most unwholesome and drink himself immoderately, doth he not as well reprove his own folly as rebuke his son's? Age alway ought to be a mirror for youth, for where old age is impudent, there certainly youth must needs be shameless; where the aged have no respect of their honourable and grey hairs, there the young gallants have little regard of their honest behaviours; and in one word to conclude all, where age is past gravity, there youth is past grace.

The sum of all wherewith I would have my Ephebus endued and how I would have him instructed shall briefly appear in this following: first, that he be of honest parents, nursed of his mother, brought up in such a place as is incorrupt both for the air and manners, with such a person as is undefiled, of great zeal, of profound knowledge, of absolute perfection; that [he] be instructed in philosophy, whereby he may attain learning, and have in all sciences a smack,[1] whereby he may readily dispute of anything; that his body be kept in his pure strength by honest exercise, his wit and memory by diligent study; that he abandon all allurements of vice and continually incline to virtue. Which if it shall, as it may, come to pass, then do I hope that if ever Plato's commonweal shall flourish, that my Ephebus shall be a citizen; that if Aristotle find any happy man, it will be my child; if Tully confess any to be an absolute orator,[2] it will be my young youth.

I am here therefore, gentlemen, to exhort you that with all industry you apply your minds to the study of philosophy; that as you profess yourselves students, so you may be students; that as you disdain not the name of a scholar, so you will not be found void of the duty of scholars. Let not your minds be carried away with vain delights, as with travelling into far and strange countries, where you shall see more wickedness than learn virtue and wit; neither with costly attire of the new cut,[3] the Dutch hat, the French hose, the Spanish rapier, the Italian hilt, and I know not what. Cast not your eyes on the beauty of women lest ye cast away your hearts with folly, let not that fond love wherewith youth fatteth himself as fat as a fool infect you; for as a sinew being cut though it be healed there will always remain a scar, or as fine linen stained with black ink though it be washed never so often will have an iron-mole,[4] so the mind once mangled or maimed with love, though it be

---

1 *smack*] basic knowledge
2 *Plato ... orator*] see p. 100n.
3 *cut*] fashion
4 *iron-mole*] blemish

never so well cured with reason or cooled by wisdom, yet there will appear a scar by the which one may guess the mind hath been pierced, and a blemish whereby one may judge the heart hath been stained. Refrain from dicing which was the only cause that Pyreus was stricken to the heart,[1] and from dancing which was the means that lost John Baptist's head.[2] I am not he that will disallow honest recreation, although I detest the abuses. I speak boldly unto you because I myself know you. What Athens hath been; what Athens is; what Athens shall be, I can guess. Let not every inn and ale-house in Athens be as it were your chamber, frequent not those ordinary[3] tables where either for the desire of delicate cates[4] or the meeting of youthful companions ye both spend your money vainly and your time idly. Imitate him in life whom ye honour for his learning, Aristotle, who was never seen in the company of those that idly bestowed their time. There is nothing more swifter than time, nothing more sweeter. We have not, as Seneca[5] saith, little time to live, but we leese[6] much; neither have we a short life by nature, but we make it shorter by naughtiness.[7] Our life is long if we know how to use it. Follow Apelles, that cunning and wise painter, which would let no day pass over his head without a line, without some labour.[8]

It was prettily said of Hesiodus,[9] 'Let us endeavour by reason to excel beasts, seeing beasts by nature excel men,' although, strictly taken it be not so, for that man is endued with a soul, yet taken touching their perfection of senses in their kind it is most certain. Doth not the lion for strength, the turtle[10] for love, the ant for labour excel man? Doth not the eagle see clearer, the vulture smell better, the mole hear lightlier? Let us, therefore, endeavour to excel in virtue, seeing in qualities of the body we are inferior to beasts.

And here I am most earnestly to exhort you to modesty in your behaviour, to duty to your elders, to diligence in your studies. I was of late[11] in Italy where mine ears glowed and my heart was galled to hear the abuses that reign in Athens. I cannot tell whether those things sprang by the lewd and lying lips of the ignorant, which are always enemies to learning, or by the reports of such as saw them and sorrowed at them. It was openly reported of an old man in Naples that there was more lightness in Athens than in all Italy, more wanton youths of scholars than in all Europe, besides more papists, more atheists, more sects, more schisms than in all the monarchies in the world. Which things, although I think they be not true, yet can I not but lament that

---

1 *Pyreus ... heart*] No source has been found for this allusion.

2 *dancing ... head*] The reward requested by Salome for dancing before King Herod was the head of John the Baptist.

3 *ordinary*] tavern

4 *cates*] provisions

5 *Seneca*] philosopher, and tutor to the Emporer Nero (d. AD 65). One of his discourses is on the brevity of life.

6 *leese*] lose

7 *naughtiness*] wickedness

8 *Apelles ... labour*] Apelles (see p. 27n.) was renowned for his dedication to his art.

9 *Hesiodus*] one of the earliest of the Greek poets (fl. 735 BC). The passage quoted is from *Works and Days* (see Bond, I, p. 363). *of* = by

10 *turtle*] turtle-dove

11 *late*] recently

they should be deemed to be true, and I fear me they be not altogether false; there can no great smoke arise but there must be some fire, no great report without great suspicion. Frame, therefore, your lives to such integrity, your studies to attaining of such perfection, that neither the might of the strong, neither the malice of the weak, neither the swift reports of the ignorant be able to spot[1] you with dishonesty or note you of ungodliness. The greatest harm that you can do unto the envious is to do well, the greatest corrosive that you can give unto the ignorant is to prosper in knowledge, the greatest comfort that you can bestow on your parents is to live well and learn well, the greatest commodity that you can yield unto your country is with wisdom to bestow that talent that by grace was given you.

And here I cannot choose but give you that counsel that an old man in Naples[2] gave me most wisely, although I had then neither grace to follow it, neither will to give ear to it; desiring you not to reject it because I did once despise it. It is this, as I can remember, word for word. 'Descend into your own consciences. Consider with yourselves the great difference between staring and stark-blind, wit and wisdom, love and lust. Be merry, but with modesty; be sober, but not too sullen; be valiant, but not too venturous. Let your attire be comely, but not too costly; your diet wholesome, but not excessive; use pastime as the word importeth—to pass the time in honest recreation. Mistrust no man without cause, neither be ye credulous without proof. Be not light to follow every man's opinion, neither obstinate to stand in your own conceits.[3] Serve God, fear God, love God, and God will bless you as either your hearts can wish, or your friends desire.' This was his grave and godly advice whose counsel I would have you all to follow.

Frequent[4] lectures, use disputations openly, neglect not your private studies, let not degrees be given for love but for learning, not for money but for knowledge. And because you shall be the better encouraged to follow my counsel, I will be as it were an example myself, desiring you all to imitate me.

Euphues having ended his discourse and finished those precepts which he thought necessary for the instructing of youth, gave his mind to the continual study of philosophy, insomuch as he became Public Reader[5] in the university, with such commendation as never any before him, in the which he continued for the space of ten years, only searching out the secrets of nature and the hidden mysteries of philosophy. And having collected into three volumes his lectures, thought for the profit of young scholars to set them forth in print, which if he had done, I would also in this his *Anatomy* have inserted. But he, altering his determination, fell into this discourse with himself:

'Why, Euphues, art thou so addicted to the study of the heathen that thou hast forgotten thy God in heaven? Shall thy wit be rather employed

---

1 *spot*] besmirch
2 *an old man in Naples*] Eubulus. For his advice to Euphues see pp. 35ff.
3 *obstinate . . . conceits*] stubborn in adhering to your own views
4 *Frequent*] go to
5 *Public Reader*] lecturer (approximating to modern professor)

to the attaining of human wisdom than divine knowledge? Is Aristotle
more dear to thee with his books than Christ with his blood? What
comfort canst thou find in philosophy for thy guilty conscience, what
hope of the resurrection, what glad tidings of the gospel? Consider with
thyself that thou art a gentleman, yea, and a Gentile, and if thou neglect
thy calling thou art worse than a Jew. Most miserable is the estate[1] of
those gentlemen which think it a blemish to their ancestors and a blot to
their own gentry to read or practise divinity. They think it now sufficient
for their felicity to ride well upon a great horse,[2] to hawk, to hunt, to
have a smack in[3] philosophy, neither thinking of the beginning of wisdom,
neither the end, which is Christ; only they account divinity most contemptible, which is, and ought to be, most noble. Without this there is
no lawyer be he never so eloquent, no physician be he never so excellent,
no philosopher be he never so learned, no king, no kaiser, be he never so
royal in birth, so politic in peace, so expert in war, so valiant in prowess,[4]
but he is to be detested and abhorred.

'Farewell, therefore, the fine and filed phrases of Cicero, the pleasant
elegies of Ovid, the depth and profound knowledge of Aristotle.[5] Farewell
rhetoric, farewell philosophy, farewell all learning which is not sprung
from the bowels of the holy Bible. In this learning shall we find milk for
the weak and marrow for the strong; in this shall we see how the ignorant may be instructed, the obstinate confuted, the penitent comforted,
the wicked punished, the godly preserved. Oh, I would gentlemen would
sometimes sequester themselves from their own delights and employ their
wits in searching these heavenly and divine mysteries! It is common, yea,
and lamentable, to see that if a young youth have the gifts of nature, as
a sharp wit, or of fortune, as sufficient wealth to maintain them, he
employeth the one in the vain inventions of love, the other in the vile
bravery of pride, the one in the passions of his mind and praises of his
lady, the other in furnishing of his body and furthering of his lust. Hereof
it cometh that such vain ditties, such idle sonnets, such enticing songs
are set forth to the gaze of the world and grief of the godly. I myself know
none so ill as myself, who in times past have been so superstitiously
addicted that I thought no heaven to the paradise of love, no angel to be
compared to my lady; but as repentance hath caused me to leave and
loathe such vain delights, so wisdom hath opened unto me the perfect
gate to eternal life.

'Besides this, I myself have thought that in divinity there could be no
eloquence which I might imitate, no pleasant invention which I might
follow, no delicate phrase that might delight me; but now I see that in the

---

1 *estate*] condition
2 *great horse*] war horse
3 *smack in*] slight knowledge of
4 *prowess*] acts of daring
5 *fine and filed . . . Aristotle*] rhetoric, poetry and philosophy (i.e. the liberal arts)

sacred knowledge of God's will the only eloquence, the true and perfect phrase, the testimony of salvation doth abide. And seeing without this all learning is ignorance, all wisdom m[e]re folly, all wit plain bluntness, all justice iniquity, all eloquence barbarism, all beauty deformity, I will spend all the remainder of my life in studying the Old Testament, wherein is prefigured the coming of my Saviour, and the New Testament, wherein my Christ doth suffer for my sins and is crucified for my redemption; whose bitter agonies should cast every good Christian into a shivering ague to remember His anguish, whose sweating of water and blood should cause every devout and zealous Catholic to shed tears of repentance in remembrance of His torments.'

Euphues, having discoursed this with himself, did immediately abandon all light company, all the disputations in schools, all philosophy, and gave himself to the touchstone of holiness in divinity, accounting all other things as most vile and contemptible.

EUPHUES TO THE GENTLEMEN SCHOLARS IN ATHENS

The merchant that travaileth[1] for gain, the husbandman[2] that toileth for increase, the lawyer that pleadeth for gold, the craftsman that seeketh to live by his labour, all these after they have fatted themselves with sufficient either take their ease or less pain than they were accustomed. Hippomenes ceased to run when he had gotten the goal, Hercules to labour when he had obtained the victory, Mercury[3] to pipe when he had cast Argus in a slumber. Every action hath his end, and then we leave to sweat when we have found the sweet. The ant, though she toil in summer, yet in winter she leaveth to travail. The bee, though she delight to suck the fair flower, yet is she at last cloyed with honey. The spider that weaveth the finest thread ceaseth at the last, when she hath finished her web.

But in the action and study of the mind, gentlemen, it is far otherwise, for he that tasteth the sweet of learning endureth all the sour of labour. He that seeketh the depth of knowledge is as it were in a labyrinth, in the which the further he goeth, the further he is from the end; or like the bird in the lime-bush,[4] which the more she striveth to get out, the faster she sticketh in. And certainly it may be said of learning as it was feigned of nectar, the drink of the gods, the which the more it was drunk the more it would overflow the

---

1 *travaileth*] labours (with a pun on *travel* = to journey)
2 *husbandman*] farmer
3 *Hippomenes / Hercules / Mercury*] suitor to Atalanta who won her by out-running her in a race by causing her to be distracted by three golden apples / celebrated hero of antiquity required to perform twelve seemingly impossible tasks (his 'labours') / son of Jupiter who abducted Io for his father by charming her guardian, Argus, to sleep with his flute
4 *bird ... lime-bush*] A reference to the practice of catching small birds by covering the twigs of bushes with a sticky substance known as 'bird-lime'.

brim of the cup; neither is it far unlike the stone that groweth in the river of Caria,[1] the which the more it is cut the more it increaseth. And it fareth with[2] him that followeth it as with him that hath the dropsy, who the more he drinketh the more he thirsteth. Therefore, in my mind, the student is at less ease than the ox that draweth or the ass that carrieth his burden, who neither at the board when others eat is void of labour, neither in his bed when others sleep is without meditation.

But as in manuary crafts,[3] though they be all good, yet that is accounted most noble that is most necessary, so in the actions and studies of the mind, although they be all worthy, yet that deserveth greatest praise which bringeth greatest profit. And so we commonly do make best account of that which doth us most good. We esteem better of the physician that ministereth the potion than of the apothecary that selleth the drugs. How much more ought we with all diligence, study, and industry spend our short pilgrimage in the seeking out of our salvation? Vain is philosophy, vain is physic, vain is law, vain is all learning without the taste of divine knowledge.

I was determined to write notes of philosophy, which had been to feed you fat with folly; yet that I might seem neither idle, neither you evil employed, I have here set down a brief discourse which of late I had with an heretic, which kept me from idleness and may, if you read it, deter you from heresy. It was with an atheist, a man in my opinion monstrous, yet tractable to be persuaded. By this shall you see the absurd dotage of him that thinketh there is no God, or an insufficient God; yet here shall you find the sum of faith which justifieth only in Christ, the weakness of the law, the strength of the gospel, and the knowledge of God's will. Here shall ye find hope, if you be in despair; comfort, if ye be distressed; if ye thirst, drink; meat, if ye hunger. If ye fear Moses who saith, 'Without you fulfil the law you shall perish,' behold Christ which saith, 'I have overcomen the law.' And that in these desperate days wherein so many sects are sown, and in the waning of the world wherein so many false Christs are come, you might have a certainty of your salvation, I mean to set down the touchstone whereunto everyone ought to trust, and by the which everyone should try himself; which, if you follow, I doubt not but that as you have proved learned philosophers, you will also proceed excellent divines, which God grant.

EUPHUES AND ATHEOS

Atheos. I am glad, Euphues, that I have found thee at leisure, partly that we might be merry, and partly that I might be persuaded in a thing that much troubled my conscience. It is concerning God. There be many that are of this mind, that there is a God whom they term the Creator of all things, a God whom they call the Son, the Redeemer of the world, a God whom they name the Holy Ghost, the Worker of all things, the Comforter, the Spirit; and yet are they of this opinion also, that they be but one God, coequal in power,

---

1 *river of Caria*] see p. 56n.
2 *fareth with*] happens to
3 *manuary crafts*] manual occupations

coeternal, incomprehensible, and yet a Trinity in person. I, for my part, although I am not so credulous to believe their curious opinions, yet am I desirous to hear the reasons that should drive them into such fond and frantic imaginations. For as I know nothing to be so absurd which some of the philosophers have not defended, so think I nothing so erroneous which some of our Catholics[1] have not maintained. If there were, as divers[2] dream, a God that would revenge the oppression of the widows and fatherless, that would reward the zeal of the merciful, pity the poor, and pardon the penitent, then would the people either stand in greater awe or owe more love towards their God.

I remember Tully,[3] disputing of the nature of gods, bringeth Dionysius as a scoffer of such vain and devised deities, who, seeing Aesculapius with a long beard of gold and Apollo, his father, beardless, played the barber and shaved it from him, saying it was not decent that the son should have a beard and the father none. Seeing also Jupiter with an ornament of gold, took it from him jesting thus, 'In summer this array is too heavy, in winter too cold; here I leave one of woollen, both warmer for the cold and lighter for the heat.' He coming also into the temple, where certain of the gods with golden gifts stretched out their hands, took them all away, saying, 'Who will be so mad as to refuse things so gently offered?' Dost thou not see, Euphues, what small account he made of their gods, for at the last, sailing into his country with a prosperous wind, he laughing said, 'Lo, see you not, my masters, how well the gods reward our sacrilege?'

I could rehearse infinite opinions of excellent men who in this point hold on my side, but especially Protagoras.[4] And in my judgement if there be any god it is the world wherein we live, that is the only god. What can we behold more noble than the world, more fair, more beautiful, more glorious? What more majestical to the sight, or more constant in substance? But this by the way, Euphues; I have greater and more forcible arguments to confirm my opinion and to confute the errors of those that imagine that there is a God. But first I would gladly hear thee shape an answer to that which I have said, for well I know that thou art not only one of those which believe that there is a God, but of them also which are so precise in honouring Him that they be scarce wise in helping themselves.

Euphues. If my hope, Atheos, were not better to convert thee than my hap[5] was here to confer with thee, my heart would break for grief, which beginneth freshly to bleed for sorrow. Thou hast stricken me into such a shivering and cold terror at the rehearsing of this thy monstrous opinion that I look

---

1 *Catholics*] members of the Christian faith (not simply members of the Roman Catholic church)

2 *divers*] many

3 *Tully*] Cicero (see p. 32n.). The passage that follows derives from his *De natura deorum* (see Bond, I, pp. 365–6). Though Apollo and Aesculapius were father and son, the former was invariably depicted clean-shaven and the latter (the god of medicine) with a beard. Dionysius, tyrant of Syracuse (b. 430 BC) was the most powerful Greek ruler before Alexander the Great.

4 *Protagoras*] celebrated Sophist (b. circa 480 BC) who was impeached for doubting the existence of the gods

5 *hap*] luck, fortune

every minute when the ground should open to swallow thee up, and that God which thou knowest not should with thunder from heaven strike thee to hell. Was there ever barbarian so senseless, ever miscreant so barbarous, that did not acknowledge a living and everlasting Jehovah? I cannot but tremble at the remembrance of His majesty; and dost thou make it a mockery? Oh iniquity of times! Oh corruption of manners! Oh blasphemy against the heavens! The heathen man saith, yea, that Tully whom thou thyself allegest, that there is no nation so barbarous, no kind of people so savage, in whom resteth not this persuasion that there is a God. And even they that in other parts of their life seem very little to differ from brute beasts do continually keep a certain seed of religion, so throughly has this common principle possessed all men's minds, and so fast it sticketh in all men's bowels. Yea, idolatry itself is sufficient proof of this persuasion, for we see how willingly man abaseth himself to honour other creatures, to do homage to stocks,[1] to go on pilgrimages to images. If, therefore, man rather than he would have no God do worship a stone, how much more art thou duller than a stone, which goest against the opinion of all men!

Plato, a philosopher, would often say, 'There is one whom we may call God, omnipotent, glorious, immortal, unto whose similitude we that creep here on the earth have our souls framed.'[2] What can be said more of a heathen, yea, what more of a Christian? Aristotle, when he could not find out by the secrecy of nature the cause of the ebbing and flowing of the sea, cried out with a loud voice, 'O thing of things, have mercy upon me!' Cleanthes[3] alleged four causes which might induce man to acknowledge a God: the first by the foreseeing of things to come; the second by the infinite commodities which we daily reap, as by the temperature of the air, the fatness of the earth, the fruitfulness of trees, plants, and herbs, the abundance of all things that may either serve for the necessity of many or the superfluity of a few; the third by the terror that the mind of man is stricken into by lightnings, thunderings, tempests, hails, snow, earthquakes, pestilence, by the strange and terrible sights which cause us to tremble, as the raining of blood, the fiery impressions in the element,[4] the overflowing of floods in the earth, the prodigious shapes and unnatural forms of men, of beasts, of birds, of fishes, of all creatures, the appearance of blazing comets which ever prognosticate some strange mutation, the sight of two suns which happened in the consulship of Tuditanus and Aquilius[5]— with these things mortal men being afrighted are enforced to acknowledge an immortal and omnipotent God; the fourth by the equality in moving in the heaven, the course of the sun, the order of the stars, the beautifulness of the element, the sight whereof might sufficiently induce us to believe they proceed not by chance, by nature, or by destiny, but by the eternal and divine purpose of some omnipotent deity. Hereof it came that, when the philosophers could give no reason by nature, they would say there is one above

---

1 *stocks*] inanimate objects
2 *Plato . . . framed*] a summary of Plato's position rather than a direct quotation. Similarly there is no direct source for the following quotation from Aristotle.
3 *Cleanthes*] Stoic philosopher (b. circa 300 BC). Lyly's summary is drawn from Cicero (see Bond, I, pp. 366–7). *fatness* in the same sentence = fertility
4 *element*] air
5 *Tuditanus and Aquilius*] Roman consuls in 129 BC

nature, another would call him the first mover, another the aider of nature—
and so forth.

But why go I about in a thing so manifest to use proofs so manifold? If
thou deny the truth, who can prove it? If thou deny that black is black, who
can by reason reprove thee, when thou opposest thyself against reason? Thou
knowest that manifest truths are not to be proved but believed, and that he
that denieth the principles of any art is not to be confuted by arguments, but
to be left to his own folly. But I have a better opinion of thee, and therefore
I mean not to trifle with philosophy but to try this by the touchstone of the
Scriptures.

We read in the second of Exodus[1] that when Moses desired of God to know
what he should name Him to the children of Israel, He answered, 'Thou shalt
say, I am that I am.' Again, 'He that is hath sent me unto you, the Lord, even
your God. He is God in the heaven above and in the earth beneath. I am the
first and the last I am. I am the Lord and there is none other besides me.'
Again, 'I am the Lord, and there is none other. I have created the light and
made darkness, making peace and framing evil.' If thou desire to understand
what God is, thou shalt hear. He is even a consuming fire, the Lord of revenge,
the God of judgement, the living God, the searcher of the reins,[2] He that made
all things of nothing, Alpha and Omega,[3] the beginning and yet without beginning, the end and yet everlasting; one at whose breath the mountains shall
shake, whose seat is the lofty cherubins, whose footstool is the earth, invisible yet seeing all things, a jealous God, a loving God, miraculous in all points,
in no part monstrous.

Besides this, thou shalt well understand that He is such a God as will punish
him, whosoever he be, that blasphemeth His name, for holy is the Lord. It is
written, 'Bring out the blasphemer without the tents, and let all those that
heard him lay their hands upon his head, and let all the people stone him. He
that blasphemeth the name of the Lord shall die the death.' Such a jealous
God that whosoever committeth idolatry with strange gods He will strike with
terrible plagues. 'Turn not to idols, neither make gods with hands. I am the
Lord your God. Thou shalt make no image which the Lord thy God abhorreth. Thou shalt have no new god, neither worship any strange idol, for all
the gods of the gentiles are devils. My sons keep yourselves from images, the
worshipping of idols is the cause of all evil, the beginning and the end. Cursed
be that man that engraveth any images, it as an abomination before the Lord.
They shall be confounded that worship graven images or glory in idols. I will
not give my glory to another, nor my praises to graven images.'

If all these testimonies of the Scriptures cannot make thee to acknowledge
a living God, hearken what they say of such as be altogether incredulous.
'Every unbeliever shall die in his incredulity. Woe be to those that be loose in
heart; they believe there is no God, and therefore they shall not be protected
of Him. The wrath of the Lord shall kindle against an unbelieving nation. If
ye believe not, ye shall not endure. He that believeth shall not be damned. He

---

1 *second of Exodus*] properly the third, rather than the second chapter (i.e. 3.14). The
paragraphs that follow consist of a tissue of quotations from the Old and New
Testaments.
2 *reins*] kidneys (and, by extension, loins), the seat of the feelings
3 *Alpha and Omega*] first and last letters of the Greek alphabet

that believeth not is judged already. The portion[1] of the unbelievers shall be in the lake that burneth with fire and brimstone, which is the second death.'

If thou feel in thyself, Atheos, any spark of grace, pray unto the Lord and He will cause it to flame; if thou have no feeling of faith, yet pray and the Lord will give abundance. For as He is a terrible God whose voice is like the rushing of many waters, so is He a merciful God whose words are as soft as oil; though He breathe fire out of his nostrils against sinners, yet is He mild to those that ask forgiveness. But if thou be obstinate, that seeing thou wilt not see, and knowing thou wilt not acknowledge, then shall thy heart be hardened with Pharaoh, and grace shall be taken away from thee with Saul.[2] Thus saith the Lord, 'Whoso believeth not shall perish, heaven and earth shall pass, but the word of the Lord shall endure for ever.' Submit thyself before the throne of His majesty and His mercy shall save thee. Honour the Lord and it shall be well with thee. Besides Him fear no strange god. Honour the Lord with all thy soul. Offer unto God the sacrifice of praise. Be not like the hypocrites which honour God with their lips but be far from Him with their hearts, neither like the fool which saith in his heart there is no God.

But if thou wilt still persevere in thine obstinacy, thine end shall be worse than thy beginning. The Lord, yea, thy Saviour, shall come to be thy Judge. When thou shalt behold Him come in glory, with millions of angels and archangels, when thou shalt see Him appear in thunderings and lightnings and flashings of fire, when the mountains shall melt and the heavens be wrapped up like a scroll, when all the earth shall tremble, with what face wilt thou behold His glory that deniest His Godhead? How canst thou abide His presence that believest not His essence? What hope canst thou have to be saved which didst never acknowledge any to be thy Saviour? Then shall it be said to thee and to all those of thy sect, unless ye repent, 'Depart all ye workers of iniquity.' There shall be weeping and gnashing of teeth when you shall see Abraham, Isaac and Jacob, and all the prophets in the kingdom of God, and ye to be thrust out. You shall conceive heat and bring forth wood; your own consciences shall consume you like fire.

Here dost thou see, Atheos, the threatenings against unbelievers, and the punishment prepared for miscreants. What better or sounder proof canst thou have that there is a God than thine own conscience, which is unto thee a thousand witnesses? Consider with thyself that thy soul is immortal, made to the image of the Almighty God. Be not curious to inquire of God, but careful to believe; neither be thou desperate if thou see thy sins abound, but faithful to obtain mercy, for the Lord will save thee because it is His pleasure. Search, therefore, the Scriptures, for they testify of Him.

Atheos.   Truly, Euphues, you have said somewhat, but you go about contrary to the customs of schools, which, methinks, you should diligently observe, being a professed philosopher. For when I demand by what reason men are induced to acknowledge a God, you confirm it by course of Scripture, as who should say there were not a relation between God and the Scripture; because as the old fathers define, without Scripture there were no God,

---

1 *portion*] inheritance
2 *Saul*] The kingship of Israel was withheld from Saul after he transgressed God's command to destroy the Amalekites and all their possessions.

no Scripture without a God. Whosoever, therefore, denieth a Godhead denieth also the Scriptures which testify of Him. This is in my opinion *absurdum per absurdius*, to prove one absurdity by another.

If thou canst as substantially by reason prove thy authority of Scriptures to be true, as thou hast proved by Scriptures there is a God, then will I willingly with thee both believe the Scriptures and worship thy God. I have heard that Antiochus commanded all the copies of the Testament to be burned.[1] From whence, therefore, have we these new books? I think thou wilt not say by revelation. Therefore go forward.

Euphues. I have read of the milk of a tigress that the more salt there is thrown into it the fresher it is, and it may be that thou hast either eaten of that milk or that thou art the whelp of that monster; for the more reasons that are beat into thy head, the more unreasonable thou seemest to be, the greater my authorities are, the lesser is thy belief.

As touching the authority of Scriptures, although there be many arguments which do prove, yea and enforce the wicked to confess, that the Scriptures come from God, yet by none other mean than by the secret testimony of the Holy Ghost our hearts are truly persuaded that it is God which speaketh in the law, in the prophets, in the gospel. The orderly disposition of the wisdom of God, the doctrine savouring nothing of earthliness, the godly agreement of all parts among themselves, and especially the baseness of contemptible words uttering the high mysteries of the heavenly kingdom are second helps to establish the Scriptures.

Moreover, the antiquity of the Scripture, whereas the books of other religions are later than the books of Moses; which yet doth not himself invent a new God but setteth forth to the Israelites the God of their fathers. Whereas Moses doth not hide the shame of Levi his father, nor the mourning of Aaron his brother and of Mary his sister,[2] nor doth advance his own children; the same are arguments that in his book is nothing feigned by man. Also the miracles that happened, as well at the publishing of the law as in all the rest of time, are infallible proofs that the Scriptures proceeded from the mouth of God. Also whereas Moses, speaking in the person of Jacob, assigneth government to the tribe of Judah,[3] and where he telleth before of the calling of the Gentiles,[4] whereof the one came to pass four hundred years after, the other almost two thousand years, these are arguments that it is God Himself that speaketh in the books of Moses. Whereas Isaiah telleth before of the captivity of the Jews and their restoring by Cyrus (which was born an hundred years

---

1 *Antiochus ... burned*] Antiochus Epiphanes (King of Syria), who occupied Jerusalem in 168 BC, attempted to extirpate the Jewish religion by burning the books of the Law.

2 *Moses ... sister*] instances of Moses' objectivity, indicating that God was the ultimate author of his work. Levi (Moses' grandfather rather than his father) killed Shechem dishonourably in revenge for the rape of his sister, Dinah. Aaron and Mary (Miriam) spoke against Moses for taking an Ethiopian wife.

3 *Also whereas Moses ... Judah*] Moses, reputed to be the author of the book of Genesis, records Jacob's pronouncement that the tribe of Judah (Jacob's fourth son), would lead the people of Israel.

4 *calling of the Gentiles*] following the ministry of Christ

after the death of Isaiah),[1] and whereas Jeremiah, before the people were led away, appointed their exile to continue threescore and ten years; whereas Jeremiah and Ezekiel,[2] being far distant in places the one from the other, do agree in all their sayings; where Daniel[3] telleth of things to come six hundred years after—these are most certain proofs to establish the authority of the books of the prophets.

The simplicity of the speech of the first three evangelists containing heavenly mysteries, the praise of John[4] thundering from on high with weighty sentences, the heavenly majesty shining in the writings of Peter and Paul,[5] the sudden calling of Matthew[6] from the receipt of custom, the calling of Peter and John[7] from their fisher boats to the preaching of the gospel, the conversion and calling of Paul[8] being an enemy to the apostleship, are signs of the Holy Ghost speaking in them.

The consent[9] of so many ages, of so sundry nations, and of so divers minds in embracing the Scriptures, and the rare godliness of some, ought to establish the authority thereof amongst us. Also the blood of so many martyrs, which for the confession thereof have suffered death with a constant and sober zeal, are undoubted testimonies of the truth and authority of the Scriptures.

The miracles that Moses recounteth are sufficient to persuade us that God, yea the God of hosts, set down the Scriptures. For this, that he[10] was carried in a cloud up into the mountain, that there even until the fortieth day he continued without the company of men, that in the very publishing[11] of the law his face did shine as it were beset with sunbeams, that lightnings flashed round about, that thunder and noises were each where heard in the air, that a trumpet sounded being not sounded with any mouth of man, that the entry of the tabernacle,[12] by a cloud set between, was kept from the sight of the people, that his authority was so miraculously revenged with the horrible destruction of Korah, Dathan and Abiram,[13] and all that wicked faction, that the rock stricken with a rod did by and by pour forth a river, that at his prayer

---

1 *captivity of the Jews . . . death of Isaiah*] The captivity of the Jews by the Egyptians took place in 588 BC, their liberation by Cyrus, founder of the Persian empire, in 536 BC. Isaiah died circa 710–695 BC.

2 *Jeremiah / Ezekiel*] Old Testament prophets, living in different lands and at different ent times, who prophesied the restoration of the Jews. Jeremiah lived in Jerusalem, Ezekiel in a Jewish settlement north of Babylon.

3 *Daniel*] Old Testament prophet who foretold the death of the Messiah

4 *John*] author of the fourth gospel

5 *writings of Peter and Paul*] the epistles of the two principal exponents of the Christian faith

6 *Matthew*] a tax collector, called by Christ to be one of the Apostles

7 *Peter / John*] fisherman of Bethsaida, called by Christ to be chief of the Apostles / son of Zebedee, a fisherman on the sea of Galilee

8 *Paul*] a persecutor of the Christians, converted to Christianity by a spiritual experience on the road to Damascus (see also note 5 above)

9 *consent*] agreement

10 *he*] Moses

11 *publishing*] making known, announcement

12 *tabernacle*] portable sanctuary containing the ark of the covenant (sacred symbol of God's presence among the Jewish people)

13 *Korah, Dathan and Abiram*] swallowed up when the ground opened beneath them for disputing the authority of Moses

it rained manna from heaven. Did not God herein commend him from heaven as an undoubted prophet?

Now as touching the tyranny of Antiochus which commanded all the books to be burned, herein God's singular providence is seen, which hath always kept His word both from the mighty, that they could never extinguish the same, and from the malicious, that they could never diminish it. There were divers copies which God of His great goodness kept from the bloody proclamation of Antiochus, and by and by followed the translating of them into Greek, that they might be published unto the whole world. The Hebrew tongue lay not only unesteemed but almost unknown, and surely, had it not been God's will to have His religion provided for, it had altogether perished.

Thou seest, Atheos, how the Scriptures come from the mouth of God and are written by the finger of the Holy Ghost in the consciences of all the faithful. But if thou be so curious to ask other questions, or so quarrelous to strive against the truth, I must answer thee as an old father answered a young fool, which needs would know what God did before he made heaven, to whom he said, 'Hell, for such curious inquisitors of God's secrets, whose wisdom is not to be comprehended.' For who is he that can measure the wind, or weigh the fire, or attain unto the unsearchable judgements of the Lord?

Besides this, where the Holy Ghost hath ceased to set down, there ought we to cease to inquire, seeing we have the sufficiency of our salvation contained in Holy Scripture. It were an absurdity in schools if one, being urged with a place[1] in Aristotle, could find none other shift to avoid a blank[2] than in doubting whether Aristotle spake such words or no. Shall it then be tolerable to deny the Scriptures, having no other colour[3] to avoid an inconvenience but by doubting whether they proceed from the Holy Ghost? But that such doubts arise among many in our age, the reason is their little faith, not the insufficient proof of the cause. Thou mayst as well demand how I prove white to be white or black black, and why it should be called white rather than green. Such gross questions are to be answered with slender reasons, and such idle heads should be scoffed with addle[4] answers.

He that hath no motion of God in his mind, no feeling of the Spirit, no taste of heavenly things, no remorse in conscience, no spark of zeal, is rather to be confounded by torments than reasons, for it is an evident and infallible sign that the Holy Ghost hath not sealed[5] his conscience, whereby he might cry 'Abba,[6] Father.' I could allege Scripture to prove that the godly should refrain from the company of the wicked, which although thou wilt not believe yet will it condemn thee. St Paul saith,[7] 'I desire you, brethren, that you abstain from the company of those that walk inordinately.'[8] Again, 'My son, if sinners shall flatter thee give no ear unto them. Fly from the evil, and evils shall fly from thee.'

---

1 *urged with a place*] challenged over a passage
2 *shift to avoid a blank*] strategy to cover an inability to reply
3 *colour*] pretext
4 *addle*] empty
5 *sealed*] placed His seal upon (i.e. as a mark of ownership)
6 *Abba*] father
7 *St Paul saith*] The following lines paraphrase (rather than directly quote) a passage from Paul's epistle to the Thessalonians.
8 *walk inordinately*] follow intemperate paths

And surely, were it not to confute thy detestable heresy and bring thee, if it might be, to some taste of the Holy Ghost, I would abandon all place of thy abode; for I think the ground accursed whereon thou standest. Thine opinions are so monstrous that I cannot tell whether thou wilt cast a doubt, also, whether thou have a soul or no; which if thou do, I mean not to waste wind[1] in proving that which thine infidelity will not permit thee to believe. For if thou hast, as yet, felt no taste of the Spirit working in thee, then sure I am that to prove the immortality of the soul were bootless;[2] if thou have a secret feeling, then it were needless. And God grant thee that glowing and sting in conscience that thy soul may witness to thyself that there is a living God, and thy heart shed drops of blood as a token of repentance in that thou hast denied that God. And so I commit thee to God; and that which I cannot do with any persuasion I will not leave to attempt with my prayer.

Atheos. Nay, stay a while, good Euphues, and leave not him perplexed with fear whom thou mayst make perfect by faith. For now I am brought into such a double and doubtful distress that I know not how to turn me. If I believe not the Scriptures then shall I be damned for unbelief, if I believe them then I shall be confounded for my wicked life. I know the whole course of the Bible which, if I should believe, then must I also believe that I am an abject.[3] For thus saith Eli[4] to his sons, 'If man sin against man, God can forgive it; if against God, who shall entreat for him? He that sinneth is of the devil; the reward of sin is death; thou shalt not suffer the wicked to live. Take all the princes of the people and hang them up against the sun on gibbets, that my anger may be turned from Israel.' These sayings of Holy Scripture cause me to tremble and shake in every sinew. Again, this saith the Holy Bible,[5] 'Now shall the scourge fall upon thee for thou hast sinned. Behold, I set a curse before you today, if you shall not hearken to the commandments of the Lord. All they that have forsaken the Lord shall be confounded.'

Furthermore, where threats are poured out against sinners, my heart bleedeth in my belly to remember them. 'I will come unto you in judgement,' saith the Lord, 'and I will be a swift and a severe witness: offenders, adulterers, and those that have committed perjury and retained the duty of hirelings, oppressed the widows, misused the stranger, and those that have not feared me, the Lord of Hosts.' Out of his mouth shall come a two-edged sword. 'Behold, I come quickly and bring my reward with me, which is to yield everyone according to his deserts.' Great is the day of the Lord and terrible, and who is he that may abide[6] Him? What shall I then do when the Lord shall arise to judge, and when He shall demand what shall I answer?

Besides this, the names that in Holy Scripture are attributed to God bring a terror to my guilty conscience. He is said to be a terrible God, a God of

---

1 *wind*] my breath
2 *bootless*] in vain
3 *abject*] outcast
4 *Eli*] high priest at Shiloh whose sons rebelled against God. The quotations that follow are not all drawn, however, from Eli's reproof to his sons (1 Samuel, 2).
5 *this saith the Holy Bible*] As before, the lines that follow are a tissue of Old and New Testament phrases rather than direct quotations from one specific passage.
6 *abide*] withstand

revenge, whose voice is like the thunder, whose breath maketh all the corners of the earth to shake and tremble. These things, Euphues, testify unto my conscience that if there be a God, He is the God of the righteous, and one that will confound the wicked. Whither, therefore, shall I go, and who may avoid the day of vengeance to come? If I go to heaven that is His seat, if into the earth, that is His footstool, if into the depth there He is also. Who can shroud himself from the face of the Lord, or where can one hide him that the Lord cannot find him? His words are like fire and the people like dry wood and shall be consumed.

Euphues.   Although I cannot but rejoice to hear thee acknowledge a God, yet must I needs lament to see thee so much distrust Him. The devil, that roaring lion, seeing his prey to be taken out of his jaws, allegeth all Scripture that may condemn the sinner,[1] leaving all out that should comfort the sorrowful; much like unto the deceitful physician, which recounteth all things that may endamage his patient, never telling anything that may recure[2] him.

Let not thy conscience be aggrieved,[3] but with a patient heart renounce all thy former iniquities, and thou shalt receive eternal life. Assure thyself that as God is a lord, so He is a father; as Christ is a judge, so He is a saviour; as there is a law, so there is a gospel. Though God have leaden hands which when they strike pay home,[4] yet hath He leaden feet which are as slow to overtake a sinner. Hear, therefore, the great comfort flowing in every leaf and line of the Scripture,[5] if thou be patient:

'I myself am even He which doth blot out thy transgressions and that for mine own sake, and I will not be mindful of thy sins. Behold the Lord's hand is not shortened that it cannot save, neither His ear heavy that it cannot hear. If your sins were as crimson, they shall be made whiter than snow; and though they were as red as scarlet they shall be made like white wool. If we confess our offences He is faithful and just, so that He will forgive us our sins. God hath not appointed[6] us unto wrath but unto salvation, by the means of our Lord, Jesus Christ. The earth is filled with the mercy of the Lord. It is not the will of your Father which is in heaven that any one of the little ones should perish. God is rich in mercy. I will not the death of a sinner, saith the Lord God; return and live. The Son of man came not to destroy but to save. God hath mercy on all because He can do all. God is merciful, long-suffering, and of much mercy. If the wicked man shall repent of his wickedness, which he hath committed, and keep my commandments, doing justice and judgement, he shall live the life and shall not die. If I shall say unto the sinner, "Thou shalt die the death," yet if he repent and do justice he shall not die.'

Call to thy mind the great goodness of God in creating thee, His singular love in giving His Son for thee. 'So God loved the world that He gave His

---

1 *allegeth ... sinner*] adduces all those passages of the Bible that damn the unrighteous
2 *endamage / recure*] have a detrimental effect on / heal
3 *aggrieved*] troubled
4 *pay home*] exact full retribution
5 *every leaf ... Scripture*] The following paragraphs are again a synthesis of biblical extracts rather than direct quotations.
6 *appointed*] destined

only begotten Son that whosoever believed in Him might not perish but have everlasting life. God hath not sent His Son to judge the world, but that the world might be saved by Him. Can the mother,' saith the prophet, 'forget the child of her womb? And though she be so unnatural, yet will I not be unmindful of thee. There shall be more joy in heaven for the repentance of one sinner than for ninety and nine just persons. I came not,' saith Christ, 'to call the righteous but sinners to repentance. If any man sin, we have an advocate with the Father, Jesus Christ the righteous; He is the propitiation for our sins, and not for our sins only but the sins of the whole world. I write unto you, little children, because your sins be forgiven for His name's sake.' Doth not Christ say that whatsoever we shall ask the Father in His name we shall obtain? Doth not God say, 'This is my beloved Son in whom I am well pleased; hear Him?'

I have read of Themistocles[1] which, having offended Philip the King of Macedonia and could no way appease his anger, meeting his young son Alexander took him in his arms and met Philip in the face. Philip, seeing the smiling countenance of the child, was well pleased with Themistocles. Even so, if through thy manifold sins and heinous offences thou provoke the heavy displeasure of thy God, insomuch as thou shalt tremble for horror, take His only begotten and well-beloved Son, Jesus, in thine arms, and then He neither can nor will be angry with thee. If thou have denied thy God, yet if thou go out with Peter and weep bitterly, God will not deny thee. Though with the prodigal son thou wallow in thine own wilfulness, yet if thou return again sorrowful thou shalt be received. If thou be a grievous offender, yet if thou come unto Christ with the woman in Luke and wash His feet with thy tears, thou shalt obtain remission.[2]

Consider with thyself the great love of Christ and the bitter torments that He endured for thy sake, which was enforced through the horror of death to cry with a loud voice, 'Eloi, Eloi, lama sabachthani? My God, my God, why hast thou forsaken me?' And with a groaning spirit to say, 'My soul is heavy even unto the death: tarry here and watch.' And again, 'Father, if it be possible, let this cup pass from me.' Remember how He was crowned with thorns, crucified with thieves, scourged and hanged for thy salvation, how He sweat water and blood for thy remission, how He endured even the torments of the damned spirits for thy redemption, how He overcame death that thou shouldst not die, how He conquered the devil that thou mightst not be damned. When thou shalt record what He hath done to purchase thy freedom, how canst thou dread bondage? When thou shalt behold the agonies and anguish of mind that He suffered for thy sake, how canst thou doubt of the release of thy soul? When thy Saviour shall be thy judge, why shouldst thou

---

1 *Themistocles*] celebrated commander of the Athenian fleet (see p. 101n.), who preserved himself from the anger of Admetus, King of the Molossi (not Philip of Macedonia) by taking his child in his arms. The story as Lyly tells it is anachronistic.

2 *If thou have denied . . . remission*] all examples of sinners who repented and were pardoned. Peter, having denied Christ three times, wept and was forgiven. The prodigal son demanded his inheritance and having been brought to penury was received home by his father with joy. The woman in the gospel of St Luke who anointed Christ's feet in the house of a Pharisee was absolved of her sins.

tremble to hear of judgement? When thou hast a continual mediator with
God the Father, how canst thou distrust of His favour?

Turn, therefore unto Christ with a willing heart and a wailing mind for thy
offences, who hath promised that at what time soever a sinner repenteth him
of his sins he shall be forgiven, who calleth all those that are heavy laden that
they might be refreshed, who is the door to them that knock, the way to
them that seek the truth, the rock, the corner-stone, the fulness of time; it is
He that can, and will, pour oil into thy wounds. Who absolved Mary
Magdalene[1] from her sins but Christ? Who forgave the thief his robbery and
manslaughter but Christ? Who made Matthew, the publican and toll-
gatherer, an apostle and preacher but Christ? Who is that good shepherd that
fetcheth home the stray sheep so lovingly upon His shoulders but Christ? Who
received home the lost son? Was it not Christ? Who made of Saul, a persecutor, Paul,[2] an apostle? Was it not Christ? I pass over divers other histories
both of the Old and New Testament which do abundantly declare what great
comfort the faithful penitent sinners have always had in hearing the comfortable[3] promises of God's mercy.

Canst thou then, Atheos, distrust thy Christ who rejoiceth at thy repentance? Assure thyself that through His passion and bloodshedding death hath
lost his sting, the devil his victory, and that the gates of hell shall not prevail
against thee. Let not, therefore, the blood of Christ be shed in vain by thine
obstinate and hard heart. Let this persuasion rest in thee that thou shalt
receive absolution freely, and then shalt thou feel thy soul even as it were to
hunger and thirst after righteousness.

Atheos.   Well, Euphues, seeing the Holy Ghost hath made thee the mean to
make me a man (for before the taste of the gospel I was worse than a beast),
I hope the same Spirit will also lighten my conscience with His word and
confirm it to the end in constancy that I may not only confess my Christ faithfully but also preach Him freely, that I may not only be a minister of His
word but also a martyr for it, if be His pleasure. Oh Euphues, how much am
I bound to the goodness of Almighty God, which hath made me of an infidel
a believer, of a castaway a Christian, of an heathenly pagan an heavenly
Protestant! Oh how comfortable is the feeling and taste of grace, how joyful
are the glad tidings of the gospel, the faithful promises of salvation, the
free redemption of the soul! I will endeavour by all means to confute those
damnable—I know not by what names to term them—but blasphemers I am
sure; which if they be no more, certainly they can be no less. I see now the
odds betwixt light and darkness, faith and frowardness,[4] Christ and Belial.[5]
Be thou, Euphues, a witness of my faith, seeing thou hast been the instrument
of my belief, and I will pray that I show it in my life. As for thee, I account
myself so much in thy debt as I shall never be able with the loss of my life to
render thee thy due; but God, which rewardeth the zeal of all men, will, I
hope, bless thee, and I will pray for thee.

---

1 *Mary Magdalene*] a prostitute and faithful follower of Christ
2 *Matthew / Paul*] see p. 129nn.
3 *comfortable*] reassuring, inspiriting
4 *frowardness*] apostasy
5 *Belial*] the devil

Euphues. Oh Atheos, little is the debt thou owest me, but great is the comfort that I have received by thee. Give the praise to God, whose goodness hath made thee a member of the mystical body of Christ, and not only a brother with His Son but also coheritor with thy Saviour. There is no heart so hard, no heathen so obstinate, no miscreant or infidel so impious, that by grace is not made as supple as oil, as tractable as a sheep, as faithful as any. The adamant,[1] though it be so hard that nothing can bruise it, yet if the warm blood of a goat be poured upon it, it bursteth; even so, although the heart of the atheist and unbeliever be so hard that neither reward nor revenge can mollify it, so stout that no persuasion can break it, yet if the grace of God purchased by the blood of Christ do but once touch it, it renteth in sunder and is enforced to acknowledge an omnipotent and everlasting Jehovah. Let us, therefore, both (Atheos I will not now call thee, but Theophilus)[2] fly unto that Christ which hath through His mercy, not our merits, purchased for us the inheritance of everlasting life.

---

1 *adamant*] diamond. For another reference to its capacity to be softened by blood see p. 56.

2 *Theophilus*] beloved of God

EUPHUES TO PHILAUTUS

If the course of youth had any respect to the staff of age or the living man
any regard to the dying mould,[1] we would with greater care when we were
young shun those things which should grieve us when we be old, and
with more severity direct the sequel of our life for the fear of present death.
But such is either the unhappiness of man's condition, or the untowardness[2]
of his crooked nature, or the wilfulness of his mind, or the blindness of his
heart, that in youth he surfeiteth with delights preventing age,[3] or, if he live,
continueth in dotage forgetting death. It is a world to see how in our flourishing time, when we best may, we be worst willing to thrive; and how in
the fading of our days, when we most should, we have least desire to remember our end.

Thou wilt muse, Philautus, to hear Euphues to preach, who of late had
more mind to serve his lady than to worship his Lord. Ah, Philautus, thou
art now a courtier in Italy, I a scholar in Athens, and as hard it is for thee to
follow good counsel as for me to enforce thee, seeing in thee there is little will
to amend and in me less authority to command. Yet will I exhort thee as a
friend—I would I might compel thee as a father. But I have heard that it is
peculiar to an Italian to stand in his own conceit,[4] and to a courtier never to
be controlled,[5] which causeth me to fear that in thee which I lament in others;
that is, that either thou seem too wise in thine own opinion, thinking scorn
to be taught, or too wild in thine attempts[6] in rejecting admonishment. The
one proceedeth of self-love, and so thy name importeth, the other of mere
folly, and that thy nature showeth.

Thou lookest I should crave pardon for speaking so boldly. No, Philautus,
I mean not to flatter thee, for then should I incur the suspicion of fraud;
neither am I determined to fall out with thee, for then might the wise convince[7] me of folly. But thou art in great credit in the court! And what then?
Shall thy credit with the Emperor[8] abate my courage to my God, or thy

---

1 *mould*] body
2 *untowardness*] perversity
3 *preventing age*] bringing himself to an early death
4 *stand in his own conceit*] adhere to his own views
5 *controlled*] rebuked
6 *attempts*] undertakings
7 *convince*] convict
8 *Emperor*] Possibly an allusion to Philip II of Spain, within whose jurisdiction Naples
 fell (see Croll and Clemens, p. 164n.), but the term may simply be construed as 'head
 of state'.

haughty looks quench my kindled love, or thy gallant show aslake[1] my goodwill? Hath the courtier any prerogative above the clown[2] why he should not
be reprehended? Doth his high calling not only give him a commission to sin
but remission also if he offend? Doth his pre-eminence in the court warrant
him to oppress the poor by might and acquit him of punishment? No,
Philautus. By how much the more thou excellest others in honours, by so
much the more thou oughtst to exceed them in honesty, and the higher thy
calling is, the better ought thy conscience to be; and as far it beseemeth a gentleman to be from pride as he is from poverty, and as near to gentleness in
condition[3] as he is in blood.

But I will descend with thee to particulars. It is reported here for a truth
that Philautus hath given over himself to all deliciousness, desiring rather to
be dandled in the laps of ladies than busied in the study of good letters. And
I would this were all, which is too much, or the rest a lie, which is too monstrous. It is now in every man's mouth that thou, yea, thou, Philautus, art so
void of courtesy that thou hast almost forgotten common sense and humanity, having neither care of religion (a thing too common in a courtier), neither
regard of honesty, or any virtuous behaviour.

Oh Philautus, dost thou live as thou shouldst never die, and laugh as thou
shouldst never mourn; art thou so simple as thou dost not know from whence
thou camest, or so sinful that thou carest not whither thou goest? What is in
thee that should make thee so secure,[4] or what can there be in any that may
cause him to glory? Milo, that great wrestler, began to weep when he saw his
arms brawnfallen and weak, saying, 'Strength, strength, is but vanity.' Helen,[5]
in her new glass viewing her old face, with a smiling countenance cried,
'Beauty, where is thy blaze?' Croesus[6] with all his wealth, Aristotle with all
his wit, all men with all their wisdom, have and shall perish and turn to dust.
But thou delightest to have the new fashion, the Spanish felt,[7] the French ruff,
thy crew of ruffians, all thy attire misshapen to make thee a monster, and all
thy time misspent to show thee unhappy.

What should I go about to decipher thy life, seeing the beginning showeth
the end to be nought? Art not thou one of those, Philautus, which seekest
to win credit with thy superiors by flattery and wring out wealth from
thy inferiors by force and undermine thy equals by fraud? Dost thou not
make the court not only a cover to defend thyself from wrong, but a colour[8]
also to commit injury? Art not thou one of those that, having gotten on
their sleeve the cognizance[9] of a courtier, have shaken from thy skirts
the regard of courtesy? I cannot but lament (I would I might remedy) the
great abuses that reign in the eyes of the Emperor. I fear me the poet say too
truly,

1 *aslake*] lessen
2 *clown*] peasant
3 *condition*] disposition
4 *secure*] free from apprehension
5 *Milo / Helen*] For Milo's strength and its decline pp. 35 and 102 / see p. 27n.
6 *Croesus*] King of Lydia (reigned 560–546 BC), noted for his extreme wealth
7 *Spanish felt*] type of hat
8 *colour*] justification
9 *cognizance*] badge

exeat aula
qui vult esse pius. virtus & summa potestas
non coeunt.[1]

Is not piety turned all to policy, faith to foresight, rigour to justice? Doth not
he best thrive that worst deserveth, and he rule all the country that hath no
conscience? Doth not the Emperor's court grow to this insolent blindness, that
all that see not their folly they account fools, and all that speak against it
precise;[2] laughing at the simplicity of the one, and threatening the boldness
of the other? Philautus, if thou wouldst with due consideration weigh how
far a courtier's life is from a sound belief, thou wouldst either frame thyself
to a new trade or else amend thine old manners; yea, thou wouldst with Crates
leave all thy possessions, taking thy books, and trudge to Athens, and with
Anaxagoras[3] despise wealth to attain wisdom. If thou hadst as great respect
to die well as thou hast care to live wantonly, thou wouldst with Socrates
seek how thou mightst yield to death, rather than with Aristippus[4] search how
to prolong thy life.

Dost thou not know that where the tree falleth, there it lieth, and everyone's death's day is his doomsday;[5] that the whole course of life is but a
meditation of death, a pilgrimage, a warfare? Hast thou not read, or dost
thou not regard what is written, that we shall all be cited before the tribunal
seat of God to render a strait account of our stewardship? If then the reward
be to be measured by thy merits, what boot[6] canst thou seek for but eternal
pain, which here livest in continual pleasure? So shouldst thou live as thou
mayst die, and then shalt thou die to live. Wert thou as strong as Samson, as
wise as Solomon, as holy as David, as faithful as Abraham, as zealous as
Moses, as good as any that ever lived, yet shalt thou die as they have done,
but not rise again to life with them, unless thou live as they did.

But thou wilt say that no man ought to judge thy conscience but thyself,
seeing thou knowest it better than any. Oh Philautus, if thou search thyself and
see not sin, then is thy case almost cureless. The patient, if physicians are to be
credited and common experience esteemed, is the nearest death when he thinketh himself past his disease, and the less grief he feeleth the greater fits he
endureth; the wound that is not searched because it little smarteth[7] is fullest of

---

1 *the poet ... coeunt*] The quotation is from Lucan's *Pharsalia*: 'He leaves the
palace / Who wishes to be a just man. Virtue and supreme power / Cannot go
together.'
2 *precise*] excessively punctilious
3 *Crates / Anaxagoras*] Cynic philosopher, heir to a large fortune, who renounced his
wealth to live with only the absolute necessities (see also p. 106n.) / celebrated
philosopher of the Ionian school (b. 500 BC) who gave his property to his relatives
in order to devote himself to higher things.
4 *Socrates / Aristippus*] celebrated Greek philosopher (b. 469 BC) who declined to
escape, having been sentenced to death, and took his own life by swallowing hemlock
(see also p. 108n.) / a pupil of Socrates who departed from his master's teaching to
embrace the life of the senses (see also p. 32n.)
5 *doomsday*] judgement day
6 *boot*] reward
7 *that is ... smarteth*] which is not probed because it barely hurts

dead flesh, and the sooner it skinneth,[1] the sorer it festereth. It is said that thunder bruiseth the tree but breaketh not the bark, and pierceth the blade, and never hurteth the scabbard; even so doth sin wound the heart but never hurt the eyes, and infect the soul though outwardly it nothing afflict the body.

Descend, therefore, into thine own conscience, confess thy sins, reform thy manners, contemn[2] the world, embrace Christ, leave the court, follow thy study, prefer holiness before honour, honesty before promotion, religion and uprightness of life before the overlashing[3] desires of the flesh. Resemble the bee, which out of the driest and bitterest thyme sucketh moist and sweet honey; and, if thou canst, out of the court, a place of more pomp than piety, suck out the true juice of perfection. But if thou see in thyself a will rather to go forward in thy looseness than any mean to go backward, if the glistering faces of fair ladies, or the glittering show of lusty gallants, or courtly fair, or any delicate thing, seem to entice thee to further lewdness, come from the court to Athens, and so in shunning the causes of evil thou shalt soon escape the effect of thy misfortune. The more those things please thee, the more thou displeasest God; and the greater pride thou takest in sin, the greater pain thou heapest to thy soul. Examine thine own conscience and see whether thou hast done as is required; if thou have, thank the Lord and pray for increase of grace, if not, desire God to give thee a willing mind to attain faith and constancy to continue to the end.

EUPHUES TO EUBULUS

I salute thee in the Lord etc. Although I was not so witty to follow thy grave advice when I first knew thee, yet do I not lack grace to give thee thanks since I tried thee.[4] And if I were as able to persuade thee to patience as thou wert desirous to exhort me to piety, or as wise to comfort thee in thine age as thou willing to instruct me in my youth, thou shouldst now with less grief endure thy late loss and with little care lead thy aged life.

Thou weepest for the death of thy daughter, and I laugh at the folly of the father; for greater vanity is there in the mind of the mourner than bitterness in the death of the diseased. But she was amiable; but yet sinful. But she was young and might have lived; but she was mortal and must have died. Aye, but her youth made thee often merry; aye, but thine age should once make thee wise. Aye, but her green years were unfit for death; aye, but thy hoary hairs should despise life. Knowest thou not, Eubulus, that life is the gift of God, death the due of nature; as we receive the one as a benefit, so must we abide the other of necessity. Wise men have found that by learning which old men should know by experience, that in life there is nothing sweet, in death nothing sour. The philosophers accounted it the chiefest felicity never to be born, the second soon to die. And what hath death in it so hard that we

---

1 *skinneth*] is superficially healed
2 *contemn*] despise
3 *overlashing*] unbridled
4 *so witty / tried thee*] wise enough / put your advice to the test

should take it so heavily? Is it strange to see that cut off which by nature is made to be cut, or that molten which is fit to be melted, or that burnt which is apt to be burnt, or man to pass that is born to perish?

But thou grantest that she should have died, and yet art thou grieved that she is dead. Is the death the better if the life be longer? No, truly. For as neither he that singeth most, or prayeth longest, or ruleth the stern[1] oftenest, but he that doth it best deserveth greatest praise, so he, not that hath most years, but many virtues, nor he that hath greyest hairs, but greatest goodness, livest longest. The chief beauty of life consisteth not in the numbering of many days but in the using of virtuous doings. Amongst plants those be best esteemed that in shortest time bring forth much fruit. Be not the fairest flowers gathered when they be freshest, the youngest beasts killed for sacrifice because they be finest? The measure of life is not length but honesty; neither do we enter into life to the end we should set down the day of our death, but therefore do we live that we may obey Him that made us and be willing to die when He shall call us.

But I will ask thee this question—whether thou wail the loss of thy daughter for thine own sake or hers? If for thine own sake, because thou didst hope in thine age to recover comfort, then is thy love to her but for thy commodity,[2] and therein thou art but an unkind father; if for hers, then dost thou mistrust her salvation, and therein thou showest thy unconstant faith. Thou shouldst not weep that she hath run fast, but that thou hast gone so slow; neither ought it to grieve thee that she is gone to her home with a few years, but that thou art to go with many.

But why go I about to use a long process to a little purpose? The bud is blasted as soon as the blown rose, the wind shaketh off the blossom as well as the fruit, death spareth neither the golden locks nor the hoary head. I mean not to make a treatise in the praise of death, but to note the necessity; neither to write what joys they receive that die, but to show what pains they endure that live. And thou which art even in the wane of thy life, whom nature hath nourished so long that now she beginneth to nod, mayst well know what griefs, what labours, what pains are in age; and yet wouldst thou be either young to endure many, or elder to bide more. But thou thinkest it honourable to go to the grave with a grey head, but I deem it more glorious to be buried with an honest name. 'Age,' sayest thou, 'is the blessing of God'—yet the messenger of death. Descend, therefore, into thine own conscience, consider the goodness that cometh by the end and the badness which was by the beginning, take the death of thy daughter patiently and look for thine own speedily; so shalt thou perform both the office of an honest man, and the honour of an aged father. And so farewell.

EUPHUES TO PHILAUTUS, TOUCHING
THE DEATH OF LUCILLA

I have received thy letters, and thou hast deceived mine expectation, for thou seemest to take more thought for the loss of an harlot than the life of

---

1 *ruleth the stern*] steers the ship
2 *commodity*] convenience

an honest woman. Thou writest that she was shameful in her trade and shameless in her end. I believe thee. It is no marvel that she which living practised sin should dying be void of shame, neither could there be any great hope of repentance at the hour of death where there was no regard of honesty in time of life. She was stricken suddenly, being troubled with no sickness; it may be, for it is commonly seen that a sinful life is rewarded with a sudden death, and a sweet beginning with a sour end. Thou addest, moreover, that she being in great credit with the states,[1] died in great beggary in the streets; certes, it is an old saying that whoso liveth in the court shall die in the straw. She hoped there by delights to gain money, and by her deserts purchased misery; they that seek to climb by privy sin shall fall with open shame, and they that covet to swim in vice shall sink in vanity to their own perils. Thou sayest that for beauty she was the Helen of Greece,[2] and I durst swear that for beastliness she might be the monster of Italy. In my mind, greater is the shame to be accounted an harlot than the praise to be esteemed amiable. But where thou art, in the court, there is more regard of beauty than honesty, and more are they lamented that die viciously than they loved that live virtuously; for thou givest, as it were, a sigh, which all thy companions in the court seem by thee to sound also,[3] that Lucilla, being one of so great perfection in all parts of the body and so little piety in the soul, should be, as it were, snatched out of the jaws of so many young gentlemen.

Well, Philautus, thou takest not so much care for the loss of her as I grieve for thy lewdness; neither canst thou sorrow more to see her die suddenly than I to hear thee live shamefully. If thou mean to keep me as a friend, shake off those vain toys[4] and dalliances with women. Believe me, Philautus—I speak it with salt tears trickling down my cheeks—the life thou livest in court is no less abhorred than the wicked death of Lucilla detested, and more art thou scorned for thy folly than she hated for her filthiness. The evil end of Lucilla should move thee to begin a good life. I have often warned thee to shun thy wonted trade;[5] and if thou love me, as thou protesteth in thy letters, then leave all thy vices and show it in thy life. If thou mean not to amend thy manners, I desire thee to write no more to me, for I will neither answer thee nor read them. The jennet is broken as soon with a wand as with the spur,[6] a gentleman as well allured with a word as with a sword.

Thou concludest in the end that Livia is sick. Truly I am sorry; for she is a maiden of no less comeliness than modesty, and hard it is to judge whether she deserves more praise for her beauty with the amorous or admiration for her honesty of the virtuous. If thou love me, embrace her, for she is able both to satisfy thine eye for choice and instruct thy heart with learning. Commend me unto her, and as I praise her to thee so will I pray for her to God, that either she may have patience to endure her trouble or deliverance to scape her peril.

Thou desirest me to send thee the sermons which were preached of late in Athens. I have fulfilled thy request, but I fear me thou wilt use them as St

---

1 *great credit . . . states*] well-regarded by those in power
2 *Helen of Greece*] see p. 27n.
3 *seem . . . also*] appear, according to you, to give too
4 *toys*] triflings
5 *wonted trade*] customary course of conduct
6 *jennet . . . spur*] for the same analogy see p. 117

George doth his horse, who is ever on his back but never rideth.[1] But if thou wert as willing to read them as I was to send them, or as ready to follow them as desirous to have them, it shall not repent thee of thy labour nor me of my cost. And thus farewell.

EUPHUES TO BOTONIO, TO TAKE HIS
EXILE PATIENTLY[2]

If I were as wise to give thee counsel as I am willing to do thee good, or as able to set thee at liberty as desirous to have thee free, thou shouldst neither want good advice to guide thee, nor sufficient help to restore thee. Thou takest it heavily that thou shouldst be accused without colour[3] and exiled without cause; and I think thee happy to be so well rid of the court and be so void of crime. Thou sayest banishment is bitter to the free-born; and I deem it the better, if thou be without blame. There be many meats which are sour in the mouth and sharp in the maw,[4] but if thou mingle them with sweet sauces they yield both a pleasant taste and wholesome nourishment. Divers colours offend the eyes, yet having green among them whet the sight. I speak this to this end, that though thy exile seem grievous to thee, yet guiding thyself with the rules of philosophy it shall be more tolerable. He that is cold doth not cover himself with care, but with clothes; he that is washed in the rain drieth himself by the fire, not by his fancy; and thou which art banished oughtst not with tears to bewail thy hap, but with wisdom to heal thy hurt.

Nature hath given no man a country, no more than she hath a house, or lands, or livings. Socrates would neither call himself an Athenian, neither a Grecian, but a citizen of the world. Plato would never account him banished that had the sun, fire, air, water and earth that he had before, where he felt the winter's blast and the summer's blaze, where the same sun and the same moon shined; whereby he noted that every place was a country to a wise man, and all parts a palace to a quiet mind.

But thou art driven out of Naples? That is nothing. All the Athenians dwell not in Collytus, nor every Corinthian in Graecia, nor all the Lacedaemonians in Pitane.[5] How can any part of the world be distant far from the other, whenas the mathematicians set down that the earth is but a point being compared to the heavens? Learn of the bee as well to gather honey of the weed as the flower, and out of far countries to live as well as in thine own. He is to be laughed at which thinketh the moon better at Athens than at Corinth, or the honey of the bee sweeter that is gathered in Hybla than that which is made in Mantua. When it was cast in Diogenes' teeth that the Sinoponetes

---

1 *St George ... rideth*] for the same analogy see p. 100n.
2 *EUPHUES TO BOTONIO ... PATIENTLY*] The content of the following letter is largely derived from Plutarch's *De exilio*, but the name Botonio appears to be Lyly's invention.
3 *colour*] show of reason
4 *maw*] stomach
5 *Collytus / Pitane*] district of Athens where Plato resided / the most important of the five districts of Sparta

had banished him Pontus,[1] 'Yea,' said he, 'I them of Diogenes.' I may say to thee as Stratonicus said to his guest, who demanded what fault was punished with exile; and he answering, 'Falsehood,' 'Why then,' said Stratonicus, 'dost not thou practise deceit to the end thou mayst avoid the mischiefs that flow in thy country?'[2] And surely if conscience be the cause thou art banished the court, I account thee wise in being so precise that by the using of virtue thou mayst be exiled the place of vice. Better it is for thee to live with honesty in the country than with honour in the court, and greater will thy praise be in flying vanity than thy pleasure in following trains.[3]

Choose that place for thy palace which is most quiet; custom will make it thy country, and an honest life will cause it a pleasant living. Philip, falling in the dust and seeing the figure of his shape perfect in show, 'Good God!' said he, 'we desire the whole earth, and see how little serveth.' Zeno,[4] hearing that this only bark[5] wherein all his wealth was shipped to have perished, cried out, 'Thou hast done well, Fortune, to thrust me into my gown again to embrace philosophy.' Thou hast, therefore, in my mind, great cause to rejoice that God by punishment hath compelled thee to strictness of life, which by liberty might have grown to lewdness.

When thou hast not one place assigned thee wherein to live but one forbidden thee which thou must leave, then thou being denied but one, that excepted, thou mayst choose any. Moreover, this dispute with thyself: 'I bear no office, whereby I should either for fear please the noble or for gain oppress the needy. I am no arbiter in doubtful cases, whereby I should either pervert justice or incur displeasure. I am free from the injuries of the strong and malice of the weak. I am out of the broils of the seditious, and have escaped the threats of the ambitious.'

But as he that having a fair orchard, seeing one tree blasted, recounteth the discommodity[6] of that and passeth over in silence the fruitfulness of the other, so he that is banished doth always lament the loss of his house and the shame of his exile, not rejoicing at the liberty, quietness, and pleasure that he enjoyeth by that sweet punishment. The kings of Persia were deemed happy in that they passed their winter in Babylon, in Media their summer, and their spring in Susa; and certainly the exile in this may be as happy as any king in Persia, for he may at his leisure, being at his own pleasure, lead his winter in Athens, his summer in Naples, his spring in Argos. But if he have any business in hand, he may study without trouble, sleep without care, and wake at his will without controlment. Aristotle must dine when it pleaseth Philip, Diogenes when it listeth Diogenes.[7] The courtier suppeth

---

1 *Sinoponetes / Pontus*] people of Sinope, a Greek colony on the Black Sea / district on the coast of the Black sea. For *Diogenes* see p. 38n.

2 *I may say ... country*] No source has been traced for this anecdote.

3 *trains*] intrigues

4 *Philip / Zeno*] King of Macedonia (b. 382 BC) and father of Alexander the Great (about whom the same story is frequently told) / Stoic philosopher (fl. 260 BC) renowned for his simplicity of life

5 *bark*] ship

6 *discommodity*] inconvenience

7 *Aristotle ... Diogenes*] Aristotle, tutor to Alexander, was subject to the will of Philip of Macedonia (Alexander's father). Diogenes refused to participate in court life.

when the king is satisfied, but Botonio may now eat when Botonio is anhungered.

But thou sayest that banishment is shameful. No, truly; no more than poverty to the content, or grey hairs to the aged. It is the cause that maketh thee shame. If thou wert banished upon choler, greater is thy credit in sustaining wrong than thy en[em]ies in committing injury, and less shame is it to thee to be oppressed by might than theirs that wrought it for malice. But thou fearest thou shalt not thrive in a strange nation. Certainly, thou art more afraid than hurt. The pine-tree groweth as soon in Pharos as in Ida,[1] the nightingale singeth as sweetly in the deserts as in the woods of Crete, the wise man liveth as well in a far country as in his own home. It is not the nature of the place but the disposition of the person that maketh the life pleasant. Seeing, therefore, Botonio, that all the sea is apt for any fish, that it is a bad ground where no flower will grow, that to a wise man all lands are as fertile as his own inheritance, I desire thee to temper the sharpness of thy banishment with the sweetness of the cause, and to measure the clearness of thine own conscience with the spite of thy enemies' quarrel; so shalt thou revenge their malice with patience, and endure thy banishment with pleasure.

EUPHUES TO A YOUNG GENTLEMAN IN NAPLES
NAMED ALCIUS, WHO, LEAVING HIS STUDY,
FOLLOWED ALL LIGHTNESS AND LIVED BOTH
SHAMEFULLY AND SINFULLY, TO THE GRIEF
OF HIS FRIENDS AND DISCREDIT OF THE
UNIVERSITY

If I should talk in words of those things which I have to confer with thee in writings, certes thou wouldst blush for shame and I weep for sorrow; neither could my tongue utter that with patience which my hand can scarce write with modesty, neither could thy ears hear that without glowing which thine eyes can hardly view without grief. Ah, Alcius, I cannot tell whether I should most lament in thee thy want of learning or thy wanton living; in the one thou art inferior to all men, in the other superior to all beasts—insomuch as who seeth thy dull wit and marketh thy froward[2] will may well say that he never saw smack of learning in thy doings, nor spark of religion in thy life.

Thou only vauntest of thy gentry.[3] Truly, thou wast made a gentleman before thou knewest what honesty meant, and no more hast thou to boast of thy stock than he who being left rich by his father dieth a beggar by his folly. Nobility began in thine ancestors and endeth in thee; and the generosity[4] that they gained by virtue thou hast blotted with vice. If thou claim gentry by pedigree, practise gentleness[5] by thine honesty, that as thou

---

1 *Pharos / Ida*] small island adjacent to Alexandria / wooded mountain, celebrated in Greek mythology as a seat of the gods
2 *froward*] perverse
3 *Thou . . . gentry*] you boast of your good birth
4 *generosity*] nobility
5 *gentleness*] gentlemanly behaviour

challengest[1] to be noble in blood thou mayst also prove noble by knowledge; otherwise shalt thou hang like a blast[2] among the fair blossoms, and like a stain in a piece of white lawn. The rose that is eaten with the canker is not gathered because it groweth on that stalk that the sweet doth, neither was Helen made a star because she came of that egg with Castor,[3] nor thou a gentleman in that thy ancestors were of nobility. It is not the descent of birth but the consent of conditions[4] that maketh gentlemen, neither great manors but good manners that express the true image of dignity. There is copper coin of the stamp that gold is, yet is it not current; there cometh poison of the fish as well as good oil, yet is it not wholesome; and of man may proceed an evil child, and yet no gentleman. For as the wine that runneth on the lees is not therefore to be accounted neat because it was drawn of the same piece,[5] or as the water that springeth from the fountain's head and floweth into the filthy channel is not to be called clear because it came of the same stream, so neither is he that descendeth of noble parentage, if he desist from noble deeds, to be esteemed a gentleman in that he issued from the loins of a noble sire, for that he obscureth the parents he came of and discrediteth his own estate.[6] There is no gentleman in Athens but sorroweth to see thy behaviour so far to disagree from thy birth; for this say they all (which is the chiefest note of a gentleman) that thou shouldst as well desire honesty in thy life as honour by thy lineage, that thy nature should not swerve from thy name, that as thou by duty wouldst be regarded for thy progeny,[7] so thou wouldst endeavour by deserts to be reverenced for thy piety. The pure coral is chosen as well by his virtue[8] as his colour, a king is known better by his courage than his crown, a right gentleman is sooner seen by the trial of his virtue than blazing of his arms.[9]

But I let pass[10] thy birth, wishing thee rather with Ulysses to show it in works than with Ajax to boast of it with words;[11] thy stock shall not be the less, but thy modesty the greater. Thou livest in Athens as the wasp doth among bees, rather to sting than to gather honey, and thou dealest with most of thy acquaintance as the dog doth in the manger, who neither suffereth the horse to eat hay nor will himself; for thou, being idle, wilt not permit any (as far as in thee lieth) to be well-employed. Thou art an heir to fair living. That is nothing if thou be disherited of learning; for better were it to thee to inherit

---

1 *thou challengest*] you claim
2 *blast*] blighted bud
3 *Helen / Castor*] born of the same egg from the union between Leda and Zeus in the form of a swan. For *Helen* see p. 27n. Castor was turned into a star after his death because of his heroic life.
4 *consent of conditions*] conformity of manners
5 *runneth on the lees . . . piece*] is drawn to the dregs is not regarded as free from impurities because it was drawn from the same cask (i.e. as the rest of the wine drawn from the barrel)
6 *estate*] rank
7 *progeny*] ancestry
8 *virtue*] properties. (Coral was thought to repel lightning: see Croll and Clemons, p. 177n.)
9 *blazing of his arms*] proclaiming his heraldry
10 *let pass*] pass over
11 *Ulysses . . . words*] see p. 78 for a variation of the same comparison

righteousness than riches, and far more seemly were it for thee to have thy study full of books than thy purse full of money. To get goods is the benefit of fortune, to keep them the gift of wisdom. As, therefore, thou art to possess them by thy father's will, so art thou to increase them by thine own wit.

But, alas, why desirest thou to have the revenues of thy parent and nothing regardest to have his virtues? Seekest thou by succession to enjoy thy patrimony and by vice to obscure his piety? Wilt thou have the title of his honour and no touch of his honesty? Ah, Alcius, remember that thou art born not to live after thine own lust but to learn to die, whereby thou mayst live after thy death. I have often heard thy father say, and that with a deep sigh, the tears trickling down his grey hairs, that thy mother never longed more to have thee born when she was in travail than he to have thee dead to rid him of trouble. And not seldom hath thy mother wished that either her womb had been thy grave or the ground hers. Yea, all thy friends with open mouth desire either that God will send thee grace to amend thy life or grief to hasten thy death. Thou wilt demand of me in what thou dost offend; and I ask thee in what thou dost not sin. Thou swearest thou art not covetous; but I say thou art prodigal, and as much sinneth he that lavisheth without mean[1] as he that hoardeth without measure. But canst thou excuse thyself of vice in that thou art not covetous? Certainly no more than the murderer would therefore be guiltless because he is no coiner.

But why go I about to debate reason with thee when thou hast no regard of honesty? Though I leave here to persuade thee, yet will I not cease to pray for thee. In the mean season, I desire thee, yea, and in God's name command thee, that if neither the care of thy parents whom thou shouldst comfort, nor the counsel of thy friends which thou shouldst credit, nor the rigour of the law which thou oughtst to fear, nor the authority of the magistrate which thou shouldst reverence, can allure thee to grace, yet the law of thy Saviour, who hath redeemed thee, and the punishment of the Almighty, who continually threateneth thee, draw thee to amendment. Otherwise, as thou livest now in sin, so shalt thou die with shame and remain with Satan, from whom He that made thee keep thee.

LIVIA, FROM THE EMPEROR'S COURT, TO EUPHUES AT ATHENS

If sickness had not put me to silence and the weakness of my body hindered the willingness of my mind, thou shouldst have had a more speedy answer, and I no cause of excuse. I know it expedient to return an answer, but not necessary to write in post;[2] for that in things of great importance we commonly look before we leap, and where the heart droopeth through faintness, the hand is enforced to shake through feebleness.

Thou sayest thou understandest how men live in the court, and of me thou desirest to know the estate[3] of women. Certes, to dissemble with thee were

---

1 *mean*] moderation
2 *in post*] in haste
3 *estate*] condition

to deceive myself, and to cloak the vanities in court were to clog mine own conscience with vices. The Empress keepeth her estate royal and her maidens will not leese[1] an inch of their honour; she endeavoureth to set down good laws, and they to break them; she warneth them of excess, and they study to exceed; she sayeth that decent attire is good though it be not costly, and they swear unless it be dear it is not comely. She is here accounted a slut that cometh not in her silks, and she that hath not every fashion hath no man's favour. They that be most wanton are reputed most wise, and they that be the idlest livers are deemed the finest lovers. There is great quarrelling for beauty, but no question of honesty.[2] To conclude, both women and men have fallen here in court to such agreement that they never jar[3] about matters of religion because they never mean to reason of them. I have wished oftentimes rather in the country to spin than in the court to dance; and truly a distaff doth better become a maiden than a lute, and fitter it is with the needle to practise how to live than with the pen[4] to learn how to love.

The Empress giveth example of virtue and the ladies have no leisure to follow her. I have nothing else to write. Here is no good news; as for bad, I have told sufficient. Yet this I must add, that some there be which for their virtue deserve praise, but they are only commended for their beauty; for this think courtiers, that to be honest is a certain kind of count[r]y modesty, but to be amiable[5] the courtly courtesy.

I mean shortly to sue to the Empress to be dismissed of the court, which, if I obtain, I shall think it a good reward for my service to be so well rid from such severity;[6] for, believe me, there is scarce one in court that either feareth God or meaneth good. I thank thee for the book thou didst send me, and as occasion shall serve I will requite thee. Philautus beginneth a little to listen to counsel. I wish him well, and thee too, of whom to hear so much good it doth me not a little good. Pray for me as I do for thee; and if opportunity be offered, write to me. Farewell.

EUPHUES TO HIS FRIEND LIVIA

Dear Livia,

I am as glad to hear of thy welfare as sorrowful to understand thy news, and it doth me as much good that thou art recovered as harm to think of those which are not to be recured. Thou hast satisfied my request and answered my expectation; for I longed to know the manners of women and looked[7] to have them wanton. I like thee well that thou wilt not conceal their vanities, but I love thee the better that thou dost not follow them; to reprove sin is the sign of true honour, to renounce it the part of honesty. All good

---

1 *leese*] lose
2 *question of honesty*] thought for chastity
3 *jar*] disagree
4 *with the needle / with the pen*] by sewing (i.e. by useful employment) / by writing (e.g. sonnets). For *distaff* see p. 68n.
5 *honest / amiable*] chaste / loving
6 *severity*] rigours
7 *looked*] expected

men will account thee wise for thy truth and happy for thy trial; for they say
to abstain from pleasure is the chiefest piety, and I think in court to refrain
from vice is no little virtue. Strange[1] it is that the sound eye viewing the sore
should not be dimmed, that they that handle pitch should not be defiled,
that they that continue in court should not be infected. And yet it is no great
marvel; for by experience we see that the adamant cannot draw iron if the
diamond lie by it,[2] nor vice allure the courtier if virtue be retained.

Thou praisest the Empress for instituting good laws, and grievest to see
them violated by the ladies. I am sorry to think it should be so, and I sigh in
that it cannot be otherwise. Where there is no heed taken of a commandment,
there is small hope to be looked for of amendment. Where duty can have no
show, honesty can bear no sway. They that cannot be enforced to obedience
by authority will never be won by favour; for, being without fear, they commonly are void of grace, and as far be they careless from honour as they be
from awe, and as ready to despise the good counsel of their peers as to
contemn the good laws of their Prince. But the breaking of laws doth not
accuse the Empress of vice, neither shall her making of them excuse the ladies
of vanities. The Empress is no more to be suspected of erring than the car-
penter that buildeth the house be accused because thieves have broken it, or
the mint-master condemned for his coin because the traitor hath clipped it.[3]
Certainly God will both reward the godly zeal of the Prince and revenge the
godless doings of the people.

Moreover, thou sayest that in the court all be sluts that swim not in silks
and that the idlest livers are accounted the bravest lovers. I cannot tell whether
I should rather laugh at their folly or lament their frenzy, neither do I know
whether the sin be greater in apparel which moveth to pride, or in affection
which enticeth to peevishness;[4] the one causeth them to forget themselves, the
other to forgo their senses. Each do deceive[5] their soul. They that think
one cannot be cleanly without pride will quickly judge none to be honest
without pleasure, which is as hard to confess as to say no mean to be without
excess.

Thou wishest to be in the country with thy distaff rather than to continue
in the court with thy delights. I cannot blame thee; for Greece is as much to
be commended for learning as the court for bravery, and here mayst thou live
with as good report for thine honesty as they with renown for their beauty.
It is better to spin with Penelope all night than to sing with Helen[6] all day.
Housewifery in the country is as much praised as honour in the court. We
think it as great mirth to sing psalms as you melody to chant sonnets, and
we account them as wise that keep their own lands with credit as you those
that get others' livings by craft. Therefore, if thou wilt follow my advice and

---

1 *Strange*] rare
2 *adamant . . . lie by it*] apparantly contradictory in view of the references on pp. 98
and 135 where *adamant* = diamond. Here, however, as Bond points out (I, pp.
373-4), the word probably translates Latin 'magnes' (magnet).
3 *mint-master . . . clipped it*] The edges of coins were clipped by the unscrupulous in
the sixteenth century for the precious metals of which they were made.
4 *peevishness*] folly
5 *deceive*] betray
6 *spin . . . night / Helen*] see p. 57n. / see p. 27n.

prosecute thine own determination, thou shalt come out of a warm sun into God's blessing.[1]

Thou addest (I fear me also thou errest) that in the court there be some of great virtue, wisdom and sobriety. If it be so, I like it; and in that thou sayest it is so, I believe it. It may be, and, no doubt, it is in the court as in all rivers, some fish some frogs; and as in all gardens, some flowers some weeds; and as in all trees, some blossoms some blasts.[2] Nylus breedeth the precious stone and the poisoned serpent;[3] the court may as well nourish virtuous matrons as the lewd minion.[4] Yet this maketh me muse, that they should rather be commended for their beauty than for their virtue, which is an infallible argument that the delights of the flesh are preferred before the holiness of the spirit.

Thou sayest thou wilt sue to leave thy service and I will pray for thy good success. When thou art come into the country, I would have thee first learn to forget all those things which thou hast seen in the court. I would Philautus were of thy mind to forsake his youthful course, but I am glad thou writest that he beginneth to amend his conditions. He runneth far that never returneth, and he sinneth deadly that never repenteth. I would have him end as Lucilla began, without vice, and not begin as she ended, without honesty. I love the man well, but I cannot brook his manners.[5] Yet I conceive a good hope that in his age he will be wise, for that in his youth I perceived him witty. He hath promised to come to Athens, which if he do I will so handle the matter that either he shall abjure the court for ever or absent himself for a year. If I bring the one to pass, he shall forgo his old course; if the other, forget his ill conditions. He that in court will thrive to reap wealth and live wary to get worship must gain by good conscience and climb by wisdom; otherwise his thrift is but theft, where there is no regard of gathering,[6] and his honour but ambition, where there is no care but of promotion. Philautus is too simple to understand the wiles in court, and too young to undermine any by craft. Yet hath he shown himself as far from honesty as he is from age, and as full of craft as he is of courage. If it were for thy preferment and his amendment I wish you were both married; but if he should continue his folly, whereby thou shouldst fall from thy duty, I rather wish you both buried. Salute him in my name and hasten his journey, but forget not thine own.

I have occasion to go to Naples that I may with more speed arrive in England, where I have heard of a woman that in all qualities excelleth any man;[7] which if it be so, I shall think my labour as well bestowed as Saba[8] did hers when she travelled to see Solomon. At my going, if thou be in Naples I will visit thee—and at my return I will tell thee my judgement. If Philautus

---

1 *prosecute / warm sun ... blessing*] pursue / exchange your present state for a better (proverbial)
2 *blasts*] blighted buds
3 *Nylus ... serpent*] the river Nile yields both the jewel and the asp
4 *lewd minion*] vicious hussy
5 *brook his manners*] tolerate his behaviour
6 *no regard of gathering*] indifference to the means of acquisition
7 *a woman ... man*] Queen Elizabeth
8 *Saba*] queen of the kingdom of the Sabeans, a wealthy people trading in precious substances. For the visit of the queen (also known as the Queen of Sheba) to Solomon see 1 Kings, 10.1–13.

come this winter, he shall in this my pilgrimage be a partner. A pleasant companion is a bait[1] in a journey. We shall there, as I hear, see a court both braver in show and better in substance, more gallant courtiers, more godly consci[ence]s, as fair ladies, and fairer conditions.[2] But I will not vaunt before the victory, nor swear it is so until I see it be so. Farewell unto whom above all I wish well.

I have finished the first part of *Euphues*, whom now I left ready to cross the seas to England. If the wind send him a short cut,[3] you shall in the second part hear what news he bringeth, and I hope to have him returned within one summer. In the mean season I will stay for him in the country, and as soon as he arriveth you shall know of his coming.

FINIS

---

1 *bait*] refreshment
2 *conditions*] moral natures
3 *cut*] passage

There is no privilege that needeth a pardon, neither is there any remission to be asked where a commission is granted.[1] I speak this, gentlemen, not to excuse the offence which is taken, but to offer a defence where I was mistaken. A clear conscience is a sure card, truth hath the prerogative to speak with plainness and the modesty to bear with patience. It was reported by some, and believed of many, that in the education of Ephebus, where mention was made of universities, that Oxford was too much either defaced or defamed. I know not what the envious have picked out by malice, or the curious[2] by wit, or the guilty by their own galled[3] consciences; but this I say, that I was as far from thinking ill as I find them from judging well. But if I should now go about to make amends, I were then faulty in somewhat amiss,[4] and should show myself like Apelles' prentice,[5] who, coveting to mend the nose, marred the cheek; and not unlike the foolish dyer, who never thought his cloth black until it was burned. If any fault be committed impute it to Euphues who knew you not, not to Lyly who hates you not.

Yet may I of all the rest most condemn Oxford of unkindness[6]—of vice I cannot—who seemed to wean me before she brought me forth, and to give me bones to gnaw before I could get the teat to suck;[7] wherein she played the nice[8] mother, in sending me into the country to nurse, where I tired[9] at a dry breast three years and was, at the last, enforced to wean myself. But it was destiny; for if I had not been gathered from the tree in the bud I should, being blown, have proved a blast,[10] and as good it is to be an addle egg as an idle bird.

Euphues at his arrival (I am assured) will view Oxford, where he will either recant his sayings or renew his complaints. He is now on the seas, and how he hath been tossed I know not; but whereas I had thought to receive

---

1 *There is no . . . granted*] No pardon can be required for exercising a privilege, and there is no need to ask for a concession where a right has been granted
2 *curious*] over-ingenious
3 *galled*] chaffed
4 *faulty in somewhat amiss*] guilty of some fault
5 *Apelles' prentice*] an apprentice to the Greek master-painter (for *Apelles* see p. 27n.)
6 *unkindness*] unnatural behaviour
7 *bones . . . suck*] an inappropriate and unrewarding education. The paragraph as a whole refers to Lyly's dissatisfaction with his studies at Oxford, but the biographical details remain obscure (see Introduction, p. 2).
8 *nice*] over-fastidious
9 *tired*] tugged
10 *being blown / blast*] having flowered / blighted blossom

him at Dover, I must meet him at Hampton.[1] Nothing can hinder his coming but death, neither anything hasten his departure but unkindness.

Concerning myself, I have always thought so reverently of Oxford, of the scholars, of the manners, that I seemed to be rather an idolater than a blasphemer. They that invented this toy[2] were unwise, and they that reported it unkind; and yet none of them can prove me unhonest. But suppose I glanced at some abuses. Did not Jupiter's egg bring forth as well Helen, a light huswife in earth, as Castor a light star in heaven?[3] The ostrich, that taketh the greatest pride in her feathers, picketh some of the worst out and burneth them. There is no tree but hath some blast,[4] no countenance but hath some blemish; and shall Oxford, then, be blameless? I wish it were so, yet I cannot think it is so. But as it is, it may be better; and were it badder, it is not the worst. I think there are few universities that have less faults than Oxford, many that have more, none but hath some.

But I commit my cause to the consciences of those that either know what I am or can guess what I should be; the one will answer themselves in construing friendly, the other, if I knew them, I would satisfy reasonably.

Thus, loath to incur the suspicion of unkindness[5] in not telling my mind, and not willing to make any excuse where there need no amends, I can neither crave pardon lest I should confess a fault, nor conceal my meaning lest I should be thought a fool. And so I end.

Yours assured to use,
John Lyly.

---

1 *Hampton*] Southampton (with some allusion to Lyly's personal circumstances that is now obscure)
2 *toy*] fooolish tale
3 *Jupiter's egg ... heaven*] for the same analogy see above p. 145.
4 *blast*] diseased bud
5 *unkindness*] ill-will

¶Euphues and his England.

CONTAINING

his voyage and aduentures , myxed with
sundry pretie discourses of honest
Loue , the discription of the
countrey, the Court,and
the manners of that
life.

DELIGHTFVL TO

be read,and nothing hurtfull to be regarded : wher-in there is small offence
by lightnesse giuen to the wise,
and lesse occasion of loose-
nes proffered to the
wanton.

¶By Iohn Lyly , Maister
of Arte.

Commend it,or amend it.

❧Imprinted at London for
Gabriell Cawood,dwelling in
Paules Church-yard.
1580.

Title-page of *Euphues and His England* (1580)
Harry Ransom Humanities Research Center,
University of Texas at Austin (Pforz 629.5)

EUPHUES
AND HIS ENGLAND

TO THE RIGHT HONOURABLE MY VERY
GOOD LORD AND MASTER EDWARD DE VERE,
EARL OF OXFORD, VISCOUNT BULBECK,
LORD OF ESCALES AND BADLESMERE,
AND LORD GREAT CHAMBERLAIN
OF ENGLAND,
JOHN LYLY WISHETH LONG LIFE
WITH INCREASE OF HONOUR[1]

The first picture that Phidias, the first painter, shadowed[2] was the portraiture of his own person, saying thus: 'If it be well, I will paint many
besides Phidias; if ill, it shall offend none but Phidias.' In the like manner
fareth it with me, Right Honourable, who, never before handling the
pencil, did for my first counterfeit colour mine own Euphues, being of
this mind that if it were liked I would draw more besides Euphues, if
loathed grieve none but Euphues.

Since that, some there have been that, either dissembling[3] the faults they
saw for fear to discourage me, or not examining them for the love they
bore me, that praised mine old work and urged me to make a new, whose
words I thus answered: 'If I should coin a worse, it would be thought that
the former was framed by chance, as Protogenes did the foam of his dog;[4]
if a better, for flattery, as Narcissus did, who only was in love with his
own face;[5] if none at all, as froward as the musician, who being entreated
will scarce sing sol fa, but not desired strain above e la.'[6]

But their importunity admitted no excuse, insomuch that I was enforced
to prefer their friendship before mine own fame, being more careful to
satisfy their requests than fearful of others' reports. So that at the last I
was content to set another face to Euphues, yet just behind the other, like

---

1 *RIGHT HONOURABLE . . . HONOUR*] For Oxford's patronage of Lyly see Introduction, pp. 2ff.
2 *Phidias / shadowed*] the most celebrated sculptor of the antique world (circa
490–432 BC), reputed to be the founder of classical art / drew
3 *dissembling*] disguising
4 *Protogenes . . . dog*] noted Greek painter (fl. 332 BC), reputed to have accidentally
created the effect of foam at a dog's mouth by throwing a sponge full of paint at the
picture in frustration at his failed attempts
5 *Narcissus*] beautiful son of Cephissus and Liriope, punished by Nemesis for his indifference to the nymph Echo by being made to fall in love with his own reflection
6 *sol fa / e la*] notes of the musical scale, the last at the very top of the register. (For
froward in the same sentence see p. 144n.)

the image of Janus,[1] not running together, like the Hopplitides of Parrhasius,[2] lest they should seem so unlike brothers that they might be both thought bastards. The picture whereof I yield as common [for] all to view, but the patronage only to your Lordship, as able to defend; knowing that the face of Alexander stamped in copper doth make it current,[3] that the name of Caesar wrought in canvas is esteemed as cambric,[4] that the very feather of an eagle is of force to consume the beetle.[5]

I have brought into the world two children; of the first I was delivered before my friends thought me conceived, of the second I went a whole year big,[6] and yet when everyone thought me ready to lie down, I did then quicken.[7] But good housewives shall make my excuse, who know that hens do not lay eggs when they cluck but when they cackle, nor men set forth books when they promise but when they perform. And in this I resemble the lapwing, who, fearing her young ones to be destroyed by passengers,[8] flieth with a false cry far from their nests, making those that look for them seek where they are not. So I, suspecting that Euphues would be carped of some curious[9] reader, thought by some false show to bring them in hope of that which then I meant not, leading them with a longing of a second part that they might speak well of the first, being never further from my study than when they thought me hovering over it.

My first burden, coming before his time, must needs be a blind whelp;[10] the second, brought forth after his time, must needs be a monster. The one I sent to a noble man to nurse,[11] who with great love brought him up for a year; so that wheresoever he wander, he hath his nurse's name in his forehead, where sucking his first milk, he cannot forget his first master. The other, Right Honourable, being but yet in his swathe-clouts,[12] I commit most humbly to your Lordship's protection, that in his infancy

---

1 *Janus*] guardian deity of gateways, depicted with two faces to signify the two directions in which doors face

2 *Hopplitides of Parrhasius*] companion pictures of runners in full armour painted by Parrhasius (see p. 27n.), one in process of running, the other removing his armour after the race

3 *face of Alexander . . . current*] the image of a king stamped on worthless metal turns it into valuable coin

4 *canvas / cambric*] coarse unbleached cloth (i.e. the meanest fabric) / fine white linen

5 *feather . . . beetle*] a variation on the tradition that eagles' feathers consume those of other birds (see p. 52n.)

6 *of the second . . . big*] I was pregnant with the second for a year

7 *lie down / quicken*] give birth / conceive

8 *passengers*] travellers on foot

9 *carped / curious*] criticized / over-particular

10 *my first . . . whelp*] proverbial (signifying that things undertaken prematurely are doomed to failure). *burden* = unborn child

11 *noble man to nurse*] Lord Delaware, to whom *Euphues: The Anatomy of Wit* is dedicated

12 *swathe-clouts*] cloth in which a new-born infant is wrapped

he may be kept by your good care from falls, and in his youth by your great countenance shielded from blows, and in his age by your gracious continuance[1] defended from contempt. He is my youngest and my last, and the pain that I sustained for him in travail hath made me past teeming;[2] yet do I think myself very fertile in that I was not altogether barren.

Glad I was to send them both abroad[3] lest, making a wanton of my first with a blind conceit, I should resemble the ape and kill it by culling[4] it, and not able to rule the second, I should with the viper lose my blood with mine own brood.[5] Twins they are not, but yet brothers, the one nothing resembling the other, and yet (as all children are nowadays) both like the father. Wherein I am not unlike unto the unskilful painter,[6] who, having drawn the twins of Hippocrates (who were as like as one pease[7] is to another), and being told of his friends that they were no more like than Saturn and Apollo, he had no other shift to manifest what his work was than over their heads to write, 'The Twins of Hippocrates'. So may it be that had I not named Euphues, few would have thought it had been Euphues; not that in goodness the one so far excelleth the other, but that both being so bad, it is hard to judge which is the worst.

This unskilfulness is no ways to be covered but as Accius[8] did his shortness, who, being a little poet, framed for himself a great picture; and I, being a naughty painter, have gotten a most noble patron, being of Ulysses' mind, who thought himself safe under the shield of Ajax.[9]

I have now finished both my labours, the one being hatched in the hard winter with the halcyon,[10] the other not daring to bud till the cold were past like the mulberry. In either of the which, or in both, if I seem to glean after another's cart for a few ears of corn, or of the tailor's shreds to make me a livery, I will not deny but that I am one of those poets which the

---

1 *great countenance / gracious continuance*] eminent position / continued favour
2 *travail / teeeming*] child-birth / child-bearing
3 *abroad*] from home
4 *blind conceit / culling*] undiscerning estimation / embracing
5 *viper ... brood*] It was thought that vipers were born by eating their way out of their mothers' bodies.
6 *unskilful painter*] It is not clear to whom this alludes. Hippocrates is referred to as an artist on p. 217 and may therefore himself be the 'unskilful painter'. Alternatively the Hippocrates of this passage may be the celebrated physician, in which case he is the father of the twins rather than the inept painter of their portraits.
7 *pease*] pea
8 *Accius*] Roman tragic poet and dramatist (b. 170 BC). For Lyly's probable source for his shortness of stature see Croll and Clemons, p. 194n.
9 *Ulysses' mind ... Ajax*] possibly a reference to the rescue of Ulysses effected by Menelaus and Ajax in the *Iliad*, bk xi (*naughty* in the same sentence = bad)
10 *halcyon*] fabulous bird believed to breed at sea on a floating nest during the winter solstice

painters feign to come unto Homer's basin, there to lap up that he doth cast up.[1]

In that I have written, I desire no praise of others, but patience; altogether unwilling, because every way unworthy, to be accounted a workman. It sufficeth me to be a water bough,[2] no bud, so I may be of the same root; to be the iron, not steel, so I be in the same blade; to be vinegar, not wine, so I be in the same cask; to grind colours for Apelles, though I cannot garnish, so I be of the same shop. What I have done was only to keep myself from sleep, as the crane doth the stone in her foot; and I would also, with the same crane, I had been silent holding a stone in my mouth.[3]

But it falleth out with me as with the young wrestler that came to the games of Olympia, who, having taken a foil,[4] thought scorn to leave till he had received a fall; or him that being pricked in the finger with a bramble, thrusteth his whole arm among the thorns for anger. For I, seeing myself not able to stand on the ice, did nevertheless adventure to run; and being with my first book stricken into disgrace, could not cease until I was brought into contempt by the second—wherein I resemble those that having once wet their feet care not how deep they wade. In the which my wading, Right Honourable, if the envious shall clap lead to my heels to make me sink, yet if your Lordship with your little finger do but hold me up by the chin I shall swim, and be so far from being drowned that I shall scarce be ducked.

When Bucephalus was painted, Apelles craved the judgement of none but Zeuxis;[5] when Jupiter was carved, Prisius asked the censure of none but Lysippus;[6] now Euphues is shadowed, only I appeal to your Honour, not meaning thereby to be careless what others think, but knowing that if your Lordship allow[7] it there is none but will like it, and if there be any so nice[8] whom nothing can please, if he will not commend it, let him

---

1 *I will not . . . cast up*] I am willing to admit my indebtedness to others. Literally: I am one of those represented by painters as going to ingest that which Homer has regurgitated into his bowl.
2 *water bough*] side shoot
3 *as the crane doth . . . mouth*] Cranes were reputed to stand guard with a stone in their claws in order to be wakened by the sound of it falling if they dropped asleep. In flight, by contrast, they carried stones in their beaks to ensure their silence, for fear their cries would attract eagles (see Bond, II, p. 488, and Croll and Clemons, p. 195n.).
4 *taken a foil*] received a repulse
5 *When Bucephalus . . . Zeuxis*] Apelles (see p. 27n.) sought the opinion of no one but Zeuxis (outstanding Greek painter fl. 424–400 BC) when he painted the war horse of Alexander
6 *when Jupiter . . . Lysippus*] Prisius (of whom nothing is known) sought the judgement of no one but Lysippus (outstanding Greek sculptor, particularly favoured by Alexander) when he carved the chief of the gods
7 *allow*] approve
8 *nice*] over-particular

amend it. And here, Right Honourable, although the history seem unperfect, I hope your Lordship will pardon it.

Apelles died not before he could finish Venus, but before he durst; Nicomachus left Tyndarides rawly for fear of anger, not for want of art; Timomachus[1] broke off Medea scarce half-coloured, not that he was not willing to end it, but that he was threatened. I have not made Euphues to stand without legs for that I want matter to make them, but might to maintain them; so that I am enforced with the old painters to colour my picture but to the middle, or as he that drew Cyclops, who in a little table[2] made him to lie behind an oak, where one might perceive but a piece yet conceive that all the rest lay behind the tree; or as he that painted an horse in the river with half legs, leaving the pasterns for the viewer to imagine as in the water. For he that vieweth Euphues will say that he is drawn but to the waist, that he peepeth as it were behind some screen, that his feet are yet in the water; which maketh me present your Lordship with the mangled body of Hector as it appeared to Andromache,[3] and with half a face as the painter did him that had but one eye,[4] for I am compelled to draw a hose on before I can finish the leg, and instead of a foot to set down a shoe. So that whereas I had thought to show the cunning of a chirurgeon by mine anatomy[5] with a knife, I must play the tailor on the shop-board with a pair of shears. But whether Euphues limp with Vulcan as born lame, or go on stilts with Amphionax[6] for lack of legs, I trust I may say that his feet should have been old Helena;[7] for the poor fisherman that was warned he should not fish did yet at his door make nets, and the old vintner of Venice that was forbidden to sell wine did notwithstanding hang out an ivy-bush.[8]

This pamphlet, Right Honourable, containing the estate[9] of England, I know none more fit to defend it than one of the nobility of England, nor

---

1 *Apelles / Nicomachus / Timomachus*] all celebrated classical artists. Apelles (see p. 27n.) was at work on a portrait of Venus at his death. Nicomachus, a Theban (fl. 360 BC) was noted for the perfection of his work (hence the uncharacteristic nature of leaving a painting 'rawly'), Timomachus (of Byzantium) sold his painting of Medea to Julius Caesar. There is no historical evidence that any of them feared to complete their works.
2 *Cyclops / table*] Polyphemus, chief of a race of giants, each of whom had only one eye / design
3 *the mangled . . . Andromache*] Andromache, wife of Hector (see p. 33n.), foresaw his death and mutilation in a dream.
4 *the painter . . . eye*] Apelles drew King Antigonus (one of Alexander's generals) with his head averted, to avoid representing his blind eye.
5 *chirurgeon / anatomy*] surgeon / dissection
6 *Vulcan / Amphionax*] see p. 27n. / No such figure has been traced.
7 *old Helena*] beyond compare
8 *Apelles . . . ivy-bush*] The purport of this paragraph is that Lyly was deterred by the hostile reception of his work from speaking as plainly as he wished. The precise circumstances, however, remain unclear. For *ivy-bush* see p. 29n.
9 *estate*] condition

any of the nobility more ancient or more honourable than your Lordship. Besides that, describing the condition of the English court and the majesty of our dread sovereign, I could not find one more noble in court than your Honour, who is, or should be, under Her Majesty, chiefest in court, by birth born to the greatest office,[1] and therefore methought by right to be placed in great authority. For whoso compareth the honour of your Lordship's noble house with the fidelity of your ancestors may well say, which no other can truly gainsay, 'Vero nihil verius.'[2] So that I commit the end of all my pains unto your most honourable protection, assuring myself that the little cock-boat is safe when it is hoised[3] into a tall ship, that the cat dare not fetch the mouse out of the lion's den, that Euphues shall be without danger by your Lordship's patronage; otherwise I cannot see where I might find succour in any noble personage.

Thus, praying continually for the increase of your Lordship's honour, with all other things that either you would wish or God will grant, I end.

Your Lordship's most dutifully to command.
John Lyly.

---

1 *by birth . . . greatest office*] Oxford held the hereditary office of Lord Great Chamberlain.

2 *Vero nihil verius*] Nothing truer than the truth (with a pun on de Vere), the motto of the de Vere family

3 *cock-boat / hoised*] light craft towed behind a coasting vessel / raised by ropes (nautical)

Arachne[1] having woven in cloth of Arras[2] a rainbow of sundry silks, it was objected unto her by a lady, more captious than cunning,[3] that in her work there wanted some colours; for that in a rainbow there should be all. Unto whom she replied, 'If the colours lack thou lookest for, thou must imagine that they are on the other side of the cloth; for in the sky we can discern but one side of the rainbow, and what colours are in the other, see we cannot, guess we may.'

In the like manner, Ladies and Gentlewomen, am I to shape an answer in the behalf of Euphues, who, framing divers questions and quirks of love, if by some, more curious than needeth, it shall be told him that some sleights are wanting, I must say they are noted on the backside of the book. When Venus is painted we cannot see her back but her face; so that all other things that are to be recounted in love, Euphues thinketh them to hang at Venus' back in a budget,[4] which because he cannot see, he will not set down.

These discourses I have not clapped[5] in a cluster, thinking with myself that ladies had rather be sprinkled with sweet water than washed; so that I have sowed them here and there like strawberries, not in heaps like hops, knowing that you take more delight to gather flowers one by one in a garden than to snatch them by handfuls from a garland.

It resteth,[6] Ladies, that you take the pains to read it, but at such times as you spend in playing with your little dogs; and yet will I not pinch you of that pastime, for I am content that your dogs lie in your laps, so Euphues may be in your hands, that when you shall be weary in reading of the one you may be ready to sport with the other. Or handle him as you do your junkets,[7] that when you can eat no more you tie some in your napkin for children; for if you be filled with the first part, put the

---

1 *Arachne*] Lydian maiden whose skill in weaving was so great she challenged Athena to a contest. The goddess, enraged by the flawlessness of her work, destroyed it and changed the despairing Arachne into a spider. No source has been found for the story Lyly relates.
2 *cloth of Arras*] a tapestry
3 *more captious than cunning*] more critical than knowledgeable
4 *budget*] pouch, bag
5 *clapt*] brought together
6 *resteth*] remains
7 *junkets*] sweetmeats

second in your pocket for your waiting maids. Euphues had rather lie shut in a lady's casket than open in a scholar's study.

Yet after dinner you may overlook him to keep you from sleep, or if you be heavy[1] to bring you asleep; for to work upon a full stomach is against physic, and therefore better it were to hold Euphues in your hands, though you let him fall when you be willing to wink, than to sew in a clout[2] and prick your fingers when you begin to nod.

Whatsoever he hath written it is not to flatter, for he never reaped any reward by your sex but repentance; neither can it be to mock you, for he never knew anything by your sex but righteousness.

But I fear no anger for saying well when there is none but thinketh she deserveth better. She that hath no glass to dress her head[3] will use a bowl of water, she that wanteth a sleek-stone[4] to smooth her linen will take a pebble, the country dame girdeth herself as strait in the waist with a coarse caddis[5] as the madam of the court with a silk riband; so that seeing everyone so willing to be pranked,[6] I could not think anyone unwilling to be praised.

One hand washeth another, but they both wash the face; one foot goeth by another, but they both carry the body; Euphues and Philautus praise one another, but they both extol women. Therefore in my mind you are more beholding to gentlemen that make the colours than to the painters that draw your counterfeits,[7] for that Apelles' cunning is nothing if he paint with water, and the beauty of women not much if they go unpraised.

If you think this love dreamed, not done, yet methinketh you may as well like that love which is penned and not practised as that flower that is wrought with the needle and groweth not by nature; the one you wear in your heads for the fair sight, though it have no savour, the other you may read for to pass the time, though it bring small pastime. You choose cloth that will wear whitest, not that will last longest, colours that look freshest, not that endure soundest, and I would you would read books that have more show of pleasure than ground of profit. Then should Euphues be as often in your hands, being but a toy, as lawn[8] on your heads, being but trash; the one will be scarce liked after once reading, and the other is worn out after the first washing.

There is nothing lighter than a feather, yet is it set aloft in a woman's hat, nothing slighter than hair, yet is it most frizzled in a lady's head; so that I am in good hope, though there be nothing of less account than

---

1 *heavy*] drowsy
2 *clout*] cloth
3 *dress her head*] do her hair
4 *wanteth a sleek-stone*] lacks a polishing-stone
5 *girdeth herself as strait / coarse caddis*] binds herself as tightly / worsted binding
6 *pranked*] dressed up
7 *counterfeits*] pictures
8 *lawn*] fine linen

Euphues, yet he shall be marked with ladies' eyes and liked sometimes in their ears. For this I have diligently observed, that there shall be nothing found that may offend the chaste mind with unseemly terms or uncleanly talk.

Then, Ladies, I commit myself to your courtesies, craving this only, that having read you conceal your censure, writing your judgements as you do the posies in your rings, which are always next to the finger, not to be seen of him that holdeth you by the hands, and yet known to you that wear them on your hands. If you be wrung,[1] which cannot be done without wrong, it were better to cut the shoe than burn the last.[2] If a tailor make your gown too little, you cover his fault with a broad stomacher,[3] if too great, with a number of plights,[4] if too short, with a fair guard,[5] if too long, with a false gathering. My trust is you will deal in the like manner with Euphues, that if he have not fed your humour, yet you will excuse him more than the tailor; for could Euphues take the measure of a woman's mind as the tailor doth of her body, he would go as near to fit them for a fancy as the other doth for a fashion. He that weighs wind must have a steady hand to hold the balance, and he that searcheth a woman's thoughts must have his own stayed.[6]

But lest I make my epistle, as you do your new-found bracelets, endless, I will frame it like a bullet, which is no sooner in the mould but it is made; committing your Ladyships to the Almighty, who grant you all you would have and should have, so your wishes stand with His will.

And so humbly I bid you farewell.
Your Ladyships' to command,
John Lyly.

---

1 *be wrung*] are pinched. The pun is more pointed in the copy-text, which reads 'wrong'.
2 *last*] wooden mould on which a shoe is constructed
3 *stomacher*] garment (often embroidered) worn under the lacing of the bodice
4 *plights*] pleats
5 *guard*] ornamental border, hem
6 *stayed*] fixed

Gentlemen, Euphues is come at the length, though too late;[1] for whose absence I hope three bad excuses shall stand instead of one good reason. First, in his travel you must think he loitered, tarrying many a month in Italy viewing the ladies in a painter's shop, when he should have been on the seas in a merchant's ship; not unlike unto an idle housewife who is catching of flies when she should sweep down cobwebs. Second, being a great start[2] from Athens to England, he thought to stay for the advantage of a leap-year; and had not this year[3] leaped with him, I think he had not yet leaped hither. Thirdly, being arrived, he was as long in viewing of London as he was in coming to it; not far differing from gentlewomen, who are longer a-dressing their heads than their whole bodies.

But now he is come, Gentlemen, my request is only to bid him welcome; for divers there are, not that they mislike the matter but that they hate the man, that will not stick to tear Euphues because they do envy[4] Lyly. Wherein they resemble angry dogs, which bite the stone not him that throweth it, or the choleric horse-rider who, being cast from a young colt, and not daring to kill the horse, went into the stable to cut the saddle.[5] These be they that thought Euphues to be drowned, and yet were never troubled with drying of his clothes; but they guessed as they wished, and I would it had happened as they desired.

They that loathe the fountain's head will never drink of the little brooks; they that seek to poison the fish will never eat the spawn; they that like not me will not allow[6] anything that is mine. But as the serpent porphirius, though he be full of poison, yet having no teeth, hurteth none but himself, so the envious, though they swell with malice till they burst, yet having no teeth to bite, I have no cause to fear.

Only my suit is to you, Gentlemen, that if anything be amiss, you pardon it; if well, you defend it; and howsoever it be, you accept it. Faults escaped in the printing, correct with your pens; omitted by my negligence, overslip with patience; committed by ignorance, remit with favour.

---

1 *at length . . . late*] Though the imminent publication of *Euphues and His England* was announced in 1578, the book did not appear until 1580 (see Introduction, p. 2)

2 *start*] leap

3 *this year*] 1580 (the date of the book's publication)

4 *do envy*] bear malice to

5 *But now . . . saddle*] The inference here and in the following paragraph is that *Euphues* was attacked because of hostility to the author, whereas the address 'To My Very Good Friends the Gentlemen Scholars of Oxford' (pp. 151–2) suggests that it was the work itself that occasioned offence.

6 *allow*] approve

If in every part it seem not alike, you know that it is not for him that fashioneth the shoe to make the grain of the leather. The old hermit will have his talk savour of his cell; the old courtier,[1] his love taste of Saturn; yet the last lover may haply come somewhat near Jupiter.[2] Lovers when they come into a garden, some gather nettles, some roses, one thyme, another sage, and everyone that for his lady's favour that she favoureth; insomuch as there is no weed almost but it is worn. If you, Gentlemen, do the like in reading, I shall be sure all my discourses shall be regarded, some for the smell, some for the smart, all for a kind of a loving smack.[3] Let everyone follow his fancy and say that is best which he liketh best.

And so I commit every man's delight to his own choice, and myself to all your courtesies.

Yours to use,
John Lyly.

---

1 *the old hermit / the old courtier*] Cassander (see pp. 171ff.) / Fidus (see pp. 185ff.)
2 *Saturn / Jupiter*] deity inducing leaden spirits / deity inducing feelings of joy
3 *loving smack*] taste of love

Euphues, having gotten all things necessary for his voyage into England, accompanied only with Philautus, took shipping the first of December, 1579, by our English computation.[1] Who, as one resolved to see that with his eyes which he had oftentimes heard with his ears, began to use this persuasion to his friend Philautus, as well to counsel him how he should behave himself in England, as to comfort him being now on the seas:

'As I have found thee willing to be a fellow in my travel, so would I have thee ready to be a follower of my counsel; in the one shalt thou show thy good will, in the other manifest thy wisdom. We are now sailing into an island of small compass, as I guess by their maps, but of great civility, as I hear by their manners; which, if it be so, behoveth us to be more inquisitive of their conditions[2] than of their country, and more careful to mark the natures of their men than curious to note the situation of the place. And surely methinketh we cannot better bestow our time on the sea than in advice how to behave ourselves when we come to the shore; for greater danger is there to arrive in a strange country where the inhabitants be politic,[3] than to be tossed with the troublesome waves where the mariners be unskilful. Fortune guideth men in the rough sea, but wisdom ruleth them in a strange land.

'If travellers in this our age were as wary of their conditions[4] as they be venturous of their bodies, or as willing to reap profit by their pains as they are to endure peril for their pleasure, they would either prefer their own soil before a strange land, or good counsel before their own conceit. But as the young scholar in Athens went to hear Demosthenes' eloquence at Corinth and was entangled with Lais' beauty,[5] so most of our travellers which pretend to get a smack of strange language to sharpen their wits are infected with vanity by following their wills. Danger and delight grow both upon one stalk, the rose and the canker in one bud, white and black are commonly in one border. Seeing then, my good Philautus, that we are not to conquer wild beasts by fight, but to confer with wise men by policy, we ought to take greater heed that we be not entrapped in folly than fear to be subdued by force.

'And here, by the way, it shall not be amiss, as well to drive away the tediousness of time as to delight ourselves with talk, to rehearse an old

---

1 *by our English computation*] i.e. by the Julian rather than the Gregorian calendar
2 *conditions*] characters
3 *politic*] discerning, socially adroit
4 *wary of their conditions*] concerned about their dispositions
5 *Demosthenes / Lais*] see p. 108n. / see p. 83n. Their anachronistic association does not originate with Lyly but is found in Painter's *Palace of Pleasure* (1566).

EUPHUES AND HIS ENGLAND   167

treatise of an ancient hermit, who, meeting with a pilgrim at his cell, uttered a strange and delightful tale; which if thou, Philautus, art disposed to hear, and these present attentive to have, I will spend some time about it, knowing it both fit for us that be travellers to learn wit, and not unfit for these that be merchants to get wealth.'

Philautus, although the stumps of love so sticked in his mind that he rather wished to hear an elegy in Ovid than a tale of an hermit, yet was he willing to lend his ear to his friend, who[1] had left his heart with his lady. For you shall understand that Philautus, having read the 'Cooling Card' which Euphues sent him, sought rather to answer it than allow it.[2] And I doubt not but if Philautus fall into his old vein in England, you shall hear of his new device in Italy.[3] And although some shall think it impertinent to the history, they shall not find it repugnant, no more than in one nosegay to set two flowers or in one counterfeit two colours, which bringeth more delight than disliking.

Philautus answered Euphues in this manner:

'My good Euphues, I am as willing to hear thy tale as I am to be partaker of thy travel. Yet I know not how it cometh to pass that my eyes are either heavy against foul weather, or my head so drowsy against[4] some ill news, that this tale shall come in good time to bring me asleep; and then shall I get no harm by the hermit, though I get no good.'

The other that were then in the ship flocked about Euphues, who began in this manner:

There dwelt sometimes in the island Scyros[5] an ancient gentleman called Cassander, who, as well by his being a long gatherer[6] as his trade being a lewd usurer, waxed so wealthy that he was thought to have almost all the money in that country in his own coffers; being both aged and sickly, found such weakness in himself that he thought nature would yield to death and physic to his diseases. This gentleman had one only son who nothing resembled the father either in fancy or favour, which the old man perceiving, dissembled with him both in nature and honesty; whom he caused to be called unto his bedside and, the chamber being voided, he brake with him[7] in these terms:

'Callimachus,' (for so was he called) 'thou art too young to die, and I too old to live. Yet as nature must of necessity pay her debt to death, so must she also show her devotion to thee, whom I alive had to be the comfort of mine age, and whom alone I must leave behind me for to be the only maintainer of all mine honour. If thou couldst as well conceive the care of a father as I can level at the nature of a child, or were I as able to utter my affection

---

1 *who*] referring back to 'he', i.e. Philautus
2 *answer it than allow it*] quarrel with it than agree with it
3 *his new device in Italy*] i.e. his amorous adventures following those recounted in *The Anatomy of Wit*
4 *heavy against / drowsy against*] sleepy in expectation of
5 *Scyros*] an island in the Aegean sea
6 *long gatherer*] a thrifty man over many years
7 *brake with him*] revealed his thoughts to him

towards a son as thou oughtst to show thy duty to thy sire, then wouldst thou
desire my life to enjoy my counsel and I should correct thy life to amend thy
conditions;[1] yet so tempered as neither rigour might detract anything from
affection in me, or fear any whit from thee in duty. But seeing myself so feeble
that I cannot live to be thy guide, I am resolved to give thee such counsel as
may do thee good; wherein I shall show my care and discharge my duty.

'My good son, thou art to receive by my death wealth, and by my counsel
wisdom; and I would thou wert as willing to imprint the one in thy heart, as
thou wilt be ready to bear the other in thy purse. To be rich is the gift of
fortune, to be wise the grace of God. Have more mind on thy books than my
bags, more desire of godliness than gold, greater affection[2] to die well than
to live wantonly.

'But as the cypress-tree the more it is watered the more it withereth, and
the oftener it is lopped the sooner it dieth, so unbridled youth the more it is
also by grave advice counselled or due correction controlled[3] the sooner it
falleth to confusion, hating all reasons that would bring it from folly, as that
tree doth all remedies that should make it fertile.

'Alas, Callimachus, when wealth cometh into the hands of youth before
they can use it, then fall they to all disorder that may be, tedding[4] that with
a fork in one year which was not gathered together with a rake in twenty.

'But why discourse I with thee of worldly affairs, being myself going to
heaven? Here, Callimachus, take the key of yonder great barred chest, where
thou shalt find such store of wealth that if thou use it with discretion thou
shalt become the only rich man of the world.'

Thus turning him on his left side,[5] with a deep sigh and pitiful groan, gave
up the ghost.

Callimachus, having more mind to look to the lock than for a shrouding
sheet, the breath being scarce out of his father's mouth, and his body yet
panting with heat, opened the chest; where he found nothing but a letter,
written very fair, sealed up with his signet of arms,[6] with this superscription:
In finding nothing, thou shalt gain all things. Callimachus, although he were
abashed at sight of the empty chest, yet hoping this letter would direct him
to the golden mine, he boldly opened it. The contents whereof follow in these
terms:

> Wisdom is great wealth. Sparing is good getting.[7] Thrift consisteth not
> in gold but grace. It is better to die without money than to live without
> modesty. Put no more clothes on thy back than will expel cold, neither any
> more meat in thy belly than may quench hunger. Use not change in attire,
> nor variety in thy diet; the one bringeth pride, the other surfeits. Each vain,
> void of piety; both costly, wide of profit.

---

1 *conditions*] habits
2 *affection*] inclination
3 *controlled*] rebuked
4 *tedding*] spreading (specifically new-mown hay for drying in the sun)
5 *turning him ... side*] a sign of approaching death (the left being the weaker side of
   the body)
6 *signet of arms*] seal set in a ring, engraved with a coat of arms
7 *Sparing is good getting*] Frugality is a prime means of acquisition

Go to bed with the lamb and rise with the lark. Late watching in the night breedeth unquiet, and long sleeping in the day ungodliness. Fly both; this as unwholesome, that as unhonest.

Enter not into bands;[1] no, not for thy best friends. He that payeth another man's debt seeketh his own decay. It is as rare to see a rich surety as a black swan; and he that lendeth to all that will borrow showeth great goodwill but little wit. Lend not a penny without a pawn, for that will be a good gage[2] to borrow.

Be not hasty to marry. It is better to have one plough going than two cradles; and more profit to have a barn filled than a bed. But if thou canst not live chastely, choose such an one as may be more commended for humility than beauty. A good housewife is a great patrimony;[3] and she is most honourable that is most honest.

If thou desire to be old, beware of too much wine; if to be healthy, take heed of many women; if to be rich, shun playing at all games. Long quaffing maketh a short life; fond lust causeth dry bones; and lewd pastimes naked purses. Let the cook be thy physician and the shambles thy apothecary's shop.[4] He that for every qualm will take a receipt,[5] and cannot make two meals unless Galen be his God's good,[6] shall be sure to make the physician rich and himself a beggar; his body will never be without diseases, and his purse ever without money.

Be not too lavish in giving alms. The charity of this country is, 'God help thee,' and the courtesy, 'I have the best wine in town for you.'[7]

Live in the country, not in the court, where neither grass will grow nor moss[8] cleave to thy heels.

Thus hast thou, if thou canst use it, the whole wealth of the world, and he that cannot follow good counsel never can get commodity. I leave thee more than my father left me. For he dying gave me great wealth without care how I might keep it; and I give thee good counsel, with all means how to get riches. And no doubt whatso is gotten with wit will be kept with wariness and increased with wisdom.

God bless thee, and I bless thee; and as I tender thy safety, so God deal with my soul.

Callimachus was stricken into such a maze at this his father's last will that he had almost lost his former wit. And being in an extreme rage, renting[9] his clothes and tearing his hair, began to utter these words:

---

1 *bands*] bonds, binding agreements on behalf of others
2 *gage*] security
3 *patrimony*] inheritance
4 *Let the cook ... shop*] Let properly cooked food and fresh meat obviate the need for a doctor or medicines (*shambles* = meat market)
5 *receipt*] doctor's prescription
6 *Galen be his God's good*] a doctor is his yeast, i.e. makes his food digestible (with a possible pun on *God's good* = blessing)
7 *The charity ... for you*] Charity in this country consists in consigning the needy to the care of God, while no expense is spared between those of equal status
8 *moss*] pun (species of plant / money)
9 *renting*] rending

'Is this the nature of a father to deceive his son, or the part of crabbed age to delude credulous youth? Is the death-bed, which ought to be the end of devotion, become the beginning of deceit? Ah Cassander, friend I cannot term thee, seeing thee so unkind; and father I will not call thee, whom I find so unnatural. Whoso shall hear of this ungratefulness will rather lament thy dealing than thy death, and marvel that a man affected[1] outwardly with such great gravity should inwardly be infected with so great guile. Shall I then show the duty of a child when thou hast forgotten the nature of a father? No, no! For as the torch turned downward is extinguished with the self-same wax which was the cause of his light, so nature turned to unkindness[2] is quenched by those means it should be kindled, leaving no branch of love where it found no root of humanity.

'Thou hast carried to thy grave more grey hairs than years, and yet more years than virtues. Couldst thou, under the image of so precise holiness, harbour the express[3] pattern of barbarous cruelty? I see now that as the canker soonest entereth into the white rose, so corruption doth easiliest creep into the white head. Would Callimachus could as well digest thy malice with patience as thou didst disguise it with craft; or would I might either bury my care with thy carcass, or that thou hadst ended thy defame with thy death. But as the herb moly hath a flower as white as snow and a root as black as ink, so age hath a white head, showing piety, but a black heart swelling with mischief; whereby I see that old men are not unlike unto old trees, whose barks seemeth to be sound when their bodies are rotten.

'I will mourn not that thou art now dead, but because thou hast lived so long; neither do I weep to see thee without breath, but to find thee without money.

'Instead of coin thou hast left me counsel. O politic old man! Didst thou learn by experience that an edge[4] can be anything worth if it have nothing to cut, or that miners could work without metals, or wisdom thrive without where-with? What availeth it to be a cunning lapidary[5] and have no stones, or a skilful pilot and have no ship, or a thrifty man and have no money? Wisdom hath no mint; counsel is no coiner. He that in these days seeketh to get wealth by wit without friends, is like unto him that thinketh to buy meat in the market for honesty without money; which thriveth on either side so well that the one hath a witty head and an empty purse, the other a godly mind and an empty belly.

'Yea, such a world it is that gods can do nothing without gold, and who of more might? Nor princes anything without gifts, and who of more majesty? Nor philosophers anything without gilt, and who of more wisdom? For as among the Egyptians there was no man esteemed happy that had not a beast full of spots,[6] so amongst us there is none accounted wise that hath not a

---

1 *affected*] possessed, seized (with medical implications, cf. *infected* in the same sentence)
2 *unkindness*] unnaturalness
3 *express*] exact
4 *edge*] sharp instrument
5 *lapidary*] worker in precious stones
6 *beast full of spots*] an Apis (sacred bull with markings on the face and chest, worshipped by the Egyptians)

purse full of gold. And hadst thou not loved money so well, thou wouldst never have lived so warily and died so wickedly; who, either burying thy treasure dost hope to meet it in hell, or borrowing it of the devil hast rendered him the whole, the interest whereof, I fear me, cometh to no less than the price of thy soul.

'But whither art thou carried, Callimachus? Rage can neither reduce[1] thy father's life nor recover his treasure. Let it suffice thee that he was unkind and thou unfortunate, that he is dead and heareth thee not, that thou art alive and profitest nothing.

'But what did my father think? That too much wealth would make me proud, and feared not too great misery would make me desperate—?'

Whilst he was beginning afresh to renew his complaints and revile his parents, his kinsfolk assembled, who caused him to bridle his lavish tongue, although they marvelled at his piteous tale; for it was well known to them all that Cassander had more money than half the country and loved Callimachus better than his own self.

Callimachus by the importunity of his allies repressed his rage, setting order for all things requisite for his father's funerals; who being brought with due reverence unto the grave, he returned home, making a short inventory to his father's long will. And having made ready money of such movables as were in his house, put both them and his house into his purse,[2] resolving now with himself in this extremity either with the hazard of his labour to gain wealth, or by misfortune to seek death, accounting it great shame to live without travel as grief to be left without treasure. And although he were earnestly entreated, as well by good proffers of gentle persuasions, to wean himself from so desolate (or rather desperate) life, he would not hearken either to his own commodities[3] or their counsels. 'For seeing,' said he, 'I am left heir to all the world, I mean to execute my authority and claim my lands in all places of the world. Who now so rich as Callimachus, who had as many revenues everywhere as in his own country!'

Thus, being in a readiness to depart, apparelled in all colours as one fit for all companies and willing to see all countries, journeyed three or four days very devoutly like a pilgrim. Who, straying out of his pathway and somewhat weary (not used to such day labours), rested himself upon the side of a silver stream, even almost in the grisping[4] of the evening; where, thinking to steal a nap, began to close his eyes.

As he was thus between slumbering and waking, he heard one cough piteously, which caused him to start; and seeing no creature, he searched diligently in every bush and under every shrub. At the last he lighted on a little cave where, thrusting in his head (more bold than wise), he espied an old man clad all in grey, with a head as white as alabaster, his hoary beard hanging down well near to his knees; with him no earthly creature saving only a mouse sleeping in a cat's ear. Over the fire this good old man sat, leaning his head to look into a little earthen vessel which stood by him. Callimachus, delighted

---

1 *reduce*] bring back
2 *put both them . . . purse*] sold up his property
3 *commodities*] interests
4 *grisping*] twilight

more than abashed at this strange sight, thought to see the manner of his host
before he would be his guest.

This old man immediately took out of his pot certain roots on the which
he fed hungerly, having no other drink than fair water. But that which was
most of all to be considered and noted, the mouse and the cat fell to their
victuals, being such relics[1] as the old man had left; yea, and that so lovingly
as one would have thought them both married, judging the mouse to be very
wild, or the cat very tame.

Callimachus could not refrain laughter to behold the solemn feast, at the
voice whereof the old man arose and demanded who was there. Unto whom
Callimachus answered:

'Father, one that wisheth thee both greater cheer and better servants.'

Unto whom he replied, shoring up his eyes:

'By Jis,[2] son, I account the cheer good, which maintaineth health, and the
servants honest, whom I find faithful. And if thou neither think scorn of my
company nor my cell, enter and welcome.'

The which offer Callimachus accepted with great thanks, who thought his
lodging would be better than his supper.

The next morning, the old man being very inquisitive of Callimachus what
he was, where he dwelt, and whither he would,[3] Callimachus discoursed with
him in particulars as before, touching his father's death and despite; against
whom he uttered so many bitter and burning words as the old hermit's ears
glowed to hear them, and my tongue would blister if I should utter them.
Moreover, he added that he was determined to seek adventures in strange
lands, and either to fetch the golden fleece[4] by travel or sustain the force of
fortune by his own wilful folly.

Now, Philautus, thou shalt understand that this old hermit, which was
named also Cassander, was brother to Callimachus' father and uncle to
Callimachus; unto whom Cassander had before his death conveyed the sum
of ten thousand pounds to the use of his son in his most extremity and necessity, knowing, or at the least foreseeing, that his young colt will never bear a
white mouth without a hard bridle.[5] Also he assured himself that his brother
so little tendered[6] money, being a professed hermit, and so much tendered and
esteemed Callimachus, being his near kinsman, as he put no doubt to stand
to his devotion.[7]

Cassander, this old hermit, hearing it to be Callimachus his nephew and
understanding of the death of his brother, dissembled his grief, although he
were glad to see things happen out so well, and determined with himself to
make a cozen[8] of his young nephew until he had bought wit with the price

---

1 *relics*] scraps
2 *By Jis*] contracted form of 'By Jesus'
3 *whither he would*] where he was going
4 *golden fleece*] some wonder of inestimable value (originally the prize achieved by
  Jason and the Argonauts)
5 *never bear . . . bridle*] would never become docile without harsh treatment
6 *tendered*] cared about
7 *put no doubt . . . . devotion*] did not hestitate to rely on his trustworthiness
8 *cozen*] pun (kinsman / dupe)

of woe; wherefore he assayed first to stay him from travel and to take some other course more fit for a gentleman.

'And to the intent,' said he, 'that I may persuade thee, give ear unto my tale.'

And this is the tale, Philautus, that I promised thee, which the hermit, sitting now in the sun, began to utter to Callimachus.

'When I was young as thou now art, I never thought to be old as now I am, which caused lusty blood to attempt those things in youth which aching bones have repented in age. I had one only brother, which also bore my name, being both born at one time as twins; but so far disagreeing in nature as had not as well the respect of the just time, as also the certainty and assurance of our mother's fidelity, persuaded the world we had one father, it would very hardly have been thought that such contrary dispositions could well have been bred in one womb, or issued from one's loins. Yet as out of one and the self-same root cometh as well the wild olive as the sweet, and as the palm Persian fig-tree[1] beareth as well apples as figs, so our mother thrust into the world at one time the blossom of gravity and lightness.

'We were nursed both with one teat, where my brother sucked a desire of thrift, and I of theft; which evidently showeth that as the breath of the lion engendereth as well the serpent as the ant, and as the self-same dew forceth the earth to yield both the darnel[2] and wheat, or as the easterly wind maketh the blossoms to blast and the buds to blow, so one womb nourished contrary wits, and one milk divers manners—which argueth something in nature, I know not what, to be marvellous, I dare not say monstrous.

'As we grew old in years, so began we to be more opposite in opinions. He grave, I gamesome; he studious, I careless; he without mirth, and I without modesty. And verily, had we resembled each other as little in favour[3] as we did in fancy, or disagreed as much in shape as we did in sense, I know not what Daedalus[4] would have made a labyrinth for such monsters, or what Apelles could have coloured such misshapes. But as the painter Timanthes could no way express the grief of Agamemnon, who saw his only daughter sacrificed, and therefore drew him with a veil over his face, whereby one might better conceive his anguish than he colour it, so some Timanthes,[5] seeing us, would be constrained with a curtain to shadow that deformity which no counterfeit could portray lively.

'But nature recompensed the dissimilitude of minds with a sympathy of bodies, for we were in all parts one so like the other that it was hard to distinguish, either in speech, countenance, or height, one from the other; saving that either carried the motion of his mind in his manners, and that the affects of the heart were bewrayed by the eyes, which made us known manifestly.

---

1 *palm Persian fig-tree*] The word *palm* here appears to be superflous, and may be an error Lyly intended to delete. It is not corrected, however, in later editions.
2 *darnel*] weed commonly found in wheat fields
3 *favour*] appearance
4 *Daedalus*] legendary craftsman of supreme skill who constructed the labyrinth where the Minotaur was kept (see p. 83n.)
5 *Timanthes*] celebrated Greek painter (fl. 400 BC). The picture of the sacrifice of Iphigenia alluded to here was his masterpiece.

For as two rubies be they never so like, yet if they be brought together one staineth[1] the other, so we being close one to the other, it was easy to imagine by the face whose virtue deserved most favour; for I could never see my brother but his gravity would make me blush, which caused me to resemble the thrush who never singeth in the company of the nightingale. For whilst my brother was in presence, I durst not presume to talk, lest his wisdom might have checked my wildness; much like to Roscius, who was always dumb when he dined with Cato.[2]

'Our father, being on his death-bed, knew not whom to ordain his heir, being both of one age. To make both would breed, as he thought, unquiet; to appoint but one were, as he knew, injury; to divide equally were to have no heir; to impart more to one than to the other were partiality; to disherit me of his wealth, whom nature had disherited of wisdom, were against reason; to bar my brother from gold, whom God seemed to endue with grace, were flat impiety. Yet, calling us before him, he uttered, with watery eyes, these words: "Were it not, my sons, that nature worketh more in me than justice, I would disherit the one of you who promiseth by his folly to spend all, and leave the other nothing whose wisdom seemeth to purchase all things. But I well know that a bitter root is amended with a sweet graft, and crooked trees prove good cammocks,[3] and wild grapes make pleasant wine. Which persuadeth me that thou—" pointing to me, "wilt in age repent thy youthly affections[4] and learn to die as well as thou hast lived wantonly. As for thee–" laying his hand on my brother's head, "although I see more than commonly in any of thy years, yet knowing that those that give themselves to be bookish are oftentimes so blockish that they forget thrift (whereby the old saw is verified that the greatest clerks are not the wisest men, who dig still at the root while others gather the fruit), I am determined to help thee forward, lest having nothing thou desire nothing, and so be accounted as nobody."

'He, having thus said, called for two bags, the one full of gold, the other stuffed with writings; and casting them both unto us, said this: "There, my sons, divide all as between you it shall be best agreed," and so rendered up his ghost with a pitiful groan.

'My brother, as one that knew his own good and my humour, gave me leave to choose which bag I liked. At the choice I made no great curiosity, but snatching the gold let go the writings, which were, as I knew, evidences for land,[5] obligations for debt, too heavy for me to carry, who determined (as now thou dost, Callimachus) to seek adventures.

'My purse now swelling with a tympany,[6] I thought to search all countries for a remedy, and sent many gold angels[7] into every quarter of the world, which never brought news again to their master, being either soared into heaven where I cannot fetch them, or sunk into hell for pride where I mean

---

1 *staineth*] exposes the inferiority of
2 *Roscius / Cato*] celebrated Roman comic actor (d. 62 BC) / Stoic philosopher noted for his rigid morality (b. 95 BC)
3 *cammocks*] shepherds' crooks (i.e. useful commodities in course of time)
4 *affections*] favoured pursuits, inclinations
5 *evidences for land*] title deeds
6 *swelling with a tympany*] swollen as if with dropsy
7 *angels*] pun (messengers: from Latin *angelus* / coins)

not to follow them. This life I continued the space of fourteen years, until I had visited and viewed every country and was a stranger in mine own; but finding no treasure to be wrapped in travel, I returned with more vices than I went forth with pence, yet with so good a grace as I was able to sin both by experience and authority, use framing me to the one and the countries to the other. There was no crime so barbarous, no murder so bloody, no oath so blasphemous, no vice so execrable, but that I could readily recite where I learned it, and by rote repeat the peculiar crime of every particular country, city, town, village, house, or chamber.

'If I met with one of Crete, I was ready to lie with him for the whetstone;[1] if with a Grecian, I could dissemble with Sinon. I could court it with the Italian, carouse it with the Dutchman. I learned all kind of poisons, yea, and such as were fit for the Pope's holiness. In Egypt I worshipped their spotted god at Memphis;[2] in Turkey their Mahomet; in Rome their Mass, which gave me not only a remission for my sins past without penance, but also a commission to sin ever after without prejudice. There was no fashion but fitted my back, no fancy but served my turn.

'But now my barrel of gold, which pride set abroach, love began to set a-tilt; which in short time ran so on the lees[3] that the devil danced in the bottom, where he found never a cross.[4] It were too tedious to utter my whole life in this my pilgrimage, the remembrance whereof doth nothing but double my repentance.

'Then to grow to an end, I, seeing my money wasted, my apparel worn, my mind infected with as many vices as my body with diseases, and my body with more maladies than the leopard hath marks, having nothing for amends[5] but a few broken languages, which served me in no more stead than to see one meat served in divers dishes, I thought it best to return into my native soil. Where, finding my brother as far now to exceed others in wealth as he did me in wit, and that he had gained more by thrift than I could spend by pride, I neither envied his estate nor pitied mine own, but opened[6] the whole course of my youth, not thinking thereby to recover that of him by request which I had lost myself by riot. For casting in my mind the misery of the world with the mischiefs of my life, I determined from that unto my life's end to lead a solitary life in this cave, which I have done the term of full forty winters; from whence neither the earnest entreaty of my brother, nor the vain pleasures of the world could draw me—neither shall anything but death.

'Then, my good Callimachus, record with thyself[7] the inconveniences that come by travelling, when on the seas every storm shall threaten death, and

---

1 *whetstone*] the proverbial prize for skill in lying. For the national characteristics of Cretans, Greeks, Italians and Dutchmen see pp. 34 and 110nn. For *Sinon* see p. 76n.
2 *spotted god at Memphis*] see p. 170n.
3 *set abroach / set a-tilt / on the lees*] first tapped / tilted up (to allow the contents to flow out / to the dregs
4 *found never a cross*] both 'found no impulse to good' and 'found no coins left' (many Renaissance coins had a cross on the reverse)
5 *for amends*] in recompense
6 *opened*] revealed
7 *record with thyself*] remember

every calm a danger; when either thou shalt be compelled to board others as a pirate, or fear to be boarded of others as a merchant; when at all times thou must have the back of an ass to bear all, and the snout of a swine to say nothing. Thy hand on thy cap to show reverence to every rascal, thy purse open to be prodigal to every boor, thy sword in thy sheath, not once daring either to strike or ward[1]—which maketh me think that travellers are not only framed not to commit injuries but also to take them.

'Learn, Callimachus, of the bird acanthis,[2] who being bred in the thistles will live in the thistles, and of the grasshopper, who being sprung of the grass will rather die than depart from the grass. I am of this mind with Homer, that as the snail that crept out of her shell was turned eftsoons into a toad and thereby was forced to make a stool to sit on, disdaining her own house,[3] so the traveller that straggleth[4] from his own country is in short time transformed into so monstrous a shape that he is fain to alter his mansion with his manners, and to live where he can, not where he would. What did Ulysses wish in the midst of his travelling but only to see the smoke of his own chimney?[5] Did not all the Romans say that he that wandered did nothing else but heap sorrows to his friends and shame to himself, and resembled those that seeking to light a link[6] quenched a lamp; imitating the barbarous Goths, who thought the roots in Alexandria sweeter than the raisins in Barbary?[7]

'But he that leaveth his own home is worthy no home. In my opinion it is a homely[8] kind of dealing to prefer the courtesy of those he never knew before the honesty of those among whom he was born. He that cannot live with a groat[9] in his own country shall never enjoy a penny in another nation. Little dost thou know, Callimachus, with what wood travellers are warmed, who must sleep with their eyes open lest they be slain in their beds, and wake with their eyes shut lest they be suspected by their looks, and eat with their mouths close lest they be poisoned with their meats. Where if they wax wealthy [they shall] be envied, not loved; if poor punished, not pitied; if wise, accounted espials;[10] if foolish, made drudges. Every gentleman will be [their] peer, though they be noble; and every peasant their lord, if they be gentle.[11] He, therefore, that leaveth his own house to seek adventures is like the quail that forsaketh the mallows to eat hemlock,[12] or the fly that shunneth the rose to light in a cow-shard.[13]

---

1 *ward*] defend yourself from a blow
2 *acanthis*] goldfinch
3 *Homer . . . house*] Bond notes that 'in reality these curious facts in natural history seem to have escaped Homer' (II, p. 494). *eftsoons* = soon afterwards
4 *straggleth*] strays
5 *Ulysses . . . chimney*] For Ulysses' travels see p. 57n.
6 *link*] torch used to light dark streets
7 *Barbary*] the lands held by the barbarians (not exclusively a region of North Africa)
8 *homely*] simple
9 *groat*] coin worth four pence in pre-decimalization English currency
10 *espials*] spies
11 *gentle*] gentlemen by birth
12 *mallows / hemlock*] varieties of plant, the second poisonous
13 *cow-shard*] cowpat (i.e. patch of cow dung)

'No, Callimachus. There will no moss stick to the stone of Sisyphus; no grass hang on the heels of Mercury;[1] no butter cleave on the bread of a traveller. For as the eagle at every flight loseth a feather, which maketh her bald in her age, so the traveller in every country loseth some fleece, which maketh him a beggar in his youth; buying that with a pound which he cannot sell again for a penny—repentance.

'But why go I about to dissuade thee from that which I myself followed, or to persuade thee to that which thou thyself fliest? My grey hairs are like unto a white frost, thy red blood not unlike unto a hot fire; so that it cannot be that either thou shouldst follow my counsel, or I allow thy conditions.[2] Such a quarrel hath there always been between the grave and the cradle, that he that is young thinketh the old man fond,[3] and the old knoweth the young man to be a fool. But, Callimachus, for the towardness I see in thee I must needs love thee, and for thy frowardness[4] of force counsel thee; and do in the same sort as Phoebus did that daring boy Phaethon.[5] Thou goest about a great matter, neither fit for thy years, being very young, nor thy profit, being left so poor. Thou desirest that which thou knowest not, neither can any perform that which thou seemest to promise. If thou covet to travel strange countries, search the maps; there shalt thou see much with great pleasure and small pains. If to be conversant in all courts, read histories, where thou shalt understand both what the men have been, and what their manners are; and methinketh there must be much delight when there is no danger. And if thou have any care either of the green bud which springeth out of the tender stalk, or the timely fruit which is to grow of so good a root, seek not to kill the one or hasten the other; but let time so work that grafts may be gathered off the tree rather than sticks to burn. And so I leave thee, not to thyself, but to Him that made thee; who guide thee with His grace, whether thou go as thou wouldst or tarry at home as thou shouldst.'

Callimachus, obstinate in his fond conceit,[6] was so far from being persuaded by this old hermit that he rather made it a greater occasion of his pilgrimage; and with an answer between scorning and reasoning, he replied thus:

'Father or friend (I know not very well how to term you), I have been as attentive to hear your good discourse as you were willing to utter it. Yet methinketh you deal marvellously with youth in seeking by sage counsel to put grey hairs on their chins before nature hath given them almost any hairs on their heads; wherein you have gone so far that, in my opinion, your labour had been better spent in travelling where you have not lived, than in talking where you cannot be believed.

---

1 *Sisyphus / Mercury*] King of Corinth, punished in the underworld for his wicked life by being obliged to roll a huge stone to the top of a hill from where it immediately rolled back again to the bottom / winged messenger of the gods noted for his swiftness

2 *allow thy conditions*] approve your behaviour

3 *fond*] foolish

4 *towardness / frowardness*] promise / perversity

5 *Phoebus . . . Phaethon*] Phaethon begged his father, Phoebus, to allow him to drive the chariot of the sun and was killed by Zeus with a flash of lightning when he lost control of the horses.

6 *fond conceit*] foolish fancy

'You have been a traveller and tasted nothing but sour; therefore whosoever travelleth shall eat of the same sauce! An argument it is that your fortune was ill, not that others' should be as bad; and a warning to make you wise, not a warning to prove others unfortunate. Shall a soldier that hath received a scar in the battle give out that all warriors shall be maimed; or the merchant that hath lost by the seas be a cause that no other should venture; or a traveller that hath sustained harm by sinister[1] fortune, or been infected by his own folly, dissuade all gentlemen to rest at their own home till they come to their long home? Why then, let all men abstain from wine because it made Alexander tipsy, let no man love a woman for that Tarquin was banished,[2] let not a wise man play at all for that a fool hath lost all; which in my mind would make such medley[3] that we should be enforced to leave things that were best for fear they may be bad—and that were as fond as not to cut one's meat with that knife that another hath cut his finger. Things are not to be judged by the event but by the end, nor travelling to be condemned by yours, or many's, unlucky success, but by the common and most approved wisdom of those that can better show what it is than I, and will better speak of it than you do.

'Where you allege Ulysses, that he desired nothing so much as to see the smoke of Ithaca, it was not because he loved not to travel but that he longed to see his wife[4] after his travel. And greater commendation brought his travel to him than his wit; the one taught but to speak, the other what he should speak. And in this you turn the point of your own bodkin[5] into your own bosom. Ulysses was no less esteemed for knowledge he had of other countries than for the revenues he had in his own. And where in the end you seem to refer me to that viewing of maps, I was never of that mind to make my ship in a painter's shop; which is like those who have great skill in a wooden globe, but never behold the sky. And he that seeketh to be a cunning traveller by seeing the maps, and an expert astronomer by turning the globe, may be an apprentice for Apelles but no page for Ulysses.

'Another reason you bring that travelling is costly. I speak for myself—he that hath little to spend hath not much to lose, and he that hath nothing in his own country cannot have less in any. Would you have me spend the flower of my youth as you do the withered race[6] of your age? Can the fair blood of youth creep into the ground as it were frost-bitten? No, father hermit, I am of Alexander's mind: if there were as many worlds as there be cities in the world, I would never leave until I had seen all the worlds and each city in every world.[7] Therefore, to be short, nothing shall alter my mind, neither penny nor paternoster.'[8]

---

1 *sinister*] adverse
2 *Alexander tipsy / Tarquin was banished*] see p. 28n. / Tarquin was banished from Rome following his rape of Lucretia (see p. 57n.).
3 *medley*] confusion
4 *his wife*] Penelope (see p. 57n.)
5 *bodkin*] dagger
6 *race*] possibly a pun, both 'course of life' and 'root' (specifically of ginger)
7 *Alexander's mind . . . . world*] For *Alexander* see p. 27n. His desire to conquer the world is frequently alluded to by Lyly, particularly in *Campaspe*.
8 *penny nor paternoster*] money nor prayer (proverbial)

This old man seeing him so resolute, resolved to let him depart, and gave him this farewell:

'My good son, though thou wilt not suffer me to persuade thee, yet shalt thou not let me to pity thee,[1] yea, and to pray for thee; but the time will come when, coming home by weeping cross,[2] thou shalt confess that it is better to be at home in the cave of an hermit than abroad in the court of an emperor, and that a crust with quietness shall be better than quails with unrest. And to the end thou mayst prove my sayings as true as I know thyself to be wilful, take the pains to return by this poor cell, where thy fare shall be amended if thou amend thy fault. And so farewell.'

Callimachus courteously took his leave and went his way; but we will not leave him till we have him again at the cell where we found him.

Now Philautus and gentlemen all, suppose that Callimachus had as ill fortune as ever had any; his mind infected with his body, his time consumed with his treasure, nothing won but what he cannot lose though he would— misery. You must imagine (because it were too long to tell all his journey) that he was seasick (as thou beginnest to be, Philautus), that he hardly escaped death, that he endured hunger and cold, heat without drink, that he was entangled with women, entrapped, deceived, that every stool he sat on was penniless bench,[3] that his robes were rags, that he had as much need of a chirurgeon as a physician,[4] and that thus he came home to the cell and with shame and sorrow began to say as followeth:

'I find too late, yet at length, that in age there is a certain foresight which youth cannot search, and of a kind of experience unto which unripened years cannot come; so that I must, of necessity, confess that youth never reineth well but when age holdeth the bridle. You see, my good father, what I would say by outward show, and I need not tell what I have tried,[5] because before you told me I should find it. This I say, that whatsoever misery happened either to you or any, the same hath chanced to me alone. I can say no more, I have tried no less.'

The old hermit, glad to see this ragged colt returned yet grieved to see him so tormented, thought not to add sour words to augment his sharp woes. But taking him by the hand and sitting down, began after a solemn manner from the beginning to the end to discourse with him of his father's affairs, even after the sort that before I rehearsed, and delivered unto him his money, think-ing now that misery would make him thrifty; desiring also that as well for the honour of his father's house as his own credit, he would return again to the island, and there be a comfort to his friends and a relief to his poor neigh-bours, which would be more worth than his wealth and the fulfilling of his father's last will.

Callimachus, not a little pleased with this tale and, I think, not much dis-pleased with the gold, gave such thanks as to such a friend appertained; and following the counsel of his uncle, which ever after he obeyed as a com-mandment, he came to his own house, lived long with great wealth, and as

---

1 *let me to pity thee*] prevent me from pitying you
2 *by weeping cross*] in shame and remorse (proverbial)
3 *every stool ... bench*] he was constantly in need (proverbial)
4 *of a chirurgeon ... physician*] of surgery as medicine
5 *tried*] experienced

much worship as any one in Scyros. And whether he be now living I know not; but whether he be or no, it skilleth not.[1]

'Now, Philautus, I have told this tale to this end: not that I think travelling to be ill if it be used well, but that such advice be taken that the horse carry not his own bridle, nor youth rule himself in his own conceits.[2] Besides that such places are to be chosen wherein to inhabit as are as commendable for virtue as buildings, where the manners are more to be marked than the men seen. And this was my whole drift, either never to travel, or so to travel as although the purse be weakened the mind may be strengthened. For not he that hath seen most countries is most to be esteemed, but he that learned best conditions;[3] for not so much are the situation of the places to be noted as the virtues of the persons. Which is contrary to the common practice of our travellers, who go either for gain and return without knowledge, or for fashion sake and come home without piety; whose estates[4] are as much to be lamented as their follies are to be laughed at. This causeth youth to spend their golden time without either praise or profit, pretending a desire of learning when they only follow loitering. But I hope our travel shall be better employed, seeing virtue is the white[5] we shoot at, not vanity; neither the English tongue, which (as I have heard) is almost barbarous, but the English manners, which (as I think) are most precise. And to thee, Philautus, I begin to address my speech, having made an end of mine hermit's tale; and if these few precepts I give thee be observed, then doubt not but we both shall learn that we best like. And these they are:

'At thy coming into England be not too inquisitive of news, neither curious in matters of state; in assemblies ask no questions, either concerning manners or men. Be not lavish of thy tongue, either in causes of weight, lest thou show thyself an espial,[6] or in wanton talk, lest thou prove thyself a fool.

'It is the nature of that country to sift[7] strangers. Everyone that shaketh thee by the hand is not joined to thee in heart. They think Italians wanton and Grecians subtle. They will trust neither, they are so incredulous, but undermine both, they are so wise. Be not quarrelous for every light occasion. They are impatient in their anger of any equal; ready to revenge an injury, but never wont to proffer any. They never fight without provoking, and once provoked they never cease. Beware thou fall not into the snares of love. The women there are wise, the men crafty. They will gather love by thy looks and pick thy mind out of thy

---

1 *skilleth not*] doesn't matter
2 *in his own conceits*] by his own fancies
3 *conditions*] habits of mind and behaviour
4 *estates*] conditions
5 *white*] target (metaphor drawn from archery)
6 *espial*] intelligencer, spy (a matter of concern in Elizabethan England)
7 *sift*] narrowly scrutinize, probe

hands.[1] It shall be there better to hear what they say, than to speak what thou thinkest. They have long ears and short tongues, quick to hear and slow to utter; broad eyes and light fingers, ready to espy and apt to strike. Every stranger is a mark for them to shoot at; yet this must I say, which in no country I can tell the like, that it is as seldom to see a stranger abused there as it is rare to see any well used elsewhere. Yet presume not too much of the courtesies of those, for they differ in natures. Some are hot, some cold, one simple and other wily; yet if thou use few words and fair speeches thou shalt command anything thou standest in need of.

'Touching the situation of the soil I have read in my study, which I partly believe (having no worse authority than Caesar); yet at my coming, when I shall confer[2] the things I see with those I have read, I will judge accordingly. And this have I heard,[3] that the inner part of Britain is inhabited by such as were born and bred in the isle, and the sea-coast by such as have passed thither out of Belgia to search booties and to make war. The country is marvellously replenished with people, and there be many buildings almost like in fashion to the buildings of Gallia.[4] There is great store of cattle; the coin they use is either of brass or else rings of iron, sized at[5] a certain weight instead of money. In the inner parts of the realm groweth tin, and in the sea-coast groweth iron. The brass that they occupy[6] is brought in from beyond-sea. The air is more temperate in those places than in France, and the cold lesser.

'The island is in fashion three-cornered, whereof one side is toward France. The one corner of this side, which is in Kent (where for the most part ships arrive out of France), is in the east, and the other nethermore[7] is towards the south. This side containeth about five hundred miles. Another side lieth toward Spain and the sun going down, on the which side is Ireland, less than Britain, as is supposed, by the one half; but the cut[8] between them is like the distance that is between France and Britain. In the middest of this course[9] is an island called Man. The length of this side is (according to the opinion of the inhabiters) seven hundred miles. The third side is northward, and against it lieth no land; but the point of that side butteth most upon[10] Germany. This they esteem to be eight

---

1 *pick thy . . . . hands*] deduce your thoughts from your gestures
2 *confer*] compare
3 *And this have I heard*] The account that follows is translated from Caesar's *Gallic Wars* and does not correct the inaccuracies of the source. Hence the confusion over the angle of the south coast and the position of the west coast relative to Spain (see Croll and Clemons, p. 227n.). The inaccuracies reflect the status of the two travellers as strangers.
4 *Gallia*] Gaul
5 *sized at*] regulated to
6 *occupy*] use
7 *nethermore*] lower down
8 *cut*] channel
9 *course*] channel
10 *butteth most upon*] comes closest to

hundred miles long, and so the circuit of the whole island is two thousand miles.

'Of all the inhabitants of this isle, the Kentish men are most civilest, the which country marcheth[1] altogether upon the sea and differeth not greatly from the manner of France. They that dwell more in the heart of the realm sow corn, but live by milk and flesh, and clothe themselves in leather. All the Britons do dye themselves with woad, which setteth a bluish colour upon them, and it maketh them more terrible to behold in battle. They wear their hair long, and shave all parts of their bodies, saving the head and the upper lip.

'Divers other uses and customs [are] among them as I have read, Philautus, but whether these be true or no I will not say. For methinketh an island so well governed in peace then, and so famous in victories, so fertile in all respects, so wholesome and populous, must needs in the term of a thousand years be much better. And I believe we shall find it such as we never read the like of any; and until we arrive there we will suspend our judgements. Yet do I mean at my return from thence to draw the whole description of the land, the customs, the nature of the people, the state, the government, and whatsoever deserveth either marvel or commendation.'

Philautus, not accustomed to these narrow seas, was more ready to tell what wood the ship was made of[2] than to answer to Euphues' discourse; yet, between waking and winking[3] as, one half sick and somewhat sleepy, it came in his brains, answered thus:

'In faith, Euphues, thou hast told a long tale. The beginning I have forgotten, the middle I understand not, and the end hangeth not together. Therefore I cannot repeat it as I would, nor delight in it as I ought; yet if at our arrival thou wilt renew thy tale, I will rub my memory. In the mean season, would I were either again in Italy or now in England. I cannot brook[4] these seas, which provoke my stomach sore. I have an appetite[5] it were best for me to take a nap, for every word is brought forth with a nod.'

Euphues replied:

'I cannot tell, Philautus, whether the sea make thee sick or she that was born of the sea;[6] if the first thou hast a queasy[7] stomach, if the latter a wanton desire. I well believe thou rememberest nothing that may do thee good, nor forgettest anything which can do thee harm, making more of a sore than a plaster, and wishing rather to be cursed than cured. Wherein

---

1 *marcheth*] borders
2 *more ready to . . . . made of*] better able to report on the construction of the ship (i.e. hanging over the side because of seasickness)
3 *winking*] sleeping
4 *brook*] tolerate
5 *appetite*] urge
6 *she that . . . . sea*] Venus (i.e. he is not sure if Philautus is seasick or lovesick)
7 *queasy*] easily upset

thou agreest with those which having taken a surfeit seek the means rather
to sleep than purge, or those that having the green-sickness[1] and are
brought to death's door follow their own humour and refuse the physician's remedy. And such, Philautus, is thy disease; who, pining in thine
own follies, choosest rather to perish in love than to live in wisdom. But
whatsoever be the cause, I wish the effect may answer my friendly care;
then, doubtless, thou shalt neither die being seasick or dote being lovesick. I would the sea could as well purge thy mind of fond conceits as thy
body of gross humours.'

Thus ending, Philautus again began to urge:

'Without doubt, Euphues, thou dost me great wrong in seeking a scar
in a smooth skin, thinking to stop a vein where none opened,[2] and to cast
love in my teeth which I have already spit out of my mouth. Which I must
needs think proceedeth rather for lack of matter than any good meaning,
else wouldst thou never harp on that string which is burst in my heart
and yet ever sounding in thy ears. Thou art like those that procure one
to take physic before he be sick, and to apply a cerecloth[3] to his body
when he feeleth no ache, or a vomit for a surfeit when his stomach is
empty. If ever I fall to mine old bias, I must put thee in the fault[4] that
talks of it, seeing thou didst put me in the mind to think of it. Whereby
thou seemest to blow the coal which thou wouldst quench, setting a
teen[5] edge where thou desirest to have a sharp point, imping[6] a feather
to make me fly when thou oughtst rather to cut my wing for fear of
soaring.

'Lucilla is dead, and she upon whom I guess thou harpest is forgotten;[7]
the one not to be redeemed, the other not to be thought on. Then, good
Euphues, wring not a horse on the withers with a false[8] saddle, neither
imagine what I am by thy thoughts but by mine own doings; so shalt thou
have me both willing to follow good counsel and able hereafter to give
thee comfort. And so I rest, half sleepy with the seas.'

With this answer Euphues held himself content; but as much wearied
with talk as the other was with travel, made a pillow of his hand.
And there let them both sleep their fill and dream with their fancies, until
either a storm cause them to wake, or their hard beds, or their journey's
end.

---

1 *green-sickness*] illness arising from iron deficiency (once common in adolescence and
   thought to be associated with the sexual appetite)
2 *stop a vein where none opened*] close up the vein where there is no incision
   (metaphor drawn from bleeding for medical purposes)
3 *cerecloth*] impregnated cloth used as a plaster for wounds
4 *put thee in the fault*] blame you
5 *teen*] sharp
6 *imping*] grafting on
7 *she upon whom . . . harpest*] the object of Philautus' frustrated desires after Lucilla.
   See p. 292 for a further allusion to this incident.
8 *wring not / false*] do not pinch / ill-fitting

Thus for the space of an eight weeks Euphues and Philautus sailed on the seas from their first shipping; between whom divers speeches were uttered, which to recite were nothing necessary in this place and, weighing the circumstances, scarce expedient. What tempests they endured, what strange sights in the element,[1] what monstrous fishes were seen, how often they were in danger of drowning, in fear of boarding,[2] how weary, how sick, how angry, it were tedious to write; for that whosoever hath either read of travelling, or himself used it, can sufficiently guess what is to be said. And this I leave to the judgement of those that in the like journey have spent their time from Naples to England; for if I should feign more than others have tried[3] I might be thought too poetical, if less partial. Therefore I omit the wonders, the rocks, the marks, the gulfs, and whatsoever they passed or saw, lest I should trouble divers with things they know, or may shame myself with things I know not. Let this suffice, that they are safely come within a ken[4] of Dover; which the master[5] espying, with a cheerful voice waking them, began to utter these words unto them:

'Gentlemen and friends, the longest summer's day hath his evening, Ulysses arriveth at last,[6] and rough winds in time bring the ship to safe road.[7] We are now within four hours' sailing of our haven[8] and, as you will think, of an earthly heaven. Yonder white cliffs, which easily you may perceive, are Dover hills, whereunto is adjoining a strong and famous castle into the which Julius Caesar[9] did enter, where you shall view many goodly monuments, both strange and ancient. Therefore pull up your hearts. This merry wind will immediately bring us to an easy bait.'[10]

Philautus was glad he slept so long and was awaked in so good time, being as weary of the seas as he that never used them. Euphues, not sorrowful of this good news, began to shake his ears,[11] and was soon apparalled. To make short, the winds were so favourable, the mariners so skilful, the way so short, that I fear me they will land before I can describe the manner how; and therefore suppose them now in Dover town in the noble isle of England, somewhat benighted, and more apt to sleep than sup. Yet for manners' sake they entertained their master and the rest of the merchants and mariners, where having in due time both recorded[12]

---

1 *element*] air
2 *boarding*] boarding by pirates
3 *tried*] endured
4 *ken*] distance of approximately twenty miles
5 *master*] captain of the ship
6 *Ulysses . . . . last*] see p. 57n.
7 *road*] anchorage
8 *haven*] harbour
9 *Julius Caesar*] the traditional founder of Dover castle
10 *bait*] stopping place for a rest
11 *shake his ears*] rouse himself
12 *recorded*] recalled

their travels past and ended their repast, everyone went to his lodging—
where I will leave them, soundly sleeping, until the next day.

The next day they spent in viewing the castle of Dover, the pier, the
cliffs, the road,[1] and town; receiving as much pleasure by the sight of
ancient monuments as by their courteous entertainment, no less praising
the persons for their good minds than the place for the goodly buildings.
And in this sort they refreshed themselves three or four days, until they
had digested the seas and recovered again their healths. Yet so warily they
behaved themselves as they were never heard either to enquire of any news
or point to any fortress, beholding the bulwarks with a slight and
careless regard,[2] but the other places of peace with admiration. Folly it
were to show what they saw, seeing hereafter in the description of
England[3] it shall most manifestly appear. But I will set them forward in
their journey, where now, within this two hours, we shall find them in
Canterbury.

Travelling thus like two pilgrims, they thought it most necessary to
direct their steps toward London, which they heard was the most royal
seat of the Queen of England. But first they came to Canterbury, an
old city, somewhat decayed yet beautiful to behold; most famous for a
cathedral church, the very majesty whereof struck them into a maze,
where they saw many monuments and heard tell of greater than either
they ever saw or easily would believe.[4]

After they had gone long, seeing themselves almost benighted determined to make the next house their inn, and espying in their way,
even at hand, a very pleasant garden, drew near; where they saw a
comely old man as busy as a bee among his bees, whose countenance
bewrayed his conditions.[5] This ancient father Euphues greeted in this
manner:

'Father, if the courtesy of England be answerable to[6] the custom of
pilgrims, then will the nature of the country excuse the boldness of
strangers. Our request is to have such entertainment, being almost tired[7]
with travel, not as divers have for acquaintance, but as all men have for
their money; which courtesy if you grant, we will ever remain in your
debt, although everyway discharge our due. And rather we are importunate for that we are no less delighted with the pleasures of your garden
than the sight of your gravity.'

---

1 *road*] harbour
2 *Yet so warily . . . . careless regard*] A further instance of the sensitivity to spying
   noted above, functioning in part to prepare the reader for the travellers' reception
   by Fidus (see pp. 187ff.)
3 *description of England*] i.e. in Euphues' 'Glass' with which the work concludes
4 *Canterbury . . . . believe*] For Lyly's association with Canterbury see Introduction,
   p. 2.
5 *countenance . . . . conditions*] whose appearance was indicative of his disposition
6 *be answerable to*] accords with
7 *tired*] exhausted

Unto whom the old man said:

'Gentlemen (you are no less I perceive by your manners, and you can be no more being but men), I am neither so uncourteous to mislike your request, nor so suspicious to mistrust your truths; although it be no less perilous to be secure than peevish to be curious.[1] I keep no victualling,[2] yet is my house an inn, and I an host to every honest man, so far as they with courtesy will and I may with ability. Your entertainment shall be as small for cheer as your acquaintance is for time, yet in my house ye may haply find some one thing cleanly, nothing courtly; for that wisdom provideth things necessary, not superfluous, and age seeketh rather a modicum for sustenance than feasts for surfeits. But until something may be made ready, might I be so bold as enquire your names, countries, and the cause of your pilgrimage; wherein, if I shall be more inquisitive than I ought, let my rude[3] birth excuse my bold request, which I will not urge as one importunate, I might say impudent.'

Euphues, seeing this fatherly and friendly sire (whom we will name Fidus) to have no less inward courtesy than outward comeliness, conjectured (as well he might) that the proffer of his bounty noted the nobleness of his birth, being well assured that as no Thersites could be transformed into Ulysses, so no Alexander could be couched in Damocles.[4] Thinking therefore now with more care and advisedness to temper his talk, lest either he might seem foolish or curious,[5] he answered him in these terms:

'Good sir, you have bound us unto you with a double chain, the one in pardoning our presumption, the other in granting our petition; which great and undeserved kindness though we cannot requite with the like, yet, if occasion shall serve, you shall find us hereafter as willing to make amends as we are now ready to give thanks.

'Touching your demands, we are not so unwise to mislike them, or so ungrateful to deny them; lest in concealing our names it might be thought for some trespass, and covering our pretence[6] we might be suspected of treason. Know you then, sir, that this gentleman my fellow is called Philautus, I Euphues; he an Italian, I a Grecian; both sworn friends by just trial, both pilgrims by free will. Concerning the cause of our coming into this island, it was only to glue our eyes to our ears, that we might justify[7] those things by sight which we have oftentimes with incredible

---

1 *perilous to be secure / peevish to be curious*] dangerous to be careless / foolish to be over-suspicious
2 *keep no victualling*] do not sell provisions
3 *rude*] lowly
4 *no Thersites . . . Ulysses / no Alexander . . . Damocles*] no impudent talker could take on the shape of the embodiment of discretion / no magnanimous ruler lie hidden in a sycophant
5 *curious*] affected
6 *covering our pretence*] concealing our purposes
7 *justify*] confirm

admiration understood by hearing: to wit, the rare qualities, as well of
the body as the mind, of your most dread sovereign and Queen, the bruit[1]
of the which hath filled every corner of the world, insomuch as there is
nothing that moveth either more matter or more marvel[2] than her excellent Majesty. W[hich] fame when we saw without comparison and almost
above credit, we determined to spend some part of our time and treasure
in the English court, where if we could find the report but to be true in
half, we should not only think our money and travel well employed, but
returned with interest more than infinite. This is the only end of our
coming, which we are nothing fearful to utter, trusting as well to the courtesy of your country as the equity of our cause.

'Touching the court, if you can give us any instructions, we shall think
the evening well spent; which procuring our delight, can no way work
your disliking.'

'Gentlemen,' answered this old man, 'if because I entertain you you
seek to undermine me, you offer me great discourtesy. You must needs
think me very simple, or yourselves very subtle, if upon so small acquaintance I should answer to such demands as are neither for me to utter,
being a subject, nor for you to know, being strangers. I keep hives for
bees, not houses for busybodies (pardon me, gentlemen, you have moved
my patience), and more welcome shall a wasp be to my honey than a
privy enemy to my house.

'If the rare report of my most gracious Lady have brought you hither,
methinketh you have done very ill to choose such a house to confirm your
minds as seemeth more like a prison than a palace, whereby in my opinion
you mean to derogate from the worthiness of the person by the vileness
of the place;[3] which argueth your pretences to savour of malice more than
honest meaning. They use to consult of Jove in the Capitol,[4] of Caesar
in the senate, of our noble Queen in her own court. Besides that,
Alexander must be painted of none but Apelles, nor engraven of any but
Lysippus,[5] nor our Elizabeth set forth of everyone that would in duty,
which are all, but of those that can in skill, which are few. So far hath
nature overcome art, and grace eloquence, that the painter draweth a veil
over that he cannot shadow,[6] and the orator holdeth a paper in his hand
for that he cannot utter.

'But whither am I wandering, rapt further by devotion than I can wade
through with discretion! Cease then, gentlemen, and know this, that an

---

1 *bruit*] report
2 *moveth either . . . . marvel*] provokes more discussion or wonder
3 *derogate . . . . place*] detract from the honour of the person about whom you are
  asking by the humbleness of the place in which you make your enquiries
4 *consult of Jove in the Capitol*] speak of Jupiter in the Capitolium (temple of Jupiter
  in Rome)
5 *Alexander . . . . Lysippus*] see pp. 27 and 221nn.
6 *the painter draweth . . . . shadow*] an allusion to Timanthes' handling of the grief of
  Agamemnon, see p. 173.

Englishman learneth to speak of men and to hold his peace of the gods. Enquire no further than beseemeth you, lest you hear that which cannot like[1] you. But if you think the time long before your repast, I will find some talk which shall breed your delight touching my bees.'

And here Euphues brake him off and replied, though not as bitterly as he would, yet as roundly as he durst, in this manner:

'We are not a little sorry, sir, not that we have opened our minds but that we are taken amiss, and where we meant so well, to be entreated[2] so ill; having talked of no one thing unless it be of good will towards you, whom [we] reverenced for age, and of duty toward your sovereign, whom we marvelled at for virtue. Which good meaning of ours, misconstrued by you, hath bred such a distemperature in our heads[3] that we are fearful to praise her whom all the world extolleth, and suspicious to trust you whom above any in the world we loved. And whereas your greatest argument is the baseness of your house, methinketh that maketh most against you. Caesar never rejoiced more than when he heard that they talked of his valiant exploits in simple cottages, alleging this, that a bright sun shineth in every corner, which maketh not the beams worse, but the place better. When (as I remember) Agesilaus' son[4] was set at the lower end of the table and one cast it in his teeth as a shame, he answered, "This is the upper end where I sit, for it is not the place that maketh the person but the person that maketh the place honourable." When it was told Alexander that he was much praised of a miller, "I am glad," quoth he, "that there is not so much as a miller but loveth Alexander." Among other fables, I call to my remembrance one not long but apt and, as simple as it is, so fit it is that I cannot omit it for the opportunity of the time, though I might over-leap it for the baseness of the matter. When all the birds were appointed to meet to talk of the eagle, there was great contention at whose nest they should assemble, everyone willing to have it at his own home; one preferring[5] the nobility of his birth, another the stateliness of his building; some would have it for one quality, some for another. At the last the swallow said they should come to his nest (being commonly of filth) which all the birds, disdaining, said, "Why, thy house is nothing else but dirt!" "And therefore," answered the swallow, "would I have talk there of the eagle; for being the basest, the name of an eagle will make it the bravest."[6] And so, good father, may I say of thy cottage, which thou seemest to account of so homely, that moving but speech of thy sovereign it will be more like a court than a cabin, and of a prison the name of Elizabeth will make it a palace. The image of a prince stamped

1 *like*] please (for another example of this usage see p. 72)
2 *entreated*] treated
3 *distemperature in our heads*] disturbance of mind
4 *Agesilaus' son*] Archidamus (d. 338 BC), son of a noted king of Sparta
5 *preferring*] putting forward
6 *bravest*] most splendid

in copper goeth as current;[1] and a crow may cry, "Ave Caesar,"[2] without any rebuke.

'The name of a prince is like the sweet dew which falleth as well upon low shrubs as high trees, and resembleth a true glass wherein the poor may see their faces with the rich, or a clear stream wherein all may drink that are dry, not they only that are wealthy. Where you add that we should fear to move any occasion touching talk of so noble a prince, truly our reverence taketh away the fear of suspicion. The lamb feareth not the lion but the wolf, the partridge dreadeth not the eagle but the hawk, a true and faithful heart standeth more in awe of his superior whom he loveth for fear, than of his prince whom he feareth for love. A clear conscience needeth no excuse, nor feareth any accusation.

'Lastly, you conclude that neither art nor heart can so set forth your noble Queen as she deserveth. I grant it, and rejoice at it; and that is the cause of our coming to see her, whom none can sufficiently commend. And yet doth it not follow that because we cannot give her as much as she is worthy of, therefore we should not owe her any. But in this we will imitate the old painters in Greece, who drawing in their tables[3] the portraiture of Jupiter, were every hour mending it but durst never finish it. And being demanded why they began that which they could not end, they answered, "In that we show him to be Jupiter, whom everyone may begin to paint but none can perfect." In the like manner mean we to draw in part the praises of her whom we cannot throughly portray, and in that we signify her to be Elizabeth; who enforceth every man to do as much as he can, when, in respect of her perfection, it is nothing. For as he that beholdeth the sun steadfastly, thinking thereby to describe it more perfectly, hath his eyes so dazzled that he can discern nothing, so fareth it with those that seek marvellously to praise those that are without the compass of their judgements[4] and all comparison, that the more they desire, the less they discern, and the nearer they think themselves in good will, the further they find themselves off in wisdom, thinking to measure that by the inch which they cannot reach with the ell.[5]

'And yet, father, it can be neither hurtful to you nor hateful to your prince to hear the commendation of a stranger, or to answer his honest request who will wish in heart no less glory to her than you do, although they can wish no more. And, therefore, methinketh you have offered a little discourtesy not to answer us, and to suspect us great injury; having neither might to attempt anything which may do you harm, nor malice

---

1 *goeth as current*] is accepted as coinage
2 *Ave Caesar*] hail Caesar. Croll and Clemons note that a crow trained to say 'Ave Caesar victor, Imperator' was presented to Augustus after his defeat of Antony (p. 236n.).
3 *tables*] pictures
4 *without the compass of their judgements*] beyond the range of their understanding
5 *ell*] unit of length, equivalent to 45 inches

to revenge where we find help.[1] For mine own part this I say, and for my friend present the like I dare swear, how boldly I cannot tell, how truly I know, that there is not anyone, whether he be bound by benefit or duty or both, whether linked by zeal or time or blood or all, that more humbly reverenceth Her Majesty, or marvelleth at her wisdom, or prayeth for her long, prosperous and glorious reign, than we; than whom we acknowledge none more simple, and yet dare avow none more faithful. Which we speak not to get service by flattery, but to acquit ourselves of suspicion by faith; which is all that either a prince can require of his subject or a vassal yield to his sovereign, and that which we owe to your Queen, and all others should offer, that either for fear of punishment dare not offend or for love of virtue will not.'

Here old Fidus interrupted young Euphues, being almost induced by his talk to answer his request. Yet, as one neither too credulous nor altogether mistrustful, he replied as a friend; and so wisely as he glanced from the mark Euphues shot at and hit at last the white[2] which Philautus set up, as shall appear hereafter. And thus he began:

'My sons (mine age giveth me the privilege of that term, and your honesties cannot refuse it), you are too young to understand matters of state, and were you elder to know them it were not for your estates.[3] And therefore methinketh the time were but lost in pulling Hercules' shoe upon an infant's foot, or in setting Atlas' burden[4] on a child's shoulder, or to bruise your backs with the burden of a whole kingdom. Which I speak not that either I mistrust you (for your reply hath fully resolved that fear), or that I malice you[5] (for my good will may clear me of that fault), or that I dread your might (for your small power cannot bring me into such a folly), but that I have learned by experience that to reason of kings or princes hath ever been much misliked of the wise, though much desired of fools, especially where old men which should be at their beads[6] be too busy with the court, and young men which should follow their books be too inquisitive in the affairs of princes. We should not look at that we cannot reach, nor long for that we should not have. Things above us are not for us; and therefore are princes placed under the gods, that they should not see what they do, and we under princes, that we might not enquire what they do. But as the foolish eagle that seeing the sun coveteth to build her nest in the sun, so fond youth which viewing the glory and gorgeousness

---

1 *malice . . . . help*] ill-will to do injury where we find succour
2 *white*] see p. 180n.
3 *to know them . . . . estates*] it would not be appropriate to those of your social position to know them
4 *Hercules' shoe / Atlas' burden*] the shoe of the mightiest of men / the world (which Atlas carried on his shoulder)
5 *malice you*] bear you ill-will
6 *at their beads*] at their prayers (*beads* = rosary)

of the court longeth to know the secrets in the court. But as the eagle burneth out her eyes with that proud lust, so doth youth break his heart with that peevish conceit.[1] And as Satyrus, not knowing what fire was, would needs embrace it and was burned, so these fond Satyri,[2] not understanding what a prince is, run boldly to meddle in those matters which they know not and so feel worthily the heat they would not. And therefore, good Euphues and Philautus, content yourselves with this, that, to be curious in things you should not enquire of, if you know them they appertain not unto you, if you knew them not they cannot hinder you.

'And let Apelles' answer to Alexander be an excuse for me. When Alexander would needs come to Apelles' shop[3] and paint, Apelles placed him at his back; who, going to his own work, did not so much as cast an eye back to see Alexander's devices. Which being well marked, Alexander said thus unto him, "Art not thou a cunning painter, and wilt thou not over-look my picture and tell me wherein I have done well and wherein ill?" Whom he answered wisely, yet merrily, "In faith, O King, it is not for Apelles to enquire what Alexander hath done, neither if he show it me to judge how it is done. And therefore did I set your Majesty at my back, that I might not glance towards a king's work, and that you looking over my head might see mine; for Apelles' shadows are to be seen of Alexander, but not Alexander's of Apelles." So ought we, Euphues, to frame ourselves in all our actions and devices as though the king stood over us to behold us, and not to look what the king doth behind us. For whatsoever he painteth it is for his pleasure, and, we must think, for our profit; for Apelles had his reward, though he saw not the work.

'I have heard of a magnifico[4] in Milan (and I think, Philautus, you being an Italian do remember it), who hearing his son inquisitive of the Emperor's life and demeanour, reprehended him sharply, saying that it beseemed not one of his house to enquire how an Emperor lived, unless he himself were an Emperor; for that the behaviour and usage of so honourable personages are not to be called in question of everyone that doubteth, but of such as are their equals.

'Alexander, being commanded of Philip his father to wrestle in the games of Olympia, answered he would if there were a king to strive with him. Whereby I have noted (that others seem to enforce) that as kings' pastimes are no plays for everyone, so their secrets, their counsels, their dealings are not to be either scanned or enquired of any way, unless of those that are in the like place or serve the like person.

---

1 *proud lust / peevish conceit*] arrogant desire / foolish notion
2 *Satyrus / Satyri*] Satyrus, drawn to the fire brought into the world by Prometheus, kissed it and was burned / satyrs
3 *shop*] workshop. Alexander's patronage of Apelles is well-attested but this incident appears to be Lyly's invention. (For *Alexander* and *Apelles* see p. 27n.)
4 *magnifico*] nobleman

'I cannot tell whether it be a Canterbury tale[1] or a fable in Aesop (but pretty it is and true in my mind), that the Fox and the Wolf, going both a-filching[2] for food, thought it best to see whether the Lion were asleep or awake, lest being too bold they should speed too bad. The Fox, entering into the King's den (a king I call the Lion), brought word to the Wolf that he was asleep, and went himself to his own kennel. The Wolf, desirous to search in the Lion's den, that he might espy some fault or steal some prey, entered boldly, whom the Lion caught in his paws and asked what he would. The silly Wolf (an unapt term for a wolf, yet fit, being in a lion's hands) answered that understanding by the Fox he was asleep, he thought he might be at liberty to survey his lodging. Unto whom the princely Lion, with great disdain though little despite[3] (for that there can be no envy in a king), said thus, "Dost thou think that a Lion, thy prince and governor, can sleep though he wink; or darest thou enquire whether he wink or wake? The Fox had more craft than thou, and thou more courage (courage I will not say, but boldness—and bold-ness is too good—I may say desperateness), but you shall both well know, and to your griefs feel, that neither the wiliness of the Fox, nor the wildness[4] of the Wolf, ought either to see, or to ask, whether the Lion either sleep or wake, be at home or abroad, dead or alive. For this is sufficient for you to know, that there is a Lion, not where he is or what he doth."

'In like manner, Euphues, is the government of a monarchy (though homely be the comparison, yet apt it is); that it is neither the wise Fox nor the malicious Wolf should venture so far as to learn whether the Lion sleep or wake in his den, whether the prince fast or feast in his court. But this should be their order, to understand there is a king; but what he doth is for the gods to examine, whose ordinance[5] he is, not for men, whose overseer he is. Then how vain is it, Euphues (too mild a word for so mad a mind), that the foot should neglect his office to correct the face, or that subjects should seek more to know what their princes do than what they are. Wherein they show themselves as bad as beasts, and much worse than my bees, who in my conceit, though I may seem partial, observe more order than they, and (if I might say so of my good bees) more honesty. Honesty my old grandfather called that when men lived by law not list,[6] observing in all things the mean, which we name virtue; and virtue we account nothing else but to deal justly and temperately.

---

1 *Canterbury tale*] traditional story (not specifically one of Chaucer's *Canterbury Tales*)
2 *a-filching*] stealing
3 *despite*] malice
4 *wildness*] boldness
5 *ordinance*] providential appointment
6 *list*] will

'And if I might crave pardon, I would a little acquaint you with the commonwealth of my bees, which is neither impertinent to the matter we have now in hand, nor tedious to make you weary.'

Euphues, delighted with the discourses of old Fidus, was content to hear anything so he might hear him speak something; and consenting willingly he desired Fidus to go forward. Who now removing himself nearer to the hives, began as followeth:

'Gentlemen, I have for the space of this twenty years dwelt in this place, taking no delight in anything but only in keeping my bees and marking[1] them. And this I find, which had I not seen I should hardly have believed, that they use as great wit by indution,[2] and art by workmanship, as ever man hath or can, using between themselves no less justice than wisdom, and yet not so much wisdom as majesty. Insomuch as thou wouldst think that they were a kind of people, a commonwealth for Plato,[3] where they all labour, all gather honey, fly all together in a swarm, eat in a swarm, and sleep in a swarm, so neat and finely, that they abhor nothing so much as uncleanness, drinking pure and clear water, delighting in sweet and sound music, which if they hear but once out of tune, they fly out of sight—and therefore are they called the Muses' birds, because they follow not the sound so much as the consent.[4]

'They live under a law, using great reverence to their elder, as to the wiser. They choose a king, whose palace they frame both braver in show and stronger in substance; whom, if they find to fall, they establish again in his throne, with no less duty than devotion, guarding him continually as it were for fear he should miscarry and for love he should not; whom they tender with such faith and favour that whithersoever he flieth they follow him, and if he cannot fly they carry him; whose life they so love that they will not for his safety stick[5] to die, such care have they for his health on whom they build all their hope. If their prince die, they know not how to live. They languish, weep, sigh, neither intending[6] their work nor keeping their old society. And that which is most marvellous (and almost incredible), if there be any that hath disobeyed his commandments, either of purpose or unwittingly, he killeth himself with his own sting, as executioner of his own stubbornness. The king himself hath his sting, which he useth rather for honour than punishment. And yet, Euphues,

---

1 *marking*] observing
2 *use as great . . . . indution*] Obscure. Possibly 'employ as much intelligence in inferring the general from the specific'. The account of the bees' commonwealth that follows is drawn from Pliny's *Historia naturalis* but is clearly designed from its context to reflect upon Elizabethan England.
3 *commonwealth for Plato*] see p. 100n.
4 *consent*] harmony
5 *stick*] hesitate
6 *intending*] giving their attention to

albeit they live under a prince, they have their privilege and as great liberties as strait[1] laws.

'They call a parliament wherein they consult for laws, statutes, penalties; choosing officers, and creating their king, not by affection[2] but reason, not by the greater part but the better. And if such a one by chance be chosen (for among men sometimes the worst speed best) as is bad, then is there such civil war and dissension that until he be plucked down there can be no friendship, and, overthrown, there is no enmity—not fighting for quarrels but quietness.

'Everyone hath his office, some trimming the honey, some working the wax, one framing hives, another the combs, and that so artificially[3] that Daedalus could not with greater art or excellency better dispose the orders, measures, proportions, distinctions, joints, and circles. Divers hew, others polish, all are careful to do their work so strongly as they may resist the craft of such drones as seek to live by their labours; which maketh them to keep watch and ward, as living in a camp to others and as in a court to themselves. Such a care of chastity that they never engender; such a desire of cleannness that there is not so much as meat in all their hives.

'When they go forth to work they mark the wind, the clouds, and whatsoever doth threaten[4] either their ruin or reign, and having gathered out of every flower honey, they return laden in their mouths, thighs, wings and all the body; whom they that tarried at home receive readily, as easing their backs of so great burdens. The King himself, not idle, goeth up and down, entreating, threatening, commanding, using the counsel of a sequel[5] but not losing the dignity of a prince, preferring[6] those that labour to greater authority, and punishing those that loiter with due severity.

'All which things being much admirable, yet this is most: that they are so profitable, bringing unto man both honey and wax, each so wholesome that we all desire it, both so necessary that we cannot miss[7] them. Here, Euphues, is a commonwealth which, oftentimes calling to my mind, I cannot choose but commend above any that either I have heard or read of; where the king is not for everyone to talk of, where there is such homage, such love, such labour, that I have wished oftentimes rather be a bee than not be as I should be.

'In this little garden, with these hives, in this house, have I spent the better part of my life, yea, and the best. I was never busy in matters of

---

1 *strait*] strict
2 *affection*] emotion, bias
3 *artificially*] skilfully. For *Daedalus* see p. 173n.
4 *threaten*] portend (with *ruin*) / endanger (with *reign*)
5 *sequel*] train of attendants
6 *preferring*] promoting
7 *miss*] do without

state, but referring all my cares unto the wisdom of grave counsellors, and my confidence in the noble mind of my dread sovereign and Queen; never asking what she did but always praying she may do well, not enquiring whether she might do what she would but thinking she would do nothing but what she might. Thus, contented with a mean estate and never curious of the high estate, I found such quiet that methinketh he which knoweth least liveth longest; insomuch that I choose rather to be an hermit in a cave than a counsellor in the court.'

Euphues, perceiving old Fidus to speak what he thought, answered him in these short words:

'He is very obstinate whom neither reason nor experience can persuade, and truly seeing you have alleged both I must needs allow[1] both. And if my former request have bred any offence, let my latter repentance make amends. And yet this I know, that I enquired nothing that might bring you into danger or me into trouble; for, as young as I am,[2] this have I learned, that one may point at a star but not pull at it, and see a prince but not search[3] him. And for mine own part, I never mean to put my hand between the bark and the tree,[4] or in matters which are not for me to be over-curious.

'The commonwealth of your bees did so delight me that I was not a little sorry that either their estate have not been longer, or your leisure more; for in my simple judgement there was such an orderly government that men may not be ashamed to imitate them, nor you weary to keep them.'

They having spent much time in these discourses were called in to supper. Philautus, more willing to eat than hear their tales, was not the last that went in. Where, being all set down, they were served all in earthen dishes, all things so neat and cleanly that they perceived a kind of courtly majesty in the mind of their host, though he wanted matter to show it in his house. Philautus, I know not whether of nature melancholy, or feeling love in his bosom, spake scarce ten words since his coming into the house of Fidus; which the old man well noting, began merrily thus to parley with him:

'I marvel, gentleman, that all this time you have been tongue-tied, either thinking not yourself welcome, or disdaining so homely entertainment. In the one you do me wrong, for I think I have not showed myself strange;[5] for the other you must pardon me, for that I have not to do as I would but as I may. And though England be no grange,[6] but yieldeth everything,

---

1 *allow*] agree to
2 *young as I am*] For the discrepancies between Euphues' age at the close of *The Anatomy of Wit* and the beginning of *Euphues and His England* see Introduction, p. 9.
3 *search*] examine
4 *put my hand . . . . tree*] intrude where there is no place for me (proverbial)
5 *strange*] unwelcoming, distant
6 *grange*] isolated farmhouse

yet is it here, as in every place, all for money. And if you will but accept a willing mind instead of a costly repast, I shall think myself beholding unto you, and if time serve or my bees prosper, I will make you part of amends with a better breakfast.'

Philautus thus replied:

'I know, good father, my welcome greater than anyways I can requite and my cheer more bountiful than ever I shall deserve; and though I seem silent for matters that trouble me, yet I would not have you think me so foolish that I should either disdain your company or mislike your cheer. Of both the which I think so well that, if time might answer my true meaning, I would exceed in cost, though in courtesy I know not how to compare with you. For (without flattery be it spoken) if the common courtesy of England be no worse than this toward strangers, I must needs think them happy that travel into these coasts, and the inhabitants the most courteous of all countries.'

Here began Euphues to take the tale out of Philautus' mouth and to play with him in his melancholic mood, beginning thus:

'No, father, I durst swear for my friend that both he thinketh himself welcome and his fare good. But you must pardon a young courtier who in the absence of his lady thinketh himself forlorn. And this vile dog, Love, will so rankle where he biteth that I fear my friend's sore will breed to a fistula;[1] for you may perceive that he is not where he lives but where he loves, and more thoughts hath he in his head than you bees in your hives. And better it were for him to be naked among your wasps, though his body were all blistered, than to have his heart stung so with affection, whereby he is so blinded. But believe me, Fidus, he taketh as great delight to course a cogitation[2] of love as you do to use your time with honey. In this plight hath he been ever since his coming out of Naples, and so hath it wrought with him (which I had thought impossible) that pure love did make him seasick; insomuch as in all my travel with him, I seemed to everyone to bear with me the picture of a proper man, but no living person—the more pity, and yet no force.'[3]

Philautus, taking Euphues' tale by the end and the old man by the arm, between grief and game,[4] jest and earnest, answered him thus:

'Euphues would die if he should not talk of love once in a day, and therefore you must give him leave after every meal to close his stomach with love as with marmalade.[5] And I have heard not those that say nothing, but they that kick oftenest against love, are ever in love. Yet doth he use me as the mean to move the matter, and as the man to make his

---

1 *fistula*] abscess
2 *course a cogitation*] pursue a consideration
3 *no force*] no matter
4 *game*] sport
5 *close his stomach / marmalade*] round off his appetite / a newly introduced delicacy in the sixteenth century

mirror, he himself knowing best the price of corn not by the market-folks but his own footsteps.[1] But if he use this speech either to make you merry or to put me out of conceit,[2] he doth well; you must thank him for the one, and I will think on him for the other. I have oftentimes sworn that I am as far from love as he, yet will he not believe me; as incredulous as those who think none bald till they see his brains.'

As Euphues was making answer, Fidus prevented him in this manner: 'There is no harm done, Philautus, for whether you love or Euphues jest this shall breed no jar.[3] It may be when I was as young as you, I was as idle as you (though in my opinion there is none less idle than a lover). For to tell the truth, I myself was once a courtier, in the days of that most noble king of famous memory, Henry VIII, father to our most gracious lady, Elizabeth.'

Where, and with that, he paused, as though the remembrance of his old life had stopped his new speech. But Philautus, itching to hear what he would say, desired him to go forward; unto whom Fidus, fetching a great sigh, said 'I will'—and there again made a full point.[4] Philautus, burning as it were in desire of this discourse, urged him again with great entreaty. Then the old man commanded the board to be uncovered,[5] grace being said, called for stools, and sitting all by the fire, uttered the whole discourse of his love; which brought Philautus abed and Euphues asleep.

And now, gentlemen, if you will give ear to the tale of Fidus, it may be some will be as watchful as Philautus, though many as drowsy as Euphues. And thus he began, with a heavy countenance (as though his pains were present, not past), to frame his tale:

I was born in the Weald of Kent, of honest parents and worshipful, whose tender cares (if the fondness of parents may be so termed) provided all things even from my very cradle until their graves that might either bring me up in good letters or make me heir to great livings. I (without arrogancy be it spoken) was not inferior in wit to many; which finding in myself, I flattered myself, but in the end deceived myself. For being of the age of twenty years, there was no trade or kind of life that either fitted my humour or served my turn but the court, thinking that place the only means to climb high and sit sure. Wherein I followed the vein of young soldiers, who judge nothing sweeter than war till they feel the weight.

I was there entertained as well by the great friends my father made as by mine own forwardness. Where, it being now but honeymoon,[6] I endeavoured to court it with a grace (almost past grace), laying more on my back than my

---

1 *knowing best . . . . footsteps*] knowing all about the matter not by hearsay but experience
2 *put me out of conceit*] discountenance me
3 *jar*] quarrel
4 *point*] stop
5 *board to be uncovered*] table to be cleared
6 *honeymoon*] the joyful early days of my career

friends could well bear, having many times a brave cloak and a threadbare purse. Who so conversant[1] with the ladies as I? Who so pleasant? Who more prodigal? Insomuch as I thought the time lost which was not spent either in their company with delight, or for their company in letters.

Among all the troop of gallant gentlemen, I singled out one (in whom I misliked nothing but his gravity) that above all I meant to trust; who, as well for the good qualities he saw in me as the little government he feared in me, began one night to utter these few words:

'Friend Fidus (if Fortune allow a term so familiar), I would I might live to see thee as wise as I perceive thee witty; then should thy life be so seasoned as neither too much wit might make thee proud, nor too great riot poor. My acquaintance is not great with thy person; but such insight have I into thy conditions[2] that I fear nothing so much as that there thou catch thy fall where thou thinkest to take thy rising. There belongeth more to a courtier than bravery,[3] which the wise laugh at, or personage, which the chaste mark not, or wit, which the most part see not. It is sober and discreet behaviour, civil and gentle demeanour, that in court winneth both credit and commodity;[4] which counsel thy unripened years think to proceed rather of the malice of age than the good meaning. To ride well is laudable, and I like it; to run at the tilt not amiss, and I desire it; to revel much to be praised, and I have used it. Which things as I know them all to be courtly, so for my part I account them necessary; for where greatest assemblies are of noble gentlemen, there should be the greatest exercise of true nobility. And I am not so precise but that I esteem it as expedient in feats of arms and activity to employ the body as in study to waste the mind; yet so should the one be tempered with the other as it might seem as great a shame to be valiant and courtly without learning, as to be studious and bookish without valour.[5]

'But there is another thing, Fidus, which I am to warn thee of and (if I might) to wrest thee from, not that I envy thy estate[6] but that I would not have thee forget it. Thou usest too much (a little I think to be too much) to dally with women, which is the next way to dote on them. For as they that angle for the tortoise, having once caught him, are driven into such a litherness[7] that they lose all their spirits, being benumbed; so they that seek to obtain the good will of ladies, having once a little hold of their love, they are driven into such a trance that they let go the hold of their liberty, bewitched like those that view the head of Medusa,[8] or the viper tied to the bough of the beech tree, which keepeth him in a dead sleep, though it begin with a

---

1 *conversant*] familiar
2 *conditions*] nature
3 *bravery*] finery
4 *credit and commodity*] a good name and tangible benefits
5 *To ride well . . . without valour*] The range of physical and mental accomplishments seen here as requisite to the courtly life conforms to the ideals of the period as defined in Castiglione's *Il cortegiano* and exemplified by Sir Philip Sidney (*run at the tilt* = take part in jousts).
6 *estate*] position
7 *litherness*] state of inertia. Croll and Clemons (p. 249n.) note a comparable association between the tortoise and lethargy in Pliny (xxxii. 14).
8 *head of Medusa*] see p. 69n.

sweet slumber.[1] I myself have tasted new wine, and find it to be more pleasant than wholesome; and grapes gathered before they be ripe may set the eyes
on lust but they make the teeth an edge;[2] and love desired in the bud, not
knowing what the blossom were, may delight the conceits of the head but it
will destroy the contemplature of the heart.

'What I speak now is of mere good will, and yet upon small presumption;
but in things which come on the sudden one cannot be too wary to prevent
or too curious to mistrust. For thou art in a place either to make thee hated
for vice or loved for virtue; and as thou reverencest the one before the other,
so in uprightness of life show it. Thou hast good friends which by thy lewd
delights thou mayst make great enemies, and heavy foes which by thy well
doing thou mayst cause to be earnest abettors of thee in matters that now
they canvass[3] against thee. And so I leave thee, meaning hereafter to bear the
rein of thy bridle in mine hands[4] if I see thee headstrong.'

And so he departed.

I gave him great thanks, and glad I was we were parted. For his putting
love into my mind was like the throwing of bugloss[5] into wine, which
increaseth in him that drinketh it a desire of lust, though it mitigate the force
of drunkenness.

I now fetching a windlass, that I might better have a shoot, was prevented[6]
with ready game; which saved me some labour but gained me no quiet. And
I would, gentlemen, that you could feel the like impressions in your minds at
the rehearsal of my mishap as I did passions at the entering into it. If ever
you loved, you have found the like; if ever you shall love, you shall taste no
less.

But he,[7] so eager of an end, as one leaping over a stile before he come to
it, desired few parentheses, or digressions, or glosses, but the text, where
he himself was coting in the margent.[8]

'Then,' said Fidus, 'thus it fell out.'

It was my chance (I know not whether chance or destiny) that being invited
to a banquet where many ladies were—and too many by one as the end tried,
though then too many by all saving that one, as I thought—I cast mine eyes
so earnestly upon her that my heart vowed her the mistress of my love; and
so fully was I resolved to prosecute my determination, as I was earnest to
begin it.

---

1 *the viper . . . . slumber*] Bond (II, p. 500) traces the source of this property of the
    viper to Plutarch.
2 *set the eyes on lust / make the teeth an edge*] make the eyes desire them / set the
    teeth on edge
3 *abettors / canvass*] supporters / raise
4 *bear the rein . . . . hands*] curb your conduct
5 *bugloss*] borage (a plant with a variety of culinary uses and properties)
6 *fetching a windlass . . . . shoot / prevented*] making a circuit to give myself a better
    sight of the target / forestalled
7 *he*] Philautus
8 *coting in the margent*] marking off chapter and verse in the margin (i.e. glossing it
    in the light of his own experience)

Now gentlemen, I commit my case to your considerations, being wiser than I was then and somewhat, as I guess, elder. I was but in court a novice, having no friend but him before rehearsed, whom in such a matter I was likelier to find a bridle than a spur. I never before that time could imagine what love should mean, but used the term as a flout[1] to others, which I found now as a fever in myself; neither know[ing] from whence the occasion should arise, nor where I might seek the remedy. This distress I thought youth would have worn out, or reason, or time, or absence, or if not every one of them, yet all. But as fire getting hold in the bottom of a tree never leaveth till it come to the top, or as strong poison antidotum[2] being but chafed in the hand pierceth at the last the heart, so love, which I kept but low, thinking at my will to leave, entered at the last so far that it held me conquered. And then, disputing with myself, I played this on the bit:[3]

'Fidus, it standeth thee upon[4] either to win thy love or to wean thy affections; which choice is so hard that thou canst not tell whether the victory will be the greater in subduing thyself or conquering her. To love and to live well is wished of m[any], but incident to few. To live and to love well is incident to few, but indifferent to all.[5] To love without reason is an argument of lust, to live without love a token of folly. The measure of love is to have no mean, the end to be everlasting.

'Theseus had no need of Ariadne's thread[6] to find the way into the labyrinth, but to come out; nor thou of any help how to fall into these brakes[7] but to fall from them. If thou be witched with eyes, wear the eye of a weasel in a ring, which is an enchantment against such charms, and reason with thyself whether there be more pleasure to be accounted amorous or wise. Thou art in the view of the whole court, where the jealous will suspecteth upon every light occasion, where of the wise thou shalt be accounted fond,[8] and of the foolish amorous. The ladies themselves, howsoever they look, will thus imagine: that if thou take thought for love thou art but a fool, if take it lightly, no true servant.[9]

'Besides this, thou art to be bound as it were an apprentice, serving seven years for that which if thou win is lost in seven hours. If thou love thine equal, it is no contest; if thy superior, thou shalt be envied; if thine inferior, laughed at. If one that is beautiful, her colour will change before thou get thy desire; if one that is wise, she will over-reach thee so far that thou shalt never touch her; if virtuous, she will eschew such fond affection; if one deformed, she is not worthy of any affection; if she be rich, she needeth thee not; if poor, thou

---

1 *flout*] taunt
2 *antidotum*] presumably an error, but not corrected in later editions
3 *played this on the bit*] chewed over the constraints of my situation
4 *standeth thee upon*] is incumbent upon you
5 *indifferent to all*] of no consequence to any (because a true lover knows no moderation)
6 *Ariadne's thread*] Theseus was aided in his quest to slay the Minotaur (see p. 83n.) by Ariadne, daughter of the King of Crete, who supplied him with a thread to enable him to find his way out of the labyrinth in which the monster was kept.
7 *brakes*] thickets
8 *jealous / fond*] suspicious / foolish
9 *true servant*] faithful lover

needest not her; if old, why shouldst thou love her; if young, why should she love thee?'

Thus, gentlemen, I fed myself with mine own devices, thinking by piece-meal to cut off that which I could not diminish. For the more I strived with reason to conquer mine appetite, the more against reason I was subdued of mine affections.

At the last, calling to my remembrance an old rule of love, which a courtier then told me; of whom when I demanded what was the first thing to win my lady, he answered, 'Opportunity,' asking what was the second, he said, 'Opportunity,' desirous to know what might be the third, he replied, 'Opportunity'—which answers I marking, as one that thought to take mine aim of so cunning an archer, conjectured that to the beginning, continuing and ending of love nothing could be more convenient than opportunity. To the getting of the which I applied my whole study, and wore my wits to the hard stumps, assuring myself that as there is a time when the hare will lick the hound's ear, and the fierce tigress play with the gentle lamb, so there was a certain season when women were to be won, in the which moment they have neither will to deny nor wit to mistrust. Such a time, I have read, a young gentleman found to obtain the love of the Duchess of Milan; such a time, I have heard, that a poor yeoman chose to get the fairest lady in Mantua.[1] Unto the which time I trusted so much that I sold the skin before the beast was taken, reckoning without mine host, and setting down that in my books as ready money which afterwards I found to be a desperate debt.[2]

It chanced that this my lady (whom although I might name for the love I bore her, yet I will not for the reverence I owe her, but in this story call her Iffida) for to recreate her mind as also to solace her body went into the country, where she determined to make her abode for the space of three months, having gotten leave of those that might best give it. And in this journey I found good fortune so favourable that her abiding was within two miles of my father's mansion house, my parents being of great familiarity with the gentleman where my Iffida lay. Who now so fortunate as Fidus? Who so frolic? She being in the country, it was no being for me in the court, where every pastime was a plague to the mind that lived in melancholy. For as the turtle[3] having lost her mate wandereth alone, joying in nothing but in soli-tariness, so poor Fidus in the absence of Iffida walked in his chamber, as one not desolate for lack of company but desperate.

To make short of the circumstances, which hold you too long from that you would hear and I fain utter, I came home to my father; where, at mine entrance, supper being set on the table, I espied Iffida—Iffida, gentlemen, whom I found before I sought and lost before I won. Yet lest the alteration of my face might argue[4] some suspicion of my follies, I as courtly as I could,

---

1 *Such a time . . . Mantua*] Bond suggests (II, pp. 500–1) that this may be an allusion to the lost play *The Duke of Milan and the Marquis of Mantua* performed at Whitehall on St Stephen's Day, 1579.

2 *I sold the skin . . . desperate debt*] all proverbial, signifying to take something for granted. The skin sold prematurely is usually that of a lion. For *reckoning without mine host* see p. 72n.

3 *turtle*] turtle dove, emblematic of constancy

4 *argue*] evince

though God knows but coarsely, at that time behaved myself as though nothing pained me, when in truth nothing pleased me.

In the middle of supper, Iffida, as well for the acquaintance we had in court as also the courtesy she used in general to all, taking a glass in her hand filled with wine, drank to me in this wise:

'Gentleman, I am not learned, yet have I heard that the vine beareth three grapes; the first altereth, the second troubleth, the third dulleth. Of what grape this wine is made I cannot tell, and therefore I must crave pardon if either this draught change you, unless it be to the better, or grieve you, except it be for greater gain, or dull you, unless it be your desire; which long preamble I use to no other purpose than to warn you from wine hereafter, being so well counselled before.'

And with that she, drinking, delivered me the glass.

I, now taking heart at grass[1] to see her so gamesome, as merrily as I could pledged her in this manner:

'It is a pity, lady, you want a pulpit, having preached so well over the pot. Wherein you both show the learning which you profess you have not, and a kind of love, which would you had; the one appeareth by your long sermon, the other by the desire you have to keep me sober. But I will refer mine answer till after supper, and in the mean season be so temperate as you shall not think my wit to smell of the wine; although in my opinion such grapes set rather an edge upon wit than abate the point.'

'If I may speak in your cast,'[2] quoth Iffida (the glass being at my nose), 'I think wine is such a whetstone for wit that if it be often set in that manner it will quickly grind all the steel out, and scarce leave a back where it found an edge.'[3]

With many like speeches we continued our supper, which I will not repeat, lest you should think us Epicures[4] to sit so long at our meat. But all being ended, we arose, where, as the manner is, thanks and courtesy made to each other, we went to the fire. Where I, boldened now, without blushing took her by the hand, and thus began to kindle the flame which I should rather have quenched, seeking to blow a coal when I should have blown out the candle.

'Gentlewoman, either thou thought[est] my wits very short, that a sip of wine could alter me, or else yours very sharp, to cut me off so roundly; whenas I (without offence be it spoken) have heard that as deep drinketh the goose as the gander.'

'Gentleman,' quoth she, 'in arguing of wits you mistake mine and call your own into question. For what I said proceeded rather of a desire to have you in health than of malice to wish you harm. For you well know that wine to a young blood is in the spring-time flax to fire,[5] and at all times either

---

1 *taking heart at grass*] plucking up my spirits (see p. 58 for another example of the phrase in a similar context)
2 *speak in your cast*] interrupt you
3 *edge*] blade
4 *Epicures*] see p. 34n.
5 *flax to fire*] proverbial, signifying to heighten a dangerous potentiality (flax, a plant grown for both its seeds and fibre, being highly combustible)

unwholesome or superfluous, and so dangerous that more perish by a surfeit than the sword. I have heard wise clerks say that Galen,[1] being asked what diet he used that he lived so long, answered, "I have drunk no wine, I have touched no woman, I have kept myself warm."

'Now, sir, if you will license me to proceed, this I thought: that if one of your years should take a dram of magis,[2] whereby consequently you should fall to an ounce of love, and then upon so great heat take a little cold, it were enough to cast you away or turn you out of the way.[3] And although I be no physician, yet have I been used to attend sick persons, where I found nothing to hurt them so much as wine, which always drew with it, as the adamant[4] doth the iron, a desire of women. How hurtful both have been, though you be too young to have tried it, yet you are old enough to believe it. Wine should be taken as the dogs of Egypt drink water, by snatches, and so quench their thirst and not hinder their running; or as the daughters of Lysander[5] used it, who with a drop of wine took a spoonful of water; or as the virgins in Rome, who drink but their eye-full,[6] contenting themselves as much with the sight as the taste.

'Thus to excuse myself of unkindness you have made me almost impudent, and I you (I fear me) impatient, in seeming to prescribe a diet where there is no danger, giving a preparative[7] when the body is purged. But seeing all this talk came of drinking, let it end with drinking.'

I, seeing myself thus ridden, thought either she should sit fast or else I would cast[8] her. And thus I replied:

'Lady, you think to wade deep where the ford is but shallow, and to enter into the secrets of my mind when it lieth open already. Wherein you use no less art to bring me in doubt of your good will, than craft to put me out of doubt, having baited your hook both with poison and pleasure; in that, using the means of physic (whereof you so talk), mingling sweet syrups with bitter dregs. You stand in fear that wine should inflame my liver and convert me to a lover. Truly, I am framed of that metal that I can mortify any affections, whether it be in drink or desire; so that I have no need of your plasters,[9] though I must needs give thanks for your pains.'

And now, Philautus, for I see Euphues begin to nod, thou shalt understand that in the midst of my reply my father, with the rest of the company, interrupted me, saying they would all fall to some pastime. Which, because it groweth late, Philautus, we will defer till the morning, for age must keep a strait diet,[10] or else a sickly life.

---

1 *Galen*] celebrated Greek physician (b. AD 130) who had a profound influence on the development of European medicine
2 *dram of magis*] a sixteenth of an ounce (i.e. the smallest quantity) of a love potion
3 *cast you away . . . way*] kill you or lead you astray
4 *adamant*] magnet
5 *Lysander*] see p. 68n.
6 *the virgins in Rome . . . . eye-full*] satisfy themselves with the sight like Roman women (who were not permitted to drink wine)
7 *preparative*] draught administered before a medicine to prepare the system
8 *cast*] throw (metaphor drawn from horse-riding)
9 *mortify / plasters*] subdue / salves
10 *strait diet*] strict regimen

Philautus, tickled in every vein with delight, was loath to leave so, although not willing the good old man should break his accustomed hour,[1] unto whom sleep was the chiefest sustenance. And so waking Euphues, who had taken a nap, they all went to their lodging, where I think Philautus was musing upon the event of Fidus his love. But there I will leave them in their beds till the next morning.

Gentlemen and gentlewomen, in the discourse of this love it may seem I have taken a new course; but such was the time then that it was strange to love, as it is now common, and then less used in the court than it is now in the country. But having respect to the time past, I trust you will not condemn my present time, whom am enforced to sing after their plainsong that was then used, and will follow hereafter the crotchets[2] that are in these days cunningly handled.

For the minds of lovers alter with the mad moods of the musicians. And so much are they within few years changed that we account their old wooing and singing to have so little cunning that we esteem it barbarous; and were they living to hear our new coyings, they would judge it have so much curiosity[3] they would term it foolish.

In the time of Romulus all heads were rounded[4] of his fashion; in the time of Caesar curled of his manner. When Cyrus lived everyone praised the hooked nose, and when he died they allowed[5] the straight nose. And so it fareth with love. In times past they used to woo in plain terms, now in picked sentences,[6] and he speedeth best that speaketh wisest. Everyone following the newest way, which is not ever the nearest way; some going over the stile when the gate is open, and other keeping the right beaten path when he may cross over better by the fields. Everyone followeth his own fancy, which maketh divers leap short for want of good rising,[7] and many shoot over for lack of true aim.

And to that pass it is come that they make an art of that which was wont to be thought natural. And thus it standeth, that it is not yet determined whether in love Ulysses more prevailed with his wit, or Paris with his personage, or Achilles with his prowess.[8] For every of them have Venus by the hand, and they are all assured and certain to win her heart.

But I had almost forgotten the old man, who useth not to sleep compass,[9] whom I see with Euphues and Philautus now already in the

---

1 *break his accustomed hour*] depart from his usual schedule
2 *after their plainsong / crotchets*] according to their unadorned style / intricacies (the musical metaphor is sustained in the following paragraph)
3 *coyings / curiosity*] dallyings / nicety
4 *rounded*] close-cropped (for *Romulus* see p. 34n.)
5 *allowed*] approved (for *Cyrus* see p. 27 and note)
6 *picked sentences*] exquisite pronouncements
7 *rising*] take off
8 *personage / prowess*] physical beauty / bravery (for *Ulysses*, *Paris* and *Achilles* see p. 76n., p. 33n. and p. 106n. respectively)
9 *compass*] round the clock

garden, ready to proceed with his tale. Which, if it seem tedious, we will break off again when they go to dinner.

Fidus, calling these gentlemen up, brought them into his garden, where under a sweet arbour of eglantine, the birds recording their sweet notes, he also strained his old pipe,[1] and thus began:

Gentlemen, yesternight I left off abruptly and therefore I must now begin in the like manner.

My father placed us all in good order, requesting either by questions[2] to whet our wits or by stories to try our memories; and Iffida, that might best there be bold, being the best[3] in the company, and at all assays too good for me, began again to preach in this manner:

'Thou art a courtier, Fidus, and therefore best able to resolve any question, for I know thy wit good to understand and ready to answer. To thee, therefore, I address my talk.

'There was sometime in Siena a Magnifico, whom God blessed with three daughters, but by three wives, and of three sundry[4] qualities. The eldest was very fair, but a very fool; the second marvellous witty, but yet marvellous wanton; the third as virtuous as any living, but more deformed than any that ever lived.

'The noble gentleman their father disputed for the bestowing of them with himself thus: "I thank the gods that have given me three daughters who in their bosoms carry their dowries, insomuch as I shall not need to disburse one mite[5] for all their marriages. Maidens be they never so foolish yet, being fair, they are commonly fortunate; for that men in these days have more respect to the outward show than the inward substance. Wherein they imitate good lapidaries,[6] who choose the stones that delight the eye, measuring the value not by the hidden virtue but by the outward glistering; or wise painters, who lay their best colours upon their worst counterfeit. And in this methinketh Nature hath dealt indifferently,[7] that a fool whom everyone abhorreth should have beauty which everyone desireth, that the excellency of the one might excuse the vanity of the other; for as we in nothing more differ from the gods than when we are fools, so in nothing do we come near them so much as when we are amiable.[8] This caused Helen to be snatched up for a star, and Ariadne[9] to be placed in the heavens; not that they were wise but

---

1 *recording / pipe*] warbling, piping / voice
2 *questions*] subjects for debate. Participating in the discusion of a set topic constituted one of the conversational arts during this period and was a customary form of amusement in cultivated circles (cf. the topics propounded after dinner at the Lady Flavia's house, pp. 298ff.)
3 *best*] person of highest rank
4 *sundry*] different
5 *disburse one mite*] spend the smallest of sums (i.e. as a dowry)
6 *lapidaries*] jewellers
7 *indifferently*] even-handedly
8 *amiable*] beautiful
9 *Helen / Ariadne*] according to classical tradition, it was Helen's brother, not Helen herself, who became a star / the crown given to Ariadne (see p. 67) at her marriage to Dionysus was placed among the stars after her death

fair, fitter to add a majesty to the sky than bear a majesty in earth. Juno, for all her jealousy, beholding Io[1] wished to be no goddess so she might be so gallant.[2] Love cometh in at the eye, not at the ear; by seeing Nature's works, not by hearing women's words. And such effects and pleasure doth sight bring unto us that divers have lived by looking on fair and beautiful pictures, desiring no meat[3] nor hearkening to any music. What made the gods so often to truant from heaven and miche[4] here on earth but beauty? What made men to imagine that the firmament was God but beauty, which is said to bewitch the wise and enchant them that made it? Pygmalion for beauty loved an image of ivory, Apelles the counterfeit of Campaspe;[5] and none we have heard of so senseless that the name of beauty cannot either break or bend. It is this only that princes desire in their houses, gardens, orchards, and beds; following Alexander, who more esteemed the face of Venus not yet finished, than the table of the nine Muses perfected.[6] And I am of that mind that there can be nothing given unto mortal men by the immortal gods either more noble or more necessary than beauty. For as when the counterfeit of Ganymede[7] was shown at a market, everyone would fain buy it, because Zeuxis had therein showed his greatest cunning, so when a beautiful woman appeareth in a multitude, every man is drawn to sue to her, for that the gods (the only painters of beauty) have in her expressed the art of their deity. But I will here rest myself, knowing that if I should run so far as beauty would carry me, I should sooner want breath to tell her praises than matter to prove them. Thus I am persuaded that my fair daughter shall be well married, for there is none that will or can demand a greater jointure[8] than beauty.

' "My second child is witty, but yet wanton; which in my mind rather addeth a delight to the man, than a disgrace to the maid. And so linked are those two qualities together that to be wanton without wit is apishness, and to be thought witty without wantonness preciseness.[9] When Lais, being very pleasant, had told a merry jest, 'It is pity,' said Aristippus, 'that Lais, having so good a wit, should be a wanton.' 'Yea,' quoth Lais, 'but it were more pity that Lais should be a wanton and have no good wit.'[10] Osiris, King of the Egyptians, being much delighted with pleasant conceits, would often affirm that he had rather have a virgin that could give a quick answer that might cut him than a mild speech that might claw him.[11] When it was objected to a

---

1 *Juno / Io*] Queen of the gods and wife of Jupiter / mortal loved by Jupiter
2 *gallant*] fine-looking
3 *meat*] sustenance
4 *miche*] skulk
5 *Pygmalion ... Campaspe*] Alexander's commissioning of the portrait of his Theban captive, Campaspe, and Apelles' love for the sitter is the subject of Lyly's first play. For *Pygmalion* see p. 36n.
6 *following Alexander ... perfected*] No source has been found for this preference.
7 *counterfeit of Ganymede*] picture of the youthful cup-bearer to the gods (for *Zeuxis* see p. 158n.)
8 *jointure*] marriage portion
9 *apishness / preciseness*] foolishness / scrupulosity
10 *When Lais ... no good wit*] For the relationship between Lais and Aristippus see p. 97n.
11 *Osirus / claw him*] legendary figure reputed to have brought civilization to Egypt and spread it to neighbouring lands / flatter him. (The story related here appears to be Lyly's invention.)

gentlewoman that she was neither fair nor fortunate, 'And yet,' quoth she, 'wise and well-favoured,' thinking it the chiefest gift that Nature could bestow to have a nut-brown hue[1] and an excellent head. It is wit that allureth, when every word shall have his weight, when nothing shall proceed but it shall either savour of a sharp conceit or a secret conclusion.[2] And this is the greatest thing, to conceive readily[3] and answer aptly, to understand whatsoever is spoken and to reply as though they understood nothing. A gentleman that once loved a lady most entirely, walking with her in a park, with a deep sigh began to say, 'Oh, that women could be constant!' She replied, 'Oh, that they could not,' pulling her hat over her head. 'Why,' quoth the gentleman, 'doth the sun offend your eyes?' 'Yea,' answered she, 'the son of your mother.' Which quick and ready replies being well marked of him, he was enforced to sue for that which he was determined to shake off.

' "A nobleman in Siena, disposed to jest with a gentlewoman of mean birth yet excellent qualities, between game and earnest gan thus to salute her: 'I know not how I should commend your beauty, because it is somewhat too brown, nor your stature, being somewhat too low, and of your wit I cannot judge.' 'No,' quoth she, 'I believe you, for none can judge of wit but they that have it.' 'Why then,' quoth he, 'dost thou think me a fool?' 'Thought is free, my lord,' quoth she. 'I will not take you at your word.' He, perceiving all outward faults to be recompensed with inward favour, chose this virgin for his wife. And in my simple opinion he did a thing both worthy his stock and her virtue.

' "It is wit that flourisheth when beauty fadeth, that waxeth young when age approacheth, and resembleth the ivy leaf, who although it be dead continueth green. And because of all creatures the woman's wit is most excellent, therefore have the poets feigned the Muses[4] to be women, the nymphs, the goddesses; examples of whose rare wisdoms and sharp capacities would nothing but make me commit idolatry with my daughter. I never heard but of three things which argued a fine wit: invention, conceiving, answering. Which have all been found so common in women that, were it not I should flatter them, I should think them singular.[5]

' "Then this sufficeth me that my second daughter shall not lead apes in hell,[6] though she have not a penny for the priest, because she is witty; which bindeth weak things, and looseth strong things, and worketh all things in those that have either wit themselves or love wit in others.

' "My youngest, though no pearl to hang at one's ear,[7] yet so precious she is to a well-disposed mind that grace seemeth almost to disdain nature. She is deformed in body, slow of speech, crabbed in countenance, and almost in all parts crooked; but in behaviour so honest, in prayer so devout, so precise in all her dealings, that I never heard her speak anything that either concerned

---

1 *nut-brown hue*] dark colouring (not generally regarded as a mark of beauty in the Renaissance)
2 *secret conclusion*] hidden meaning
3 *conceive readily*] grasp ideas quickly
4 *Muses*] the nine daughters of Zeus and Mnemosyne, who presided over the arts and sciences
5 *singular*] incomparable
6 *lead apes in hell*] be an old maid (see p. 65n.)
7 *no pearl to hang at one's ear*] not one to be paraded for her beauty

not good instruction or godly mirth. Who never delighteth in costly apparel but ever desireth homely attire, accounting no bravery[1] greater than virtue; who beholding her ugly shape in a glass, smiling said, 'This face were fair if it were turned,' noting that the inward motions would make the outward favour but counterfeit. For as the precious stone sandastros[2] hath nothing in outward appearance but that which seemeth black, but being broken poureth forth beams like the sun, so virtue showeth but bare to the outward eye, but being pierced with inward desire shineth like crystal. And this dare I avouch, that as the Troglodytae which digged in the filthy ground for roots and found the inestimable stone topazon,[3] which enriched them ever after, so he that seeketh after my youngest daughter, which is deformed, shall find the greatest treasure of piety to comfort him during his life. Beautiful women are but like the ermine,[4] whose skin is desired, whose carcass is despised; the virtuous, contrariwise, are then most liked when their skin is least loved.

' "Then ought I to take least care for her whom everyone that is honest will care for; so that I will quiet myself with this persuasion, that every one shall have a wooer shortly. Beauty cannot live without a husband; wit will not; virtue shall not."

'Now, gentleman, I have propounded my reasons, for every one I must now ask you the question. If it were your chance to travel to Siena and to see as much there as I have told you here, whether would you choose for your wife, the fair fool, the witty wanton, or the crooked saint?'

When she had finished I stood in a maze, seeing three hooks laid in one bait, uncertain to answer what might please her, yet compelled to say somewhat lest I should discredit myself. But seeing all were whist[5] to hear my judgement, I replied thus:

'Lady Iffida and gentlewomen all, I mean not to travel to Siena to woo beauty, lest in coming home the air change it and then my labour be lost; neither to seek so far for wit, lest she account me a fool when I might speed as well nearer hand; nor to sue to virtue, lest in Italy I be infected with vice, and so looking to get Jupiter by the hand I catch Pluto by the heel.[6] But if you will imagine that great Magnifico to have sent his three daughters into England, I would thus debate with them before I would bargain with them.

'I love beauty well, but I could not find it in my heart to marry a fool; for if she be impudent I shall not rule her, and if she be obstinate she will rule me. And myself none of the wisest, methinketh it were no good match; for two fools in one bed are too many.

'Wit of all things setteth my fancies on edge, but I should hardly choose a wanton. For be she never so wise, if always she want one when she hath me,

---

1 *bravery*] finery
2 *sandastros*] species of onyx found in India and Asia
3 *Troglodytae / topazon*] cave-dwelling, Ethiopian people who sustained themselves with roots / topaz
4 *ermine*] variety of stoat valued only for its winter (white) fur
5 *whist*] hushed
6 *looking to get ... heel*] seeking to achieve the best I gain the worst (*Jupiter / Pluto* = supreme deity dwelling on Mount Olympus / god of the underworld)

I had as lief she should want me too; for of all my apparel I would have my cap fit close.[1]

'Virtue I cannot mislike, which hitherto I have honoured, but such a crooked apostle I never brooked.[2] For virtue may well fat my mind, but it will never feed mine eye; and in marriage, as market folks tell me, the husband should have two eyes and the wife but one.[3] But in such a match it is as good to have no eye as no appetite.

'But to answer of three inconveniences which I would choose (although each threaten a mischief), I must needs take the wise wanton; who if by her wantonness she will never want where she likes, yet by her wit she will ever conceal whom she loves. And to wear a horn and not know it will do me no more harm than to eat a fly and not see it.'[4]

Iffida, I know not whether stung with mine answer, or not content with my opinion, replied in this manner:

'Then, Fidus, when you match, God send you such a one as you like best, but be sure always that your head be not higher than your hat.'[5]

And thus, feigning an excuse, departed to her lodging, which caused all the company to break off their determined pastimes, leaving me perplexed with a hundred contrary imaginations.

For this, Philautus, thought I, that either I did not hit the question which she would, or that I hit it too full against her will. For to say the truth, witty she was and somewhat merry, but God knoweth so far from wantonness as myself was from wisdom; and I as far from thinking ill of her as I found her from taking me well.

Thus all night tossing in my bed, I determined the next day, if any opportunity were offered, to offer also my importunate service. And found the time fit, though her mind so froward[6] that to think of it my heart throbbeth, and to utter it will bleed freshly.

The next day, I coming to the gallery where she was solitarily walking with her frowning-cloth, as sick lately of the sullens,[7] understanding my father to be gone on hunting, and all other the gentlewomen either walked abroad to take the air or not yet ready to come out of their chambers, I adventured in one ship to put all my wealth, and at this time to open my long-concealed love; determining either to be a knight, as we say, or a knitter of caps.[8] And in this manner I uttered my first speech:

---

1 *I had as lief ... too / of all my apparel ... close*] I would prefer her to be without me also / I am most concerned that of all my clothes my hat should be tight-fitting (an allusion to the horns conventionally associated with a deceived husband)

2 *brooked*] endured

3 *in marriage ... but one*] an adaptation of the proverb 'who buys wants a hundred eyes, who sells needs have but one'

4 *eat a fly ... see it*] a variation of the proverb 'the blind man eats many a fly'

5 *your head ... hat*] your horns don't protrude through your cap (i.e. that you are not a manifest cuckold)

6 *froward*] contrarily disposed

7 *frowning-cloth / sick ... sullens*] a binding for the head worn by women when sick (used metaphorically to signify a state of displeasure) / in a mood of gloomy ill-humour

8 *a knight ... caps*] a hero or the humblest of men (proverbial)

'Lady, to make a long preamble to a short suit would seem superfluous, and to begin abruptly in a matter of great weight might be thought absurd; so as I am brought into a doubt whether I should offend you with too many words, or hinder myself with too few.'

She, not staying for a longer treatise, brake me off thus roundly:

'Gentleman, a short suit is soon made, but great matters not easily granted. If your request be reasonable, a word will serve; if not, a thousand will not suffice. Therefore if there be anything that I may do you pleasure in, see it be honest, and use not tedious discourses or colours of rhetoric;[1] which though they be thought courtly, yet are they not esteemed necessary. For the purest emerald shineth brightest when it hath no oil,[2] and truth delighteth best when it is apparelled worst.'

Then I thus replied:

'Fair lady, as I know you wise, so have I found you courteous; which two qualities, meeting in one of so rare beauty, must foreshow some great marvel, and works such effects in those that either have heard of your praise or seen your person that they are enforced to offer themselves unto your service. Among the number of which your vassals, I, though least worthy yet most willing, am now come to proffer both my life to do you good and my livings to be at your command; which frank offer proceeding of a faithful mind can neither be refused of you nor misliked. And because I would cut off speeches which might seem to savour either of flattery or deceit, I conclude thus: that as you are the first unto whom I have vowed my love, so you shall be the last; requiring nothing but a friendly acceptance of my service and goodwill for the reward of it.'

Iffida, whose right ear began to glow and both whose cheeks waxed red, either with choler or bashfulness, took me up thus for stumbling:

'Gentleman, you make me blush as much for anger as shame, that seeking to praise me and proffer yourself, you both bring my good name into question and your ill meaning into disdain; so that thinking to present me with your heart, you have thrust into my hands the serpent amphisbena,[3] which having at each end a sting hurteth both ways. You term me fair, and therein you flatter; wise, and therein you mean witty; courteous, which in other plain words, if you durst have uttered it, you would have named wanton.

'Have you thought me, Fidus, so light that none but I could fit your looseness? Or am I the witty wanton which you harped upon yesternight, that would always give you the sting in the head?[4] You are much deceived in me, Fidus, and I as much in you; for you shall never find me for your appetite, and I had thought never to have tasted you so unpleasant to mine. If I be amiable,[5] I will do those things that are fit for so good a face; if deformed, those things which shall make me fair. And howsoever I live I pardon your

---

1 *colours of rhetoric*] elaborate artificial terms
2 *For the purest . . . oil*] Some precious stones were thought to be enhanced by the application of oil (see the comparison between a true woman and a sapphire, p. 225).
3 *the serpent amphisbena*] serpent found in Libya, able to move backwards as well as forwards, hence the belief in the sting at each end of its body
4 *give you the sting in the head*] make you a cuckold (*sting* = smart resulting from the growth of the horns traditionally associated with the cuckold)
5 *amiable*] lovely

presumption, knowing it to be no less common in court than foolish to tell a fair tale to a foul lady; wherein they sharpen, I confess, their wits, but show, as I think, small wisdom. And you among the rest, because you would be accounted courtly, have assayed to feel the vein you cannot see. Wherein you follow not the best physicians, yet the most, who, feeling the pulses, do always say it betokeneth an ague; and you, seeing my pulses beat pleasantly, judge me apt to fall into a fool's fever. Which lest it happen to shake me hereafter, I am minded to shake you off now, using but one request where I should seek oft to revenge: that is, that you never attempt by word or writing to solicit your suit, which is no more pleasant to me than the wringing of a strait shoe.'[1]

When she had uttered these bitter words, she was going into her chamber; but I, that now had no stay of myself, began to stay[2] her, and thus again to reply:

'I perceive, Iffida, that where the stream runneth smoothest the water is deepest; and where the least smoke is there to be the greatest fire; and where the mildest countenance is there to be the melancholiest conceits. I swear to thee by the gods—'

And there she interrupted me again, in this manner:

'Fidus, the more you swear the less I believe you. For that it is a practice in love to have as little care of their own oaths as they have of others' honours; imitating Jupiter, who never kept oath he swore to Juno, thinking it lawful in love to have as small regard of religion as he had of chastity.[3] And because I will not feed you with delays, nor that you should comfort yourself with trial, take this for a flat answer: that as yet I mean not to love any; and if I do, it is not you. And so I leave you.'

But once again I stayed her steps, being now throughly heated, as well with love as with choler. And thus I thundered:

'If I had used the policy that hunters do in catching of hyena,[4] it might be also I had now won you. But coming of the right side, I am entangled myself, and had it been on the left side, I should have inveigled thee. Is this the guerdon for good will, is this the courtesy of ladies, the life of courtiers, the food of lovers? Ah, Iffida, little dost thou know the force of affection, and therefore thou rewardest it lightly, neither showing courtesy like a lover, nor giving thanks like a lady.

'If I should compare my blood with thy birth, I am as noble; if my wealth with thine, as rich; if confer[5] qualities, not much inferior; but in good will as far above thee as thou art beyond me in pride. Dost thou disdain me because thou art beautiful? Why, colours fade when courtesy flourisheth. Dost thou reject me for that thou art wise? Why, wit having told[6] all his cards lacketh

---

1 *wringing . . . shoe*] pinching of a tight shoe
2 *stay / stay*] control / detain
3 *imitating Jupiter . . . chastity*] Though married to Juno, goddess of marriage, Jupiter had numerous amorous affairs.
4 *the policy . . . hyena*] Bond (II, p. 504) cites Pliny's assertion that if a hyena swerve to the right when pursued it will catch the hunters, if to the left its strength will fail. Hence the craft of the hunter depends on exploiting the weaker side (*guerdon* in the next sentence = reward).
5 *confer*] compare
6 *told*] counted

many an ace of wisdom. But this is incident to women: to love those that least care for them and to hate those that most desire them, making a stake of that which they should use for a stomacher.[1]

'And seeing it is so, better lost they are with a little grudge[2] than found with much grief; better sold for sorrow than bought for repentance; and better to make no account of love than an occupation—where all one's service, be it never so great, is never thought enough, when were it never so little it is too much.'

When I had thus raged, she thus replied:

'Fidus, you go the wrong way to the wood in making a gap when the gate is open, or in seeking to enter by force when your next[3] way lieth by favour. Wherein you follow the humour of Ajax, who, losing Achilles' shield by reason, thought to win it again by rage.[4] But it fell out with him as it doth commonly with all those that are choleric, that he hurt no man but himself; neither have you moved any to offence but yourself. And in my mind (though simple be the comparison yet seemly it is), that your anger is like the wrangling of children, who when they cannot get what they would have by play, they fall to crying; and not unlike the use of foul gamesters, who having lost the main[5] by true judgement, think to face it out with a false oath; and you missing of my love, which you required in sport, determine to hit it by spite. If you have a commission[6] to take up ladies, let me see it; if a privilege, let me know it; if a custom, I mean to break it.

'You talk of your birth, when I know there is no difference of bloods in a basin; and as little do I esteem those that boast of their ancestors and have themselves no virtue, as I do of those that crake[7] of their love and have no modesty. I know Nature hath provided, and I think our laws allow it, that one may love when they see their time, not that they must love when others appoint it.

'Whereas you bring in a rabble of reasons as it were to bind me against my will, I answer that in all respects I think you so far to excel me that I cannot find in my heart to match with you. For one of so great good will as you are to encounter with one of such pride as I am were neither commendable nor convenient, no more than a patch of fustian in a damask[8] coat. As for my beauty and wit, I had rather make them better than they are, being now

---

1 *making a stake . . . stomacher*] obscure. Bond suggests (unconvincingly) 'treating marriage as a gambler's throw, instead of a wise investment in what may comfort and protect' (II, p. 504). Croll and Clemons propose 'stock' i.e. 'hose' for *stake*, implying keeping at a distance something that should be close to the heart (p. 269). It is possible, however, that *stake* may be something that impales, as opposed to a *stomacher* something that protects.

2 *grudge*] complaint

3 *next*] readiest

4 *humour of Ajax . . . rage*] a further reference to the dispute over Achilles' armour in which Ulysses defeated Ajax through his superior eloquence (see p. 78n.)

5 *main*] wager (in the game of hazard)

6 *commission*] warrant

7 *in a basin / crake*] i.e. in the physician's bowl after bleeding for medical purposes / vaunt

8 *fustian / damask*] coarse cloth made from cotton and flax / reversible fabric usually of silk

but mean, by virtue, than worse than they are, which would be nothing, by love.

'Now whereas you bring in (I know not by what proof, for I think you were never so much of women's counsels) that there women best like where they be least beloved, then ought they more to pity us, not to oppress us, seeing we have neither free will to choose nor fortune to enjoy. Then, Fidus, since your eyes are so sharp that you cannot only look through a millstone[1] but clean through the mind, and so cunning that you can level at the dispositions of women whom you never knew, methinketh you should use the mean if you desire to have the end, which is to hate those whom you would fain have to love you; for this have you set for a rule (yet out of square), that women then love most when they be loathed most. And to the end I might stoop to your lure, I pray begin to hate me that I may love you.

'Touching your losing and finding, your buying and selling, it much skilleth not,[2] for I had rather you should lose me so you might never find me again, than find me that I should think myself lost; and rather had I be sold of you for a penny than bought for you with a pound.

'If you mean either to make an art or an occupation of love,[3] I doubt not but you shall find work in the court sufficient, but you shall not know the length of my foot until by your cunning you get commendation.[4] A phrase now there is which belongeth to your shop-board,[5] that is 'to make love', and when I shall hear of what fashion it is made, if I like the pattern you shall cut me a partlet[6]—so as you cut it not with a pair of left-handed shears.[7] And I doubt not, though you have marred your first love in the making, yet by the time you have made three or four loves you will prove an expert workman; for as yet you are like the tailor's boy, who thinketh to take measure before he can handle the shears. And thus I protest unto you, because you are but a young beginner, that I will help you to as much custom as I can, so as you will promise me to sew no false stitches; and when mine old love is worn threadbare, you shall take measure of a new.

'In the mean season, do not discourage yourself. Apelles was no good painter the first day, for in every occupation one must first endeavour to begin. He that will sell lawn must learn to fold it, and he that will make love must learn first to court it.'[8]

As she was in this vein very pleasant, so I think she would have been very long, had not the gentlewomen called her to walk, being so fair a day. Then,

---

1 *look through a millstone*] proverbial (said of those who unjustifiably lay claim to sharpness of sight)
2 *it much skilleth not*] it doesn't particularly matter
3 *art or an occupation of love*] The paragraphs that follow turns on the idea of 'making' love as an occupation analogous to tailoring, and Fidus as an inexperienced craftsman yet to learn his trade.
4 *know the length of my foot / by your cunning . . . commendation*] discover my weaknesses (but Lyly plays on the literal sense) / you have proved your skill by receiving testimonies from others
5 *shop-board*] trade (literally 'work bench')
6 *partlet*] garment covering the neck and shoulders
7 *left-handed shears*] dishonestly (in this context, with a view to my dishonour)
8 *lawn / to court it*] fine linen / the art of courtship

taking her leave very courteously, she left me alone; yet turning again she said:
'Will you not man[1] us, Fidus, being so proper a man?'
'Yes,' quoth I, 'and without asking too, had you been a proper[2] woman.'
Then, smiling, she said:
'You should find me a proper woman had you been a proper workman.'
And so she departed.

Now, Philautus and Euphues, what a trance was I left in, who bewailing
my love was answered with hate; or if not with hate, such a kind of heat as
almost burnt the very bowels within me! What greater discourtesy could there
possibly rest in the mind of a gentlewoman than with so many nips, such
bitter girds, such disdainful gleeks[3] to answer him that honoured her? What
cruelty more unfit for so comely a lady than to spur him that galloped, or to
let him blood in the heart whose vein she should have staunched in the liver?[4]
But it fared with me as with the herb basil, the which the more it is crushed
the sooner it springeth; or the rue, which the oftener it is cut the better it
groweth; or the poppy, which the more it is trodden with the feet the more
it flourisheth. For in these extremities, beaten as it were to the ground with
disdain, my love reacheth to the top of the house with hope; not unlike unto
a tree which, though it be often felled to the hard root, yet it buddeth again
and getteth a top.

But to make an end both of my tale and my sorrows, I will proceed; only
craving a little patience if I fall into mine old passions.

With that Philautus came in with his spoke,[5] saying:
'In faith, Fidus, methinketh I could never be weary in hearing this discourse; and I fear me the end will be too soon, although I feel in myself
the impression of thy sorrows.'
'Yea,' quoth Euphues, 'you shall find my friend Philautus so kind-
hearted that before you have done he will be further in love with her than
you were; for as your lady said, Philautus will be bound to make love, as
warden of that occupation.'[6]
Then Fidus:

Well, God grant Philautus better success than I had, which was too bad. For
my father being returned from hunting and the gentlewomen from walking,
the table was covered and we all set down to dinner; none more pleasant than
Iffida, which would not conclude her mirth, and I not melancholy, because I
would cover my sadness—lest either she might think me to dote or my father
suspect me to desire her. And thus we both in table-talk began to rest.[7] She
requesting me to be her carver and I, not attending well to that she craved,
gave her salt; which when she received she gan thus to reply:

---

1 *man*] escort
2 *proper / proper*] handsome / true
3 *girds / gleeks*] taunts / jibes
4 *liver*] seat of the passions and thus analogous to the heart, the domain of love
5 *came in with his spoke*] interrupted
6 *warden of that occuption*] chief officer of that profession (metaphor drawn from the
organization of sixteenth-century guilds)
7 *began to rest*] took a pause (with a pun on 'wrest', i.e. twist words)

'In sooth, gentleman, I seldom eat salt for fear of anger; and if you give it me in token that I want wit, then will you make me choleric before I eat it.[1] For women, be they never so foolish, would ever be thought wise.'

I stand not long for mine answer, but as well quickened by her former talk and desirous to cry quittance for her present tongue,[2] said thus:

'If to eat store of salt cause one to fret and to have no salt signify lack of wit, then do you cause me to marvel that eating no salt you are so captious, and loving no salt you are so wise; when indeed so much wit is sufficient for a woman as when she is in the rain can warn her to come out of it.'[3]

'You mistake your aim,' quoth Iffida, 'for such a shower may fall as did once into Danae's lap,[4] and then that woman were a fool that would come out of it. But it may be your mouth is out of taste, therefore you were best season it with salt.'

'Indeed,' quoth I, 'your answers are so fresh that without salt I can hardly swallow them.'

Many nips were returned that time between us, and some so bitter that I thought them to proceed rather of malice, to work despite,[5] than of mirth, to show disport.

My father, very desirous to hear questions asked,[6] willed me after dinner to use some demand; which, after grace, I did in this sort:

'Lady Iffida, it is not unlikely but that you can answer a question as wisely as the last night you asked one wilily, and I trust you will be as ready to resolve any doubt by entreaty as I was by commandment.

'There was a lady in Spain who after the decease of her father had three suitors, and yet never a good archer.[7] The one excelled in all gifts of the body, insomuch that there could be nothing added to his perfection, and so armed in all points as his very looks were able to pierce the heart of any lady, especially of such a one as seemed herself to have no less beauty than she had personage.[8] For that as between the similitude of manners there is a friendship in every respect absolute, so in the composition of the body there is a certain love engendered by one look, where both the bodies resemble each other as woven both in one loom.

'The other had nothing to commend him but a quick wit, which he had always so at his will that nothing could be spoken but he would wrest it to his own purpose; which wrought such delight in this lady, who was no less witty than he, that you would have thought a marriage to be solemnized before the match could be talked of. For there is nothing in love more requi-

---

1 *I seldom . . . eat it*] Two properties of salt are played on both here and in the following paragraphs, its tendency to heighten irascibility and its association with mental acuity. The former property is not widely attested.

2 *cry quittance . . . tongue*] revenge myself for her fresh taunts

3 *so much wit . . . out of it*] i.e. intelligence is all but unnecessary in a woman. Iffida's riposte turns on the literal meaning of the words.

4 *such a shower . . . Danae's lap*] i.e. a shower of gold (the form in which Jupiter gained access to Danae)

5 *to work despite*] to create ill-will

6 *to hear questions asked*] see p. 205n.

7 *never a good archer*] not one among them who could hit the target (with a pun on *suitor*, pronounced 'shooter' in the sixteenth century)

8 *personage*] distinction of rank

site or more delectable than pleasant and wise conference; neither can there arise any storm in love which by wit is not turned to a calm.

'The third was a gentleman of great possessions, large revenues, full of money, but neither the wisest that ever enjoyed so much, nor the properest[1] that ever desired so much. He had no plea in his suit but gilt,[2] which rubbed well in a hot hand is such a grease as will supple a very hard heart. And who is so ignorant that knoweth not gold be a key for every lock, chiefly with his lady, who herself was well-stored and a[s] yet infected with a desire of more that she could not but lend him a good countenance[3] in this match.

'Now, Lady Iffida, you are to determine this Spanish bargain—or, if you please, we will make it an English controversy. Supposing you to be the lady, and three such gentlemen to come unto you a-wooing, in faith, who should be the speeder?'

'Gentleman,' quoth Iffida, 'you may answer your own question by your own argument if you would. For if you conclude the lady to be beautiful, witty, and wealthy, then no doubt she will take such a one as should have comeliness of body, sharpness of wit, and store of riches. Otherwise I would condemn that wit in her, which you seem so much to commend, herself excelling in three qualities, she should take one which was endued but with one. In perfect love the eye must be pleased, the ear delighted, the heart comforted; beauty causeth the one, wit the other, wealth the third.

'To love only for comeliness were lust; to like for wit only, madness; to desire chiefly for goods, covetousness. And yet can there be no love without beauty, but we loathe it; nor without wit, but we scorn it; nor without riches, but we repent it. Every flower hath his blossom, his savour, his sap; and every desire should have to feed the eye, to please the wit, to maintain the root.

'Ganymede may cast an amiable countenance,[4] but that feedeth not; Ulysses tell a witty tale, but that fatteth not; Croesus bring bags of gold, and that doth both. Yet without the aid of beauty he cannot bestow it, and without wit he knows not how to use it. So that I am of this mind: there is no lady but in her choice will be so resolute that either she will live a virgin till she have such a one as shall have all these three properties, or else die for anger if she match with one that wanteth[5] any one of them.'

I, perceiving her to stand so stiffly, thought, if I might, to remove her footing, and replied again:

'Lady, you now think by policy to start[6] where you bound me to answer by necessity; not suffering me to join three flowers in one nosegay, but to choose one or else to leave all. The like must I crave at your hands; that if of force[7] you must consent to any one, whether would you have the proper man, the wise, or the rich?'

---

1 *properest*] most handsome
2 *no plea . . . gilt*] nothing to advance his case but money
3 *lend him . . . countenance*] look favourably upon him
4 *Ganymede . . . countenance*] the cup-bearer of the gods may turn a lovely face towards you. For *Ulysses* and *Croesus* in the following clauses see p. 78n. and p. 137n.
5 *wanteth*] lacks
6 *by policy to start*] to evade by craft
7 *of force*] by necessity

She, as not without an answer, quickly requited me.

'Although there be no force which may compel me to take any, neither a proffer whereby I might choose all, yet to answer you flatly, I would have the wealthiest. For beauty without riches goeth a-begging, and wit without wealth cheapeneth[1] all things in the fair, but buyeth nothing.'

'Truly, lady,' quoth I, 'either you speak not as you think or you be far over-shot. For methinketh that he that hath beauty shall have money of ladies for alms, and he that is witty will get it by craft; but the rich having enough, and neither loved for shape nor sense, must either keep his gold for those he knows not [or] spend it on them that cares not.'

'Well,' answered Iffida, 'so many men, so many minds.[2] Now you have my opinion, you must not think to wring me from it; for I had rather be, as all women are, obstinate in mine own conceit, than apt to be wrought to others' constructions.'[3]

My father liked her choice, whether it were to flatter her, or for fear to offend her, or that he loved money himself better than either wit or beauty. And our conclusions thus ended, she, accompanied with her gentlewomen and other her servants, went to her uncle's, having tarried a day longer with my father than she appointed, though not so many with me as she was welcome.

Ah Philautus, what torments didst thou think poor Fidus endured, who now felt the flame even to take full hold of his heart! And thinking by soli-tariness to drive away melancholy, and by imagination to forget love, I laboured no otherwise than he that to have his horse stand still pricketh him with the spur, or he that having sore eyes rubbeth them with salt water. At the last, with continual abstinence from meat, from company, from sleep, my body began to consume and my head to wax idle;[4] insomuch that the sus-tenance which perforce was thrust into my mouth was never digested, nor the talk which came from my addle brains liked. For ever in my slumber methought Iffida presented herself, now with a countenance pleasant and merry, straightways with a colour full of wrath and mischief.

My father, no less sorrowful for my disease than ignorant of the cause, sent for divers physicians, among the which there came an Italian, who feeling my pulses, casting my water,[5] and marking my looks, commanded the chamber to be voided and, shutting the door, applied this medicine to my malady:

'Gentleman, there is none that can better heal your wound than he that made it, so that you should have sent for Cupid, not Aesculapius;[6] for al-though they be both gods, yet will they not meddle in each other's office. Apelles will not go about to amend Lysippus' carving, yet they both wrought Alexander;[7] nor Hippocrates busy himself with Ovid's art,[8] and yet they both

---

1 *cheapeneth*] haggles over
2 *so many men . . . minds*] everyone has their own opinion (proverbial)
3 *constructions*] views
4 *wax idle*] become unhinged, grow light
5 *casting my water*] analysing my urine
6 *Cupid, not Aesculapius*] the god of love, not the god of medicine
7 *Apelles will not . . . Alexander*] though both the painter Apelles and the sculptor Lysippus represented Alexander, the former would not presume to correct the latter's work
8 *nor Hippocrates . . . Ovid's art*] neither did the painter Hippocrates (see p. 157n.) concern himself with poetry like Ovid although both took Venus as their subject

described Venus. Your humour is to be purged not by the apothecary's confections,[1] but by the following of good counsel.

'You are in love, Fidus, which if you cover in a close chest will burn every
place before it burst the lock. For as we know by physic that poison will dis-
perse itself into every vein before it part the heart, so I have heard by those
that in love could say somewhat that it maimeth every part before it kill the
liver.[2] If, therefore, you will make me privy to all your devices, I will procure
such means as you shall recover in short space; otherwise if you seek to
conceal the party, and increase your passions, you shall but shorten your life,
and so lose your love for whose sake you live.'

When I heard my physician so pat to hit my disease, I could not dissemble
with him lest he should bewray it;[3] neither would I, in hope of remedy. Unto
him I discoursed the faithful love which I bore to Iffida, and described in every
particular, as to you I have done. Which he hearing, procured within one day
Lady Iffida to see me, telling my father that my disease was but a consuming
fever which he hoped in short time to cure.

When my lady came and saw me so altered in a month, wasted to the hard
bones, more like a ghost than a living creature, after many words of comfort
(as women want none about sick persons), when she saw opportunity she
asked me whether the Italian were my messenger, or if he were whether his
embassage were true; which question I thus answered:

'Lady, to dissemble with the world when I am departing from it would
profit me nothing with man and hinder me much with God; to make my
death-bed the place of deceit might hasten my death and increase my danger.

'I have loved you long, and now at the length must leave you, whose hard
heart I will not impute to discourtesy[4] but destiny. It contenteth me that I died
in faith, though I could not live in favour; neither was I ever more desirous
to begin my love than I am now to end my life. Things which cannot be
altered are to be borne not blamed; follies past are sooner remembered than
redressed; and time lost may well be repented but never recalled. I will not
recount the passions I have suffered, I think the effect show them, and now
it is more behoveful for me to fall to praying for a new life than to remember the old. Yet this I add (which though it merit no mercy to save, it deserveth
thanks of a friend), that only I loved thee, and lived for thee, and now die
for thee.'

And so turning on my left side,[5] I fetched a deep sigh.

Iffida, the water standing in her eyes, clasping my hand in hers, with a sad
countenance answered me thus:

'My good Fidus, if the increasing of my sorrows might mitigate the extremity of thy sickness, I could be content to resolve myself into tears to rid thee
of trouble. But the making of a fresh wound in my body is nothing to the
healing of a festered sore in thy bowels, for that such diseases are to be cured
in the end by the means of their original. For as by basil the scorpion is engen-

---

1 *confections*] compounds
2 *liver*] see p. 214n.
3 *pat / bewray it*] exactly / reveal it
4 *discourtesy*] lack of courtly generosity
5 *turning . . . side*] see p. 168n.

dered and by the means of the same herb destroyed,[1] so love which by time and fancy is bred in an idle head is by time and fancy banished from the heart; or as the salamander which being a long space nourished in the fire, at the last quencheth it,[2] so affection having taken hold of the fancy, and living as it were in the mind of the lover, in tract of time altereth and changeth the heat and turneth it to chillness.

'It is no small grief to me, Fidus, that I should be thought to be the cause of thy languishing and cannot be remedy of thy disease. For unto thee I will reveal more than either wisdom would allow[3] or my modesty permit; and yet so much as may acquit me of ungratitude towards thee, and rid thee of the suspicion conceived of me.

'So it is, Fidus, and my good friend, that about a two years past there was in court a gentleman, not unknown unto thee, nor, I think, unbeloved of thee, whose name I will not conceal lest thou shouldst either think me to forge or him not worthy to be named. This gentleman was called Thirsus, in all respects so well qualified, as had he not been in love with me I should have been enamoured of him.

'But his hastiness prevented my heat, who began to sue for that which I was ready to proffer; whose sweet tale, although I wished it to be true, yet at the first I could not believe it, for that men in matters of love have as many ways to deceive as they have words to utter. I seemed strait-laced, as one neither accustomed to such suits nor willing to entertain such a servant;[4] yet so warily, as putting him from me with my little finger I drew him to me with my whole hand. For I stood in a great mammering[5] how I might behave myself, lest being too coy[6] he might think me proud, or using too much courtesy he might judge me wanton. Thus long time I held him in a doubt, thinking thereby to have just trial of his faith or plain knowledge of his falsehood.

'In this manner I led my life almost one year; until with often meeting and divers conferences I felt myself so wounded that though I thought no heaven to my hap,[7] yet I lived as it were in hell till I had enjoyed my hope. For as the tree ebenus,[8] though it in no way be set in a flame, yet it burneth with sweet savours, so my mind, though it could not be fired for that I thought myself wise, yet was it almost consumed to ashes with pleasant delights and sweet cogitations. Insomuch as it fared with me as it doth with the trees stricken with thunder, which having the barks sound are bruised in the

---

1 *by basil . . . destroyed*] Scorpions were reputed to breed in the leaves of basil if the plant was exposed to the sun. Their sting was thought to be relieved by the same herb (see Croll and Clemons, p. 279n.).
2 *the salamander . . . quencheth it*] The belief that the salamander ultimately cools the fire in which it lives (see p. 64n.) is noted by a number of classical writers including Pliny.
3 *allow*] approve
4 *strait-laced / servant*] reserved / lover
5 *mammering*] state of uncertainty
6 *coy*] aloof
7 *no heaven to my hap*] no heaven comparable to my lot
8 *ebenus*] ebony

body;[1] for finding my outward parts without blemish, looking into my mind could not see it without blows.

'I now perceiving it high time to use the physician who was always at hand,[2] determined at the next meeting to conclude such faithful and inviolable league of love as neither the length of time, nor the distance of place, nor the threatening of friends, nor the spite of fortune, nor the fear of death should either alter or diminish; which, accordingly, was then finished, and hath hitherto been truly fulfilled.

'Thirsus, as thou knowest, hath ever since been beyond the seas, the remembrance of whose constancy is the only comfort of my life. Neither do I rejoice in anything more than the faith of my good Thirsus. Then, Fidus, I appeal in this case to thy honesty, which shall determine of mine honour. Wouldst thou have me inconstant to my old friend, and faithful to a new? Knowest thou not that as the almond-tree beareth most fruit when he is old, so love hath greatest faith when it groweth in age? It falleth out in love as it doth in vines; for the young vines bring the most wine, but the old the best. So tender love maketh greatest show of blossoms, but tried love bringeth forth sweetest juice.

'And yet I will say thus much (not to add courage to thy attempts),[3] that I have taken as great delight in thy company as ever I did in any's (my Thirsus only excepted), which was the cause that oftentimes I would either by questions move thee to talk or by quarrels incense thee to choler; perceiving in thee a wit answerable to my desire, which I thought throughly to whet by some discourse. But wert thou in comeliness Alexander and my Thirsus Thersites, wert thou Ulysses he Midas, thou Croesus he Codrus,[4] I would not forsake him to have thee—no, not if I might thereby prolong thy life or save mine own. So fast a root hath true love taken in my heart that the more it is digged at the deeper it groweth, the oftener it is cut the less it bleedeth, and the more it is loaden the better it beareth.

'What is there in this vile earth that more commendeth a woman than constancy? It is neither his wit, though it be excellent, that I esteem, neither his birth, though it be noble, nor his bringing up, which hath always been courtly; but only his constancy and my faith, which no torments, no tyrant, not death shall dissolve. For never shall it be said that Iffida was false to Thirsus, though Thirsus be faithless (which the gods forfend) unto Iffida.

'For as Amulius, the cunning painter, so portrayed Minerva[5] that which way soever one cast his eye she always beheld him, so hath Cupid so exquisitely drawn the image of Thirsus in my heart that what way soever I glance methinketh he looketh steadfastly upon me; insomuch that when I have seen any to gaze on my beauty (simple, God wot,[6] though it be), I have wished to

---

1 *it fared with me . . . body*] an effect usually attributed to lightning rather than thunder
2 *the physician who was always at hand*] i.e. Thirsus
3 *add courage . . . attempts*] encourage your courtship
4 *Alexander . . . Thersites / Ulysses . . . Midas / Croesus . . . Codrus*] all polar opposites in some respects (physical prowess as opposed to deformity / wisdom as opposed to folly / wealth as opposed to poverty)
5 *Amulius / Minerva*] Roman artist patronized by the Emperor Nero / goddess of wisdom
6 *wot*] knows

have the eyes of Augustus Caesar to dim their sights with the sharp and scorching beams.[1]

'Such force hath time and trial wrought that if Thirsus should die I would be buried with him; imitating the eagle which Sesta, a virgin, brought up, who seeing the bones of the virgin cast into the fire threw himself in with them and burnt himself with them,[2] or Hippocrates' twins,[3] who were born together, laughed together, wept together, and died together. For as Alexander would be engraven of no one man in a precious stone but only of Pyrgoteles,[4] so would I have my picture imprinted in no heart but in his by Thirsus.

'Consider with thyself, Fidus, that a fair woman without constancy is not unlike unto a green tree without fruit; resembling the counterfeit that Praxiteles made for Flora,[5] before the which if one stood directly it seemed to weep, if on the left side to laugh, if on the other side to sleep, whereby he noted the light behaviour of her which could not in one constant shadow be set down. And yet for the great good will thou bearest me I cannot reject thy service, but I will not admit[6] thy love. But if either my friends or myself, my goods or my good will may stand thee in stead, use me, trust me, command me, as far forth as thou canst with modesty and I may grant with mine honour. If to talk with me or continually to be in thy company may in any respect satisfy thy desire, assure thyself I will attend on thee as diligently as thy nurse, and be more careful for thee than thy physician. More I cannot promise without breach of my faith; more thou canst not ask without suspicion of folly.

'Here, Fidus, take this diamond, which I have heard old women say to have been of great force against idle thoughts, vain dreams, and frantic imaginations; which if it do thee no good, assure thyself it can do thee no harm, and better I think it against such enchanted fantasies than either Homer's moly or Pliny's centaurio.'[7]

When my lady had ended this strange discourse, I was stricken into such a maze that for the space almost of half an hour I lay as it had been in a trance,

---

1 *eyes of Augustus Caesar ... beams*] Croll and Clemons (p. 282n.) quote Suetonius, *De caesaribus*: 'He had clear and bright eyes, in which he loved to think there was something of a divine virtue, and rejoiced if anyone lowered his countenance when he looked sharply at him, as if overcome by the brightness of the sun.'

2 *imitating the eagle ... them*] Bond notes that Lyly transfers the name of the town (Sestos), in which this story (derived from Pliny) is set, to the virgin herself (II, pp. 506–7).

3 *Hippocrates' twins*] see p. 157n.

4 *Pyrgoteles*] The most celebrated gem engraver of the antique world, particularly favoured by Alexander who would permit no one else to make his seal-rings, cf. the comparable status of Apelles (painting) and Lysippus (sculpture).

5 *Praxiteles / for Flora*] distinguished sculptor (fl. circa 364 BC), who excelled in the representation of the female form / of the goddess of spring. (The qualities Lyly associates with the statue may derive from the later Roman association of the goddess with a courtesan.)

6 *admit*] accept

7 *Homer's moly / Pliny's centaurio*] magic herb given by Hermes to Ulysses to nullify the enchantments of Circe / remedy by which, in some traditions, Charon (one of the Centaurs) was cured of a wound in the foot inflicted by one of Hercules' arrows

mine eyes almost standing in my head without motion, my face without colour, my mouth without breath; insomuch that Iffida began to screech out and call company, which called me also to myself. And then, with a faint and trembling tongue, I uttered these words:

'Lady, I cannot use as many words as I would, because you see I am weak; nor give so many thanks as I should, for that you deserve infinite. If Thirsus have planted the vine, I will not gather the grapes; neither is it reason that he having sowed with pain, that I should reap the pleasure. This sufficeth me, and delighteth me not a little, that you are so faithful and he so fortunate. Yet, good lady, let me obtain one small suit, which derogating[1] nothing from your true love must needs be lawful: that is, that I may in this my sickness enjoy your company, and if I recover be admitted as your servant;[2] the one will hasten my health, the other prolong my life.'

She courteously granted both, and so carefully tended me in my sickness that, what with her merry sporting and good nourishing, I began to gather up my crumbs[3] and in short time to walk into a gallery near adjoining unto my chamber, where she disdained not to lead me, and so at all times to use me as though I had been Thirsus. Every evening she would put forth either some pretty question or utter some merry conceit, to drive me from melancholy. There was no broth that would down but of her making, no meat but of her dressing,[4] no sleep enter into mine eyes but by her singing; insomuch as she was both my nurse, my cook, and my physician. Being thus by her for the space of one month cherished, I waxed strong, and so lusty as though I had never been sick.

'Now, Philautus, judge not partially: whether was she, a lady of greater constancy towards Thirsus or courtesy towards me?'

Philautus thus answered:

'Now surely, Fidus, in my opinion she was no less to be commended for keeping her faith inviolable, than to be praised for giving such alms unto thee; which good behaviour differeth far from the nature of our Italian dames, who if they be constant they despise all other that seem to love them. But I long yet to hear the end; for methinketh a [mat]ter begun with such heat should not end with a bitter cold.'

'Oh Philautus, the end is short and lamentable; but as it is have it.'

She, after long recreating of herself in the country, repaired again to the court, and so did I also; where I lived as the elephant doth by air,[5] with the sight of my lady, who ever used me in all her secrets as one that she most trusted. But my joys were too great to last, for even in the middle of my bliss there came tidings to Iffida that Thirsus was slain by the Turks,[6] being then in pay with

---

1 *derogating*] detracting
2 *admitted as your servant*] accepted as your admirer
3 *to gather up my crumbs*] recover my strength
4 *no meat but of her dressing*] no food unless prepared by her
5 *as the elephant doth by air*] No source has been traced for this belief.
6 *the Turks*] a major threat to western Europe throughout the sixteenth century. The circumstances of Thirsus' death may have been inspired by the battle of Lepanto in 1571, though Fidus' tale is set in the reign of Henry VIII.

the King of Spain; which battle was so bloody that many gentlemen lost their lives.

Iffida, so distraught of her wits with these news, fell into a frenzy, having nothing in her mouth but always this, 'Thirsus slain! Thirsus slain!' Ever doubling this speech with such pitiful cries and screeches as it would have moved the soldiers of Ulysses[1] to sorrow. At the last, by good keeping and such means as by physic were provided, she came again to herself; unto whom I writ many letters to take patiently the death of him whose life could not be recalled. Divers she answered, which I will show you at my better leisure.

But this was most strange, that no suit could allure her again to love, but ever she lived all in black, not once coming where she was most sought for. But within the term of five years she began a little to listen to mine old suit, of whose faithful meaning she had such trial as she could not think that either my love was builded upon lust or deceit. But destiny cut off my love by the cutting of her life; for, falling into a hot pestilent fever, she died. And how I took it, I mean not to tell it. But forsaking the court presently,[2] I have here lived ever since; and so mean until death shall call me.

'Now, gentlemen, I have held you too long I fear me, but I have ended at the last. You see what love is: begun with grief, continued with sorrow, ended with death; a pain full of pleasure, a joy replenished with misery, a heaven, a hell, a god, a devil, and what not that either hath in it solace or sorrow; where the days are spent in thoughts, the nights in dreams, both in danger; either beguiling us of that we had, or promising us that we had not; full of jealousy without cause, and void of fear when there is cause; and so many inconveniences hanging upon it as to reckon them all were infinite, and to taste one of them intolerable.

'Yet in these days it is thought the signs of a good wit, and the only virtue peculiar to a courtier. For love they say is in young gentlemen; in clowns it is lust, in old men dotage; when it is in all men madness. But you, Philautus, whose blood is in his chiefest heat, are to take great care, lest being over-warmed with love it so inflame the liver as it drive you into a consumption.'

And thus the old man brought them into dinner; where they having taken their repast, Philautus, as well in the name of Euphues as his own, gave this answer to the old man's tale, and these or the like thanks for his cost and courtesy:

'Father, I thank you no less for your talk, which I found pleasant, than for your counsel, which I account profitable; and so much for your great cheer and courteous entertainment as it deserveth of those that cannot deserve any.

'I perceive in England the women and men are in love constant, to

---

1 *soldiers of Ulysses*] hardened warriors rarely touched by emotion. Bond (II, p. 507) compares the opening of the *Aeneid*, bk II, in which Aeneas' tale is described as capable of moving even a 'soldier of stern Ulysses' to tears.
2 *presently*] immediately

strangers courteous, and bountiful in hospitality; the two latter we have tried to your cost, the other we have heard to your pains, and may justify them all wheresoever we become[1] to your praises and our pleasure. This only we crave, that necessity may excuse our boldness, and for amends we will use such means as although we cannot make you gain much, yet you shall lose little.'

Then Fidus, taking Philautus by the hand, spake thus to them both:

'Gentlemen and friends, I am ashamed to receive so many thanks for so small courtesy; and so far off it is for me to look for amends for my cost, as I desire nothing more than to make you amends for your company, and your good wills in accounting well of ill fare. Only this I crave, that at your return, after you shall be feasted of great personages, you vouchsafe to visit the cottage of poor Fidus, where you shall be no less welcome than Jupiter was to Bacchus.'[2]

Then Euphues:

'We have troubled you too long, and high time it is for poor pilgrims to take the day before them, lest being benighted they strain courtesy in another place. And as we say in Athens, "Fish and g[uests] in three days are stale." Notwithstanding, we will be bold to see you, and in the mean season we thank you; and ever, as we ought, we will pray for you.'

Thus after many farewells, with as many welcomes of the one side as thanks of the other, they departed, and framed their steps towards London. And to drive away the time, Euphues began thus to instruct Philautus:

'Thou seest, Philautus, the courtesy of England to surpass, and the constancy (if the old gentleman told the truth) to excel; which warneth us both to be thankful for the benefits we receive and circumspect in the behaviour we use, lest being unmindful of good turns we be accounted ingrate, and being dissolute[3] in our lives we be thought impudent.

'When we come into London we shall walk in the garden of the world, where among many flowers we shall see some weeds, sweet roses and sharp nettles, pleasant lilies and pricking thorns, high vines and low hedges; all things (as the fame goeth) that may either please the sight or dislike the smell, either feed the eye with delight or fill the nose with infection.

'Then, good Philautus, let the care I have of thee be instead of grave counsel, and my good will towards thee in place of wisdom. I had rather thou shouldst walk among the beds of wholesome pot-herbs than the

---

1 *justify / become*] confirm / come
2 *no less welcome . . . Bacchus*] No traditional story accords with this reference. It is possible that Bacchus here is a slip for 'Baucis', the wife of a poor man who gave hospitality to Jupiter and Mercury disguised as strangers. Lyly refers to this story in *Campaspe* (Prologue at the Court, 8–9).
3 *accounted ingrate / dissolute*] thought ungrateful / careless

knots[1] of pleasant flowers, and better shalt thou find it to gather garlic for thy stomach than a sweet violet[2] for thy senses.

'I fear me, Philautus, that seeing the amiable faces of the English ladies thou wilt cast off all care both of my counsel and thine own credit. For well I know that a fresh colour doth easily dim a quick sight, that a sweet rose doth soonest pierce a fine scent, that pleasant syrups doth chiefliest infect a delicate taste, that beautiful women do first of all allure them that have the wantonest eyes and the whitest mouths.[3]

'A strange tree there is, called alpina, which bringeth forth the fairest blossoms of all trees; which the bee, either suspecting to be venomous, or misliking because it is so glorious, neither tasteth it nor cometh near it. In the like case, Philautus, would I have thee to imitate the bee, that when thou shalt behold the amiable[4] blossoms of the alpine tree in any woman, thou shun them as a place infected either with poison to kill thee or honey to deceive thee. For it were more convenient thou shouldst pull out thine eyes and live without love, than to have them clear and be infected with lust.

'Thou must choose a woman as the lapidary doth a true sapphire, who when he seeth it to glister covereth it with oil,[5] and then if it shine he alloweth it, if not he breaketh it. So if thou fall in love with one that is beautiful, cast some kind of colour in her face,[6] either as it were misliking her behaviour, or hearing of her lightness; and then if she look as fair as before,[7] woo her, win her, and wear her.

'Then, my good friend, consider with thyself what thou art—an Italian; where thou art—in England; whom thou shalt love if thou fall into that vein—an angel.[8] Let not thy eye go beyond thy ear, nor thy tongue so far as thy feet. And thus I conjure thee, that of all things that thou refrain from the hot fire of affection. For as the precious stone anthracitis being thrown into the fire looketh black and half dead, but being cast into the water glistereth like the sunbeams, so the precious mind of man once put into the flame of love is as it were ugly and loseth his virtue, but sprinkled with the water of wisdom and detestation of such fond delights it shineth like the golden rays of Phoebus.[9]

---

1 *pot-herbs / knots*] plants grown for culinary purposes / intricate ornamental gardens (both figurative here)
2 *garlic / violet*] vegetable noted for its medicinal properties / ironically the 'flower' Philautus finally picks with Euphues' encouragement
3 *whitest mouths*] most fastidious tastes
4 *amiable*] fair
5 *lapidary . . . oil*] see p. 210n.
6 *cast some . . . face*] pretend to discern some fault in her
7 *if she look . . . before*] if she remains unchanged in her demeanour
8 *angel*] pun, originally ascribed to Gregory the Great (Angle, i.e. member of the Anglian = English people / heavenly being)
9 *anthracitis / Phoebus*] species of carbuncle known as the 'coal-carbuncle' / the sun

'And it shall not be amiss, though my physic be simple, to prescribe a strait diet before thou fall into thine old disease. First, let thy apparel be but mean, neither too brave to show thy pride nor too base to bewray[1] thy poverty. Be as careful to keep thy mouth from wine as thy fingers from fire. Wine is the glass of the mind, and the only sauce that Bacchus gave Ceres when he fell in love.[2] Be not dainty mouthed. A fine taste noteth the fond appetites that Venus said her Adonis to have,[3] who, seeing him to take chiefest delight in costly cates, smiling said this: "I am glad that my Adonis hath a sweet tooth in his head—and who knoweth not what followeth?"

'But I will not wade too far, seeing heretofore, as well in my "Cooling Card" as at divers other times, I have given thee a caveat[4] in this vanity of love to have a care. And yet methinketh the more I warn thee the less I dare trust thee; for I know not how it cometh to pass that every minute I am troubled in mind about thee.'

When Euphues had ended, Philautus thus began:

'Euphues, I think thou wast born with this word "love" in thy mouth, or that thou art bewitched with it in mind, for there is scarce three words uttered to me but the third is "love". Which how often I have answered thou knowest, and yet that I speak as I think thou never believest, either thinking thyself a god to know thoughts, or me worse than a devil not to acknowledge them. When I shall give any occasion, warn me; and that I should give none, thou hast already armed me. So that this persuade thyself, I will stick as close to thee as the sole doth to the shoe.

'But truly, I must needs commend the courtesy of England, and old Fidus for his constancy to his Lady Iffida, and her faith to her friend Thirsus; the remembrance of which discourse did often bring into my mind the hate I bore to Lucilla, who loved all and was not found faithful to any. But I let that pass, lest thou come in again with thy faburden and hit me in the teeth[5] with love, for thou hast so charmed me that I dare not speak any word that may be wrested[6] to charity, lest thou say I mean love. And in truth, I think there is no more difference between them than between a broom and a besom.[7]

'I will follow thy diet and thy counsel. I thank thee for thy good will; so that I will now walk under thy shadow and be at thy commandment.'

---

1 *mean / brave / bewray*] modest / gaudy / indicate
2 *Bacchus gave . . . love*] As cultivator and guardian of the vine Bacchus comes into close proximity with Ceres, protectress of the fruits of the earth, hence the 'love' between them (*sauce* = love potion).
3 *noteth . . . her Adonis to have*] is indicative of the wanton desires Venus noted in the mortal youth with whom she fell in love (*costly cates* = expensive delicacies)
4 *caveat*] warning
5 *faburden / hit me in the teeth*] refrain / accuse
6 *wrested*] twisted
7 *besom*] broom made of twigs

'Not so,' answered Euphues, 'But if thou follow me, I dare be thy warrant we will not offend much.'

Much talk there was in the way, which much shortened their way. And at last they came to London, where they met divers strangers of their friends,[1] who in small space brought them familiarly acquainted with certain English gentlemen; who much delighted in the company of Euphues, whom they found both sober and wise, yet sometimes merry and pleasant. They were brought into all places of the city, and lodged at the last in a merchant's house, where they continued till a certain breach.[2] They used continually[3] the court, in the which Euphues took such delight that he accounted all the praises he heard of it before rather to be envious[4] than otherwise, and to be partial in not giving so much as it deserved, and yet to be pardoned because they could not.

It happened that these English gentlemen conducted these two strangers to a place where divers gentlewomen were, some courtiers, others of the country. Where, being welcome, they frequented almost every day for the space of one month, entertaining of time in courtly pastimes, though not in the court; insomuch that if they came not they were sent for, and so used as they had been countrymen[5] not strangers. Philautus, with this continual access and often conference with gentlewomen, began to wean himself from the counsel of Euphues, and to wed his eyes to the comeliness of ladies, yet so warily as neither his friend could by narrow watching discover it, neither did he by any wanton countenance bewray it; but carrying the image of love engraven in the bottom of his heart, and the picture of courtesy imprinted in his face, he was thought to Euphues courtly, and known to himself comfortless.[6]

Among a number of ladies he fixed his eyes upon one, whose countenance seemed to promise mercy and threaten mischief, intermeddling a desire of liking with a disdain of love; showing herself in courtesy to be familiar with all, and with a certain comely pride to accept none; whose wit would commonly taunt without despite but not without disport,[7] as one that seemed to abhor love worse than lust, and lust worse than murder; of greater beauty than birth, and yet of less beauty than honesty, which gat her more honour by virtue than nature could by art, or fortune might by promotion. She was ready of answer, yet wary; shrill of speech, yet sweet; in all her passions so temperate as in her greatest mirth none would think her wanton, neither in her deepest grief solemn; but always

---

1 *divers strangers of their friends*] many foreigners of their acquaintance
2 *breach*] quarrel between them (the details of which emerge in the course of the narrative)
3 *used continually*] constantly frequented
4 *envious*] grudging
5 *countrymen*] compatriots
6 *he was thought ... comfortless*] he appeared to Euphues to be merely well-mannered, while knowing himself to be beyond help
7 *despite / disport*] malice / gaiety

to look with so sober cheerfulness as it was hardly thought whe[the]r she were more commended for her gravity of the aged or for her courtliness of the youth; oftentimes delighted to hear discourses of love, but ever desirous to be instructed in learning; somewhat curious[1] to keep her beauty, which made her comely, but more careful to increase her credit, which made her commendable; not adding the length of a hair to courtliness that might detract the breadth of a hair from chastity; in all her talk so pleasant, in all her looks so amiable, so grave modesty joined with so witty mirth, that they that were entangled with her beauty were enforced to prefer her wit before their wills; and they that loved her virtue were compelled to prefer their affections before her wisdom;[2] whose rare qualities caused so strange events that the wise were allured to vanity and the wantons to virtue, much like the river in Arabia which turneth gold to dross and dirt to silver.[3] In conclusion, there wanted nothing in this English angel that nature might add for perfection, or fortune could give for wealth, or God doth commonly bestow on mortal creatures. And more easy it is in the description of so rare a personage to imagine what she had not, than to repeat all she had. But such a one she was as almost they all are that serve so noble a Prince; such virgins carry lights before such a Vesta, such nymphs arrows with such a Diana.[4] But why go I about to set her in black and white, whom Philautus is now with all colours importraying in the table[5] of his heart? And surely I think by this he is half mad, whom long since I left in a great maze.

Philautus, viewing all these things and more than I have uttered (for that the lover's eye pierceth deeper), withdrew himself secretly into his lodging, and locking his door began to debate with himself in this manner:

'Ah, thrice unfortunate is he that is once faithful, and better it is to be a merciless soldier than a true lover; the one liveth by another's death, the other dieth by his own life. What strange fits be these, Philautus, that burn thee with such a heat that thou shakest for cold, and all thy body in a shivering sweat, in a flaming ice, melteth like wax and hardeneth like the adamant?[6] Is it love? Then would it were death! For likelier it is that I should lose my life, than win my love.

'Ah Camilla! But why do I name thee, when thou dost not hear me? Camilla, name thee I will, though thou hate me! But alas, the sound of

1 *somewhat curious*] taking some pains
2 *they that were entangled . . . wisdom*] those who fell in love with her appearance were obliged to give her wisdom priority over their own desires, and those who loved her moral character found their passions overriding their regard for her wisdom
3 *the river in Arabia . . . silver*] Croll and Clemons (p. 291n.) suggest this may refer to the river Pactolus in Asia Minor which was reputed to contain a stone resembling silver obscured by crumbled gold floating on the surface.
4 *Vesta / Diana*] both associated with chastity and thus frequently appropriated in the sixteenth century to the cult of the Virgin Queen
5 *importraying in the table*] painting in the picture
6 *adamant*] diamond (see p. 98n.)

thy name doth make me sound[1] for grief. What is in me that thou shouldst not despise; and what is there not in thee that I should not wonder at? Thou a woman, the last thing God made and therefore the best; I a man that could not live without thee, and therefore the worst. All things were made for man as a sovereign, and man made for woman as a slave.[2] O Camilla, would either thou hadst been bred in Italy, or I in England; or would thy virtues were less than thy beauty, or my virtues greater than my affections.

'I see that India bringeth gold, but England breedeth goodness. And had not England been thrust into a corner[3] of the world it would have filled the whole world with woe; where such women are as we have talked of in Italy, heard of in Rome, read of in Greece, but never found but in this island. And for my part (I speak softly because I will not hear myself), would there were none such here, or such everywhere.

'Ah fond Euphues, my dear friend but a simple fool if thou believe now thy "Cooling Card", and an obstinate fool if thou do not recant it. But it may be thou layest that card for the elevation of Naples, like an astronomer.[4] If it were so I forgive thee, for I must believe thee; if for the whole world, behold England where Camilla was born, the flower of courtesy, the picture of comeliness, one that shameth Venus, being some- what fairer but much more virtuous, and staineth Diana, being as chaste but much more amiable.[5]

'Aye but, Philautus, the more beauty she hath, the more pride; and the more virtue, the more preciseness. The peacock is a bird for none but Juno, the dove for none but Vesta. None must wear Venus in a tablet but Alexander, none Pallas in a ring but Ulysses.[6] For as there is but one phoenix[7] in the world, so is there but one tree in Arabia wherein she buildeth; and as there is but one Camilla to be heard of, so is there but one Caesar that she will like of. Why then, Philautus, what resteth for

---

1 *sound*] swoon
2 *Thou a woman . . . slave*] Philautus' stance here runs counter to Renaissance ortho-
   doxy which places man above woman both in perfection and in the social order.
3 *corner*] pun (not original to Lyly) on angle + land (i.e. England, a land 'thrust into
   a corner of the world')
4 *it may be . . . astronomer*] The sense turns on a pun on *card* (playing card / compass).
   Hence 'you set your compass for the latitude of Naples as an astronomer (i.e.
   astrologer) charts the future (or the skies) according to certain fixed points.'
5 *staineth Diana / amiable*] dims Diana by comparison / beautiful
6 *The peacock . . . Ulysses*] all properties peculiar to (and having an emblematic association with) their owners. The peacock (sacred to Juno) signifies her jealousy by the
   eyes in its tail. The dove, noted for its constancy, embodies the virtues fostered by
   the goddess of the hearth. The *tablet* (picture in a locket) worn by Alexander and
   engraved ring worn by Ulysses denote their supremacy in the fields of love and
   wisdom through divine favour (*Pallas* = Pallas Athene, goddess of wisdom)
7 *phoenix*] legendary bird, only one of which was said to exist, which was thought
   to be consumed by fire every five hundred years and to arise renewed from its own
   ashes

thee but to die with patience, seeing thou mayst not live with pleasure;
when thy disease is so dangerous that the third letting of blood is not able
to recover thee;[1] when neither Ariadne's thread, nor Sibylla's bough, nor
Medea's seed[2] may remedy thy grief. Die, die, Philautus, rather with a
secret scar than an open scorn. Patroclus cannot mask in Achilles' armour
without a mai[m],[3] nor Philautus in the English court without a mock.

'Aye, but there is no pearl so hard but vinegar breaketh it, no diamond
so stony but blood mollifieth,[4] no heart so stiff but love weakeneth it.
And what then? Because she may love one, is it necessary she should love
thee? Be there not infinite in England who as far exceed thee in wealth
as she doth all the Italians in wisdom, and are as far above thee in all
qualites of the body as she is above them in all gifts of the mind? Dost
thou not see every minute the noble youth of England frequent the court,
with no less courage than thou cowardice? If courtly bravery may allure
her, who more gallant than they? If personage,[5] who more valiant? If wit,
who more sharp? If birth, who more noble? If virtue, who more devout?
When there are all things in them that should delight a lady, and no one
thing in thee that is in them, with what face, Philautus, canst thou desire
[that] which they cannot deserve, or with what service deserve that which
so many desire before thee? The more beauty Camilla hath, the less hope
shouldst thou have; and think not but the bait that caught thee hath
beguiled other Englishmen or[6] now. Infants they can love;[7] neither so
hard-hearted to despise it, nor so simple not to discern it.

'It is likely then, Philautus, that the fox will let the grapes hang for
the goose, or the Englishman bequeath beauty to the Italian? No, no,
Philautus, assure thyself, there is no Venus but she hath her temple, where
on the one side Vulcan may knock but Mars shall enter;[8] no saint but
hath her shrine, and he that cannot win with a paternoster must offer a
penny.[9] And as rare it is to see the sun without a light as a fair woman
without a lover; and as near is fancy to beauty as the prick to the rose,
as the stalk to the rind, as the earth to the root. Dost thou not think that
hourly she is served and sued unto of thy betters in birth, thy equals in
wealth, thy inferiors in no respect?

1 *the third letting of blood / recover*] literally the third bleeding for medical purposes
   (i.e. extreme remedy) / cure
2 *Ariadne's thread / Sibylla's bough / Medea's seed*] all aids to heroes in times of need.
   For *Ariadne's thread* see p. 200n. Sibylla's golden bough enabled Aeneas to enter the
   underworld. The charms and herbal compounds of Medea (daughter of the King of
   Colchis, noted for her magic potions) assisted Jason.
3 *Patroclus ... maim*] Patroclus was killed at Troy while wearing the armour of
   Achilles, who had withdrawn from the conflict.
4 *diamond ... mollifieth*] see p. 56n.
5 *bravery / personage*] display / bearing
6 *or*] before
7 *Infants they can love*] young knights can fall in love
8 *there is no Venus ... Mars shall enter*] see p. 29n.
9 *cannot win ... penny*] who cannot achieve his goal by prayer must offer money

'If then she have given her faith, darest thou call her honour into suspicion of falsehood? If she refuse such vain delights, wilt thou bring her wisdom into the compass of folly? If she love so beautiful a piece,[1] then will she not be unconstant. If she vow virginity, so chaste a lady cannot be perjured. And of two things the one of these must be true: that either her mind is already so weaned from love that she is not to be moved, or so settled in love that she is not to be removed.

'Aye, but it may be that so young and tender a heart hath not yet felt the impression of love. Aye, but it cannot be that so rare perfection should want that which they all wish, affection. A rose is sweeter in the bud than full blown, young twigs are sooner bent than old trees, white snow sooner melted than hard ice; which proveth that the younger she is the sooner she is to be wooed, and the fairer she is the likelier she is to be won. Who will not run with Atalanta, though he be lame? Who would not wrestle with Cleopatra, though he were sick? Who feareth to love Camilla, though he were blind? Ah beauty, such is thy force that Vulcan courteth Venus; she for comeliness a goddess, he for ugliness a devil, more fit to strike with a hammer in his forge than to hold a lute in thy chamber.[2]

'Whither dost thou wade, Philautus, in lancing the wound thou shouldst taint[3] and pricking the heart which asketh a plaster. For in deciphering what she is, thou hast forgotten what thou thyself art, and being dazzled with her beauty thou seest not thine own baseness. Thou art an Italian, poor Philautus, as much misliked for the vice of thy country, as she marvelled at for the virtue of hers, and with no less shame dost thou hear, than know with grief, how if any Englishman be infected with any misdemeanour they say with one mouth, "He is Italianated."[4] So odious is that nation to this that the very man is no less hated for the name, than the country for the manners.

'O Italy, I must love thee because I was born in thee, but if the infection of the air be such as whosoever breed in thee is poisoned by thee, then had I rather be a bastard to the Turk Ottomo than heir to the Emperor Nero.[5] Thou which heretofore wast most famous for victories art become most infamous by thy vices, as much disdained now for thy beastliness in peace as once feared for thy battles in war, thy Caesar being turned to a vicar,[6] thy consuls to cardinals, thy sacred senate of three hundred grave counsellors to a shameless synod of three thousand greedy

---

1 *piece*] person
2 *Who will not run . . . lute in thy chamber*] For *Atalanta* see p. 122n., for *Venus* and *Vulcan* p. 27n.
3 *lancing the wound . . . taint*] making an incision in (i.e. aggravating) the wound to which you should apply ointment
4 *"He is Italianated"*] Bond notes the Italian proverb quoted in Ascham's *The School-master* (1570): 'Englese Italionato, e un diabolo incarnato' (II, p. 509).
5 *Turk Ottomo / Emporer Nero*] the embodiment of Turkish barbarity (from *Ottoman* = Turkish) / one of the most vicious of the Roman emperors (b. AD 37)
6 *vicar*] the Pope (Vicar of Christ)

caterpillars; where there is no vice punished, no virtue praised, where none is long loved if he do not ill, where none shall be long loved if he do well. But I leave to name thy sins, which no ciphers can number; and I would I were as free from the infection of some of them, as I am from the reckoning of all of them, or would I were as much envied for good, as thou art pitied for ill. Philautus, would thou hadst never lived in Naples, or never left it.

'What new skirmishes dost thou now feel between reason and appetite, love and wisdom, danger and desire? Shall I go and attire myself in costly apparel? Tush, a fair pearl in a Morian's[1] ear cannot make him white. Shall I ruffle[2] in new devices with chains, with bracelets, with rings and robes? Tush, the precious stones of Mausolus' sepulchre[3] cannot make the dead carcass sweet. Shall I curl my hair, colour my face, counterfeit courtliness? Tush, there is no painting can make a picture sensible.[4] No, no, Philautus, either swallow the juice of mandrake, which may cast thee into a dead sleep, or chew the herb chervil,[5] which may cause thee to mistake everything; so shalt thou either die in thy slumber, or think Camilla deformed by thy potion. No, I cannot do so though I would, neither would I though I could.

'But suppose thou think thyself in personage comely, in birth noble, in wit excellent, in talk eloquent, of great revenues, yet will this only be cast in thy teeth as an obloquy—"Thou art an Italian." Aye, but all that be black dig not for coals, all things that breed in the mud are not efts,[6] all that are born in Italy be not ill. She will not think what most are, but enquire what I am. Everyone that sucketh a wolf is not ravening;[7] there is no country but hath some as bad as Italy, many that have worse, none but hath some.

'And canst thou think that an English gentleman will suffer an Italian to be his rival? No, no. Thou must either put up a quarrel with shame or try the combat[8] with peril. An Englishman hath three qualities: he can suffer no partner in his love, no stranger to be his equal, nor to be dared by any. Then, Philautus, be as wary of thy life as careful for thy love.

---

1 *Morian's*] Moor's
2 *ruffle*] swagger
3 *Mausolus' sepulchre*] elaborate monument erected by Artemisia in memory of her husband Mausolus (d. 353 BC), one of the seven wonders of the world
4 *sensible*] capable of perception
5 *juice of mandrake / chervil*] mandragora, a powerful narcotic prepared from the root of the mandrake, a plant with many fabulous properties / aromatic plant, used in salads but also for medicinal purposes. Hence, perhaps, its otherwise obscure capacity to blur the senses.
6 *efts*] newts
7 *Everyone that sucketh ... ravening*] all that are suckled by wolves are not rapacious (an allusion to the virtue of Romulus, who was suckled by a she-wolf)
8 *put up a quarrel / try the combat*] accept injury (and thus endure shame) / suffer trial by force of arms

Thou must at Rome reverence Romulus, in Boeotia[1] Hercules, in England those that dwell there, else shalt thou not live there.

'Ah Love, what wrong dost thou me, which once beguiledest me with that I had,[2] and now beheadest me for that I have not! The love I bore to Lucilla was cold water, the love I owe Camilla hot fire; the first was ended with defame, the last must begin with death. I see now that as the resiluation[3] of an ague is desperate, and the second opening of a vein deadly, so the renewing of love is—I know not what to term it—worse than death, and as bad as what is worst. I perceive at the last the punishment of love is to live. Thou art here a stranger without acquaintance, no friend to speak for thee, no one to care for thee. Euphues will laugh at thee if he know it, and thou wilt weep if he know it not. O infortunate Philautus, born in the wane of the moon,[4] and as likely to obtain thy wish as the wolf is to catch the moon! But why go I about to quench fire with a sword or with affection to mortify my love?[5]

'O my Euphues, would I had thy wit, or thou my will! Shall I utter this to thee? But thou art more likely to correct my follies with counsel, than to comfort me with any pretty conceit. Thou wilt say that she is a lady of great credit, and I, here, of no countenance. Aye but, Euphues, low trees have their tops, small sparks their heat, the fly his spleen, the ant her gall, Philautus his affection, which is neither ruled by reason nor led by appointment.[6] Thou broughtest me into England, Euphues, to see and [I] am blind, to seek adventures and I have lost myself, to remedy love and I am now past cure; much like Seriphuis, that old drudge in Naples, who, coveting to heal his bleared eye, put it out.[7] My thoughts are high, my fortune low; and I resemble that foolish pilot who hoiseth up all his sails and hath no wind, and lanceth out[8] his ship and hath no water. Ah Love, thou takest away my taste and provokest mine appetite; yet if Euphues would be as willing to further me now, as he was once wily to hinder me, I should think myself fortunate and all that are not amorous to be fools. There is a stone in the flood of Thracia that whosoever findeth it is never after grieved.[9] I would I had that stone in my mouth, or that my body were in that river, that either I might be without grief, or without life.'

---

1 *Boeotia*] Hercules' birthplace
2 *with that I had*] i.e. Lucilla
3 *resiluation*] recurrence
4 *wane of the moon*] The last quarter of the moon is conventionally associated with misfortune.
5 *go I about / with affection ... love*] do I attempt / to deaden my love with passion
6 *appointment*] direction
7 *Seriphuis ... out*] No source has been found for this allusion.
8 *lanceth out*] launches
9 *There is a stone ... grieved*] pausilypus, a fabulous stone said to be found in the river Strymon in Thrace (see Croll and Clemons, p. 299n.)

And with these words, Euphues knocked at the door; which Philautus opened pretending drowsiness, and excusing his absence by idleness. Unto whom Euphues said:

'What, Philautus, dost thou shun the court to sleep in a corner, as one either cloyed with delight or having surfeited with desire? Believe me, Philautus, if the wind be in that door,[1] or thou so devout to fall from beauty to thy beads,[2] and to forsake the court to live in a cloister, I cannot tell whether I should more wonder at thy fortune or praise thy wisdom. But I fear me if I live to see thee so holy I shall be an old man before I die, or if thou die not before thou be so pure, thou shalt be more marvelled at for thy years than esteemed for thy virtues.

'In sooth, my good friend, if I should tarry a year in England, I could not abide an hour in my chamber, for I know not how it cometh to pass that in earth I think no other paradise; such variety of delights to allure a courtly eye, such rare purity to draw a well-disposed mind, that I know not whether they be in England more amorous or virtuous, whether I should think my time best bestowed in viewing goodly ladies or hearing godly lessons. I had thought no woman to excel Livia in the world, but now I see that in England they be all as good, none worse, many better; insomuch that I am enforced to think that it is as rare to see a beautiful woman in England without virtue, as to see a fair woman in Italy without pride. Courteous they are without coyness, but not without a care; amiable without pride, but not without courtliness; merry without curiosity,[3] but not without measure—so that conferring[4] the ladies of Greece with the ladies of Italy, I find the best but indifferent, and comparing both countries with the ladies of England, I account them all stark nought.

'And truly, Philautus, thou shalt not shrive me like a ghostly father,[5] for to thee I will confess in two things my extreme folly: the one in loving Lucilla, who in comparison of these had no spark of beauty, the other for making a "Cooling Card" against women, when I see these to have so much virtue; so that in the first I must acknowledge my judgement raw to discern shadows, and rash in the latter to give so peremptory sentence.[6] In both I think myself to have erred so much that I recant both, being ready to take any penance thou shalt enjoin me, whether it be a faggot[7]

---

1 *if the wind be in that door*] if that is how you are disposed (cf. if that's the way the wind blows)
2 *beads*] prayers
3 *curiosity*] undue refinement (*amiable* in the previous clause = lovely)
4 *conferring*] comparing
5 *shrive me like a ghostly father*] hear my confession and give me absolution like a priest (either because Euphues is willing to confess without compulsion, or because, as Croll and Clemons suggest (p. 300n.), he intends to make a full confesssion, unlike the formal acts of contrition condemned in Protestant anti-Catholic polemic)
6 *raw to discern shadows / peremptory sentence*] insufficiently mature to recognize false appearance / hasty judgement
7 *a faggot*] to be burned at the stake

for heresy or a fine for hypocrisy. An heretic I was by mine invective against women, and no less than an hypocrite for dissembling with thee; for now, Philautus, I am of that mind that women—'

But Philautus, taking hold of this discourse, interrupted him with a sudden reply, as followeth:

'Stay, Euphues, I can level at the thoughts of thy heart by the words of thy mouth; for that commonly the tongue uttereth the mind, and the outward speech bewrayeth[1] the inward spirit. For as a good root is known by a fair blossom, so is the substance of the heart noted by the show of the countenance. I can see day at a little hole; thou must halt cunningly if thou beguile a cripple.[2] But I cannot choose but laugh to see thee play with the bait that I fear thou hast swallowed, thinking with a mist to make my sight blind because I should not perceive thy eyes bleared. But in faith, Euphues, I am now as well acquainted with thy conditions[3] as with thy person, and use hath made me so expert in thy dealings that well thou mayst juggle with the world, but thou shalt never deceive me.

'A burnt child dreadeth the fire; he that stumbleth twice at one stone is worthy to break his shins; thou mayst haply forswear thyself, but thou shalt never delude me. I know thee now as readily by thy vizard as thy visage.[4] It is a blind goose that knoweth not a fox from a fern bush, and a foolish fellow that cannot discern craft from conscience being once co[zened].[5] But why should I lament thy follies with grief, when thou seemest to colour them with deceit? Ah Euphues, I love thee well, but thou hatest thyself, and seekest to heap more harms on thy head by a little wit than thou shalt ever claw off by thy great wisdom. All fire is not quenched by water, thou hast not love in a string,[6] affection is not thy slave, thou canst not leave when thou listest. With what face, Euphues, canst thou return to thy vomit, seeming with the greedy hound to lap up that which thou didst cast up? I am ashamed to rehearse the terms that once thou didst utter of malice against women, and art thou not ashamed now again to recant them? They must needs think thee either envious[7] upon small occasion or amorous upon a light cause; and then will they all be as ready to hate thee for thy spite as to laugh at thee for thy looseness.

'No, Euphues, so deep a wound cannot be healed with so light a plaster; thou mayst by art recover[8] the skin but thou canst never cover the scar,

---

1 *bewrayeth*] reveals
2 *I can see ... hole / thou must halt ... cripple*] both proverbial. It is not difficult to recognize the blindingly obvious / you cannot deceive those who know more about a subject than you do.
3 *conditions*] nature
4 *vizard / visage*] mask / face
5 *being once co[zened]*] having been deceived once
6 *in a string*] on a lead
7 *envious*] malicious
8 *recover*] heal

thou mayst flatter with fools because thou art wise but the wise will ever mark thee for a fool. Then, sure, I cannot see what thou gainest if the simple condemn thee of flattery and the grave of folly.

'Is thy "Cooling Card" of this property, to quench fire in others and to kindle flames in thee, or is it a whetstone to make thee sharp and us blunt, or a sword to cut wounds in me and cure them in Euphues? Why didst thou write that against them thou never thoughtest; or if thou didst it, why dost thou not follow it? But it is lawful for the physician to surfeit, for the shepherd to wander, for Euphues to prescribe what he will and do what he list. The sick patient must keep a strait diet, the silly[1] sheep a narrow fold, poor Philautus must believe Euphues, and all lovers (he only accepted) are cooled with a card of ten[2] or rather fooled with a vain toy.

'Is this thy professed purity, to cry "Peccavi,"[3] thinking it as great sin to be honest as shame not to be amorous? Thou that didst blaspheme the noble sex of women without cause, dost thou now commit idolatry with them without care, observing as little gravity then in thine unbridled fury as thou dost now reason by thy disordinate[4] fancy? I see now that there is nothing more smooth than glass, yet nothing more brittle; nothing more fair than snow, yet nothing less firm; nothing more fine than wit, yet nothing more fickle. For as polypus upon what rock soever he liketh turneth himself into the same likeness, or as the bird pyralis[5] sitting upon white cloth is white, upon green green, and changeth her colour with every cloth, or as our changeable silk turned to the sun hath many colours and turned back the contrary, so wit shippeth itself to every conceit, being constant in nothing but inconstancy. Where is now thy conference with Atheos, thy devotion, thy divinity? Thou sayest that I am fallen from beauty to my beads, and I see thou art come from thy book to beastliness, from coting[6] of the Scriptures to courting with ladies, from Paul to Ovid,[7] from the prophets to poets; resembling the wanton Diophantus,[8] who refused his mother's blessing to hear a song, and thou forsakest God's blessing to sit in a warm sun.[9]

'But thou, Euphues, thinkest to have thy prerogative (which others

---

1 *strait / silly*] restricted / innocent, helpless
2 *cooled with . . . ten*] gambling term signifying to have one's hopes dashed by a turn of play involving the highest of the numbered cards (see p. 88n.)
3 *Peccavi*] I have sinned
4 *disordinate*] ungoverned
5 *polypus / pyralis*] see p. 64n. / winged insect capable of living in fire (also known as pyrausta). No source has been found for its capacity to change colour.
6 *coting*] marking off chapter and verse of the scriptures (see p. 199n.)
7 *from Paul to Ovid*] from the Christian advocate of sexual morality to the author of the *Art of Love*
8 *Diophantus*] spoilt son of Themistocles (see p. 101n.)
9 *thou forsakest . . . sun*] a variation on the proverb used on p. 149 (signifying here to exchange a happy state for a superficially pleasant but ultimately worse one)

will not grant thee for a privilege) that under the colour of wit thou mayst be accounted wise, and being obstinate thou art to be thought singular.[1] There is no coin good silver but thy halfpenny,[2] if thy glass glister it must needs be gold, if thou speak a sentence it must needs be a law, if give a censure an oracle, if dream a prophecy, if conjecture a truth; insomuch that I am brought into a doubt whether I should more lament in thee thy want of government or laugh at thy feigned gravity. But as that rude poet Cherilus had nothing to be noted in his verses but only the name of Alexander, nor that rural poet Daretus[3] anything to cover his deformed ape but a white curtain, so Euphues hath no one thing to shadow his shameless wickedness but only a show of wit.

'I speak all this, Euphues, not that I envy thy estate[4] but that I pity it; and in this I have discharged the duty of a friend, in that I have not winked at thy folly. Thou art in love, Euphues, contrary to thine oath, thine honour, thine honesty; neither would any, professing that thou dost, live as thou dost, which is no less grief to me than shame to thee. Excuse thou mayst make to me, because I am credulous; but amends to the world thou canst not frame, because thou art come out of Greece to blaze[5] thy vice in England, a place too honest for thee, and thou too dishonest for any place. And this is my flat and friendly dealing—if thou wilt not take as I mean, take as thou wilt. I fear not thy force, I force not[6] thy friendship. And so I end.'

Euphues, not a little amazed with the discourteous speech of Philautus whom he saw in such a burning fever, did not apply warm clothes to continue his sweat, but gave him a cold drink to make him shake; either thinking so strange a malady was to be cured with a desperate medicine, or determining to use as little art in physic as the other did honesty in friendship. And therefore instead of a pill to purge his hot blood, he gave him a choke-pear[7] to stop his breath, replying as followeth:

'I had thought, Philautus, that a wound healing so fair could never have bred to a fistula,[8] or a body kept so well from drink to a dropsy; but I

---

1 *singular*] set apart by virtue of pre-eminence
2 *There is no coin . . . halfpenny*] there is nothing of any value except that which you have to offer
3 *Cherilus / Daretus*] mediocre writer regarded with some favour by Alexander (see Croll and Clemons, p. 303n. / possibly Dares, reputed author of an *Iliad* claimed to be of greater antiquity than Homer's, but known only through a purported translation by Cornelius Nepos, a poor imitation ('deformed ape') of major classical works
4 *envy thy estate*] feel resentment at your condition
5 *blaze*] openly exhibit
6 *force not*] do not care about
7 *choke-pear*] a species of inedible fruit (here used metaphorically as a reproof, something designed to be unpalatable rather than to assuage)
8 *fistula*] abscess. The passage turns on the idea that Philautus is inwardly infected with the disease of love, though outwardly cured of it.

well perceive that thy flesh is as rank as the wolf's, who as soon as he is stricken[1] recovereth a skin but rankleth inwardly until it come to the liver, and thy stomach as queasy as old Nestor's,[2] unto whom pap was no better than poison, and thy body no less distempered than Hermogineus'[3] whom abstinence from wine made oftentimes drunken. I see thy humour is love, thy quarrel jealousy; the one I gather by thine addle head, the other by thy suspicious nature. But I leave them both to thy will and thee to thine own wickedness.

'Prettily to cloak thine own folly thou callest me thief first; not unlike unto a curst wife, who, deserving a check,[4] beginneth first to scold. There is nothing that can cure the king's evil[5] but a prince, nothing ease a pleurisy but letting blood, nothing purge thy humour[6] but that which I cannot give thee, nor thou get of any other—liberty. Thou seemest to colour craft by a friendly kindness, taking great care for my bondage that I might not distrust thy follies; which is as though the thrush in the cage should be sorry for the nightingale which singeth on the tree, or the bear at the stake lament the mishap of the lion in the forest.

'But in truth, Philautus, though thy skin show thee a fox, thy little skill trieth thee[7] a sheep. It is not the colour that commendeth a good painter but the good countenance, nor the cutting that valueth the diamond but the virtue, nor the gloze of the tongue that trieth a friend but the faith.[8] For as all coins are not good that have the image of Caesar, nor all gold that are coined with the king's stamp, so all is not truth that beareth the show of godliness, nor all friends that bear a fair face. If thou pretend such love to Euphues, carry thy heart on the back of thy hand and thy tongue in the palm, that I may see what is in thy mind and thou with thy fingers clasp thy mouth.

'Of a stranger I can bear much, because I know not his manners; of an enemy more, for that all proceedeth of malice; all things of a friend if it be to try me—nothing if it be to betray me. I am of Scipio's mind, who had rather that Hannibal should eat his heart with salt than Laelius grieve it with unkindness, and of the like with Laelius, who chose rather to be

---

1 *stricken*] injured
2 *old Nestor's*] that of the oldest of the Greek heroes who fought at Troy (*pap* in the same sentence = *baby food*)
3 *Hermogineus'*] Obscure. Possibly the celebrated Greek rhetorician Hermogenes (fl. AD 161) whose body was so 'distempered' that his heart was found, after his death, to be covered with hair.
4 *check*] rebuke
5 *king's evil*] scrofula, a disease thought to be capable of cure by a king's touch
6 *humour*] excess of one of the four chief fluids (humours) thought to govern health and the human disposition (used metaphorically to imply an obsessive state)
7 *skin / trieth thee*] outward appearance / proves you to be
8 *nor the cutting . . . faith*] nor the way in which a diamond is cut that gives it value but the properties of the stone itself, nor fine phrases that are indicative of a friend but fidelity

slain with the Spaniards than suspected of Scipio.[1] I can better take a blister of a nettle than a prick of a rose, more willing that a raven should peck out mine eyes than a turtle[2] peck at them. To die of the meat one liketh not is better than to surfeit of that he loveth, and I had rather an enemy should bury me quick[3] than a friend belie me when I am dead.

'But thy friendship, Philautus, is like a new fashion, which being used in the morning is accounted old before noon. Which variety of changing being oftentimes noted of a grave gentleman in Naples, who having bought a hat of the newest fashion and best block[4] in all Italy, and wearing but one day it was told him that it was stale, he hung it up in his study; and viewing all sorts, all shapes, perceived at the last his old hat again to come into the new fashion; wherewith, smiling to himself, he said, "I have now lived compass,[5] for Adam's old apron must make Eve a new kirtle," noting this, that when no new thing could be devised nothing could be more new than the old.

'I speak this to this end, Philautus, that I see thee as often change thy head as other do their hats; now being friend to Ajax because he should cover thee with his buckler,[6] now to Ulysses that he may plead for thee with his eloquence, now to one, and now to another. And thou dealest with thy friends as that gentleman did with his felt;[7] for seeing not my vein answerable to thy vanities,[8] thou goest about (but yet the nearest way) to hang me up for holidays, as one neither fitting thy head nor pleasing thy humour. But when, Philautus, thou shalt see that change of friendships shall make thee a fat calf and a lean coffer,[9] that there is no more hold in a new friend than a new fashion, that hats alter as fast as the turner[10] can turn his block, and hearts as soon as one can turn his back, when seeing everyone return to his old wearing and find it the best, then compelled rather for want of others than good will of me thou wilt retire to Euphues, whom thou laidst by the walls, and seek him again as a new

---

1 *Scipio's mind . . . suspected of Scipio*] The friendship between Scipio Africanus Major (b. 234 BC) and Laelius the elder (fl. 190 BC) was exemplary as was that between the grandson of the former and son of the latter (see pp. 45 and 96nn.). The allusion to Hannibal, military opponent of Scipio Africanus Major, suggests that the elder pair is intended, though no source has been found for the incidents alluded to here.

2 *turtle*] turtle dove

3 *quick*] alive

4 *block*] fashion, design (literally the mould on which a hat is constructed)

5 *compass*] full circle

6 *cover thee . . . buckler*] a further reference to the rescue of Ulysses by Menelaus and Ajax (see p. 157n.) implying Philautus' tendency to curry favour with the great (*buckler* = shield)

7 *felt*] hat (commonly made of felt)

8 *seeing not . . . vanities*] perceiving my attitudes to be at odds with your frivolous proceedings

9 *a fat calf . . . coffer*] a great fool and a poor man

10 *turner*] manufacturer

friend, saying to thyself, "I have lived compass. Euphues' old faith must make Philautus a new friend." Wherein thou resemblest those that at the first coming of new wine leave the old, yet, finding that grape more pleasant than wholesome, they begin to say as Callisthenes[1] did to Alexander, that he had rather carouse old grains with Diogenes in his dish than new grapes with Alexander in his standing cup. "For of all gods," said he, "I love not Aesculapius."

'But thou art willing to change, else wouldst thou be unwilling to quarrel. Thou keepest only company out of my sight with Reynaldo, thy countryman, which I suspecting concealed, and now proving it do not care. If he have better deserved the name of a friend than I, God knoweth; but as Achilles' shield[2] being lost on the seas by Ulysses was tossed by the sea to the tomb of Ajax as a manifest token of his right, so thou being forsaken of Reynaldo wilt be found in Athens by Euphues' door as the true owner—which I speak not as one loath to lose thee, but careful[3] thou lose not thyself.

'Thou thinkest an apple may please a child, and every odd answer appease a friend. No, Philautus. A plaster is a small amends for a broken head, and a bad excuse will not purge an ill accuser. A friend is long a-getting and soon lost, like a merchant's riches, who by tempest loseth as much in two hours as he hath gathered together in twenty years. Nothing so fast knit as glass, but once broken it can never be joined; nothing fuller of metal than steel, yet over-heated it will never be hardened. Friendship is the best pearl, but by disdain thrown into vinegar it bursteth rather in pieces than it will bow to any softness. It is a salt fish that water cannot make fresh, sweet honey that is not made bitter with gall, hard gold that is not to be mollified with fire, and a miraculous friend that is not made an enemy with contempt.

'But give me leave to examine the cause of thy discourse to the quick, and, omitting the circumstance, I will to the substance. The only thing thou layest to my charge is love, and that is a good ornament;[4] the reasons to prove it is my praising of women, but that is no good argument. Am I in love, Philautus? With whom it should be thou canst not conjecture, and that it should not be with thee thou givest occasion. Priamus began to be jealous of Hecuba when he knew none did love her, but when he loved many;[5] and thou of me when thou art assured I love none, but thou

---

1 *Callisthenes*] relative and pupil of Aristotle noted for his outspoken opposition to Alexander. Bond (II, p. 511) traces the origins of his rejection of Alexander's wine to Plutarch. (For *Diogenes* and *Aesculapius* see p. 38n. and p. 124n.)
2 *Achilles' shield*] won by Ulysses by means of his eloquence rather than Ajax to whom it should have descended for his courage (see p. 78n.)
3 *careful*] concerned
4 *ornament*] pretence
5 *Priamus . . . loved many*] Priam, King of Troy, was father of fifty sons, only nineteen of whom were by his wife, Hecuba.

thyself everyone. But whether I love or no, I cannot live in quiet unless I be fit for thy diet. Wherein thou dost imitate Sciron and Procrustes,[1] who, framing a bed of brass to their own bigness, caused it to be placed as a lodging for all passengers, insomuch that none could travel that way but he was enforced to take measure of their sheets. If he were too long for the bed, they cut off his legs for catching cold—it was no place for a longis;[2] if too short, they racked him at length—it was no pallet for a dwarf. And certes, Philautus, they are no less to be discommended for their cruelty than thou for thy folly. For in like manner hast thou built a bed in thine own brains, wherein everyone must be of thy length. If he love, thou cuttest him shorter, either with some odd device or grave counsel; swearing (rather than thou wouldst not be believed) that Protogenes[3] portrayed Venus with a sponge sprinkled with sweet water, but if once she wrung it it would drop blood, that her ivory comb would at the first tickle the hairs, but at the last turn all the hairs into adders, so that nothing is more hateful than love. If he love not, th[ou] stretchest out like a wiredrawer,[4] making a wire as long as thy finger longer than thine arm; pulling on with the pincers with the shoemaker a little shoe on a great foot, till thou crack thy credit as he doth his stitches; alleging that love followeth a good wit as the shadow doth the body, and as requisite for a gentleman as steel in a weapon.

'A wit, sayest thou, without love is like an egg without salt; and a courtier void of affection[5] like salt without savour. Then as one pleasing thyself in thine own humour, or playing with others for thine own pleasure, thou rollest all thy wits to sift love from lust, as the baker doth the bran from his flour; bringing in Venus with a tortoise under her foot as slow to harms, her chariot drawn with white swans as the cognizance of Vesta, her birds to be pigeons noting piety,[6] with as many inventions to make Venus current as the ladies use sleights in Italy to make themselves counterfeit.[7] Thus with the Egyptian[8] thou playest fast or loose, so that there is nothing more certain than that thou wilt love, and nothing more uncertain than when; turning at one time thy tail to the wind with the

<del>___</del>

1 *Sciron and Procrustes*] both persecutors of travellers killed by Theseus. Sciron obliged passers-by to wash his feet before kicking them into the sea. Procrustes made travellers fit his bed in the way Lyly describes. Lyly partners the two (contrary to tradition) both here and in *Pappe with an Hatchet*.
2 *longis*] tall man
3 *Protogenes*] see p. 155n. No source has been found for the emblematic representations of Venus ascribed to him here.
4 *wiredrawer*] manufacturer of wire by a process of extension
5 *affection*] passion
6 *bringing in Venus ... piety*] all common emblematic representations of Venus exhibiting facets of the amatory state (*as the cognizance of Vesta* = to denote her affinity with the chaste goddess of the hearth)
7 *current / counterfeit*] creditable / embodiments of deceit
8 *Egyptian*] gipsy (but Cleopatra may also be intended here)

hedgehog, and thy nose in the wind with the weather-cock, in one gale both hoising sail and weighing[1] anchor, with one breath making an alarm and a parley,[2] discharging in the same instant both a bullet and a false fire.[3] Thou hast racked me and curtailed me.[4] Sometimes I was too long, sometimes too short, now too big, then too little; so that I must needs think thy bed monstrous or my body, either thy brains out of temper, or my wits out of tune; insomuch as I can liken thy head to Mercury's pipe, who with one stop[5] caused Argus to stare and wink. If this fault be in thy nature counsel can do little good, if in thy disease physic can do less; for nature will have her course, so that persuasions are needless, and such a malady in the marrow will never out of the bones, so that medicines are bootless.[6]

'Thou sayest that all this is for love, and that I being thy friend thou art loath to wink at[7] my folly. Truly, I say with Tully,[8] with fair words thou shalt yet persuade me. For experience teacheth me that straight trees have crooked roots, smooth baits sharp hooks, that the fairer the stone is in the toad's head the more pestilent the poison is in her bowels,[9] that talk the more it is seasoned with fine phrases the less it savoureth of true meaning. It is a mad hare that will be caught with a tabor, and a foolish bird that stayeth the laying salt on her tail,[10] and a blind goose that cometh to the fox's sermon; Euphues is not entangled with Philautus' charms. If all were in jest it was too broad, weighing[11] the place; if in earnest too bad, considering the person. If to try thy wit, it was folly to be so hot; if thy friendship, malice to be so hasty.

'Hast thou not read since thy coming into England a pretty discourse of one Phialo concerning the rebuking of a friend?[12] Whose reasons, although they were but few, yet were they sufficient; and if thou desire more, I could rehearse infinite. But thou art like the Epicure,[13] whose belly is sooner filled than his eye. For he coveteth to have twenty dishes at his table when he cannot digest one in his stomach, and thou desirest many

---

1 *hoising / weighing*] hoisting / beginning the process of dropping
2 *making an alarm . . . parley*] sounding a call to arms and an invitation to peace talks
3 *false fire*] blank shot (i.e. a salute)
4 *racked / curtailed me*] stretched me / cut me off short
5 *stop*] note (for the charming of Argus see p. 122n.)
6 *bootless*] of no avail
7 *wink at*] close your eyes to (i.e. overlook)
8 *Tully*] Cicero. Bond (II, p. 512) notes that the source is *De amicitia*.
9 *the fairer the stone . . . bowels*] see p. 48n.
10 *a foolish bird . . . tail*] an allusion to the playful advice offered to children that birds could be caught by putting salt on their tails. (For *it is a mad hare . . . tabor* see p. 41n.)
11 *weighing*] considering
12 *a pretty discourse . . . friend*] Stephen Gosson's *Ephemerides of Phialo* (1579), an instance of Lyly's topicality
13 *Epicure*] see p. 34n.

reasons to be brought when one might serve thy turn; thinking it no rainbow that hath [not] all colours, nor ancient armoury that are not quartered with sundry coats,[1] nor perfect rules that have not [a] thousand reasons. And of all the reasons would thou wouldst follow but one, not to check thy friend in a bravery;[2] knowing that rebukes ought not to weigh a grain more of salt than sugar, but to be so tempered as like pepper they might be hot in the mouth, but like treacle[3] wholesome at the heart; so shall they at the first make one blush if he were pale, and well considered better if he were not past grace. If a friend offend he is to be whipped with a good nurse's rod; who when her child will not be still giveth it together both the twig[4] and the teat, and bringeth it asleep when it is wayward as well with rocking it as rating[5] it. The admonition of a true friend should be like the practice of a wise physician, who wrappeth his sharp pills in fine sugar, or the cunning chirurgeon, who lancing the wound with an iron immediately applieth to it soft lint, or as mothers deal with their children for worms, who put their bitter seeds into sweet raisins. If this order had been observed in thy discourse, that interlacing sour taunts with sugared counsel, bearing as well a gentle rein as using a hard snaffle, thou mightst have done more with the whisk of a wand[6] than now thou canst with the prick of the spur, and avoided that which now thou mayst not—extreme unkindness. But thou art like that kind judge which Propertius[7] noteth, who condemning his friend caused him for the more ease to be hanged with a silken twist; and thou like a friend cuttest my throat with a razor not with a hatchet, for my more honour. But why should I set down the office of a friend when thou, like our Athenians, knowest what thou shouldst do, but like them never dost it?[8]

'Thou sayest I eat my own words in praising women. No, Philautus, I was never either so wicked or so witless to recant truths or mistake colours.[9] But this I say, that the ladies in England as far excel all other countries in virtue as Venus doth all other women in beauty. I flatter not those of whom I hope to reap benefit, neither yet so praise them but that I think them women. There is no sword made of steel but hath iron, no

1 *armoury . . . coats*] heraldic devices that are not subdivided into many coats of arms (indicating the antiquity of the family name and the many noble houses associated with it by marriage)
2 *check thy friend . . . bravery*] reprimand your friend in a fit of bravado
3 *treacle*] noted for its medicinal properties
4 *the twig*] a light cane (i.e. light physical correction, a tap). The lines that follow look back to the discussion of the rearing of children in *Euphues and his Ephebus*.
5 *rating*] scolding
6 *whisk of a wand*] light stroke of a riding switch
7 *Propertius*] see p. 59n. Bond reports that the story related here is not to be found among his works (II, p. 512).
8 *like our Athenians . . . dost it*] see pp. 111–12
9 *mistake colours*] either be deceived by appearances or unwittingly change sides (by confusing the flags of one army with those of another)

fire made of wood but hath smoke, no wine made of grapes but hath lees, no woman created of flesh but hath faults. And if I love them, Philautus, they deserve it.

'But it grieveth not thee, Philautus, that they be fair, but that they are chaste; neither dost thou like me the worse for commending their beauty, but thinkest they will not love thee well, because so virtuous. Wherein thou followest those who better esteem the sight of the rose than the savour, preferring fair weeds before good herbs, choosing rather to wear a painted flower in their bosoms than to have a wholesome root in their broths; which resembleth the fashion of your maidens in Italy, who buy that for the best cloth that will wear whitest, not that will last longest. There is no more praise to be given to a fair face than to a false glass; for as the one flattereth us with a vain shadow to make us proud in our own conceits, so the other feedeth us with an idle hope to make us peevish[1] in our own contemplations.

'Chirurgeons affirm that a white vein being stricken, if at the first there spring out blood it argueth[2] a good constitution of body; and I think if a fair woman, having heard the suit of a lover, if she blush at the first brunt[3] and show her blood in her face, showeth a well-disposed mind. So as virtuous women, I confess, are for to be chosen by the face—not when they blush for the shame of some sin committed, but for fear she should commit any. All women shall be as Caesar would have his wife, not only free from sin but from suspicion.[4] If such be in the English court, if I should not praise them thou wouldst say I care not for their virtue; and now I give them their commendation, thou swearest I love them for their beauty. So that it is no less labour to please thy mind than a sick man's mouth, who can relish nothing by the taste, not that the fault is in the meat but in his malady; nor thou like of anything in thy head, not that there is any disorder in my sayings, but in thy senses.

'Thou dost last of all object that which silence might well resolve, that I am fallen from prophets to poets, and returned again with the dog to my vomit; which God knoweth is as far from truth as I know thou art from wisdom. What have I done, Philautus, since my going from Naples to Athens? Speak no more than the truth, utter no less; flatter me not to make me better than I am, belie me not to make me worse; forge nothing of malice, conceal nothing for love. Did I ever use any unseemly talk to corrupt youth? Tell me where. Did I ever deceive those that put me in trust? Tell me whom. Have I committed any fact worthy either of death or defame?[5] Thou canst not reckon what. Have I abused myself[6] towards

---

1 *conceits / peevish*] opinion / foolish
2 *argueth*] is indicative of
3 *brunt*] assault
4 *All women . . . suspicion*] from Plutarch's biography of Julius Caesar and frequently cited as a definition of rectitude in public life
5 *defame*] dishonour
6 *abused myself*] misconducted myself

my superiors, equals, or inferiors? I think thou canst not devise when. But as there is no wool so white but the dyer can make black, no apple so sweet but a cunning grafter can change into a crab, so there is no man so void of crime that a spiteful tongue cannot make him to be thought a caitiff.[1]

'Yet commonly it falleth out so well that the cloth weareth the better being dyed, and the apple eateth pleasanter being grafted, and the innocent is more esteemed and thriveth sooner being envied for virtue and belied for malice. For as he that struck Jason on the stomach thinking to kill him, brake his impostume with the blow whereby he cured him,[2] so oftentimes it fareth with those that deal maliciously, who instead of a sword apply a salve, and thinking to be one's priest they become his physician. But as the traitor that clippeth the coin of his prince maketh it lighter to be weighed,[3] not worse to be touched, so he that by sinister reports seemeth to pare[4] the credit of his friend may make him lighter among the common sort, who by weight oftentimes are deceived with counterfeits, but nothing impaireth his good name with the wise, who try all gold by the touchstone.

'A stranger coming into the Capitol of Rome,[5] seeing all the gods to be engraven, some in one stone, some in another, at the last he perceived Vulcan to be wrought in ivory, Venus to be carved in jet. Which long time beholding with great delight, at the last he burst out in these words: "Neither can this white ivory, Vulcan, make thee a white smith, neither this fair woman, jet, make thee a fair stone." Whereby he noted that no cunning could alter the nature of the one, nor no nature transform the colour of the other. In like manner say I, Philautus, although thou have shadowed my guiltless life with a defamed counterfeit,[6] yet shall not thy black Vulcan make either thy accusations of force[7] or my innocency faulty, neither shall the white Venus which thou hast portrayed upon the black jet of thy malice make thy conditions amiable;[8] for Vulcan cannot make ivory black, nor Venus change the colour of jet, the one having received such course by nature, the other such force by virtue.

'What cause have I given thee to suspect me, and what occasion hast thou not offered me to detest thee? I was never wise enough to give thee

---

1 *crab / caitiff*] sour apple used for preserves / villain
2 *he that struck ... cured him*] a story told by Cicero (see Bond, II, p. 513) of Jason, Tyrant of Pherae (d. 370 BC), not the hero who won the golden fleece (*impostume* = abscess)
3 *clippeth the coin ... weighed*] see p. 148n.
4 *pare*] diminish
5 *Capitol of Rome*] temple of Jupiter Optimus Maximus. For *Vulcan* and *Venus* see p. 29n.
6 *shadowed my guiltless ... counterfeit*] represented my innocent life by a dishonoured picture (with a pun on *shadowed* = obscured)
7 *of force*] weighty
8 *conditions amiable*] nature attractive

counsel, yet ever willing to wish thee well, my wealth small to do thee good, yet ready to do my best; insomuch as thou couldst never accuse me of any discourtesy, unless it were in being more careful of thee than of myself. But as all flowers that are in one nosegay are not of one nature, nor all rings that are worn upon one hand are not of one fashion, so all friends that associate at bed and at board are not of one disposition. Scipio must have a noble mind, Laelius an humble spirit; Titus must lust after Sempronia, Gysippus must leave her; Damon must go take order for his lands, Pythias must tarry behind as a pledge for his life;[1] Philautus must do what he will, Euphues not what he should.

'But it may be that as the sight of divers colours make divers[2] beasts mad, so my presence doth drive thee into this melancholy. And seeing it is so, I will absent myself, hire another lodging in London, and for a time give myself to my book; for I have learned this by experience, though I be young,[3] that bavins are known by their bands,[4] lions by their claws, cocks by their combs, envious minds by their manners. Hate thee I will not, and trust thee I may not. Thou knowest what a friend should be, but thou wilt never live to try what a friend is. Farewell, Philautus, I will not stay to hear thee reply, but leave thee to thy list.[5] Euphues carrieth this posy written in his hand and engraven in his heart, "A faithful friend is a wilful fool." And so I taking leave till I hear thee better-minded, England shall be my abode for a season. Depart when thou wilt. And again, farewell.'

Euphues, in a great rage, departed, not suffering Philautus to answer one word, who stood in a maze after the speech of Euphues; but taking courage by love, went immediately to the place where Camilla was dancing. And there will I leave him, in a thousand thoughts hammering in his head; and Euphues seeking a new chamber, which by good friends he quickly got, and there fell to his paternoster,[6] where a while I will not trouble him in his prayers.

Now you shall understand that Philautus, furthered as well by the opportunity of the time as the requests of certain gentlemen his friends, was entreated to make one in a masque; which Philautus, perceiving to be at the gentleman's house where Camilla lay, assented as willingly

---

1 *Scipio . . . pledge for his life*] all pairs of friends who differed in nature or conduct. Scipio Africanus the younger was noted for his adherence to austere Roman virtues, his friend Laelius for his prudent and reflective character. Gysippus surrendered his proposed bride to Titus on discovering his friend was in love with her. Pythias stood surety for Damon (condemned to death on a charge of spying) to permit his friend to return home to settle his affairs (see also p. 34n.).
2 *divers / divers*] certain / different
3 *though I be young*] See Introduction, p. 9 for a discussion of the discrepancies between Euphues' age at the close of *The Anatomy of Wit* and at the start of *Euphues and His England*.
4 *bavins . . . bands*] bundles of brushwood are distinguished by their bindings
5 *thy list*] your own inclination
6 *fell to his paternoster*] began to pray

to go as he desired to speed. And all things being in a readiness, they went with speed.[1] Where being welcomed they danced, Philautus taking Camilla by the hand; and as time served, began to board[2] her in this manner:

'It hath been a custom, fair lady, how commendable I will not dispute, how common you know, that masquers do therefore cover their faces that they may open[3] their affections, and under the colour of a dance discover their whole desires; the benefit of which privilege I will not use except you grant it, neither can you refuse except you break it. I mean only with questions[4] to try your wit, which shall neither touch your honour to answer, nor my honesty to ask.'

Camilla took him up short, as one not to seek[5] how to reply, in this manner:

'Gentleman, if you be less, you are too bold, if so, too broad in claiming a custom where there is no prescription.[6] I know not your name because you fear to utter it, neither do I desire it; and you seem to be ashamed of your face else would you not hide it, neither do I long to see it. But as for any custom, I was never so superstitious that either I thought it treason to break them or reason to keep them.

'As for the proving of my wit, I had rather you should account me a fool by silence, than wise by answering. For such questions in these assemblies move[7] suspicion where there is no cause, and therefore are not to be resolved lest there be cause.'

Philautus, who ever as yet but played with the bait, was now struck with the hook;[8] and no less delighted to hear her speak than desirous to obtain his suit, trained her by the blood[9] in this sort:

'If the patience of men were not greater than the perverseness of women I should then fall from a question to a quarrel, for that I perceive you draw the counterfeit of that I would say by the conceit[10] of that you think others have said. But whatsoever the colour be, the picture is as it pleaseth the painter; and whatsoever were pretended, the mind[11] is as the heart doth intend. A cunning archer is not known by his arrow, but by his aim; neither a friendly affection by the tongue, but by the faith. Which if it be

---

1 *speed / speed*] be successful (in his suit) / quickly
2 *board*] court
3 *open*] disclose
4 *questions*] topics for debate (see p. 205n.)
5 *to seek*] at a loss
6 *claiming a custom . . . prescription*] insisting upon a social convention to which there is no obligation to conform
7 *move*] arouse
8 *but played . . . hook*] who had formerly simply toyed with the idea was now wholly captivated
9 *trained her by the blood*] roused her to the chase (metaphor drawn from giving hunting animals a taste of blood)
10 *counterfeit / conceit*] picture / notion
11 *pretended / mind*] falsely alleged / meaning

so, methinketh common courtesy should allow that which you seek to cut off by courtly coyness, as one either too young to understand, or obstinate to overthwart;[1] your years shall excuse the one, and my humour pardon [the] other.

'And yet, lady, I am not of that faint mind that though I wink with a flash of lightning I dare not open mine eyes again, or having once suffered a repulse I should not dare to make fresh assault. He that striketh sail in a storm, hoiseth[2] them higher in a calm; which maketh me the bolder to utter that which you disdain to hear. But as the dove seemeth angry as though she had a gall,[3] yet yieldeth at the last to delight, so ladies pretend a great skirmish at the first, yet are boarded willingly[4] at the last. I mean, therefore, to tell you this, which is all—that I love you.'

And so, wringing[5] her by the hand, he ended; she beginning as followeth:

'Gentleman (I follow my first term, which showeth rather my modesty than your desert), seeing you resemble those which having once wet their feet care not how deep they wade, or those that breaking the ice weigh not how far they slip, thinking it lawful, if one suffer you to tread awry, no shame to go slipshod,[6] if I should say nothing, then would you vaunt that I am won, for that they that are silent seem to consent, if anything, then would you boast that I would be wooed, for that castles that come to parley and women that delight in courting are willing to yield. So that I must either hear those things which I would not, and seem to be taught by none, or to hold you talk which I should not, and run into the suspicion of others. But certainly, if you knew how much your talk displeaseth me and how little it should profit you, you would think the time as vainly lost in beginning your talk, as I account over-long until you end it.

'If you build upon custom that masquers have liberty to speak what they should not, you shall know that women have reason to make them hear what they would not; and though you can utter by your vizard whatsoever it be without blushing, yet cannot I hear it without shame. But I never looked for a better tale of so ill a face. You say a bad colour may make a good countenance, but he that conferreth your disordered discourse [with] your deformed attire may rightly say that he never saw so crabbed a visage, nor heard so crooked a vein.[7] An archer, say you, is to be known by his aim, not by his arrow; but your aim is so ill that if you

---

1 *overthwart*] cross
2 *hoiseth*] hoists
3 *as though ... gall*] The dove was thought to lack a gall because of its gentle nature.
4 *boarded willingly*] content to be wooed
5 *wringing*] squeezing
6 *go slipshod*] wear slippers (i.e. abandon the social proprieties altogether)
7 *conferreth your disordered discourse ... vein*] compares your confused speech with your grotesque costume may rightly remark that he never saw such a contorted face or heard such a tortuous discourse

knew how far wide from the white[1] your shaft sticketh, you would hereafter rather break your bow than bend it. If I be too young to understand
your destinies,[2] it is a sign I cannot like; if too obstinate, it is a token I
will not. Therefore, for you to be displeased, it either needeth not or
booteth not.[3]

'Yet go you further, thinking to make a great virtue of your little valour,
seeing that lightning may cause you wink but it shall not strike you blind,
that a storm may make you strike sail but never cut the mast, that a hot
skirmish may cause you to retire but never to run away. What your
cunning is I know not, and likely it is your courage is great; yet have I
heard that he that hath escaped burning with lightning hath been spoiled[4]
with thunder, and one that often hath wished drowning hath been hanged
once for all, and he that shrinketh from a bullet in the main battle hath
been stricken with a bill[5] in the rearward. You fall from one thing to
another using no decorum except this, that you study to have your discourse as far void of sense as your face is of favour, to the end that your
disfigured countenance might supply[6] the disorder of your ill-couched sentences. Among the which you bring in a dove without a gall, as far from
the matter you speak of as you are from the mastery you would have;
who although she cannot be angry with you in that she hath no gall, yet
can she laugh at you for that she hath a spleen.

'I will end where you began, hoping you will begin where I end. You
let fall[7] your question which I looked for, and picked a quarrel which I
thought not of, and that is love. But let her that is disposed to answer
your quarrel, be curious to demand your question. And this, gentleman,
I desire you, all questions and other quarrels set apart: you think me as
a friend so far forth as I can grant with modesty or you require with good
manners; and as a friend I wish you that you blow no more this fire of
love, which will waste you before it warm me, and make a coal in you
before it can kindle in me. If you think otherwise, I may as well use a
shift[8] to drive you off, as you did a show to draw me on. I have answered
your custom, lest you should argue[9] me of coyness, no otherwise than I
might, mine honour saved and your name unknown.'

By this time entered another masque, but almost after the same manner,
and only for Camilla's love; which Philautus quickly espied. And seeing
his Camilla to be courted with so gallant a youth, departed, yet within a
corner, to the end he might decipher the gentleman; whom he found to

1 *white*] centre of the target
2 *destinies*] prognostications
3 *it either needeth . . . not*] is either needless or unavailing
4 *spoiled*] killed
5 *bill*] long-handled weapon tipped with a point and/or blade
6 *supply*] reinforce
7 *let fall*] dropped, abandoned
8 *shift*] device
9 *argue*] accuse

be one of the bravest youths in all England, called Surius. Then, wounded
with grief, he sounded[1] with weakness; and going to his chamber began
afresh to recount his miseries, in this sort:

'Ah miserable and accursed Philautus, the very monster of nature and
spectacle of shame! If thou live, thou shalt be despised; if thou die, not
missed; if woo, pointed at; if win, loathed; if lose, laughed at. Bred either
to live in love and be forsaken, or die with love and be forgotten!

'Ah Camilla! Would either I had been born without eyes not to see thy
beauty, or without ears not to hear thy wit. The one hath inflamed me
with the desire of Venus, the other with the gifts of Pallas;[2] both with the
fire of love. Love? Yea love, Philautus—than the which nothing can
happen unto man more miserable.

'I perceive now that the chariot of the sun is for Phoebus not for
Phaethon, that Bucephalus will stoop to none but Alexander, that none
can sound Mercurius' pipe but Orpheus,[3] that none shall win Camilla's
liking but Surius; a gentleman, I confess, of greater birth than I, and yet
I dare say not of better faith. It is he, Philautus, that will fleet all the fat
from thy beard,[4] insomuch as she will disdain to look upon thee if she
but once think upon him. It is he, Philautus, that hath wit to try her,
wealth to allure her, personage to entice her, and all things that either
nature or fortune can give to win her. For as the Phrygian harmony being
moved to the Celaenes maketh a great noise, but being moved to Apollo
it is still and quiet,[5] so the love of Camilla desired of me moveth I know
not how many discords, but proved of Surius it is calm and consenteth.

'It is not the sweet flower that ladies desire, but the fair; which maketh
them wear that in their heads wrought forth with the needle, not brought
forth by nature. And in the like manner they account of that love which
art can colour,[6] not that the heart doth confess; wherein they imitate the
maidens (as Euphues often hath told me) of Athens, who took more
delight to see a fresh and fine colour than to taste a sweet and wholesome
syrup.

'Aye, but how knowest thou that Surius' faith is not as great as thine,
when thou art assured thy virtue is no less than his? He is wise, and that

---

1 *sounded*] swooned
2 *gifts of Pallas*] wisdom (the blessing bestowed by Pallas Athene)
3 *the chariot of the sun . . . Orpheus*] all attributes or capabilities unique to an individual. For *Phoebus* and *Phaethon* see p. 177n. Alexander alone could ride his war-
   horse, Bucephalus. Orpheus, the mythical poet and musician, was instructed by the
   Muses, and was thus able to play the pipe of a god.
4 *fleet . . . beard*] proverbial, signifying to be robbed of something desirable
5 *For as the . . . quiet*] The comparison refers to the outcome of a musical contest
   between Apollo and Marsyas of Phrygia (a rustic figure associated with the earliest
   period of Greek music). The skin of the vanquished Marsyas, flayed by the god, was
   hung up in a cave at Celaenae, which thus rings with sound when Phrygian music is
   played but is still when music is played that would please Apollo.
6 *art can colour*] that may be expressed in fine terms

thou seest; valiant, and that thou fearest; rich, and that thou lackest; fit to please her, and displace thee; and, without spite be it said, worthy to do the one, and willing to attempt the other.

'Ah Camilla, Camilla, I know not whether I should more commend thy beauty or thy wit, neither can I tell whether thy looks have wounded me more or thy words; for they both have wrought such an alteration in my spirits that seeing thee silent thy comeliness maketh me in a maze, and hearing thee speaking thy wisdom maketh me stark mad.

'Aye, but things above thy height are to be looked at, not reached at.[1] Aye, but if now I should end, I had been better never to have begun. Aye, but time must wear away love. Aye, but time may win it. Hard stones are pierced with soft drops, great oaks hewn down with many blows, the stoniest heart mollified by continual persuasions or true perseverance.

'If deserts can nothing prevail I will practise deceits, and what faith cannot do conjuring shall. What sayest thou, Philautus? Canst thou imagine so great mischief against her thou lovest? Knowest thou not that fish caught with medicines[2] and women gotten with witchcraft are never wholesome? No, no, the fox's wiles shall never enter into the lion's head, nor Medea's charms[3] into Philautus' heart. Aye, but I have heard that extremities are to be used where the mean[4] will not serve, and that as in love there is no measure of grief so there should be no end of guile. Of two mischiefs the least is to be chosen, and therefore I think it better to poison her with the sweet bait of love, than to spoil[5] myself with the bitter sting of death.

'If she be obstinate, why should not I be desperate? If she be void of pity, why should I not be void of piety? In the ruling of empires there is required as great policy as prowess; in governing an estate close cruelty doth more good than open clemency; for the obtaining of a kingdom as well mischief as mercy is to be practised.[6] And then in the winning of my love, the very image of beauty, courtesy, and wit, shall I leave anything unsought, unattempted, undone? He that desireth riches must stretch the string that will not reach, and practise all kinds of getting. He that coveteth honour and cannot climb by the ladder must use all colours of lustiness.[7] He that thirsteth for wine must not care how he get it, but where he may get it; nor he that is in love be curious[8] what means he

---

1 *things above . . . reached at*] see pp. 43 and 190 for variations on this maxim
2 *medicines*] poisoned bait
3 *Medea's charms*] see p. 230n. Many of Medea's charms were terrible in effect.
4 *the mean*] moderation
5 *spoil*] destroy
6 *In the ruling . . . practised*] These sentiments would be regarded as Machiavellian by a contemporary audience and thus both appropriate to an Italian and indicative of Philautus' decline from virtue when estranged from Euphues (*policy as prowess* = cunning as courage).
7 *all colours of lustiness*] every appearance of vigorous capability
8 *curious*] over-scrupulous about

ought to use, but ready to attempt any. For slender affection do I think that which either the fear of law or care of religion may diminish.

'Fie, Philautus, thine own words condemn thee of wickedness. Tush, the passions I sustain are neither to be quieted with counsel nor eased by reason. Therefore I am fully resolved either by art to win her love, or by despair to lose my own life.

'I have heard here in London of an Italian, cunning in mathematic, named Psellus,[1] of whom in Italy I have heard in such cases can do much by magic, and will do all things for money. Him will I assay, as well with gold as other good turns, and I think there is nothing that can be wrought but shall be wrought for gilt, or good will, or both.'

And in this rage, as one forgetting where he was and whom he loved, he went immediately to seek physic for that which only was to be found by fortune.

Here, gentlemen, you may see into what open sins the heat of love driveth man, especially where one loving is in despair, either of his own imperfection or his lady's virtues, to be beloved again; which causeth man to attempt those things that are contrary to his own mind, to religion, to honesty. What greater villainy can there be devised than to enquire of sorcerers, soothsayers, conjurers, or learned clerks for the enjoying of love? But I will not refel[2] that here which shall be confuted hereafter.

Philautus hath soon found this gentleman, who conducting him into his study and demanding of him the cause of his coming, Philautus beginneth in this manner, as one past shame, to unfold his suit:[3]

'Master Psellus and Countryman, I neither doubt of your cunning to satisfy my request, nor of your wisdom to conceal it; for were either of them wanting in you, it might turn me to trouble and yourself to shame. I have heard of your learning to be great in magic, and somewhat in physic; your experience in both to be exquisite. Which caused me to seek to you for a remedy of a certain grief, which by your means may be eased, or else no ways cured. And to the end such cures may be wrought, God hath stirred up in all times clerks[4] of great virtue, and in these our days men of no small credit; among the which I have heard no one more commended than you, which although haply your modesty will deny (for that the greatest clerks do commonly dissemble their knowledge), or your preciseness[5] not grant it (for that cunning men are often dangerous),

---

1 *Psellus*] Croll and Clemons note a Psellus Platonicus, who wrote on magic, from whom the name of Lyly's magus may derive (p. 323n.). There was also a celebrated eleventh-century philosopher (Michael Constantius Psellus), however, who was noted for the breadth of his learning.

2 *refel*] refute

3 *unfold his suit*] explain his request

4 *clerks*] scholars

5 *preciseness*] scrupulous correctness of behaviour. (The need for secrecy among those thought to possess occult powers and their fear of being exploited by those in high office recur in jocular form in *Gallathea*.)

yet the world doth well know it, divers have tried it, and I must needs believe it.'

Psellus, not suffering him to range[1] yet desirous to know his errand, answered him thus:

'Gentleman, and Countryman as you say (and I believe, but of that hereafter), if you have so great confidence in my cunning as you protest, it may be your strong imagination shall work that in you which my art cannot; for it is a principle among us that a vehement thought is more available than the virtue of our figures, forms, or characters.[2] As for keeping your counsel, in things honest it is no matter, and in causes unlawful I will not meddle. And yet, if it threaten no man harm and may do you good, you shall find my secrecy to be great, though my science be small. And therefore say on.'

'There is, not far hence, a gentlewoman whom I have long time loved, of honest parents, great virtue, and singular beauty; such a one as neither by art I can describe, nor by service deserve. And yet, because I have heard many say that where cunning must work the whole body must be coloured,[3] this is her shape.

'She is a virgin of the age of eighteen years; of stature neither too high nor too low, and such was Juno; her hair black yet comely, and such had Leda; her eyes hazel yet bright, and such were the lights[4] of Venus. And although my skill in physiognomy be small, yet in my judgement she was born under Venus; her forehead, nose, lips, and chin foreshowing (as by such rules we guess) both a desire to live and a good success in love. In complexion of pure sanguine, in condition a right saint,[5] seldom given to play, often to prayer, the first letter of whose name (for that also is necessary) is Camilla.[6]

'This lady I have served long and often sued unto, insomuch that I have melted like wax against the fire, and yet lived in the flame with the fly pyrausta.[7] Oh Psellus, the torments sustained by her presence, the griefs endured by her absence, the pining thoughts in the day, the pinching dreams in the night, the dying life, the living death, the jealousy at all times, and the despair at this instant can neither be uttered of me without

---

1 *suffering him to range*] allowing him to develop his subject more broadly
2 *vehement thought . . . characters*] a strong conviction is more efficacious than the properties of our magic symbols
3 *coloured*] depicted
4 *Leda / lights*] see p. 27n. / eyes
5 *In complexion . . . sanguine / in condition . . . saint*] in temperament of the sanguine humour (one of the four medieval humours thought to govern the disposition) / in nature an absolute saint
6 *the first letter . . . Camilla*] a common formulation (cf. Middleton's *The Family of Love*, 'Her name begins with Mistress Purge, does it not?' (II.iii.53–4). Philautus supplies in this sentence the principal information needed to draw up a horoscope or cast a spell—the planet under which the subject was born, her predominant humour, temperament and name.
7 *the fly pyrausta*] see p. 236n.

floods of tears, nor heard of thee without grief. No, Psellus, not the tortures of hell are either to be compared or spoken of in the respect of my torments; for what they all had severally, all that and more do I feel jointly. Insomuch that with Sisyphus I roll the stone even to the top of the hill, when it tumbleth both itself and me into the bottom of hell;[1] yet never ceasing I attempt to renew my labour, which was begun in death and cannot end in life. What drier thirst could Tantalus endure than I, who have almost every hour the drink I dare not taste and the meat I cannot? Insomuch that I am torn upon the wheel with Ixion,[2] my liver gnawn of the vultures and harpies;[3] yea, my soul troubled even with the unspeakable pains of Megaera, Tisiphone, Alecto.[4] Which secret sorrows although it were more meet to enclose them in a labyrinth than to set them on a hill,[5] yet where the mind is past hope the face is past shame.

'It fareth with me, Psellus, as with the ostrich, who pricketh none but herself, which causeth her to run when she would rest; or as it doth with the pelican, who striketh blood out of her own body to do others good; or with the wood-culver, who plucketh off her feathers in winter to keep others from cold; or as with the stork, who when she is least able carrieth the greatest burden.[6] So I practise all things that may hurt me to do her good that never regardeth my pains, so far is she from rewarding them.

'For as it is impossible for the best adamant to draw iron unto it if the diamond[7] be near it, so is it not to be looked for that I, with all my service, suit, deserts, and what else soever that may draw a woman, should win Camilla as long as Surius, a precious stone in her eyes and an eyesore in mine, be present; who loveth her (I know) too well, and she him (I fear me) better. Which love will breed between us such a deadly hatred that

---

1 *with Sisyphus ... hell*] see p. 177n.
2 *Tantalus / Ixion*] king who revealed the divine secrets entrusted to him and was punished in the underworld by being unable to assuage his hunger and thirst with the food and drink by which he was surrounded as it constantly receded from his reach / king who, having been purged of his crimes by Zeus and invited to sit at his table, treacherously attempted to seduce the queen of the gods and was punished by being chained to an ever-turning wheel
3 *my liver ... harpies*] the fate of Prometheus, who stole fire from the gods (*harpies* = monstrous birds with the heads of maidens, long claws and faces pale with hunger)
4 *Megaera, Tisiphone, Alecto*] the Eumenides, who punished crimes by inflicting prolonged and terrible suffering
5 *to enclose ... hill*] to conceal rather than publish them
6 *the ostrich ... burden*] all instances of perverse or self-sacrificing natural behaviour. The ostrich was thought to have goads on its wing tips with which it spurred itself when running, the pelican was believed to feed its young with the blood from its own breast, the wood-culver (i.e. woodpigeon) was said to pluck out its feathers in winter to keep its young warm, while young storks were reputed to carry their parents when they grew infirm (see Croll and Clemons, pp. 325–6nn.).
7 *adamant ... diamond*] see p. 148n.

being dead our blood cannot be mingled together, like florus and aegithus, and being burnt the flames shall part, like Polynices and Eteocles.[1]
Such a mortal enmity is kindled that nothing can quench it but death,
and yet death shall not end [it].

'What counsel can you give me in this case? What comfort? What
hope? When Acontius[2] could not persuade Cydippe to love, he practised
fraud; when Tarquinius could not win Lucretia by prayer, he used force;
when the gods could not obtain their desires by suit, they turned themselves into new shapes, leaving nothing undone for fear they should be
undone.[3]

'The disease of love, Psellus, is impatient, the desire extreme; whose
assaults neither the wise can resist by policy, nor the valiant by strength.
Julius Caesar, a noble conqueror in war, a grave counsellor in peace, after
he had subdued France, Germany, Britain, Spain, Italy, Thessaly, Egypt,
yea, entered with no less puissance than good fortune into Armenia, into
Pontus, into Africa, yielded in his chiefest victories to love,[4] Psellus, as
a thing fit for Caesar, who conquered all things saving himself; and a
deeper wound did the small arrow of Cupid make than all the spears
of his enemies. Hannibal,[5] not less valiant in arms nor more fortunate in
love, having spoiled Ticinum, Trebia, Trasimenus, and Cannae, sub-
mitted himself in Apulia to the love of a woman, whose hate was a terror
to all men, and became so bewitched that neither the fear of death, nor
the desire of glory, could remove him from the lap of his lover. I omit
Hercules, who was constrained to use a distaff for the desire of his love;
Leander, who ventured to cross the seas for Hero; Iphis, that hanged
himself; Pyramus,[6] that killed himself; and infinite more which could
not resist the hot skirmishes of affection. And so far hath this humour
crept into the mind that Byblis loved her brother, Myrrha her father,

1 *florus and aegithus / Polynices and Eteocles*] yellow wagtail and red linnet, mutu-
ally antipathetic birds / sons of Oedipus and Jocasta who agreed to govern Thebes
by turns but slew one another in single combat after disputes broke out between
them. (The divided smoke from their funeral pyres signifies their enmity beyond
death.)
2 *Acontius*] beautiful youth from Ceos who won Cydippe by throwing an apple into
the temple of Diana where she was sitting inscribed with the words, 'I swear by the
sanctuary of Diana to marry Acontius.' Cydippe, having read the words aloud, was
obliged to keep her pledge by Diana. (For *Tarquinius* in the next clause see p. 57n.)
3 *undone / undone*] unperformed / brought to ruin
4 *yielded . . . love*] Caesar fell in love with Cleopatra after his defeat of Pompey.
5 *Hannibal*] Carthaginian general (b. 247 BC). Croll and Clemons (p. 327n.) suggest
that Lyly may be indebted for this story to North's *Diall of Princes* (1557).
6 *Hercules / Leander / Iphis / Pyramus*] all lovers driven to extremes. Hercules, sold
as a slave to Omphale, consented to dress as a woman and spin wool to please
her. Leander, a youth living in Abydos, swam nightly across the Hellespont to visit
Hero and was drowned one night in a storm. Iphis hanged himself at the door of
Anaxarete who did not reciprocate his love. Pyramus killed himself in the belief
that Thisbe, a Babylonian maiden with whom he was in love, had been killed by a
lioness.

Canace[1] her nephew; insomuch as there is no reason to be given for so strange a grief, nor no remedy so unlawful but is to be sought for so monstrous a disease. My disease is strange, I myself a stranger; and my suit no less strange than my name. Yet lest I be tedious in a thing that requireth haste, give ear to my tale.

'I have heard oftentimes that in love there are three things for to be used: if time serve, violence; if wealth be great, gold; if necessity compel, sorcery. But of these three but one can stand me in stead, the last, but not the least; which is able to work the minds of all women like wax, when the other can scarce wind them like withy.[2] Medicines there are that can bring it to pass, and men there are that have—some by potions, some by verses, some by dreams, all by deceit. The examples were tedious to recite, and you know them; the means I come to learn, and you can give them; which is the only cause of my coming, and may be the occasion of my pleasure, and certainly the way both for your praise and profit.

'Whether it be an enchanted leaf,[3] a verse of Pythia,[4] a figure of Amphion,[5] a character of Osthanes,[6] an image of Venus, or a branch of Sibylla,[7] it skilleth not. Let it be either the seeds of Medea, or the blood of Phyllis;[8] let it come by oracle of Apollo, or by prophecy of Tiresias;[9] either by the entrails of a goat,[10] or what else soever, I care not; or by all these in one, to make sure incantation and spare not.[11]

'If I win my love, you shall not lose your labour; and whether it redound or no to my greater peril, I will not yet forget your pains. Let this potion be of such force that she may dote in her desire and I delight in her distress. And if in this case you either reveal my suit or deny it, you shall soon perceive that Philautus will die as desperately in one minute as he hath lived this three months carefully,[12] and this your study shall be my grave, if by your study you ease not my grief.'

---

1 *Byblis / Myrrha / Canace*] all instances of perverse love. For Byblis and Myrrha see p. 75n. Canace, daughter of Aeolus, had an unnatural love for her brother (rather than her nephew as Lyly states) and was killed by her father.

2 *withy*] flexible willow stems

3 *enchanted leaf*] possibly a page from the prophetic book of the Sibyl of Cumae, endued with magical powers

4 *verse of Pythia*] pronouncement of the priestess (Pythia) of Apollo at Delphi

5 *Amphion*] son of Zeus and Antiope who built the walls of Thebes by raising the stones by playing on his harp (*figure* = cabalistic symbol)

6 *Osthanes*] early writer in magic, contemporary with Xerxes (*character* = cabalistic symbol)

7 *branch of Sibylla*] see p. 230n.

8 *seeds of Medea / blood of Phyllis*] see p. 230n. / see p. 67

9 *oracle of Apollo / Tiresias*] pronouncement of the god of prophecy / blind seer, one of the most renowned soothsayers of antiquity

10 *entrails of a goat*] examining the entrails (for divination purposes) of a slaughtered sacrificial animal

11 *Whether it be . . . spare not*] The rhymes, numerous proper names, and rhythmic structure of this paragraph mimic the casting of a spell, enacting Philautus' request.

12 *carefully*] full of care

When he had thus ended, he looked so sternly upon Psellus that he wished him further off; yet taking him by the hand, and walking into his chamber, this good man began thus to answer him:

'Gentleman, if the inward spirit be answerable to the outward speech, or the thoughts of your heart agreeable to the words of your mouth, you shall breed to yourself great discredit, and to me no small disquiet. Do you think, gentleman, that the mind, being created of God, can be ruled by man, or that anyone can move the heart but He that made the heart? But such hath been the superstition of old women, and such the folly of young men, that there could be nothing so vain but the one would invent, nor anything so senseless but the other would believe; which then brought youth into a fool's paradise, and hath now cast age into an open mockage.

'What the force of love is, I have known; what the effects have been, I have heard; yet could I never learn that ever love could be won by the virtues of herbs, stones, or words. And though many there have been so wicked to seek such means, yet was there never any so unhappy to find them.

'Parrhasius painting Hopplitides[1] could neither make him that ran to sweat nor the other that put off his armour to breathe; adding this, as it were for a note, "No further than colours," meaning that to give life was not in his pencil but in the gods. And the like may be said of us that give our minds to know the course of the stars, the planets, the whole globe of heaven, the simples,[2] the compounds, the bowels of the earth, that something we may guess by the outward shape, something by the nativity;[3] but to wrest the will of man, or to wreath his heart to our humours, it is not in the compass of art but in the power of the Most Highest.

'But for because there have been many, without doubt, that have given credit to the vain illusions of witches, or the fond inventions of idle persons, I will set down such reasons as I have heard and you will laugh at; so, I hope, I shall both satisfy your mind and make you a little merry, for methinketh there is nothing that can more delight than to hear the things which have no weight to be thought to have wrought wonders.

'If you take pepper, the seed of a nettle, and a pretty quantity of pyretum,[4] beaten or pounded all together and put into wine of two years old, whensoever you drink to Camilla, if she love you not you lose your labour.[5] The cost is small, but if your belief be constant, you win the goal; for this receipt standeth in a strong conceit.[6] Eggs and honey blended with

---

1 *Parrhasius painting Hopplitides*] see p. 156n.
2 *simples*] plants with medicinal properties
3 *nativity*] place and time of birth together with the disposition of the planets
4 *pyretum*] possibly feverfew, a plant widely used for medical purposes in the sixteenth century
5 *you . . . labour*] your efforts are wasted
6 *standeth in a strong conceit*] depends on a powerful imagination

the nuts of a pine-tree, and laid to your left side, is of as great force when you look upon Camilla to bewitch the mind as the quintessence of stock-fish is to nourish the body.[1] An herb there is called anacamsoritis,[2] a strange name and doubtless of a strange nature, for whosoever toucheth it falleth in love with the person she next seeth. It groweth not in England, but here you shall have that which is not half so good that will do as much good and yet truly no more. The herb carisium,[3] moistened with the blood of a lizard and hanged about your neck, will cause Camilla (for her you love best) to dream of your services, suits, desires, deserts, and whatsoever you would wish her to think of you, but being wakened she shall not remember what she dreamed of. And this herb is to be found in a lake near Boeotia, of which water whoso drinketh shall be caught in love, but never find the herb; and if he drink not, the herb is of no force.

'There is in the frog's side a bone called apocynon,[4] and in the head of a young colt a bunch named hippomanes;[5] both so effectual for the obtaining of love that whoso getteth either of them shall win any that are willing. But so injuriously both craft and nature dealt with young gentlemen that seek to gain good will by these means, that the one is licked off before it can be gotten, the other breaketh as soon as it is touched. And yet unless hippomanes be licked it cannot work, and except apocynon be sound it is nothing worth.

'I omit the thistle eryngium, the herbs catanance and piteuma,[6] Juba his charitoblepharon, and Orpheus' staphylinus,[7] all of such virtue in cases of love that if Camilla should but taste any one of them in her mouth she would never let it go down her throat, lest she should be poisoned; for well you know, gentleman, that love is a poison, and therefore by poison it must be maintained. But I will not forget, as it were the mithridate[8] of the magicians, the beast hyena; of whom there is no part so small or so vile but it serveth for their purpose. Insomuch that they account hyena their god that can do all, and their devil that will do all. If you take seven hairs of hyena's lips and carry them six days in your teeth, or a piece of her skin next your bare heart, or her belly girded to [your]

---

1 *of as great force . . . body*] i.e. of no potency whatsoever
2 *anacamsoritis*] anacampseros, credited by Pliny with being efficacious in amatory affairs (see Croll and Clemons, p. 330n.)
3 *carisium*] a love philtre mentioned by Aristotle (see Croll and Clemons, p. 331n.)
4 *apocynon*] small bone on the left side of a venomous frog, noted by Pliny
5 *bunch named hippomanes*] small black membrane on the forehead of a foal, used in making love potions
6 *eryngium / catanance / piteuma*] spotted yellow thistle / plant used in love potions mentioned by Pliny / No such plant as piteuma has been traced.
7 *Juba his charitoblepharon / Orpheus' staphylinus*] marine plant used in love potions, described by Juba (King of Mauretania and author of a biological treatise) / species of parsnip to which Orpheus (legendary father of the study of plants and stones) was said to have ascribed the power to excite the passions
8 *mithridate*] sovereign resource

left side, if Camilla suffer you not to obtain your purpose, certainly she cannot choose but thank you for your pains.

'And if you want medicines to win women, I have yet more: the lungs of a vulture, the ashes of stellio,[1] the left stone[2] of a cock, the tongue of a goose, the brain of a cat, the last hair of a wolf's tail—things easy to be had and commonly practised, so that I would not have thee stand in doubt of[3] thy love, when either a young swallow famished, or the shrouding sheet of a dear friend, or a waxen taper that burned at his feet, or the enchanted needle that Medea hid in Jason's sleeve[4] are able not only to make them desire love but also die for love.

'How do you now feel yourself, Philautus? If the least of these charms be not sufficient for thee, all exorcisms and conjurations in the world will not serve thee.

'You see, gentleman, into what blind and gross errors in old time we were led, thinking every old wives' tale to be a truth, and every merry word a very witchcraft. When the Egyptians fell from their god to their priests of Memphis, and the Grecians from their moral questions to their disputations of Pyrrho, and the Romans from religion to policy,[5] then began all superstition to breed and all impiety to bloom; and to be so great they have both grown that the one being then an infant is now an elephant, and the other being then a twig is now a tree. They invented as many enchantments for love as they did for the toothache; but he that hath tried both will say that the best charm for a tooth is to pull it out, and the best remedy for love to wear it out.

'If incantations, or potions, or amorous sayings could have prevailed, Circe[6] would never have lost Ulysses, nor Phaedra Hippolytus, nor Phyllis Demophon. If conjurations, characters, circles, figures, fiends, or furies might have wrought anything in love, Medea would not have suffered Jason to alter his mind.[7] If the syrups of Macaonias, or the verses of Aeus, or the Satyren of Dipsas[8] were of force to move the mind, they all three

---

1 *stellio*] species of lizard found (among other places) in Greece
2 *stone*] testicle
3 *stand in doubt of*] be uncertain of achieving
4 *the enchanted ... sleeve*] see p. 230n.
5 *When the Egyptians ... policy*] all examples of a decline from an adherence to absolutes to an engagement with intellectual subleties (*Pyrrho* = founder of the Sceptical school of philosophy and a contemporary of Alexander the Great)
6 *Circe*] mythical sorceress with whom Ulysses lingered for a year in the course of his travels (for *Phaedra* and *Hippolytus* see p. 75n. and for *Phyllis* and *Demophon* p. 67n.)
7 *Medea ... mind*] Jason deserted Medea after she had helped him to obtain the golden fleece (see p. 67n).
8 *If the syrups ... Dipsas*] obscure. Macaonias may be derived from Machaon, son of Aesculapius, to whom 'syrups' would clearly have been available. Aeus is another name for Circe (see note 6 above) derived from her island, Aeaea. Dipsas reappears as a sorceress in Lyly's *Endymion*. Bond (II, pp. 515–16) traces the conjunction of the names in an amatory context to Ovid's *Ars amatoria*.

would not have been martyred with the torments of love. No, no, Philautus, thou mayst well poison Camilla with such drugs, but never persuade her. For I confess that such herbs may alter the body from strength to weakness, but to think that they can move the mind from virtue to vice, from chastity to lust, I am not so simple to believe, neither would I have thee so sinful as to doubt it.

'Lucilla, ministering an amorous potion unto her husband Lucretius,[1] procured his death, whose life she only desired. Aristotle noteth one that being inflamed with the beauty of a fair lady thought by medicine to procure his bliss, and wrought in the end her bane. So was Caligula slain of Caesonia, and Lucius Lucullus of Calistine.[2]

'Persuade thyself, Philautus, that to use herbs to win love will weaken the body, and to think that herbs can further[3] doth hurt the soul; for as great force have they in such cases as noble men thought them to have in the old time. Achaemenis the herb was of such force that it was thought if it were thrown into the battle it would make all the soldiers tremble. But where was it when the Humbri and Teutoni[4] were exiled by war? Where grew achaemenis, one of whose leaves would have saved a thousand lives? The kings of Persia gave their soldiers the plant latace, which whoso had should have plenty of meat, and money, and men, and all things. But why did the soldiers of Caesar endure such famine in Pharsalia,[5] if one herb might have eased so many hearts? Where is balis that Juba[6] so commendeth, the which could call the dead to life, and yet he himself died? Democritus made a confection that whosoever drank it should have a fair, a fortunate, and a good child. Why did not the Persian kings swill this nectar, having such deformed and unhappy issue?[7] Cato

---

1 *Lucretius*] Roman poet (d. AD 51 or 52) who was driven mad by a love potion but actually died by his own hand. No source has been found for a Lucilla.

2 *Aristotle noteth . . . Calistine*] all three examples differ in some respect from Lyly's sources. Croll and Clemons note that in the instance cited by Aristotle the woman is the giver rather than the recipient of the potion (p. 334n.). Caligula (d. AD 41) was killed by a tribune rather than by the love philtre given to him by Caesonia (his last wife). Lucius Lucullus (b. 110 BC) fell into dotage before his death and was attended by a freedman, Callisthenes, who was suspected of occasioning his death (see Bond, II, p. 516).

3 *further*] do more

4 *Achaemenis / Humbri and Teutoni*] amber-coloured plant from India / barbarian peoples defeated by the Roman consul Marius (b. 157 BC). *Humbri* = Cimbri

5 *latace / Pharsalia*] plant with magical properties about which very little is known / district of Thessaly, site of the decisive battle between Caesar and Pompey (48 BC)

6 *balis / Juba*] possibly belion, a strong-smelling plant also known as polion / see p. 258n.

7 *Democritus / deformed and unhappy issue*] celebrated Greek philosopher (see p. 114n.) with an extensive knowledge of the natural sciences / Xerxes II, for example, having reigned for only two months, was murdered by his half-brother, who was killed by his brother seven months later.

was of that mind that three enchanted words could heal the eyesight,[1] and Varro[2] that a verse of Sibylla could ease the gout; yet the one was fain to use running water, which was but a cold medicine, the other patience, which was but a dry plaster.

'I would not have thee think, Philautus, that love is to be obtained by such means; but only by faith, virtue, and constancy. Philip, King of Macedon,[3] casting his eye upon a fair virgin, became enamoured; which Olympias, his wife, perceiving thought him to be enchanted, and caused one of her servants to bring the maiden unto her, whom she thought to thrust both to exile and shame. But viewing her fair face without blemish, her chaste eyes without glancing, her modest countenance, her sober and womanly behaviour, finding also her virtues to be no less than her beauty, she said, "In [th]yself there are charms"—meaning that there was no greater enchantment in love than temperance, wisdom, beauty and chastity. Fond,[4] therefore, is the opinion of those that think the mind to be tied to magic, and the practice of those filthy that seek those means.

'Love dwelleth in the mind, in the will, and in the hearts, which neither conjurer can alter nor physic. For as credible it is that Cupid shooteth his arrow and hitteth the heart, as that herbs have the force to bewitch the heart; only this difference there is, that the one was a fiction of poetry, the other of susperstition. The will is placed in the soul, and who can enter there but He that created the soul?

'No, no, gentleman, whatsoever you have heard touching this, believe nothing; for they (in mine opinion) which imagine that the mind is either by incantation or excantation[5] to be ruled are as far from truth as the east from the west, and as near impiety against God as they are to shame among men, and so contrary is it to the profession of a Christian as paganism. Suffer not yourself to be led with that vile conceit. Practise in your love all kind of loyalty. Be not mute, nor full of babble; be sober, but avoid sullenness; use no kind of riot, either in banqueting, which procureth surfeits, nor in attire, which hasteth beggary. If you think well of your wit, be always pleasant; if ill, be often silent. In the one, thy talk shall prove thee sharp; in the other, thy modesty wise.

'All fish are not caught with flies, all women are not allured with personage.[6] Frame letters, ditties, music, and all means that honesty may allow; for he wooeth well that meaneth no ill, and he speedeth sooner[7] that

---

1 *Cato ... eyesight*] Bond notes (II, p. 516) that Cato names in his *De re rustica* three varieties of cabbage that are good for the eyes.
2 *Varro*] known as the most learned of the Romans (d. 28 BC). No source has been found for his charm to cure gout.
3 *Philip King of Macedon*] see p. 143n.
4 *Fond*] foolish
5 *excantation*] charm with power to undo or reverse a condition or spell
6 *personage*] physical appearance
7 *speedeth sooner*] is more likely to be successful

speaketh what he should than he that uttereth what he will. Believe me, Philautus, I am now old yet have I in my head a love-tooth,[1] and in my mind there is nothing that more pierceth the heart of a beautiful lady than writing; where thou mayst so set down thy passions and her perfection as she shall have cause to think well of thee and better of herself, but yet so warily as neither thou seem to praise her too much or debase thyself too lowly. For if thou flatter them without mean,[2] they loathe it; and if thou make of thyself above reason, they laugh at it. Temper thy words so well, and place every sentence so wisely, as it may be hard for her to judge whether thy love be more faithful or her beauty amiable. Lions fawn when they are clawed, tigers stoop when they are tickled, Bucephalus lieth down when he is curried,[3] women yield when they are courted. This is the poison, Philautus, the enchantment, the potions that creepeth by sleight into the mind of a woman and catcheth her by assurance; better than the fond devices of old dreams, as an apple with an Ave Mary,[4] or a hazel wand of a year old crossed with six characters,[5] or the picture of Venus in virgin wax, or the image of Camilla upon a mouldwarp's[6] skin.

'It is not once mentioned in the English court, nor so much as thought of in anyone's conscience, that love can be procured by such means or that any can imagine such mischief; and yet I fear me it is too common in our country, whereby they incur hate of everyone and love of none. Touching my cunning in any vile devices of magic, it was never my study; only some delight I took in the mathematics, which made me known of more than I would, and of more than think well of me, although I never did hurt any nor hindered.

'But be thou quiet, Philautus, and use those means that may win thy love, not those that may shorten her life. And if I can in any ways stand thee in stead, use me as thy poor friend and countryman; harm I will do thee none, good I cannot. My acquaintance in court is small, and therefore my dealings about the court shall be few, for I love to stand aloof from Jove and lightning.[7] Fire giveth light to things far off and burneth that which is next to it; the court shineth to me that come not there, but singeth those that dwell there. Only my counsel use, that is in writing, and me thou shalt find secret, wishing thee always fortunate; and if thou make me partaker of thy success it shall not turn to thy grief, but as much as in me lieth I will further thee.'

When he had finished his discourse, Philautus liked very well of it; and thus replied:

---

1 *love-tooth*] an inclination to love
2 *without mean*] immoderately
3 *clawed / curried*] scratched / groomed (for *Bucephalus* see p. 250n.)
4 *Ave Mary*] prayer to the Virgin Mary
5 *characters*] magic symbols
6 *mouldwarp's*] mole's
7 *Jove and lightning*] irresistible and unaccountable powers. Lyly uses the same analogy in *Campaspe* (IV.iv.36–7).

'Well, Psellus, thou hast wrought that in me which thou wishest; for if the baits that are laid for beauty be so ridiculous, I think it of as great effect in love to use a plaster as a potion. I now utterly dissent from those that imagine magic to be the means, and consent with thee that thinkest letters to be, which I will use; and how I speed I will tell thee. In the mean season, pardon me if I use no longer answer; for well you know that he that hath the fit of an ague upon him hath no lust to talk but to tumble,[1] and love pinching me I have more desire to chew upon melancholy than to dispute upon magic. But hereafter I will make repair unto you, and what I now give you in thanks I will then requite with amends.'[2]

Thus these two countrymen parted with certain Italian embracings, and terms of courtesy more than common. Philautus we shall find in his lodging, Psellus we will leave in his study, the one musing of his love, the other of his learning.

Here, gentlewomen, you may see how justly men seek to entrap you when scornfully you go about to reject them, thinking it not unlawful to use art when they perceive you obstinate. Their dealings I will not allow,[3] neither can I excuse yours; and yet what should be the cause of both I can guess.

When Phidias first painted, they used no colours but black, white, red and yellow. Zeuxis[4] added green, and everyone invented a new shadowing. At the last it came to this pass, that he in painting deserved most praise that could set down most colours; whereby there was more contention kindled about the colour than the counterfeit,[5] and greater emulation for variety in show than workmanship in substance.

In the like manner hath it fallen out in love. When Adam wooed, there was no policy[6] but plain dealing, no colours but black and white. Affection was measured by faith, not by fancy; he was not curious, nor Eve cruel;[7] he was not enamoured of her beauty, nor she allured with his personage—and yet then was she the fairest woman in the world and he the properest[8] man. Since that time every lover hath put to a link, and made of a ring a chain and an odd corner,[9] and framed of a plain alley a crooked knot,[10] and of Venus' temple Daedalus' labyrinth.[11] One curleth his hair, thinking love to be moved with fair locks, another layeth all his

---

1 *tumble*] toss and turn
2 *make repair unto you / requite with amends*] visit you / recompense
3 *allow*] sanction
4 *Phidias / Zeuxis*] see p. 155n. / see p. 158n. (*shadowing* = style of representation)
5 *counterfeit*] drawing, picture
6 *policy*] craft
7 *curious / cruel*] affected / disdainful
8 *properest*] most handsome
9 *put to / odd corner*] added / pun (idiosyncratic turn or angle / private, out-of-the-way place)
10 *plain alley / crooked knot*] straight walk / intricate formal garden
11 *Daedalus' labyrinth*] see p. 173n.

living upon his back, judging that women are wedded to bravery,[1] some use discourses of love to kindle affection, some ditties to allure the mind, some letters to stir the appetite, divers fighting to prove their manhood, sundry sighing to show their maladies,[2] many attempt with shows to please their lady's eyes, not few with music to entice the ear; insomuch that there is more strife now who shall be the finest lover than who is the faithfullest.

This causeth you, gentlewomen, to pick out those that can court you, not those that love you; and he is accounted the best in your conceits that useth most colours,[3] not that showeth greatest courtesy. A plain tale of faith you laugh at, a picked[4] discourse of fancy you marvel at, condemning the simplicity of truth and preferring the singularity of deceit; wherein you resemble those fishes that rather swallow a fair bait with a sharp hook than a foul worm breeding in the mud.

Hereof it cometh that true lovers, receiving a flout for their faith and a mock for their good meaning, are enforced to seek such means as might compel you; which you knowing impossible maketh you the more disdainful, and them the more desperate. This, then, is my counsel: that you use your lovers like friends and choose them by their faith; not by the show, but by the sound; neither by the weight, but by the touch, as you do gold—so shall you be praised as much for virtue as beauty.

But return we again to Philautus, who thus began to debate with himself:

'What hast thou done, Philautus, in seeking to wound her that thou desirest to win? With what face canst thou look on her whom thou soughtest to lose?[5] Fie, fie, Philautus, thou bringest thy good name into question and her life into hazard, having neither care of thine own credit nor her honour. Is this the love thou pretendest, which is worse than hate? Didst not thou seek to poison her that never pinched thee?

'But why do I recount those things which are past and I repent? I am now to consider what I must do, not what I would have done. Follies past shall be worn out with faith to come, and my death shall show my desire. Write, Philautus! What sayest thou, write? No, no, thy rude style will bewray thy mean estate,[6] and thy rash attempt will purchase thine overthrow. Venus delighteth to hear none but Mercury, Pallas will be stolen

---

1 *layeth . . . back / wedded to bravery*] spends his entire substance on clothes / enamoured of finery
2 *maladies*] love sickness
3 *accounted the best . . . colours*] is held the most worthy in your estimation who uses most art
4 *picked*] refined
5 *lose*] destroy
6 *rude style . . . estate*] unrefined style will betray your low condition

of none but Ulysses, it must be a smooth tongue and a sweet tale that can enchant Vesta.[1]

'Besides that, I dare not trust a messenger to carry it, nor her to read it, lest in showing my letter she disclose my love; and then shall I be pointed at of those that hate me, and pitied of those that like me, of her scorned, of all talked of. No, Philautus, be not thou the byword of the common people, rather suffer death by silence than derision by writing. Aye, but it is better to reveal thy love than conceal it; thou knowest not what bitter poison lieth in sweet words. Remember Psellus, who by experience hath tried that in love one letter is of more force than a thousand looks. If they like writings they read them often, if dislike them run them over once; and this is certain, that she that readeth such toys will also answer them. Only this, be secret in conveyance, which is the thing they chiefliest desire. Then write, Philautus! Write! He that feareth every bush must never go a-birding, he that casteth all doubts[2] shall never be resolved in anything. And this assure thyself, that be thy letter never so rude and barbarous she will read it, and be it never so loving she will not show it; which were a thing contrary to her honour, and the next way to call her honesty[3] into question. For thou hast heard, yea and thyself knowest, that ladies that vaunt of their lovers or show their letters are accounted in Italy counterfeit, and in England they are not thought current.'[4]

Thus Philautus determined, hab nab,[5] to send his letters, flattering himself with the success which he to himself feigned; and after long musing, he thus began to frame the minister[6] of his love:

To the fairest Camilla,

Hard is the choice, fair lady, when one is compelled either by silence to die with grief or by writing to live with shame. But so sweet is the desire of life, and so sharp are the passions of love, that I am enforced to prefer an unseemly suit before an untimely death. Loath I have been to speak, and in despair to speed; the one proceeding of mine own cowardice, the other of thy cruelty. If thou enquire my name, I am the same Philautus which for thy sake of late came disguised in a masque, pleading custom for a privilege and courtesy for a pardon; the same Philautus which then in secret terms coloured his love, and now with bitter tears bewrays it. If thou nothing esteem the brinish water that falleth from mine eyes, I would thou couldst see the warm blood that

---

1 *Venus delighteth . . . Vesta*] only the most nimble-tongued of the gods will gain the attention of the goddess of love, only the wisest of mortals be loved by the goddess of wisdom, and extreme eloquence is required to enrapture a goddess associated with chastity
2 *a-birding / casteth all doubts*] hunting for birds / raises every objection
3 *next / honesty*] readiest / chastity
4 *counterfeit / current*] of doubtful virtue / creditable
5 *hab nab*] win or lose
6 *minister*] envoy

droppeth from my heart. Oftentimes I have been in thy company, where easily thou mightst have perceived my wan cheeks, my hollow eyes, my scalding sighs, my trembling tongue to foreshow that then which I confess now. Then consider with thyself, Camilla, the plight I am in by desire, and the peril I am like to fall into by denial.

To recount the sorrows I sustain or the service I have vowed would rather breed in thee an admiration[1] than a belief; only this I add for the time, which the end shall try for a truth, that if thy answer be sharp my life will be short. So far love hath wrought in my pining and almost consumed body that thou only mayst breathe into me a new life, or bereave me of the old.

Thou art to weigh[2] not how long I have loved thee but how faithfully, neither to examine the worthiness of my person but the extremity of my passions; so preferring my deserts before the length of time, and my disease before the greatness of my birth, thou wilt either yield with equity or deny with reason. Of both the which, although the greatest be on my side, yet the least shall not dislike me; for that I have always found in thee a mind neither repugnant to right nor void of reason. If thou wouldst but permit me to talk with thee, or by writing suffer me at large to discourse with thee, I doubt not but that both the cause of my love would be believed and the extremity rewarded, both proceeding of thy beauty and virtue, the one able to allure, the other ready to pity. Thou must think that God hath not bestowed those rare gifts upon thee to kill those that are caught, but to cure them. Those that are stung with the scorpion are healed with the scorpion,[3] the fire that burneth taketh away the heat of the burn, the spider phalangium[4] that poisoneth doth with her skin make a plaster for poison; and shall thy beauty which is of force to win all with love be of the cruelty to wound any with death? No, Camilla, I take no less delight in thy fair face than pleasure in thy good conditions assuring myself that for affection without lust thou wilt not render[5] malice without cause.

I commit my care to thy consideration, expecting thy letter either as a cullis[6] to preserve or as a sword to destroy, either as antidotum or as aconitum.[7] If thou delude me, thou shalt not long triumph over me living, and small will thy glory be when I am dead. And I end.

Thine ever, though he be never thine,
Philautus.

This letter being coined, he studied how he might convey it, knowing it to be no less perilous to trust those he knew not in so weighty a case, than difficult for himself to have opportunity to deliver it in so suspicious a company. At the last, taking out of his closet a fair

---

1 *admiration*] wonder
2 *Thou art to weigh*] you must consider
3 *Those that are stung ... scorpion*] see p. 89n.
4 *phalangium*] species of venomous spider. Pliny notes (see Bond, II, p. 517) that an antidote for its sting can be made from its own body (*plaster* = remedy, literally one externally applied)
5 *conditions / render*] qualities / return
6 *care / cullis*] suffering / rich broth
7 *aconitum*] aconite. The dried root was used as a poison.

pomegranate[1] and pulling all the kernels out of it, he wrapped his letter in it, closing the top of it finely, that it could not be perceived whether nature again had knit it of purpose to further him, or his art had overcome nature's cunning. This pomegranate he took, being himself both messenger of his letter and the master, and insinuating himself into the company of the gentlewomen, among whom was also Camilla, he was welcomed as well for that he had been long time absent as for that he was at all times pleasant. Much good communication there was touching many matters, which here to insert were neither convenient, seeing it doth not concern the history, nor expedient, seeing it is nothing to the delivery of Philautus' letter. But this it fell out in the end: Camilla, whether longing for so fair a pomegranate, or willed to ask it yet loath to require it,[2] she suddenly complained of an old disease wherewith she many times felt herself grieved, which was an extreme heat in the stomach; which advantage Philautus marking, would not let slip, when it was purposely spoken that he should not give them the slip. And therefore as one glad to have so convenient a time to offer both his duty and his devotion, he began thus:

'I have heard, Camilla, of physicians, that there is nothing either more comfortable or more profitable for the stomach or inflamed liver than a pomegranate. Which if it be true, I am glad that I came in so good time with a medicine, seeing you were in so ill a time surprised with your malady; and verily this will I say, that there is not one kernel but is able both to ease your pain and to double your pleasure.'

And with that he gave it her, desiring that as she felt the working of the potion so she would consider of the physician.

Camilla, with a smiling countenance, neither suspecting the craft nor the conveyer, answered him with these thanks:

'I thank you, gentleman, as much for your counsel as your courtesy, and if your cunning be answerable[3] to either of them, I will make you amends for all of them. Yet I will not open so fair a fruit as this is until I feel the pain that I so much fear.'

'As you please,' quoth Philautus, 'yet if every morning you take one kernel, it is the way to prevent your disease; and methinketh that you should be as careful to work means before it come that you have it not, as to use means to expel it when you have it.'

'I am content,' answered Camilla, 'to try your physic; which as I know it can do me no great harm, so it may do me much good.'

---

1 *pomegranate*] fruit with positive and negative connotations, both of which Lyly exploits. Pluto, having abducted Proserpine, gave her part of a pomegranate to eat before allowing her to visit her mother on earth, obliging her to return, having eaten there, to Hades. The fruit is thus associated with duplicitous and destructive love. It is also noted for its medicinal properties, particularly in relation to gastric conditions.

2 *willed to ... require it*] wanting to ask for it but reluctant to demand it

3 *answerable*] equal

'In truth,' said one of the gentlewomen then present, 'I perceive this gentleman is not only cunning in physic, but also very careful for his patient.'

'It behoveth,' quoth Philautus, 'that he that ministereth to a lady be as desireth of her health as his own credit; for that there redoundeth more praise to the physician that hath a care to his charge, than to him that hath only a show of his art. And I trust Camilla will better accept of the good will I have to rid her of her disease, than the gift which must work the effect.'

'Otherwise,' quoth Camilla, 'I were very much to blame, knowing that in many the behaviour of the man hath wrought more than the force of the medicine. For I would always have my physician of a cheerful countenance, pleasantly conceited,[1] and well proportioned, that he might have his sharp potions mixed with sweet counsel, and his sour drugs mitigated with merry discourses. And this is the cause that in old time they painted the god of physic not like Saturn[2] but Aesculapius, of a good complexion, fine wit, and excellent constitution. For this I know by experience, though I be but young to learn and have not often been sick, that the sight of a pleasant and quick-witted physician hath removed that from my heart with talk that he could not with all his treacle.'[3]

'That might well be,' answered Philautus, 'for the man that wrought the cure did perchance cause the disease, and so secret might the grief be that none could heal you but he that hurt you; neither was your heart to be eased by any inward potion, but by some outward persuasion. And then it is no marvel if the ministering of a few words were more available than mithridate.'[4]

'Well, gentleman,' said Camilla, 'I will neither dispute in physic wherein I have no skill, neither answer you to your last surmise which you seem to level at; but thanking you once again both for your gift and good will, we will use other communication,[5] not forgetting to ask for your friend Euphues, who hath not long time been where he might have been welcomed at all times; and that he came not with you at this time we both marvel and would fain know.'

This question, so earnestly asked of Camilla and so hardly to be answered of Philautus, nipped him in the head.[6] Notwithstanding, lest he should seem by long silence to incur some suspicion, he thought a bad excuse better than none at all, saying that Euphues nowadays became so studious (or, as he termed it, susperstitious) that he could not himself so much as have his company.

---

1 *pleasantly conceited*] full of agreeable ideas
2 *Saturn*] associated with leaden spirits and therefore dour
3 *treacle*] see p. 243n.
4 *more available than mithridate*] more efficacious than the most sovereign remedy
5 *use other communication*] talk of something else
6 *so hardly / nipped him . . . head*] with such difficulty / brought him to a stand (cf. p. 80 for another example of the phrase)

'Belike,' quoth Camilla, 'he hath either espied some new faults in the women of England, whereby he seeketh to absent himself, or some old haunt, that will cause him to spoil[1] himself.'

'Not so,' said Philautus, 'and yet that it was said so I will tell him.'

Thus after much conference, many questions, and long time spent, Philautus took his leave. And being in his chamber, we will there leave him with such cogitations as they commonly have that either attend the sentence of life or death at the bar, or the answer of hope or despair of their loves; which none can set down but he that hath them, for that they are not to be uttered by the conjecture of one that would imagine what they should be, but by him that knoweth what they are.

Camilla the next morning opened the pomegranate and saw the letter; which reading, pondering and perusing, she fell into a thousand contrarities[2] whether it were best to answer it or not. At the last, inflamed with a kind of choler, for that she knew not what belonged to the perplexities of a lover, she requited his fraud and love with anger and hate, in these terms or the like:

To Philautus,

I did long time debate with myself, Philautus, whether it might stand[3] with mine honour to send thee an answer. For comparing my place with thy person,[4] methought thy boldness more than either good manners in thee would permit, or I with modesty could suffer. Yet at the last, casting with myself[5] that the heat of thy love might clean be razed with the coldness of my letter, I thought it good to commit an inconvenience that I might prevent a mischief, choosing rather to cut thee off short by rigour than to give thee any jot of hope by silence. Green sores are to be dressed roughly lest they fester, tetters[6] to be drawn in the beginning lest they spread, ring worms to be anointed when they first appear lest they compass the whole body, and the assaults of love to be beaten back at the first siege lest they undermine at the second. Fire is to be quenched in the spark, weeds are to be rooted in the bud, follies in the blossom.

Thinking this morning to try thy physic, I perceived thy fraud; insomuch as the kernel that should have cooled my stomach with moistness hath kindled it with choler, making a flaming fire where it found but hot embers, converting like the spider a sweet flower into bitter poison.[7] I am, Philautus, no Italian lady, who commonly are wooed with leasings[8] and won with lust, entangled with deceit and enjoyed with delight, caught with sin and cast off with shame.

---

1 *spoil*] ruin (editions after 1595 have 'soil', used of a hunted animal which takes refuge)
2 *contrarities*] opposing arguments
3 *stand*] be consonant
4 *person*] social standing
5 *casting with myself*] reckoning
6 *tetters*] eruptions of the skin, boils
7 *converting . . . poison*] Spiders were believed to make poison from honey.
8 *leasings*] lies

For mine own part, I am too young to know the passions of a lover and too wise to believe them, and so far from trusting any that I suspect all; not that there is in everyone a practice to deceive, but that there wanteth in me a capacity to conceive.[1] Seek not then, Philautus, to make the tender twig crooked by art which might have grown straight by nature. Corn is not to be gathered in the bud but in the ear, nor fruit to be pulled from the tree when it is green but when it is mellow, nor grapes to be cut for the press when they first rise but when they are full ripe; nor young ladies to be sued unto that are fitter for a rod[2] than a husband, and meeter to bear blows than children.

You must not think of us as of those in your own country, that are no sooner out of the cradle but they are sent to the court, and wooed sometimes before they are weaned; which bringeth both the nation and their names not in question only of dishonesty[3] but into obloquy. This I would have thee to take for a flat answer: that I neither mean to love thee, nor hereafter, if thou follow thy suit, to hear thee. Thy first practice in the masque I did not allow,[4] the second by thy writing I mislike; if thou attempt the third means, thou wilt enforce me to utter that which modesty now maketh me to conceal.

If thy good will be so great as thou tellest, seek to mitigate it by reason or time. I thank thee for it, but I cannot requite it, unless either thou wert not Philautus or I not Camilla. Thus pardoning thy boldness upon condition, and resting thy friend if thou rest thy suit, I end.

Neither thine, nor her own,
Camilla.

This letter Camilla stitched into an Italian *Petrarch* which she had, determining at the next coming of Philautus to deliver it under the pretence of asking some question, or the understanding of some word. Philautus, attending hourly the success of his love, made his repair according to his accustomable use;[5] and finding the gentlewomen sitting in an arbour saluted them courteously, not forgetting to be inquisitive[6] how Camilla was eased by his pomegranate. Which oftentimes asking of her, she answered him thus:

'In faith, Philautus, it had a fair coat but a rotten kernel; which so much offended my weak stomach that the very sight caused me to loathe it, and the scent to throw it into the fire.'

'I am sorry,' quoth Philautus (who spake no less than truth), 'that the medicine could not work that which my mind wished.'

And with that stood as one in a trance; which Camilla perceiving, thought best to rub no more on that gall, lest the standers-by should espy where Philautus' shoe wrung[7] him.

---

1 *wanteth in me . . . conceive*] I lack the understanding to take their meaning
2 *a rod*] parental discipline
3 *dishonesty*] unchaste behaviour
4 *allow*] approve
5 *made his repair . . . use*] paid his visit according to his usual practice
6 *to be inquisitive*] to enquire
7 *gall / wrung*] sore / pinched

'Well,' said Camilla, 'let it go. I must impute it to my ill fortune, that where I looked for a restority[1] I found a consumption.'

And with that she drew out her *Petrarch*, requesting him to conster her a lesson,[2] hoping his learning would be better for a schoolmaster than his luck was for a physician.

Thus, walking in the alley, she listened to his construction; who, turning the book, found where the letter was enclosed. And dissembling that he suspected, he said he would keep her *Petrarch* until the morning.

'Do you,' quoth Camilla.

With that the gentlewomen clustered about them both, either to hear how cunningly Philautus could conster, or how readily Camilla could conceive.[3] It fell out that they turned to such a place as turned them all to a blank, where it was reasoned whether love came at the sudden view of beauty or by long experience of virtue. A long disputation was like to ensue had not Camilla cut it off before they could join issue, as one not willing in the company of Philautus either to talk of love or think of love, lest either he should suspect she had been wooed or might be won; which was not done so closely but it was perceived of Philautus, though dissembled. Thus after many words they went to their dinner, where I omit their table-talk, lest I lose mine.

After their repast, Surius came in with a great train,[4] which lightened Camilla's heart and was a dagger to Philautus' breast; who tarried no longer than he had leisure to take his leave, either desirous to read his lady's answer or not willing to enjoy Surius his company. Whom also I will now forsake and follow Philautus, to hear how his mind is quieted with Camilla's courtesy.

Philautus no sooner entered his chamber but he read her letter; which wrought such skirmishes in his mind that he had almost forgot reason, falling into the old vein of his rage in this manner:

'Ah cruel Camilla and accursed Philautus! I see now that it fareth with thee as it doth with the [harpy], which having made one astonied[5] with her fair sight, turneth him into a stone with her venomous savour; and with me as it doth with those that view the basilisk,[6] whose eyes procure delight to the looker at the first glimpse, and death at the second glance.

'Is this the courtesy of England towards strangers, to entreat them so despitefully? Is my good will not only rejected without cause, but also disdained without colour?[7] Aye, but Philautus, praise at the

---

1 *restority*] restorative
2 *conster her a lesson*] construe a passage for her
3 *conster / conceive*] explicate / understand
4 *great train*] large following
5 *harpy / astonied*] see p. 254n. / pun (astonished / turned to stone)
6 *basilisk*] fabulous reptile hatched from a cock's egg, capable of blasting the beholder with its gaze
7 *colour*] excuse. *entreat* in the previous sentence = treat.

parting;[1] if she had not liked thee, she would never have answered thee. Knowest thou not that where they love much, they dissemble most; that as fair weather cometh after a foul storm, so sweet terms succeed sour taunts? Assay once again, Philautus, by letters to win her love; and follow not the unkind hound who leaveth the scent because he is rated,[2] or the bastard spaniel which being once rebuked never retrieveth his game. Let Atalanta run never so swiftly, she will look back upon Hippomenes; let Medea be as cruel as a fiend to all gentlemen, she will at the last respect Jason.[3] A denial at the first is accounted a grant,[4] a gentle answer a mockery. Ladies use their lovers as the stork doth her young ones, who pecketh them till they bleed with her bill, and then healeth them with her tongue.[5] Cupid himself must spend one arrow, and thinkest thou to speed with one letter? No, no, Philautus, he that looketh to have clear water must dig deep, he that longeth for sweet music must set his strings at the highest, he that seeketh to win his love must stretch his labour and hazard his life. Venus blesseth lions in the fold and lambs in the chamber, eagles at the assault and foxes in counsel, so that thou must be hardy[6] in the pursuit and meek in victory, venturous in obtaining and wise in concealing, so that thou win that with praise which otherwise thou wilt lose with peevishness.[7] Faint heart, Philautus, neither winneth castle nor lady. Therefore endure all things that shall happen with patience, and pursue with diligence; thy fortune is to be tried not by the accidents but by the end.'[8]

Thus, gentlewomen, Philautus resembleth the viper, who being stricken with a reed lieth as he were dead, but stricken the second time recovereth his strength.[9] Having his answer at the first in the masque he was almost amazed, and now again denied he is animated; presuming thus much upon the good disposition and kindness of women, that the higher they sit the lower they look, and the more they seem at the first to loathe the more they love at the last. Whose judgement, as I am not altogether to allow,[10] so can I not in some respect mislike. For in this they resemble the crocodile, who when one approacheth near unto him gathereth up himself into the roundness of a ball, but running from him stretcheth himself into the

---

1 *praise at the parting*] don't judge your host until your visit is over, i.e. don't judge too rashly (proverbial)

2 *unkind / rated*] degenerate / reproved

3 *Let Atalanta . . . Jason*] see p. 122n. and p. 230n. Medea was noted for the ruthlessness with which she achieved her aims and treated her enemies.

4 *accounted a grant*] deemed to be an acceptance

5 *the stork . . . tongue*] No source has been found for this belief.

6 *hardy*] daring

7 *peevishness*] folly

8 *thy fortune . . . end*] your success is to be judged not by individual events but by the outcome

9 *the viper . . . recovereth his strength*] translated from Montuus, *De admirandis facultatibus*, 1556 (see Croll and Clemons, p. 349n.)

10 *I am not altogether to allow*] I cannot entirely agree with

length of a tree. The willing resistance of women was the cause that made Arellius (whose art was only to draw women) to paint Venus Cnidia[1] catching at the ball with her hand which she seemed to spurn at with her foot. And in this point they are not unlike unto the myrrh tree, which being hewed gathereth in his sap, but not moved poureth it out like syrup. Women are never more coy than when they are beloved, yet in their minds never less constant; seeming to tie themselves to the mast of the ship with Ulysses[2] when they are wooed, with a strong cable, which being well discerned is a twine thread; throwing a stone at the head of him unto whom they immediately cast out an apple. Of which their gentle nature Philautus being persuaded, followed his suit again in this manner:

Philautus to the fair Camilla,

I cannot tell, Camilla, whether thy ingratitude be greater or my misfortune; for perusing the few lines thou gavest me, I found as small hope of my love as of thy courtesy. But so extreme are the passions of love that the more thou seekest to quench them by disdain, the greater flame thou increasest by desire; not unlike unto Jupiter's well, which extinguisheth a fiery brand and kindleth a wet stick.[3] And no less force hath thy beauty over me than the fire hath over naplytia,[4] which leapeth into it wheresoever it seeth it.

I am not he, Camilla, that will leave the rose because I pricked my finger, or forsake the gold that lieth in the hot fire for that I burnt my hand, or refuse the sweet chestnut for that it is covered with sharp husks. The mind of a faithful lover is neither to be daunted with despite nor affrighted with danger. For as the loadstone, what wind soever blow, turneth always to the north, or as Aristotle's quadratus,[5] which way soever you turn it, is always constant, so the faith of Philautus is evermore applied to the love of Camilla, neither to be removed with any wind, or rolled with any force.

But to thy letter. Thou sayest green wounds are to be dressed roughly lest they fester. Certainly, thou speakest like a good chirurgeon, but dealest like one unskilful; for making a great wound, thou puttest in a small tent,[6] cutting the flesh that is sound before thou cure the place that is sore, striking the vein with a knife which thou shouldst stop with lint. And so hast thou drawn my tetter[7] (I use thine own term), that in seeking to spoil it in my chin thou hast spread it over my body.

---

1 *Arellius / Venus Cnidia*] Roman painter in the time of Augustus / the Venus at Cnidus (a city in Asia Minor). The only representation of Venus known by this name, a statue by Praxiteles, does not accord with this description.
2 *tie themselves ... Ulysses*] Ulysses was advised by Circe (see p. 259n.) to order his sailors to bind him to the mast of his own ship to enable him to listen to the music of the Sirens without succumbing to their enchantment (*Odyssey*, bk xii).
3 *Jupiter's well ... stick*] situated in Dodona, site of a famous oracle. The properties of the well are described by Pliny.
4 *naplytia*] naphtha, a highly inflammable, volatile liquid, issuing from the ground in certain parts of the world
5 *loadstone / quadratus*] magnetite (naturally magnetic stone) / four-sided figure, square
6 *tent*] roll of medicated material used to distend a wound in order to cleanse it or allow it to heal
7 *tetter*] see p. 269n.

Thou addest thou art no Italian lady. I answer, would thou wert; not that I would have thee wooed as thou sayest they are, but that I might win thee as thou now art. And yet this I dare say, though not to excuse all or to disgrace thee, that some there are in Italy too wise to be caught with leasings, and too honest[1] to be entangled with lust, and as wary to eschew sin as they are willing to sustain shame; so that whatsoever the most be, I would not have thee think ill of the best.

Thou allegest thy youth and allowest thy wisdom;[2] the one not apt to know the impressions of love, the other suspicious not to believe them. Truly, Camilla, I have heard that young is the goose that will eat no oats, and a very ill cock that will not crow before he be old, and no right lion that will not feed on hard meat before he taste sweet milk; and a tender virgin God knows it must be that measureth her affections by her age, whenas naturally they are inclined (which thou particularly puttest to our country) to play the brides before they be able to dress their heads.[3]

Many similitudes thou bringest in to excuse youth—thy twig, thy corn, thy fruit, thy grape, and I know not what; which are as easily to be refelled[4] as they are to be repeated. But, my good Camilla, I am as unwilling to confute anything thou speakest as I am thou shouldst utter it; insomuch as I would swear the crow were white, if thou shouldst but say it.

My good will is greater than I can express, and thy courtesy less than I deserve; thy counsel to expel it with time and reason of so little force that I have neither the will to use the mean nor the wit to conceive it. But this I say: that nothing can break off my love but death, nor anything hasten my death but thy discourtesy. And so I attend thy final sentence and my fatal destiny.

Thine ever, though he be never thine,

Philautus.

This letter he thought by no means better to be conveyed than in the same book he received hers. So omitting no time, lest the iron should cool before he could strike,[5] he presently went to Camilla; whom he found in gathering of flowers, with divers other ladies and gentlewomen, which came as well to recreate themselves for pleasure as to visit Camilla whom they all loved. Philautus, somewhat boldened by acquaintance, courteous by nature, and courtly by countenance,[6] saluted them all with such terms as he thought meet for such personages; not forgetting to call Camilla his scholar, when she had schooled him, being her master.

One of the ladies, who delighted much in mirth, seeing Philautus behold Camilla so steadfastly, said unto him:

'Gentleman, what flower like you best in all this border? Here be fair roses, sweet violets, fragrant primroses; here will be gilly-flowers, carnations, sops in wine, sweet-Johns,[7] and what may either please you for

---

1 *leasings / honest*] lies / virtuous, chaste
2 *Thou allegest . . . wisdom*] you cite your youth and approve your own wisdom
3 *dress their heads*] do their hair
4 *refelled*] rebutted
5 *lest the iron . . . strike*] proverbial (cf. 'to strike while the iron is hot')
6 *by countenance*] in demeanour
7 *gilly-flowers / sops in wine / sweet-Johns*] all pinks of different varieties

sight or delight you with savour. Loath we are you should have a posy
of all, yet willing to give you one; not that which shall look best, but such
a one as you shall like best.'

Philautus, omitting no opportunity that might either manifest his affection or commend his wit, answered her thus:

'Lady, of so many sweet flowers to choose the best it is hard, seeing
they be all so good. If I should prefer the fairest before the sweetest, you
would haply imagine that either I were stopped[1] in the nose or wanton
in the eyes; if the sweetness before the beauty, then would you guess me
either to live with savours or to have no judgement in colours. But to tell
my mind (upon correction be it spoken) of all flowers I love a fair woman.'

'Indeed,' quoth Flavia (for so was she named), 'fair women are set thick
but they come up thin;[2] and when they begin to bud they are gathered,
as though they were blown, of such men as you are, gentleman, who think
green grass will never be dry hay.[3] But when the flower of their youth,
being slipped[4] too young, shall fade before they be old, then I dare say
you would change your fair flower for a weed, and the woman you loved
then for the worst violet you refuse now.'

'Lady,' answered Philautus, 'it is a sign that beauty was no niggard of
her slips in this garden, and very envious[5] to other grounds, seeing here
are so many in one plot as I shall never find more in all Italy, whether the
reason be the heat which killeth them, or the country that cannot bear
them. As for plucking them up soon, in that we show the desire we have
to them, not the malice. Where you conjecture that men have no respect
to things when they be old, I cannot consent to your saying; for well do
they know that it fareth with women as it doth with the mulberry-tree,
which the elder it is the younger it seemeth.[6] And therefore hath it grown
to a proverb in Italy, when one seeth a woman stricken in age to look
amiable he sayeth, "She hath eaten a snake"[7]—so that I must of force[8]
follow mine old opinion that I love fresh flowers well, but fair women
better.'

Flavia would not so leave him, but thus replied to him:

'You are very amorous, gentleman, otherwise you would not take the
defence of that thing which most men contemn and women will not

---

1 *stopped*] blocked
2 *set thick . . . thin*] thickly planted but few survive
3 *blown / who think . . . dry hay*] in full bloom / who believe the young will never
grow old
4 *slipped*] both 'cut' (in order to be rooted independent of the parent plant) and 'to
be used for cuttings'. Hence taken in marriage and made a mother.
5 *no niggard of her slips / envious*] was not miserly with her cuttings / malicious
6 *mulberry-tree . . . seemeth*] Bond attributes this statement to the late-flowering habit
of the tree (II, p. 519).
7 *She hath eaten a snake*] The widely attested belief in the rejuvenating effect of eating
a snake may arise from the animal's seeming capacity to renew itself by shedding its
skin.
8 *of force*] perforce

confess. For whereas you go about to curry favour, you make a fault, either in praising us too much, which we account in England flattery, or pleasing yourself in your own mind, which wise men esteem as folly. For when you endeavour to prove that women the older they are the fairer they look, you think them either very credulous to believe or your talk very effectual to persuade. But as cunning as you are in your paternoster,[1] I will add one article more to your creed:[1] that is, you may speak in matters of love what you will, but women will believe but what they list; and in extolling their beauties, they give more credit to their own glasses than men's glozes.[2] But you have not yet answered my request touching what flower you most desire; for women do not resemble flowers, neither in show nor savour.'

Philautus, not shrinking for an April shower,[3] followed the chase in this manner:

'Lady, I neither flatter you nor please myself (although it pleaseth you so to conjecture), for I have always observed this: that to stand too much in mine own conceit would gain me little, and to claw[4] those of whom I sought for no benefit would profit me less. Yet was I never so ill brought up but that I could, when time and place should serve, give everyone I liked their just commendation, unless it were among those that were without comparison; offending in nothing but in this, that being too curious in praising my lady I was like to the painter Protogenes,[5] who could never leave when his work was well; which fault is to be excused in him because he would make it better, and may be borne with in me for that I wish it excellent.

'Touching your first demand, which you seem again to urge in your last discourse, I say of all flowers I love the rose best; yet with this condition, because I will not eat my word, I like a fair lady well.'

'Then,' quoth Flavia, 'since you will needs join the flower with the woman, among all us (and speak not partially) call her your rose that you most regard; and if she deny that name, we will enjoin her a penance for her pride, and reward you with a violet for your pains.'

Philautus, being driven to this shift,[6] wished himself in his chamber. For this he thought: that if he should choose Camilla she would not accept it, if another she might justly reject him; if he should discover his love then would Camilla think him not to be secret, if conceal it not to be fervent; besides all, the ladies would espy his love and prevent it, or Camilla despise his offer and not regard it. While he was thus in a deep meditation, Flavia wakened him, saying:

1 *cunning ... paternoster / creed*] glib as you are in rehearsing your beliefs / faith
2 *glozes*] fine phrases
3 *not shrinking for ... shower*] not easily daunted
4 *stand too much ... conceit / claw*] to be too wedded to my own opinions / flatter
5 *Protogenes*] perfectionist painter (see p. 155n.), reputed to have spent more than seven years in the creation of his masterpiece, which he repainted four times
6 *shift*] extremity

'Why, gentleman, are you in a dream, or is there none here worthy to make choice of, or are we all so indifferent that there is never a good?'

Philautus, seeing this lady so courteous, and loving Camilla so earnestly, could not yet resolve with himself what to do. But at the last, Love, which neither regardeth what it speaketh nor where, he replied thus at all adventures:

'Ladies and gentlewomen, I would I were so fortunate that I might chose every one of you for a flower, and then would I boldly affirm that I could show the fairest posy in the world, but folly it is for me to wish that, being a slave, which none can hope for that is an emperor. If I make my choice, I shall speed so well as he that enjoyeth all Europe.'

And with that, gathering a rose, he gave it to Camilla; whose colour so increased as one would have judged all her face to have been a rose, had it not been stained with a natural whiteness which made her to excel the rose.

Camilla, with a smiling countenance as though nothing grieved, yet vexed inwardly to the heart, refused the gift flatly, pretending a ready excuse—which was that Philautus was either very much over-seen[1] to take her before the Lady Flavia, or else disposed to give her a mock above the rest in the company.

'Well,' quoth Flavia to Philautus (who now stood like one that had been besmeared),[2] 'there is no harm done, for I perceive Camilla is otherwise sped. And if I be not much deceived she is a flower for Surius' wearing. The penance she shall have is to make you a nosegay, which she shall not deny thee unless she defy us; and the reward thou shalt have is this, while you tarry in England my niece shall be your violet.'

This lady's cousin was named Frances, a fair gentlewoman and a wise, young and of very good conditions,[3] not much inferior to Camilla, equal she could not be.

Camilla, who was loath to be accounted in any company coy,[4] endeavoured in the presence of the Lady Flavia to be very courteous, and gathered for Philautus a posy of all the finest flowers in the garden, saying thus unto him, 'I hope you will not be offended, Philautus, in that I could not be your rose'—but imputing the fault rather to destiny than discourtesy.

Philautus, plucking up his spirits, gave her thanks for her pains; and immediately gathered a violet which he gave Mistress Frances, which she courteously received. Thus all parties were pleased for that time.

Philautus was invited to dinner, so that he could no longer stay; but pulling out the book wherein his letter was enclosed, he delivered it to Camilla, taking his humble leave of the Lady Flavia and the rest of the

---

1 *over-seen*] mistaken
2 *besmeared*] covered with mud (or some other noxious substance), aspersed
3 *cousin/conditions*] kinswoman/qualities
4 *coy*] unsociably reserved

gentlewomen. When he was gone, there fell much talk of him between the gentlewomen, one commending his wit, another his personage, some his favour, all his good conditions;[1] insomuch that the Lady Flavia bound it with an oath that she thought him both wise and honest.

When the company was dissolved, Camilla, not thinking to receive an answer but a lecture, went to her Italian book, where she found the letter of Philautus; who without any further advice, as one very much offended, or in a great heat, sent him this bone to gnaw upon:

To Philautus,

Sufficed it not thee, Philautus, to bewray thy follies and move my patience, but thou must also procure in me a mind to revenge and to thyself the means of a further peril? Where didst thou learn that being forbidden to be bold thou shouldst grow impudent, or being suffered to be familiar thou shouldst wax hail-fellow? But to so malapert[2] boldness is the demeanour of young gentlemen come, that where they have been once welcome for courtesy they think themselves worthy to court any lady by customs; wherein they imagine they use singular audacity, which we can no otherwise term than sauciness, thinking women are to be drawn by their coined and counterfeit conceits, as the straw is by the amber, or the iron by the loadstone, or the gold by the mineral chrysocolla.[3] But as there is no serpent that can breed in the box-tree for the hardness, nor will build in the cypress-tree for the bitterness, so is there no fond or poisoned lover that shall enter into my heart which is hardened like the adamant,[4] nor take delight in my words which shall be more bitter than gall.

It fareth with thee, Philautus, as with the drone, who having lost her own wings seeks to spoil the bees of theirs, and thou being clipped of thy liberty, goest about to bereave me of mine; not far differing from the natures of dragons, who sucking blood out of the elephant kill him and with the same poison themselves.[5] And it may be that by the same means that thou takest in hand to inveigle my mind thou entrap thine own; a just reward for so unjust dealing, and a fit revenge for so unkind a regard.

But I trust thy purpose shall take no place,[6] and that thy malice shall want might; wherein thou shalt resemble the serpent porphirius, who is full of poison, but being toothless he hurteth none but himself.[7] And I doubt not but thy mind is as full of deceit as thy words are of flattery, but having no tooth to bite I have no cause to fear.

I had not thought to have used so sour words, but where a wand cannot rule the horse a spur must. When gentle medicines have no force to purge, we must use bitter potions; and where the sore is neither to be dissolved by

---

1 *personage / favour / conditions*] figure / looks / disposition
2 *malapert*] impudent
3 *chrysocolla*] a precious stone. (For the sources of its reputed power to attract gold, see Croll and Clemons, p. 357n.)
4 *adamant*] diamond
5 *not far differing ... themselves*] Pliny notes that dragons drink the blood of elephants (thought to be cold-blooded) in order to cool themselves in summer and are crushed beneath their fainting victims (for Lyly's immediate sources see Croll and Clemons, p. 358n.)
6 *take no place*] be ineffectual
7 *the serpent porphirius ... himself*] see p. 164 for the same analogy

plaster nor to be broken, it is requisite it should be lanced. Herbs that are the worse for watering are to be rooted out, trees that are less fertile for the lopping are to [be] hewn down, hawks that wax haggard by manning[1] are to be cast off; and fond lovers that increase in their follies when they be rejected are to be despised.

But as to be without hair amongst the Myconions[2] is accounted no shame because they be all born bald, so in Italy to live in love is thought no fault for that there they are all given to lust; which maketh thee to conjecture that we in England reckon love as the chiefest virtue, which we abhor as the greatest vice, which groweth like the ivy about the trees and killeth them by culling[3] them. Thou art always talking of love and applying both thy wit and thy wealth in that idle trade, only for that thou thinkest thyself amiable; not unlike unto the hedgehog, who evermore lodgeth in the thorns because he himself is full of prickles.

But take this both for a warning and an answer, that if thou prosecute thy suit thou shalt but undo thyself; for I am neither to be wooed with thy passions whilest thou livest, nor to repent me of my rigour when thou art dead. Which I would not have thee think to proceed of any hate I bear thee, for I malice[4] none, but for love to mine honour, which neither Italian shall violate nor Englishman diminish. For as the precious stone chalazias[5] being thrown into the fire keepeth still his coldness, not to be warmed with any heat, so my heart, although dented at with the arrows of thy burning affections and as it were environed with the fire of thy love, shall always keep his hardness, and be so far from being mollified that thou shalt not perceive it moved.

The violet Lady Flavia bestowed on thee I wish thee, and if thou like it I will further thee; otherwise, if thou persist in thine old follies whereby to increase my new griefs, I will neither come where thou art nor shalt thou have access to the place where I am. For as little agreement shall there be between us as is betwixt the vine and the cabbage, the oak and the olive-tree, the serpent and the ash-tree, the iron and theamedes.[6] And if ever thou didst love me manifest it in this, that hereafter thou never write to me; so shall I both be persuaded of thy faith and eased of mine own fear. But if thou attempt again to wring water out of the pumice thou shalt but bewray thy falsehood, and augment thy shame and my severity. For this I swear by her whose lights can never die, Vesta, and by her whose hests[7] are not to be broken, Diana, that I will never consent to love him whose sight (if I may so say with modesty) is more bitter unto me than death.

If this answer will not content thee I will show thy letters, disclose thy love, and make thee ashamed to undertake that which thou canst never bring to pass. And so I end.

Thine, if thou leave to be mine,
Camilla.

---

1 *wax haggard by manning*] grow wild in training to human use
2 *Myconians*] inhabitants of Myconus (an island in the Aegean sea), noted among ancient writers for their tendency to baldness
3 *culling*] embracing
4 *malice*] bear ill-will to
5 *chalazias*] hail stone
6 *the vine ... theamedes*] all traditionally regarded as antipathetic in some respect (*theamedes* = precious stone found in Ethiopia)
7 *hests*] commands

Camilla dispatched this letter with speed, and sent it to Philautus by her man; which Philautus having read, I commit the plight he was in to the consideration of you gentlemen that have been in the like. He tore his hair, rent his clothes, and fell from the passions of a lover to the pangs of frenzy. But at the last, calling his wits to him, forgetting both the charge Camilla gave him and the contents of her letter, he greeted her immediately again with an answer by her own messenger, in this manner:

To the cruel Camilla, greeting,

If I were as far in thy books[1] to be believed as thou art in mine to be beloved, thou shouldst either soon be made a wife or ever remain a virgin; the one would rid me of hope, the other acquit me of fear. But seeing there wanteth wit in me to persuade and will in thee to consent, I mean to manifest the beginning of my love by the end of my life; the affects of the one shall appear by the effects of the other. Whenas neither solemn oath, nor sound persuasion, nor any reason can work in thee a remorse, I mean by death to show my desire; the which the sooner it cometh the sweeter it shall be, and the shortness of the force[2] shall abate the sharpness of the sorrow.

I cannot tell whether thou laugh at my folly or lament my frenzy; but this I say, and with salt tears trickling down my cheeks I swear, that thou never foundest more pleasure in rejecting my love than thou shalt feel pain in remembering my loss, and as bitter shall life be to thee as death to me, and as sorrowful shall my friends be to see thee prosper as thine glad to see me perish.

Thou thinkest all I write of course,[3] and makest all I speak of small account; but God who revengeth the perjuries of the dissembler is witness of my truth, of whom I desire no longer to live than I mean simply to love. I will not use many words, for if thou be wise few are sufficient, if froward[4] superfluous. One line is enough if thou be courteous, one word too much if thou be cruel. Yet this I add, and that in bitterness of soul, that neither my hand dareth write that which my heart intendeth, nor my tongue utter that which my hand shall execute. And so farewell, unto whom only I wish well.

Thine ever, though shortly never,

Philautus.

This letter, being written in the extremity of his rage, he sent by him that brought hers. Camilla, perceiving a fresh reply, was not a little melancholy; but digesting it with company[5] and burning the letter, she determined never to write to him nor after that to see him, so resolute was she in her opinion—I dare not say obstinate, lest you gentlewomen should take pepper in the nose[6] when I put but salt to your mouths. But this I dare boldly affirm, that ladies are to be wooed with Apelles' pencil,

---

1 *thy books*] your favour
2 *force*] rigour
3 *of course*] a matter of custom
4 *froward*] wilfully perverse
5 *digesting it with company*] coming to terms with it in the society of others
6 *pepper in the nose*] offence

Orpheus' harp, Mercury's tongue, Adonis' beauty, Croesus' wealth,[1] or else never to be won; for their beauties being blazed, their ears tickled, their minds moved, their eyes pleased, their appetite satisfied, their coffers filled, when they have all things they should have and would have, then men need not to stand in doubt of their coming but of their constancy.

But let me follow Philautus, who now, both loathing his life and cursing his luck, called to remembrance his old friend Euphues, whom he was wont to have always in mirth a pleasant companion, in grief a comforter, in all his life the only stay of his liberty. The discourtesy which he offered him so increased his grief that he fell into these terms of rage, as one either in an ecstasy or in a lunacy:

'Now, Philautus, dispute no more with thyself of thy love, but be desperate to end thy life. Thou hast cast off thy friend, and thy lady hath forsaken thee; thou, destitute of both, canst neither have comfort of Camilla whom thou seest obstinate, nor counsel of Euphues whom thou hast made envious.[2]

'Ah, my good friend Euphues! I see now at length, though too late, that a true friend is of more price than a kingdom, and that the faith of thee is to be preferred before the beauty of Camilla. For as safe being is it in the company of a trusty mate as sleeping in the grass trifoly,[3] where there is no serpent so venomous that dare venture. Thou wast ever careful for my estate[4] and I careless for thine; thou didst always fear in me the fire of love, I ever flattered myself with the bridle of wisdom. When thou wast earnest to give me counsel, I waxed angry to hear it; if thou didst suspect me upon just cause, I fell out with thee for every light occasion. Now, now, Euphues, I see what it is to want a friend, and what it is to lose one. Thy words are come to pass, which once I thought thou spakest in sport, but now I find them as a prophesy, that I should be constrained to stand at Euphues' door as the true owner.

'What shall I do in this extremity? Which way shall I turn me? Of whom shall I seek remedy? Euphues will reject me, and why should he not? Camilla hath rejected me, and why should she? The one I have offended with too much grief, the other I have served with too great good will; the one is lost with love, the other with hate; he for that I cared not for him, she because I cared for her.

'Aye, but though Camilla be not to be moved, Euphues may be mollified. Try him, Philautus! Sue to him, make friends, write to him, leave nothing undone that may either show in thee a sorrowful heart or move in him a mind that is pitiful. Thou knowest he is of nature courteous, one

1 *with Apelles' pencil ... wealth*] by means of outstanding gifts (artistry, musicianship, eloquence, physical perfection, affluence). *blazed* in the next clause = published.
2 *envious*] resentful
3 *trifoly*] plant of the genus trifolium. The power to repel the serpent may derive from an emblematic association with the Trinity.
4 *estate*] condition

that hateth none, that loveth thee, that is tractable in all things. Lions spare those that couch to them, the tigress biteth not when she is clawed, Cerberus[1] barketh not if Orpheus pipe sweetly. Assure thyself that if thou be penitent he will be pleased, and the old friendship will be better than the new.'

Thus Philautus, joying now in nothing but only in the hope he had to recover the friendship with repentance which he had broken off by rashness, determined to greet his friend Euphues, who all this while lost no time at his book in London. But how he employed it he shall himself utter, for that I am neither of his counsel nor court; but what he hath done he will not conceal, for rather he wisheth to bewray his ignorance than his idleness, and willinger you shall find him to make excuse of rudeness[2] than laziness.

But thus Philautus saluted him:

Philautus to Euphues,

The sharp north-east wind, my good Euphues, doth never last three days, tempests have but a short time, and the more violent the thunder is the less permanent it is. In the like manner it falleth out with the jars[3] and crossings of friends, which, begun in a minute, are ended in a moment. Necessary it is that among friends there should be some over-thwarting, but to continue in anger not convenient.[4] The camel first troubleth the water before he drink, the frankincense is burned before it smell, friends are tried before they are to be trusted; lest shining like the carbuncle[5] as though they had fire, they be found, being touched, to be without fire. Friendship should be like the wine which Homer, much commending, calleth Maroneum,[6] whereof one pint being mingled with five quarts of water yet it keepeth his old strength and virtue, not to be qualified by any discourtesy. Where salt doth grow nothing else can breed; where friendship is built no offence can harbour. Then, good Euphues, let the falling out of friends be a renewing of affection; that in this we may resemble the bones of the lion, which lying still and not moved begin to rot, but being stricken one against another break out like fire and wax green.[7]

The anger of friends is not unlike unto the physician's cucurbitae,[8] which drawing all the infection in the body into one place doth purge all diseases; and the rages of friends, reaping up all the hidden malices, or suspicions, or

---

1 *clawed / Cerberus*] gently scratched / the dog that guarded the entrance to Hades, charmed by the music of Orpheus when he sought to reclaim his dead wife, Eurydice
2 *court / rudeness*] circle / simplicity
3 *jars*] disagreements
4 *over-thwarting / convenient*] crossing of one another / fitting
5 *carbuncle*] gemstone, fiery in colour
6 *Maroneum*] a wine of singular strength and quality given to Ulysses by the priest Maron (*Odyssey*, bk ix)
7 *wax green*] grow young. (For the origins of the simile, see Croll and Clemons, p. 364n.)
8 *cucurbitae*] cupping glass (used for bleeding for medical purposes)

follies that lay lurking in the mind, maketh the knot more durable. For as the body being purged of melancholy waxeth light and apt to all labour, so the mind as it were scoured of mistrust becometh fit ever after for belief.

But why do I not confess that which I have committed, or knowing myself guilty why use I to gloze?[1] I have unjustly, my good Euphues, picked a quarrel against thee, forgetting the counsel thou gavest me, and despising that which I now desire; which as often as I call to my mind I cannot but blush to myself for shame, and fall out with myself for anger. For in falling out with thee I have done no otherwise than he that desiring to sail safely killeth him at the helm, resembling him that having need to alight spurreth his horse to make him stand still, or him that swimming upon another's back seeketh to stop his breath.

It was in thee, Euphues, that I put all my trust, and yet upon thee that I poured out all my malice; more cruel than the crocodile who suffereth the bird to breed in her mouth that scoureth her teeth, and nothing so gentle as the princely lion who saved his life that helped his foot.[2] But if either thy good nature can forget that which my ill tongue doth repent, or thy accustomable kindness forgive that my unbridled fury did commit, I will hereafter be as willing to be thy servant as I am now desirous to be thy friend, and as ready to take an injury as I was to give an offence.

What I have done in thine absence I will certify at thy coming, and yet I doubt not but thou canst guess by my condition. Yet this I add, that I am as ready to die as to live, and were I not animated with the hope of thy good counsel I would rather have suffered the death I wish for than sustained the shame I sought for. But now in these extremities, reposing both my life in thy hands and my service at thy commandment, I attend thine answer.

And rest thine to use more than his own,
Philautus.

This letter he dispatched by his boy; which Euphues reading could not tell whether he should more rejoice at his friend's submission or mistrust his subtlety. Therefore, as one not resolving himself to determine anything as yet, answered him thus immediately by his own messenger:

Euphues to him that was his Philautus,

I have received thy letter and know the man. I read it and perceived the matter, which I am as far from knowing how to answer as I was from looking for such an errand.

Thou beginnest to infer a necessity that friends should fall out, whenas I cannot allow a convenience.[3] For if it be among such as are faithful there should be no cause of breach, if between dissemblers no care of reconciliation. The camel, sayest thou, loveth water when it is troubled, and I say the hart thirsteth for the clear stream. And fitly didst thou bring it in against thyself (though applied it, I know not how aptly, for thyself), for such friendship dost thou like where brawls may be stirred not quietness sought.

---

1 *use I to goze*] do I palliate with fine words
2 *more cruel than . . . teeth / nothing so gentle . . . foot*] see p. 41n. / Androcles, having removed a thorn from the paw of a lion, was subsequently saved by the same beast when thrown to the lions in the Roman circus.
3 *allow a convenience*] agree to the propriety

The wine Maroneum which thou commendest and the salt ground which thou inferrest, the one is neither fit for thy drinking nor the other for thy taste; for such strong wines will overcome such light wits, and so good salt cannot relish[1] in so unsavoury a mouth, neither as thou desirest to apply them, can they stand thee in stead. For oftentimes have I found much water in thy deeds but not one drop of such wine, and the ground where salt should grow but never one corn that had savour.

After many reasons to conclude that jars were requisite, thou fallest to a kind of submission which I marvel at. For if I gave no cause, why didst thou pick a quarrel? If any, why shouldst thou crave a pardon? If thou canst defy thy best friend, what wilt thou do to thine enemy? Certainly this must needs ensue, that if thou canst not be constant to thy friend when he doth thee good, thou wilt never bear with him when he shall do thee harm; thou that seekest to spill the blood of the innocent canst show small mercy to an offender; thou that treadest a worm on the tail wilt crush a wasp on the head; thou that art angry for no cause wilt, I think, run mad for a light occasion.

Truly, Philautus, that once I loved thee I cannot deny, that now I should again do so I refuse;[2] for small confidence shall I repose in thee when I am guilty, that can find no refuge in innocency. The malice of a friend is like the sting of an asp, which nothing can remedy; for being pierced in the hand it must be cut off, and a friend thrust to the heart it must be pulled out. I had as lief,[3] Philautus, have a wound that inwardly might lightly grieve me, than a scar that outwardly should greatly shame me.

In that thou seemest so earnest to crave atonement thou causest me the more to suspect thy truth; for either thou art compelled by necessity and then it is not worth thanks, or else disposed again to abuse me and then it deserveth revenge. Eels cannot be held in a wet hand, yet are they stayed with a bitter fig leaf; the lamprey is not to be killed with a cudgel, yet is she spoiled[4] with a cane; so friends that are so slippery and wavering in all their dealings are not to be kept with fair and smooth talk, but with rough and sharp taunts; and contrariwise, those which with blows are not to be reformed are oftentimes won with light persuasions. Which way I should use thee I know not; for now a sharp word moved thee when otherwiles a sword will not, then a friendly check[5] killeth thee when a razor cannot raze[6] thee.

But to conclude, Philautus, it fareth with me now as with those that have been once bitten with the scorpion, who never after feel any sting, either of the wasp, or the hornet, or the bee; for I, having been pricked with thy falsehood, shall never I hope again be touched with any other dissembler, flatterer, or fickle friend.

Touching thy life in my absence, I fear me it hath been too loose; but seeing my counsel is no more welcome unto thee than water into a ship, I will not waste wind[7] to instruct him that wasteth himself to destroy others. Yet if I

---

1 *relish*] taste well
2 *refuse*] decline to agree to
3 *had as lief*] would as willingly
4 *spoiled*] killed
5 *moved / check*] angered / reproof
6 *raze*] pun (slash / entirely obliterate)
7 *wind*] breath

were as fully persuaded of thy conversion as thou wouldst have me of thy confession, I might haply do that which now I will not.

And so farewell, Philautus; and though thou little esteem my counsel, yet have respect to thine own credit. So, in working thine own good, thou shalt keep me from harm.

Thine once,
Euphues.

This letter pinched Philautus at the first. Yet trusting much to the good disposition of Euphues, he determined to persevere both in his suit and amendment; and therefore, as one beating his iron that he might frame it while it were hot, answered him in this manner:

To mine only friend, Euphues,

There is no bone so hard but being laid in vinegar it may be wrought, nor ivory so tough but seasoned with zythum it may be engraven, nor box[1] so knotty that dipped in oil cannot be carved; and can there be a heart in Euphues which neither will yield to softness with gentle persuasions nor true perseverance? What canst thou require at my hand that I will deny thee? Have I broken the league of friendship? I confess it. Have I misused thee in terms?[2] I will not deny it. But being sorrowful for either, why shouldst not thou forgive both?

Water is praised for that it savoureth of nothing, fire for that it yieldeth to nothing; and such should the nature of a true friend be that it should not savour of any rigour, and such the effect that it may not be conquered with any offence. Otherwise, faith put into the breast that beareth grudges, or contracted with him that can remember griefs, is not unlike unto wine poured into fir vessels,[3] which is present death to the drinker.

Friends must be used as the musicians tune their strings, who finding them in a discord do not break them, but either by intention or remission frame them to a pleasant consent;[4] or as riders handle their young colts, who finding them wild and untractable bring them to a good pace with a gentle rein, not with a sharp spur; or as the Scythians[5] ruled their slaves, not with cruel weapons, but with the show of small whips. Then, Euphues, consider with thyself what I may be, not what I have been, and forsake me not for that I deceived thee; if thou do, thy discourtesy will breed my destruction. For as there is no beast that toucheth the herb whereon the bear hath breathed,[6] so there is no man that will come near him upon whom the suspicion of deceit is fastened.

Concerning my life passed, I conceal it, though to thee I mean hereafter to confess it; yet hath it not been so wicked that thou shouldst be ashamed,

---

1 *zythum / box*] malt liquor used by the Egyptians / wood notorious for its dense, knotty character, and therefore its resistance to being worked
2 *misused thee in terms*] verbally abused you
3 *fir vessels*] small barrels made of yew, once used, according to Pliny, when travelling (see Croll and Clemons, p. 368n.)
4 *intention or remission / consent*] tightening or slackening / harmony
5 *Scythians*] Mongol people, whose social customs, including their treatment of slaves, were described by the Greek historian Herodotus
6 *For as there ... breathed*] a belief recorded by Pliny

though so infortunate that I am grieved. Consider we are in England, where our demeanour will be narrowly marked if we tread awry, and our follies mocked if [we] use wrangling. I think thou art willing that no such thing should happen, and I know thou art wise to prevent it.

I was of late in the company of divers gentlewomen, among whom Camilla was present; who marvelled not a little that thou soughtest either to absent thyself of some conceived injury, where there was none given, or of set purpose, because thou wouldst give one. I think it requisite, as well to avoid the suspicion of malice as to shun the note of ingratitude, that thou repair thither, both to purge thyself of the opinion may be conceived, and to give thanks for the benefits received.

Thus, assuring myself thou wilt answer my expectation and renew our old amity, I end.

Thine assured to command,
Philautus.

Philautus did not sleep about his business, but presently[1] sent this letter; thinking that if once he could fasten friendship again upon Euphues, that by his means he should compass[2] his love with Camilla. And yet this I durst affirm, that Philautus was both willing to have Euphues, and sorrowful that he lost him by his own lavishness.[3]

Euphues perused this letter oftentimes, being in a mammering what to answer. At the last, he determined once again to lie aloof,[4] thinking that if Philautus meant faithfully he would not desist from his suit, and therefore he returned salutations in this manner:

Euphues to Philautus,

There is an herb in India, Philautus, of pleasant smell, but whoso cometh to it feeleth present smart,[5] for that there breed in it a number of small serpents. And it may be that though thy letter be full of sweet words, there breed in thy heart many bitter thoughts; so that in giving credit to thy letters I may be deceived with thy leasings.[6] The box-tree is always green, but the seed is poison; tilia[7] hath a sweet rind and a pleasant leaf, but the fruit so bitter that no beast will bite it; a dissembler hath evermore honey in his mouth, and gall in his mind; which maketh me to suspect their wiles, though I cannot ever prevent them.

Thou settest down the office of a friend, which if thou couldst as well perform as thou canst describe, I would be as willing to confirm our old league as I am to believe thy new laws. Water that savoureth nothing (as thou sayest) may be heated and scald thee, and fire which yieldeth to nothing may be quenched when thou wouldst warm thee. So the friend in whom there was no intent to offend may through the sinister dealings of his fellow be turned

---

1 *sleep / presently*] delay / immediately
2 *compass*] achieve
3 *lavishness*] ungoverned conduct
4 *in a mammering / lie aloof*] uncertain / keep his distance
5 *present smart*] instant pain
6 *leasings*] lies
7 *tilia*] the linden-tree

to heat, being before cold, and the faith which wrought like a flame in him be quenched and have no spark.

The pouring of wine into fir vessels serveth thee to no purpose; for if it be good wine there is no man so foolish to put into fir, if bad who would pour into better than fir. Musty casks are fit for rotten grapes, a barrel of poisoned ivy is good enough for a tun of stinking oil, and cruelty too mild a medicine for craft.

How musicians tune their instruments I know, but how a man should temper his friend I cannot tell. Yet oftentimes the string breaketh that the musician seeketh to tune, and the friend cracketh which good counsel should tame. Such colts are to be ridden with a sharp snaffle, not with a pleasant bit, and little will the Scythian whip be regarded where the sharpness of the sword is derided.

If thy luck have been infortunate, it is a sign thy living hath not been godly; for commonly there cometh an ill end where there was a naughty[1] beginning. But learn, Philautus, to live hereafter as though thou shouldst not live at all. Be constant to them that trust thee, and trust them that thou hast tried; dissemble not with thy friend, either for fear to displease him or for malice to deceive him. Know this, that the best simples are very simple[2] if the physician could not apply them, that precious stones were no better than pebbles if lapidaries[3] did not know them, that the best friend is worse than a foe if a man do not use him. Mithridate must be taken inwardly, not spread on plasters; purgations must be used like drink, not like baths; the counsel of a friend must be fastened to the mind, not to the ear, followed, not praised, employed in good living, not talked of in good meaning.

I know, Philautus, we are in England, but I would we were not; not that the place is too base, but that we are too bad. And God grant thou have done nothing which may turn thee to discredit or me to displeasure. Thou sayest thou wert of late with Camilla; I fear me too late, and yet perhaps too soon. I have always told thee that she was too high for thee to climb, and too fair for others to catch, and too virtuous for any to inveigle. But wild horses break high hedges though they cannot leap over them, eager wolves bark at the moon though they cannot reach it, and Mercury whistleth for Vesta[4] though he cannot win her.

For absenting myself I hope they can take no cause of offence, neither (that I know) have I given any. I love not to be bold, yet would I be welcome; but guests and fish, say we in Athens, are ever stale within three days.[5] Shortly I will visit them and excuse myself; in the mean season, I think so well of them as it is possible for a man to think of women—and how well that is I appeal to thee, who always madest them no worse than saints in heaven, and shrines in no worse place than thy heart.

For answering thy suit I am not yet so hasty; for accepting thy service I am

---

1 *naughty*] wicked
2 *best simples are very simple*] most efficacious herbal remedies are without potency
3 *lapidaries*] those skilled in the handling of precious stones
4 *Mercury whistleth for Vesta*] see p. 122n. for Mercury's skill with the flute
5 *guests and fish . . . days*] see p. 224 for another example of Lyly's use of this proverb

not so imperious. For in friendship there must be an equality of estates, and be that may be[1] in us; also a similitude of manners, and that cannot, unless thou learn a new lesson and leave the old. Until which time I leave thee.
Wishing thee well as to myself,
Euphues.

This letter was written in haste, sent with speed, and answered again in post.[2] For Philautus, seeing so good counsel could not proceed of any ill conceit, thought once again to solicit his friend, and that in such terms as he might be most agreeable to Euphues' tune. In this manner:

To Euphues, health in body and quietness in mind,
In music there are many discords before there can be framed a diapason,[3] and in contracting of good will many jars before there be established a friendship; but by these means the music is more sweet, and the amity more sound. I have received thy letter, wherein there is as much good counsel contained as either I would wish or thou thyself couldst give; but ever thou harpest on that string which long since was out of tune, but now is broken—my inconstancy. Certes, my good Euphues, as I cannot but commend thy wisdom in making a stay of reconciliation (for that thou findest so little stay[4] in me), so can I not but marvel at thy incredulity in not believing me, since that thou seest a reformation in me.
But it may be thou dealest with me as the philosopher did with his knife; who being many years in making of it, always dealing by the observation of the stars, caused it at the last to cut the hard whetstone, saying that it skilled not[5] how long things were a-doing but how well they were done. And thou holdest me off with many delays, using I know not what observations, thinking thereby to make me a friend at the last that shall last. I praise thy good meaning, but I mislike thy rigour. Me thou shalt use in what thou wilt, and do that with a slender twist that none can do with a tough withy.[6]
As for my being with Camilla, good Euphues, rub there no more lest I wince; for deny I will not that I am wrung on the withers.[7] This one thing touching myself I say, and before Him that seeth all things I swear, that hereafter I will neither dissemble to delude thee, nor pick quarrels to fall out with thee. Thou shalt find me constant to one, faithless to none, in prayer devout, in manners reformed, in life chaste, in words modest, not framing my fancy to the humour of love, but my deeds to the rule of zeal.[8] And such a man as heretofore merrily thou saidst I was,[9] but now truly thou shalt see I am, and as I know thou art.

---

1 *estates / be that may be*] social position / The first 'be' does not appear in later editions and may be a compositor's error.
2 *in post*] with speed
3 *diapason*] harmonious combination of notes
4 *making a stay / stay*] pausing over / steadfastness
5 *dealing by . . . the stars / skilled not*] working according to the disposition of the planets (i.e. in propitious circumstances) / did not matter
6 *twist / withy*] thread / willow twig (see p. 256n.)
7 *wrung on the withers*] feel pain in that quarter
8 *zeal*] religious fervour
9 *such a man . . . I was*] see Euphues' jesting salutation, p. 234

Then, Euphues, appoint the place where we may meet and reconcile the minds which I confess by mine own follies were severed. And if ever after this I shall seem jealous over thee,[1] or blinded towards myself, use me as I deserve—shamefully. Thus attending thy speedy answer, for that delays are perilous, especially as my case now standeth, I end.

              Thine ever to use as thine own,
                   Philautus.

Euphues, seeing such speedy return of another answer, thought Philautus to be very sharp set[2] for to recover him. And weighing with himself that often in marriages there have fallen out brawls, where the chiefest love should be, and yet again reconciliations, that none ought at any time so to love that he should find in his heart at any time to hate, furthermore casting in his mind the good he might do to Philautus by his friendship, and the mischief that might ensue by his fellow's folly, answered him thus again speedily, as well to prevent the course he might otherwise take as also to prescribe what way he should take.

Euphues to his friend Philautus,
    Nettles, Philautus, have no prickles, yet they sting; and words have no points, yet they pierce. Though outwardly thou protest great amendment, yet oftentimes the softness of wool which the Seres send[3] sticketh so fast to the skin that when one looketh it should keep him warm it fetcheth blood; and thy smooth talk, thy sweet promises, may, when I shall think to have them performed to delight me, be a corrosive to destroy me. But I will not cast beyond the moon,[4] for that in all things I know there must be a mean.
    Thou swearest now that thy life shall be led by my line, that thou wilt give no cause of offence by thy disorders, nor take any by my good meaning; which if it be so, I am as willing to be thy friend as I am to be mine own. But this take for a warning: if ever thou jar[5] when thou shouldst jest, or follow thine own will when thou art to hear my counsel, then will I depart from thee, and so display thee[6] as none that is wise shall trust thee, nor any that is honest shall live with thee.
    I now am resolved by thy letter of that which I was almost persuaded of by mine own conjecture touching Camilla. Why, Philautus, art thou so mad, without acquaintance of thy part or familiarity of hers to attempt a thing which will not only be a disgrace to thee but also a discredit to her? Thinkest thou thyself either worthy to woo her, or she willing to wed thee? Either thou able to frame thy tale[7] to her content, or she ready to give ear to thy conclusions? No, no, Philautus, thou art too young to woo in England, though old enough to win in Italy; for here they measure more the man by the qual-

---

1 *jealous over thee*] suspicious of you
2 *sharp set*] eager
3 *wool which the Seres send*] silk, obtained in early times from the people of Serica in eastern Asia
4 *cast beyond the moon*] expect too much
5 *jar*] quarrel
6 *display thee*] advertise your conduct
7 *frame thy tale*] court her

ities of his mind than the proportion of his body. They are too expert in love, having learned in this time of their long peace every wrinkle that is to be seen or imagined. It is neither an ill tale well told nor a good history made better, neither invention of new fables nor the reciting of old, that can either allure in them an appetite to love, or almost an attention to hear. It fareth not with them as it doth with those in Italy, who prefer a sharp wit before sound wisdom, or a proper[1] man before a perfect mind. They live not by shadows, nor feed of the air, nor lust after wind. Their love is not tied to art but reason, not to the precepts of Ovid[2] but to the persuasions of honesty.

But I cannot but marvel at thy audacity, that thou didst once dare to move her to love whom I always feared to solicit in questioning; as well doubting to be gravelled[3] by her quick and ready wit as to be confuted by her grave and wise answers. But thou wilt say she was of no great birth, of meaner parentage than thyself. Aye but, Philautus, they be most noble who are commended more for their perfection than their pedigree; and let this suffice thee, that her honour consisted in virtue, beauty, wit—not blood, ancestors, antiquity.

But more of this at our next meeting, where I think I shall be merry to hear the discourse of thy madness; for I imagine to myself that she handled thee very hardly, considering both the place she served in and the person that served her. And sure I am she did not hang for thy mowing.[4]

A phoenix[5] is no food for Philautus. That dainty tooth of thine must be pulled out, else wilt thou surfeit with desire; and that eagle's eye pecked out, else wil[l i]t be dazzled with delight. My counsel must rule thy conceit,[6] lest thou confound us both.

I will this evening come to thy lodging, where we will confer. And till then I commend me to thee.

Thine ever to use, if thou be thine own,
Euphues.

This letter was so thankfully received of Philautus that he almost ran beyond himself for joy, preparing all things necessary for the entertainment of his friend, who at the hour appointed failed not.

Many embracings there were, much strange courtesy, many pretty glances; being almost for the time but strangers because of their long absence. But growing to questioning one with another, they fell to the whole discourse of Philautus' love, who left out nothing that before I put in—which I must omit lest I set before you coleworts twice sodden,[7] which will both offend your ears which I seek to delight, and trouble my hand which I covet to ease.[8] But this I am sure, that Euphues' conclusion was

---

1 *proper*] handsome
2 *precepts of Ovid*] i.e. the *Ars amatoria* (*Art of Love*)
3 *solicit in questioning / gravelled*] address in debate / confounded
4 *hang for thy mowing*] was not ready to be harvested (i.e. won) by you
5 *phoenix*] the ultimate delicacy for the refined palate, in that only one was believed to exist
6 *conceit*] fancy
7 *coleworts twice sodden*] twice-boiled cabbage (i.e. an uninteresting rehash of what went before)
8 *covet to ease*] desire to relieve

this, between waking and winking:[1] that our English ladies and gentle-women were so cunning in love that the labour were more easy in Italy to wed one and bury her, than here to woo one and marry her. And thus they with long talking waxed weary; where I leave them, not willing to talk any longer but to sleep their fills till morning.

Now, gentlewomen, I appeal in this controversy to your consciences, whether there be in you an art to love, as Euphues thinketh, or whether it breed in you as it doth in men—by sight if one be beautiful, by hearing if one be witty, by deserts if one be courteous, by desire if one be virtu-ous.[2] Which I would not know to this intent that I might be instructed how to win any of you, but to the end I might wonder at you all. For if there be in love an art, then do I not marvel to see men that every way are to be beloved so oftentimes to be rejected. But so secret is this matter that, pertaining nothing to our sex, I will not further enquire of it; lest haply in guessing what art women use in love, I should minister[3] an art they never before knew; and so in thinking to bewray the bait that hath caught one, I give them a net to draw many, putting a sword into the hand where there is but a sheath, teaching them to strike that put us to our tryings by warding.[4] Which would double our peril who without art cannot allure them, and increase their tyranny who without they torment will come to no parley.[5]

But this I admonish you, that as your own beauties make you not cov-etous of your alms[6] towards true lovers, so other men's flattery make you not prodigal of your honours towards dissemblers. Let not them that speak fairest be believed soonest; for true love lacketh a tongue, and is tried[7] by the eyes, which in a heart that meaneth well are as far from wanton glances as the mind is from idle thoughts.

And this art I will give you, which we men do commonly practise: if you behold anyone that either your courtesy hath allured, or your beauty, or both, triumph not over him; but the more earnest you see him, the more ready be to follow him, and when he thinketh himself nearest, let him be furthest off. Then if he take that with patience, assure yourself he cannot be faithless. He that angleth plucketh the bait away when he is near a bite, to the end the fish may be more eager to swallow the hook; birds are trained with a sweet call, but caught with a broad net; and lovers come with fair looks, but are entangled with disdainful eyes. The spaniel that fawneth when he is beaten will never forsake his master; the man that doteth when he is disdained will never forgo his mistress.

---

1 *winking*] sleeping
2 *by deserts . . . virtuous*] The sense here would seem to require the transposition of 'deserts' and 'desire'.
3 *minister*] furnish
4 *put us to . . . warding*] oblige us to exert ourselves to the extreme by their defence
5 *parley*] truce
6 *covetous of your alms*] niggardly of your generosity
7 *tried*] tested

But too much of this string, which soundeth too much out of square.[1]
And return we to Euphues and Philautus.

The next morning, when they were risen, they went into a gallery, where
Euphues, who perceived Philautus grievously perplexed for the love of
Camilla, began thus between jest and earnest to talk with him:

'Philautus, I have well-nigh all this night been disputing with myself of
thy distress, yet can I resolve myself in nothing that either may content
me or quiet thee.

'What metal art thou made of, Philautus, that thinkest of nothing but
love, and art rewarded with nothing less than love? Lucilla was too bad,
yet didst thou court her; thy sweetheart now in Naples is none of the best,
yet didst thou follow her; Camilla, exceeding all, where thou wast to have
least hope, thou hast wooed not without great hazard to thy person and
grief to mine.

'I have perused her letters, which in my simple judgement are so far
from allowing thy suit that they seem to loathe thy service. I will not
flatter thee in thy follies; she is no match for thee nor thou for her, the
one wanting living to maintain a wife, the other birth to advance[2] an
husband. Surius, whom I remember thou didst name in thy discourse, I
remember in the court a man of great birth and noble blood, singular wit
and rare personage. If he go about to get credit, I muse what hope thou
couldst conceive to have a good countenance.[3]

'Well, Philautus, to set down precepts against thy love will nothing
prevail, to persuade thee to go forward were very perilous; for I know in
the one love will regard no laws, and in the other persuasions can purchase no liberty. Thou art too heady[4] to enter in where no heed can help
one out. Theseus would not go into the labyrinth without a thread that
might show him the way out, neither any wise man enter into the crooked
corners of love unless he knew by what means he might get out. Love,
which should continue for ever, should not be begun in an hour, but
slowly be taken in hand and by length of time finished; resembling
Zeuxis,[5] that wise painter, who in things that he would have last long
took greatest leisure.

'I have not forgotten one Mistress Frances, which the Lady Flavia gave
thee for a violet; and by thy description, though she be not equal with
Camilla, yet is she fitter for Philautus. If thy humour be such that nothing
can feed it but love, cast thy mind on her, confer[6] the impossibility thou
hast to win Camilla with the likelihood thou mayst have to enjoy thy
violet. And in this I will endeavour both my wit and my good will, so

---

1 *soundeth . . . out of square*] is disproportionately developed
2 *wanting living / birth to advance*] lacking the means / high rank to raise the status
of
3 *have a good countenance*] receive a favourable reception
4 *heady*] headlong (for *Theseus* in the next sentence see p. 200n.)
5 *Zeuxis*] see p. 158n.
6 *confer*] compare

that nothing shall want in me that may work ease in thee. Thy violet, if she be honest, is worthy of thee; beautiful thou sayest she is, and therefore too worthy. Hot fire is not only quenched by the clear fountain, nor love only satisfied by the fair face. Therefore in this tell me thy mind, that either we may proceed in that matter or seek a new medicine.'

Philautus thus replied:

'Oh my good Euphues, I have neither the power to forsake mine own Camilla, nor the heart to deny thy counsel. It is easy to fall into a net but hard to get out. Notwithstanding, I will go against the hair[1] in all things, so I may please thee in anything. Oh my Camilla—'

With that Euphues stayed him, saying:

'He that hath sore eyes must not behold the candle, nor he that would leave his love fall to the remembering of his lady; the one causeth the eye to smart, the other the heart to bleed.'

'Well,' quoth Philautus, 'I am content to have the wound searched,[2] yet unwilling to have it cured; but sithence that sick men are not to prescribe diets but to keep them, I am ready to take potions, and if wealth serve to pay thee for them. Yet one thing maketh [me] to fear, that in running after two hares I catch neither.'

'And certainly,' quoth Euphues, 'I know many good hunters that take more delight to have the hare on foot and never catch it, than to have no cry and yet kill in the form.[3] Whereby I guess there cometh greater delight in the hunting than in the eating.'

'It may be,' said Philautus, 'but I were then very unfit for such pastimes; for what sport soever I have all the day, I love to have the game in my dish at night.'

'And truly,' answered Euphues, 'you are worse made for a hound than a hunter, for you mar your scent with carrion before you start your game, which maketh you hunt oftentimes counter;[4] whereas if you had kept it pure you might ere this time have turned the hare you winded, and caught the game you coursed.'[5]

'Why then, I perceive,' quoth Philautus, 'that to talk with gentlewomen touching the discourses of love, to eat with them, to confer with them, to laugh with them, is as great pleasure as to enjoy them; to the which thou mayst by some fallacy drive me, but never persuade me. For then were it as pleasant to behold fruit as to eat them, or to see fair bread as to taste it.'

'Thou errest, Philautus,' said Euphues, 'if thou be not of that mind. For he that cometh into fine gardens is as much recreated to smell the flower

---

1 *against the hair*] contrary to my natural inclination
2 *searched*] probed
3 *cry / form*] chase / hollow inhabited by a hare
4 *mar your scent with carrion / counter*] literally, blunt your capacity to follow a scent by sniffing dead meat before the game has been roused (i.e. hinder your amatory ambitions by pursuing inappropriate women) / in the wrong direction
5 *coursed*] pursued

as to gather it. And many we see more delighted with pictures than desirous to be painters. The effect of love is faith not lust, delightful conference not detestable concupiscence, which beginneth with folly and endeth with repentance. For mine own part, I would wish nothing (if again I should fall into that vein), than to have the company of her in common conference that I best loved, to hear her sober talk, her wise answers, to behold her sharp capacity, and to be persuaded of her constancy. And in these things do we only differ from brute beasts, who have no pleasure but in sensual appetite.'

'You preach heresy,' quoth Philautus, 'and besides so repugnant to the text you have taken that I am more ready to pull thee out of thy pulpit than to believe thy glosses.[1] I love the company of women well, yet to have them in lawful matrimony I like much better. If thy reasons should go as current, then were love no torment; for hardly[2] doth it fall out with him that is denied the sight and talk of his lady. Hungry stomachs are not to be fed with sayings against surfeitings, nor thirst to be quenched with sentences against drunkenness. To love women and never enjoy them is as much as to love wine and never taste it, or to be delighted with fair apparel and never wear it. An idle love is that, and fit for him that hath nothing but ears, that is satisfied to hear her speak, not desirous to have himself speed.[3] Why then, Euphues, to have the picture of his lady is as much as to enjoy her presence, and to read her letters of as great force as to hear her answers. Which if it be, my suit in love should be as much to the painter to draw her with an amiable face, as to my lady to write an amorous letter; both which with little suit being obtained, I may live with love and never wet my foot,[4] nor break my sleeps, nor waste my money, nor torment my mind.

'But this worketh as much delight in the mind of a lover as the apples that hang at Tantalus' nose, or the river that runneth close by his chin.[5] And in one word, it would do me no more good to see my lady and not embrace her in the heat of my desire, than to see fire and not to warm me in the extremity of my cold.

'No, no, Euphues, thou makest love nothing but a continual wooing if thou bar it of the effect, and then is it infinite; or if thou allow it and yet forbid it, a perpetual warfare—and then is it intolerable. From this opinion no man shall withdraw me: that the end of fishing is catching, not angling; of birding taking, not whistling; of love wedding, not wooing. Otherwise it is no better than hanging.'

Euphues, smiling to see Philautus so earnest, urged him again in this manner:

---

1 *glosses*] interpretation
2 *go as current / hardly*] be widely accepted / grievously
3 *speed*] achieve his goal
4 *never wet my foot*] put myself to any inconvenience
5 *the apples that hang . . . chin*] see p. 254n.

'Why, Philautus, what harm were it in love if the heart should yield his right to the eye, or the fancy his force to the ear? I have read of many, and some I know, between whom there was as fervent affection as might be, that never desired anything but sweet talk and continual company at banquets, at plays, and other assemblies; as Phrigius and Pieria,[1] whose constant faith was such that there was never word nor thought of any uncleanness. Pygmalion loved his ivory image, being enamoured only by the sight, and why should not the chaste love of others be builded rather in agreeing in heavenly meditations than temporal actions? Believe me, Philautus, if thou knewest what it were to love, thou wouldst be as far from the opinion thou holdest as I am.'

Philautus, thinking no greater absurdity to be held in the world than this, replied before the other could end, as followeth:

'Indeed, Euphues, if the king would resign his right to his legate, then were it not amiss for the heart to yield to the eyes. Thou knowest, Euphues, that the eye is the messenger of love, not the master; that the ear is the carrier of news, the heart the digester. Besides this, suppose one have neither ears to hear his lady speak, nor eyes to see her beauty, shall he not therefore be subject to the impression of love? If thou answer no, I can allege divers both deaf and blind that have been wounded;[2] if thou grant it, then confess the heart must have his hope, which is neither seeing nor hearing—and what is the third?

'Touching Phrigius and Pieria, think them both fools in this; for he that keepeth a hen in his house to cackle and not lay, or a cock to crow and not to tread,[3] is not unlike unto him that having sown his wheat never reapeth it, or reaping it never thresheth it, taking more pleasure to see fair corn than to eat fine bread. Pygmalion maketh against this,[4] for Venus, seeing him so earnestly to love, and so effectually to pray, granted him his request; which had he not by importunate suit obtained, I doubt not but he would rather have hewed her[5] in pieces than honoured her with passions, and set her up in some temple for an image, not kept her in his house for a wife. He that desireth only to talk and view without any further suit is not far different from him that liketh to see a painted rose better than to smell to a perfect violet, or to hear a bird sing in a bush rather than to have her home in his own cage.

'This will I follow, that to plead for love and request nothing but looks, and to deserve works and live only by words, is as one should plough his ground and never sow it, grind his colours and never paint, saddle his horse and never ride.'

As they were thus communing, there came from the Lady Flavia a gen-

---

1 *Phrigius and Pieria*] see p. 98n. (For *Pygmalion* in the following sentence see p. 36n.)
2 *wounded*] smitten by love
3 *tread*] mate
4 *maketh against this*] argues against your position
5 *her*] the statue he had created and with which he was in love

tleman who invited them both that night to supper; which they, with humble thanks given, promised to do so. And till supper time I leave them debating their question.

Now, gentlewomen, in this matter I would I knew your minds, and yet I can somewhat guess at your meanings. If any of you should love a gentleman of such perfection as you can wish, would it content you only to hear him, to see him dance, to mark his personage, to delight in his wit, to wonder at all his qualities, and desire no other solace?[1] If you like to hear his pleasant voice to sing, his fine fingers to play, his proper personage[2] to undertake any exploit, would you covet no more of your love? As good it were to be silent and think 'No,' as to blush and say 'Aye.'

I must needs conclude with Philautus, though I should cavil[3] with Euphues, that the end of love is the full fruition of the party beloved, at all times and in all places. For it cannot follow in reason that because the sauce is good which should provoke mine appetite, therefore I should forsake the meat for which it was made. Believe me, the qualities of the mind, the beauty of the body, either in man or woman, are but the sauce to whet our stomachs, not the meat to fill them. For they that live by the view of beauty still look very lean, and they that feed only upon virtue at board[4] will go with an hungry belly to bed.

But I will not crave herein your resolute answer because between them it was not determined; but everyone as he liketh, and then—!

Euphues and Philautus being now again sent for to the Lady Flavia her house, they came presently,[5] where they found the worthy gentleman Surius, Camilla, Mistress Frances, with many other gentlemen and gentlewomen.

At their first entrance doing their duty,[6] they saluted all the company and were welcomed. The Lady Flavia entertained them both very lovingly, thanking Philautus for his last company, saying:

'Be merry, gentleman; at this time of the year a violet is better than a rose.'

And so she arose and went her way, leaving Philautus in a muse at her words, who before was in a maze at Camilla's looks. Camilla came to Euphues in this manner:

'I am sorry, Euphues, that we have no green rushes,[7] considering you have been so great a stranger. You make me almost to think that of you, which commonly I am not accustomed to judge of any, that either you

---

1 *solace*] pleasure
2 *proper personage*] handsome figure
3 *cavil*] quibble
4 *board*] the dinner table
5 *presently*] at once
6 *doing their duty*] paying their respects
7 *rushes*] used as a floor covering in the sixteenth century. The arrival of a stranger or an honoured guest was marked by the strewing of green (i.e. fresh) rushes.

thought yourself too good or our cheer too bad; other cause of absence I cannot imagine, unless seeing us very idle you sought means to be well employed. But I pray you hereafter be bold, and those things which were amiss shall be redressed; for we will have quails to amend your commons,[1] and some questions to sharpen your wits, so that you shall neither find fault with your diet for the grossness, nor with your exercise for the easiness. As for your fellow and friend, Philautus, we are bound to him for he would oftentimes see us, but seldom eat with us; which made us think that he cared more for our company than our meat.'

Euphues, as one that knew his good,[2] answered her in this wise:

'Fair lady, it were unseemly to strew green rushes for his coming whose company is not worth a straw, or to account him a stranger whose boldness hath been strange[3] to all those that knew him to be a stranger. The small ability in me to requite, compared with the great cheer I received, might haply make me refrain; which is contrary to your conjecture. [Nei]ther was I ever so busied in any weighty affairs which I accounted not as lost time in respect of the exercise I always found in your company; which maketh me think that your latter objection proceeded rather to convince me for[4] a truant than to manifest a truth.

'As for the quails you promise me, I can be content with beef, and for the questions, they must be easy else shall I not answer them. For my wit will show with what gross diet I have been brought up, so that conferring my rude replies[5] with my base birth you will think that mean cheer will serve me, and reasonable questions deceive me; so that I shall neither find fault for my repast, nor favour for my reasons. Philautus, indeed, taketh as much delight in good company as in good cates;[6] who shall answer for himself.'

With that, Philautus said:

'Truly, Camilla, where I think myself welcome I love to be bold, and when my stomach is filled I care for no meat; so that I hope you will not blame [me] if I came[7] often and eat little.'

'I do not blame you, by my faith,' quoth Camilla, 'you mistake me. For the oftener you come the better welcome, and the less you eat the more is saved.'

Much talk passed, which being only as it were a repetition of former things I omit as superfluous. But this I must note: that Camilla earnestly desired Surius to be acquainted with Euphues, who very willingly accomplished her request, desiring Euphues, for the good report he had heard

---

1 *quails / commons*] game bird regarded as a delicacy / fare (for *questions* in the same sentence see p. 205n.)
2 *knew his good*] was well-schooled in manners
3 *strange*] a matter of surprise
4 *convince me for*] prove me guilty of being
5 *conferring my rude replies*] comparing my unpolished responses
6 *cates*] provisions
7 *came*] emended to 'come' in later editions

of him, that he would be as bold[1] with him as with anyone in England. Euphues, humbly showing his duty, promised also as occasion should serve to try him.

It now grew toward supper time, when, the table being covered and the meat served in, Lady Flavia placed Surius over against Camilla, and Philautus next Mistress Frances; she took Euphues and the rest and placed them in such order as she thought best. What cheer they had I know not, what talk they used I heard not; but supper being ended they sat still, the Lady Flavia speaking as followeth:

'Gentlemen and gentlewomen, these Lenten evenings be long, and a shame it were to go to bed; cold they are, and therefore folly it were to walk abroad; to play at cards is common, at chess tedious, at dice unseemly, with Christmas games untimely. In my opinion, therefore, to pass away these long nights I would have some pastime that might be pleasant but not unprofitable, rare but not without reasoning; so shall we all account the evening well spent, be it never so long, which otherwise would be tedious, were it never so short.'

Surius, the best in the company[2] and therefore best worthy to answer, and the wisest and therefore best able, replied in this manner:

'Good madam, you have prevented my request with your own. For as the case now standeth, there can be nothing either more agreeable to my humour or these gentlewomen's desires [than] to use some discourse; as well to renew old traditions, which have been heretofore used, as to increase friendship, which hath been by the means of certain odd persons defaced.'[3]

Everyone gave his consent with Surius, yielding the choice of that night's pastime to the discretion of the Lady Flavia, who thus proposed her mind:

'Your task, Surius, shall be to dispute with Camilla, and choose your own argument; Philautus shall argue with Mistress Frances; Martius with myself. And all having finished their discourses, Euphues shall be as judge who hath done best; and whatsoever he shall allot, either for reward to the worthiest or for penance to the worst, shall be presently accomplished.'

This liked them all exceedingly. And thus Surius, with a good grace and pleasant speech, began to enter the lists[4] with Camilla:

'Fair lady, you know I flatter not. I have read that the sting of an asp were incurable had not nature given them dim eyes,[5] and the beauty of a woman no less infectious had not nature bestowed upon them gentle

---

1 *bold*] familiarly acquainted

2 *the best in the company*] the person of highest rank (cf. p. 205 where the same phrase is used of Iffida in a similar situation)

3 *which hath been ... defaced*] Bond (II, p. 522) suggests that this comment may allude to Puritan opposition to social pursuits.

4 *enter the lists*] embark on a contest (metaphor drawn from jousting)

5 *had not nature ... eyes*] i.e. they are unaware of potential prey

hearts; which maketh me ground my reason upon this commonplace, that beautiful women are ever merciful, if merciful virtuous, if virtuous constant, if constant though no more than goddesses yet no less than saints. All these things granted, I urge my question without condition.

'If, Camilla, one wounded with your beauty (for under that name I comprehend all other virtues) should sue to open his affection, serve to try[1] it, and drive you to so narrow a point that were you never so incredulous he should prove it, yea so far to be from suspicion of deceit that you would confess he were clear from distrust, what answer would you make if you gave your consent, or what excuse if you deny his courtesy?'

Camilla, who desired nothing more than to be questioning with Surius, with a modest countenance yet somewhat bashful (which added more commendation to her speech than disgrace), replied in this manner:

'Though there be no cause, noble gentleman, to suspect an injury where a good turn hath been received, yet is it wisdom to be careful what answer be made where the question is difficult.

'I have heard that the tortoise[2] in India when the sun shineth swimmeth above the water with her back, and being delighted with the fair weather forgetteth herself until the heat of the sun so harden her shell that she cannot sink when she would, whereby she is caught. And so may it fare with me, that in this good company displaying my mind, having more regard to my delight in talking than to the ears of the hearers, I forget what I speak and so be taken in something I should not utter; which haply the itching ears of young gentlemen would so canvass that when I would call it in I cannot, and so be caught with the tortoise when I would not. Therefore, if anything be spoken either unwares or unjustly, I am to crave pardon for both, having but a weak memory and a worse wit. Which you cannot deny me, for that we say women are to be borne withal if they offend against their wills, and not much to be blamed if they trip with their wills; the one proceeding of forgetfulness, the other of their natural weakness.[3] But to the matter.

'If my beauty (which God knows how simple it is) should entangle any with desire, then should I thus think: that either he were inflamed with lust rather than love (for that he is moved by my countenance, not enquiring of my conditions), or else that I gave some occasion of lightness (because he gathereth a hope to speed[4] where he never had the heart to speak). But if at the last I should perceive that his faith were tried like gold in the fire, that his affection proceeded from a mind to please not from a mouth to delude, then would I either answer his love with liking or wean him from it by reason. For I hope, sir, you will not think this,

---

1 *open his affection / try*] disclose his love / prove
2 *tortoise*] turtle
3 *natural weakness*] innate inferiority in relation to men (an orthodox Renaissance view)
4 *conditions / speed*] character / prosecute his suit with success

but that there should be in a woman as well a tongue to deny as in a man to desire; that as men have reason to like for beauty where they love, so women have wit to refuse for sundry causes where they love not. Otherwise were we bound to such an inconvenience that whosoever served us we should answer his suit, when in every respect we mislike his conditions; so that nature might be said to frame us for others' humours, not for our own appetites.[1] Wherein to some we should be thought very courteous, but to the most scarce honest.

'For mine own part, if there be anything in me to be liked of any, I think it reason to bestow on such a one as hath also somewhat to content me; so that where I know myself loved and do love again, I would upon just trial of his constancy take him.'

Surius, without any stop or long pause, replied presently:

'Lady, if the tortoise you spake of in India were as cunning in swimming as you are in speaking, he would neither fear the heat of the sun nor the gin[2] of the fisher. But that excuse was brought in rather to show what you could say than to crave pardon for that you have said. But to your answer.

'What your beauty is I will not here dispute, lest either your modest ears should glow to hear your own praises, or my smooth tongue trip in being curious to[3] your perfection; so that what I cannot commend sufficiently, I will not cease continually to marvel at.

'You wander in one thing out of the way, where you say that many are inflamed with the countenance, not enquiring of the conditions; when this position was before grounded,[4] that there was none beautiful but she was also merciful, and so drawing by the face of her beauty all other moral virtues. For as one ring being touched with the loadstone[5] draweth another, and that his fellow, till it come to a chain, so a lady endued with beauty pulleth on courtesy, courtesy mercy, and one virtue links itself to another until there be a rare perfection.

'Besides, touching your own lightness, you must not imagine that love breedeth in the heart of man by your looks, but by his own eyes; neither by your words when you speak wittily, but by his own ears which conceive aptly. So that were you dumb and could not speak, or blind and could not see, yet should you be beloved; which argueth plainly that the eye of the man is the arrow, the beauty of the woman the white,[6] which shooteth not but receiveth, being the patient not the agent.

'Upon trial you confess you would trust, but what trial you require you conceal; which maketh me suspect that either you would have a trial

---

1 *appetites*] desires
2 *gin*] trap
3 *curious to*] excessively punctilious in seeking to define
4 *this position ... grounded*] it was established at the outset
5 *loadstone*] magnet
6 *white*] target

without mean or without end, either not to be sustained being impossible or not to be finished being infinite. Wherein you would have one run in a circle where there is no way out, or build in the air where there is no means how. This trial, Camilla, must be sifted to narrower points, lest in seeking to try your lover like a jennet you tire him like a jade.[1]

'Then you require this liberty (which truly I cannot deny you) that you may have the choice as well to refuse as the man hath to offer; requiring by that reason some qualities in the person you would bestow your love on, yet craftily hiding what properties either please you best or like women well. Wherein again you move a doubt whether personage, or wealth, or wit, or all are to be required. So that what with the close trial of his faith, and the subtle wishing of his qualities, you make either your lover so holy that for faith he must be made all of truth, or so exquisite that for shape he must be framed in wax. Which if it be your opinion, the beauty you have will be withered before you be wedded, and your wooers good old gentlemen before they be speeders.'

Camilla, not permitting Surius to leap over the hedge which she set for to keep him in, with a smiling countenance shaped him this answer:

'If your position be granted, that where beauty is there is also virtue, then might you add that where a fair flower is there is also a sweet savour; which how repugnant it is to our common experience there is none but knoweth, and how contrary the other is to truth there is none but seeth. Why then do you not set down this for a rule, which is as agreeable to reason, that Rhodopis being beautiful (if a good complexion and fair favour be termed beauty) was also virtuous? That Lais excelling was also honest? That Phryne,[2] surpassing them both in beauty, was also courteous? But it is a reason among your philosophers that the disposition of the mind followeth the composition of the body. How true in arguing it may be, I know not; how false in trial it is, who knoweth not? Beauty, though it be amiable, worketh many things contrary to her fair show; not unlike unto silver which being white draweth black lines, or resembling the tall trees in Ida which allured many to rest in them under their shadow and then infected them with their scent.[3]

'Now whereas you set down that love cometh not from the eyes of the woman but from the glances of the man, under correction be it spoken, it is as far from the truth as the head from the toe. For were a lady blind in what can she be beautiful, if dumb in what manifest her wit, whenas the eye hath ever been thought the pearl of the face and the tongue the ambassador of the heart? If there were such a lady in this company, Surius,

---

1 *sifted to narrower points / jade*] more narrowly defined / ill-conditioned hack (for *jennet* see p. 117n.)

2 *Rhodopis / Lais / Phryne*] all celebrated Greek courtesans

3 *resembling the tall trees ... scent*] Croll and Clemons (p. 389n.) suggest that 'Ida' may be a mistake for 'India' and that the allusion is to the near destruction of Alexander's cavalry by a stand of poisonous trees.

that should wink with both eyes when you would have her see your amorous looks, or be no blab of her tongue[1] when you would have her answer of your questions, I cannot think that either her virtuous conditions or her white and red complexion could move you to love; although this might somewhat procure your liking, that doing what you list she will not see it, and speaking what you would she will not utter it—two notable virtues and rare in our sex, patience and silence!

'But why talk I about ladies that have no eyes, when there is no man that will love them if he himself have eyes? More reason there is to woo one that is dumb, for that she cannot deny your suit; and yet having ears to hear she may as well give an answer with a sign as a sentence. But to the purpose.

'Love cometh not from him that loveth, but from the party loved; else must he make his love upon no cause, and then it is lust, or think himself the cause, and then it is no love. Then must you conclude thus: if there be not in women the occasion, they are fools to trust men that praise them; if the cause be in them, then are not men wise to arrogate it to themselves. It is the eye of the woman that is made of adamant,[2] the heart of the man that is framed of iron; and I cannot think you will say that the virtue attractive is in the iron which is drawn by force, but in the adamant that searcheth it[3] perforce. And this is the reason that many men have been entangled against their wills with love, and kept in it with their wills. You know, Surius, that the fire is in the flint that is stricken, not in the steel that striketh, the light in the sun that lendeth, not in the moon that borroweth, the love in the woman that is served, not in the man that sueth.

'The similitude you brought in of the arrow flew nothing right to beauty,[4] wherefore I must shoot that shaft at your own breast. For if the eye of man be the arrow and beauty the white (a fair mark for him that draweth in Cupid's bow), then must it necessarily ensue that the archer desireth with an aim to hit the white, not the white the arrow, that the mark allureth the archer, not the shooter[5] the mark; and therefore is Venus said in one eye to have two apples,[6] which is commonly applied to those that witch with the eyes, not to those that woo with their eyes.

'Touching trial, I am neither so foolish to desire things impossible, nor so froward to request that which hath no end. But words shall never make me believe without works, lest in following a fair shadow I lose the firm substance. And in one word [to] set down the only trial that a lady

---

1 *blab of her tongue*] chatterer
2 *adamant*] magnetic material
3 *virtue attractive / searcheth it*] power to attract / penetrates it
4 *flew ... beauty*] was misdirected in relation to beauty
5 *shooter*] For the probable pun here see p. 215n.
6 *apples*] pupils

requireth of her lover, it is this: that he perform as much as he swore, that every oath be a deed, every gloze a gospel,[1] promising nothing in his talk that he perform not in his trial.

'The qualities that are required of the mind are good conditions; as temperence not to exceed in diet, chastity not to sin in desire, constancy not to covet change, wit to delight, wisdom to instruct, mirth to please without offence, and modesty to govern without preciseness.[2]

'Concerning the body, as there is no gentlewoman so curious to have him in print, so is there no one so careless to have him a wretch; only his right shape to show him a man, his Christendom to prove his faith, indifferent[3] wealth to maintain his family, expecting all things necessary, nothing superfluous. And to conclude with you, Surius, unless I might have such a one I had as lief[4] be buried as married, wishing rather to have no beauty and die a chaste virgin than no joy and live a cursed wife.'

Surius, as one daunted, having little to answer, yet delighted to hear her speak, with a short speech uttered these words:

'I perceive, Camilla, that be your cloth never so bad it will take some colour,[5] and your cause never so false it will bear some show of probability; wherein you manifest the right nature of a woman, who having no way to win thinketh to overcome with words. This I gather by your answer: that beauty may have fair leaves and foul fruit, that all that are amiable[6] are not honest, that love proceedeth of the woman's perfection and the man's follies, that the trial looked for is to perform whatsoever they promise, that in mind he be virtuous, in body comely. Such a husband, in my opinion, is to be wished for, but not looked for. Take heed, Camilla, that seeking all the wood for a straight stick you choose not at the last a crooked staff, or prescribing a good counsel to others thou thyself follow the worst; much like to Chius, who, selling the best wine to others, drank himself of the lees.'[7]

'Truly,' quoth Camilla, 'my wool was black and therefore it could take no other colour, and my cause good and therefore admitteth no cavil; as for the rules I set down of love, they were not coined of me but learned and, being so true, believed. If my fortune be so ill that searching for a wand I gather a cammock,[8] or selling wine to other I drink vinegar myself,

---

1 *every gloze a gospel*] every eloquent speech the absolute truth
2 *preciseness*] over-nicety
3 *so curious to . . . print / indifferent*] so fastidious to require him to be a model of perfection / moderate
4 *had as lief*] would as willingly
5 *will take some colour*] is capable of being dyed (i.e. can appear to be something better than it is)
6 *amiable*] beautiful
7 *much like to Chius . . . lees*] a simile derived from Erasmus, though the ultimate source is Plutarch (see Croll and Clemons, p. 392n.)
8 *cammock*] crook

I must be content that of the worst poor help patience; which by so much the more is to be borne, by how much the more it is perforce.'[1]

As Surius was speaking, the Lady Flavia prevented him, saying: 'It is time that you break off your speech, lest we have nothing to speak; for should you wade any further you would both waste the night and leave us no time, and take our reasons and leave us no matter. That everyone, therefore, may say somewhat, we command you to cease; that you have both said so well we give you thanks.'

Thus, letting Surius and Camilla to whisper by themselves (whose talk we will not hear), the lady began in this manner to greet Martius:

'We see, Martius, that where young folks are they treat of love, when soldiers meet they confer of war, painters of their colours, musicians of their crotchets, and everyone talketh of that most he liketh best. Which seeing it is so, it behoveth us that have more years to have more wisdom, not to measure our talk by the affections we have had, but by those we should have.

'In this, therefore, I would know thy mind, whether it be convenient for women to haunt such places where gentlemen are, or for men to have access to gentlewomen; which methinketh in reason cannot be tolerable, knowing that there is nothing more pernicious to either than love, and that love breedeth by nothing sooner than looks. They that fear water will come near no wells, they that stand in dread of burning fly from the fire; and ought not they that would not be entangled with desire to refrain company? If love have the pangs which the passionate set down, why do they not abstain from the cause? If it be pleasant, why do they dispraise it? We shun the place of pestilence for fear of infection, the eyes of cathritius[2] because of diseases, the sight of the basilisk for dread of death; and shall we not eschew the company of them that may entrap us in love, which is more bitter than any destruction? If we fly thieves that steal our goods, shall we follow murderers that cut our throats? If we be heedy to come where wasps be, lest we be stung, shall we hazard to run where Cupid is, where we shall be stifled?

'Truly, Martius, in my opinion there is nothing either more repugnant to reason or abhorring from nature than to seek that we should shun, leaving the clear stream to drink of the muddy ditch, or in the extremity of heat to lie in the parching sun when he may sleep in the cold shadow, or being free from fancy to seek after love; which is as much as to cool a hot liver with strong wine, or to cure a weak stomach with raw flesh.

---

1 *of the worst . . . patience / perforce*] a corruption of the proverb that plain patience is the best help of those in worst state / play on the common expression 'patience perforce'

2 *cathritius*] unknown. Bond emends to 'catoblepas' (a wild Ethiopian animal, possibly a buffalo or gnu), cited by Pliny in conjunction with the basilisk. (For *basilisk* see p. 271n.)

'In this I would hear thy sentence,[1] induced the rather to this discourse
for that Surius and Camilla have begun it, than that I like it. Love in me
hath neither power to command nor persuasion to entreat. Which how
idle a thing it is, and how pestilent to youth, I partly know, and you, I
am sure, can guess.'

Martius, not very young to discourse of these matters, yet desirous to
utter his mind, whether it were to flatter Surius in his will or to make trial
of the lady's wit, began thus to frame his answer:

'Madam, there is in Chios[2] the image of Diana, which to those that
enter seemeth sharp and sour, but returning after their suits made looketh
with a merry and pleasant countenance. And it may be that at the entrance
of my discourse ye will bend your brows as one displeased, but hearing
my proof be delighted and satisfied.

'The question you move is whether it be requisite that gentlemen
and gentlewomen should meet. Truly, among lovers it is convenient to
augment desire, amongst those that are firm[3] necessary to maintain
society. For to take away all meeting for fear of love were to kindle
amongst all the fire of hate. There is greater danger, madam, by absence,
which breedeth melancholy, than by presence, which engendereth
affection.

'If the sight be so perilous that the company should be barred, why
then admit you those to see banquets that may thereby surfeit, or suffer
them to eat their meat by a candle that have sore eyes? To be separated
from one I love would make me more constant, and to keep company
with her I love not would not kindle desire. Love cometh as well in at the
ears, by the report of good conditions, as in at the eyes, by the amiable
countenance; which is the cause that divers have loved those they never
saw, and seen those they never loved.

'You allege that those that fear drowning come near no wells, nor they
that dread burning near no fire. Why then, let them stand in doubt also
to wash their hands in a shallow brook, for that Serapus falling into a
channel was drowned, and let him that is cold never warm his hands, for
that a spark fell into the eyes of Actina[4] whereof she died. Let none come
into the company of women, for that divers have been allured to love,
and, being refused, have used violence to themselves. Let this be set down
for a law, that none walk abroad in the day but men, lest meeting a beautiful woman he fall in love and lose his liberty.

'I think, madam, you will not be so precise to cut off all conference

---

1 *sentence*] judgement
2 *Chios*] one of the largest of the Aegean islands, noted for its fine marble. The changing aspect of the statue of Diana (presumably located in a temple) is described in
Erasmus' *Similia* in very similar terms to those that Lyly employs (see Croll and
Clemons, p. 394n.).
3 *convenient / firm*] appropriate / not in the grip of passion
4 *Serapus / Actina*] No source has been found for either allusion, though the name
'Actina' signifies 'full of rays'.

because love cometh by often communication; which if you do, let us all now presently depart, lest in seeing the beauty which dazzleth our eyes and hearing the wisdom which tickleth our ears we be inflamed with love. But you shall never beat the fly from the candle though he burn, nor the quail from hemlock though it be poison, nor the lover from the company of his lady though it be perilous.

'It falleth out sundry times that company is the cause to shake off love; working the effects of the root rhubarb, which being full of choler purgeth choler, or of the scorpion's sting, which being full of poison is a remedy for poison.[1]

'But this I conclude: that to bar one that is in love of the company of his lady maketh him rather mad than mortified; for him to refrain that never knew love is either to suspect him of folly without cause, or the next[2] way for him to fall into folly when he knoweth the cause. A lover is like the herb heliotropium, which always inclineth to that place where the sun shineth, and being deprived of the sun dieth. For as lunaris[3] herb as long as the moon waxeth bringeth forth leaves, and in the waning shaketh them off, so a lover whilst he is in the company of his lady, where all joys increase, uttereth many pleasant conceits, but banished from the sight of his mistress, where all mirth decreaseth, either liveth in melancholy or dieth with desperation.'

The Lady Flavia, speaking in his cast,[4] proceeded in this manner:

'Truly, Martius, I had not thought that as yet your colt's tooth stuck in your mouth,[5] or that so old a truant in love could hitherto remember his lesson. You seem not to infer that it is requisite they should meet, but being in love that it is convenient, lest falling into a mad mood they pine in their own peevishness.[6] Why then, let it follow that the drunkard which surfeiteth with wine be always quaffing because he liketh it, or the Epicure which glutteth himself with meat be ever eating for that it contenteth him; not seeking at any time the means to redress their vices, but to renew them.

'But it fareth with the lover as it doth with him that poureth in much wine, who is ever more thirsty than he that drinketh moderately. For having once tasted the delights of love, he desireth most the thing that hurteth him most, not laying a plaster to the wound but a corrosive. I am of this mind, that if it be dangerous to lay flax[7] to the fire, salt to the eyes, sulphur to the nose, that then it cannot be but perilous to let one lover come in presence of the other.'

---

1 *scorpion's sting . . . poison*] see p. 89n.
2 *next*] readiest
3 *heliotropium / lunaris*] heliotrope, a plant that turns its flowers to the sun / moon-wort, a plant thought to possess a variety of magical properties
4 *speaking in his cast*] interrupting him (see also p. 202)
5 *your colt's tooth . . . mouth*] you retained such youthful leanings
6 *peevishness*] folly
7 *flax*] see p. 202n.

Surius,[1] overhearing the lady and seeing her so earnest, although he were more earnest in his suit to Camilla, cut her off with these words:

'Good madam, give me leave either to depart or to speak; for in truth you gall me more with these terms than you wist,[2] in seeming to inveigh so bitterly against the meeting of lovers which is the only marrow of love. And though I doubt not but that Martius is sufficiently armed to answer you, yet would I not have those reasons refelled[3] which I loathe to have repeated. It may be you utter them not of malice you bear to love, but only to move controversy where there is no question. For if thou envy to have lovers meet, why did you grant us? If allow it, why seek you to separate us?'

The good lady could not refrain from laughter when she saw Surius so angry, who in the midst of his own tale was troubled with hers. Whom she thus again answered:

'I cry you mercy, gentleman, I had not thought to have catched you when I fished for another;[4] but I perceive now that with one bean it is easy to get two pigeons, and with one bait to have divers bites. I see that others may guess where the shoe wrings besides him that wears it.'

'Madam,' quoth Surius, 'you have caught a frog,[5] if I be not deceived, and therefore as good it were not to hurt him as not to eat him. But if all this while you angled to have a bite at a lover, you should have used no bitter medicines but pleasant baits.'

'I cannot tell,' answered Flavia, 'whether my bait were bitter or not, but sure I am I have the fish by the gill. That doth me good.'

Camilla, not thinking to be silent, put in her spoke, as she thought into the best wheel,[6] saying:

'Lady, your cunning may deceive you in fishing with an angle, therefore to catch him you would have you were best to use a net.'

'A net?' quoth Flavia, 'I need none; for my fish playeth in a net already.'

With that, Surius began to wince, replying immediately:

'So doth many a fish, good lady, that slippeth out when the fisher thinketh him fast in; and it may be that either your net is too weak to hold him, or your hand too wet.'

'A wet hand,' quoth Flavia, 'will hold a dead herring.'[7]

'Aye,' quoth Surius, 'but eels are no herrings.'

'But lovers are,' said Flavia.

---

1 *Surius*] The sentence begins 'For Surius' in the copy text, but the first word is omitted in later editions and was probably intended for deletion.

2 *wist*] know

3 *refelled*] answered

4 *another*] i.e. Philautus

5 *caught a frog*] expended effort for no useful purpose (proverbial expression drawn from fishing)

6 *put in her spoke / best wheel*] intervened / better side

7 *dead herring*] Croll and Clemons suggest the allusion may be to the common equation between salt (including salt fish) and the sexual appetite (pp. 397–8n.)

Surius, not willing to have the grass mown whereof he meant to make his hay, began thus to conclude:

'Good lady, leave off fishing for this time; and though it be Lent,[1] rather break a statute which is but penal, than sew a pond that may be perpetual.'[2]

'I am content,' quoth Flavia, 'rather to fast for once than to want a pleasure for ever. Yet, Surius, betwixt us two I will at large prove that there is nothing in love more venomous than meeting, which filleth the mind with grief and the body with diseases. For having the one, he cannot fail of the other. But now, Philautus and niece Frances, since I am cut off, begin you. But be short, because the time is short, and that I was more short than I would.'

Frances, who was ever of wit quick and of nature pleasant, seeing Philautus all this while to be in his dumps,[3] began thus to play with him:

'Gentleman, either you are musing who shall be your second wife or who shall father your first child, else would you not all this while hang your head, neither attending to the discourses that you have heard nor regarding the company you are in. Or it may be (which of both conjectures is likeliest) that hearing so much talk of love you are either driven to the remembrance of the Italian ladies which once you served, or else to the service of those in England which you have since your coming seen. For as Andromache whensoever she saw the tomb of Hector could not refrain from weeping, or as Laodamia[4] could never behold the picture of Protesilaus in wax but she always fainted, so lovers whensoever they view the image of their ladies, though not the same substance yet the similitude in shadow, they are so benumbed in their joints and so bereft of their wits that they have neither the power to move their bodies to show life nor their tongues to make answer. So that I, thinking that with your other senses you had also lost your smelling, thought rather to be a thorn whose point might make you feel somewhat, than a violet whose savour could cause you to smell nothing.'

Philautus, seeing this gentlewoman so pleasantly disposed, replied in this manner:

'Gentlewoman, to study for a second wife before I know my first were to resemble the good housewife in Naples, who took thought to bring forth her chickens before she had hens to lay eggs; and to muse who should father my first child were to doubt when the cow is mine who

---

1 *Lent*] a time of abstinence, and therefore appropriate to the catching of fish
2 *break a statute . . . perpetual*] violate a law (i.e. that against eating meat during Lent) which attracts a legal penalty, rather than drain the water from a pond (in order to catch the fish) which may have more enduring consequences
3 *in his dumps*] melancholy
4 *Laodamia*] devoted wife of Protesilaus, who begged the gods to be allowed to talk with her husband for three hours after his death at Troy and caused an effigy, to which she paid divine honours, to be subsequently made of him. (For *Andromache* see p. 159n.)

should own the calf.[1] But I will neither be so hasty to beat my brains about two wives before I know where to get one, nor so jealous to mistrust her fidelity when I have one. Touching the view of ladies or the remembrance of my loves, methinketh it should rather sharp the point in me than abate the edge. My senses are not lost, though my labour be; and therefore, my good violet, prick not him forward with sharpness whom thou shouldst rather comfort with savours.

'But to put you out of doubt that my wits were not all this while a-wool-gathering, I was debating with myself whether in love it were better to be constant, bewraying all the counsels, or secret, being ready every hour to flinch.[2] And so many reasons came to confirm either that I could not be resolved of any. To be constant, what thing more requisite in love; when it shall always be green like the ivy though the sun parch it, that shall ever be hard like the true diamond though the hammer beat it, that still groweth with the good vine though the knife cut it? Constancy is like unto the stork, who wheresoever she fly cometh into no nest but her own, or the lapwing, whom nothing can drive from her young ones but death. But to reveal the secrets of love, the counsels, the conclusions, what greater despite[3] to his lady or more shameful discredit to himself can be imagined; when there shall no letter pass but it shall be disclosed, no talk uttered but it shall be again repeated, nothing done but it shall be revealed? Which when I considered, methought it better to have one that should be secret though fickle, than a blab[4] though constant.

'For what is there in the world that more delighteth a lover than secrecy, which is void of fear, without suspicion, free from envy, the only hope a woman hath to build both her honour and her honesty upon? The tongue of a lover should be like the point in the dial, which though it go none can see it going, or a young tree, which though it grow none can perceive it growing; having always the stone in their mouth which the cranes use when they fly over mountains lest they make a noise.[5] But to be silent and lightly esteem of his lady, to shake her off though he be secret, to change for everything though he bewray nothing, is the only thing that cutteth the heart in pieces of a true and constant lover. Which deeply weighing with myself, I preferred him that would never remove though he revealed all, before him that would conceal all and ever be sliding. Thus, wafting to and fro, I appeal to you, my good violet, whether in love be more required, secrecy or constancy?'

Frances, with her accustomable boldness, yet modestly, replied as followeth:

---

1 *were to doubt . . . calf*] a common analogy in sixteenth-century paternity cases (cf. Shakespeare, *King John*, I.i.123–4)

2 *bewraying / flinch*] revealing / be unfaithful

3 *despite*] injury

4 *blab*] one unable to govern his tongue

5 *having always the stone . . . noise*] see p. 158n.

'Gentleman, if I should ask you whether in the making of a good sword iron were more to be required or steel, sure I am you would answer that both were necessary; or if I should be so curious to demand whether, in a tale told to your ladies, disposition[1] or [inv]ention [be] most convenient, I cannot think but you would judge them both expedient. For as one metal is to be tempered with another in fashioning a good blade, lest either being all of steel it quickly break or all of iron it never cut, so fareth it in speech, which if it be not seasoned as well with wit to move delight as with art to manifest cunning, there is no eloquence. And in no other manner standeth it with love; for to be secret and not constant, or constant and not secret, were to build a house of mortar without stones, or a wall of stones without mortar. There is no lively picture drawn without colour, no curious[2] image wrought with one tool, no perfect music played with one string; and wouldst thou have love, the pattern of eternity, coloured either with constancy alone or only secrecy?

'There must in every triangle be three lines: the first beginneth, the second augmenteth, the third concludeth it a figure. So, in love, three virtues: affection which draweth the heart, secrecy which increaseth the hope, constancy which finish[eth] the work. Without any of these lines there can be no triangle, without any of these virtues no love. There is no man that runneth with one leg, no bird that flieth with one wing, no love that lasteth with one limb. Love is likened to the emerald, which cracketh rather than consenteth to any disloyalty,[3] and can there be any greater villainy than being secret not to be constant, or being constant not to be secret? But it falleth out with those that being constant and yet full of babble as it doth with the serpent jaculus[4] and the viper, who burst with their own brood, as these are torn with their own tongues.

'It is no question, Philautus, to ask which is best when, being not joined, there is never a good. If thou make a question where there is no doubt, thou must take an answer where there is no reason. Why then also dost thou not enquire whether it were better for a horse to want his forelegs or his hinder, when having not all he cannot travel? Why art thou not inquisitive whether it were more convenient for the wrestlers in the games of Olympia to be without arms or without feet, or for trees to want roots or lack tops, when either is impossible? There is no true lover, believe me, Philautus—sense telleth me so, not trial—that hath not faith, secrecy, and constancy. If thou want either, it is lust, no love; and that thou hast not them all thy profound question assureth me. Which if thou didst ask to try my wit, thou thoughtest me very dull; if t[o] resolve thyself of a doubt, I cannot think thee very sharp.'

---

1 *disposition*] artistry
2 *curious*] exquisitely worked
3 *which cracketh . . . disloyalty*] a traditional property of the emerald
4 *jaculus*] a snake said to dart from trees to attack its prey. For the birth of serpents
   see p. 157n.

Philautus, that perceived her to be so sharp, thought once again like a whetstone to make her sharper, and in these words returned his answer:

'My sweet violet, you are not unlike unto those who, having gotten the start in a race, think none to be near their heels because they be foremost. For having the tale in your mouth you imagine it is all truth, and that none can control[1] it.'

Frances, who was not willing to hear him go forward in so fond an argument, cut him off before he should come to his conclusion:

'Gentleman, the faster you run after me, the further you are from me. Therefore I would wish you to take heed that in seeking to strike at my heels you trip not up your own. You would fain with your wit cast a white upon black, wherein you are not unlike unto those that seeing their shadow very short in the sun think to touch their head with their heel, and putting forth their leg are further from it than when they stood still. In my opinion, it were better to sit on the ground with little ease, than to rise and fall with great danger.'

Philautus, being in a maze to what end this talk should tend, thought that either Camilla had made her privy to his love or that she meant by suspicion to entrap him. Therefore, meaning to leave his former question and to answer her speech, proceeded thus:

'Mistress Frances, you resemble in your sayings the painter Timanthes,[2] in whose pictures there was ever more understood than painted; for with a gloze you seem to shadow that which in colours you will not show. It cannot be, my violet, that the faster I run after you the further I should be from you, unless that either you have wings tied to your heels or I thorns thrust into mine. The last dog oftentimes catcheth the hare, though the fleetest turn him;[3] the slow snail climbeth the tower at last, though the swift swallow mount it; the laziest winneth the goal sometimes, though the lightest[4] be near it. In hunting I had as lief stand at the receipt as at the loosing,[5] in running rather endure long with an easy amble than leave off being out of wind with a swift gallop; especially when I run as Hippomenes did with Atalanta, who was the last in the course but first at the crown.[6] So that I guess that women are either easy to be out-stripped, or willing.

'I seek not to trip at you, because I might so hinder you and hurt myself; for in letting your course by striking at your short heels, you would, when

---

1 *control*] refute
2 *Timanthes*] see p. 173n. The allusion is to his masterpiece, the sacrifice of Iphigenia, in which Agamemnon's face is veiled to permit the spectator to imagine his grief.
3 *turn him*] overtake and deflect him from his course
4 *lightest*] swiftest
5 *as lief ... loosing*] as soon take up my position at the point of interception as at the start
6 *Hippomenes ... crown*] see p. 122n.

I should crave pardon, show me a high instep.[1] As for my shadow, I never go about to reach it but when the sun is at the highest, for then is my shadow at the shortest; so that it is not difficult to touch my head with my heel, when it lieth almost under my heel.

'You say it is better to sit still than to arise and fall, and I say he that never climbeth for fear of falling is like unto him that never drinketh for fear of surfeiting. If you think either the ground so slippery wherein I run that I must needs fall, or my feet so chill that I must needs founder, it may be I will change my course hereafter, but I mean to end it now. For I had rather fall out of a low window to the ground than hang in midway by a brier.'

Frances, who took no little pleasure to hear Philautus talk, began to come on roundly[2] in these terms:

'It is a sign, gentleman, that your footmanship is better than your stomach; for, whatsoever you say, methinketh you had rather be held in a slip than let slip.[3] Wherein you resemble the greyhound that seeing his game leapeth upon him that holdeth him, not running after that he is held for; or the hawk which being cast off at a partridge taketh a stand to prune[4] her feathers, when she should take her flight. For [it] seem you bear good will to the game you cannot play at, or will not, or dare not; wherein you imitate the cat that leaveth the mouse to follow the milk pan. For I perceive that you let the hare go by to hunt the badger.'

Philautus, astonied at this speech, knew not which way to frame his answer, thinking now that she perceived his tale to be addressed to her, though his love were fixed on Camilla. But to rid her of suspicion, though loath that Camilla should conceive any inkling, he played fast and loose in this manner:

'Gentle[wo]man, you mistake me very much, for I have been better taught than fed,[5] and therefore I know how to follow my game, if it be for my gain. For were there two hares to run at, I would endeavour not to catch the first that I followed but the last that I started; yet so as the first should not scape, nor the last be caught.'

'You speak contraries,' quoth Frances, 'and you will work wonders. But take heed your cunning in hunting make you not to lose both.'

'Both?' said Philautus. 'Why, I seek but for one.'

'And yet of two,' quoth Frances, 'you cannot tell which to follow. One runneth so fast you will never catch her, the other is so at the squat[6] you can never find her.'

---

1 *letting your course / high instep*] hindering your progress / act disdainfully towards me (*short heels* carries implications of wantonness)

2 *come on roundly*] respond directly

3 *footmanship ... stomach / held in a slip ... let slip*] ability as a runner is greater than your desire to run / leashed than set free

4 *prune*] preen

5 *taught than fed*] trained than allowed to satisfy my hunger (of dogs, kept hungry to encourage them to the chase)

6 *at the squat*] crouched to the ground

The Lady Flavia, whether desirous to sleep or loath these jests should be too broad, as moderator commanded them both to silence, willing Euphues as umpire in these matters briefly to speak his mind. Camilla and Surius are yet talking, Frances and Philautus are not idle, yet all attentive to hear Euphues, as well for the expectation they had of his wit as to know the drift of their discourses. Who thus began the conclusion of all their speeches:

'It was a law among the Persians that the musician should not judge of the painter, nor anyone meddle in that handicraft wherein he was not expert; which maketh me marvel, good madam, that you should appoint him to be an umpire in love who never yet had skill in his laws. For although I seemed to consent by my silence before I knew the argument whereof you would dispute, yet hearing nothing but reasons for love I must either call back my promise or call in your discourses; and better it were, in my opinion, not to have your reasons concluded than to have them confuted. But sure I am that neither a good excuse will serve where authority is rigorous, nor a bad one be heard where necessity compelleth. But lest I be longer in breaking a web than the spider is in weaving it, your pardons obtained if I offend in sharpness, and your patience granted if molest in length, I thus begin to conclude against you all; not as one singular in his own conceit,[1] but to be tried by your gentle constructions.

'Surius beginneth with love which proceedeth by beauty (under the which he comprehendeth all other virtues). Lady Flavia moveth a question whether the meeting of lovers be tolerable. Philautus cometh in with two branches in his hand, as though there were no more leaves on that tree, asking whether constancy or secrecy be most to be required. Great hold[2] there hath been who should prove his love best, when in my opinion there is none good. But such is the vanity of youth that it thinketh nothing worthy either of commendation or conference but only love; whereof they sow much and reap little, wherein they spend all and gain nothing, whereby they run into dangers before they wist,[3] and repent their desires before they would. I do not discommend honest affection, which is grounded upon virtue as the mean, but disordinate[4] fancy, which is builded upon lust as an extremity; and lust I must term that which is begun in an hour and ended in a minute, the common love in this our age, where ladies are courted for beauty not for virtue, men loved for proportion in body not perfection in mind. It fareth with lovers as with those that drink of the river Gallus[5] in Phrygia, whereof sipping moderately is a medicine, but swilling with excess it breedeth madness.

---

1 *singular in his own conceit*] above all in his own estimation
2 *hold*] contention
3 *wist*] are aware
4 *disordinate*] ungoverned
5 *Gallus*] river said by Pliny to be beneficial for gallstones (see Bond, II, p. 525) but thought to occasion madness in those who drank of it

'Lycurgus[1] set it down for a law that where men were commonly drunken the vines should be destroyed, and I am of that mind that where youth is given to love the means should be removed. For as the earth wherein the mines of silver and gold are hidden is profitable for no other thing but metals, so the heart wherein love is harboured receiveth no other seed but affection. Lovers seek not those things which are most profitable but most pleasant, resembling those that make garlands, who choose the fairest flowers not the wholesomest; and being once entangled with desire they always have the disease, not unlike unto the goat who is never without an ague.[2] Then being once in, they follow the note of the nightingale, which is said with continual straining to sing to perish in her sweet lays, as they do in their sugared lives. Where is it possible either to eat, or drink, or walk, but he shall hear some question of love? Insomuch that love is become so common that there is no artificer of so base a craft, no clown so simple, no beggar so poor, but either talketh of love, or liveth in love, when they neither know the means to come by it, nor the wisdom to increase it. And what can be the cause of these loving worms[3] but only idleness?

'But to set down as a moderator the true perfection of love, not like an enemy to talk of the infection (which is neither the part of my office nor pleasant to your ears), this is my judgement.

'True and virtuous love is to be grounded upon time, reason, favour, and virtue. Time to make trial; not at the first glance so to settle his mind as though he were willing to be caught when he might escape, but so by observation and experience to build and augment his desires that he be not deceived with beauty but persuaded with constancy. Reason, that all his doings and proceedings seem not to flow from a mind inflamed with lust, but a true heart kindled with love. Favour, to delight his eyes, which are the first messengers of affection. Virtue, to allure the soul, for the which all things are to be desired.

'The arguments of faith in a man are constancy not to be removed, secrecy not to utter, security not to mistrust, credulity to believe; in a woman, patience to endure, jealousy to suspect, liberality to bestow, fervency, faithfulness. One of the which branches if either the man want or the woman, it may be a liking between them for the time, but no love to continue for ever.

'Touching Surius his question, whether love come from the man or the woman, it is manifest that it beginneth in both, else can it not end in both. To the Lady Flavia's demand concerning company, it is requisite they should meet; and though they be hindered by divers means, yet is it

---

1 *Lycurgus*] see p. 32n.
2 *the goat . . . ague*] a belief derived from Pliny (see Bond, II, p. 525)
3 *loving worms*] The phrase recurs in *Campaspe* (V.iv.142) and *Mother Bombie* (II.ii.15), and is used in both instances by characters who, like Euphues, are in some way superior or indifferent to passion.

impossible but that they will meet. Philautus must this think, that constancy without secrecy availeth little, and secrecy without constancy profiteth less.

'Thus have I, good madam, according to my simple skill in love, set down my judgement, which you may, at your Ladyship's pleasure, correct; for he that never took the oar in hand must not think scorn to be taught.'

'Well,' quoth the lady, 'you can say more if you list, but either you fear to offend our ears or to bewray your own follies. One may easily perceive that you have been of late in the painter's shop by the colours that stick in your coat.[1] But at this time I will urge nothing, though I suspect somewhat.'

Surius gave Euphues thanks, allowing[2] his judgement in the description of love, especially in this, that he would have a woman if she were faithful to be also jealous, which is as necessary to be required in them as constancy.

Camilla, smiling, said that Euphues was deceived, for he would have said that men should have been jealous; and yet that had been but superfluous, for they are never otherwise.

Philautus, thinking Camilla to use that speech to gird[3] him, for that all that night he viewed her with a suspicious eye, answered that jealousy in a man was to be pardoned, because there is no difference in the look of a lover that can distinguish a jealous eye from a loving.

Frances, who thought her part not to be the least, said that in all things Euphues spake gospel, saving in that he bound a woman to patience, which is to make them fools.

Thus everyone gave his verdict, and so with thanks to the Lady Flavia they all took their leave for that night. Surius went to his lodging, Euphues and Philautus to theirs. Camilla, accompanied with her women and her waiting-maid, departed to her home; whom I mean to bring to her chamber, leaving all the rest to their rest.

Camilla no sooner had entered in her chamber but she began in strange terms to utter this strange tale, her door being close shut and her chamber voided:

'Ah Camilla, ah wretched wench Camilla! I perceive now that when the hop groweth high it must have a pole, when the ivy spreadeth it cleaveth to the flint, when the vine riseth it wreatheth about the elm, when virgins wax in years they follow that which belongeth to their appetites— love. Love? Yea, love, Camilla, the force[4] whereof thou knowest not, and yet must endure the fury. Where is that precious herb panacea which

---

1 *One may easily . . . coat*] it is easy to see you have experience of these matters by the signs you still bear about you
2 *allowing*] approving
3 *gird*] taunt
4 *force*] pun (power / true import)

cureth all diseases? Or that herb nepenthes[1] that procureth all delights? No, no, Camilla. Love is not to be cured by herbs which cometh by fancy, neither can plasters take away the grief which is grown so great by persuasions. For as the stone draconites can by no means be polished unless the lapidary[2] burn it, so the mind [of] Camilla can by no means be cured except Surius ease it.

'I see that love is not unlike unto the stone pantura,[3] which draweth all other stones be they never so heavy, having in it the three roots which they attribute to music—mirth, melancholy, madness.[4]

'Aye but, Camilla, dissemble thy love, though it shorten thy life; for better it were to die with grief, than live with shame. The sponge is full of water, yet is it not seen; the herb adiantum,[5] though it be wet, looketh always dry; and a wise lover, be she never so much tormented, behaveth herself as though she were not touched.

'Aye, but fire cannot be hidden in the flax without smoke, nor musk in the bosom without smell, nor love in the breast without suspicion. Why then, confess thy love to Surius, Camilla, who is ready to ask before thou grant. But it fareth in love as it doth with the root of the reed, which being put unto the fern taketh away all his strength, and likewise the root of the fern put to the reed depriveth it of all his force.[6] So the looks of Surius having taken all freedom from the eyes of Camilla, it may be the glances of Camilla have bereaved Surius of all liberty. Which if it were so, how happy shouldst thou be; and that it is so, why shouldst not thou hope?

'Aye, but Surius is noble. Aye, but love regardeth no birth. Aye, but his friends will not consent. Aye, but love knoweth no kindred. Aye, but he is not willing to love, nor thou worthy to be wooed. Aye, but love maketh the proudest to stoop, and to court the poorest.'

Whilst she was thus debating, one of her maidens chanced to knock, which she hearing left off that which all you gentlewomen would gladly hear; for no doubt she determined to make a long sermon had not she been interrupted. But by the preamble you may guess to what purpose the drift tended. This I note, that they that are most wise, most virtuous, most beautiful, are not free from the impressions of fancy. For who would have thought that Camilla, who seemed to disdain love, should so soon

---

1 *panacea / nepenthes*] herb thought to be a universal cure / a plant reputed to exhilarate when mixed with wine
2 *draconites / lapidary*] see p. 101n. / jeweller
3 *pantura*] identified by Croll and Clemons (p. 408n.) with the pantarbe (known as the stone of the sun), thought to attract gold
4 *having in it . . . madness*] for the power of music to move stones, see p. 256n. The three elements or 'roots' of music were defined by Plutarch.
5 *adiantum*] maidenhair
6 *the root of the reed . . . force*] a variation on Pliny's assertion that the root of a reed could be used to extract fern prickles, and that splinters of reed could be removed by a compound made from the root of a fern (see Bond, II, p. 526)

be entangled? But as the straightest wands are to be bent when they be small, so the precisest virgins are to be won when they be young. But I will leave Camilla, with whose love I have nothing to meddle, for that it maketh nothing to my matter. And return we to Euphues, who must play the last part.

Euphues, bestowing his time in the court, began to mark diligently the men and their manners; not as one curious to misconstrue,[1] but desirous to be instructed. Many days he used speech with the ladies, sundry times with the gentlewomen, with all became so familiar that he was of all earnestly beloved.

Philautus had taken such a smack in the good entertainment of the Lady Flavia that he began to look askew upon Camilla, driving out the remembrance of his old love with the recording of[2] the new. Who now but his violet, who but Mistress Frances?—whom if once every day he had not seen, he would have been so sullen that no man should have seen him.

Euphues, who watched his friend, demanded how his love proceeded with Camilla; unto whom Philautus gave no answer but a smile, by the which Euphues thought his affection but small. At the last, thinking it both contrary to his oath and his honesty to conceal anything from Euphues, he confessed that his mind was changed from Camilla to Frances.

'Love,' quoth Euphues, 'will never make thee mad; for it cometh by fits, not like a quotidian but a tertian.'[3]

'Indeed,' quoth Philautus, 'if ever I kill myself for love, it shall be with a sigh, not with a sword.'

Thus they passed the time many days in England, Euphues commonly in the court to learn fashions, Philautus ever in the country to love Frances—so sweet a violet to his nose that he could hardly suffer it to be an hour from his nose.

But now came the time that Euphues was to try Philautus' truth. For it happened that letters were directed from Athens to London concerning serious and weighty affairs of his own, which incited him to hasten his departure. The contents of the which when he had imparted to Philautus and requested his company, his friend was so fast tied by the eyes that he found thorns in his heel,[4] which Euphues knew to be thoughts in his heart—and by no means he could persuade him to go into Italy, so sweet was the very smoke of England.

Euphues, knowing the tide would tarry for no man, and seeing his business to require such speed, being for his great preferment, determined suddenly to depart; yet not without taking of his leave courteously,

---

1 *curious to misconstrue*] concerned to place a false construction on
2 *smack / the recording of*] delight / descanting on
3 *a quotidian . . . tertian*] a fever that recurs daily but one that returns every other day
4 *so fast tied . . . heel*] so bound to the sight of Frances that he discovered impediments to leave

and giving thanks to all those which since his coming had used him friendly. Which that it might be done with one breath, he desired the merchant with whom all this while he sojourned to invite a great number to dinner, some of great calling, many of good credit, among the which Surius as chief, the Lady Flavia, Camilla, and Mistress Frances were not forgotten.

The time being come of meeting, he saluted them all in this manner:

'I was never more desirous to come into England than I am loath to depart, such courtesy have I found, which I looked not for, and such qualities, as I could not look for; which I speak not to flatter any, when in truth it is known to you all. But now the time is come that Euphues must pack from those whom he best loveth, and go to the seas which he hardly brooketh.[1] But I would fortune had dealt so favourably with a poor Grecian that he might have either been born here or able to live here. Which seeing the one is past and cannot be, the other unlikely and therefore not easy to be, I must endure the cruelty of the one, and with patience bear the necessity of the other.

'Yet this I earnestly crave of you all, that you will instead of a recompense accept thanks, and of him that is able to give nothing take prayer for payment. What my good mind is to you all my tongue cannot utter, what my true meaning is your hearts cannot conceive; yet, as occasion shall serve, I will show that I have not forgotten any, though I may not requite one.

'Philautus, not wiser than I in this though bolder, is determined to tarry behind; for he saith that he had as lief be buried in England as married in Italy, so holy doth he think the ground here, or so homely[2] the women there. Whom although I would gladly have with me, yet seeing I cannot I am most earnestly to request you all, not for my sake who ought to desire nothing, nor for his sake who is able to deserve little, but for the courtesy's sake of England, that you use him, not so well as you have done, which would make him proud, but no worse than I wish him, which will make him pure. For though I speak before his face, you shall find true behind his back that he is yet but wax which must be wrought whilst the water is warm, and iron which, being hot, is apt either to make a key or a lock.

'It may be, ladies and gentlewomen all, that though England be not for Euphues to dwell in, yet it is for Euphues to send to.'

When he had thus said, he could scarce speak for weeping. All the company were sorry to forgo[3] him. Some proffered him money, some lands, some houses, but he refused them all, telling them that not the necessity of lack caused him not[4] to depart, but of importance.

1 *pack / hardly brooketh*] depart / is barely able to endure
2 *as lief / homely*] as willingly / plain
3 *forgo*] lose
4 *not*] possibly a printer's error. Omitted in later editions.

This done, they sat down all to dinner; but Euphues could not be merry for that he should so soon depart. The feast being ended, which was very sumptuous, as merchants never spare for cost when they have full coffers, they all heartily took their leaves of Euphues. Camilla, who liked very well of his company, taking him by the hand desired him that being in Athens he would not forget his friends in England. 'And the rather for your sake,' quoth she, 'your friend shall be better welcome.' 'Yea, and to me for his own sake,' quoth Flavia. Whereat Philautus rejoiced, and Frances was not sorry, who began a little to listen to the lure of love.

Euphues, having all things in a readiness, went immediately toward Dover, whither Philautus also accompanied him; yet not forgetting by the way to visit the good old father Fidus, whose courtesy they received at their coming. Fidus, glad to see them, made them great cheer according to his ability, which had it been less would have been answerable to [their] desires. Much communication they had of the court; but Euphues cried quittance,[1] 'For,' he said, 'things that are commonly known it were folly to repeat, and secrets it were against mine honesty to utter.'

The next morning they went to Dover; where Euphues being ready to take ship, he first took his farewell of Philautus, in these words:

'Philautus, the care that I have had of thee from time to time hath been tried[2] by the counsel I have always given thee; which, if thou have forgotten, I mean no more to write in water, if thou remember, imprint it still. But seeing my departure from thee is as it were my death, for that I know not whether ever I shall see thee, take this as my last testament of my good will.

'Be humble to thy superiors, gentle to thy equals, to thy inferiors be favourable; envy not thy betters, jostle not thy fellows,[3] oppress not the poor.

'The stipend that is allowed to maintain thee use wisely; be neither prodigal to spend all, nor covetous to keep all. Cut thy coat according to thy cloth, and think it better to be accounted thrifty among the wise than a good companion among the riotous.

'For thy study or trade of life, use thy book in the morning, thy bow after dinner—or what other exercise shall please thee best. But always have an eye to the main, whatsoever thou art chanced at the by.[4]

'Let thy practice be law; for the practice of physic is too base for so fine a stomach as thine, and divinity too curious[5] for so fickle a head as thou hast.

---

1 *cried quittance*] had his revenge (in adopting the stance Fidus formerly advocated)
2 *tried*] proved
3 *gentle / favourable / jostle not thy fellows*] courteous / gracious / do not be competitive with your companions
4 *have an eye . . . by*] focus on the most important matters whatever incidental opportunities may arise (see also p. 87n.)
5 *curious*] abstruse

'Touching thy proceedings in love, be constant to one and try but one; otherwise thou shalt bring thy credit into question and thy love into derision. Wean thyself from Camilla, deal wisely with Frances; for in England thou shalt find those that will decipher thy dealings, be they never so politic. Be secret to thyself, and trust none in matters of love as thou lovest thy life.

'Certify me of th[y] proceedings by thy letters; and think that Euphues cannot forget Philautus, who is as dear to me as myself. Commend me to all my friends. And so farewell, good Philautus; and well shalt thou fare, if thou follow the counsel of Euphues.'

Philautus, the water standing in his eyes, not able to answer one word until he had well wept, replied at the last as it were in one word, saying that his counsel should be engraven in his heart and he would follow everything that was prescribed him, certifying him of his success as either occasion or opportunity should serve. But when friends at departing would utter most, then tears hinder most; which brake off both his answer, and stayed Euphues' reply. So after many millions of embracings, at the last they departed,[1] Philautus to London, where I leave him, Euphues to Athens, where I mean to follow him; for he it is that I am to go with, not Philautus.

There was nothing that happened on the seas worthy the writing. But within few days Euphues, having a merry wind, arrived at Athens; where, after he had visited his friends and set an order in his affairs, he began to address his letters to Livia, touching the state of England, in this manner:

Livia,
I salute thee in the Lord etc. I am at length returned out of England, a place in my opinion (if any such may be in the earth) not inferior to a paradise.

I have here enclosed sent thee the description, the manners, the conditions, the government, and entertainment of that country. I have thought it good to dedicate it to the ladies of Italy. If thou think it worthy, as thou canst not otherwise, cause it to be imprinted, that the praise of such an isle may cause those that dwell elsewhere both to commend it and marvel at it.

Philautus I have left behind me, who like an old dog followeth his old scent, love. Wiser he is than he was wont, but as yet nothing more fortunate. I am in health, and that thou art so I hear nothing to the contrary; but I know not how it fareth with me, for I cannot as yet brook[2] mine own country, I am so delighted with another.

Advertise me by letters what estate[3] thou art in, also how thou likest the state of England which I have sent thee. And so farewell.
Thine to use,
Euphues.

---

1 *departed*] went their separate ways
2 *brook*] bear
3 *estate*] state

TO THE LADIES AND GENTLEWOMEN
OF ITALY, EUPHUES WISHETH HEALTH
AND HONOUR

If I had brought, ladies, little dogs from Malta, or strange stones[1] from India, or fine carpets from Turkey, I am sure that either you would have wooed me to have them or wished to see them. But I am come out of England with a glass,[2] wherein you shall behold the things which you never saw, and marvel at the sights when you have seen. Not a glass to make you beautiful but to make you blush, yet not at your vices but others' virtues; not a glass to dress your hairs but to redress your harms, by the which if you every morning correct your manners, being as careful to amend faults in your hearts as you are curious to find faults in your heads,[3] you shall in short time be as much commended for virtue of the wise as for beauty of the wanton.

Yet at the first sight [if] you seem deformed by looking in this glass, you must not think that the fault is in the glass but in your manners; not resembling Lavia,[4] who, seeing her beauty in a true glass to be but deformity, washed her face and broke the glass.

Here shall you see beauty accompanied with virginity, temperance, mercy, justice, magnanimity, and all other virtues whatsoever; rare in your sex, and but one,[5] and rarer than the phoenix where I think there is not one.

In this glass shall you see that the glasses[6] which you carry in your fans of feathers show you to be lighter than feathers, that the glasses wherein you carouse your wine make you to be more wanton than Bacchus, that the new-found glass chains that you wear about your necks argue you to be more brittle than glass. But your eyes being too old to judge of so rare a spectacle, my counsel is that you look with spectacles; for ill can you abide the beams of the clear sun, being scant able to view the blaze of a dim candle. The spectacles I would have you use are, for the one eye, judgement without flattering yourselves, for the other eye, belief without mistrusting of me. And then I doubt not but you shall both thank me for this glass (which I send also into all places of Europe), and think worse of your garish glasses, which maketh you of no more price than broken glasses.

Thus, fair ladies, hoping you will be as willing to pry in this glass for amendment of manners as you are to prank yourselves in a looking-glass for commendation of men, I wish you as much beauty as you would have, so as you would endeavour to have as much virtue as you should have. And so farewell.

Euphues.

---

1 *little dogs from Malta / strange stones*] fashionable ladies' pets in the sixteenth century / exotic jewels
2 *glass*] looking-glass
3 *curious to find . . . heads*] at pains to detect faults in your hair-styles
4 *Lavia*] The name is derived from Latin *lavare* (to wash), hence 'washed her face', but no source has been found for the allusion.
5 *but one*] i.e. Elizabeth
6 *glasses*] looking-glasses, mirrors

There is an isle, lying in the Ocean Sea directly against that part of France which containeth Picardy and Normandy, called now England, heretofore named Britain. It hath Ireland upon the west side, on the north the main sea, on the east side the Germany Ocean. This island is in circuit 1,720 miles, in form like unto a triangle, being broadest in the south part, and gathering narrower and narrower till it come to the furthest point of Caithness northward, where it is narrowest; and there endeth in manner of a promontory.

To repeat the ancient manner of this island, or what sundry nations have inhabited there, to set down the giants, which in bigness of bone have passed the common size and almost common credit, to rehearse what diversities of languages have been used, into how many kingdoms it hath been divided, what religions have been followed before the coming of Christ, although it would breed great delight to your ears yet might it happily seem tedious; for that honey taken excessively cloyeth the stomach, though it be honey. But my mind is briefly to touch such things as at my being there I gathered by mine own study and enquiry, not meaning to write a chronicle, but to set down in a word what I heard by conference.[1]

It hath in it twenty six cities, of which the chiefest is named London; a place both for the beauty of building, infinite riches, variety of all things, that excelleth all the cities in the world, insomuch that it may be called the storehouse and mart of all Europe. Close by this city runneth the famous river called the Thames, which from the head where it riseth, named Isis, unto the fall Medway[2] it is thought to be an hundred and fourscore miles. What can there be in any place under the heavens that is not in this noble city either to be bought or borrowed?

It hath divers hospitals[3] for the relieving of the poor, six score fair churches for divine service, a glorious burse,[4] which they call the Royal Exchange, for the meeting of merchants of all countries where any traffic is to be had. And among all the strange and beautiful shows, methinketh there is none so notable as the bridge which crosseth the Thames; which is in manner of a continual street, well replenished with large and stately houses on both sides, and situate upon twenty arches, whereof each one is made of excellent free-stone[5] squared, every one of them being three score foot in height, and full twenty in distance one from another.

---

1 *not meaning to write . . . conference*] A more humorous observation than appears at first sight, in that Lyly relies heavily in the account that follows on William Harrison's 'Description of England' in Holinshed's *Chronicles* (1577, revised 1587).
2 *fall Medway*] the point at which the river Medway falls into it
3 *hospitals*] charitable institutions for the relief of the needy
4 *burse*] meeting place for merchants for the transaction of business (*traffic* in the same sentence = trade)
5 *free-stone*] fine-grained stone (particularly sandstone or limestone) that can be cut or worked in any direction without fracturing

To this place the whole realm hath his recourse, whereby it seemeth so populous that one would scarce think so many people to be in the whole island as he shall see sometimes in London. This maketh gentlemen brave and merchants rich, citizens to purchase and sojourners to mortgage,[1] so that it is to be thought that the greatest wealth and substance of the whole realm is couched within the walls of London; where they that be rich keep it from those that be riotous,[2] not detaining it from the lusty youths of England by rigour, but increasing it until young men shall savour of reason, wherein they show themselves treasurers for others, not hoarders for themselves. Yet although it be sure enough, would they[3] had it; in my opinion it were better to be in the gentleman's purse than in the merchant's hands.

There are in this isle two and twenty bishops, which are as it were superintendents over the church; men of great zeal and deep knowledge, diligent preachers of the Word, earnest followers of their doctrine, careful watchmen that the wolf devour not the sheep,[4] in civil government politic, in ruling the spiritual sword (as far as to them under their prince appertaineth)[5] just, cutting off those members from the church by rigour that are obstinate in their heresies and instructing those that are ignorant, appointing godly and learned ministers in every of their sees that in their absence may be lights to such as are in darkness, salt to those that are unsavoury, leaven[6] to such as are not seasoned. Visitations[7] are holden oftentimes, whereby abuses and disorders, either in the laity for negligence or in the clergy for superstition or in all for wicked living, there are punishments, by due execution whereof the divine service of God is honoured with more purity and followed with greater sincerity.

There are also in this island two famous universities, the one Oxford, the other Cambridge; both for the profession of all sciences, for divinity, physic, law, and all kind of learning, excelling all the universities in Christendom. I was myself in either[8] of them, and like them both so well that I mean not in the way of controversy to prefer any for the better in England, but both for the best in the world; saving this, that colleges in Oxford are much more stately for the building, and Cambridge much more sumptuous for the houses in the town. But the learning neither lieth in the free-stones of the one nor the fine streets of the other, for out of them both do daily proceed men of great wisdom to rule in the commonwealth, of learning to instruct the common people, of all singular kind of professions to do good to all. And let this suffice, not to enquire which of them is the superior, but that neither of

---

1 *mortgage*] i.e. to mortgage their estates in order to meet their costs (*brave* = finely dressed)
2 *they that be rich ... riotous*] wealthy merchants hold lands in trust for prodigal young heirs
3 *sure / they*] safe / the young gentlemen
4 *the wolf devour not the sheep*] the Christian flock does not fall prey to malign forces (more specifically to the Roman Catholic Church)
5 *as far to them ... appertaineth*] The monarch, as head of the Anglican church, had ultimate authority in spiritual matters.
6 *leaven*] see p. 100n.
7 *Visitations*] official visits by a bishop to a diocese for the purpose of inspection
8 *either*] both (derived from Lyly's source and not necessarily to be taken as a biographical reference)

them have their equal; neither to ask which of them is the most ancient, but whether any other be so famous.

But to proceed in England. Their buildings are not very stately, unless it be the houses of noblemen, and here and there the place of a gentleman, but much amended,[1] as they report that have told me. For their munition, they have not only great store, but also great cunning to use them and courage to practise them. Their armour is not unlike unto that which in other countries they use, as corselets, Almain rivets, shirts of mail, jacks[2] quilted and covered over with leather, fustian,[3] or canvas, over thick plates of iron that are sewed in the same. The ordnance they have is great, and thereof great store.

Their navy is divided as it were into three sorts, of the which the one serveth for wars, the other for burden,[4] the third for fishermen. And some vessels there be (I know not by experience, and yet I believe by circumstance) that will sail nine hundred miles in a week, when I should scarce think that a bird could fly four hundred.

Touching other commodities, they have four baths, the first called St Vincent's, the second Holywell,[5] the third Buxton, the fourth (as in old time they read) Cair Bledud, but now, taking his name of a town near adjoining it, is called the Bath. Besides this, many wonders there are to be found in this island, which I will not repeat because I myself never saw them, and you have heard of greater.

Concerning their diet, in number of dishes and change of meat[6] the nobility of England do exceed most, having all things that either may be bought for money or gotten for the season. Gentlemen and merchants feed very finely, and a poor man it is that dineth with one dish, and yet so content with a little that having half dined they say, as it were in a proverb, that they are as well satisfied as the Lord Mayor of London, whom they think to fare best, though he eat not most. In their meals there is great silence and gravity, using wine rather to ease the stomach than to load it; not like unto other nations, who never think that they have dined till they be drunken.

The attire they use is rather led by the imitation of others than their own invention, so that there is nothing in England more constant than the inconstancy of attire. Now using the French fashion, now the Spanish, then the Morisco[7] gowns, then one thing, then another—insomuch that in drawing of an Englishman the painter setteth him down naked, having in the one hand a pair of shears, in the other a piece of cloth,[8] who having cut his collar after

---

1 *amended*] improved
2 *corselets / Almain rivets / jacks*] armour for the upper body / armour of German origin consisting of overlapping plates connected by rivets sliding in slot-holes (see Bond, II, pp. 527–8) / sleeveless protective coat worn by foot soldiers
3 *fustian*] coarse cloth made of cotton and flax
4 *burden*] the transport of goods
5 *St Vincent's / Holywell*] Bond notes that 'the St Vincent Rocks near the Clifton suspension-bridge preserve the name of the hot springs once frequented there' (II, p. 528) / located on the Dee in Flintshire (Wales)
6 *change of meat*] variety of food
7 *Morisco*] Moorish
8 *in drawing of an Englishman . . . cloth*] Such a picture was painted in 1570 for the Earl of Lincoln (see Bond, II, p. 528), but Lyly is relying here on his source (see p. 322n.)

the French guise is ready to make his sleeve after the Barbarian[1] manner. And although this were the greatest enormity that I could see in England, yet is it to be excused; for they that cannot maintain this pride must leave of necessity, and they that be able will leave when they see the vanity.

The laws they use are different from ours, for although the common[2] and civil law be not abolished, yet are they not had in so great reputation as their own common laws, which they term the laws of the Crown. The regiment[3] that they have dependeth upon statute law, and that is by Parliament, which is the highest court, consisting of three several sorts of people, the nobility, clergy, and commons of the realm; so as whatsoever be among them enacted, the Queen striketh the stroke,[4] allowing such things as to Her Majesty seemeth best. Then upon common law, which standeth upon maxims and principles, years and terms. The cases in this law are called pleas or actions, and they are either criminal or civil; the means to determine are writs, some original, some judicial.[5] Their trials and recoveries are either by verdict or demur, confession or default;[6] wherein if any fault hath been committed either in process or form, matter or judgement, the party grieved may have a writ of error.[7] Then upon customable law, which consisteth upon laudable customs used in some private country.[8] Last of all upon prescription, which is a certain custom continued time out of mind, but it is more particular than their customary law. Murderers and thieves are hanged, witches burned, all other villainies that deserve death punished with death; insomuch that there are very few heinous offences practised, in respect of those that in other countries are commonly used.

Of savage beasts and vermin they have no great store, nor any that are noisome.[9] The cattle they keep for profit are oxen, horses, sheep, goats, and swine, and such like, whereof they have abundance. Wildfowl and fish they want none, nor anything that either may serve for pleasure or profit. They have more store of pasture than tillage, their meadows better than their corn field; which maketh more graziers than cornmongers, yet sufficient store of both. They excel for one thing, their dogs of all sorts—spaniels, hounds, mastiffs and divers such. The one they keep for hunting and hawking, the other for necessary uses about their houses, as to draw water, to watch thieves, etc. And thereof they derive the word mastiff, of 'mase' and 'thief'.[10]

---

1 *after the French guise / Barbarian*] in the French fashion / see p. 176n.
2 *common*] possibly a mistake for 'canon' but not corrected in later editions
3 *regiment*] system of government
4 *striketh the stroke*] has the ultimate authority
5 *some original, some judicial*] some from a plaintiff, some from a criminal proceeding
6 *demur / default*] a plea which admits the facts of a case but denies that the plaintiff is entitled to redress / failure to perform a legal requirement (e.g. failure to attend the court on the day assigned)
7 *writ of error*] writ brought to procure the reversal of a judgement on the grounds of some procedural fault
8 *customable / used in some private country*] customary / exclusive to a particular land
9 *noisome*] poisonous
10 *And thereof they derive . . . 'thief'*] erroneous derivation from Harrison's 'Description of England' where *mase* = master

There is in that isle salt made, and saffron. There are great quarries of stone for building, sundry minerals of quicksilver, antimony, sulphur, black lead, and orpiment red and yellow.[1] Also there groweth[2] the finest alum that is, vermilion, bitumen, chrysocolla, copperas,[3] the mineral stone whereof petroleum is made, and that which is most strange, the mineral pearl, which as they are for greatness and colour most excellent, so are they digged out of the mainland, in places far distant from the shore. Besides these, though not strange, yet necessary, they have coal mines, saltpetre[4] for ordnance, salt-soda for glass. They want no tin, nor lead; there groweth iron, steel, and copper—and what not? So hath God blessed that country as it should seem not only to have sufficient to serve their own turns but also others' necessities; whereof there was an old saying, 'All countries stand in need of Britain, and Britain of none.'

Their air is very wholesome and pleasant, their civility not inferior to those that deserve best, their wits very sharp and quick; although I have heard that the Italian and the Frenchman have accounted them but gross and dull-pated, which I think came not to pass by the proof they made of their wits but by the Englishman's report. For this is strange (and yet how true it is there is none that ever travelled thither but can report) that it is always incident to an Englishman to think worst of his own nation, either in learning, experience, common reason, or wit; preferring always a stranger rather for the name than the wisdom. I for mine own part think that in all Europe there are not lawyers more learned, divines more profound, physicians more expert than are in England. But that which most allureth a stranger is their courtesy, their civility, and good entertainment. I speak this by experience, that I found more courtesy in England among those I never knew in one year, than I have done in Athens or Italy among those I ever loved in twenty.

But having entreated sufficiently of[5] the country and their conditions, let me come to the glass I promised, being the court. Where although I should, as order requireth, begin with the chiefest, yet I am enforced with the painter to reserve my best colours to end Venus, and to lay the ground with the basest.

First, then, I must tell you of the grave and wise counsellors, whose foresight in peace warrenteth safety in war, whose provision in plenty maketh sufficient in dearth, whose care in health is as it were a preparative against sickness; how great their wisdom hath been in all things the twenty-two years' peace[6] doth both show and prove. For what subtlety hath there been wrought so closely, what privy attempts so craftily, what rebellions stirred up so disorderly, but they have by policy bewrayed, prevented by wisdom, repressed by justice? What conspiracies abroad, what confederacies at home, what injuries in any place hath there been contrived, the which they have not either foreseen before they could kindle, or quenched before they could flame? If any wily Ulysses should feign madness, there was among them always some Palamedes to reveal him; if any Thetis went about to keep her son from the doing of his country service, there was also a wise Ulysses in the court to bewray it; if Sinon came with a smooth tale to bring in the horse into Troy, there hath been always some courageous Laocoon to throw his spear against the bowels, which being not bewitched with Laocoon hath unfolded that which Laocoon suspected.[1] If Argus with his hundred eyes went prying to undermine Jupiter, yet met he with Mercury who whistled all his eyes out; insomuch as there could never yet any craft prevail against their policy, or any challenge against their courage. There hath always been Achilles at home to buckle[2] with Hector abroad, Nestor's gravity to countervail Priam's counsel, Ulysses' subtleties to match with Antenor's policies.[3] England hath all those that can and have wrestled with all others, whereof we can require no greater proof than experience.

Besides, they have all a zealous care for the increasing of true religion, whose faiths for the most part hath been tried through the fire which they had felt had not they fled over the water.[4] Moreover, the great study they bend towards schools of learning doth sufficiently declare that they are not only furtherers of learning but fathers of the learned. O thrice happy England, where such counsellors are, where such people live, where such virtue springeth!

Among these shall you find Zopyrus that will mangle himself to do his country good, Achates that will never start an inch from his Prince Aeneas, Nausicaa that never wanted a shift in extremity, Cato that ever counselled to the best, Ptolemaeus Philadelphus[5] that always maintained learning. Among the number of all which noble and wise counsellors, I cannot but for his honour's sake remember the most prudent and right honourable the Lord Burghley, High Treasurer of that realm, no less reverenced for his wisdom

---

1 *If any wily Ulysses should feign . . . Laocoon suspected*] all instances of the revealing of duplicity prejudicial to a national interest. Ulysses pretended to be mad in
  order to avoid taking part in the Trojan war but was detected by a stratagem propounded by Palamedes; Thetis disguised her son, Achilles, as a maiden to prevent
  him being called upon to fight at Troy but was thwarted by Ulysses who discovered
  his place of concealment; Laocoon attempted to dissuade the Trojans from taking
  the horse devised by Sinon into Troy, and threw a spear, to exhibit its dangerous
  nature, into its side. (For *Argus* and *Mercury* in the following sentence see p. 122n.)
2 *buckle*] combat
3 *Antenor's policies*] the stratagems of one of the wisest of the Trojan elders. (For
  Achilles, Hector, Nestor and *Priam* see pp. 106, 33, 238 and 33nn.)
4 *whose faiths . . . water*] i.e. the majority were victims of persecution under Mary
5 *Zopyrus / Achates / Nausicaa / Ptolemaeus Philadelphus*] probably exemplary figures
  (representative of patriotism, fidelity, wisdom and learning) rather than allusions to
  specific courtiers. Zopyrus, a Persian, mutilated himself in order to gain the confidence of and then betray the Babylonians, representing himself as a victim of Persian
  cruelty; Achates was the armour-bearer and faithful friend of Aeneas; Nausicaa refers
  to Ulysses, aided by a princess of that name in the Odyssey, bk vi. Ptolemaeus
  Philadelphus, son of Ptolemy I, was renowned as a patron of the arts. (For *Cato* see
  p. 174n.)

than renowned for his office, more loved at home than feared abroad, and
yet more feared for his counsel among other nations than sword or fire; in
whom the saying of Agamemnon may be verified, who rather wished for one
such as Nestor than many such as Ajax. This noble man I have found so
ready, being but a stranger, to do me good,[1] that neither I ought to forget him
neither cease to pray for him, that as he hath the wisdom of Nestor so he
may have the age, that having the policies of Ulysses he may have his honour;
worthy to live long by whom so many live in quiet, and not unworthy to be
advanced by whose care so many have been preferred.

Is not this a glass, fair ladies, for all other countries to behold, where there
is not only an agreement in faith, religion, and counsel, but in friendship,
brotherhood, and living? By whose good endeavours vice is punished, virtue
rewarded, peace established, foreign broils repressed, domestical cares
appeased? What nation can of counsellors desire more? What dominion,
that excepted, hath so much, when neither courage can prevail against their
chivalry, nor craft take place[2] against their counsel, nor both joined in one be
of force to undermine their country?

When you have dazzled your eyes with this glass, behold here another.
It was my fortune to be acquainted with certain English gentlemen, which
brought me to the court; where when I came I was driven into a maze to
behold the lusty and brave gallants, the beautiful and chaste ladies, the rare
and godly orders, so as I could not tell whether I should most commend virtue
or bravery.[3] At the last, coming oftener thither than it beseemed one of my
degree, yet not so often as they desired my company, I began to pry after their
manners, natures and lives; and that which followeth I saw, whereof whoso
doubteth I will swear.

The ladies spend the morning in devout prayer; not resembling the gentlewomen in Greece and Italy, who begin their morning at midnoon and make
their evening at midnight, using sonnets for psalms and pastimes for prayers,
reading the epistle of a lover when they should peruse the gospel of our Lord,
drawing wanton lines when death is before their face, as Archimedes[4] did triangles and circles when the enemy was at his back. Behold, ladies, in this
glass that the service of God is to be preferred before all things. Imitate the
English damsels, who have their books tied to their girdles, not feathers, who
are as cunning in the scriptures as you are in Ariosto or Petrarch,[5] or any
book that liketh you best and becometh you worst.

For bravery I cannot say that you exceed them, for certainly it is the most
gorgeous court that ever I have seen, read, or heard of. But yet do they not
use their apparel so nicely[6] as you in Italy, who think scorn to kneel at service

---

1 *This noble man . . . good*] For Lyly's relations with Burghley see Introduction, p. 2
   and 19n.
2 *take place*] be effectual
3 *orders / bravery*] observances / magnificence
4 *drawing wanton lines / Archimedes*] making up their faces (by drawing lines with
   cosmetics) / celebrated Greek mathematician (b. 287 BC), killed when Syracuse fell
   to the Romans, being too intent on a mathematical problem to make his escape
5 *Ariosto or Petrarch*] both Italian writers concerned with love. Ariosto's *Orlando
   Furioso* (pub. 1532) was widely known in England, while the statement that English
   ladies were indifferent to Petrarch runs counter to pp. 270–1 above.
6 *so nicely*] with such fastidiousness

for fear of wrinkles in your silks, who dare not lift up your head to heaven for fear of rumpling the ruffs in your neck; yet your hands, I confess, are holden up, rather I think to show your rings than to manifest your right-eousness. The bravery they use is for the honour of their Prince,[1] the attire you wear for the alluring of your prey; the rich apparel maketh their beauty more seen, your disguising causeth your faces to be more suspected; they resemble in their raiment the ostrich, who being gazed on closeth her wings and hideth her feathers, you in your robes are not unlike the peacock, who being praised spreadeth her tail and bewrayeth her pride. Velvets and silks in them are like gold about a pure diamond, in you like a green hedge about a filthy dunghill.

Think not, ladies, that because you are decked with gold you are endued with grace; imagine not that shining like the sun in earth ye shall climb the sun in heaven. Look diligently into this English glass, and then shall you see that the more costly your apparel is the greater your courtesy should be, that you ought to be as far from pride as you are from poverty, and as near to princes in beauty as you are in brightness. Because you are brave disdain not those that are base. Think with yourselves that russet coats have their Christendom,[2] that the sun when he is at his height shineth as well upon coarse kersey as cloth of tissue.[3] Though you have pearls in your ears, jewels in your breasts, precious stones on your fingers, yet disdain not the stones in the street, which although they are nothing so noble, yet are they much more necessary. Let not your robes hinder your devotion; learn of the English ladies that God is worthy to be worshipped with the most price, to whom you ought to give all praise. Then shall you be like stars to the wise, who now are but staring-stocks[4] to the foolish, then shall you be praised of most, who are now pointed at of all, then shall God bear with your folly, who now abhorreth your pride.

As the ladies in this blessed island are devout and brave,[5] so are they chaste and beautiful; insomuch that when I first beheld them I could not tell whether some mist had bleared mine eyes or some strange enchantment altered my mind. 'For it may be,' thought I, 'that in this island either some Artemidorus, or Lisimandro,[6] or some odd necromancer did inhabit, who would show me fairies, or the body of Helen, or the new shape of Venus.' But coming to myself and seeing that my senses were not changed, but hindered, that the place where I stood was no enchanted castle, but a gallant court, I could scarce restrain my voice from crying, 'There is no beauty but in England!' There did I behold them of pure complexion exceeding the lily and the rose, of favour (wherein the chiefest beauty consisteth) surpassing the pictures that were feigned or the magician that would feign. Their eyes piercing like the sun-

1 *bravery / Prince*] finery / monarch (i.e. Elizabeth)
2 *russet coats have their Christendom*] poor men are part of the Christian church as you are (*russet* = reddish-brown homespun fabric worn by peasants)
3 *kersey / cloth of tissue*] rough woollen cloth / fine cloth interwoven with threads of gold or silver
4 *staring-stocks*] objects to be gazed at
5 *brave*] splendid in appearance
6 *Artemidorus / Lisimandro*] author of a lengthy work on dreams, written in the mid second century, designed to demonstrate that they foretell the future / untraced

beams, yet chaste; their speech pleasant and sweet, yet modest and courteous; their gait comely, their bodies straight, their hands white. All things that man could wish or woman would have; which how much it is none can set down, whenas the one desireth as much as may be, the other more. And to these beautiful moulds,[1] chaste minds; to these comely bodies, temperance, modesty, mildness, sobriety. Whom I often beheld merry, yet wise; conferring with courtiers, yet warily; drinking of wine, yet moderately; eating of delicates, yet but their ear full;[2] listing to discourses of love, but not without reasoning of learning. For there it more delighteth them to talk of Robin Hood than to shoot in his bow,[3] and greater pleasure they take to hear of love than to be in love.

Here ladies is a glass that will make you blush for shame and look wan for anger. Their beauty cometh by nature, yours by art; they increase their favours with fair water, you maintain yours with painters' colours; the hair they lay out groweth upon their own heads, your seemliness hangeth upon others; theirs is always in their own keeping, yours often in the dyer's; their beauty is not lost with a sharp blast, yours fadeth with a soft breath: not unlike unto paper flowers which break as soon as they are touched, resembling the birds in Egypt called ibis who being handled lose their feathers, or the serpent serapie[4] which being but touched with a brake bursteth. They use their beauty because it is commendable, you because you would be common;[5] they if they have little do not seek to make it more, you that have none endeavour to bespeak most. If theirs wither by age they nothing esteem it,[6] if yours waste by years you go about to keep it; they know that beauty must fail if life continue, you swear that it shall not fade if colours last.

But to what end, ladies, do you alter the gifts of nature by the shifts[7] of art? Is there no colour good but white, no planet bright but Venus, no linen fair but lawn? Why go ye about to make the face fair by those means that are most foul, a thing loathsome to man and therefore not lovely, horrible before God and therefore not lawful? Have you not heard that the beauty of the cradle is most brightest, that paintings are for pictures without sense, not for persons with true reason? Follow at the last, ladies, the gentlewomen of England, who being beautiful do those things as shall become so amiable faces, if of an indifferent hue those things as they shall make them lovely, not adding an ounce to beauty that may detract a dram from virtue.

Besides this, their chastity and temperance is as rare as their beauty; not going in your footsteps that drink wine before you rise to increase your colour, and swill it when you are up to provoke your lust. They use their needle to

---

1 *moulds*] bodies
2 *but their ear full*] Bond suggests (II, p. 531) that the phrase denotes a very small quantity, but Lyly may intend that the attention of the ladies is on conversation (i.e. food for the mind) rather than delicacies.
3 *to talk of Robin Hood . . . bow*] proverbial, signifying to know about a subject without being actively engaged in it
4 *ibis / serapie*] No source has been found either for the ibis' aversion to being touched or for a serapie. Pliny does, however, note a cerastes, a horned worm injurious to trees (*brake* = bush).
5 *common*] a matter of public talk
6 *they nothing esteem it*] they do not consider it important
7 *shifts*] devices

banish idleness, not the pen to nourish it; not spending their times in answering the letters of those that woo them, but forswearing the company of those that write them; giving no occasion, either by wanton looks, unseemly gestures, unadvised speech, or any uncomely behaviour, of lightness or liking; contrary to the custom of many countries where filthy words are accounted to savour of a fine wit, broad speech of a bold courage, wanton glances of a sharp eyesight, wicked deeds of a comely gesture, all vain delights of a right courteous[1] courtesy. And yet are they not in England precise but wary, not disdainful to confer but careful to offend, not without remorse[2] where they perceive truth but without replying where they suspect treachery; whenas among other nations there is no tale so loathsome to chaste ears but it is heard with great sport and answered with great speed.

Is it not then a shame, ladies, that that little island should be a mirror to you, to Europe, to the whole world? Where is the temperance you profess when wine is more common than water? Where the chastity when lust is thought lawful? Where the modesty when your mirth turneth to uncleanness, uncleannness to shamelessness, shamelessness to all sinfulness? Learn, ladies, though late yet at length, that the chiefest title of honour in earth is to give all honour to Him that is in heaven, that the greatest bravery in this world is to be burning lamps in the world to come, that the clearest beauty in this life is to be amiable to Him that shall give life eternal.

Look in the glass of England, too bright I fear me for your eyes. What is there in your sex that they have not, and what that you should not have? They are in prayer devout, in bravery humble,[3] in beauty chaste, in feasting temperate, in affection wise, in mirth modest, in all their actions though courtly because women, yet angels because virtuous.

Ah, good ladies—good, I say, for that I love you—I would ye could a little abate that pride of your stomachs, that looseness of mind, that licentious behaviour, which I have seen in you with no small sorrow and cannot remedy with continual sighs. They in England pray when you play, sew when you sleep, fast when you feast, and weep for their sins when you laugh at your sensuality. They frequent the church to serve God, you to see gallants; they deck themselves for cleanliness, you for pride; they maintain their beauty for their own liking, you for others' lust; they refrain wine because they fear to take too much, you because you can take no more. Come ladies, with tears I call you, look in this glass, repent your sins past, refrain your present vices, abhor vanities to come. Say thus with one voice, 'We can see our faults only in the English glass,' a glass of grace to them, of grief to you, to them in the stead of righteousness, to you in place of repentance.

The lords and gentlemen in that court are also an example for all others to follow, true types of nobility, the only stay and staff to honour, brave courtiers, stout soldiers, apt to revel in peace and ride in war; in fight fierce not dreading death, in friendship firm not breaking promise, courteous to all that deserve well, cruel to none that deserve ill. Their adversaries they trust not, that showeth their wisdom; their enemies they fear not, that argueth[4]

---

1 *right courteous*] over sexually familiar
2 *precise / remorse*] over-nice / pity
3 *bravery humble*] sumptuousness without pride
4 *argueth*] testifies to

their courage. They are not apt to proffer injuries, nor fit to take any; loath to pick quarrels, but longing to revenge them. Active they are in all things, whether it be to wrestle in the games of Olympia or to fight at barriers in Palaestra, able to carry as great burdens as Milo, of strength to throw as big stones as Turnus,[1] and what not that either man hath done or may do; worthy of such ladies, and none but they, and ladies willing to have such lords, and none but such.

This is a glass for our youth in Greece, for your young ones in Italy—the English glass. Behold it, ladies and lords and all that either mean to have piety, use bravery, increase beauty, or that desire temperancy, chastity, wit, wisdom, valour, or anything that may delight yourselves or deserve praise of others.

But another sight there is in my glass, which maketh me sigh for grief I cannot show it; and yet had I rather offend in derogating from my glass than my good will.[2]

Blessed is that land that hath all commodities to increase the common-wealth, happy is that island that hath wise counsellors to maintain it, virtu-ous courtiers to beautify it, noble gentlemen to advance it; but to have such a Prince to govern it as is their sovereign Queen, I know not whether I should think the people to be more fortunate or the Prince famous, whether their felicity be more to be had in admiration that have such a ruler, or her virtues to be honoured that hath such royalty. For such is their estate there, that I am enforced to think that every day is as lucky to the Englishmen as the sixth day of February[3] hath been to the Grecians.

But I see you gaze until I show this glass, which you having once seen will make you giddy. Oh ladies, I know not when to begin nor where to end. For the more I go about to express the brightness, the more I find mine eyes bleared, the nearer I desire to come to it, the further I seem from it; not unlike unto Simonides,[4] who being curious to set down what God was, the more leisure he took the more loath he was to meddle, saying that in things above reach it was easy to catch a strain but impossible to touch a star, and there-fore scarce tolerable to point at that which one can never pull at.

When Alexander had commanded that none should paint him but Apelles, none carve him but Lysippus, none engrave him but Pyrgoteles,[5] Parrhasius framed a table squared every way two hundred foot, which in the borders he trimmed with fresh colours and limned[6] with fine gold, leaving all the other

---

1 *Palaestra / Turnus*] wrestling ground, used here as a specific place (*fight at barriers* = participate in jousts) / heroic leader of the Latin forces opposed to Aeneas (for *Milo* see p. 35n.)

2 *derogating / good will*] detracting / willing acquiescence (to the limitations placed upon him)

3 *sixth day of February*] Abraham Fleming's translation of Aelian's *Varia historia* (1576) cites 6 February as the day on which Alexander and Socrates were born and the battles of Marathon, Plataea etc. took place (see Bond, II, p. 531 and Croll and Clemons p. 432n.).

4 *Simonides*] celebrated Greek lyric poet (b. 556 BC), asked by the tyrant Hiero to define the nature of God. Having initially asked for a day in which to reflect, Simonides was driven to ask for a series of postponements, declaring that the more he thought about the matter the more complex it appeared.

5 *When Alexander . . . Pyrgoteles*] see p. 221n.

6 *table / limned*] picture / illuminated (For *Parrhasius* see p. 27n.)

room without knot or line. Which table he presented to Alexander, who, no less marvelling at the bigness than at the bareness, demanded to what end he gave him a frame without a face, being so naked, and without fashion, being so great. Parrhasius answered him, 'Let it be lawful for Parrhasius, O Alexander, to show a table wherein he would paint Alexander if it were not unlawful, and for others to square timber though Lysippus carve it, and for all to cast brass though Pyrgoteles engrave it.' Alexander, perceiving the good mind of Parrhasius, pardoned his boldness and preferred his art. Yet enquiring why he framed the table so big, he answered that he thought that frame to be but little enough for his picture, when the whole world was too little for his person; saying that Alexander must as well be praised as painted, and that all his victories and virtues were not for to be drawn in the compass of a signet but in a field.[1] This answer Alexander both liked and rewarded, insomuch that it was lawful ever after for Parrhasius both to praise that noble king and to paint him.

In the like manner I hope that though it be not requisite that any should paint their Prince in England that cannot sufficiently perfect her, yet it shall not be thought rashness or rudeness for Euphues to frame a table for Elizabeth, though he presume not to paint her. Let Apelles show his fine art, Euphues will manifest his faithful heart; the one can but prove his conceit to blaze his cunning,[2] the other his good will to grind his colours. He that whetteth the tools is not to be misliked though he cannot carve the image, the worm that spinneth the silk is to be esteemed though she cannot work the sampler, they that fell timber for ships are not to be blamed because they cannot build ships. He that carrieth mortar furthereth the building though he be no expert mason, he that diggeth the garden is to be considered though he cannot tread the knots,[3] the goldsmith's boy must have his wages for blowing the fire though he cannot fashion the jewel. Then, ladies, I hope poor Euphues shalt not be reviled, though he deserve not to be rewarded.

I will set down this Elizabeth as near as I can; and it may be that as the Venus of Apelles not finished, the Tyndarides of Nicomachus not ended, the Medea of Timomachus not perfected,[4] the table of Parrhasius not coloured brought greater desire to them to consummate them and to others to see them, so the Elizabeth of Euphues, being but shadowed for others to varnish, but begun for others to end, but drawn with a black coal for others to blaze with a bright colour, may work either a desire in Euphues hereafter if he live to end it, or a mind in those that are better able to amend it, or in all (if none can work it) a will to wish it. In the mean season, I say as Zeuxis did when he had drawn the picture of Atalanta, 'More will envy me than imitate me, and not commend it though they cannot amend it.'[5] But I come to my England.

There were for a long time civil wars in this country, by reason of several claims to the crown between the two famous and noble houses of Lancaster

1 *signet / field*] small seal bearing a device, usually on a ring / background for a picture (with a pun on *field* = battlefield)
2 *prove his conceit... cunning*] show his invention to exhibit his artistry
3 *tread the knots*] set out the formal gardens by treading out their design
4 *the Venus of Apelles... perfected*] see p. 159n.
5 *I say as Zeuxis did... amend it*] Bond notes (II, p. 531) that the picture, according to Pliny, was of an athlete rather than Atalanta (for *Zeuxis* see p. 158n.)

and York, either of them pretending[1] to be of the royal blood; which caused them both to spend their vital blood. These jars[2] continued long, not without great loss both to the nobility and commonalty, who, joining not in one but divers parts, turned the realm to great ruin, having almost destroyed their country before they could anoint a king. But the living God, who was loath to oppress England, at last began to repress injuries, and to give an end by mercy to those that could find no end of malice nor look for any end of mischief. So tender a care hath He always had of that England as of a new Israel, his chosen and peculiar people.

This peace began by a marriage solemnized by God's special providence between Henry, Earl of Richmond, heir of the house of Lancaster, and Elizabeth, daughter to Edward the Fourth, the undoubted issue and heir of the house of York; whereby (as they term it) the red rose and the white[3] were united and joined together. Out of these roses sprang two noble buds, Prince Arthur and Henry; the eldest dying without issue, the other, of most famous memory, leaving behind him three children—Prince Edward, the Lady Mary, the Lady Elizabeth.

King Edward lived not long, which could never for that realm have lived too long. But sharp frosts bite forward springs, easterly winds blasteth towardly[4] blossoms, cruel death spareth not those which we ourselves living cannot spare. The elder sister, the Princess Mary, succeeded as next heir to the crown, and, as it chanced, next heir to the grave; touching whose life I can say little because I was scarce born, and what others say of me shall be forborne.

This queen being deceased, Elizabeth, being of the age of twenty-two years,[5] of more beauty than honour, and yet of more honour than any earthly creature, was called from a prisoner to be a prince, from the castle to the crown, from the fear of losing her head to be supreme head. And here, ladies, it may be you will move a question why this noble lady was either in danger of death or cause of distress; which had you thought to have passed in silence I would notwithstanding have revealed.

This lady all the time of her sister's reign was kept close, as one that tendered not those proceedings which were contrary to her conscience.[6] Who having divers enemies endured many crosses, but so patiently as in her deepest sorrow she would rather sigh for the liberty of the gospel than her own freedom; suffering her inferiors to triumph over her, her foes to threaten her, her dissembling friends to undermine her, learning in all this misery only the patience that Zeno taught Eretricus[7] to bear and forbear, never seeking revenge, but, with good Lycurgus, to lose her own eye rather than to hurt another's eye.[8]

---

1 *either of them pretending*] both of them claiming
2 *jars*] conflicts
3 *the red rose and the white*] the emblems of the two houses (*red* = Lancaster / *white* = York)
4 *towardly*] precocious
5 *twenty-two years*] Elizabeth was in fact twenty-five at her accession.
6 *tendered not / those proceedings . . . conscience*] did not look favourably on / i.e. the reinstatement of Catholicism and persecution of Protestants
7 *Eretricus*] a philosopher of Eretria (for *Zeno* see p. 143n.)
8 *good Lycurgus . . . eye*] Lycurgus (see p. 32n.) exhibited exemplary magnanimity in his generosity to a young man who blinded him in one eye during a public disturbance.

But being now placed in the seat royal, she first of all established religion, banished popery, advanced the Word that before was so much defaced. Who, having in her hand the sword to revenge, used rather bountifully to reward, being as far from rigour when she might have killed as her enemies were from honesty when they could not; giving a general pardon when she had cause to use particular punishments, preferring the name of pity before the remembrance of perils, thinking no revenge more princely than to spare when she might spill,[1] to stay when she might strike, to proffer to save with mercy when she might have destroyed with justice. Here is the clemency worthy commendation and admiration; nothing inferior to the gentle disposition of Aristides,[2] who, after his exile, did not so much as note them that banished him, saying with Alexander that there can be nothing more noble than to do well to those that deserve ill.

This mighty and merciful queen, having many bills[3] of private persons that sought beforetime to betray her, burnt them all; resembling Julius Caesar, who, being presented with the like complaints of his commons, threw them into the fire, saying that he had rather not know the names of rebels than have occasion to revenge, thinking it better to be ignorant of those that hated him than to be angry with them. This clemency did Her Majesty not only show at her coming to the crown but also throughout her whole government, when she hath spared to shed their bloods that sought to spill hers, not racking the laws to extremity but mitigating the rigour with mercy; insomuch as it may be said of that royal monarch as it was of Antoninus,[4] surnamed the godly emperor, who reigned many years without the effusion of blood. What greater virtue can there be in a prince than mercy? What greater praise than to abate[5] the edge which she should whet, to pardon where she should punish, to reward where she should revenge?

I myself, being in England when Her Majesty was for her recreation in her barge upon the Thames, heard of a gun that was shot off, though of the party unwittingly,[6] yet to her noble person dangerously. Which fact she most graciously pardoned, accepting a just excuse before a great amends, taking more grief for her poor bargeman that was a little hurt than care for herself that stood in greatest hazard. Oh rare example of pity! Oh singular spectacle of piety![7]

Divers besides have there been which, by private conspiracies, open rebellions, close wiles, cruel witchcrafts, have sought to end her life which saveth all their lives, whose practices by the divine providence of the Almighty have

---

1 *spill*] do to death
2 *Aristides*] Athenian commander of the maritime confederacy, who refused after his ostracism in 482 BC to oppose Themistocles (see p. 101n.) who was probably responsible for his banishment. (The saying attributed to Alexander that follows is probably derived from Plutarch.)
3 *bills*] documents
4 *Antoninus*] Roman emperor (d. AD 161), noted for his care of his people and for the peaceful character of his reign
5 *abate*] blunt
6 *of the party unwittingly*] not deliberately by the person concerned
7 *I myself, being in England . . . piety*] The incident took place near Greenwich during the summer of 1579, and was seen by some as an attempt on the life of the Duke of Anjou's ambassador, who was attempting to negotiate a marriage between his master and the Queen.

ever been disclosed; insomuch that He hath kept her safe in the whale's belly when her subjects went about to throw her into the sea, preserved her in the hot oven when her enemies increased the fire,[1] not suffering a hair to fall from her, much less for any harm to fasten upon her. These injuries and treasons of her subjects, these policies and undermining of foreign nations so little moved her that she would often say, 'Let them know that though it be not lawful for them to speak what they list, yet it is lawful for us to do with them what we list,' being always of that merciful mind which was in Theodosius,[2] who wished rather that he might call the dead to life than put the living to death; saying with Augustus when she should set her hand to any condemnation, 'I would to God we could not write.'[3] Infinite were the examples that might be alleged, and almost incredible, whereby she hath showed herself a lamb in meekness when she had cause to be a lion in might, proved a dove in favour when she was provoked to be an eagle in fierceness, requiting injuries with benefits, revenging grudges with gifts, in highest majesty bearing the lowest mind, forgiving all that sued for mercy, and forgetting all that deserved justice.

Oh divine nature! Oh heavenly nobility! What thing can there more be required in a prince than in greatest power to show greatest patience, in chiefest glory to bring forth chiefest grace, in abundance of all earthly pomp to manifest abundance of all heavenly piety? Oh fortunate England that hath such a Queen! Ungrateful if thou pray not for her, wicked if thou do not love her, miserable if thou lose her!

Here, ladies, is a glass for all princes to behold, that being called to dignity they use moderation not might, tempering the severity of the laws with the mildness of love, not executing all they will but showing what they may. Happy are they, and only they, that are under this glorious and gracious sovereignty; insomuch that I account all those abjects[4] that be not her subjects.

But why do I tread still in one path when I have so large a field to walk, or linger about one flower when I have many to gather? Wherein I resemble those that being delighted with the little brook neglect the fountain's head, or that painter that being curious to colour Cupid's bow forgot to paint the string.

As this noble prince is endued with mercy, patience, and moderation, so is she adorned with singular beauty and chastity, excelling in the one Venus, in the other Vesta. Who knoweth not how rare a thing it is, ladies, to match virginity with beauty, a chaste mind with an amiable face, divine cogitations with a comely countenance? But such is the grace bestowed upon this earthly

---

1 *kept her safe in the whale's belly ... increased the fire*] instances of preservation through the favour of God. Jonah was swallowed by a whale after being thrown into the sea and kept safe in the animal's belly (see Jonah, 1 and 2), Shadrach, Meshach and Abednego were unharmed when cast into a fiery furnace for failing to worship a golden image (see Daniel, 1).

2 *Theodosius*] identified by Croll and Clemons (p. 437n.) as Theodosius the younger (Roman Emperor of the East, b. AD 401) rather than Theodosius the elder as supposed by Bond.

3 *saying with Augustus ... write*] a sentiment usually attributed to Nero but diplomatically tranferred by Lyly to a more admirable figure

4 *abjects*] outcasts

goddess that, having the beauty that might allure all princes, she hath the chastity also to refuse all, accounting it no less praise to be called a virgin than to be esteemed a Venus, thinking it as great honour to be found chaste as thought amiable. Where is now Electra, the chaste daughter of Agamemnon? Where is Lala, that renowned virgin? Where is Aemilia, that through her chastity wrought wonders in maintaining continual fire at the altar of Vesta? Where is Claudia, that to manifest her virginity set the ship on float with her finger that multitudes could not remove by force? Where is Tuccia, one of the same order, that brought to pass no less marvels by carrying water in a sieve, not shedding one drop from Tiber to the temple of Vesta?[1]

If virginity have such force, then what hath this chaste virgin Elizabeth done, who by the space of twenty and odd years with continual peace against all policies, with sundry miracles contrary to all hope, hath governed that noble island, against whom neither foreign force nor civil fraud, neither discord at home nor conspiracies abroad could prevail? What greater marvel hath happened since the beginning of the world than for a young and tender maiden to govern strong and valiant men, than for a virgin to make the whole world, if not to stand in awe of her, yet to honour her. Yea, and to live in spite of all those that spite her, with her sword in the sheath, with her armour in the Tower, with her soldiers in their gowns; insomuch as her peace may be called more blessed than the quiet reign of Numa Pompilius,[2] in whose government the bees have made their hives in the soldiers' helmets. Now is the temple of Janus[3] removed from Rome to England, whose door hath not been opened this twenty years; more to be marvelled at than the regiment of Deborah who ruled twenty years with religion, or Semiramis that governed long with power, or Zenobia[4] that reigned six years in prosperity.

This is the only[5] miracle that virginity ever wrought: for a little island environed round about with wars to stand in peace, for the walls of France to burn and the houses of England to freeze,[6] for all other nations either with civil sword to be divided or with foreign foes to be invaded, and that country neither to be molested with broils in their own bosoms nor threatened with

---

1 *Where is now Electra ... temple of Vesta?*] all examples of exemplary chastity. Electra saved the life of her brother Orestes, after the murder of their father Agamemnon, and assisted him in revenging his death; Lala was an unmarried artist living in Cyzicus (one of the most powerful cities of Asia Minor); Aemilia, a vestal virgin, rekindled the sacred fire when it had been extinguished by throwing her best garment on the ashes; Claudia (wrongly described by some authorities as a vestal virgin), who had been accused of incontinency, freed a ship grounded in the Tiber in 204 BC when soothsayers had predicted that it could be released only by a chaste woman; Tuccia carried water in a sieve to prove her innocence when charged with incest.

2 *Numa Pompilius*] successor to Romulus (and thus second King of Rome), renowned for his wisdom and the peaceful nature of his reign

3 *temple of Janus*] a passageway (rather than a place of worship), dedicated by Numa Pompilius to Janus, opened in time of war and closed in time of peace

4 *Semiramis / Zenobia*] one of the mythical founders of the Assyrian empire, in the course of whose forty-two-year reign the city of Babylon was built / Queen of Palmyra from AD 267, who aspired by her conquests to the title of Queen of the East (for *Deborah* see p. 98n.)

5 *the only*] the greatest

6 *freeze*] remain free of the fires of war

blasts of other borderers, but always, though not laughing, yet looking through an emerald at others' jars.¹ Their fields have been sown with corn, strangers theirs pitched with camps; they have their men reaping their harvest, when others are mustering in their harness;² they use their pieces to fowl for pleasure, others their calivers³ for fear of peril.

Oh blessed peace! Oh happy Prince! Oh fortunate people! The living God is only the English God, where He hath placed peace which bringeth all plenty, anointed a Virgin Queen which with a wand ruleth her own subjects and with her worthiness winneth the good wills of strangers; so that she is no less gracious among her own than glorious to others, no less loved of her people than marvelled at of other nations.

This is the blessing that Christ always gave to His people: peace. This is the curse that He giveth to the wicked: there shall be no peace to the ungodly. This was the only salutation He used to his disciples: 'Peace be unto you.' And therefore is He called the God of love and peace in holy writ. In peace was the Temple of the Lord built by Solomon; Christ would not be born until there were peace throughout the whole world; this was the only thing that Hezekiah⁴ prayed for, 'Let there be truth and peace, O Lord, in my days.' All which examples do manifestly prove that there can be nothing given of God to man more notable than peace.

This peace hath the Lord continued with great and unspeakable goodness among His chosen people of England. How much is that nation bound to such a prince, by whom they enjoy all benefits of peace; having their barns full when others famish, their coffers stuffed with gold when others have no silver, their wives without danger when others are defamed, their daughters chaste when others are deflowered, their houses furnished when others are fired, where they have all things for superfluity, others nothing to sustain their need. This peace hath God given for her virtues—pity, moderation, virginity; which peace the same God of peace continue for His name's sake.

Touching the beauty of this Prince, her countenance, her personage, her majesty, I cannot think that it may be sufficiently commended, when it cannot be too much marvelled at. So that I am constrained to say as Praxiteles⁵ did when he began to paint Venus and her son, who doubted whether the world could afford colours good enough for two such fair faces, and I whether our tongue can yield words to blaze that beauty, the perfection whereof none can imagine. Which seeing it is so, I must do like those that want a clear sight, who, being not able to discern the sun in the sky, are enforced to behold it in the water. Zeuxis,⁶ having before him fifty fair virgins of Sparta whereby to draw one amiable Venus, said that fifty more fairer than those could not minister sufficient beauty to show the goddess of beauty. Therefore, being in despair either by art to shadow her or by imagination to comprehend her, he

1 *looking through an emerald ... jars*] A reference to Nero's habit of watching gladiatorial combats through an emerald ring (see Bond, II, p. 533).
2 *strangers / harness*] foreigners / armour
3 *pieces / calivers*] firearms / muskets
4 *Solomon / Hezekiah*] see p. 33n. / see Isaiah, 39, 8
5 *Praxiteles*] see p. 221n.
6 *Zeuxis*] see p. 158n.

drew in a table a fair temple, the gates open, and Venus going in, so as nothing could be perceived but her back.[1] Wherein he used such cunning that Apelles himself, seeing this work, wished that Venus would turn her face, saying that if it were in all parts agreeable to the back, he would become apprentice to Zeuxis and slave to Venus.

In the like manner it fareth with me, for having all the ladies in Italy, more than fifty hundred, whereby to colour Elizabeth, I must say with Zeuxis that as many more will not suffice; and therefore, in as great an agony, paint her court with her back towards you, for that I cannot by art portray her beauty. Wherein though I want the skill to do it as Zeuxis did, yet viewing it narrowly and comparing it wisely, you all will say that if her face be answerable to her back you will like my handicraft and become her handmaids. In the mean season, I leave you gazing until she turn her face, imagining her to be such a one as nature framed to that end that no art should imitate; wherein she hath proved herself to be exquisite and painters to be apes.

This beautiful mould, when I beheld to be endued with chastity, temperance, mildness, and all other good gifts of nature (as hereafter shall appear), when I saw her to surpass all in beauty and yet a virgin, to excel all in piety and yet a prince, to be inferior to none in all the lineaments of the body and yet superior to everyone in all gifts of the mind, I began thus to pray: that as she hath lived forty years[2] a virgin in great majesty, so she may live fourscore years a mother with great joy, that as with her we have long time had peace and plenty, so by her we may ever have quietness and abundance; wishing this, even from the bottom of a heart that wisheth well to England, though feareth ill, that either the world may end before she die or she live to see her children's children in the world; otherwise how tickle their state is that now triumph, upon what a twist[3] they hang that now are in honour, they that live shall see, which I to think on sigh. But God for His mercy's sake, Christ for His merit's sake, the Holy Ghost for His name's sake grant to that realm comfort without any ill chance, and the prince they have without any other change; that the longer she liveth the sweeter she may smell, like the bird ibis, that she may be triumphant in victories like the palm-tree, fruitful in her age like the vine, in all ages prosperous, to all men gracious, in all places glorious; so that there be no end of her praise until the end of all flesh. This did I often talk with myself and wish with mine whole soul.

What should I talk of her sharp wit, excellent wisdom, exquisite learning, and all other qualities of the mind, wherein she seemeth as far to excel those that have been accounted singular as the learned have surpassed those that have been thought simple? In questioning not inferior to Nicaulia, the Queen of Saba,[4] that did put so many hard doubts to Solomon; equal to Nicostrata in the Greek tongue, who was thought to give precepts for the

---

1 *he drew in a table . . . back*] Bond notes (II, pp. 480 and 533) that a similar picture (not attributed) is described in Sannazarro's *Arcadia*. There appears to be no classical source for such a Venus by Zeuxis (*table* = picture).
2 *forty years*] Elizabeth was, in fact, forty-seven in 1580. The lines that follow bear witness to growing anxiety over the succession in the latter half of Elizabeth's reign.
3 *tickle / twist*] uncertain / thread
4 *Nicaulia, the Queen of Saba*] see p. 149n.

better perfection; more learned in the Latin than Amalasuntha; passing Aspasia in philosophy, who taught Pericles; exceeding in judgement Themistoclea,[1] who instructed Pythagoras. Add to these qualities those that none of these had, the French tongue, the Spanish, the Italian, not mean in every one but excellent in all, readier to correct escapes in those languages than to be controlled,[2] fitter to teach others than learn of any, more able to add new rules than err in the old. Insomuch as there is no ambassador that cometh into her court but she is willing and able both to understand his message and utter her mind; not like unto the kings of Assyria, who answer ambassades[3] by messengers, while they themselves either dally in sin or snort in sleep.

Her godly zeal to learning, with her great skill, hath been so manifestly approved that I cannot tell whether she deserve more honour for her knowledge or admiration for her courtesy, who in great pomp hath twice directed her progress unto the universities, with no less joy to the students than glory to her state. Where, after long and solemn disputations in law, physic, and divinity, not as one wearied with scholars' arguments but wedded to their orations, when everyone feared to offend in length, she, in her own person, with no less praise to Her Majesty than delight to her subjects, with a wise and learned conclusion both gave them thanks and put herself to pains.[4] Oh noble pattern of a princely mind! Not like to the kings of Persia, who in their progress did nothing else but cut sticks to drive away the time,[5] nor like the delicate lives of the Sybarites[6] who would not admit any art to be exercised within their city that might make the least noise.

Her wit so sharp, that if I should repeat the apt answers, the subtle questions, the fine speeches, the pithy sentences which on the sudden she hath uttered, they would rather breed admiration than credit.[7] But such are the gifts that the living God hath endued her withal that, look in what art or language, wit or learning, virtue or beauty anyone hath particularly excelled most, she only hath generally exceeded everyone in all; insomuch that there is nothing to be added that either man would wish in a woman or God doth give to a creature.

I let pass her skill in music, her knowledge in all the other sciences, whenas I fear lest by my simplicity I should make them less than they are, in seeking to show how great they are; unless I were praising her in the gallery of

---

1 *Nicostrata / Amalasuntha / Aspasia / Themistoclea*] all women with outstanding intellectual gifts. Nicostrata was a prophetess of a pre-Roman Arcadian colony in Italy; Amalasuntha, Queen of the Ostrogoths from AD 526, was noted for her learning; Aspasia, admired for both her wit and beauty by Pericles, was at the centre of Athenian literary and philosophical society; Themistoclea was a priestess at Delphi.
2 *escapes / controlled*] errors / corrected
3 *ambassades*] ambassadorial missions
4 *who in great pomp hath twice directed her progress . . . pains*] Elizabeth visited Cambridge in 1564 and Oxford in 1566, attending disputations and addressing her hosts in both Greek and Latin.
5 *the kings of Persia . . . time*] The Persian kings whittled wood to pass the time while travelling (cf. *Campaspe*, The Prologue at the Court, line 9).
6 *Sybarites*] people of Sybaris (founded 720 BC), a town of such wealth that its citizens were notorious for the voluptuousness of their lives
7 *admiration than credit*] wonder than belief

Olympia,[1] where giving forth one word I might hear seven. But all these graces, although they be to be wondered at, yet her politic government, her prudent counsel, her zeal to religion, her clemency to those that submit, her stoutness to those that threaten so far exceed all other virtues that they are more easy to be marvelled at than imitated.

Two and twenty years hath she borne the sword with such justice that neither offenders could complain of rigour nor the innocent of wrong, yet so tempered with mercy as malefactors have been sometimes pardoned upon hope of grace and the injured requited to ease their grief. Insomuch that in the whole course of her glorious reign it could never be said that either the poor were oppressed without remedy or the guilty repressed without cause; bearing this engraven in her noble heart, that justice without mercy were extreme injury and pity without equity plain partiality, and that it is as great tyranny not to mitigate laws as iniquity to break them.

Her care for the flourishing of the gospel hath well appeared, whenas neither the curses of the Pope (which are blessings to good people), nor the threatenings of kings (which are perilous to a prince), nor the persuasions of papists (which are honey to the mouth), could either fear her or allure her to violate the holy league contracted with Christ, or to maculate[2] the blood of the ancient lamb which is Christ. But always constant in the true faith, she hath, to the exceeding joy of her subjects, to the unspeakable comfort of her soul, to the great glory of God, established that religion, the maintenance whereof she rather seeketh to confirm by fortitude than leave off for fear, knowing that there is nothing that smelleth sweeter to the Lord than a sound spirit, which neither the hosts of the ungodly nor the horror of death can either remove or move. This gospel, with invincible courage, with rare constancy, with hot zeal, she hath maintained in her own countries without change, and defended against all kingdoms that sought change; insomuch that all nations round about her threatening alteration, shaking swords, throwing fire, menacing famine, murder, destruction, desolation, she only hath stood like a lamp on the top of a hill, not fearing the blasts of the sharp winds, but trusting in His providence that rideth upon the wings of the four winds.

Next followeth the love she beareth to her subjects, who no less tendereth them than the apple of her own eye;[3] showing herself a mother to the afflicted, a physician to the sick, a sovereign and mild governess to all. Touching her magnanimity, her majesty, her estate royal, there was neither Alexander, nor Galba the Emperor,[4] nor any that might be compared with her.

This is she that, resembling the noble Queen of Navarre,[5] useth the marigold for her flower, which at the rising of the sun openeth her leaves and at the setting shutteth them, referring all her actions and endeavours to Him

---

1 *the gallery of Olympia*] the Heptaphonon, a portico at Olympia, noted for its sevenfold echo
2 *maculate*] stain
3 *apple of her own eye*] that which is dearest to her (proverbial). For *apple* see p. 302n.
4 *Galba the Emperor*] Roman emperor, AD 68–9
5 *Queen of Navarre*] Marguerite d'Angoulême (wife of Henri II), whose religious meditations had been translated by Elizabeth into English. Croll and Clemons note (p. 446n.) that French *marguerite* = marigold during this period, hence the equation between the queen and a flower emblematic of piety.

that ruleth the sun. This is that Caesar that first bound the crocodile to the palm-tree, bridling those that sought to rein her.[1] This is that good pelican that to feed her people spareth not to rend her own person. This is that mighty eagle that hath thrown dust into the eyes of the hart that went about to work destruction to her subjects; into whose wings although the blind beetle would have crept, and so being carried into her nest destroyed her young ones, yet hath she with the virtue of her feathers consumed that fly in his own fraud.[2] She hath exiled the swallow that sought to spoil the grasshopper, and given bitter almonds to the ravenous wolves that endeavoured to devour the silly lambs,[3] burning even with the breath of her mouth, like the princely stag, the serpents that were engendered by the breath of the huge elephant.[4] So that now all her enemies are as whist as the bird attagen, who never singeth any tune after she is taken, nor they being so overtaken.[5]

But whither do I wade, ladies, as one forgetting himself, thinking to sound the depth of her virtues with a few fathoms, when there is no bottom? For I know not how it cometh to pass that being in this labyrinth I may sooner lose myself than find the end.

Behold, ladies, in this glass a Queen, a woman, a virgin; in all gifts of the body, in all graces of the mind, in all perfection of either so far to excel all men that I know not whether I may think the place too bad for her to dwell among men.

To talk of other things in that court were to bring eggs after apples, or after the setting out of the sun to tell a tale of a shadow. But this I say, that all offices are looked to with great care, that virtue is embraced of all, vice hated, religion daily increased, manners reformed; that whoso seeth the place there will think it rather a church for divine service, than a court for princes' delight.

This is the glass, ladies, wherein I would have you gaze, wherein I took my whole delight. Imitate the ladies in England, amend your manners, rub out the wrinkles of the mind, and be not curious about the wems in the face.[6] As

---

1 *that Caesar . . . rein her*] presumably an allusion to Caesar's conquest of Egypt, with reference to Elizabeth's curbing of her enemies, particularly the upholders of the Roman Catholic Church (for *pelican* in the next sentence see p. 254n.)
2 *This is that mighty eagle . . . fraud*] The analogy turns on the belief that eagles, having rolled on the ground to fill their feathers with dust, beat their wings in the eyes of stags in order to blind them (see Croll and Clemons, pp. 446–7n.) and that the feathers of eagles destroy other material placed among them. The eagle (the king of the birds) stands for Elizabeth, the stag and the beetle for her enemies, specifically the adherents of the Roman Catholic Church.
3 *She hath exiled the swallow . . . lambs*] instances of the extirpation of predators, here the representatives of the Roman Catholic Church (*bitter almonds* = sharp reproofs)
4 *burning even with the breath . . . elephant*] Croll and Clemons note (p. 447n.) that according to Pliny the breath of elephants draws serpents from their holes, and that the breath of stags burns them. The passage again alludes to the extirpation of forces hostile to the English reformation. The elephant may stand for France or Spain.
5 *as whist as the bird attagen / overtaken*] as silent as a hazel hen (European woodland game bird) / caught out
6 *be not curious . . . face*] do not concern yourself over the moles [*wems*] in your face

for their Elizabeth, sith you can neither sufficiently marvel at her, nor I praise
her, let us all pray for her; which is the only duty we can perform, and the
greatest that we can proffer.

Yours to command,
Euphues.

IOVIS ELIZABETH[1]

Pallas, Iuno, Venus, cum Nympham numine plenam
   spectarunt, 'nostra haec' quaeque triumphat 'erit.'
contendunt avide; sic tandem regia Iuno:
   'est mea; de magnis stemma petivit avis.'
'hoc leve (nec sperno tantorum insignia patrum);   5
   ingenio pollet; dos mea,' Pallas ait.
dulce Venus risit, vultusque in lumina fixit;
   'haec mea' dixit 'erit, nam quod ametur habet.
iudicio Paridis cum sit praelata venustas,
   ingenium Pallas, Iuno quid urget avos?'   10
haec Venus. impatiens veteris Saturnia damni,
   'arbiter in coelis non Paris' inquit 'erit.'
intumuit Pallas nunquam passura priorem;
   'Priamides Helen[a]m' dixit 'adulter amet.'
risit et erubuit mixto Cytherea colore;   15
   'iudicium' dixit 'Iuppiter ipse ferat.'

assensere: Iovem compellant vocibus ultro;
   incipit affari regia Iuno Iovem:
'Iuppiter, Elizabeth vestras si venit ad aures,
   (quam certe omnino coelica turba stupent)   20
hanc propriam et merito semper vult esse Monarcham
   quaeque s[u]am; namque est pulchra, diserta,[2] potens.
quod pulchra, est Veneris; quod polleat arte, Minervae;
   quod Princeps, Nympham quis neget esse meam?
arbiter istius, modo vis, certaminis esto;   25
   sin minus, est nullum lis habitura modum.'

---

1 *IOVIS ELIZABETH*] See Appendix, pp. 355ff., for a translation of and commen-
tary on the following verses.

2 *diserta*] All early editions read *deserta*, but both sense and metre support the emen-
dation adopted here.

obstupet Omnipotens; 'durum est quod poscitis,' inquit.
  'est tamen arbitrio res peragenda meo.
tu soror et coniux Iuno, tu filia Pallas,
  es quoque (quid simulem?) ter mihi chara, Venus.   30
non tua, da veniam, Iuno, nec Palladis illa est,
  nec Veneris, credas hoc licet, alma Venus.
haec Iuno, haec Pallas, Venus haec, et quaeque Dearum,
  divisum Elizabeth cum Iove numen habet.
ergo quid obstrepitis? frustra contenditis,' inquit,   35
  'ultima vox haec est, Elizabetha mea est.'

Euphues:

es Iovis Elizabeth, nec quid Iove maius habendum;
  et, Iove teste, Iovi es Iuno, Minerva, Venus.

These verses Euphues sent also under his 'Glass' which having once finished he gave himself to his book, determining to end his life in Athens, although he had a month's mind[1] to England; who at all times and in all companies was no niggard of his good speech to that nation, as one willing to live in that court and wedded to the manners of that country.

It chanced that being in Athens not passing one quarter of a year, he received letters out of England from Philautus; which I thought necessary also to insert that I might give some end to the matters in England which at Euphues' departure were but rawly left. And thus they follow:

Philautus to his own Euphues,

I have oftentimes, Euphues, since thy departure, complained of the distance of place that I am so far from thee, of the length of time that I could not hear of thee, of the spite of fortune that I might not send to thee. But time at length, and not too late because at last, hath recompensed the injuries of all, offering me both a convenient messenger by whom to send and strange news whereof to write.

Thou knowest how froward[2] matters went when thou tookest ship, and thou wouldst marvel to hear how forward they were before thou struckest sail. For I had not been long in London (sure I am thou wast not then at Athens), whenas the corn which was green in the blade began to wax ripe in the ear, when the seed which I had scarce thought to have taken root began to spring, when the love of Surius which hardly I would have guessed to have a blossom showed a bud. But so unkind[3] a year it hath been in England that we felt the heat of the summer before we could discern the temperature of the spring; insomuch that we were ready to make hay before we could mow grass, having, in effect, the ides of May before the calends of March.[4] Which seeing it is so forward in these things, I marvelled the less to see it so ready in matters of love, where oftentimes they clap hands[5] before they know the bargain, and seal the obligation before they read the condition.

At my being in the house of Camilla, it happened I found Surius accompanied with two knights, and the Lady Flavia with three other ladies. I drew back as one somewhat shamefast,[6] when I was willed to draw near, as one that was wished for. Who thinking of nothing less than to hear a contract for marriage where I only expected a conceit for mirth, I suddenly, yet solemnly, heard those words of assurance[7] between Surius and Camilla in the which I had rather have been a party than a witness. I was not a little amazed to see them strike the iron which I thought cold, and to make an end before I could hear a beginning. When they saw me as it were in a trance, Surius, taking me by the hand, began thus to jest:

'You muse, Philautus, to see Camilla and me to be assured; not that you

---

1 *month's mind*] longing for
2 *froward*] contrary
3 *unkind*] unnatural
4 *ides of May / calends of March*] 15 May / 1 March, both by the Roman calendar
5 *clap hands*] make the agreement
6 *shamefast*] shy
7 *assurance*] betrothal

doubted it unlikely to come to pass but that you were ignorant of the practices, thinking the dial to stand still because you cannot perceive it to move.
But had you been privy to all proofs, both of her good meaning towards me
and of my good will towards her, you would rather have thought great haste
to be made than long deliberation. For this understand, that my friends are
unwilling that I should match so low, not knowing that love thinketh the
juniper shrub to be as high as the tall oak, or the nightingale's lays to be more
precious than the ostrich's feathers, or the lark that breedeth in the ground
to be better than the hobby[1] that mounteth to the clouds. I have always hitherto preferred beauty before riches and honesty before blood,[2] knowing that
birth is the praise we receive of our ancestors, honesty the renown we leave
to our successors; and of two brittle goods, riches and beauty, I had rather
choose that which might delight me than destroy me. Made marriages by
friends, how dangerous they have been I know, Philautus, and some present
have proved. Which can be likened to nothing else so well than as if a man
should be constrained to pull on a shoe by another's last,[3] not by the length
of his own foot; which being too little wrings him that wears it, not him that
made it, if too big shameth him that hath it, not him that gave it. In meats I
love to carve where I like, and in marriage shall I be carved where I like not?
I had as lief another should take measure by his back of my apparel,[4] as
appoint what wife I shall have by his mind.

'In the choice of a wife sundry men are of sundry minds. One looketh high,
as one that feareth no chips,[5] saying that the oil that swimmeth in the top is
the wholesomest. Another poreth in the ground, as dreading all dangers that
happen in great stocks,[6] alleging that the honey that lieth in the bottom is
the sweetest. I assent to neither, as one willing to follow the mean, thinking
that the wine which is in the middest to be the finest. That I might therefore
match to mine own mind I have chosen Camilla, a virgin of no noble race,
nor yet the child of a base father, but between both; a gentlewoman of an
ancient and worshipful house, in beauty inferior to none, in virtue superior
to a number.

'Long time we loved, but neither durst she manifest her affection because
I was noble, nor I utter mine for fear of offence, seeing in her always a mind
more willing to carry torches before Vesta than tapers before Juno.[7] But as
fire when it bursteth out catcheth hold soonest of the driest wood, so love
when it is revealed fasteneth easiest upon the affectionate will. Which came
to pass in both us; for talking of Love, of his laws, of his delights, torments
and all other branches, I could neither so dissemble my liking but that she

---

1 *hobby*] species of falcon
2 *blood*] lineage
3 *by another's last*] made on the mould for another's foot
4 *I had as lief . . . apparel*] I would as willingly have my clothes cut according to the
size of another's back
5 *feareth no chips*] has no fear of harm by aspiring above his position (proverbial
expression drawn from wood-cutting, where it is dangerous to the eyes to cut above
the head)
6 *stocks*] families
7 *more willing to carry torches . . . Juno*] more inclined to celibacy than marriage

espied it, whereat I began to sigh, nor she so cloak her love but that I perceived it, whereat she began to blush. At the last, though long time straining
courtesy[1] who should go over the stile when we had both haste, I (for that I
knew women would rather die than seem to desire) began first to unfold the
extremities of my passions, the causes of my love, the constancy of my faith,
the which she knowing to be true easily believed, and replied in the like
manner. Which I thought not certain, not that I misdoubted her faith, but
that I could not persuade myself of so good fortune. Having thus made each
other privy to our wished desires, I frequented more often to Camilla, which
caused my friends to suspect that which now they shall find true. And this
was the cause that we all meet here, that before this good company we might
knit that knot with our tongues that we shall never undo with our teeth.'
   This was Surius' speech unto me, which Camilla with the rest affirmed. But
I, Euphues, in whose heart the stumps of love were yet sticking, began to
change colour, feeling as it were new storms to arise after a pleasant calm;
but thinking with myself that the time was past to woo her that another was
to wed, I digested the pill which had almost choked me. But time caused me
to sing a new tune, as after thou shalt hear.
   After much talk and great cheer I, taking my leave, departed, being willed
to visit the Lady Flavia at my leisure; which word was to me in stead of[2] a
welcome.
   Within a while after it was noised[3] that Surius was assured to Camilla,
which bred great quarrels. But he, like a noble gentleman, rejoicing more in
his love than esteeming the loss of his friends, maugre[4] them all was married,
not in a chamber privately, as one fearing tumults, but openly in the church,
as one ready to answer any objections. This marriage solemnized, could not
be recalled; which caused his allies[5] to consent. And so, all parties pleased, I
think them the happiest couple in the world.
   Now, Euphues, thou shalt understand that all hope being cut off from
obtaining Camilla, I began to use the advantage of the word that Lady Flavia
cast out; whom I visited more like to a sojourner than a stranger, being absent
at no time from breakfast till evening. Draff was mine errand, but drink I
would; my great courtesy[6] was to excuse my grievous torments. For I ceased
not continually to court my violet, whom I never found so coy as I thought
nor as courteous[7] as I wished. At the last, thinking not to spend all my wooing
in signs, I fell to flat sayings, revealing the bitter sweets that I sustained, the
joy at her presence, the grief at her absence, with all speeches that a lover
might frame. She, not degenerating[8] from the wiles of a woman, seemed to
accuse men of inconstancy, that the painted words were but wind, that feigned

---

1 *straining courtesy*] being overly polite
2 *in stead of*] as good as
3 *noised*] rumoured (for *assured* in the same sentence see p. 345n.)
4 *maugre*] in spite of
5 *his allies*] those related to him
6 *Draff was mine errand . . . I would / great courtesy*] my pretext was worthless, but
   my purpose was to achieve something worth gaining (proverbial) / extreme civility
7 *coy / courteous*] reserved / forthcoming
8 *degenerating*] departing in nature

sighs were but sleights, that all their love was but to laugh, laying baits to catch the fish that they meant again to throw into the river, practising only cunning to deceive not courtesy to tell truth. Wherein she compared all lovers to Mizaldus the poet, which was so light that every wind would blow him away unless he had lead tied to his heels,[1] and to the fugitive stone in Cyzicus, which runneth away if it be not fastened to some post.[2] Thus would she dally, a wench evermore given to such disport. I answered for myself as I could, and for all men as I thought.

Thus oftentimes had we conference but no conclusions, many meetings but few pastimes. Until at the last Surius, one that could quickly perceive on which side my bread was buttered, began to break with me touching Frances;[3] not as though he had heard anything, but as one that would understand something. I durst not seem strange[4] when I found him so courteous, knowing that in this matter he might almost work all to my liking. I unfolded to him from time to time the whole discourses I had with my violet, my earnest desire to obtain her, my lands, goods, and revenues. Who, hearing my tale, promised to further my suit; wherein he so bestirred his study that within one month I was in possibility to have her I most wished and least looked for.

It were too too long to write an history, being but determined to send a letter; therefore I will defer all the actions and accidents that happened until occasion shall serve either to meet thee or minister leisure to me. To this end it grew, that, conditions drawn for the performance of a certain jointure (for the which I had many Italians bound), we were both made as sure[5] as Surius and Camilla. Her dowry was in ready money a thousand pounds and a fair house, wherein I mean shortly to dwell. The jointure I must make is four hundred pounds yearly, the which I must here purchase in England and sell my lands in Italy.

Now, Euphues, imagine with thyself that Philautus beginneth to change, although in one year to marry and to thrive it be hard. But would I might once again see thee here, unto whom thou shalt be no less welcome than to thy best friend.

Surius, that noble gentleman, commendeth himself unto thee. Camilla forgetteth thee not. Both earnestly wish thy return, with great promises to do thee good, whether thou wish it in the court or in the country. And this I durst swear, that if thou come again into England thou wilt be so friendly entreated[6] that either thou wilt altogether dwell here or tarry here longer.

The Lady Flavia saluteth thee, and also my violet. Everyone wisheth thee so well as thou canst wish thyself no better. Other news here is none but that which little appertaineth to me and nothing to thee.

---

1 *Mizaldus the poet . . . heels*] a story told by Mizaldus (i.e. Antoine Mizauld, a sixteenth-century physicist) rather than of him (see Croll and Clemons, pp. 453–4n.)

2 *the fugitive stone . . . post*] Pliny notes a wandering stone (*lapis fugitivus*) but states that it was weighted with lead (see Croll and Clemons, p. 454n.). For *Cyzicus* see p. 337n.

3 *began to break . . . Frances*] broached the subject of Frances with me

4 *strange*] distant

5 *jointure / made as sure*] provision made by a husband to support his wife after his death by securing property upon her / as firmly contracted to one another

6 *so friendly entreated*] used in such a friendly fashion

Two requests I have to make, as well from Surius as myself: the one to come into England, the other to hear thine answer. And thus in haste I bid thee farewell. From London, the first of February, 1579.[1]

Thine or not his own,
Philautus.

This letter being delivered to Euphues and well perused caused him both to marvel and to joy, seeing all things so strangely concluded, and his friend so happily contracted.[2] Having, therefore, by the same means opportunity to send answer by the which he had pleasure to receive news, he dispatched his letter in this form:

Euphues to Philautus,

There could nothing have come out of England to Euphues more welcome than thy letters, unless it had been thy person. Which when I had throughly perused, I could not at the first either believe them for the strangeness or at the last for the happiness; for upon the sudden to hear such alterations of Surius passed all credit, and to understand so fortunate success to Philautus all expectation. Yet considering that many things fall between the cup and the lip,[3] that in one lucky hour more rare things come to pass than sometimes in seven year, that marriages are made in heaven though consummated in earth, I was brought both to believe the events and to allow[4] them.

Touching Surius and Camilla, there is no doubt but that they both will live well in marriage, who loved so well before their matching. And in my mind he dealt both wisely and honourably to prefer virtue before vain-glory, and the godly ornaments of nature before the rich armour of nobility. For this must we all think (how well soever we think of ourselves), that virtue is most noble by the which men became first noble.

As for thine own estate, I will be bold to counsel thee,[5] knowing it never to be more necessary to use advice than in marriage. Solon[6] gave counsel that before one assured himself he should be so wary that in tying himself fast he did not undo himself; wishing them first to eat a quince-pear, that is, to have sweet conference without brawls, then salt, to be wise without boasting. In Boeotia they covered the bride with asparagonia,[7] the nature of the which plant is to bring sweet fruit out of a sharp thorn; whereby they noted that although the virgin were somewhat shrewish at the first, yet in time she might become a sheep.

---

1 *first of February, 1579*] old style (according to which the year began on 25 March rather than 1 January). Hence 1580 in modern terms. (The date poses problems in relation to the time-scheme of the narrative which runs from 1 December 1579 and includes an eight-week sea journey (see p. 184), a year spent in England (see p. 326) and the period of something under three months in which the events related in Philautus' letter took place.)

2 *contracted*] betrothed

3 *fall between the cup and the lip*] occur in the briefest of intervals between the initiation and completion of an undertaking (proverbial)

4 *allow*] approve

5 *I will be bold . . . thee*] The advice that follows is largely derived from Plutarch's *Coniugalia praecepta*.

6 *Solon*] celebrated Athenian legislator (b. 638 BC), noted for his wisdom

7 *asparagonia*] asparagus

Therefore, Philautus, if thy violet seem in the first month either to chide or chafe, thou must hear without reply and endure it with patience. For they that cannot suffer the wranglings of young married women are not unlike unto those that, tasting the grape to be sour before it be ripe, leave to gather[1] it when it is ripe; resembling them that being stung with the bee forsake the honey. Thou must use sweet words, not bitter checks;[2] and though haply thou wilt say that wands are to be wrought when they are green, lest they rather break than bend when they be dry, yet know also that he that bendeth a twig because he would see if it would bow by strength may chance to have a crooked tree when he would have a straight.

It is prettily noted of a contention between the wind and the sun, who should have the victory. A gentleman walking abroad, the wind thought to blow off his cloak; which, with great blasts and blusterings striving to unloose it, made it to stick faster to his back. For the more the wind increased the closer his cloak clapt to his body. Then the sun shining with his hot beams began to warm this gentleman; who, waxing somewhat faint in this fair weather, did not only put off his cloak but his coat. Which the wind perceiving, yielded the conquest to the sun.

In the very like manner fareth it with young wives. For if their husbands, with great threatenings, with jars,[3] with brawls, seek to make them tractable or bend their knees, the more stiff they make them in the joints; the oftener they go about by force to rule them, the more froward they find them. But using mild words, gentle persuasions, familiar counsel, entreaty, submission, they shall not only make them to bow to their knees but to hold up their hands, not only cause them to honour them but to stand in awe of them. For their stomachs[4] are all framed of diamond, which is not to be bruised with a hammer but blood, not by force but flattery; resembling the cock, who is not to be feared by a serpent but a gleed.[5] They that fear their vines will make too sharp wine must not cut the arms but graft next to them mandrake,[6] which causeth the grape to be more pleasant. They that fear to have curst wives must not with rigour seek to calm them, but saying gentle words in every place by them, which maketh them more quiet.

Instruments sound sweetest when they be touched softest, women wax wisest when they be used mildest. The horse striveth when he is hardly reined, but having the bridle[7] never stirreth; women are stark mad if they be ruled by might, but with a gentle rein they will bear a white mouth.[8] Gall was cast out from the sacrifice of Juno,[9] which betokened that the marriage bed should be without bitterness.

Thou must be a glass to thy wife, for in thy face she must see her own. For if when thou laughest she weep, when thou mournest she giggle, the one is a

---

1 *leave to gather*] refrain from picking
2 *checks*] rebukes
3 *fareth it / jars*] it happens / quarrels
4 *stomachs*] dispositions. (For the effect of blood on diamonds see p. 56n.)
5 *gleed*] hot coal
6 *mandrake*] see p. 232n.
7 *hardly reined / having the bridle*] severely curbed / allowed to take his own way
8 *bear a white mouth*] not chafe (and hence bleed) on the bit
9 *Gall was cast out ... Juno*] The gall was removed from sacrifices offered to the goddess of marriage.

manifest sign she delighteth in others, the other a token she despiseth thee. Be in thy behaviour modest, temperate, sober, for as thou framest thy manners so will thy wife fit hers. Kings that be wrestlers cause their subjects to exercise that feat, princes that are musicians incite their people to use instruments, husbands that are chaste and godly cause also their wives to imitate their goodness.

For thy great dowry, that ought to be in thine own hands; for as we call that wine wherein there is more than half water, so do we term that the goods of the husband which his wife bringeth, though it be all. Helen gaped[1] for goods, Paris for pleasure. Ulysses was content with chaste Penelope. So let it be with thee, that whatsoever others marry for, be thou always satisfied with virtue. Otherwise may I use that speech to thee that Olympias[2] did to a young gentleman who only took a wife for beauty, saying, 'This gentleman hath only married his eyes, but by that time he have also wedded his ear, he will confess that a fair shoe wrings[3] though it be smooth in the wearing.' Lycurgus[4] made a law that there should be no dowry given with maidens, to that end that the virtuous might be married, who commonly have little, not the amorous, who oftentimes have too much.

Behave thyself modestly with thy wife before company, remembering the severity of Cato, who removed Manilius[5] from the Senate for that he was seen to kiss his wife in presence of his daughter. Old men are seldom merry before children, lest their laughter might breed in them looseness; husbands should scarce jest before their wives, lest want of modesty on their parts be cause of wantonness on their wives' part. Imitate the kings of Persia, who when they were given to riot kept no company with their wives, but when they used good order had their queens ever at their table. Give no example of lightness; for look what thou practisest most, that will thy wife follow most, though it becometh her least.

And yet would I not have thy wife so curious[6] to please thee that, fearing lest her husband should think she painted her face, she should not therefore wash it; only let her refrain from such things as she knoweth cannot well like thee. He that cometh before an elephant will not wear bright colours, nor he that cometh to a bull red, nor he that standeth by a tiger play on a tabor;[7] for that by the sight or noise of these things they are commonly much incensed. In the like manner there is no wife, if she be honest, that will practise those things that to her mate shall seem displeasant, or move him to choler.

Be thrifty and wary in thy expenses; for in old time they were as soon condemned by law that spent their wives' dowry prodigally, as they that divorced them wrongfully. Fly that vice which is peculiar to all those of thy country, jealousy; for if thou suspect without cause, it is the next[8] way to have cause.

---

1 *gaped for*] hungered after
2 *Olympias*] mother of Alexander the Great
3 *wrings*] may give pain
4 *Lycurgus*] see p. 32n.
5 *Manilius*] a tribune of the plebians. (For *Cato* see p. 174n.)
6 *curious*] anxious
7 *tabor*] small drum
8 *next*] readiest

Women are to be ruled by their own wits; for be they chaste no gold can win them, if immodest no grief can amend them—so that all mistrust is either needless or bootless. Be not too imperious over her, that will make her to hate thee; nor too submiss, that will cause her to disdain thee. Let her neither be thy slave nor thy sovereign; for if she lie under thy foot she will never love thee, if climb above thy head never care for thee. The one will breed thy shame to love her too little, the other thy grief to suffer too much.

In governing thy household use thine own eye and her hand; for house-wifery consisteth as much in seeing things as settling things. And yet in that go not above thy latchet,[1] for cooks are not to be taught in the kitchen, nor painters in their shops, nor housewives in their houses. Let all the keys hang at her girdle, but the purse at thine; so shalt thou know what thou dost spend and how she can spare.[2]

Break nothing of thy stock; for as the stone thyrrenus[3] being whole swim-meth, but never so little diminished sinketh to the bottom, so a man having his stock full is ever afloat, but wasting of his store becometh bankrupt.

Entertain such men[4] as shall be trusty; for if thou keep a wolf within thy doors to do mischief, or a fox to work craft and subtlety, thou shalt find it as perilous as if in thy barns thou shouldst maintain mice, or in thy grounds moles. Let thy maidens[5] be such as shall seem readier to take pains than follow pleasure, willinger to dress up their house than their heads, not so fine-fingered to call for a lute when they should use the distaff, nor so dainty-mouthed that their silken throats should swallow no pack-thread.[6]

For thy diet, be not sumptuous nor yet simple. For thy attire, not costly nor yet clownish,[7] but cutting thy coat by thy cloth. Go no further than shall become thy estate lest thou be thought proud, and so envied; nor debase not thy birth lest thou be deemed poor, and so pitied.

Now thou art come to that honourable estate forget all thy former follies, and debate[8] with thyself that heretofore thou didst but go about the world and that now thou art come into it; that love did once make thee to follow riot, that it must now enforce thee to pursue thrift; that then there was no pleasure to be compared to the courting of ladies, that now there can be no greater delight than to have a wife.

Commend me humbly to that noble man, Surius, and to his good lady, Camilla. Let my duty to the Lady Flavia be remembered, and to thy violet. Let nothing that may be added be forgotten.

Thou wouldst have me come again into England. I would but I cannot. But

---

1 *go not above thy latchet*] do not trespass beyond your sphere (cf. p. 28 for the same image). Literally *latchet* = shoelace.
2 *spare*] save
3 *Break nothing of thy stock / stone thyrrenus*] do not break into your capital / a stone known by a variety of names, but ultimately deriving from Pliny's *syrium lapidem* (see Croll and Clemons, p. 460n.)
4 *entertain such men*] employ such male servants
5 *maidens*] maidservants
6 *nor so dainty-mouthed . . . pack-thread*] nor too fastidious to undertake coarse work (for *distaff* see p. 68n.)
7 *simple / clownish*] too plain / below your station (literally 'peasant-like')
8 *debate*] consider

if thou desire to see Euphues, when thou art willing to visit thine uncle I will meet thee. In the mean season,[1] know that it is as far from Athens to England as from England to Athens.

Thou sayest I am much wished for, that many fair promises are made to me. Truly, Philautus, I know that a friend in the court is better than a penny in the purse; but yet I have heard that such a friend cannot be gotten in the court without pence. Fair words fat few,[2] great promises without performance delight for the time but yerk[3] ever after.

I cannot but thank Surius who wisheth me well, and all those that at my being in England liked me well. And so, with my hearty commendations, until I hear from thee I bid thee farewell.

Thine to use if marriage change not manners,
Euphues.

This letter dispatched, Euphues gave himself to solitariness, determining to sojourn in some uncouth place until time might turn white salt into fine sugar;[4] for surely he was both tormented in body and grieved in mind. And so I leave him, neither in Athens nor elsewhere that I know. But this order he left with his friends, that if any news came, or letters, that they should direct them to the Mount of Silixsedra,[5] where I leave him either to his musing or his muses.

Gentlemen, Euphues is musing in the bottom of the Mountain Silixsedra, Philautus married in the isle of England. Two friends parted; the one living in the delights of his new wife, the other in contemplation of his old griefs. What Philautus doth they can imagine that are newly married; how Euphues liveth they may guess that are cruelly martyred. I commit them both to stand to their own bargains. For if I should meddle any further with the marriage of Philautus it might haply make him jealous, if with the melancholy of Euphues it might cause him to be choleric;[6] so the one would take occasion to rub his head, sit his hat never so close,[7] and the other offence to gall his heart, be his case never so quiet. I, gentlewomen, am indifferent, for it may be that Philautus would not have his life known which he leadeth in marriage, nor Euphues his love descried which he beginneth in solitariness;[8] lest either the one being too

---

1 *In the mean season*] meanwhile
2 *Fair words fat few*] kind words do not fill the stomach
3 *yerk*] either 'inflict sharp blows' or (less probably given the variant spellings in later editions) a variant of the unrelated 'irk' = weary or disgust
4 *uncouth / turn white salt . . . sugar*] unknown / had effected a beneficial transformation in his state (with the implication that the process would be of infinite duration)
5 *Silixsedra*] literally 'seat of flint', but no such location has been traced
6 *choleric*] For the association between choler and salt (cf. 'turn white salt' in the previous paragraph), see p. 215.
7 *take occasion to rub . . . close*] suspect himself of being a cuckold however faithful his wife
8 *his love descried . . . solitariness*] see Introduction, pp. 10–11

kind might be thought to dote, or the other too constant might be judged to be mad. But were the truth known, I am sure, gentlewomen, it would be a hard question among ladies whether Philautus were a better wooer or a husband, whether Euphues were a better lover or a scholar. But let the one mark the other. I leave them both to confer at their next meeting, and commit you to the Almighty.

FINIS

APPENDIX

LYLY'S 'IOVIS ELIZABETH'

The poem in celebration of Elizabeth, with which Euphues' 'Glass for Europe' concludes, has its source in the story of the judgement of Paris,[1] specifically Ovid's version of the tale in his *Heroides* (16.53–88). The elegiac metre and rhetorical tone both look back to the classical source, and Lyly's indebtedness is confirmed by a number of verbal echoes.[2] The handling of both hexameter and pentameter conforms to Augustan[3] norms, hexameters concluding with a dactyl, plus a spondee or trochee, the final word being either disyllabic or trisyllabic, and pentameters ending with a disyllabic word. The use of the caesura is orthodox throughout and the practice of ending pentameters with a noun, verb or possessive adjective is strictly observed (except in the special case of *potens*, line 22). In conformity with Augustan usage couplets are self-contained and only two examples of emphatic enjambement occur between hexameter and pentameter (lines 1 and 21).[4]

While emulating the Augustans in its neatness and elegance, the poem is most effective at those points at which the context permits the deployment of stylistic devices familiar in classical literature but also highly characteristic of Lyly himself. A concise pattern of antithesis is constructed, for example, on *ingenium ... avos* (line 10), and *quod ... meam* (lines 23–4), while alliteration is functional as well as decorative in line 13 (where the spluttering plosives enact the indignation of the goddess), line 16 (where sound patterning strengthens the tone of Venus' proposed solution to the dispute), and line 27 (where the aural effect signals a key point of the narrative).[5] The effect of line 1 is enhanced by assonance (*Nym ... num ... nam*), and the word-play on *Venus* in line 7 and *venustas* in line 9 contributes to the wit of the whole. The couplet *quod pulchra ... meam* (lines 23–4) represents the highpoint of Lyly's achievement in the fusion of his own style with that of his classical models. The rival claims of the three goddesses are summed up in a single, tightly organized couplet, with significant words and phrases pointed by alliteration, and the use of the common classical device of the 'law of increasing members' (by which each successive member of a trio is longer than that which precedes it) to achieve a climax.[6] The concluding couplet also represents a significant tour de force. The poet stresses the authority of the final judgement by introducing Jupiter's name four times (in three different cases), with epigrammatic effect, bringing his compliment to a triumphant conclusion by including all four deities in the last five words.

Lyly's Latinity is not without its flaws. Both vocabulary and grammar deviate at times from classical norms, e.g. *spectarunt* indicative (line 2), *triumphat* (line 2), *obstupet* (line 27), *simulem* (line 30). Phrasing is also occasionally clumsy or uneconomical, e.g. *hanc...suam* (lines 21–2), and there are occasional metrical errors, e.g. *turba stupent* (line 20). The poem is deft, nevertheless, in its enlistment of classical cultural authority to the service of Elizabethan panegyric. A translation is appended below.

Jupiter's Elizabeth

When Pallas, Juno and Venus looked upon a nymph filled with
    divine majesty,
Each of them boasted, 'This nymph shall be mine.'
They argued passionately; at length royal[7] Juno spoke thus:
    'She is mine; she has claimed her descent from mighty ancestors.'[8]
'That's unimportant (not that I despise the emblems of such great
    forefathers);   5
She is outstanding in intellect; that is *my* gift,' said Pallas.
Venus smiled sweetly,[9] and fixed her gaze upon the nymph's eyes;
    'This nymph,' she said, 'will be mine; for she possesses desirability.
Since loveliness was preferred by Paris's verdict,[10]
    Why does Pallas press the claims of intellect, and Juno ancestry?'   10
Thus Venus. Saturn's daughter, chafing at her ancient injury,[11] said:
    'In heaven,[12] the judge is not going to be Paris.'
Pallas, never willing to let herself be bettered, swelled with rage;
    'Let Priam's son,' she said, 'pursue his adulterous affair with Helen.'[13]
The goddess of Cythera[14] smiled and blushed, blending her colour;[15]   15
    'Let Jupiter himself,' she said, 'cast the verdict.'

They agreed: readily they appealed to Jupiter with their words;
    It was royal Juno who began to address Jupiter:
'Jupiter, if the name of Elizabeth has come to your ears,
    (At whom the heavenly throng are certainly struck entirely dumb
    with awe)   20
Each of us, at all times, with good cause, wants this Queen to belong
    to her
And be her own; for she is beautiful, eloquent and powerful.
Because she is beautiful, she belongs to Venus; because she excels in
    the arts, she belongs to Minerva;
Because she is a Prince, who would deny the nymph is mine?
Be the judge in this dispute, if you please;   25
    Otherwise the argument is going to have no end.'

The Almighty was dumbfounded; 'What you demand is painfully
    hard,' he said.
'Nevertheless, the problem has to be settled by my decision.
You, Juno, are my sister and wife; you, Pallas, are my daughter;
    You too, Venus, (why make a pretence?) are trebly dear to me.[16]   30

Forgive me, Juno, that nymph does not belong to you, nor to Pallas,
  Nor to Venus, even though you, life-giving[17] Venus, believe it so.
This nymph is Juno, she is Pallas, she is Venus, she is each of the
    goddesses;
  Elizabeth has a divine majesty shared with Jupiter.
Therefore what is the point of your loud protests? You argue in vain,'
    he said;   35
  'This is my last word: Elizabeth is mine.'

Euphues:

You are Jupiter's Elizabeth, and nothing should be thought
    greater than Jupiter;
  And on Jupiter's testimony you are (in Jupiter's eyes) Juno, Minerva
    and Venus.

NOTES

1 The story turns on a dispute between Venus, Juno, and Minerva (Pallas Athene).
  The three goddesses, unable to agree which of them was the most beautiful, applied
  to Jupiter for arbitration, who in turn deputed Paris, then a shepherd on Mount
  Ida, to pass judgement. In order to influence his decision, Juno offered him power,
  Minerva glory and renown in war, and Venus the love of the most beautiful woman
  in the world. Paris awarded the prize (a golden apple) to Venus and was rewarded
  with the love of Helen, wife of Menelaus (see p. 27n.), giving rise to the Trojan war.
2 Notably in lines 7 (*dulce Venus risit*, Ovid, *Her.* 16.83; *vult*[*us*], Ovid 16.74), 8
  (*quod ame*[*tur*], Ovid 16.85), and 27 (*obstup*[*et*], Ovid 16.67). Other items of
  shared vocabulary, e.g. *iudici*[*um*] (Lyly 9 and 16, Ovid 16.80), *potens* (Lyly 22,
  Ovid 16.82), *arbiter* and *certam*[*inis*] (Lyly 25, Ovid 16.69), and *coniux . . . filia*
  (Lyly 29, Ovid 16.81), while attributable in isolation to shared subject matter,
  heighten the case for Lyly's dependency through their conjunction.
3 i.e. the period during the reign of the Emperor Augustus (27 BC–AD 14), when
  Virgil, Ovid, Horace, Tibullus etc. flourished.
4 Lyly exhibits, in fact, a greater strictness than his classical predecessors in his frequent use of the single line as the unit of composition.
5 Ovid similarly uses alliteration to mark a narrative climax.
6 Compare *tu soror . . . Venus* (lines 29–30) where a very similar device is employed.
7 *royal*] Latin *regia*, a traditional epithet for Juno (as wife of the king of the gods),
  frequently applied to her in the *Aeneid*. The references to her as 'royal' pave the
  way for the claim that Elizabeth, as a member of a royal line, rightly belongs to
  her.
8 *she has claimed . . . ancestors*] A more politically significant assertion than might
  appear at first sight in that the legitimacy of both the Tudor dynasty and Elizabeth
  herself were subject to challenge in the sixteenth century.
9 *Venus smiled sweetly*] Latin *dulce Venus risit*, a direct borrowing from Ovid's
  Heroides and an echo of a well-known tag in Catullus and Horace (*dulce riden-
  tem*). Homer refers to Aphrodite / Venus as 'laughter-loving'.
10 *Paris's verdict*] An explicit reference to the judgement of Paris (see note 1) on which
  the conceit governing Lyly's poem is based.
11 *Saturn's daughter / ancient injury*] Juno / Paris' decision to award the golden apple
  to Venus rather than to Juno
12 *in heaven*] In opposition to Mount Ida, where the judgement of Paris took place.

13 *Let Priam's son . . . Helen*] A further example of the ambivalent time-scheme of *Euphues and His England* (see Introduction, p. 9). Though the deities dispute ownership of a sixteenth-century monarch, the Trojan war, by implication, is not yet over.

14 *The goddess . . . Cythera*] Venus (born from the sea at Cythera)

15 *blending her colour*] marrying her natural white with a blush. The blending of white and red in the female face was an index of beauty in the sixteenth century.

16 *trebly dear to me*] An allusion to Jupiter's notorious susceptibility to beauty.

17 *life-giving*] Latin *alma*, a conventional epithet of Venus (see the opening lines of Lucretius' *De rerum natura*)

Lightning Source UK Ltd.
Milton Keynes UK
UKHW011045160520
363106UK00013B/101